bibliographie

DE LA COUR INTERNATIONALE
DE JUSTICE

2004-2009 **58**

bibliography

OF THE INTERNATIONAL COURT
OF JUSTICE

CIJ LA HAYE 2018 ICJ THE HAGUE

ISBN 978-92-1-003868-3
ISSN 0085-2139

N° de vente:
Sales number: **1207**

IMPRIMÉ AUX PAYS-BAS
PRINTED IN THE NETHERLANDS

PRÉFACE

La présente publication contient les données bibliographiques relatives aux ouvrages faisant référence à la Cour internationale de Justice publiés de 2004 à 2009 (n° 58) et parvenus au Greffe. La *Bibliographie* a paru annuellement sous la forme d'une publication officielle de 1946 à 2003 (n°s 1-57), les numéros annuels étant périodiquement regroupés dans des recueils.

Pour des raisons pratiques, le Greffe tient à présent la liste officielle des références bibliographiques dans une base de données. La présente publication est une version imprimée des entrées qui s'y trouvent ; elle reprend la présentation du dernier numéro de la série officielle et vise à faciliter l'accès aux documents faisant référence à la Cour.

La *Bibliographie*, préparée par la bibliothèque privée de la Cour, qui est un service du Greffe, n'engage la Cour en aucune façon. La présente édition n'a fait l'objet d'aucune révision formelle. Les lecteurs sont priés de bien vouloir porter toute publication pertinente qui n'y figure pas à la connaissance de *M. le Greffier de la Cour internationale de Justice, Palais de la Paix, 2517 KJ La Haye, Pays-Bas.* Tél. (+3170) 302 23 23. Courriel : library@icj-cij.org

PREFACE

This work contains bibliographical references concerning the International Court of Justice received by the Registry of the Court and published during the years 2004 to 2009 (No. 58). The *Bibliography* was prepared as an official publication on an annual basis from 1946 to 2003, as Nos. 1-57, with the annual issues periodically collected in cumulative volumes.

For practical reasons, the Registry now maintains the official record of bibliographical references in a database. This work is a printed version of records found in that database, following the style of the last number in the official series and prepared in order to facilitate greater access to works referencing the Court.

The *Bibliography*, which is prepared by the Court's private library (a division of the Registry), in no way involves the responsibility of the Court. This edition has not been formally edited. Readers are requested kindly to draw any relevant publications which have not been included to the attention of *The Registrar, International Court of Justice, Peace Palace, 2517 KJ The Hague, Netherlands.* Tel. (+3170) 302 23 23. E-mail : library@icj-cij.org

TABLE DES MATIÈRES

TABLE OF CONTENTS

A. LA COUR ET LE SYSTÈME JUDICIAIRE INTERNATIONAL

A. THE COURT AND THE INTERNATIONAL JUDICIAL SYSTEM

1. Ouvrages sur la Cour en général
1. Writings on the Court in general

ABILA Committee on Intergovernmental Settlement of Disputes: Reforming the United Nations: what about the International Court of Justice? (In: Chinese Journal of International Law, 2006, v. 5, p. 39-65.)

Abraham, Ronny: La Cour internationale de Justice, juge constitutionnel? (Dans: La Charte des Nations Unies, constitution mondiale?, sous la dir. de Régis Chemain; Alain Pellet. Paris: Pedone, 2006, p. 105-108.)

Anand, Ram Prakash: Studies in international law and history: an Asian perspective. Leiden [etc.]: Nijhoff, 2004. (Developments in International Law; 49.) [P.C.I.J., p. 145-146, 154, 159-161, 166, 244; I.C.J., p. xiii, 11-12, 142, 144-179, 210-212, 230.]

Angehr, Mark: The International Court of Justice's advisory jurisdiction and the review of Security Council and General Assembly resolutions. (In: Northwestern University Law Review, 2009, v. 103, no. 2, p. 1007-1036.)

Angelet, Nicolas et Clavé, Corinne: L'argumentation devant la Cour internationale de Justice: une plaidoirie de Jean Salmon confrontée à sa pensée théorique. (Dans: Droit du pouvoir, pouvoir du droit: mélanges offerts à Jean Salmon. Bruxelles: Bruylant, 2007, p. 53-65.)

Apostolidis, Charalambos: Préface. (Dans: Les arrêts de la Cour internationale de Justice, sous la dir. de Charalambos Apostolidis. Dijon: Ed. universitaires de Dijon, 2005, p. 5-7.)

Apostolidis, Charalambos (sous la dir. de): Les arrêts de la Cour internationale de Justice. Dijon: Ed. universitaires de Dijon, 2005. (Institutions.)

Arone, Charikleia: Elegchos ton apofaseon tou Sumbouliou Asfaleias ton Enomenon ethnon apo to Diethnes Dikasterio. Athènes: Sakkoula, 2006.

Bederman, David J.: Tibor Várady's advocacy before the International Court of Justice. (In: Resolving international conflicts: liber amicorum Tibor Várady, ed. by Peter Hay; Lajos Vékás; Yehuda Elkana; Nenad Dimitrijevic. Budapest: Central European University Press, 2009, p. 21-44.)

Bedi, Shiv R. S.: The development of human rights law by the judges of the International Court of Justice. Oxford [etc.]: Hart Publishing, 2007. (Studies in International Law; 10.)

Béranger, Anne-Hélène: La relecture de l'article 38 du Statut par la Cour internationale de Justice. (Dans: Les arrêts de la Cour internationale de

Justice, sous la dir. de Charalambos Apostolidis. Dijon : Ed. universitaires de Dijon, 2005, p. 109-121.)

Biehler, Gernot: International law and legal procedures before the International Court of Justice in arbitration and diplomatic methods : an analysis of the limits of international law. (In : Dublin University Law Journal, 2007, v. 29, p. 209-230.)

Bourilhon, Grégory: Les avis consultatifs obligatoires de la Cour permanente de Justice internationale et de la Cour internationale de Justice. Toulon : Université du Sud Toulon-Var; UFR Faculté de droit, 2005.

Braasch, Patrick and Fuhrmann, Sirko: Die Rechtsprechung des Internationalen Gerichtshofes im Jahre 2008. (In : German Yearbook of International Law, 2009, v. 52, p. 497-546.)

Brant, Leonardo Nemer Caldeira : A competência da Corte Internacional de Justiça na busca de uma paz durával. (Dans : O Brasil e os novos desafios do direito internacional, sous la dir. de Brant, Leonardo Nemer Caldeira. Rio de Janeiro : Editora Forense, 2004, p. 39-92.)

Brant, Leonardo Nemer Caldeira: L'autorité des arrêts de la Cour internationale de Justice. (Dans : Les arrêts de la Cour internationale de Justice, sous la dir. de Charalambos Apostolidis. Dijon : Ed. universitaires de Dijon, 2005, p. 141-168.) [C.P.J.I., p. 141, 144-145, 149, 153-154, 156, 158, 161.]

Briggs, Herbert W.: Unilateral denunciation of treaties : the Vienna Convention and the International Court of Justice. (In : The law of treaties, ed. by Scott Davidson. Aldershot [etc.] : Ashgate/Dartmouth, 2004, p. 517-534.)

Brownlie, Ian: State responsibility and the International Court of Justice. (In : Issues of State responsibility before international judicial institutions, ed. by Malgosia A. Fitzmaurice ; Danesh Sarooshi. Oxford : Hart, 2004, p. 11-18.)

Buergenthal, Thomas: The I.C.J., human rights and extraterritorial jurisdiction. (In : Human rights, democracy and the rule of law : liber amicorum Luzius Wildhaber, ed. by Stephan Breitenmoser ; Bernhard Ehrenzeller ; Marco Sassòli ; Walter Stoffel ; Beatrice Wagner Pfeifer. Zürich [etc.] : Dike : Nomos, 2007, p. 143-150.)

Burgis, Michelle: Boundaries of discourse in the International Court of Justice : mapping arguments in Arab territorial disputes. Leiden ; Boston : Martinus Nijhoff, 2009.

Cahin, Gérard et Guillaume, Gilbert, cont.: La motivation des décisions de la Cour internationale de Justice. (Dans : La motivation des décisions des juridictions internationales, sous la dir. d'Hélène Ruiz Fabri ; Jean-Marc Sorel. Paris : Pedone, 2008, p. 9-99.)

Calliess, Gralf-Peter: Judicial independence and impartiality in international courts : a comment on Posner. (In : International conflict resolution, ed. by Stefan Voigt; Max Albert; Dieter Schmidtchen. Tübingen: Mohr Siebeck, 2006, p. 143-153.) [I.C.J., passim.]

Cassel, Douglass : Is there a new world court? (In : Northwestern University journal of international human rights, 2003, v. 1, p. 1-7.)

Chemillier-Gendreau, Monique: Conclusions. (Dans: Les arrêts de la Cour internationale de Justice, sous la dir. de Charalambos Apostolidis. Dijon : Ed. universitaires de Dijon, 2005, p. 199-206.)

Chinkin, Christine M. : Article 62. (In : The Statute of the International Court of Justice: a commentary, ed. by Andreas Zimmermann; Christian Tomuschat; Karin Oellers-Frahm. 2006, p. 1331-1368.) [I.C.J., passim.]

Condé, Pierre-Yves : Causes de la justice internationale, causes judiciaires internationales: notes de recherche sur la remise en question de la Cour internationale de Justice. (Dans : Pacifier et punir, 2008, v. 2, p. 25-32.)

Corell, Hans: The role of public international law and the I.C.J. in a changing world. (In: Freedom from nuclear weapons through legal accountability and good faith: conference report, ed. by George Farebrother. Nottingham: Spokesman; World Court Project, 2007, p. 12-22.)

Corten, Olivier: Le juge international, le droit et la guerre. (Dans: Liber amicorum Paul Martens : l'humanisme dans la résolution des conflits : utopie ou réalité ? Bruxelles : Larcier, 2007, p. 213-221.)

Cour internationale de Justice: La Cour internationale de Justice. [S.l.]: United Nations, 2006.

Couvreur, Philippe: The International Court of Justice at The Hague: the keystone of the edifice of the "legal capital of the world". (In: The Hague legal capital? Liber in honorem W. J. Deetman, ed. by Vriesendorp, David; Nelissen, Frans A.; Wladimiroff, Michaïl. The Hague: Hague Academic Press, 2008, p. 181-189.)

Couvreur, Philippe: Una mirada hacia la Corte Internacional de Justicia. (Dans: Cursos de derecho internacional y relaciones internacionales de Vitoria-Gasteiz, 2007, p. 95-98.)

Couvreur, Philippe : Una mirada hacia la Corte Internacional de Justicia : el balance histórico-sociológico de la Corte. (Dans: Cursos de derecho internacional y relaciones internacionales de Vitoria-Gasteiz, 2007, p. 99-132.)

Couvreur, Philippe : Una mirada hacia la Corte Internacional de Justicia : la obra de la Corte Internacional de Justicia. (Dans: Cursos de derecho internacional y relaciones internacionales de Vitoria-Gasteiz, 2007, p. 133-174.)

Crawford, James and Pellet, Alain: Anglo Saxon and continental approaches to pleading before the ICJ. (In: International law between universalism and fragmentation: festschrift in honour of Gerhard Hafner, sous la dir. d'Isabelle Buffard ; James Crawford ; Alain Pellet ; Stephan Wittich. Leiden [etc.] : Martinus Nijhoff, 2008, p. 831-867.)

Crawford, James : International Court of Justice. (In : The Oxford handbook on the United Nations, ed. by Thomas G. Weiss ; Sam Daws. 2007, p. 193-213.)

Cronin-Furman, Kathleen Renée : The International Court of Justice and the United Nations Security Council : rethinking a complicated relationship. (In : Columbia Law Review, 2006, v. 106, no. 2, p. 435-463.)

d'Aspremont, Jean : The recommendations made by the International Court of Justice. (In : International and Comparative Law Quarterly, 2007, v. 56, no. 1, p. 185-198.)

Decaux, Emmanuel : La Cour internationale de Justice et les droits de l'homme. (Dans : Studi di diritto internazionale in onore di Gaetano Arangio-Ruiz, sous la dir. de Giovanni Battaglini ; Paolo Benvenuti ; Antonio Cassese ; Giorgio Gaja. Napoli : Editoriale Scientifica, 2004, v. 2, p. 921-970.)

Deiseroth, Dieter : Stärkung des Völkerrechts durch Anrufung des Internationalen Gerichtshofs ? Münster [etc.] : Lit, 2004.

Détais, Julien : Les critères du droit de légitime défense dans la jurisprudence de la Cour internationale de Justice. (Dans : Légitimes défenses : colloque international, sous la dir. de Rahim Kherad. Paris : LGDJ, 2007, p. 149-171.)

Divac Öberg, Marko : The legal effects of resolutions of the UN Security Council and General Assembly in the jurisprudence of the ICJ. (In : European Journal of International Law, 2005, v. 16, no. 5, p. 879-906.)

Dupuy, Pierre-Marie : Le droit des Nations Unies et sa pratique dans la jurisprudence de la Cour internationale de Justice. (Dans : La pratique et le droit international : colloque de Genève. Paris : A. Pedone, 2004, p. 139-157.)

Erne, Jaanika : Link of jurisdiction in Article 62 proceedings before the ICJ : developments of the requirement for link of jurisdiction in Article 62 intervention proceedings before the International Court of Justice. Köln : Lambert Academic Publishing, 2009. [I.C.J., passim.]

Fitzmaurice, Malgosia A. : The International Court of Justice and the environment. (In : Non-State actors and international law, 2004, v. 4, no. 3, p. 173-197.)

Fleischhauer, Carl-August : Deutschland und der Internationale Gerichtshof. (In : Deutschland und die internationale Gerichtsbarkeit : Vortragsreihe am Walther-Schücking-Institut für Internationales Recht and der Universität Kiel im Wintersemester 2002/03 und Sommersemester 2003, ed. by Zimmermann, Andreas. Berlin : Duncker & Humblot, 2004, p. 29-43.)

Fox, Hazel: State immunity in the International Court of Justice: the courts list at January 2010. (In: L'observateur des Nations Unies, 2009, v. 27, no. 2, p. 107-119.)

Franck, Thomas M.: The future relationship between a new administration and the International Court of Justice. (In: ILSA Journal of International and Comparative Law, 2009, v. 15, no. 2, p. 315-318.)

Green, Fergus: Fragmentation in two dimensions: the ICJ's flawed approach to non-state actors and international legal personality. (In: Melbourne Journal of International Law, 2008, v. 9, no. 1, p. 47-77.)

Green, James A.: Fluctuating evidentiary standards for self-defence in the International Court of Justice. (In: International and Comparative Law Quarterly, 2009, v. 58, no. 1, p. 163-179.)

Green, James A.: The International Court of Justice and self-defence in international law. Oxford; Portland: Hart Publishing, 2009. (Studies in international law; 25.)

Guillaume, Gilbert: La Corte Internacional de Justicia: situación presente, balance y perspectivas. (Dans: Diálogos sobre la justicia internacional, sous la dir. de Bernardo Sepúlveda Amor. Monterrey: Comité Regional Norte de Cooperación con la UNESCO, 2009, p. 72-107.)

Guillaume, Gilbert: La Cour internationale de Justice et le droit international de l'environnement: introduction. (Dans: The role of the judiciary in the implementation and enforcement of environmental law, sous la dir. d'Amedeo Postiglione. Bruxelles: Bruylant, 2008, p. 3-15.)

Guillaume, Gilbert: L'autorité de la Cour internationale de Justice. (Dans: L'autorité, sous la dir. de Jean Foyer; Gilles Lebreton; Catherine Puigelier. Paris: Presses universitaires de France, 2008, p. 181-186.)

Guillaume, Gilbert: L'Organisation des Nations Unies et ses juges. (Dans: L'ONU. Paris: Seuil, 2004, p. 89-102.) [C.I.J., passim.]

Higgins, Rosalyn: " ... To save succeeding generations from the scourge of war": the role of the International Court of Justice. (In: The United Nations and its future in the 21st century, by Vijay Mehta. Nottingham: Spokesman Books, 2005, p. 84-101.)

Higgins, Rosalyn: Departing thoughts on the International Court of Justice. (In: Proceeding of the annual meeting, 2009, v. 103, p. 408-412.)

Higgins, Rosalyn: Human rights in the International Court of Justice. (In: Leiden Journal of International Law, 2007, v. 20, p. 745-751.)

Higgins, Rosalyn: Issues of State responsibility before the International Court of Justice. (In: Issues of State responsibility before international judicial institutions, ed. by Malgosia A. Fitzmaurice; Dan Sarooshi. Oxford [etc.]: Hart, 2004, p. 1-9.)

Higgins, Rosalyn: MacDermott lecture 2008: litigating international disputes: the work of the International Court of Justice in a changing world: given at Queen's University Belfast on 16 April 2008 by H. E. Judge Rosalyn Higgins, President of the International Court of Justice. (In: Northern Ireland Legal Quarterly, 2008, v. 59, no. 4, p. 339-347.)

Higgins, Rosalyn: The role of the International Court of Justice in the contemporary world. Abu Dhabi: The Emirates Center for Strategic Studies and Research, 2008. (Emirates lecture series; 72.)

Higgins, Rosalyn: Some misconceptions about the judicial settlement of international disputes. (In: Hague Yearbook of International Law, 2007, v. 20, p. 13-18.)

International Court of Justice: Legal maxims: summaries and extracts from selected case law: case concerning Certain Property (Liechtenstein v. Germany), preliminary objections, judgment, 10 February 2005. (In: Global Community: Yearbook of International Law and Jurisprudence, 2006, v. 6, no. 1, p. 225-234.)

Jacovides, Andrew A.: U.N. reform and the International Court of Justice: introductory statement. (In: ILSA Journal of International and Comparative Law, 2006, v. 12, no. 2, p. 547-553.)

Jiménez Piernas, Carlos: Spanish diplomatic and parliamentary practice in public international law: 2004. (In: Spanish Yearbook of International Law, 2004, v. 10, p. 123-144.) [I.C.J., p. 139-141.]

Kamto, Maurice: Considérations actuelles sur l'inexécution des décisions de la Cour internationale de Justice. (Dans: Law of the sea, environmental law and settlement of disputes: liber amicorum Judge Thomas A. Mensah, ed. by Tafsir Malick Ndiaye; Rüdiger Wolfrum. Leiden; Boston: Martinus Nijhoff, 2007, p. 215-233.)

Karmali, Ayla: The influence of sharia norms of dispute settlement and international law: the International Court of Justice, room for accommodation? (In: Arbitration, 2009, v. 75, no. 3, p. 309-326.)

Kawano, Mariko: The administration of justice by the International Court of Justice and the parties. (In: Multiculturalism and international law: essays in honour of Edward McWhinney, ed. by Yee, Sienho; Morin, Jacques-Yvan. Leiden; Boston: Martinus Nijhoff, 2009, p. 285-300.)

Keith, Kenneth: The ICJ: some reflections on my first year. (In: New Zealand Journal of Public and International Law, 2007, v. 5, no. 2, p. 201-210.)

Kempen, Bernhard and Zan, He: The practice of the International Court of Justice on provisional measures: the recent development. (In: Zeitschrift für ausländisches öffentliches Recht und Völkerrecht, 2009, v. 69, no. 3, p. 919-929.)

Khan, Muhammad Zafrulla: The International Court and the maintenance of world peace. (In: Pakistan Horizon, 2009, v. 62, no. 1, p. 73-80.)

Klatte, Saskia and Dörschner, Jonas: Die Rechtsprechung des Internationalen Gerichtshofes im Jahre 2007. (In: German Yearbook of International Law, 2007, v. 50, p. 589-627.)

Koh, Steven Arrigg: "Respectful consideration" after "Sanchez-Llamas v. Oregon": why the Supreme Court owes more to the International Court of Justice. (In: Cornell Law Review, 2007, v. 93, no. 1, p. 243-273.)

Kooijmans, Pieter H.: The ICJ in the 21st century: judicial restraint, judicial activism, or proactive judicial policy. (In: International and Comparative Law Quarterly, 2007, v. 56, no. 4, p. 741-754.)

Koroma, Abdul G.: Pacta sunt servanda in the jurisprudence of the International Court of Justice. (In: Medunarodnoe pravo XXI veka: k 80-letju professora doktora juridieskich nauk, Laureata Gosudarstvennoj premii Rossijskoj Federacii, zasluennogo dejatelja nauki Rossijskoj Federacii Igorja Ivanovia Lukauka, ed. by V. G. Butkevic. Kiev: Promeni, 2006, p. 473-487.)

Kreß, Claus: The International Court of Justice and the elements of the crime of genocide. (In: European Journal of International Law, 2007, v. 18, p. 619-629.)

Labrecque, Georges: Les différends territoriaux en Europe: jurisprudence de la Cour internationale de Justice. Paris: L'Harmattan, 2009. (Logiques juridiques.)

Le Boeuf, Romain: La saisine de la Cour internationale de Justice pour faits de guerre. (Dans: Revue belge de droit international, 2009, v. 42, no. 1, p. 52-77.)

Le Floch, Guillaume: Le sommet mondial de Tunis sur la société de l'information. (Dans: Annuaire français de droit international, 2005, v. 51, p. 464-486.) [I.C.J., p. 468, 469.]

Lee, Yoshiyuki: The concretization of "Petitum" in the International Court of Justice. (In: Kokusaiho Gaiko Zassi, 2009, v. 107, no. 4, p. 19-41.)

Llamzon, Aloysius P.: Jurisdiction and compliance in recent decisions of the International Court of Justice. (In: European Journal of International Law, 2007, v. 18, no. 5, p. 815-852.)

Locatelli, Liliana: Corte Internacional de Justiça. (Dans: Tribunais internacionais: mecanismos contemporâneos de solução de controvérsias, sous la dir. de Welber Barral. Florianópolis: Fundação Boiteux, 2004, p. 13-30.)

M'rad, Hatem: La Cour internationale de Justice et le recours à la force. (Dans: Le droit international à la croisée des chemins: force du droit et droit de la force: VIe rencontre internationale de la Faculté des Sciences juridiques, politiques et sociales de Tunis, 14, 15 et 16 avril 2004. Paris: Pedone, 2004, p. 207-231.) [C.P.J.I., p. 213; C.I.J., passim.]

Maia, Catherine: L'appel au droit impératif: le jus cogens dans la jurisprudence de la Cour internationale de Justice. (Dans: Les arrêts de la Cour internationale de Justice, sous la dir. de Charalambos Apostolidis. Dijon: Ed. universitaires de Dijon, 2005, p. 123-138.)

Manouvel, Mita: Les opinions séparées à la Cour internationale: un instrument de contrôle du droit international prétorien par les Etats. Paris [etc.]: L'Harmattan, 2005. (Logiques juridiques.)

Martel, Charles F.: Give peace a chance: how considering peace process obligations would have improved the rulings of the International Court of Justice and the Israeli Supreme Court on the Israeli security barrier. (In: Duke Journal of Comparative and International Law, 2007, v. 17, no. 2, p. 305-359.)

Mathias, Stephen: The 2006 judicial activity of the International Court of Justice. (In: American Journal of International Law, 2007, v. 101, no. 3, p. 602-615.)

Mathias, Stephen: The 2008 judicial activity of the International Court of Justice. (In: American Journal of International Law, 2009, v. 104, no. 3, p. 527-542.)

McKeever, David: The contribution of the International Court of Justice to the law on the use of force: missed opportunities or unrealistic expectations? (In: Nordic Journal of International Law, 2009, v. 78, p. 361-396.)

McWhinney, Edward: The International Court of Justice and international law-making: the judicial activism / self-restraint antinomy. (In: Chinese Journal of International Law, 2006, v. 5, p. 3-13.) [P.C.I.J., p. 3-8; I.C.J., passim.]

McWhinney, Edward: Separation or complementary of constitutional law-making powers of United Nations Security Council, General Assembly and International Court of Justice. (In: Studi di diritto internazionale in onore di Gaetano Arangio-Ruiz, ed. by Giovanni Battaglini; Paolo Benvenuti; Antonio Cassese; Giorgio Gaja. Napoli: Editoriale Scientifica, 2004, v. 1, p. 339-354.)

Merrills, John G.: Decisions of international courts and tribunals in 2002: the International Court of Justice in 2002: introductory note. (In: Global Community: Yearbook of International Law and Jurisprudence, 2003, v. 3, no. 1, p. 277-294.)

Merrills, John G.: The International Court of Justice in 2005: introductory note. (In: Global Community: Yearbook of International Law and Jurisprudence, 2006, v. 6, no. 1, p. 211-222.)

Morin, Delphine: La motivation des arrêts de la Cour internationale de Justice. (Dans: Les arrêts de la Cour internationale de Justice, sous la dir. de Charalambos Apostolidis. Dijon: Ed. universitaires de Dijon, 2005, p. 93-105.)

Murphy, Sean D. : The United States and the International Court of Justice : coping with antinomies. (In : The sword and the scales : the United States and international courts and tribunals, ed. by Romano, Cesare P. R.. New York, NY [etc.] : Cambridge University Press, 2009, p. 46-111.)

Nanopoulos, David K. : Remarques sur l'incidence d'une réforme du Conseil de sécurité sur la Cour internationale de Justice. (Dans : African Yearbook of International Law, 2005, v. 13, p. 215-233.)

Ndulo, Muna : The International Court of Justice. (In : From global apartheid to global village : Africa and the United Nations, ed. by Adekeye Adebajo. Scottsville : University of KwaZulu-Natal Press, 2009, p. 139-166.)

Nollkaemper, André : The role of domestic courts in the case law of the International Court of Justice. (In : Chinese Journal of International Law, 2006, v. 5, p. 301-322.) [P.C.I.J., p. 303, 305, 311, 314; I.C.J., passim.]

Oda, Shigeru : International Court of Justice : its myth and reality. (In : Japanese Yearbook of International Law, 2008, v. 51, p. 427-437.)

Oellers-Frahm, Karin : The International Court of Justice and Article 51 of the UN Charter. (In : Weltinnenrecht : liber amicorum Jost Delbrück, ed. by Dicke, Klaus ; Hobe, Stephan ; Meyn, Karl-Ulrich ; Peters, Anne ; Riedel, Eibe H. ; Schütz, Hans-Joachim ; Tietje, Christian. Berlin : Duncker & Humblot, 2005, p. 503-517.)

Oellers-Frahm, Karin : The part of the International Court of Justice in solving disputes between American States. (In : L'observateur des Nations Unies, 2008, v. 24, no. 1, p. 7-35.)

Olivier, Michèle Emily : The International Court of Justice and the development of international law over the past ten years. (In : South African Yearbook of International Law, 2004, v. 29, p. 23-31.)

Ollivier, Antoine et Savoie, Pierre-Olivier : La Cour internationale de Justice (C.I.J.). (Dans : Revue québécoise de droit international, 2004, v. 17, no. 2, p. 217-229.)

Orakhelashvili, Alexander : The International Court and "its freedom to select the ground upon which it will base its judgment". (In : International and Comparative Law Quarterly, 2007, v. 56, p. 171-184.) [P.C.I.J., p. 179-180; I.C.J., passim.]

Ouechtati, Sana : L'hétérogénéité dans la justice internationale : le cas de la Cour internationale de Justice. (Dans : Select proceedings of the European Society of International Law, sous la dir. d'Hélène Ruiz Fabri ; Rüdiger Wolfrum ; Jana Gogolin. 2008, v. 2, p. 412-440.)

Oumba, Parfait : La prise en compte de la règle de droit humanitaire dans la jurisprudence de la Cour internationale de Justice. (Dans : La responsabilité de protéger. Paris : Ed. des archives contemporaines, 2008, p. 69-83.)

Ovchar, Alexander: Estoppel in the jurisprudence of the ICJ: a principle promoting stability threatens to undermine it. (In: Bond Law Review, 2009, v. 21, no. 1, p. 124-158.)

Owada, Hisashi: The changing docket of the International Court of Justice and the significance of the change going forward. (In: Proceedings of the American Society of International Law, 2009, v. 103, p. 399-403.)

Owada, Hisashi: International environmental law and the International Court of Justice. (In: Iustum Aequum Salutare, 2006, v. 3-4, p. 5-32.) [I.C.J., passim.]

Palchetti, Paolo: The activity of the International Court of Justice in 2008. (In: Italian Yearbook of International Law, 2008, v. 18, p. 201-217.)

Palombino, Fulvio Maria: Les arrêts de la Cour internationale de Justice devant le juge interne. (Dans: Annuaire français de droit international, 2005, v. 51, p. 121-139.) [C.P.J.I., p. 124, 130; C.I.J., passim.]

Papa, Maria Irene: I rapporti tra la Corte internazionale di giustizia e il Consiglio di sicurezza. Padova: CEDAM, 2006. (Diritto internazionale e ordine mondiale; 10.) [I.C.J., passim.]

Patel, Bimal N.: International Court of Justice and India. (In: India and international law, ed. by Bimal N. Patel. Leiden; Boston: Martinus Nijhoff, 2005, p. 289-318.) [P.C.I.J., p. 312, 317-318; I.C.J., p. 289-318.]

Patel, Bimal N.: Recommendations on the enhancement of the role and effectiveness of the International Court of Justice and State practice: the gap between recommendation and practice (1917-2006). (In: Singapore Year Book of International Law, 2007, v. 11, p. 99-122.)

Paulson, Colter: Compliance with final judgments of the International Court of Justice since 1987. (In: American Journal of International Law, 2004, v. 98, no. 3, p. 434-461.)

Payandeh, Mehrdad: Die verfassungsrechtliche Stärkung der internationalen Gerichtsbarkeit: zur Bindung deutscher Gerichte an Entscheidungen des Internationalen Gerichtshofs. (In: Archiv des Völkerrechts, 2007, v. 45, no. 2, p. 244-257.)

Pellet, Alain: Article 38. (In: The Statute of the International Court of Justice: a commentary, by Andreas Zimmermann. Oxford: Oxford University Press, 2006, p. 677-792.)

Pellet, Alain: Lotus que de sottises on profère en ton nom ! Remarques sur le concept de souveraineté dans la jurisprudence de la Cour mondiale. (Dans: L'Etat souverain dans le monde d'aujourd'hui: mélanges en l'honneur de Jean-Pierre Puissochet, par Edwige Belliard. Paris: Pedone, 2008, p. 215-230.)

Pellet, Alain: Strengthening the role of the International Court of Justice as the principal judicial organ of the United Nations. (In: Law and Practice of International Courts and Tribunals, 2004, v. 3, no. 2, p. 159-180.)

Perrin, Delphine: La Cour internationale de Justice et l'Afrique. Aix-en-Provence : Presses universitaires d'Aix-Marseille – PUAM, 2005.

Petculescu, Ioana: The review of the United Nations Security Council decisions by the International Court of Justice. (In : Netherlands International Law Review, 2005, v. 52, no. 2, p. 167-195.)

Pinto, M. C. W.: Some thoughts on the International Court of Justice and the power of judicial review. (In : Reflections on emerging international law : essays in memory of late Subrata Roy Chowdhury. Bangalore : National Law School of India University, 2004, p. 127-133.)

Posner, Eric A.: The decline of the International Court of Justice. (In : International conflict resolution, ed. by Stefan Voigt ; Max Albert ; Dieter Schmidtchen. Tübingen : Mohr Siebeck, 2006, p. 111-142.)

Posner, Eric A. and Figueiredo, Miguel F. P. de : Is the International Court of Justice biased ? (In : Journal of Legal Studies, 2005, v. 34, p. 599-625.)

Post, Harry H. G.: The state of international law in The Hague : much activity at the International Court of Justice and some reflection on other matters. (In : Hague Justice Journal, 2009, v. 4, no. 1, p. 1-4.)

Quintana Aranguren, Juan José: La impugnación de la competencia en asuntos contenciosos ante la Corte Internacional de Justicia. (Dans : Anuario Colombiano de Derecho Internacional : ACDI, 2008, v. 1, no. 1, p. 12-48.)

Raimondo, Fabián O.: The International Court of Justice as a guardian of the unity of humanitarian law. (In : Leiden Journal of International Law, 2007, v. 20, no. 3, p. 593-611.)

Ranjeva, Raymond: La genèse d'un arrêt de la Cour internationale de Justice. (Dans : Les arrêts de la Cour internationale de Justice, sous la dir. de Charalambos Apostolidis. Dijon : Ed. universitaires de Dijon, 2005, p. 83-92.)

Rasilla del Moral, Ignacio de la: Nihil novum sub sole since the South West Africa cases ? On ius standi, the ICJ and community interests. (In : International Community Law Review, 2008, v. 10, no. 2, p. 171-197.) [I.C.J., passim.]

Remiro Brotons, Antonio: La Corte Internacional de Justicia come órgano judicial principal de las Naciones Unidas : algunas luces, algunas sombras. (Dans : Diálogos sobre la justicia internacional, sous la dir. de Bernardo Sepúlveda Amor. Monterrey : Comité Regional Norte de Cooperación con la UNESCO, 2009, p. 108-159.) [C.I.J., passim.]

Rosenne, Shabtai: The law and practice of the International Court, 1920-2005. Leiden : Nijhoff, 2006. 4th ed.

Rosenne, Shabtai: A role for the International Court of Justice in crisis management ? (In : Essays on international law and practice, by Shabtai Rosenne. Leiden ; Boston : Martinus Nijhoff, 2007, p. 35-63.)

Rosenne, Shabtai: The Secretary-General of the United Nations and the International Court of Justice. (In: Essays on international law and practice, by Shabtai Rosenne. Leiden; Boston: Martinus Nijhoff, 2007, p. 209-219.)

Runavot, Marie-Clotilde: La fonction consultative de la Cour internationale de Justice. (Dans: La fonction consultative des juridictions internationales, sous la dir. d'Alain Ondoua; David Szymczak. Paris: Pedone, 2009, p. 21-45.)

Sánchez Rodríguez, Luis Ignacio and López Martín, Ana Gemma: The travails of poor countries in gaining access to the International Court of Justice. (In: The legal practice in international law and European Community law: a Spanish perspective, ed. by Carlos Jiménez Piernas. Leiden; Boston: Martinus Nijhoff, 2007, p. 81-102.)

Sánchez, Victor M. (sous la dir. de): Corte Internacional de Justicia. (Dans: Derecho internacional público ed. Barcelona: Huygens, 2009, 343-350.)

Schrijver, Nico J.: From The Hague to San Francisco and back to The Hague: the ban on the use of force in international relations. (In: The Hague legal capital? Liber in honorem W. J. Deetman, ed. by Vriesendorp, David; Nelissen, Frans A.; Wladimiroff, Michaïl. The Hague: Hague Academic Press, 2008, p. 149-162.)

Schulte, Constanze: Compliance with decisions of the International Court of Justice. Oxford [etc.]: Oxford University Press, 2004. (International courts and tribunals.)

Selbmann, Frank: The International Court of Justice. (In: Mechanisms for the implementation of minority rights. Strasbourg: Council of Europe, 2004, p. 71-81.)

Shaw, Malcolm N.: The International Court, responsibility and remedies. (In: Issues of State responsibility before international judicial institutions, ed. by Malgosia A. Fitzmaurice; Dan Sarooshi. Oxford [etc.]: Hart, 2004, p. 19-33.)

Shi, Jiuyong: The role of the International Court of Justice in the peaceful settlement of international disputes. (In: Collected Courses of the Xiamen Academy of International Law, 2006, v. 1, p. 1-13.)

Simma, Bruno: How has Article 36(2) of the ICJ Statute fared? (In: A wiser century? Judicial dispute settlement, disarmament and the laws of war 100 years after the second Hague Peace Conference, by Thomas Giegerich. Berlin: Duncker & Humblot, 2009, p. 455-459.)

Smith, Adam M.: "Judicial nationalism" in international law: national identity and judicial autonomy at the I.C.J. (In: Texas International Law Journal, 2005, v. 40, no. 2, p. 197-231.)

Sorel, Jean-Marc: L'émergence de la personne humaine en droit international: l'exemple de la jurisprudence de la Cour internationale de Justice. (Dans: Studi di diritto internazionale in onore di Gaetano Arangio-

Ruiz, sous la dir. de Giovanni Battaglini; Paolo Benvenuti; Antonio Cassese; Giorgio Gaja. Napoli: Editoriale Scientifica, 2004, v. 3, p. 2169-2198.)

Spielmann, Dean: La Cour internationale de Justice et le droit de l'environnement. (Dans: Annuaire international des droits de l'homme, 2006, v. 1, p. 39-56.)

Statute of the International Court of Justice. (In: International courts and tribunals: selected documents and materials, ed. by Elin Hilwig; Relinde van Laar; Willem-Jan van der Wolf. Nijmegen: Wolf Legal Publishers (WLP), 2004, p. 255-267.)

Steinhardt, Ralph G.: The International Court of Justice at several crossroads. (In: Proceedings of the American Society of International Law, 2009, v. 103, p. 397-398.)

Sumner, Brian Taylor: Territorial disputes at the International Court of Justice. (In: Duke Law Journal, 2004, v. 53, no. 6, p. 1779-1812.)

Tams, Christian J.: Article 49. (In: The Statute of the International Court of Justice: a commentary, ed. by Andreas Zimmermann; Christian Tomuschat; Karin Oellers-Frahm. Oxford: Oxford University Press, 2006, p. 1099-1108.) [I.C.J., passim.]

Thirlway, Hugh: The contribution of the International Court of Justice to the development of international law. (In: WuDa guojifa yanjiang ji (diyi juan). Wuhan: Wuhan University Press, 2006, p. 32-49.)

Thirlway, Hugh: Injured and non-injured States before the International Court of Justice. (In: International responsibility today: essays in memory of Oscar Schachter, ed. by Maurizio Ragazzi. Leiden; Boston: Martinus Nijhoff, 2005, p. 311-328.) [P.C.I.J., p. 324; I.C.J., passim.]

Thirlway, Hugh: The law and procedure of the International Court of Justice 1960-1989 (supplement 2005) (parts one and two). (In: British Year Book of International Law, 2005, v. 76, p. 1-119.) [P.C.I.J., p. 16, 43-44, 51, 67, 71, 115, 117; I.C.J., passim.]

Thirlway, Hugh: The law and procedure of the International Court of Justice 1960-1989 (supplement 2009) (parts seven and eight). (In: British Year Book of International Law, 2009, v. 80, p. 13-216.)

Thirlway, Hugh: The law and procedure of the International Court of Justice 1960-1989: supplement, 2005: parts one and two. (In: British Year Book of International Law, 2005, v. 76, p. 1-118.)

Thirlway, Hugh: The law and procedure of the International Court of Justice 1960-1989: supplement, 2006: part three. (In: British Year Book of International Law, 2006, v. 77, p. 1-82.)

Thirlway, Hugh: The recommendations made by the International Court of Justice: a sceptical view. (In: International and Comparative Law Quarterly, 2009, v. 58, no. 1, p. 151-162.)

Tourard, Hélène: Le champ opératoire: nouvelles perspectives? (Dans: Les arrêts de la Cour internationale de Justice, sous la dir. de Charalambos Apostolidis. Dijon: Ed. universitaires de Dijon, 2005, p. 11-20.)

Tourme-Jouannet, Emmanuelle: Existe-t-il de grands arrêts de la Cour internationale de Justice? (Dans: Les arrêts de la Cour internationale de Justice, sous la dir. de Charalambos Apostolidis. Dijon: Ed. universitaires de Dijon, 2005, p. 169-197.)

Un dialogue à la Cour: actes du colloque CIJ/UNITAR organisé à l'occasion du soixantième anniversaire de la Cour internationale de Justice, au Palais de la Paix, les 10 et 11 avril 2006. La Haye – The Hague: Greffe de la Cour – Registry of the Court: UNITAR, 2006.

Vacas Fernández, Félix: La confianza de los estados de América latina en la Corte Internacional de Justicia en especial para la solución de controversias territoriales y marítimas. (Dans: Tribunales internacionales y espacio iberoamericano, sous la dir. de Fernández Liesa, Carlos R. Cizur Menor: Thomas Reuters, 2007, p. 215-229.)

Vasseur, Aude: L'influence des traditions juridiques nationales sur la motivation des décisions de la Cour internationale de Justice. (Dans: Revue belge de droit international, 2007, v. 40, no. 2, p. 474-501.)

Vereshchetin, Vladlen S.: Medunarodnyj Sud OON na novom tape. (In: Rossijskij eegodnik medunarodnogo prava, 2007, v, 2006, p. 13-22.)

Vereshchetin, Vladlen S.: On the expanding reach of the rulings of the International Court of Justice. (In: Völkerrecht als Wertordnung: Festschrift für Christian Tomuschat, ed. by Pierre-Marie Dupuy; Bardo Fassbender; Malcolm N. Shaw; Karl-Peter Sommermann. Kehl: N. P. Engel, 2006, p. 621-633.)

Vereshchetin, Vladlen S.: Praktika Mezdunarodnogo Suda OON po sporam, svjazannym s primeneniem sily. (In: Medunarodnoe pravo XXI veka: k 80-letju professora doktora juridieskich nauk, Laureata Gosudarstvennoj premii Rossijskoj Federacii, zasluennogo dejatelja nauki Rossijskoj Federacii Igorja Ivanovia Lukauka, ed. by V. G. Butkevic. Kiev: Promeni, 2006, p. 488-510.)

Verhoeven, Joe: Jura novit curia et le juge international. (Dans: Völkerrecht als Wertordnung: Festschrift für Christian Tomuschat, sous la dir. de Pierre-Marie Dupuy; Bardo Fassbender; Malcolm N. Shaw; Karl-Peter Sommermann. Kehl: N. P. Engel, 2006, p. 635-653.)

Vieira, Daniela Rodrigues et Brant, Leonardo Nemer Caldeira: Os desafios da Corte Internacional de Justiça na atualidade. (Dans: Anuário brasileiro de direito internacional, 2009, v. 1, p. 113-125.)

Viñuales, Jorge E.: The contribution of the International Court of Justice to the development of international environmental law: a contemporary assessment. (In: Fordham International Law Journal, 2008, v. 32, p. 232-258.)

Vukas, Budislav : Some provisions of the Statute of the International Court of Justice which deserve amendments. (In : Multiculturalism and international law : essays in honour of Edward McWhinney, ed. by Yee, Sienho ; Morin, Jacques-Yvan. Leiden ; Boston : Martinus Nijhoff, 2009, p. 277-283.)

Waters, Melissa A. : The U.S. Supreme Court and the International Court of Justice : what does respectful consideration mean ? (In : The sword and the scales : the United States and international courts and tribunals, ed. by Romano, Cesare P. R.. New York, NY [etc.] : Cambridge University Press, 2009, p. 112-130.)

Weckel, Philippe : La CIJ et la fragmentation du droit international. (Dans : L'influence des sources sur l'unité et la fragmentation du droit international : travaux du séminaire tenu à Palma, les 20-21 mai 2005, sous la dir. de Rosario Huesa Vinaixa ; Karel Wellens. Bruxelles : Bruylant, 2006, p. 167-185.)

Weeramantry, Christopher G. : "Internationaler Gerichtshof kann sehr rasch handeln" : Völkerrechtler Weeramantry über dir Macht der UN-Institutionen und die Kraft der weltöffentlichen Meinung. (In : Der Irak-Krieg und das Völkerrecht, ed. by Kai Ambos ; Jörg Arnold. Berlin : Berliner Wissenschafts-Verlag, 2004, p. 429-432.)

Weisburd, Arthur M. : The International Court of Justice and the concept of State practice. (In : University of Pennsylvania Journal of International Law, 2009, v. 31, no. 2, p. 295-372.)

Wellens, Karel C. : L'autorité des prononcés de la Cour internationale de Justice. (Dans : Droit du pouvoir, pouvoir du droit : mélanges offerts à Jean Salmon. Bruxelles : Bruylant, 2007, p. 729-781.)

Wittich, Stephan : The judicial functions of the International Court of Justice. (In : International law between universalism and fragmentation : festschrift in honour of Gerhard Hafner, ed. by Isabelle Buffard ; James Crawford ; Alain Pellet ; Stephan Wittich. Leiden [etc.] : Martinus Nijhoff, 2008, p. 981-1000.)

Yee, Sienho : Arguments for cleaning up Article 38(1)b) and (1)c) of the ICJ Statute. (In : Revista romana de drept international, 2007, v. 4, p. 33-43.)

Yee, Sienho : Notes on the International Court of Justice (part 2) : reform proposals regarding the International Court of Justice : a preliminary report for the international law associations study group on United Nations reform. (In : Chinese Journal of International Law, 2009, v. 8, no. 1, p. 181-189.)

Yee, Sienho : [Agora : the International Court of Justice at 60 (Part I):] Foreword. (In : Chinese Journal of International Law, 2006, v. 5, 1.)

Ziccardi Capaldo, Giuliana : Global trends and global court : the legitimacy of world governance. (In : Global Community : Yearbook of International Law and Jurisprudence, 2004, v. 4, no. 1, p. 127-169.) [P.C.I.J., p. 130-133, 141, 159; I.C.J., passim.]

Zimmermann, Andreas and Tomuschat, Christian and Oellers-Frahm, Karin (eds.): The Statute of the International Court of Justice: a commentary. Oxford [etc.]: Oxford University Press, 2006. (Oxford commentaries on international law.)

Zyberi, Gentian: The humanitarian face of the International Court of Justice: its contribution to interpreting and developing international human rights and humanitarian law rules and principles. [S.l.]: Intersentia, 2008. (School of human rights research series; 26.)

2. La Cour et les autres juridictions internationales
2. The Court and the other international tribunals

Amerasinghe, Chittharanjan Felix: Presumptions and inferences in evidence in international litigation. (In: Law and Practice of International Courts and Tribunals, 2004, v. 3, no. 3, p. 395-410.) [I.C.J., p. 397-401, 403, 405-408; P.C.I.J., p. 398-400.]

Anderson, David Heywood: The "disordered medley" of international tribunals and the coherence of international law. (In: International law and power: perspectives on legal order and justice: essays in honour of Colin Warbrick, ed. by Kaiyan Homi Kaikobad; Michael Bohlander. Leiden; Boston: Martinus Nijhoff, 2009, p. 389-400.)

Balcerzak, Michal: The doctrine of precedent in the International Court of Justice and the European Court of Human Rights. (In: Polish Yearbook of International Law, 2004, v. 27, p. 131-144.)

Battaglini, Giovanni: L'equità infra legem nei giudizi internazionali. (Dans: Studi di diritto internazionale in onore di Gaetano Arangio-Ruiz, sous la dir. de Giovanni Battaglini; Paolo Benvenuti; Antonio Cassese; Giorgio Gaja. Napoli: Editoriale Scientifica, 2004, v. 1, p. 265-293.)

Bellinger, John B. III: International courts and tribunals and the rule of law. (In: The sword and the scales: the United States and international courts and tribunals, ed. by Romano, Cesare P. R.. New York, NY [etc.]: Cambridge University Press, 2009, p. 1-11.)

Biehler, Gernot: International legal adjudication. (In: Procedures in international law, 2008, p. 243-293.) [P.C.I.J., p. 273, 281; I.C.J., p. 274-287, 289-293.]

Brown, Chester: A common law of international adjudication. Oxford: Oxford University Press, 2007. (International Courts and Tribunals.) [I.C.J., see index p. 297-2.]

Brown, Chester: The inherent powers of international courts and tribunals. (In: British Year Book of International Law, 2005, v. 76, p. 195-244.) [P.C.I.J., p. 201, 203-204, 209-210, 213, 216-217, 221, 224-226, 231, 233, 242; I.C.J., p. 195-197, 199-204, 208, 211-212, 214, 216-218, 220-228, 230-239, 242-244.]

Buergenthal, Thomas: Lawmaking by the ICJ and other international courts. (In: Proceedings of the Annual Meeting, 2009, v. 103, p. 403-406.)

Caflisch, Lucius: The law: substantive and procedural questions. (In: The Law and Practice of International Courts and Tribunals, 2008, v. 7, no. 3, p. 289-299.)

Cançado Trindade, A. A.: The relevance of international adjudication revisited: reflections on the need and quest for international compulsory jurisdiction. (In: Towards world constitutionalism: issues in the legal ordering of the world community, ed. by Ronald St. John Macdonald; Douglas M. Johnston. Leiden: Nijhoff, 2005, p. 515-542.) [P.C.I.J., p. 515, 517-518, 520, 530, 532; I.C.J., p. 515, 517-524, 529-530, 532-536, 538.]

Cervell Hortal, María José: El TIJ y los ríos internacionales, un desencuentro que no debería ser definitivo. (Dans: El agua como factor de cooperación y de conflicto en las relaciones internacionales contemporáneas: XXII Jornadas de la Asociación Española de Profesores de Derecho Internacional y Relaciones Internacionales, Murcia, 20 al 22 de septiembre de 2007, sous la dir. de Cesáreo Gutiérrez Espada. Murcia: Instituto Euromediterráneo del Agua, 2009, p. 173-181.)

Combs, Nancy and Nesser, Carl Magnus and Onwuamaegbu, Ucheora O. and Rees, Mark B. and Weisman, Jacqueline: International courts and tribunals. (In: International Lawyer, 2005, v. 39, no. 2, p. 259-278.)

Del Vecchio, Angela: Nuovi profili della giurisdizione internazionale. (Dans: Studi di diritto internazionale in onore di Gaetano Arangio-Ruiz, sous la dir. de Giovanni Battaglini; Paolo Benvenuti; Antonio Cassese; Giorgio Gaja. Napoli: Editoriale Scientifica, 2004, v. 2, p. 971-996.)

Dipla, Haritini: The role of the International Court of Justice and the International Tribunal for the Law of the Sea in the progressive development of the law of the sea. (In: Unresolved issues and new challenges to the law of the sea: time before and time after, ed. by Anastasia Strati; Maria Gavouneli; Nikolaos Skourtos. Leiden [etc.]: Martinus Nijhoff, 2006, p. 235-250.) [P.C.I.J., p. 235-236; I.C.J., passim.]

Gaja, Giorgio: Relationship with other courts and tribunals. (In: The Statute of the International Court of Justice: a commentary, ed. by Andreas Zimmermann; Christian Tomuschat; Karin Oellers-Frahm. Oxford: Oxford University Press, 2006, p. 533-544.) [I.C.J., passim.]

Guillaume, Gilbert: "La preuve devant les juridictions interétatiques à vocation universelle (CIJ et TIDM)" par Raphaële Rivier: commentaire. (Dans: La preuve devant les juridictions internationales, ed. by Hélène Ruiz Fabri; Jean-Marc Sorel. Paris: A. Pedone, 2007, p. 55-58.)

Guruswamy, Lakshman: Jurisdictional conflicts between international tribunals: a framework for adjudication & implementation. (In: Bringing new law to ocean waters, ed. by Caron, David D.; Scheiber, Harry N. Leiden; Boston: Martinus Nijhoff, 2004, p. 297-347.) [I.C.J., p. 320, 345-347.]

Het Vredespaleis: levend instituut van het internationaal recht. Den Haag: Carnegie Stichting, 2004.

Higgins, Rosalyn : A babel of judicial voices ? Ruminations from the bench. (In : International and Comparative Law Quarterly, 2006, v. 55, p. 791-804.)

Higgins, Rosalyn : International courts and tribunals : the challenges ahead (conference opening speech). (In : The Law and Practice of International Courts and Tribunals, 2008, v. 7, no. 3, p. 261-264.)

Higgins, Rosalyn : National courts and the International Court of Justice. (In : Tom Bingham and the transformation of the law : a liber amicorum, ed. by Mads Andenas ; Duncan Fairgrieve. New York : Oxford University Press, 2009, p. 405-417.)

Hilwig, Elin and Laar, Relinde van and Wolf, Willem-Jan van der (eds.) : International courts and tribunals : selected documents and materials. Nijmegen : Wolf Legal Publishers (WLP), 2004. [I.C.J., p. 255-302.]

Hosono, Junichi and Iwaishi, Junko : The 88th Hosinmaru case and the 53rd Tomimaru case : application to the International Tribunal for the Law of the Sea by Japan for prompt release. (In : Japanese Yearbook of International Law, 2008, v. 51, p. 438-453.)

Humbert, A. : L'attrait trompeur de la pluralité des juges internationaux : libres réflexions à partir de l'affaire du Liechtenstein devant la C.E.D.H. et la C.I.J. (Dans : Revue de droit international et de droit comparé, 2007, v. 84, p. 313-351.)

International Criminal Tribunal for Rwanda. (In : Global Community : Yearbook of International Law and Jurisprudence, 2006, v. 6, no. 1, p. 639-814.) [I.C.J., passim.]

International Criminal Tribunal for the Former Yugoslavia. (In : Global Community : Yearbook of International Law and Jurisprudence, 2006, v. 6, no. 1, p. 391-638.) [I.C.J., passim.]

Internationals courts and tribunals. (In : International Lawyer, 2005, v. 39, no. 2, p. 259-278.) [I.C.J., p. 259-269.]

Keith, Kenneth : The International Court of Justice : primus inter pares ? (In : International Organizations Law Review, 2008, v. 5, no. 1, p. 7-22.)

Krieken, Peter J. van and McKay, David (eds.) : The Hague : legal capital of the world. The Hague : T.M.C. Asser Press, 2005.

Linton, Suzannah and Kebede Tiba, Firew : The international judge in an age of multiple international courts and tribunals. (In : Chicago Journal of International Law, 2009, v. 9, no. 2, p. 407-470.)

McLachlan, Campbell : Lis pendens in international litigation. (In : Recueil des cours de l'Académie de droit international de La Haye, 2008, v. 336, p. 199-560.) [P.C.I.J., p. 210, 232, 236, 423, 456-458, 461, 462, 467, 468, 488; I.C.J., p. 211, 212, 217, 229, 230, 232, 233, 236, 414, 423, 425, 431-434, 445, 457, 459, 460, 462, 463, 465-469, 473-489, 505.]

Merrills, John G.: New horizons for international adjudication. (In: Global Community: Yearbook of International Law and Jurisprudence, 2006, v. 6, no. 1, p. 47-74.) [I.C.J., p. 47, 54, 66-74.]

Miller, Alicia Farrell: The preliminary reference procedure of the Court of Justice of the European Communities: a model for the ICJ? (In: Hastings International and Comparative Law Review, 2009, v. 32, no. 2, p. 669-692.)

Moulier, Isabelle: La notion de religion dans la jurisprudence des tribunaux pénaux internationaux et de la Cour internationale de Justice. (Dans: Religions et droit international humanitaire: colloque de Nice 18-19 juin 2007, sous la dir. d'Anne-Sophie Millet-Devalle. Paris: Pedone, 2008, p. 133-165.)

Movsesian, Mark L.: International commercial arbitration and international courts. (In: Duke Journal of Comparative and International Law, 2008, v. 18, no. 2, p. 423-448.)

Movsesian, Mark L.: Judging international judgments. (In: Journal of International Law, 2007, v. 48, no. 1, p. 65-118.)

Nanda, Ved P.: International environmental norms applicables to nuclear activities, with particular focus on decisions of international tribunals and international settlements. (In: Denver Journal of International Law and Policy, 2006, v. 35, p. 47-65.) [I.C.J., p. 54-60, 62.]

Nieto Navia, Rafael: Do international courts and tribunals have the power to "create" law? (In: Global Community: Yearbook of International Law and Jurisprudence, 2006, v. 6, no. 1, p. 75-103.) [P.C.I.J., p. 75, 78-80, 83, 85; I.C.J., p. 75, 77, 79-87, 89, 99, 101-102.]

Nieto Navia, Rafael: Do international courts and tribunals have the power to "create" law? (In: Global Community: Yearbook of International Law and Jurisprudence, 2006, v. 6, no. 1, p. 75-103.)

Niyungeko, Gérard: La preuve devant les juridictions internationales. Bruxelles: Bruylant: Université de Bruxelles, 2005. (Collection de droit international; 60.)

Oduntan, Gbenga: Africa before the international courts: the generational gap in international adjudication and arbitration. (In: Indian Journal of International Law, 2004, v. 44, no. 4, p. 701-748.) [I.C.J., p. 702-703, 707, 715, 718-720, 722-740, 742-743, 745-747.]

Oduntan, Gbenga: How international courts underdeveloped international law: political, economic and structural failings of international adjudication in relation to developing States. (In: African Journal of International and Comparative Law, 2005, v. 13, no. 2, p. 262-313.) [I.C.J., passim.]

Paulsson, Jan: International arbitration and the generation of legal norms: treaty arbitration and international law. (In: International arbitration 2006: back to basics? International arbitration congress, Montréal, 31 May – 3 June 2006, by Albert Jan Berg van den. Alphen aan den Rijn: Kluwer Law International, 2007, p. 879-889.)

Pellet, Alain: The anatomy of courts and tribunals. (In: The Law and Practice of International Courts and Tribunals, 2008, v. 7, no. 3, p. 275-287.)

Pellet, Alain: Remarques sur l'(in)efficacité de la Cour internationale de Justice et d'autres jurictions internationales. (Dans: Liber amicorum Jean-Pierre Cot: le procès international. Bruxelles: Bruylant, 2009, p. 193-213.)

Reddi, Vimalen J.: The ICC and the crime of aggression: a need to reconcile the prerogatives of the SC, the ICC and the ICJ. (In: International Criminal Law Review, 2008, v. 8, no. 4, p. 655-686.)

Rivier, Raphaële: La preuve devant les juridictions interétatiques à vocation universelle (C.I.J. et T.I.D.M.). (Dans: La preuve devant les juridictions internationales, sous la dir. d'Hélène Ruiz Fabri; Jean-Marc Sorel. Paris: A. Pedone, 2007, p. 9-54.)

Romano, Cesare P. R.: The shift from the consensual to the compulsory paradigm in international adjudication: elements for a theory of consent. (In: New York University Journal of International Law and Politics, 2007, v. 39, no. 4, p. 791-872.)

Rosenne, Shabtai: Article 95 of the Charter revisited. (In: Essays on international law and practice, by Shabtai Rosenne. Leiden; Boston: Martinus Nijhoff, 2007, p. 65-79.)

Rosenne, Shabtai: The International Criminal Court and the International Court of Justice: some points of contact. (In: The legal regime of the International Criminal Court: essays in honour of professor Igor Blishchenko: in memoriam Professor Igor Pavlovich Blishchenko (1930-2000), ed. by José Rodrigues Doria; Hans-Peter Gasser; M. Cherif Bassiouni. Leiden [etc.]: Martinus Nijhoff, 2009, p. 1003-1012.)

Rosenne, Shabtai: Provisional measures in international law: the International Court of Justice and the International Tribunal for the Law of the Sea. Oxford [etc.]: Oxford University Press, 2005. (International courts and tribunals.)

Rosenne, Shabtai: Some points of contact between the International Criminal Court and the International Court of Justice. (In: Essays on international law and practice, by Shabtai Rosenne. Leiden; Boston: Martinus Nijhoff, 2007, p. 353-366.)

Ruiz Fabri, Hélène et Sorel, Jean-Marc (sous la dir. de): La saisine des juridictions internationales. Paris: Pedone, 2006. (Contentieux international.)

Santulli, Carlo: Droit du contentieux international. Paris: Montchrestien, 2005. (Domat droit public.) [C.P.J.I. et C.I.J., passim.]

Schabas, William A.: International tribunals. (In: International protection of human rights: a textbook, ed. by Catarina Krause; Martin Scheinin. Turku/Âbo: Âbo Akademi University, Institute for Human Rights, 2009, p. 637-663.)

Shany, Yuval: Toward a general margin of appreciation doctrine in international law? (In: European Journal of International Law, 2005, v. 16, no. 5, p. 907-940.)

Shelton, Dinah: Form, function, and the powers of international courts. (In: Chicago Journal of International Law, 2009, v. 9, no. 2, p. 537-571.)

Simma, Bruno: Fragmentation in a positive light. (In: Michigan Journal of International Law, 2004, v. 25, no. 4, p. 845-847.) [I.C.J., p. 845-846.]

Swart, Mia: Gap-filling as law-making: the examples of the ad hoc international criminal tribunals. (In: Select Proceedings of the European Society of International Law, ed. by James Crawford; Sarah M. H. Nouwen. Oxford; Portland: Hart, 2008, v. 2, p. 313-330.) [I.C.J., p. 314-315, 320-321, 324-328.]

Thouvenin, Jean-Marc: The world court and the world order. (In: International law: issues and challenges. Gurgaon: Hope India Publications, 2009, v. 1, p. 127-138.)

Treves, Tullio: The International Tribunal for the Law of the Sea and other law of the sea jurisdictions (2007). (In: Italian Yearbook of International Law, 2007, v. 17, p. 175-193.) [I.C.J., p. 176-178, 187, 190-192.]

Treves, Tullio: Judicial lawmaking in an era of "proliferation" of international courts and tribunals: development or fragmentation of international law? (In: Developments of international law in treaty making, ed. by Rüdiger Wolfrum; Volker Röben. Berlin, [etc.]: Springer, 2005, p. 587-519.) [I.C.J., passim.]

Vasiliev, Sergey: Proofing the ban on "witness proofing": did the ICC get it right. (In: Criminal law forum, 2009, v. 20, no. 2-3, p. 193-261.) [I.C.J., p. 209-211, 222.]

Webb, Philippa: Scenarios of jurisdictional overlap among international courts. (In: Revue québécoise de droit international, 2006, v. 19, no. 2, p. 277-285.) [I.C.J., p. 277-282, 284-285.]

Yamagata, Hideo: Multiplication of international courts and tribunals. (In: Kokusaiho Gaiko Zassi, 2006, v. 104, no. 4, p. 37-62.) [P.C.I.J., p. 47-48, 51, 54; I.C.J., p. 38-39, 41, 47-48, 50, 52, 59, 61.]

You, Ki-Jun: Advisory opinions of the International Tribunal for the Law of the Sea: Article 138 of the rules of the Tribunal, revisited. (In: Ocean Development and International Law, 2008, v. 39, p. 360-371.)

Zarbiev, Fouad: Les politiques des vérités juridiques en droit international: propos autour d'une controverse interjuridictionnelle. (Dans: Finnish Yearbook of International Law, 2007, v. 18, p. 343-369.)

3. Cour permanente de Justice Internationale

3. Permanent Court of International Justice

Dörr, Oliver: Kompendium völkerrechtlicher Rechtsprechung: eine Auswahl für Studium und Praxis. Tübingen: Mohr Siebeck, 2004. (Mohr Lehrbuch.) [C.P.J.I. et C.I.J., passim.]

Generation Ukraine, Inc. v. Ukraine, [September 16, 2003]. (In: International Legal Materials, 2005, v. 44, no. 2, p. 404-464.) [P.C.I.J., p. 428, 457.]

Handeyside, Hugh: The Lotus principle in ICJ jurisprudence: was the ship ever afloat? (In: Michigan Journal of International Law, 2007, v. 29, no. 1, p. 71-94.)

Koskenniemi, Martti: International law in Europe: between tradition and renewal. (In: European Journal of International Law, 2005, v. 16, no. 1, p. 113-124.) [P.C.I.J., p. 116.]

Spiermann, Ole: International legal argument in the Permanent Court of International Justice: the rise of the international judiciary. Cambridge [etc.]: Cambridge University Press, 2005. (Cambridge studies in international and comparative law.) [P.C.I.J., passim.]

Spiermann, Ole: Judge Max Huber at the Permanent Court of International Justice. (In: European Journal of International Law, 2007, v. 18, no. 1, p. 115-133.) [P.C.I.J., passim; I.C.J., p. 122.]

Spiermann, Ole: Judge Wang Chung-hui at the Permanent Court of International Justice. (In: Chinese Journal of International Law, 2006, v. 5, p. 115-128.) [P.C.I.J., passim; I.C.J., p. 115, 116, 126.]

Supreme Court of Canada: R. v. Hape, 7 June 2007. (In: International Legal Materials, 2007, v. 46, p. 815-858.) [P.C.I.J., p. 831-832.]

B. ORGANISATION DE LA COUR

B. ORGANIZATION OF THE COURT

1. Composition de la Cour
1. Composition of the Court

López Contreras, Carlos: Las salas ad hoc de la Corte internacional de Justicia. (Dans: Anuario hispano-luso-americano de derecho internacional, 2007, 18, p. 445-465.)

Olarte Bacares, Diana Carolina: Les juges du tiers monde et les avis consultatifs de la Cour internationale de Justice. (Dans: International law: revista colombiana de derecho internacional, 2004, v, 2004, no. 3, p. 179-249.)

Rosenne, Shabtai: The President of the International Court of Justice. (In: Essays on international law and practice, by Shabtai Rosenne. Leiden; Boston: Martinus Nijhoff, 2007, p. 17-34.)

Smith, Adam M.: "Judicial nationalism" in international law: national identity and judicial autonomy at the I.C.J. (In: Texas International Law Journal, 2005, v. 40, no. 2, p. 197-231.)

2. Election des membres de la Cour
2. Election of Members of the Court

Bula-Bula, Sayeman: Sur les élections des juges à la Cour internationale de Justice du 6 novembre 2008 : la théorie et les réalités. (Dans : Revue de droit africain : doctrine et jurisprudence, 2009, v. 13, no. 49, p. 3-65.)

Coulée, Frédérique: Pratique française du droit international. (Dans : Annuaire français de droit international, 2005, v. 51, p. 802-842.) [C.I.J., p. 826, 831.]

Mackenzie, Ruth and Sands, Philippe: Judicial selection for international courts : towards common principles and practices. (In : Appointing judges in an age of judicial power : critical perspectives from around the world, ed. by Kate Malleson ; Peter H. Russell. Toronto : University of Toronto Press, 2006, p. 213-237.) [P.C.I.J., p. 217; I.C.J., p. 213-214, 216, 218-219, 222, 223, 224, 225-227.]

Martin, Pierre-Marie: La Cour internationale de Justice : des juges élus depuis l'origine. (Dans : La légitimité des juges : actes du colloque des 29-30 octobre 2003, Université Toulouse I, sous la dir. de Jacques Krynen ; Jacques Raibaut. Toulouse : Presses de l'Université des sciences sociales de Toulouse, 2004, p. 133-137.)

3. Juges *ad hoc*
3. Judges *ad hoc*

Charlesworth, Hilary: Judge ad hoc of the International Court of Justice. (In : Sir Ninian Stephen : a tribute, ed. by Timothy L. H. McCormack ; Cheryl Saunders. Carlton : Miegunyah Press, 2007, p. 176-189.)

Rosenne, Shabtai: Article 31 of the Statute of the International Court of Justice revisited : the judge ad hoc. (In : Essays on international law and practice, by Shabtai Rosenne. Leiden ; Boston : Martinus Nijhoff, 2007, p. 105-128.)

Scobbie, Iain: "Une hérésie en matière judiciaire" ? The role of the judge ad hoc in the International Court. (In : Law and Practice of International Court and Tribunals, 2005, v. 4, no. 3, p. 421-464.)

4. Biographies de juges
4. Biographies of judges

Adebowale, Olufolake Elias and Olusoji, Elias: Taslim Olawale Elias (1914-1991) : a biographical note. (In : Leiden Journal of International Law, 2008, v. 21, no. 2, p. 291-293.)

Ando, Nisuke and McWhinney, Edward and Wolfrum, Rüdiger and Reisman, William Michael: Presentation to his excellency Shigeru Oda : judge at the International Court of Justice : of the liber amicorum in his honor. (In : Zeitschrift für ausländisches öffentliches Recht und Völkerrecht, 2004, v. 64, no. 1, p. 145-162.)

Brus, Marcel : Judge Peter Kooijmans retires from the International Court of Justice. (In : Leiden Journal of International Law, 2006, v. 19, p. 699-717.)

Buergenthal, Thomas : Een gelukskind : van Auschwitz tot het Internationaal Gerechtshof. Leiden : Pensioen – En Uitkeringsradd, 2008.

Buergenthal, Thomas : Rosalyn Higgins : judge and president of the International Court of Justice (1995-2009). (In : Leiden Journal of International Law, 2009, v. 22, p. 703-713.)

Burci, Gian Luca and Schrijver, Nico J. : Carl-August Fleischhauer : his life and work. (In : Leiden Journal of International Law, 2006, v. 19, p. 693-698.)

Couvreur, Philippe : Charles de Visscher (1884-1973). (Dans : Juristas universales : vol. 4 : juristas del siglo XX : de Kelsen a Rawls, sous la dir. de Rafael Domingo. 2004, v. 4, p. 119-122.)

Higgins, Rosalyn : Sir Robert Yewdall Jennings 1913-2004. (In : British Year Book of International Law, 2004, v. 75, p. 1-5.)

Koskenniemi, Martti : Hersch Lauterpacht : (1897-1960). (In : Jurists uprooted : German-speaking émigré lawyers in twentieth century Britain, ed. by Beatson, Jack ; Zimmermann, Reinhard. Oxford : Oxford University Press, 2004, p. 601-661.) [P.C.I.J., p. 626-627, 650; I.C.J., p. 648-655, 658.]

Lim, Chin L. : Neither sheep nor peacocks : T. O. Elias and post-colonial international law. (In : Leiden Journal of International Law, 2008, v. 21, no. 2, p. 295-315.)

Obregón, Liliana : Noted for dissent : the international life of Alejandro Álvarez. (In : Leiden Journal of International Law, 2006, v. 19, p. 983-1016.) [I.C.J., p. 983, 1010.]

Punzhin, Sergey and Wiles, Nathalie : Judge Vereshchetin : a Russian scholar at the International Court of Justice. (In : Leiden Journal of International Law, 2006, v. 19, p. 719-740.)

Sandorski, Jan : Bohdan Winiarski : Prawo – Polityka – Sprawiedliwosc. Poznan : Wydawnictwo Poznanskie, 2004. (Magistri Nostri.)

Schindler, Dietrich : Max Huber : his life. (In : European Journal of International Law, 2007, v. 18, no. 1, p. 81-95.) [P.C.I.J., p. 81-82, 84, 89, 93; I.C.J., p. 88, 95.]

Spiermann, Ole : Judge Max Huber at the Permanent Court of International Justice. (In : European Journal of International Law, 2007, v. 18, no. 1, p. 115-133.) [P.C.I.J., passim; I.C.J., p. 122.]

Spiermann, Ole : Judge Wang Chung-hui at the Permanent Court of International Justice. (In : Chinese Journal of International Law, 2006, v. 5, p. 115-128.) [P.C.I.J., passim; I.C.J., p. 115, 116, 126.]

Thürer, Daniel: Max Huber: a portrait in outline. (In: European Journal of International Law, 2007, v. 18, no. 1, p. 69-80.) [P.C.I.J., p. 69; I.C.J., p. 69.]

Wierczyska, Karolina: Judge Manfred Lachs and his role in international adjudication. (In: Baltic Yearbook of International Law, 2007, v. 7, p. 113-119.)

Zobel, Katharina: Judge Alejandro Álvarez at the International Court of Justice (1946-1955): his theory of a "new international law" and judicial lawmaking. (In: Leiden Journal of International Law, 2006, v. 19, p. 1017-1040.) [P.C.I.J., p. 1017-1019, 1022-1023; I.C.J., passim.]

5. Greffe
5. Registry

Couvreur, Philippe: Aperçu du statut et des fonctions du greffier de la Cour internationale de Justice. (Dans: Les arrêts de la Cour internationale de Justice, sous la dir. de Charalambos Apostolidis. Dijon: Editions Universitaires de Dijon, 2005, p. 65-81.)

Couvreur, Philippe: The registrar of the International Court of Justice: status and functions. (In: The legal practice in international law and European Community law: a Spanish perspective, ed. by Carlos Jiménez Piernas. Leiden; Boston: Martinus Nijhoff, 2007, p. 7-61.)

Couvreur, Philippe: Una mirada hacia la Corte Internacional de Justicia: el papel de la Secretaría a través del procedimiento judicial ante la Corte Internacional de Justicia. (Dans: Cursos de derecho internacional y relaciones internacionales de Vitoria-Gasteiz, 2007, p. 175-204.)

International Court of Justice. Registry: Launch of the new website of the International Court of Justice. (In: The Law and Practice of International Courts and Tribunals, 2007, v. 6, no. 1, p. 355-356.)

Rosenboom, Annebeth: Publications of international courts and tribunals. (In: Law and Practice of International Courts and Tribunals, 2004, v. 3, no. 3, p. 543-551.) [I.C.J., p. 543, 546, 549.]

6. Finances, siège, privilèges et immunités
6. Finances, seat, privileges and immunities

Romano, Cesare P. R.: The price of international justice. (In: Law and Practice of International Courts and Tribunals, 2005, v. 4, no. 2, p. 281-328.) [I.C.J., p. 281, 284-288, 304-307, 310-311, 314-319.]

C. COMPÉTENCE DE LA COUR

C. JURISDICTION OF THE COURT

1. Etats admis à ester devant la Cour
1. States entitled to appear before the Court

De Schutter, Olivier et Gervasoni, Stéphane et Pingel, Isabelle et Angelet, Nicolas et La Rosa, Anne-Marie: [Le tiers à l'instance devant la

Cour de justice de l'Union européenne :] Débats. (Dans : Le tiers à l'instance devant les juridictions internationales, sous la dir. d'Hélène Ruiz Fabri ; Jean-Marc Sorel. Paris : A. Pedone, 2005, p. 115-119.)

Ruiz Fabri, Hélène et Sorel, Jean-Marc (sous la dir. de) : Le tiers à l'instance devant les juridictions internationales. Paris : A. Pedone, 2005. (Collection contentieux international ; 3.)

Treves, Tullio : [Le tiers à l'instance devant les juridictions internationales à vocation universelle (CIJ et TIDM) :] Commentaire. (Dans : Le tiers à l'instance devant les juridictions internationales, sous la dir. d'Hélène Ruiz Fabri ; Jean-Marc Sorel. Paris : A. Pedone, 2005, p. 73-78.)

2. Compétence de la Cour en matière contentieuse
2. Jurisdiction of the Court in contentious cases

Couvreur, Philippe : Le règlement juridictionnel. (Dans : Le processus de délimitation maritime : étude d'un cas fictif : colloque international, Monaco, 27-29 mars 2003, sous la dir. de Laurent Lucchini. Paris : Pedone, 2004, p. 349-388.)

Hammer, Dan : Allowing genocide ? An analysis of Armed Activities on the Territory of the Congo jurisdictional reservations and the legitimacy of the International Court of Justice. (In : Minnesota Journal of International Law, 2007, v. 16, p. 495-523.)

Orakhelashvili, Alexander : The concept of international judicial jurisdiction : a reappraisal. (In : Law and Practice of International Courts and Tribunals, 2003, v. 2, no. 3, p. 501-550.)

Protocol against the Illicit Manufacturing of and Trafficking in Firearms, Their Parts and Components and Ammunition, supplementing the United Nations Convention against Transnational Organized Crime. New York, 31 May 2001. (Dans : United Nations Treaty Series, 2005, v, 2326, p. 211-308.) [I.C.J., "Article 16".]

Rosenne, Shabtai : The framework agreement as the basis for the jurisdiction of the International Court of Justice and some problems of language. (In : Essays on international law and practice, by Shabtai Rosenne. Leiden ; Boston : Martinus Nijhoff, 2007, p. 161-170.)

Rosenne, Shabtai : The law and practice of the International Court, 1920-2005 : volume II : jurisdiction. Leiden ; Boston : Martinus Nijhoff, 2006. 4th ed.

Rosenne, Shabtai : Unilateral applications to the International Court of Justice : history revisited. (In : Essays on international law and practice, by Shabtai Rosenne. Leiden ; Boston : Martinus Nijhoff, 2007, p. 171-195.)

Sheppard, Audley : The jurisdictional threshold of a prima-facie case. (In : The Oxford handbook of international investment law, ed. by Peter Muchlinski ; Federico Ortino ; Christoph H. Schreuer. Oxford [etc.] : Oxford University Press, 2008, p. 932-961.)

Torres Bernárdez, Santiago: Presentation from the standpoint of Spanish law, on the legal process available to parties in the contentious procedure of the International Court of Justice. (In: The legal practice in international law and European Community law: a Spanish perspective, ed. by Carlos Jiménez Piernas. Leiden; Boston: Marinus Nijhoff, 2007, p. 63-80.)

Vannieuwenhuyse, Gauthier: Bringing a dispute concerning ICSID cases and the ICSID Convention before the International Court of Justice. (In: The Law and Practice of International Courts and Tribunals, 2009, v. 8, no. 1, p. 115-141.)

Versan, Rauf: Milletlerarasi adalet divaninin forum prorogatum ilkesine göre yetki kazanmasi. (In: Milletlerarasi hukuk ve milletlerarasi özel hukuk bülteni, 2004, v. 24, no. 1-2, p. 767-772.)

Voeffray, François: L'actio popularis ou la défense de l'intérêt collectif devant les juridictions internationales. Paris: Presses Universitaires de France, 2004. [C.I.J. et C.P.J.I., p. 38, 40, 45-106, 113-115, 140, 221, 240-243, 248-249, 253, 255, 275, 304-305, 308, 314-318, 320, 332, 334, 337-358, 366-370, 373, 375.]

Wyler, Eric: La détermination par la Cour de sa propre compétence. (Dans: Les arrêts de la Cour internationale de Justice, sous la dir. de Charalambos Apostolidis. Dijon: Ed. universitaires de Dijon, 2005, p. 21-43.)

3. Acceptation de la juridiction obligatoire de la Cour
3. Acceptance of the compulsory jurisdiction of the Court

Alexandrov, Stanimir A.: The compulsory jurisdiction of the International Court of Justice: how compulsory is it? (In: Chinese Journal of International Law, 2006, v. 5, p. 29-38.) [P.C.I.J., p. 30, 32, 33; I.C.J., passim.]

Australian practice in international law 2003: jurisdiction: International Court of Justice. (In: Australian Yearbook of International Law, 2005, v. 24, 349.)

Eick, Christophe N.: Die Anerkennung der obligatorischen Gerichtsbarkeit des Internationalen Gerichtshofs durch Deutschland. (In: Zeitschrift für ausländisches öffentliches Recht und Völkerrecht, 2008, v. 68, no. 3, p. 763-777.)

Kolb, Robert: La dénonciation avec effet immédiat de déclarations facultatives établissant la compétence de la Cour internationale de Justice. (Dans: Promoting justice, human rights and conflict resolution through international law: liber amicorum Lucius Caflisch, sous la dir. de Marcelo G. Kohen. Leiden: Martinus Nijhoff, 2007, p. 875-890.)

Kolb, Robert: The scope "ratione materiae" of the compulsory jurisdiction of the ICJ. (In: The UN Genocide Convention: a commentary, ed. by Paola Gaeta. Oxford [etc.]: Oxford University Press, 2009, p. 442-470.)

Lamm, Vanda: Declarations accepting the compulsory jurisdiction of the International Court of Justice. (In: Acta Juridica Hungarica, 2004, v. 45, no. 1-2, p. 25-48.)

Merrills, John G.: Does the optional clause still matter? (In: International law and power: perspectives on legal order and justice: essays in honour of Colin Warbrick, ed. by Kaiyan Homi Kaikobad; Michael Bohlander. Leiden; Boston: Martinus Nijhoff, 2009, p. 431-454.)

Mitchell, Sara McLaughlin and Powell, Emilia Justyna: Legal systems and variance in the design of commitments to the International Court of Justice. (In: Conflict Management and Peace Science, 2009, v. 26, no. 2, p. 164-190.) [P.C.I.J., passim.]

Piotrowicz, Ryszard: Reservations about jurisdiction at the International Court of Justice. (In: Australian Law Journal, 2006, v. 80, p. 351-355.)

Powell, Emilia Justyna and McLaughlin Mitchel, Sara: The International Court of Justice and the world's three legal systems. (In: Journal of Politics, 2007, v. 69, no. 2, p. 397-415.)

Tams, Christian J.: "The Federation shall accede to agreements providing for general, comprehensive and compulsory international arbitration": the German optional clause declaration of 1 May 2008. (In: German Yearbook of International Law, 2008, v. 51, p. 391-416.)

Tams, Christian J.: Unterwerfung mit Einschränkungen. (In: Vereinte Nationen, 2008, v. 56, no. 4, 153.)

Thompson-Barrow, Cheryl: Member States of the Commonwealth: their relationship with the International Court of Justice. (In: Commonwealth Law Bulletin, 2007, v. 33, no. 3, p. 423-428.)

Wood, Michael C.: The United Kingdom's acceptance of the compulsory jurisdiction of the International Court. (In: Dog fred er ej det bedste ...: festskrift til Carl August Fleischer pa° hans 70-a°rsdag 26. august 2006, ed. by Ole Kristian Fauchald; Henning Jakhelln; Aslak Syse. Oslo: Universitetsforlaget, 2006, p. 621-643.)

4. Autres instruments régissant la compétence de la Cour en matière contentieuse

4. Other texts governing the contentious jurisdiction of the Court

Convention de Stockholm sur les polluants organiques persistants (avec annexes). Stockholm, 22 mai 2001. (Dans: Recueil des Traités de l'ONU, 2004, v, 2256, p. 119-403.) [C.I.J., "Article 18".]

Kolb, Robert: The compromissory clause of the Convention. (In: The UN Genocide Convention: a commentary, ed. by Paola Gaeta. Oxford [etc.]: Oxford University Press, 2009, p. 407-424.)

O'Neill, Timothy: Dispute settlement under the Rome Statute of the International Criminal Court: Article 119 and the possible role of the International Court of Justice. (In: Chinese Journal of International Law, 2006, v. 5, p. 67-78.) [P.C.I.J., p. 70; I.C.J., passim.]

United Nations Convention against Corruption. (In: United Nations Treaty Series, 2005, v, 2349, no. 42146, p. 41-367.) [I.C.J., "Article 66, § 2".]

5. Compétence de la Cour en matière consultative
5. Advisory jurisdiction of the Court

Nagata, Takahide: Judicial activism in exercising advisory function by the International Court of Justice and "Eastern Carelia" principle. (In: Kokusaiho Gaiko Zassi, 2009, v. 107, no. 4, p. 42-68.)

Observatoire des mutations institutionnelles et juridiques de Limoges: La fonction consultative des juridictions internationales. Paris: Pedone, 2009. (Contentieux international.)

D. PROCÉDURE DEVANT LA COUR

D. PROCEDURE BEFORE THE COURT

Guillaume, Gilbert: De l'emploi des langues à la Cour internationale de Justice. (Dans: Droit du pouvoir, pouvoir du droit: mélanges offerts à Jean Salmon. Bruxelles: Bruylant, 2007, p. 1277-1292.)

Mahiou, Ahmed: La justice internationale et les droits de l'homme: brèves remarques. (Dans: Völkerrecht als Wertordnung: Festschrift für Christian Tomuschat, sous la dir. de Pierre-Marie Dupuy; Bardo Fassbender; Malcolm N. Shaw; Karl-Peter Sommermann. Kehl: N. P. Engel, 2006, p. 227-244.)

Rosenne, Shabtai: The general list of the International Court of Justice. (In: Essays on international law and practice, by Shabtai Rosenne. Leiden; Boston: Martinus Nijhoff, 2007, p. 197-208.)

Rules of Court: version of 5 December 2000. (In: International courts and tribunals: selected documents and materials, ed. by Elin Hilwig; Relinde van Laar; Willem-Jan van der Wolf. Nijmegen: Wolf Legal Publishers (WLP), 2004, p. 269-299.)

Savadogo, Louis: Le recours des juridictions internationales à des experts. (Dans: Annuaire français de droit international, 2004, v. 50, p. 231-258.) [C.P.J.I., p. 234, 238, 244, 246-247, 254-255, 257; C.I.J., p. 232-236, 238-239, 242-248, 250-257.]

1. Procédure contentieuse en général
1. Contentious procedure in general

Aurescu, Bogdan: Organizational and procedural aspects of the institution of State agent before the ECHR and ICJ: some Romanian perspectives. (In: Chinese Journal of International Law, 2007, v. 6, no. 2, p. 363-377.)

Bedjaoui, Mohammed: L'égalité des Etats dans le procès international, un mythe? (Dans: Liber amicorum Jean-Pierre Cot: le procès international. Bruxelles: Bruylant, 2009, p. 1-27.)

Brant, Leonardo Nemer Caldeira: O processo de revisão da sentença perante a Corte Internacional de Justiça à luz de suas últimas decisões (Iugoslávia vs. Bósnia e El Salvador vs. Honduras). (Dans: Anuario brasileiro de direito internacional, 2007, v. 1, p. 10-31.)

Coulée, Frédérique: Le principe du contradictoire devant la Cour internationale de Justice et le Tribunal international du droit de la mer. (Dans: Le principe du contradictoire devant les juridictions internationales, sous la dir. d'Hélène Ruiz-Fabri; Jean-Marc Sorel. Paris: Pedone, 2004, p. 7-33.)

Couvreur, Philippe: Una mirada hacia la Corte Internacional de Justicia: el papel de la Secretaría a través del procedimiento judicial ante la Corte Internacional de Justicia. (Dans: Cursos de derecho internacional y relaciones internacionales de Vitoria-Gasteiz, 2007, p. 175-204.)

Crawford, James: Advocacy before the International Court of Justice and other international tribunals in State-to-State cases. (In: The art of advocacy in international arbitration, ed. by Bishop, R. Doak. Huntington: Juris Publishing, 2004, p. 11-38.)

Franck, Thomas M.: The international judge and the principled imperative. (In: Weltinnenrecht: liber amicorum Jost Delbrück, ed. by Dicke, Klaus; Hobe, Stephan; Meyn, Karl-Ulrich; Peters, Anne; Riedel, Eibe H.; Schütz, Hans-Joachim; Tietje, Christian. Berlin: Duncker & Humblot, 2005, p. 267-278.) [I.C.J., passim.]

Galley, Jean-Baptiste Kossi: Le principe de la contradiction dans le contentieux international. (Dans: Revue de la recherche juridique: droit prospectif, 2004, v. 29, no. 4, p. 2523-2547.)

Galley, Jean-Baptiste Kossi: Le principe de la contradiction dans le contentieux international. (Dans: Revue de droit international, de sciences diplomatiques et politiques, 2007, v. 85, p. 231-267.) [C.I.J., passim.]

Ginsburg, Tom and McAdams, Richard H.: Adjudicating in anarchy: an expressive theory of international dispute resolution. (In: William and Mary Law Review. 2003-2004, v. 45, no. 4, p. 1229-1339.) [P.C.I.J., p. 1291-1292, 1294, 1297; I.C.J., p. 1229-1230, 1233, 1237-1238, 1288, 1291, 1301, 1303-1330.]

Joyce, Daniel: Fact-finding evidence at the International Court of Justice: systemic crisis, change, or more of the same? (In: Finnish Yearbook of International Law, 2007, v. 18, p. 283-306.)

Kamto, Maurice: Les moyens de preuve devant la Cour internationale de Justice à la lumière de quelques affaires récentes portées devant elle. (Dans: German Yearbook of International Law, 2006, v. 49, p. 259-292.)

Kaufmann, Inka: Wiederaufnahme von Verfahren vor dem Internationalen Gerichtshof. Baden-Baden: Nomos, 2005. (Völkerrecht und Außenpolitik; 67.)

Neff, Stephen C.: In search of clarity: non liquet and international law. (In: International law and power: perspectives on legal order and justice: essays in honour of Colin Warbrick, ed. by Kaiyan Homi Kaikobad; Michael Bohlander. Leiden; Boston: Martinus Nijhoff, 2009, p. 63-83.)

O'Brien, Killian: Representation in the doctrine of estoppel in international law. (In: Irish Yearbook of International Law, 2008, v. 3, p. 69-90.) [I.C.J., passim.]

Palchetti, Paolo: Novità in tema di partecipazione delle organizzazioni internazionali ai procedimenti davanti alla Corte internazionale di guistizia. (Dans: Rivista di diritto internazionale, 2006, v. 89, no. 1, 122-126).

Pellet, Alain: Remarks on proceedings before the International Court of Justice. (In: Law and Practice of International Courts and Tribunals, 2006, v. 5, p. 163-182.)

Quintana Aranguren, Juan José: Procedure before the ICJ: what is the exact date of the closure of the written phase of proceedings? (In: Law and Practice of International Courts and Tribunals, 2008, v. 7, p. 193-203.)

Remiro Brotons, Antonio: The international legal consultancy of governments from the outside. (In: The legal practice in international law and European Community law: a Spanish perspective, ed. by Carlos Jiménez Piernas. Leiden; Boston: Martinus Nijhoff, 2007, p. 488-520.)

Riddell, Anna and Plant, Brendan: Evidence before the International Court of Justice. London: British Institute of International and Comparative Law, 2009.

Riddell, Anna: Scientific evidence in the International Court of Justice: problems and possibilities. (In: Finnish Yearbook of International Law, 2009, v. 20, p. 229-258.)

Rose, Cecily: Questioning the silence of the bench: reflections on oral proceedings at the International Court of Justice. (In: Journal of Transnational Law and Policy, 2008, v. 18, no. 1, p. 47-64.)

Rosenne, Shabtai: Article 27 of the Statute of the International Court of Justice revisited. (In: Essays on international law and practice, by Shabtai Rosenne. Leiden; Boston: Martinus Nijhoff, 2007, p. 81-95.)

Rosenne, Shabtai: Article 59 of the Statute of the International Court of Justice revisited. (In: Essays on international law and practice, by Shabtai Rosenne. Leiden; Boston: Martinus Nijhoff, 2007, p. 129-159.)

Rosenne, Shabtai: Controlling interlocutory aspects of proceedings in the International Court of Justice. (In: Essays on international law and practice, by Shabtai Rosenne. Leiden; Boston: Martinus Nijhoff, 2007, p. 251-266.)

Rosenne, Shabtai: Fact-finding before the International Court of Justice. (In: Essays on international law and practice, by Shabtai Rosenne. Leiden; Boston: Martinus Nijhoff, 2007, p. 235-250.)

Rosenne, Shabtai: The International Court of Justice: new practice directions. (In: Law and Practice of International Courts and Tribunals, 2009, v. 8, p. 171-180.)

Rosenne, Shabtai: International Court of Justice: practice direction on agents, counsel and advocates. (In: Essays on international law and practice, by Shabtai Rosenne. Leiden; Boston: Martinus Nijhoff, 2007, p. 97-104.)

Rosenne, Shabtai: The law and practice of the International Court, 1920-2005: volume III: procedure. Leiden; Boston: Martinus Nijhoff, 2006. 4th ed.

Rosenne, Shabtai: Visit to the site by the International Court. (In: Essays on international law and practice, by Shabtai Rosenne. Leiden; Boston: Martinus Nijhoff, 2007, p. 221-233.)

Sorel, Jean-Marc et Lagrange, Evelyne et Treves, Tullio et Sainte-Rose, Jerry et Ruiz Fabri, Hélène: [Le tiers à l'instance devant les juridictions internationales à vocation universelle (CIJ et TIDM):] Débats. (Dans: Le tiers à l'instance devant les juridictions internationales, sous la dir. d'Hélène Ruiz Fabri; Jean-Marc Sorel. Paris: A. Pedone, 2005, p. 79-82.)

Stern, Brigitte: Commentary on substantive and procedural questions. (In: The Law and Practice of International Courts and Tribunals, 2008, v. 7, no. 3, p. 301-311.)

Tams, Christian J.: Article 50. (In: The Statute of the International Court of Justice: a commentary, ed. by Andreas Zimmermann; Christian Tomuschat; Karin Oellers-Frahm. Oxford [etc.]: Oxford University Press, 2006, p. 1109-1118.)

Teitelbaum, Ruth: Recent fact-finding developments at the International Court of Justice. (In: Law and Practice of International Courts and Tribunals, 2007, v. 6, p. 119-158.)

Thirlway, Hugh: The drafting of ICJ decisions: some personal recollections and observations. (In: Chinese Journal of International Law, 2006, v. 5, p. 15-28.)

Thirlway, Hugh: The law and procedure of the International Court of Justice 1960-1989 (supplement 2006) (part three). (In: British Year Book of International Law, 2006, v. 77, p. 1-82.)

Thirlway, Hugh: The law and procedure of the International Court of Justice 1960-1989 (supplement 2007) (parts four, five and six). (In: British Year Book of International Law, 2007, v. 78, p. 17-175.)

Watts, Arthur: The I.C.J.'s practice directions of 30 July 2004. (In: Law and Practice of International Courts and Tribunals, 2004, v. 3, no. 3, p. 385-394.)

Wittich, Stephan: Das Feststellungsurteil im Verfahren vor dem Internationalen Gerichtshof. (In: Archiv des Völkerrechts, 2006, v. 44, no. 1, p. 1-32.)

Yee, Sienho: Article 40. (In: The Statute of the International Court of Justice: a commentary, ed. by Andreas Zimmermann; Christian Tomuschat;

Karin Oellers-Frahm. Oxford [etc.]: Oxford University Press, 2006, p. 849-922.)

Yee, Sienho: Notes on the International Court of Justice (part 1): arguments for the publication of the rule-making materials. (In: Chinese Journal of International Law, 2008, v. 7, p. 691-698.)

Yee, Sienho: Notes on the International Court of Justice (Part 3): rule-making at the Court: integration, uniformization, keeping existing article numbers and giving public notice. (In: Chinese Journal of International Law, 2009, v. 8, no. 3, p. 681-694.)

2. Procédures incidentes
2. Incidental procedures

Bekker, Peter H. F.: Provisional measures in the recent practice of the International Court of Justice. (In: International Law FORUM du droit international, 2005, v. 7, p. 24-32.) [P.C.I.J., p. 24; I.C.J., passim.]

Chappez, Jean: Les mesures conservatoires devant la Cour internationale de Justice. (Dans: Les arrêts de la Cour internationale de Justice, sous la dir. de Charalambos Apostolidis. Dijon: Ed. universitaires de Dijon, 2005, p. 45-62.)

Distefano, Giovanni: La demande reconventionelle au fil des textes régissant le fonctionnement de la Cour de La Haye et de sa jurisprudence. (Dans: Schweizerische Zeitschrift für internationales und europäisches Recht, 2008, v. 18, no. 1-2, p. 243-263.)

Fortier, Yves: Interim measures: an arbitrator's provisional views. (In: Contemporary issues in international arbitration and mediation: the Fordham papers 2008, ed. by Arthur W. Rovine. Leiden; Boston: Martinus Nijhoff, 2009, v. 2, p. 47-57.)

Gautier, Philippe: Mesures conservatoires, préjudice irréparable et protection de l'environnement. (Dans: Liber amicorum Jean-Pierre Cot: le procès international. Bruxelles: Bruylant, 2009, p. 131-154.)

González Napolitano, Silvina S.: Obligatoriedad y eficacia de las medidas provisionales en la jurisdicción internacional. Buenos Aires: [s.n.], 2008.

Gros Espiell, Héctor: Las medidas cautelares (provisionales) en los tribunales internacionales: el caso de la Corte Internacional de Justicia y el medio ambiente. (Dans: Anuario hispano-luso-americano de derecho internacional, 2007, v. 18, p. 383-403.)

Kolb, Robert: Note on new international case-law concerning the binding character of provisional measures. (In: Nordic Journal of International Law, 2005, v. 74, no. 1, p. 117-129.) [I.C.J., p. 118-119, 123-126, 128-129; P.C.I.J., p. 128.]

Lagrange, Evelyne: Le tiers à l'instance devant les juridictions internationales à vocation universelle (CIJ et TIDM). (Dans: Le tiers à l'instance devant les juridictions internationales, sous la dir. d'Hélène Ruiz Fabri ; Jean-Marc Sorel. Paris : A. Pedone, 2005, p. 9-72.)

Mendelson, Maurice H. : State responsibility for breach of interim protection orders of the International Court of Justice. (In : Issues of State responsibility before international judicial institutions, ed. by Malgosia A. Fitzmaurice ; Danesh Sarooshi. Oxford : Hart, 2004, p. 35-53.)

Palchetti, Paolo : The power of the International Court of Justice to indicate provisional measures to prevent the aggravation of a dispute. (In : Leiden Journal of International Law, 2008, v. 21, p. 623-642.)

Parlett, Kate : A role for the I.C.J. in the ongoing armed conflict : provisional measures. (In : Cambridge Law Journal, 2009, v. 68, p. 4-6.)

Pasqualucci, Jo M. : Interim measures in international human rights : evolution and harmonization. (In : Vanderbilt Journal of Transnational Law, 2005, v. 38, no. 1, p. 1-49.)

Rosenne, Shabtai : Counter-claims in the International Court of Justice. (In : Essays on international law and practice, by Shabtai Rosenne. Leiden ; Boston : Martinus Nijhoff, 2007, p. 267-293.)

Rosenne, Shabtai : Provisional measures in international law : the International Court of Justice and the International Tribunal for the Law of the Sea. Oxford [etc.] : Oxford University Press, 2005. (International courts and tribunals.)

Sainte-Rose, Jerry : Remarques d'ensemble. (Dans : Le tiers à l'instance devant les juridictions internationales, sous la dir. d'Hélène Ruiz Fabri ; Jean-Marc Sorel. Paris : A. Pedone, 2005, p. 245-247.)

Sakai, Hironobu : New developments of the orders on provisional measures by the International Court of Justice. (In : Japanese Yearbook of International Law, 2009, v. 52, p. 231-280.)

Treves, Tullio : Les mesures conservatoires au Tribunal du droit de la mer et à la Cour internationale de Justice : contribution au dialogue entre cours et tribunaux internationaux. (Dans : Liber amicorum Jean-Pierre Cot : le procès international. Bruxelles : Bruylant, 2009, p. 341-348.)

Weckel, Philippe : Les mesures conservatoires devant les juridictions internationales de caractère universel. (Dans : Mesures conservatoires et droits fondamentaux, sous la dir. de Gérard Cohen-Jonathan ; Jean-Francois Flauss. Bruxelles : Bruylant ; Nemesis, 2005, p. 33-53.) [C.I.J., p. 34, 36, 37-41, 44-52.]

Wong, Jarrod : The issuance of interim measures in international disputes : a proposal requiring a reasonable possibility of success on the underlying merits. (In : Georgia Journal of International and Comparative Law, 2005, v. 33, no. 3, p. 605-620.)

Yee, Sienho: A proposal for formalizing the "no case exists" objections procedure at the International Court of Justice. (In: Chinese Journal of International Law, 2005, v. 4, p. 393-416.)

3. Procédure consultative
3. Advisory procedure

Aljaghoub, Mahasen M.: The advisory function of the International Court of Justice: 1946-2005. Berlin [etc.]: Springer, 2006.

Biesen, A. H. J. van den: The role of the I.C.J. in the international system and compliance with its judgments. (In: Freedom from nuclear weapons through legal accountability and good faith: conference report, ed. by George Farebrother. Nottingham: Spokesman; World Court Project, 2007, p. 62-64.)

Boisson de Chazournes, Laurence: La procédure consultative de la Cour internationale de Justice et la promotion de la règle de droit: remarques sur les conditions d'accès et de participation. (Dans: Völkerrecht als Wertordnung: Festschrift für Christian Tomuschat, sous la dir. de Pierre-Marie Dupuy; Bardo Fassbender; Malcolm N. Shaw; Karl-Peter Sommermann. Kehl: N. P. Engel, 2006, p. 479-492.)

Leroux, Nicolas: NGOs at the World Court: lessons from the past. (In: International Community Law Review, 2006, v. 8, p. 203-221.) [P.C.I.J., p. 203-210; I.C.J., passim.]

E. AFFAIRES PORTÉES DEVANT LA COUR
E. CASES BROUGHT BEFORE THE COURT

Abou al-Wafa, Ahmed: Commentaire de la jurisprudence de la Cour internationale de Justice (2001-2005). (In: Revue égyptienne de droit international, 2005, v. 61, p. 1-211.) [C.P.J.I. et C.I.J., passim.]

Abou al-Wafa, Ahmed: Les différends internationaux concernant les frontières terrestres dans la jurisprudence de la Cour internationale de Justice. (Dans: Recueil des cours de l'Académie de droit international de La Haye, 2009, v. 343, p. 9-570.)

Akhtarkhavari, Afshin: Power, environmental principles and the International Court of Justice. (In: Australian Yearbook of International Law, 2009, v. 28, p. 91-129.)

Aktypis, Spyridon et Boumghar, Mouloud: Chronique des activités de la Cour internationale de Justice en 2004. (Dans: African Yearbook of International Law, 2004, v. 12, p. 471-524.)

Aktypis, Spyridon et Boumghar, Mouloud: Chronique des activités de la Cour internationale de Justice en 2005. (Dans: African Yearbook of International Law, 2005, v. 13, p. 281-296.)

Barker, J. Craig: Decisions of the international tribunals: International Court of Justice. (In: International and Comparative Law Quarterly, 2006, v. 55, no. 3, p. 729-767.)

Barker, J. Craig (ed.): International Court of Justice. (In: International and Comparative Law Quarterly, 2006, v. 55, p. 729-767.)

Bekker, Peter H. F.: The 2003 record of the International Court of Justice. (In: Chinese Journal of International Law, 2004, v. 3, no. 2, p. 499-514.)

Bekker, Peter H. F.: The 2004 record of the International Court of Justice. (In: Chinese Journal of International Law, 2005, v. 4, no. 2, p. 501-513.)

Bekker, Peter H. F.: The 2005 record of the International Court of Justice. (In: Chinese Journal of International Law, 2006, v. 5, no. 2, p. 371-380.)

Bekker, Peter H. F.: The 2006 record of the International Court of Justice. (In: Chinese Journal of International Law, 2007, v. 6, no. 2, p. 379-388.)

Bekker, Peter H. F.: The 2007 record of the International Court of Justice. (In: Chinese Journal of International Law, 2008, v. 7, no. 2, p. 353-369.)

Bennouna, Mohamed: Les effectivités concurrentes dans le règlement des contentieux internationaux. (Dans: Droit international et coopération internationale: Johannis-Andrae Touscoz amicorum discipulorumque opus: hommage à Jean-André Touscoz. Nice: France Europe, 2007, p. 307-314.) [I.C.J., passim.]

Braasch, Patrick and Fuhrmann, Sirko: Die Rechtsprechung des Internationales Gerichtshofes im Jahre 2008. (In: German Yearbook of International Law, 2008, v. 51, 497-546).

Caplan, Lee M. and Combs, Nancy and Nesser, Carl Magnus and Onwuamaegbu, Ucheora O. and Romano, Cesare P. R.: International courts and tribunals. (In: International Lawyer, 2007, v. 41, p. 291-316.) [I.C.J., p. 291-297.]

Cara, Jean-Yves de: Les principes généraux de droit au sens de l'article 38 de la Cour internationale de Justice. (Dans: Les principes généraux du droit: droit français, droit des pays arabes, droit musulman (dénominateurs communs). Bruxelles: Bruylant, 2005, 243-260).

Cases before the Court. (In: International and Comparative Law Quarterly, 2005, v. 54, no. 3, p. 794-799.)

Cazala, Julien: Retour sur les méthodes de délimitation juridictionnelle d'espaces maritimes mises en oeuvre dans quelques affaires récentes. (Dans: Annuaire français de droit international, 2008, v. 54, p. 411-427.)

Combs, Nancy and Onwuamaegbu, Ucheora O. and Rees, Mark B. and Weisman, Jacqueline: International courts and tribunals. (In: International Lawyer, 2004, v. 38, no. 2, p. 451-468.) [I.C.J., p. 451-461.]

Cour internationale de Justice: Résumé des arrêts, avis consultatifs et ordonnances de la Cour internationale de Justice: 1997-2002. New York: Nations Unies, 2006.

Crook, John R.: The 2004 judicial activity of the International Court of Justice. (In: American Journal of International Law, 2005, v. 99, p. 450-459.) [P.C.I.J., p. 453.]

Crook, John R.: Current developments: the 2003 judicial activity of the International Court of Justice. (In: American Journal of International Law, 2004, v. 98, no. 2, p. 309-317.)

Distefano, Giovanni: The conceptualization (construction) of territorial title in the light of the International Court of Justice case law. (In: Leiden Journal of International Law, 2006, v. 19, p. 1041-1075.)

Dominicé, Christian: La jurisprudence de la Cour internationale de Justice en 2003. (Dans: Schweizerische Zeitschrift für internationales und europäisches Recht, 2004, v. 14, p. 69-101.)

Dominicé, Christian: La jurisprudence de la Cour internationale de Justice en 2004. (Dans: Schweizerische Zeitschrift für internationales und europäisches Recht, 2005, v. 15, p. 79-114.)

Dörr, Oliver: Kompendium völkerrechtlicher Rechtsprechung: eine Auswahl für Studium und Praxis. Tübingen: Mohr Siebeck, 2004. (Mohr Lehrbuch.) [C.P.J.I. et C.I.J., passim.]

Eisemann, Pierre Michel et Pazartzis, Photini (sous la dir. de): La jurisprudence de la Cour internationale de Justice. Paris: Pedone, 2008.

Fischer, Dana D.: Decisions to use the International Court of Justice: four recent cases. (In: Conflict resolution. London; Thousand Oaks; ew Delhi: SAGE Publications, 2006, v. 5, p. 139-158.)

Grimheden, Jonas: The International Court of Justice: monitoring human rights. (In: International human rights monitoring mechanisms: essays in honour of Jakob Th. Moller, ed. by Gudmundur Alfredsson. 2009, p. 249-261.)

Groß, René and Stubbe, Sue: Die Rechtsprechung des Internationalen Gerichtshofes im Jahre 2004. (In: German Yearbook of International Law, 2004, v. 47, p. 722-759.)

International Court of Justice. (In: Global Community: Yearbook of International Law and Jurisprudence, 2004, v. 4, no. 1, p. 321-412.)

International Court of Justice. (In: Global Community: Yearbook of International Law and Jurisprudence, 2006, v. 6, no. 1, p. 209-272.)

International Court of Justice: Summaries of judgments, advisory opinions and orders of the International Court of Justice: 2003-2007. New York: United Nations, 2009.

International Court of Justice : cases before the Court. (In : International and Comparative Law Quarterly, 2004, v. 53, no. 3, p. 762-767.)

International Court of Justice. Registry : International Court of Justice : work in 2003-2004. (In : Hague Yearbook of International Law, 2004, v. 17, 139-227).

International Court of Justice. Registry : International Court of Justice : work in 2005-2006. (In : Hague Yearbook of International Law, 2006, v. 19, p. 135-162.)

International Court of Justice. Registry : International Court of Justice : work in 2007-2008. (In : Hague Yearbook of International Law, 2008, v. 21, p. 157-185.)

International Court of Justice. Registry : International Court of Justice : work in 2008-2009. (In : Hague Yearbook of International Law, 2009, v. 22, 113-139).

Jiménez García, Francisco : La reivindicación de las cuestiones procesales ¿ La jurisdicción inherente como alternativa a la ausencia de jurisdicción obligatoria sobre el fondo? Las sentencias de la Corte Internacional de Justicia en los asuntos del Incidente aéreo de 10 de agosto de 1999, Competencia (Pakistán c. India), de las Actividades armadas en el territorio del Congo (República Democrática del Congo c. Ruanda ; República Democrática del Congo c. Uganda ; República Democrática del Congo c. Burundi) y la Demanda en revisión de la sentencia de 11 de julio de 1996 en el asunto relativo a la Aplicación del Convenio para la prevención y sanción del crimen del genocidio (Bosnia-Herzegovina c. Yugoslavia), Excepciones preliminares (Yugoslavia c. Bosnia-Herzegovina). (Dans : Cuadernos de jurisprudencia internacional, 2004, v. 1, p. 47-82.)

Jötten, Sara and Machts, Felix : Die Rechtsprechung des Internationalen Gerichtshofes im Jahre 2006. (In : German Yearbook of International Law, 2006, v. 49, p. 449-475.)

Klatte, Saskia and Dörschner, Jonas : Die Rechtsprechung des Internationalen Gerichtshofes im Jahre 2007. (In : German Yearbook of International Law, 2007, v. 50, p. 589-627.)

Kohen, Marcelo G. : La relation titres/effectivités dans le contentieux territorial à la lumière de la jurisprudence récente. (Dans : Revue générale de droit international public, 2004, v. 108, p. 561-595.) [C.I.J. et C.P.J.I., passim.]

Kolb, Robert : Chronique de la jurisprudence de la Cour internationale de Justice en 2005. (Dans : Schweizerische Zeitschrift für internationales und europäisches Recht, 2006, v. 16, p. 163-192.)

Kolb, Robert : Chronique de la jurisprudence de la Cour internationale de Justice en 2006. (Dans : Schweizerische Zeitschrift für internationales und europäisches Recht, 2007, v. 17, no. 1, p. 119-145.)

Kolb, Robert: Chronique de la jurisprudence de la Cour internationale de Justice en 2007. (Dans : Schweizerische Zeitschrift für internationales und europäisches Recht, 2008, v. 18, p. 123-171.)

Kolb, Robert: Chronique de la jurisprudence de la Cour internationale de Justice en 2008. (Dans : Schweizerische zeitschrift fur internationales und europäisches recht, 2009, v. 19, no. 1, p. 127-167.)

Kolb, Robert: Note on new international case-law concerning the binding character of provisional measures. (In : Nordic Journal of International Law, 2005, v. 74, no. 1, p. 117-129.) [I.C.J., p. 118-119, 123-126, 128-129; P.C.I.J., p. 128.]

Kooijmans, Pieter H. : The legality of the use of force in the recent case law of the International Court of Justice. (In : Multiculturalism and international law : essays in honour of Edward McWhinney, ed. by Yee, Sienho ; Morin, Jacques-Yvan. Leiden ; Boston : Martinus Nijhoff, 2009, p. 455-466.)

Kwiatkowska, Barbara: Equitable maritime boundary delimitation, as exemplified in the work of the International Court of Justice during the presidency of Judge Gilbert Guillaume (2000-2003) and beyond. (In : Global Community : Yearbook of International Law and Jurisprudence, 2005, v. 5, no. 1, p. 51-171.)

Labrecque, Georges: La force et le droit : jurisprudence de la Cour internationale de Justice. Cowansville (Québec) ; Bruxelles : Yvon Blais ; Bruylant, 2008.

Lee, Karen (ed.) : International environmental law in international tribunals. Cambridge [etc.] : Cambridge University Press, 2007. Cambridge University Press (International environmental law reports ; 5.) [I.C.J., p. 1-390.]

Leitsch, Heiko: Die Rechtsprechung des Internationalen Gerichtshofes im Jahre 2005. (In : German Yearbook of International Law, 2005, v. 48, p. 391-428.)

Lombardi, Clark B. : Islamic law in the jurisprudence of the International Court of Justice : an analysis. (In : Chicago Journal of International Law, 2007, v. 8, no. 1, p. 85-118.)

Maneggia, Amina: Attori non statali, uso dello forza legittima difesa nella giurisprudenza più recente della Corte Internazionale di Giustizia. (Dans : Le nuove frontiere del diritto internazionale : attori non statali, spazio virtuale, valori fondamentali e governo multinazionale di territori, sous la dir. de Carlo Focarelli. Perugia : Morlacchi editore, 2008, p. 31-52.)

Mathias, Stephen: The 2005 judicial activity of the International Court of Justice. (In : American Journal of International Law, 2006, v. 100, p. 629-649.)

Mathias, Stephen: The 2007 judicial activity of the International Court of Justice. (In : American Journal of International Law, 2008, v. 102, no. 3, p. 588-609.)

McCarthy, Connor: Reparation for gross violations of human rights law and international humanitarian law at the International Court of Justice. (In: Reparations for victims of genocide, war crimes against humanity: systems in place and systems in the making, ed. by Carla Ferstman; Mariana Goetz; Alan Andrew Stephens. Leiden: Nijhoff, 2009, p. 283-311.)

McWhinney, Edward and Kawano, Mariko: Judge Shigeru Oda and the path to judicial wisdom: opinions (declarations, separate opinions, dissenting opinions) on the International Court of Justice, 1993-2003. Leiden [etc.]: Martinus Nijhoff, 2006. (The Judges; 4.) [P.C.I.J., p. 66, 113; I.C.J., passim.]

Merrills, John G.: Decisions of international courts and tribunals in 2008: the International Court of Justice in 2008: introductory note. (In: Global Community: Yearbook of International Law and Jurisprudence, 2009, v. 9, no. 1, p. 289-302.)

Merrills, John G.: The International Court of Justice in 2006: introductory note. (In: Global Community: Yearbook of International Law and Jurisprudence, 2007, v. 7, no. 1, p. 195-204.)

Milano, Enrico: Diplomatic protection and human rights before the International Court of Justice: re-fashioning tradition? (In: Netherlands Yearbook of International Law, 2004, v. 35, p. 85-142.)

Milano, Enrico: Territorial disputes, wrongful occupations and State responsibility: should the International Court of Justice go the extra mile? (In: Law and Practice of International Courts and Tribunals, 2004, v. 3, no. 3, p. 509-541.)

Müller, Daniel: Procedural developments at the International Court of Justice. (In: Law and Practice of International Courts and Tribunals, 2004, v. 3, no. 3, p. 553-579.)

Müller, Daniel: Procedural developments at the International Court of Justice. (In: Law and Practice of International Courts and Tribunals, 2005, v. 4, no. 1, p. 141-163.) [P.C.I.J. and I.C.J. passim.]

Müller, Daniel: Procedural developments at the International Court of Justice. (In: Law and Practice of International Courts and Tribunals, 2005, v. 4, no. 3, p. 501-513.)

Müller, Daniel: Procedural developments at the International Court of Justice. (In: Law and Practice of International Courts and Tribunals, 2006, v. 5, no. 2, p. 305-324.)

Müller, Daniel: Procedural developments at the International Court of Justice. (In: Law and Practice of International Courts and Tribunals, 2006, v. 5, no. 3, p. 529-546.)

Müller, Daniel: Procedural developments at the International Court of Justice. (In: Law and Practice of International Courts and Tribunals, 2007, v. 6, no. 1, p. 221-232.)

Müller, Daniel: Procedural developments at the International Court of Justice. (In: Law and Practice of International Courts and Tribunals, 2007, v. 6, no. 3, p. 447-493.)

Müller, Daniel and Ben Mansour, Affef: Procedural developments at the International Court of Justice. (In: Law and Practice of International Courts and Tribunals, 2009, v. 8, no. 3, p. 459-528.)

Nations Unies. Division des affaires maritimes et du droit de la mer. Bureau des affaires juridiques: Recueil de jurisprudence internationale concernant le droit de la mer. New York: Nations Unies, 2008.

Orakhelashvili, Alexander: Legal stability and claims of change: the International Court's treatment of jus ad bellum and jus in bello. (In: Nordic Journal of International Law, 2006, v. 75, p. 371-407.)

Palchetti, Paolo: The activity of the International Court of Justice in 2006. (In: Italian Yearbook of International Law, 2006, v. 16, p. 215-225.)

Palchetti, Paolo: The activity of the International Court of Justice in 2007. (In: Italian Yearbook of International Law, 2007, v. 17, p. 159-174.)

Pinto, Mónica: L'emploi de la force dans la jurisprudence des tribunaux internationaux. (Dans: Recueil des cours de l'Académie de droit international de La Haye, 2007, v. 331, p. 9-161.) [C.I.J., passim.]

Prager, Dietmar W.: Procedural developments at the International Court of Justice. (In: The Law and Practice of International Courts and Tribunals, 2004, v. 3, no. 1, p. 125-142.)

Quigley, John: International Court of Justice as a forum for genocide cases. (In: Case Western Reserve Journal of International Law, 2008, v. 40, no. 1-2, p. 243-263.)

Ranjeva, Raymond: Les îles devant la Cour internationale de Justice. (Dans: L'évolution et l'état actuel du droit international de la mer: mélanges de droit de la mer offerts à Daniel Vignes. Bruxelles: Bruylant, 2009, p. 727-734.)

Rosenne, Shabtai: Decisions of the International Court and the law of State responsibility. (In: Essays on international law and practice, ed. by Shabtai Rosenne. Leiden; Boston: Martinus Nijhoff, 2007, p. 543-555.)

Ruiz Fabri, Hélène et Sorel, Jean-Marc: Chronique de jurisprudence de la Cour internationale de Justice (2003). (Dans: Journal du droit international, 2004, v. 131, no. 3, p. 961-996.)

Ruiz Fabri, Hélène et Sorel, Jean-Marc: Chronique de jurisprudence de la Cour internationale de Justice (2004). (Dans: Journal du droit international, 2005, v. 132, no. 3, p. 875-916.)

Ruiz Fabri, Hélène et Sorel, Jean-Marc: Chronique de jurisprudence de la Cour internationale de Justice (2007). (Dans: Journal du droit international, 2008, v. 135, no. 4, p. 1135-1185.)

Ruiz Fabri, Hélène et Sorel, Jean-Marc : Chronique de jurisprudence de la Cour internationale de Justice (2008). (Dans : Journal du droit international, 2009, v. 136, no. 4, p. 1303-1353.)

Shaw, Malcolm N. : Settling territorial disputes. (In : Liber amicorum Jean-Pierre Cot : le procès international. Bruxelles : Bruylant, 2009, p. 255-281.)

Sivakumaran, Sandesh : The International Court of Justice and human rights. (In : Research handbook on international human rights law, ed. by Sarah Joseph ; Adam McBeth. Cheltenham [etc.] : Elgar, 2009, p. 299-325.)

Stürchler, Nikolas : The threat of force in international law. Cambridge : Cambridge University Press, 2007. (Cambridge Studies in International and Comparative Law.) [I.C.J., p. 4-6, 65-91, 93-94, 102-103, 105, 110-111, 124, 180-184, 192, 202, 217, 234-235, 255-256, 260, 263, 266, 276, 282.]

Tchikaya, Blaise : L'entrée historique des pays d'Afrique dans la jurisprudence internationale. (Dans : Miskolci Nemzetközi Jogi Közlemények, 2004, v. 1, no. 2, p. 242-258.) [C.P.J.I., p. 242, 249-250; C.I.J., passim.]

Torres Bernárdez, Santiago : The use of force in the jurisprudence of the International Court of Justice. (In : International law and the use of force at the turn of centuries : essays in honour of V. D. Degan, ed. by Vesna Crnic-Grotic ; Miomir Matulovic. Rijeka : Faculty of Law University of Rijeka, 2005, p. 3-37.)

Van der Vyver, J. D. : The United States and the jurisprudence of international tribunals. (In : Resolving international conflicts : liber amicorum Tibor Várady, ed. by Peter Hay ; Lajos Vékás ; Yehuda Elkana ; Nenad Dimitrijevic. Budapest : Central European University Press, 2009, p. 283-318.)

Vereetin, Vladeni St. : Reenija i zakljuenija na Medunarodnija Sd na OON po vprosite na mira i sigurnostta. (In : Pravna misal, 2007, v. 48, no. 3.)

Vereshchetin, Vladlen S. and Le Mon, Christopher J. : Immunities of individuals under international law in the jurisprudence of the International Court of Justice. (In : Global Community : Yearbook of International Law and Jurisprudence, 2004, v. 4, no. 1, p. 77-89.)

Weckel, Philippe et Aréou, Guillaume : Chronique de jurisprudence internationale. (Dans : Revue générale de droit international public, 2008, v. 112, no. 2, p. 415-428.)

Zyberi, Gentian : Assessing the validity of reservations to international human rights treaties through the lens of the International Court of Justice. (In : NJCM Bulletin : Nederlands tijdschririft voor de mensenrechten, 2008, v. 33, no. 8, p. 1121-1129.)

Zyberi, Gentian : Self-determination through the lens of the International Court of Justice. (In : Netherlands International Law Review, 2009, v. 56, no. 3, p. 429-453.)

1, 1a, 2. *Détroit de Corfou (Royaume-Uni c. Albanie)*
1, 1a, 2. *Corfu Channel (United Kingdom* v. *Albania)*

Carty, Anthony: The Corfu channel case: and the missing admiralty orders. (In: Law and Practice of International Courts and Tribunals, 2004, v. 3, no. 1, p. 1-35.)

4. *Réparation des dommages subis au service des Nations Unies*
4. *Reparation for Injuries Suffered in the Service of the United Nations*

Dupuy, Pierre-Marie: Retour sur la théorie des sujets du droit international. (Dans: Studi di diritto internazionale in onore di Gaetano Arangio-Ruiz, sous la dir. de Giovanni Battaglini; Paolo Benvenuti; Antonio Cassese; Giorgio Gaja. Napoli: Editoriale Scientifica, 2004, v. 1, p. 71-84.)

12. *Réserves à la convention pour la prévention et la répression du crime de génocide*
12. *Reservations to the Convention on the Prevention and Punishment of the Crime of Genocide*

Doria, José Rodrigues: Reservations to the ICCPR and CEDAW in the light of common but differentiated responsibility: different scenarios in different States. (In: Hague Yearbook of International Law, 2004, v. 17, p. 37-75.) [I.C.J., p. 41-43, 53.]

Klabbers, Jan: On human rights treaties, contractual conceptions and reservations. (In: Reservations to human rights treaties and the Vienna Convention regime: conflict, harmony or reconciliation, ed. by Ineta Ziemele. Leiden, [et c.]: Martinus Nijhoff, 2004, p. 149-182.) [I.C.J., p. 149-150, 155-156, 159-165, 173-174, 176, 178.]

14. *Haya de la Torre (Colombie/Pérou)*
14. *Haya de la Torre (Colombia/Peru)*

Fonseca de Paiva, Emmanuelle Christinne et Cassão de Medeiros, Naiara et Silva de Morais, Denise Carla et Pignataro de Oliveira, Diogo: Asilo diplomático e os direitos humanos: uma análise do Caso Haya de La Torre da Corte Internacional de Justiça. (Dans: Realidades: direitos humanos, meio ambiente e desenvolvimento, sous la dir. de Rosenite Alves de Oliveira; Yanko Marcius Alencar Xavier de; Jahyr-Philippe Bichara; Mônica Bulhões e Silva; Diogo Pignataro de Oliveira; Natália Bastos Bonavides. Natal: EDUFRN, 2007, p. 31-46.)

18. *Nottebohm (Liechtenstein c. Guatemala)*
18. *Nottebohm (Liechtenstein* v. *Guatemala)*

Sloane, Robert: Breaking the genuine link: the contemporary international legal regulation of nationality. (In: Harvard International Law Journal, 2009, v. 50, no. 1, p. 1-60.) [I.C.J., passim.]

41. *Barcelona Traction, Light and Power Company, Limited (Belgique c. Espagne)*
41. *Barcelona Traction, Light and Power Company, Limited (Belgium* v. *Spain)*

Paparinskis, Martins : Barcelona Traction : a friend of investment protection law. (In : Baltic Yearbook of International Law, 2008, v. 8, p. 105-133.)

45. *Temple de Préah Vihéar (Cambodge c. Thaïlande)*
45. *Temple of Preah Vihear (Cambodia* v. *Thailand)*

Chan, Phil C. W. : Acquiescence/estoppel in international boundaries : Temple of Preah Vihear revisited. (In : Chinese Journal of International Law, 2004, v. 3, no. 2, p. 421-440.)

51, 52. *Plateau continental de la mer du Nord (République fédérale d'Allemagne/Danemark ; République fédérale d'Allemagne/Pays-Bas)*
51, 52. *North Sea Continental Shelf (Federal Republic of Germany/Denmark; Federal Republic of Germany/Netherlands)*

Heidar, Tomas H. : Legal aspects of continental shelf limits. (In : Legal and scientific aspects of continental shelf limits, ed. by Myron H. Nordquist ; John Norton Moore ; Tomas H. Heidar. Leiden [etc.] : Martinus Nijhoff, 2004, p. 19-39.) [I.C.J., p. 22.]

Linderfalk, Ulf : Reservations to treaties and norms of jus cogens : a comment on human rights committee general comment No. 24. (In : Reservations to human rights treaties and the Vienna Convention regime : conflict, harmony or reconciliation, ed. by Ineta Ziemele. Leiden, [etc.] : Martinus Nijhoff, 2004, p. 213-234.) [I.C.J., p. 216.]

Spielman, Brian : "Warships" in the north sea continental shelf cases : why the definition of "warship" for determining sovereign immunity settled 25 years ago. (In : The Journal of International Maritime Law, 2009, v. 15, no. 4, p. 322-339.)

58, 59. *Essais nucléaires (Australie c. France) (Nouvelle-Zélande c. France)*
58, 59. *Nuclear Tests (Australia* v. *France) (New Zealand* v. *France)*

Torres Cazorla, María Isabel : La historia jamás contada de los actos unilaterales de los Estados : de los Ensayos nucleares al asunto de la República democrática del Congo contra Ruanda. (Dans : Revista española de derecho internacional, 2006, v. 58, p. 257-269.)

61. *Sahara occidental*
61. *Western Sahara*

Hasani, Enver : Self-determination, territorial integrity and international stability : the case of Yugoslavia. [S.l.] : National Defence Academy, Institute for Peace Support and Conflict Management, 2004. [I.C.J., p. 27-28, 104, 107-109, 196-199, 274, 287, 306, 315-316, 319, 325-326.]

Stepanova, Sasha : L'affaire du Timor Oriental devant la Cour internationale de Justice : aspects du droit à l'autodétermination applicables au Sahara occidental. (Dans : Le droit international et la question du Sahara occidental. Leiden : International Platform of Jurists for East Timor (IPJET), 2009, p. 239-247.)

62. *Plateau continental de la mer Egée (Grèce c. Turquie)*
62. *Aegean Sea Continental Shelf (Greece* v. *Turkey)*

Bölükbas, Deniz: Turkey and Greece: the Aegean disputes: a unique case in international law. London [etc.]: Cavendish, 2004. [P.C.I.J., p. 38, 814, 877, 940-941; I.C.J., p. 103-104, 144, 155-158, 205-218, 236-238, 241-246, 253-572, 725, 783-784, 790, 792-822, 863.]

Tzimitras, Harry: Europe, nationalism and Turkish Greek Aegean disputes. (In: In the long shadow of Europe: Greeks and Turks in the era of postnationalism, ed. by Othon Anastasakis; Kalypso Aude Nicolaidis; Kerem Oktem. Leiden [etc.]: Nijhoff, 2009, p. 239-262.)

64. *Personnel diplomatique et consulaire des Etats-Unis à Téhéran (Etats-Unis d'Amérique c. Iran)*
64. *United States Diplomatic and Consular Staff in Tehran (United States of America* v. *Iran)*

Terry, Patrick: US-Iran relations in international law since 1979: hostages, oil platforms, nuclear weapons and the use of force. Rangendingen: Libertas, 2009. (Libertas paper; 70.)

67. *Délimitation de la frontière maritime dans la région du golfe du Maine (Canada/Etats-Unis d'Amérique)*
67. *Delimitation of the Maritime Boundary in the Gulf of Maine Area (Canada/United States of America)*

Caron, David D.: The rule-outcome paradox, madness cascades and the fog of preemption: seeking the "best rule" for use of force. (In: Hastings International and Comparative Law Review, 2004, v. 27, no. 3, p. 481-496.) [I.C.J., p. 485.]

Kaye, Stuart B.: Lessons learned from the Gulf of Maine case: the development of maritime boundary delimitation jurisprudence since UNCLOS III. (In: Ocean and Coastal Law Journal, 2008, v. 14, no. 1, p. 73-99.)

70. *Activités militaires et paramilitaires au Nicaragua et contre celui-ci (Nicaragua c. Etats-Unis d'Amérique)*
70. *Military and Paramilitary Activities in and against Nicaragua (Nicaragua* v. *United States of America)*

Lippman, Matthew: The history, development and decline of crimes against peace. (In: The George Washington International Law Review, 2004, v. 36, no. 5, p. 957-1056.) [P.C.I.J., p. 967, 969-974, 982; I.C.J., p. 1040-1043, 1054.]

Neuhold, Hanspeter: Law and force in international relations: European and American positions. (In: Zeitschrift für ausländisches öffentliches Recht und Völkerrecht, 2004, v. 64, no. 2, p. 263-279.) [I.C.J., p. 269.]

O'Connell, Mary Ellen: The Nicaragua case: preserving world peace and the World Court. (In: International law stories, ed. by John E. Noyes; Laura Dickinson; Mark W. Janis. New York: Foundation Press, 2007, p. 339-370.)

Tasioulas, John: In defence of relative normativity: communitarian values and the Nicaragua case. (In: International law, ed. by Malcolm D. Evans; Patrick Capps. Farnham [etc.]: Ashgate, 2009, v. 1, p. 337-380.)

Zedalis, Rex J.: Circumstances justifying pre-emptive self-defence: thoughts prompted by the military action against Iraq. (In: Nordic Journal of International Law, 2005, v. 74, no. 2, p. 209-230.) [I.C.J., p. 211, 219.]

82. *Sentence arbitrale du 31 juillet 1989 (Guinée-Bissau c. Sénégal)*
82. *Arbitral Award of 31 July 1989 (Guinea-Bissau* v. *Senegal)*

Barberis, Julio A.: Algunas consideraciones sobre la decisión internacional en dos sentencias arbitrales recientes. (Dans: Estudios de derecho internacional: libro homenaje al profesor Santiago Benadava, sous la dir. de Llanos Mansilla, Hugo. 2008, v. 1, p. 33-49.) [C.P.J.I., p. 45-46; C.I.J., passim.]

Schwebel, Stephen M.: May the majority vote of an international arbitral tribunal be impeached? (In: Arbitration insights: twenty years of the Annual Lecture of the School of International Arbitration, ed. by Julian D. M. Lew; Loukas A. Mistelis. Alphen aan den Rijn: Kluwer Law International, 2007, p. 201-212.)

84. *Timor oriental (Portugal c. Australie)*
84. *East Timor (Portugal* v. *Australia)*

Stepanova, Sasha: The Portugal-Australia Timor gap case at the International Court of Justice: aspects of self-determination relevant to the Western Sahara. (In: International law and the question of Western Sahara, ed. by Karin Arts; Pedro Pinto Leite. Leiden: International Platform of Jurists for East Timor (IPJET), 2007, p. 239-247.) [I.C.J., passim.]

87. *Délimitation maritime et questions territoriales entre Qatar et Bahreïn (Qatar c. Bahreïn)*
87. *Maritime Delimitation and Territorial Questions between Qatar and Bahrain (Qatar* v. *Bahrain)*

Conde Pérez, Elena: Pasado colonial y otras rencillas entre vecinos: la sentencia de la Corte Internacional de Justicia de 16 de marzo de 2001 en el asunto de la Delimitación marítima y de las cuestiones territoriales entre Qatar y Bahrein (Qatar c. Bahrein, fondo). (Dans: Cuadernos de jurisprudencia internacional, 2004, v. 1, p. 11-45.)

Möllers, Christoph: Transnationale Behördenkooperation: Verfassungs – und völkerrechtliche Probleme transnationaler administrativer Standardsetzung. (In: Zeitschrift für ausländisches öffentliches Recht und Völkerrecht, 2005, v. 65, no. 2, p. 351-389.) [I.C.J., p. 369.]

Rosenne, Shabtai: What is a treaty? A signatory's intentions: Qatar v. Bahrain. (In: Essays on international law and practice, by Shabtai Rosenne. Leiden; Boston: Martinus Nijhoff, 2007, p. 435-443.)

Salmon, Jean J.-A. and Sinclair, Ian: Special features of the Qatar v. Bahrein case before the ICJ: affaire de la délimitation maritime et des questions territoriales entre Qatar et Bahreïn : l'arrêt de la C.I.J du 16 mars 2001. (In : Studi di diritto internazionale in onore di Gaetano Arangio-Ruiz, ed. by Giovanni Battaglini ; Paolo Benvenuti ; Antonio Cassese ; Giorgio Gaja. Napoli : Editoriale Scientifica, 2004, v. 2, p. 1167-1242.)

Study Group on Decisions of the International Court of Justice: Maritime delimitation and territorial questions between Qatar and Bahrain (Qatar v. Bahrain) merits. (In : Kokusaiho Gaiko Zassi, 2007, v. 105, no. 4, p. 122-149.)

88, 89. *Questions d'interprétation et d'application de la convention de Montréal de 1971 résultant de l'incident aérien de Lockerbie (Jamahiriya arabe libyenne c. Royaume-Uni) (Jamahiriya arabe libyenne c. Etats-Unis d'Amérique)*

88, 89. *Questions of Interpretation and Application of the 1971 Montreal Convention arising from the Aerial Incident at Lockerbie (Libyan Arab Jamahiriya* v. *United Kingdom) (Libyan Arab Jamahiriya* v. *United States of America)*

Allain, Jean: The legacy of Lockerbie : judicial review of Security Council actions or the first manifestation of "terrorism" as a threat to international peace ? (In : Indian Journal of International Law, 2004, v. 44, no. 1, p. 74-112.)

Allain, Jean: The puzzle of the modification of customary law : the Lockerbie case as an example of a law-breaking incident turning into a law-making exercise. (In : International law : issues and challenges. Gurgaon : Hope India Publications, 2009, v. 1, p. 92-108.)

Grant, John P.: The Lockerbie trial : a documentary history. Dobbs Ferry, N.Y. : Oceana Publications, 2004. (Terrorism : documents on international and local control : second series ; 15.) [I.C.J., p. xxxix-il, 455-553.]

90. *Plates-formes pétrolières (République islamique d'Iran c. Etats-Unis d'Amérique)*

90. *Oil Platforms (Islamic Republic of Iran* v. *United States of America)*

Barthe-Gay, Clarisse: Le jeu de l'unilatéral, du bilatéral et du multilatéral en droit international : observations sous l'arrêt de la Cour internationale de Justice du 6 novembre 2003 dans l'affaire des Plates-formes pétrolières (Iran c. Etats-Unis). (Dans : Revue belge de droit international, 2004, v. 37, no. 1, p. 71-91.)

Bekker, Peter H. F.: Protecting international shipping channels during hostilities and the "Oil Platforms" case : actio popularis revisited ? (In : Yale Journal of International Law, 2004, v. 29, no. 2, p. 323-329.)

Berman, Frank: Treaty "interpretation" in a judicial context. (In : Yale Journal of International Law, 2004, v. 29, no. 2, p. 315-322.)

Cannizzaro, Enzo and Bonafè, Beatrice I.: Fragmenting international law through compromissory clauses ? Some remarks on the decision of the ICJ in the Oil Platforms case. (In : European Journal of International Law, 2005, v. 16, no. 3, p. 481-497.) [P.C.I.J., p. 487, 492-494.]

Carlowitz, Leopold von: Interpreting self-defense restrictively: the World Court In the Oil Platforms case. (In: Sicherheit und Frieden (S+F), 2005, v. 23, no. 2, p. 79-89.)

Carlowitz, Leopold von: The Oil Platforms case before the International Court of Justice: a contribution to the present debate on self-defense? (In: Schweizerische Zeitschrift für internationales und europäisches Recht, 2005, v. 15, no. 2, p. 255-280.)

Carnerero Castilla, Rubén: Libertad de comercio, uso de la fuerza y legítima defensa: la sentencia de la Corte Internacional de Justicia de 6 de noviembre de 2003 en el asunto de las Plataformas petrolíferas (República Islámica de Irán c. Estados Unidos de América). (Dans: Cuadernos de jurisprudencia internacional, 2005, v. 2, p. 45-69.)

Caron, David D.: International decisions. (In: American Journal of International Law, 2004, v. 98, no. 3, p. 550-558.)

Chenevier, Justin: Oil on troubled waters: the I.C.J. tackles use of force. (In: Cambridge Law Journal, 2004, v. 63, p. 1-4.)

Garwood-Gowers, Andrew: Case concerning Oil Platforms (Islamic Republic of Iran v. United States of America): did the I.C.J. miss the boat on the use of force? (In: Melbourne Journal of International Law, 2004, v. 5, no. 1, p. 241-255.)

Gattini, Andrea: La legittima difesa nel nuovo secolo: la sentenza della Corte internazionale di giustizia nell'affare delle Piattaforme petrolifere. (Dans: Rivista di diritto internazionale, 2004, v. 87, no. 1, p. 147-170.)

Giurisprudenza internazionale: Corte internazionale di giustizia, 6 novembre 2003: sentenza nell'affare delle Piattaforme petrolifere (Repubblica islamica d'Iran c. Stati Uniti d'America). (Dans: Rivista di diritto internazionale, 2004, v. 87, no. 1, p. 181-229.)

Green, James A.: The Oil Platforms case: an error in judgment? (In: Journal of Conflict and Security Law, 2004, v. 9, no. 3, p. 357-386.)

Heiskanen, Veijo: Oil platforms: lessons of dissensus. (In: Nordic Journal of International Law, 2005, v. 74, no. 2, p. 179-208.) [P.C.I.J., p. 183, 186, 190; I.C.J., passim.]

Henrard, K. (ed.): Hague case law: latest developments. (In: Netherlands International Law Review, 2004, v. 51, no. 1, p. 121-131.) [I.C.J., p. 121-122.]

Kammerhofer, Jörg: Oil's well that ends well? Critical comments on the merits judgement in the Oil Platforms case. (In: Leiden Journal of International Law, 2004, v. 17, no. 4, p. 695-718.)

Laursen, Andreas: The judgment by the International Court of Justice in the Oil Platforms Case. (In: Nordic Journal of International Law, 2004, v. 73, no. 1, p. 135-160.)

Momtaz, Djamchid: Did the Court miss an opportunity to denounce the erosion of the principle prohibiting the use of force? (In: Yale Journal of International Law, 2004, v. 29, no. 2, p. 307-313.)

Ochoa Ruiz, Natalia and Salamanca Aguado, Esther: Exploring the limits of international law relating to the use of force in self-defence. (In: European Journal of International Law, 2005, v. 16, no. 3, p. 499-524.) [I.C.J., passim.]

Orakhelashvili, Alexander: International Court of Justice: Oil Platforms (Islamic Republic of Iran v. United States of America), Merits, Judgment of 6 November 2003. (In: International and Comparative Law Quarterly, 2004, v. 53, no. 3, p. 753-761.)

Raab, Dominic: "Armed attack" after the Oil Platforms case. (In: Leiden Journal of International Law, 2004, v. 17, no. 4, p. 719-735.)

Rishikof, Harvey: When naked came the doctrine of "self-defense": what is the proper role of the International Court of Justice in use of force cases? (In: Yale Journal of International Law, 2004, v. 29, no. 2, p. 331-342.)

Small, David H.: The Oil Platforms Case: jurisdiction through the – closed – eye of the needle. (In: The Law and Practice of International Courts and Tribunals, 2004, v. 3, no. 1, p. 113-124.)

Symposium: reflections on the I.C.J.'s Oil Platforms decision: foreword. (In: Yale Journal of International Law, 2004, v. 29, no. 2, p. 291-293.)

Taft, William H.: Self-defense and the Oil Platforms decision. (In: Yale Journal of International Law, 2004, v. 29, no. 2, p. 295-306.)

Terry, Patrick: US-Iran relations in international law since 1979: hostages, oil platforms, nuclear weapons and the use of force. Rangendingen: Libertas, 2009. (Libertas paper; 70.)

Tourme-Jouannet, Emmanuelle: Le juge international face aux problèmes d'incohérence et d'instabilité du droit international: quelques réflexions à propos de l'arrêt C.I.J. du 6 novembre 2003, Affaire des Plates-formes pétrolières. (Dans: Revue générale de droit international public, 2004, v. 108, no. 4, p. 917-948.)

Weckel, Philippe: Chronique de jurisprudence internationale. (Dans: Revue générale de droit international public, 2004, v. 108, no. 1, p. 215-247.) [C.I.J., p. 215-234, 236, 239-241, 243, 245.]

Weil, Prosper and Richemond, Daphné: The Oil Platforms case before the International Court of Justice: a non-case of international responsibility. (In: International responsibility today: essays in memory of Oscar Schachter, ed. by Maurizio Ragazzi. Leiden; Boston: Martinus Nijhoff, 2005, p. 329-340.)

Young, Stewart M.: Destruction of property (on an international scale): the recent Oil Platforms Case and the International Court of Justice's inconsistent commentary on the use of force by the United States. (In: North

Carolina Journal of International Law and Commercial Regulation, 2004, v. 30, no. 2, p. 335-377.)

91. *Application de la convention pour la prévention et la répression du crime de génocide (Bosnie-Herzégovine c. Yougoslavie)*
91. *Application of the Convention on the Prevention and Punishment of the Crime of Genocide (Bosnia and Herzegovina* v. *Yugoslavia)*

Abass, Ademola: Proving State responsibility for genocide: the ICJ in Bosnia v. Serbia and the International Commission of Inquiry for Darfur. (In: Fordham International Law Journal, 2008, v. 31, no. 4, p. 871-910.)

Alvarez-Jiménez, Alberto: International State responsibility for acts of non-State actors: the recent standards set by the International Court of Justice in genocide and why the WTO appellate body should not embrace them. (In: Syracuse Journal of International Law and Commerce, 2007, v. 35, no. 1, p. 1-25.)

Amerasinghe, Chittharanjan Felix: The Bosnia genocide case. (In: Leiden Journal of International Law, 2008, v. 21, no. 2, p. 411-428.)

Arcari, Maurizio: L'attribuzione allo Stato di atti di genocido nella sentenza della Corte internazionale di giustizia nel caso Bosnia-Erzegovina c. Serbia. (Dans: Diritto umani e diritto internazionale, 2007, v. 1, no. 3, p. 565-578.)

Ascensio, Hervé: La responsabilité selon la Cour internationale de Justice dans l'affaire du génocide bosniaque. (Dans: Revue générale de droit international public, 2007, v. 111, no. 2, p. 285-304.)

Azari, Hadi: Regards croisés sur l'intention génocidaire: à propos de l'arrêt de la Cour internationale de Justice en l'affaire relative à l'application de la Convention pour la prévention et la répression du crime de génocide (Bosnie-Herzégovine / Serbie-et-Monténégro). (Dans: Revue de science criminelle et de droit pénal comparé, 2007, v. 4, p. 739-763.)

Azizi, Sattar: Elements of the crime of genocide in the jurisprudence of the International Court of Justice and the ad hoc international criminal courts. (In: Majalla-yi huquqi, 2007, v. 36, p. 9-34.)

Bannelier, Karine: Qu'est-ce qu'un génocide et quand un Etat est-il responsable pour ce crime? Analyse de l'arrêt rendu par la CIJ dans l'affaire Bosnie-Herzégovine c. Serbie-et-Montenégro (26 février 2007). (Dans: Revue belge de droit international, 2007, v. 40, no. 1, p. 257-299.)

Ben-Naftali, Orna and Sharon, Miri: What the I.C.J. did not say about the duty to punish genocide: the missing pieces in a puzzle. (In: Journal of International Criminal Justice, 2007, v. 5, no. 4, p. 859-874.)

Bijelic, Ana et Dumont, Hélène et Boisvert, Anne-Marie: Le système de justice des pays de l'ex-Yougoslavie et les défis de l'administration de la justice pénale internationale. (Dans: La voie vers la Cour pénale internationale: tous les chemins mènent à Rome = The highway to the International Criminal Court: all roads lead to Rome, sous la dir. de Dumont,

Hélène ; Boisvert, Anne-Marie. Montréal : Editions Thémis, 2004, p. 255-313.) [C.I.J., p. 261, 295-305, 313.]

Birkland, Berglind Halldórsdóttir : Reining in non-State actors : State responsibility and attribution in cases of genocide. (In : New York University Law Review, 2009, v. 84, no. 6, p. 1623-1655.)

Breuker, Lennert : The judgment of the I.C.J. in the Genocide case : "the State as perpetretor of genocide". (In : Griffin's View on International and Comparative Law, 2007, v. 8, no. 2, p. 39-78.)

Cassese, Antonio : The Nicaragua and Tadic tests revisited in light of the ICJ Judgment on genocide in Bosnia. (In : European Journal of International Law, 2007, v. 18, p. 649-668.) [P.C.I.J., p. 662; I.C.J., passim.]

Cassese, Antonio : On the use of criminal law notions in determining State responsibility for genocide. (In : Journal of International Criminal Justice, 2007, v. 5, no. 4, p. 875-887.)

Clearwater, Sam : Holding States accountable for the crime of crimes : an analysis of direct State responsibility for genocide in light of ICJ's 2007 decision in Bosnia v. Serbia. (In : Auckland University Law Review, 2009, v. 15, p. 1-41.)

Condé, Jean-Pierre : L'affaire du génocide : Bosnie et Serbie devant la Cour internationale de Justice ou la dénonciation à l'épreuve du droit international. (Dans : Droit et cultures, 2009, v. 58, p. 109-140.)

Corten, Olivier : L'arrêt rendu par la C.I.J. dans l'affaire du crime de génocide (Bosnie-Herzégovine c. Serbie) : vers un assouplissement des conditions permettant d'engager la responsabilité d'un Etat pour génocide ? (Dans : Annuaire français de droit international, 2007, v. 53, p. 249-279.)

David, Eric : L'arrêt de la Cour internationale de Justice en l'affaire de l'application de la Convention pour la prévention et la répression du crime de génocide : Cour internationale de Justice, Bosnie-Herzégovine c. Serbie-et-Monténégro, 26 février 2007. (Dans : Revue trimestrielle des droits de l'homme, 2008, v. 19, no. 74, p. 573-593.)

David, Eric : La responsabilité internationale de l'état après l'affaire Bosnie c. Serbie. (Dans : Frieden in Freiheit : Festschrift für Michael Bothe zum 70. Geburtstag, sous la dir. de Fischer-Lescano, Andreas ; Gasser, Hans-Peter ; Marauhn, Thilo ; Ronzitti, Natalino. Baden-Baden ; Zurich : Nomos Verlag ; Dike Verlag, 2008, p. 865-871.)

De Pooter, Hélène : The obligation to prevent genocide : a large shell yet to be filled. (In : African Yearbook of International Law, 2009, v. 17, p. 287-320.)

Dimitrijevic, Vojin : The strange story of the Bosnian genocide case. (In : Leiden Journal of International Law, 2008, v. 21, no. 1, p. 65-66.)

Dupuy, Pierre-Marie : Crime sans châtiment ou mission accomplie. (Dans : Revue générale de droit international public, 2007, v. 111, no. 2, p. 243-257.)

Epstein, Paul J. : "New facts" in the Bosnia-Herzegovina vs. Yugoslavia Genocide case : interpretation of Article 61 of the Statute of the International Court of Justice. (In : Global Community : Yearbook of International Law and Jurisprudence, 2004, v. 4, no. 1, p. 187-193.)

Franck, Thomas M. : Individual criminal liability and collective civil responsibility : do they reinforce or contradict one another ? (In : Washington University Global Studies Law Review, 2007, v. 6, no. 3, p. 567-573.)

Frulli, Micaela : Un passo avanti e due indietro : responsabilità individuale e responsabilità statale nella sentenza della Corte internazionale di giustizia nel caso Bosnia-Erzegovina c. Serbia. (Dans : Diritto umani e diritto internazionale, 2007, v. 1, no. 3, p. 579-593.)

Gaeta, Paola : Génocide d'Etat et responsabilité pénale individuelle. (Dans : Revue générale de droit international public, 2007, v. 111, no. 2, p. 273-284.)

Gaeta, Paola : The I.C.J. Judgment on genocide in Bosnia : a missed opportunity ? Foreword. (In : Journal of International Criminal Justice, 2007, v. 5, no. 4, p. 827-828.)

Gattini, Andrea : Breach of the obligation to prevent and reparation thereof in the ICJ's genocide Judgment. (In : European Journal of International Law, 2007, v. 18, p. 695-713.)

Gattini, Andrea : Evidentiary issues in the I.C.J.'s genocide Judgment. (In : Journal of International Criminal Justice, 2007, v. 5, no. 4, p. 889-904.)

Gibney, Mark : Genocide and State responsibility. (In : Human Rights Law Review, 2007, v. 7, no. 4, p. 760-773.)

Gibney, Mark : State responsibility and the "object and purpose" of the Genocide Convention. (In : International Studies Journal, 2007, v. 4, no. 2-3, p. 141-150.)

Goldstone, Richard and Hamilton, Rebecca J. : Bosnia v. Serbia : lessons from the encounter of the International Court of Justice with the International Criminal Tribunal for the former Yugoslavia. (In : Leiden Journal of International Law, 2008, v. 21, no. 1, p. 95-112.)

Groome, Dermot : Adjudication genocide : is the International Court of Justice capable of judging State criminal responsibility ? (In : Fordham International Law Journal, 2008, v. 31, no. 4, p. 911-989.)

Hasani, Enver : Self-determination, territorial integrity and international stability : the case of Yugoslavia. [S.l.] : National Defence Academy, Institute for Peace Support and Conflict Management, 2004. [I.C.J., p. 27-28, 104, 107-109, 196-199, 274, 287, 306, 315-316, 319, 325-326.]

Höpfel, Frank: Individuelle versus Staatenverantwortlichkeit im Zusammenhang mit Völkermord. (In: International law between universalism and fragmentation: festschrift in honour of Gerhard Hafner, ed. by Buffard, Isabelle; Crawford, James; Pellet, Alain; Wittich, Stephan. Leiden [etc.]: Martinus Nijhoff, 2008, p. 535-552.)

I.C.J. ruling on Serbian liability for genocide. (In: Keesing's Record of World Events, 2007, v. 53, 47763.)

International Court of Justice: Bosnia and Herzegovina v. Serbia and Montenegro. (In: International Legal Materials, 2007, v. 46, no. 2, p. 188-310.)

International Court of Justice, 26 February 2007: case concerning the application of the Convention on the Prevention and Punishment of the Crime of Genocide (Bosnia and Herzegovina v. Serbia and Montenegro), judgment. (In: International Legal Materials, 2007, v. 46, p. 188-310.)

Kamenova, Cvetana: Ustanovjavane na faktite v reenieto na Medunarodnija Sd na Organizacijata na Obedinenite Nacii ot 26 februari 2007 g. – pozovavane na reenija na drug medunaroden sd. (In: Pravna misal, 2008, v. 49, no. 1, p. 65-74.)

Knoops, Geert-Jan: Potentiële (internationale) strafrechtelijke effecten van de genocide uitspraak van het Internationaal Gerechtshof in Bosnië v. Servië op ICTY-vervolgingen. (In: Ars aequi, 2007, v. 56, no. 7-8, p. 609-614.)

Loewenstein, Andrew B. and Kostas, Stephen A.: Divergent approaches to determining responsibility for genocide: the Darfur Commission inquiry and the I.C.J.'s Judgment in the genocide case. (In: Journal of International Criminal Justice, 2007, v. 5, no. 4, p. 839-857.)

Maneggia, Amina: Sul perché c'è stato genocidio a Srebrenica ma (forse) non altrove: la prova dell'intento specifico. (Dans: Le nuove frontiere del diritto internazionale: attori non statali, spazio virtuale, valori fondamentali e governo multinazionale di territori, sous la dir. de Carlo Focarelli. Perugia: Morlacchi editore, 2008, p. 167-190.)

Marqués Rueda, Efrén Gustavo: Comentarios al fallo pronunciado por la Corte Internacional de Justicia el 14 de febrero de 2007 con relación al caso sobre la Aplicación de la convención para la prevención y sanción del delito de genocido en el asunto Bosnia-Herzegovina c. Serbia. (Dans: Anuario mexicano de derecho internacional, 2008, v. 8, p. 885-908.)

McGoldrick, Dominic: State identity and genocide: the Bosnian genocide case. (In: International law and power: perspectives on legal order and justice: essays in honour of Colin Warbrick, ed. by Kaiyan Homi Kaikobad; Michael Bohlander. Leiden; Boston: Martinus Nijhoff, 2009, p. 255-304.)

Meron, Theodor: Breaking developments in international law: a conversation on the ICJ's opinion on Bosnia and Herzegovina v. Serbia and Montenegro. (In: Proceedings of the American Society of International Law, 2007, v. 101, p. 215-228.)

Milanovic, Marko: State responsibility for genocide: a follow-up. (In: European Journal of International Law, 2007, v. 18, p. 669-694.)

Ollivier, Antoine: The judgment of the International Court of Justice in the "genocide" case between Bosnia and Herzegovina v. Serbia and Montenegro. (In: International Legal Materials, 2007, v. 46, no. 2, p. 185-187.) [I.C.J., passim.]

Palassis, Stathis: Application of the Convention on the Prevention and Punishment of the Crime of Genocide (Bosnia and Herzegovina v. Serbia and Montenegro). (In: University of New South Wales Law Journal, 2008, v. 31, no. 1, p. 80-106.)

Rajkovic, Nikolas: On "bad law" and "good politics": the politics of the I.C.J. Genocide case and its interpretation. (In: Leiden Journal of International Law, 2008, v. 21, no. 4, p. 885-910.)

Riddell, Anna: Report on the oral proceedings in the Application of the Convention on the Prevention and Punishment of the Crime of Genocide (Bosnia and Herzegovina v. Serbia and Montenegro): selected procedural aspects. (In: Leiden Journal of International Law, 2007, v. 20, no. 2, p. 405-440.)

Rosenne, Shabtai: Reflections on automatic treaty succession. (In: Essays on international law and practice, by Shabtai Rosenne. Leiden [etc.]: Martinus Nijhoff, 2007, p. 425-433.)

Schabas, William A.: Genocide and the International Court of Justice: finally, a duty to prevent the crime of crimes. (In: International Studies Journal, 2007, v. 4, no. 2-3, p. 17-64.)

Scheffer, David: The World Court's fractured ruling on genocide. (In: Genocide studies and prevention. University of Toronto Press, 2007, v. 2, no. 2, p. 123-136.)

Schmitt, Paul: The future of the genocide suits at the International Court of Justice: France's role in the Rwanda and implication in the Bosnia v. Serbia decision. (In: Georgetown Journal of International Law, 2009, v. 40, p. 585-613.)

Seymour, Jillaine: Jurisdiction and responsibility by necessary implication: genocide in Bosnia. (In: Cambridge Law Journal, 2007, v. 66, no. 2, p. 249-253.)

Shany, Yuval: Bosnia, Serbia and the politics of international adjudication. (In: Justice, 2008, no. 45, p. 21-26.)

Sivakumaran, Sandesh: Application of the Convention on the Prevention and Punishment of the Crime of Genocide (Bosnia and Herzegovina v. Serbia and Montenegro). (In: International and Comparative Law Quarterly, 2007, v. 56, no. 3, p. 695-708.)

Sivakumaran, Sandesh and Villalpando, Santiago: Application of the Convention on the Prevention and Punishment of the Crime of Genocide

(Bosnia and Herzegovina v. Serbia and Montenegro): an introduction. (In: Leiden Journal of International Law, 2008, v. 21, p. 63-64.)

Slomic, Edina: When skeletons come out of the closet: implications of the Bosnian genocide decision for Serbia's eventual EU accession. (In: Georgia Journal of International and Comparative Law, 2009, v. 37, no. 3, p. 621-658.)

Sorel, Jean-Marc: Les multiples lectures d'un arrêt: entre sentiment d'impunité et sentiment de cohérence, une décision à relativiser. (Dans: Revue générale de droit international public, 2007, v. 111, no. 2, p. 259-272.)

Souty, Vincent: La res judicata dans l'affaire du génocide (C.I.J. arrêt du 26 février 2007). (Dans: Anuario brasileiro de direito internacional, 2008, v. 3, p. 191-207.)

Spinedi, Marina: On the non-attribution of the Bosnian Serbs' conduct to Serbia. (In: Journal of International Criminal Justice, 2007, v. 5, no. 4, p. 829-838.)

Stojanovic, Radoslav (ed.): Srbija pred Medunarodnim sudom pravde: knjiga I: odbrana. Beograd: Filip Visnjic, 2007. (Diplomatske sveske.) [I.C.J., passim.]

Stojanovic, Radoslav (ed.): Srbija pred Medunarodnim sudom pravde: knjiga II: presuda. Beograd: Filip Visnjic, 2007. (Diplomatske sveske.)

Teani, Anne-Lise: L'arrêt de la Cour internationale de Justice du 26 février 2007: application de la Convention pour la prévention et la répression du crime de génocide, vecteur d'unité ou de fragmentation du droit international? (Dans: Revue de science criminelle et de droit pénal comparé, 2007, v. 4, p. 765-778.)

Tomuschat, Christian: Reparation in cases of genocide. (In: Journal of International Criminal Justice, 2007, v. 5, no. 4, p. 905-912.)

Toufayan, Mark: The World Court's distress when facing genocide: a critical commentary on the application of the Genocide Convention Case (Bosnia and Herzegovina v. Yugoslavia (Serbia and Montenegro)). (In: Texas International Law Journal, 2005, v. 40, no. 2, p. 233-261.) [P.C.I.J., p. 244; I.C.J., passim.]

Turns, David: Application of the Convention on the Prevention and Punishment of the Crime of Genocide: Bosnia and Herzegovina v Serbia and Montenegro. (In: Melbourne Journal of International Law, 2007, v. 8, no. 2, p. 398-427.)

Weckel, Philippe: L'arrêt sur le génocide: le souffle de l'avis de 1951 n'a pas transporté la Cour. (Dans: Revue générale de droit international public, 2007, v. 111, no. 2, p. 305-331.)

Wittich, Stephan: Permissible derogation from mandatory rules? The problem of party status in the genocide case. (In: European Journal of International Law, 2007, v. 18, p. 591-618.) [P.C.I.J., p. 600, 611.]

Zarbiev, Fouad: Les politiques des vérités juridiques en droit international: propos autour d'une controverse interjuridictionnelle. (Dans: Finnish Yearbook of International Law, 2007, v. 18, p. 343-369.)
North Carolina Journal of International Law and Commercial Regulation, 2004, v. 30, no. 2, p. 335-377.)

92. *Projet Gabcíkovo-Nagymaros (Hongrie/Slovaquie)*
92. *Gabcíkovo-Nagymaros Project (Hungary/Slovakia)*

Benvenisti, Eyal: Customary international law as a judicial tool for promoting efficiency. (In: The impact of international law on international cooperation: theoretical perspectives, ed. by Benvenisti, Eyal; Hirsch, Moshe. Cambridge [etc.]: Cambridge University Press, 2004, p. 85-116.) [P.C.I.J., p. 94; I.C.J., passim.]

Dupuy, Pierre-Marie: L'invocation de l'état de nécessité écologique: les enseignements tirés d'une étude de cas. (Dans: La nécessité en droit international: colloque de Grenoble. Paris: A. Pedone, 2007, p. 222-235.)

Jansky, Libor and Murakami, Masahiro and Pachova, Nevelina I.: The Danube: environmental monitoring of an international river. Tokyo [etc.]: United Nations University Press, 2004. (Water Resources Management and Policy.) [I.C.J., p. xiv-xv, xvii, 4-5, 7, 11-16, 33, 39, 42-43, 107, 150-152.]

Reichert-Facilides, Daniel: Down the Danube: the Vienna Convention on the Law of Treaties and the case concerning the Gabcikovo-Nagymaros project. (In: The law of treaties, ed. by Davidson, Scott. Aldershot; Burlington: Dartmouth; Ashgate, 2004, p. 477-494.)

Szabó, Marcel: Gabcíkovo-Nagymaros dispute: implementation of the ICJ judgment. (In: Environmental Policy and Law, 2009, v. 39, no. 2, p. 97-102.)

93, 95. *Licéité de l'utilisation des armes nucléaires par un Etat dans un conflit armé; Licéité de la menace ou de l'emploi d'armes nucléaires*
93, 95. *Legality of the Use by a State of Nuclear Weapons in Armed Conflict; Legality of the Threat or Use of Nuclear Weapons*

Bedjaoui, Mohammed: Droit international, bonne foi, et l'élimination des armes nucléaires. (Dans: Völkerrechtliche Pflicht zur nuklearen Abrüstung?, par Mohammed Bedjaoui; Karima Bennoune; Dieter Deiseroth; Elisabeth Jay Shafer. Norderstedt: Books on demand, 2009, p. 81-128.) [C.I.J., passim.]

Bedjaoui, Mohammed: Good faith, international law and elimination of nuclear weapons: keynote address. (In: Völkerrechtliche Pflicht zur nuklearen Abrüstung?, by Mohammed Bedjaoui; Karima Bennoune; Dieter Deiseroth; Elisabeth Jay Shafer. Norderstedt: Books on demand, 2009, p. 129-175.) [I.C.J., passim.]

Bedjaoui, Mohammed: Treu und Glauben, Völkerrecht und die Abschaffung der Atomwaffen. (In: Völkerrechtliche Pflicht zur nuklearen Abrüstung?, by Mohammed Bedjaoui; Karima Bennoune; Dieter Deiseroth; Elisabeth Jay Shafer. Norderstedt: Books on demand, 2009, p. 29-80.)

Bennoune, Karima: The intersection of nuclear weapons and international human rights law implication for the good-faith obligation to negotiate nuclear disarmament. (In: Völkerrechtliche Pflicht zur nuklearen Abrüstung? Legal obligation to nuclear disarmament? L'obligation de désarmement nucléaire?, by Mohammed Bedjaoui; Karima Bennoune; Dieter Deiseroth; Elisabeth Jay Shafer. Norderstedt: Books on demand, 2009, p. 207-227.) [I.C.J., p. 211, 227.]

Bennoune, Karima: Schnittpunkte zwischen den völkerrechtlichen Aspekten der Kernwaffen und den internationalen Menschenrechten: Auswirkungen auf die Verpflichtung nach dem Nichtweiterverbreitungsvertrag zu redlichen Verhandlungen über die Abrüstung der Kernwaffen. (In: Völkerrechtliche Pflicht zur nuklearen Abrüstung? Legal obligation to nuclear disarmament? L'obligation de désarmement nucléaire?, by Mohammed Bedjaoui; Karima Bennoune; Dieter Deiseroth; Elisabeth Jay Shafer. Norderstedt: Books on demand, 2009, p. 177-206.) [I.C.J., p. 182-183, 189-190, 195.]

Burroughs, John: Negotiating in "good faith". (In: Freedom from nuclear weapons through legal accountability and good faith: conference report, ed. by George Farebrother. Nottingham: Spokesman; World Court Project, 2007, p. 47-51.)

Cabasso, Jacqueline: Return to the International Court of Justice. (In: Freedom from nuclear weapons through legal accountability and good faith: conference report, ed. by George Farebrother. Nottingham: Spokesman; World Court Project, 2007, p. 83-85.)

Deiseroth, Dieter: Nutzen und Funktionen des Völkerrechts. (In: Völkerrechtliche Pflicht zur nuklearen Abrüstung? Legal obligation to nuclear disarmament? L'obligation de désarmement nucléaire?, by Mohammed Bedjaoui; Karima Bennoune; Dieter Deiseroth; Elisabeth Jay Shafer. Norderstedt: Books on demand, 2009, p. 289-318.) [I.C.J., p. 298-302.]

Dewes, Kate: The development of the World Court project. (In: Freedom from nuclear weapons through legal accountability and good faith: conference report, ed. by George Farebrother. Nottingham: Spokesman; World Court Project, 2007, p. 59-61.)

Doswald-Beck, Louise: The international humanitarian law aspects of the advisory opinion. (In: Freedom from nuclear weapons through legal accountability and good faith: conference report, ed. by George Farebrother. Nottingham: Spokesman; World Court Project, 2007, p. 23-28.)

Dwyer, Anabel: Experiences with domestic courts: defending US nuclear resisters since the I.C.J. Opinion. (In: Freedom from nuclear weapons through legal accountability and good faith: conference report, ed. by

George Farebrother. Nottingham : Spokesman ; World Court Project, 2007, p. 75-77.)

Fujita, Hisakazu : The advisory opinion of the International Court of Justice on the legality of nuclear weapons. (In : A manual of international humanitarian laws, ed. by Sanajaoba, Noarem. New Delhi : Regency Publications, 2004, p. 617-626.)

Gowlland-Debbas, Vera : The relevance of paragraph 25 of the ICJ's advisory opinion on nuclear weapons. (In : Proceedings of the American Society of International Law, 2004, v. 98, p. 358-363.)

Green, Robert : Nuclear policy concepts and self-defence. (In : Freedom from nuclear weapons through legal accountability and good faith : conference report, ed. by George Farebrother. Nottingham : Spokesman ; World Court Project, 2007, p. 43-46.)

Haines, Steven : Nuclear policy concepts and self-defence. (In : Freedom from nuclear weapons through legal accountability and good faith : conference report, ed. by George Farebrother. Nottingham : Spokesman ; World Court Project, 2007, p. 38-42.)

Jäckel, Otto : Experiences with domestic courts : nuclear weapons and German courts. (In : Freedom from nuclear weapons through legal accountability and good faith : conference report, ed. by George Farebrother. Nottingham : Spokesman ; World Court Project, 2007, p. 72-74.)

Kammerhofer, Jörg : Gaps, the "Nuclear Weapons" Advisory Opinion and the structure of international legal argument between theory and practice. (In : British Year Book of International Law, 2009, v. 80, p. 333-360.)

Klabbers, Jan : Global governance before the ICJ : re-reading the WHA opinion. (In : Max Planck Yearbook of United Nations Law, 2009, v. 13, p. 1-28.)

Koppe, Erik Vincent : The use of nuclear weapons and the protection of the environment during international armed conflict. [S.l.] : [s.n.], 2006. [P.C.I.J., p. 167, 248; I.C.J., p. 5-6, 96, 98-101, 111-112, 114, 124, 164, 167, 170-173, 195-196, 200, 204-206, 213-215, 218, 221, 226, 239, 242-243, 256-258, 262-264, 269, 275, 279, 281-283, 286-290, 296, 299-301.]

Krieger, David : Nuclear weapons and future justice. (In : The challenge of abolishing nuclear weapons, ed. by Krieger, David. New Brunswick, NJ [etc.] : Transaction Publishers, 2009, p. 109-116.) [I.C.J., p. 111-112, 114.]

Lammerant, Hans : Going to the I.C.J. and civil society : the co-ordination of direct action, political campaining and the courts. (In : Freedom from nuclear weapons through legal accountability and good faith : conference report, ed. by George Farebrother. Nottingham : Spokesman ; World Court Project, 2007, p. 97-102.) [I.C.J., p. 99.]

Lammerant, Hans : The international humanitarian law aspects of the advisory opinion. (In : Freedom from nuclear weapons through legal accountability and good faith: conference report, ed. by George Farebrother. Nottingham: Spokesman; World Court Project, 2007, p. 31-34.)

Moxley, Charles J., Jr.: The sword in the mirror: the lawfulness of North Korea's use and threat of use of nuclear weapons based on the United States' legitimization of nuclear weapons. (In: Fordham International Law Journal. 2003-2004, v. 27, no. 4, p. 1379-1489.) [I.C.J., p. 1379-1380, 1392, 1397, 1432-1433, 1441-1442, 1445-1448, 1450, 1455-1456, 1459-1460, 1463-1464, 1468-1471, 1473-1475, 1478-1481.]

Neff, Stephen C.: In search of clarity: non liquet and international law. (In: International law and power: perspectives on legal order and justice: essays in honour of Colin Warbrick, ed. by Kaiyan Homi Kaikobad; Michael Bohlander. Leiden; Boston: Martinus Nijhoff, 2009, p. 63-83.)

Shafer, Elisabeth Jay: Good faith negotiation: the nuclear disarmament obligation of Article VI of the NPT and return to the International Court of Justice. (In: Völkerrechtliche Pflicht zur nuklearen Abrüstung?, by Mohammed Bedjaoui; Karima Bennoune; Dieter Deiseroth; Elisabeth Jay Shafer. Norderstedt: Books on demand, 2009, p. 265-288.) [I.C.J., passim.]

Shafer, Elisabeth Jay: Verhandlungen in redlicher Absicht, die Verpflichtung zur nuklearen Abrüstung nach Artikel VI des Atomwaffensperrvertrages und die Rückkehr zum Internationalen Gerichtshof. (In: Völkerrechtliche Pflicht zur nuklearen Abrüstung?, by Mohammed Bedjaoui; Karima Bennoune; Dieter Deiseroth; Elisabeth Jay Shafer. Norderstedt: Books on demand, 2009, p. 229-263.)

Shiner, Phil: Going to the I.C.J. and civil society: citizens' actions and the legal case against nuclear weapons. (In: Freedom from nuclear weapons through legal accountability and good faith: conference report, ed. by George Farebrother. Nottingham: Spokesman; World Court Project, 2007, p. 94-97.)

Simon, David: Article VI of the Non-Proliferation Treaty is a pactum de contrahendo and has serious legal obligation by implication. (In: Journal of International Law and Policy, 2004, v. II, p. 1-19.) [I.C.J., p. 1-2, 9-10, 13, 15-16.]

Tchikaya, Blaise: Les récentes leçons de la Cour internationale de Justice sur les armes de destruction massive. (Dans: Les Nations Unies face aux armes de destruction massive: colloque des 5 et 6 décembre 2003, sous la dir. de Rostane Mehdi. Paris: A. Pedone, 2004, p. 113-132.)

Terry, Patrick: US-Iran relations in international law since 1979: hostages, oil platforms, nuclear weapons and the use of force. Rangendingen: Libertas, 2009. (Libertas paper; 70.)

Ware, Alyn: Return to the International Court of Justice. (In: Freedom from nuclear weapons through legal accountability and good faith: conference report, ed. by George Farebrother. Nottingham: Spokesman; World Court Project, 2007, p. 80-82.)

Weeramantry, Christopher G.: The international humanitarian law aspects of the advisory opinion. (In: Freedom from nuclear weapons through legal accountability and good faith: conference report, ed. by George Farebrother. Nottingham: Spokesman; World Court Project, 2007, p. 28-30.)

Weeramantry, Christopher G.: Main findings of the Court and legal developments since 1996. (In: Freedom from nuclear weapons through legal accountability and good faith: conference report, ed. by George Farebrother. Nottingham: Spokesman; World Court Project, 2007, p. 4-7.)

Weiss, Cora: Going to the I.C.J. and civil society: opening remarks. (In: Freedom from nuclear weapons through legal accountability and good faith: conference report, ed. by George Farebrother. Nottingham: Spokesman; World Court Project, 2007, 89.)

Weiss, Peter: Nuclear policy concepts and self-defence. (In: Freedom from nuclear weapons through legal accountability and good faith: conference report, ed. by George Farebrother. Nottingham: Spokesman; World Court Project, 2007, p. 35-37.)

Weiss, Peter: Return to the International Court of Justice. (In: Freedom from nuclear weapons through legal accountability and good faith: conference report, ed. by George Farebrother. Nottingham: Spokesman; World Court Project, 2007, p. 86-88.)

94. *Frontière terrestre et maritime entre le Cameroun et le Nigéria (Cameroun c. Nigéria; Guinée équatoriale (intervenant))*
94. *Land and Maritime Boundary between Cameroon and Nigeria (Cameroon* v. *Nigeria: Equatorial Guinea intervening)*

Christofides, Jack: How good offices changed the nature of the border dispute between Cameroon and Nigeria. (In: Conflict prevention in practice: essays in honour of James Sutterlin, ed. by Bertrand G. Ramcharan. Leiden, [etc.]: Martinus Nijhoff, 2005, p. 211-217.) [I.C.J., p. 211-213, 215.]

Daniel, Tim and Lerer, David: Cameroon-Nigeria, report no 4-1 (Add. 2): case concerning the Land and Maritime Boundary between Cameroon and Nigeria. (In: International maritime boundaries, ed. by David A. Colson; Robert W. Smith. Leiden; Boston: Martinus Nijhoff, 2005, v. 5, p. 3605-3617.)

Gray, Christine: The Eritrea/Ethiopia Claims Commission oversteps its boundaries: a partial award? (In: European Journal of International Law, 2006, v. 17, no. 4, p. 699-721.) [I.C.J., p. 713-714, 715-721.]

International Court of Justice: Case Concerning the Land and Maritime Boundary between Cameroon and Nigeria (Cameroon v. Nigeria: Equatorial Guinea intervening). Judgment of 10 October 2002. (In: International maritime boundaries, 2005, v. 5, p. 3618-3620.)

Kwiatkowska, Barbara: The Cameroon v. Nigeria; Equatorial Guinea intervening (land and maritime boundary) judgment. (In: Law in the service of human dignity: essays in honour of Florentino Feliciano, ed. by

Charnovitz, Steve ; Steger, Debra P. ; Van den Bossche, Peter. Cambridge : Cambridge University Press, 2005, p. 378-408.)

Kwiatkowska, Barbara : The contribution of the 2002 (Cameroon v. Nigeria : Equatorial Guinea intervening) Land and Maritime Boundary between Cameroon and Nigeria judgement of the International Court of Justice to equitable maritime boundary delimitation. (In : Hague Yearbook of International Law, 2004, v. 17, p. 95-135.)

López Martín, Ana Gemma : A vueltas con el título jurídico y la equidistancia : la sentencia de la Corte Internacional de Justicia de 10 de octubre de 2002 en el asunto relativo a la Frontera terrestre y marítima entre Camerún y Nigeria (Camerún c. Nigeria ; Guinea Ecuatorial interviniente). (Dans : Cuadernos de jurisprudencia internacional, 2004, v. 1, p. 105-136.)

Mbuh, Justice M. : International law and conflicts : resolving border and sovereignty disputes in Africa. New York [etc.] : iUniverse, 2004. [I.C.J., p. xix-xx, 2-3, 8, 20-21, 41-44, 47, 105, 143-144, 152, 168, 181-279.]

Mendelson, Maurice H. : The Cameroon-Nigeria case in the International Court of Justice : some territorial sovereignty and boundary delimitation issues. (In : British Year Book of International Law, 2004, v. 75, p. 223-247.)

Mohamed Salah, M. Mahmoud : La Commission mixte Cameroun/Nigéria, un mécanisme original de règlement des différends interétatiques. (Dans : Annuaire français de droit international, 2005, v. 51, p. 162-184.) [C.I.J., passim.]

Oduntan, Gbenga : The demarcation of straddling villages in accordance with the International Court of Justice jurisprudence : the Cameroon-Nigeria experience. (In : Chinese Journal of International Law, 2006, v. 5, p. 79-114.) [P.C.I.J., p. 94; I.C.J., passim.]

Tanaka, Yoshifumi : Reflections on maritime delimitation in the Cameroon/Nigeria case. (In : International and Comparative Law Quarterly, 2004, v. 53, p. 369-406.)

Tang Le Huy Quoc-Benjamin, Nguyen : La péninsule de Bakassi. (Dans : Chronique des Nations Unies (ONU), 2004, v. 41, no. 2, 16.) [C.I.J., p. 16.]

96. *Compétence en matière de pêcheries (Espagne c. Canada)*
96. *Fisheries Jurisdiction (Spain* v. *Canada)*

Study Group on Decisions of the International Court of Justice : Fisheries jurisdiction (Spain v. Canada), jurisdiction of the Court, judgment (4 December 1998). (In : Kokusaiho Gaiko Zassi, 2004, v. 103, no. 2, p. 85-104.)

99. *Convention de Vienne sur les relations consulaires (Paraguay c. Etats-Unis d'Amérique)*
99. *Vienna Convention on Consular Relations (Paraguay* v. *United States of America)*

Barrie, George N.: ICJ jurisdiction over the Vienna Convention on Consular Relations. (In: South African Yearbook of International Law, 2004, v. 29, p. 264-267.)

Naskou-Perraki, Paroula: Fairness, justice and treatment of foreign nationals before the International Court of Justice. (In: Justice in particular: festschrift in honour of professor P. J. Kozyris. Athens: Sakkoulas, 2007, p. 309-328.)

Rothenberg, Laurence E.: International law, U.S. sovereignty, and the death penalty. (In: Georgetown Journal of International Law, 2004, v. 35, no. 3, p. 547-595.) [I.C.J., p. 570-592.]

Sheik, Mani: From Breard to Medellin: Supreme Court inaction or ICJ activism in the field of international law? (In: California Law Review, 2006, v. 94, p. 531-573.)

102. *Souveraineté sur Pulau Ligitan et Pulau Sipadan (Indonésie/Malaisie)*
102. *Sovereignty over Pulau Ligitan and Pulau Sipadan (Indonesia/Malaysia)*

Faizal, Mohamed and Evangeline, Queck: The repercussions of the similarities between Sipadan/Ligitan and Pedra Branca disputes. (In: Singapore Law Review, 2004, v. 24, p. 52-65.)

Sánchez Rodríguez, Luis Ignacio: Una nueva controversia sobre soberanía insular: la sentencia de la Corte Internacional de Justicia de 17 de diciembre de 2002 en el asunto relativo a la Soberanía sobre Pulau Ligitan y Pulau Sipadan (Indonesia c. Malasia). (Dans: Cuadernos de jurisprudencia internacional, 2004, v. 1, p. 137-153.)

103. *Ahmadou Sadio Diallo (République de Guinée c. République démocratique du Congo)*
103. *Ahmadou Sadio Diallo (Republic of Guinea* v. *Democratic Republic of the Congo)*

Alvarez-Jiménez, Alberto: Foreign investors, diplomatic protection and the International Court of Justice's decision on preliminary objections in the Diallo case. (In: North Carolina Journal of International and Commercial Regulation, 2008, v. 33, no. 3, p. 437-454.)

Alvarez-Jiménez, Alberto: Minimum standard of treatment of aliens, fair and equitable treatment of foreign investors, customary international law and the Diallo case before the International Court of Justice. (In: The Journal of World Investment & Trade, 2008, v. 9, no. 1, p. 51-70.)

Dorogo, Stefano: Sulla protezione diplomatica degli azionisti: il caso Diallo di fronte alla Corte internazionale di giustizia. (Dans: Rivista di diritto internazionale, 2007, v. 90, no. 3, p. 705-737.)

Frouville, Olivier de: Affaire Ahmadou Sadio Diallo (République de Guinée c. République démocratique du Congo): exceptions préliminaires: le roman inachevé de la protection diplomatique. (Dans: Annuaire français de droit international, 2007, v. 53, p. 291-327.)

International Court of Justice: case concerning Ahmadou Sadio Diallo (Republic of Guinea v. Democratic Republic of the Congo), May 24, 2007. (In: International Legal Materials, 2007, v. 46, p. 712-734.)

Knight, Stephen J and O'Brien, Angus J: Ahmadou Sadio Diallo: Republic of Guinea v Democratic Republic of the Congo: clarifying the scope of diplomatic protection of corporate and shareholder rights. (In: Melbourne Journal of International Law, 2008, v. 9, no. 1, p. 151-170.)

Mascarenhas, Viren: Introductory note to the case concerning Ahmadou Sadio Diallo (Republic of Guinea v. Democratic Republic of Congo) (preliminary objections), May 24, 2007. (In: International Legal Materials, 2007, v. 46, p. 709-711.)

Okowa, Phoebe N.: Case concerning Ahmadou Sadio Diallo (Republic of Guinea v. Democratic Republic of Congo): preliminary objections. (In: International and Comparative Law Quarterly, 2008, v. 57, p. 219-224.)

Okowa, Phoebe N. and Barker, J. Craig: Decisions of international tribunals: case concerning Ahmadou Sadio Diallo (Republic of Guinea v Democratic Republic of Congo): preliminary objections. (In: International and Comparative Law Quarterly, 2008, v. 57, no. 1, p. 219-224.)

Parlett, Kate: Role of diplomatic protection in the protection of foreign investments. (In: Cambridge Law Journal, 2007, v. 66, no. 3, p. 533-535.)

Vermeer-Künzli, Annemarieke: Diallo and the draft articles: the application of the draft articles on diplomatic protection in the Ahmadou Sadio Diallo case. (In: Leiden Journal of International Law, 2007, v. 20, no. 4, p. 941-954.)

Weckel, Philippe: Chronique de jurisprudence internationale: Cour internationale de Justice: arrêt du 24 mai 2007 (exc. prél.), Ahmadou Sadio Diallo (Rep. de Guinée c. R.D.C.). (Dans: Revue générale de droit international public, 2007, v. 111, no. 3, p. 705-713.)

104. *LaGrand (Allemagne c. Etats-Unis d'Amérique)*
104. *LaGrand (Germany* v. *United States of America)*

Amirfar, Catherine M.: AALS panel: Mexico v. USA (Avena): arguments of Mexico. (In: German Law Journal, 2004, v. 5, no. 4, p. 375-383.) [I.C.J., passim.]

Barrie, George N.: ICJ jurisdiction over the Vienna Convention on Consular Relations. (In: South African Yearbook of International Law, 2004, v. 29, p. 264-267.)

Cançado Trindade, A. A. et Cohen-Jonathan, Gérard et Decaux, Emmanuel et Engel, Norbert et Condorelli, Luigi: Débats. (Dans: Mesures conservatoires et droits fondamentaux, sous la dir. de Gérard Cohen-Jonathan; Jean-Francois Flauss. Bruxelles: Bruylant; Nemesis, 2005, p. 57-62.) [C.I.J., p. 57-58, 60-61.]

Cohen-Jonathan, Gérard: Conclusions générales. (Dans: Mesures conservatoires et droits fondamentaux, sous la dir. de Gérard Cohen-Jonathan; Jean-Francois Flauss. Bruxelles: Bruylant; Nemesis, 2005, p. 283-307.) [C.P.J.I., p. 304-305; C.I.J., p. 285, 303-304.]

Condorelli, Luigi: Discussion. (Dans: Mesures conservatoires et droits fondamentaux, sous la dir. de Gérard Cohen-Jonathan; Jean-Francois Flauss. Bruxelles: Bruylant; Nemesis, 2005, p. 55-56.) [C.I.J., passim.]

Dominicé, Christian: Droits individuels et droits de l'homme: chevauchements et différences. (Dans: Diritti individuali e giustizia internazionale: liber Fausto Pocar, sous la dir. de Venturine, Gabriella; Bariatti, Stefania. Milano: Giuffrè, 2009, v. 1, p. 301-307.) [C.I.J., passim.]

Grzeszick, Bernd: Rechte des Einzelnen im Völkerrecht: Chancen und Gefahren völkerrechtlicher Entwicklungstrends am Beispiel der Individualrechte im allgemeinen Völkerrecht. (In: Archiv des Völkerrechts, 2005, v. 43, no. 3, p. 312-344.) [I.C.J., p. 312-317, 320-334, 339-344; P.C.I.J., p. 314, 337-338.]

Hoppe, Carsten: Implementation of LaGrand and Avena in Germany and the United States: exploring a transatlantic divide in search of a uniform interpretation of consular rights. (In: European Journal of International Law, 2007, v. 18, p. 317-336.)

Naskou-Perraki, Paroula: Fairness, justice and treatment of foreign nationals before the International Court of Justice. (In: Justice in particular: festschrift in honour of professor P. J. Kozyris. Athens: Sakkoulas, 2007, p. 309-328.)

Rothenberg, Laurence E.: International law, U.S. sovereignty, and the death penalty. (In: Georgetown Journal of International Law, 2004, v. 35, no. 3, p. 547-595.) [I.C.J., p. 570-592.]

Ruiz Colomé, Angeles: El ejercicio de la protección diplomática y la Convención de Viena de 1963 sobre Relaciones Consulares. La sentencia de la Corte Internacional de Justicia de 27 de junio de 2001 en el asunto LaGrand (Alemania c. Estados Unidos de América). (Dans: Cuardernos de jurisprudencia internacional, 2004, v. 1, p. 193-224.)

Sheik, Mani: From Breard to Medellin: Supreme Court inaction or ICJ activism in the field of international law? (In: California Law Review, 2006, v. 94, p. 531-573.)

Stirling-Zanda, Simonetta: Obtaining judicial enforcement of individual conventional rights: the Consular Convention at the ICJ and at the Inter-American Court. (In: Archiv des Völkerrechts, 2004, v. 42, no. 2, p. 184-216.)

Walter, Tonio: Der deutsche Strafprozess und das Völkerrecht. (In: Juristische Rundschau, 2007, v, 2007, no. 3, p. 99-104.) [I.C.J., p. 99-101.]

Weckel, Philippe et Condorelli, Luigi et Malinverni, Giorgio et Schabas, William A. et Condorelli, Luigi: Débats. (Dans: Mesures conservatoires et droits fondamentaux, sous la dir. de Gérard Cohen-Jonathan; Jean-Francois Flauss. Bruxelles: Bruylant; Nemesis, 2005, p. 91-92.) [C.I.J., p. 91.]

105-114. *Licéité de l'emploi de la force (Yougoslavie c. Belgique) (Yougoslavie c. Canada) (Yougoslavie c. France) (Yougoslavie c. Allemagne) (Yougoslavie c. Italie) (Yougoslavie c. Pays-Bas) (Yougoslavie c. Portugal) (Yougoslavie c. Espagne) (Yougoslavie c. Royaume-Uni) (Yougoslavie c. Etats-Unis d'Amérique)*

105-114. *Legality of Use of Force (Yugoslavia* v. *Belgium) (Yugoslavia* v. *Canada) (Yugoslavia* v. *France) (Yugoslavia* v. *Germany) (Yugoslavia* v. *Italy) (Yugoslavia* v. *Netherlands) (Yugoslavia* v. *Portugal) (Yugoslavia* v. *Spain) (Yugoslavia* v. *United Kingdom) (Yugoslavia* v. *United States of America)*

Bijelic, Ana et Dumont, Hélène et Boisvert, Anne-Marie: Le système de justice des pays de l'ex-Yougoslavie et les défis de l'administration de la justice pénale internationale. (Dans: La voie vers la Cour pénale internationale: tous les chemins mènent à Rome = The highway to the International Criminal Court: all roads lead to Rome, sous la dir. de Dumont, Hélène; Boisvert, Anne-Marie. Montréal: Editions Thémis, 2004, p. 255-313.) [C.I.J., p. 261, 295-305, 313.]

Brown, Chester: Access to international justice in the Legality of Use of Force cases: case and comment. (In: Cambridge Law Journal, 2005, v. 64, no. 2, p. 267-271.)

Escudero Espinosa, Juan Francisco: La incompetencia rationae personae de la Corte Internacional de Justicia en los asuntos relativos a la legalidad del uso de la fuerza (Serbia y Montenegro v. ocho Estados miembros de la OTAN), sentencias de 15 de diciembre de 2004. (Dans: Revista española de derecho internacional, 2005, v. 57, no. 2, p. 1122-1128.)

Frouville, Olivier de: Une harmonie dissonante de la justice internationale: les arrêts de la Cour internationale de Justice sur les exceptions préliminaires dans l'affaire relative à la Licéité de l'emploi de la force. (Dans: Annuaire français de droit international, 2004, v. 50, p. 337-369.) [C.P.J.I., p. 342, 362; C.I.J., passim.]

Gray, Christine: Legality of Use of Force (Serbia and Montenegro v. Belgium) (Serbia and Montenegro v. Canada) (Serbia and Montenegro v. France)(Serbia and Montenegro v. Germany) (Serbia and Montenegro v. Italy) (Serbia and Montenegro v. Netherlands) (Serbia and Montenegro v. Portugal) (Serbia and Montenegro v. United Kingdom): preliminary objections. Judgment of 15 December 2004. (In: International and Comparative Law Quarterly, 2005, v. 54, no. 3, p. 779-787.)

International Court of Justice: Legality of Use of Force (Serbia and Montenegro v. Portugal, United Kingdom, Netherlands, Italy, Germany, Canada, France, Belgium). (In: International Legal Materials, 2005, v. 44, no. 2, p. 299-403.)

Lamm, Vanda : A NATO-bombázások ügye a Nemzetközi Bíróság elött. (In : Dayton, 10 éu után : a kötet a Magyar Tudományos Akadémián 2005. december 9-én tartott konferencia elöadásait tartalmazza. Budapest : MTA Jogtudományi Intézet – MTA Társadalomkutató Kozpont, 2006, 63-77).

Oellers-Frahm, Karin : Jugoslawien und die NATO. (In : Vereinte Nationen, 2005, v. 53, no. 4, p. 154-156.) [C.I.J., passim.]

Olleson, Simon : "Killing three birds with one stone"? The preliminary objections judgments of the International Court of Justice in the legality of use of force cases. (In : Leiden Journal of International Law, 2005, v. 18, no. 2, p. 237-255.) [P.C.I.J., p. 252.]

Puoti, Paola : Yugoslavia dissolution before the ICJ : the need for a new approach to State succession. (In : Italian Yearbook of International Law, 2006, v. 16, p. 187-213.)

Rosenne, Shabtai : Capacity to litigate in the International Court of Justice : reflections on Yugoslavia in the Court. (In : British Year Book of International Law, 2009, v. 80, p. 217-243.)

Weckel, Philippe : Chronique de jurisprudence internationale : Cour internationale de Justice. (Dans : Revue générale de droit international public, 2005, v. 109, p. 215-221.)

106. *Licéité de l'emploi de la force (Yougoslavie c. Canada)*
106. *Legality of Use of Force (Yugoslavia* v. *Canada)*

Rouillard, Louis-Philippe F. : Canada's prevention and repression of war crimes. (In : Miskolci Nemzetközi Jogi Közlemények, 2005, v. 2, no. 1, p. 43-58.) [I.C.J., p. 56.]

Swords, Colleen and Willis, Alan : The decision of the International Court of Justice in the case concerning Legality of Use of Force (Serbia and Montenegro v. Canada). (In : Canadian Yearbook of International Law, 2004, v. 42, p. 353-383.)

109. *Licéité de l'emploi de la force (Yougoslavie c. Italie)*
109. *Legality of Use of Force (Yugoslavia* v. *Italy)*

Giurisprudenza internazionale : Corte internazionale di giustizia, 15 diciembre 2004 : sentenza nell'affare relativo alla Liceità dell'uso della forza : eccezioni preliminari (Serbia e Montenegro c. Italia). (Dans : Rivista di diritto internazionale, 2005, v. 88, no. 1, p. 166-205.) [C.P.J.I., p. 170, 197, 202; C.I.J., passim.]

110. *Licéité de l'emploi de la force (Yougoslavie c. Pays-Bas)*
110. *Legality of Use of Force (Yugoslavia* v. *Netherlands)*

Blokker, Niels : From a dispute about the use of force to a non-dispute about jurisdiction : the case concerning Legality of Use of Force (Yugoslavia v. Netherlands) before the International Court of Justice. (In : The Netherlands in court : essays in honour of Johan G. Lammers, ed. by Niels

Blokker; René Lefeber; Liesbeth Lijnzaad; Ineke Bladel van. Leiden: Martinus Nijhoff, 2006, p. 19-49.)

116. *Activités armées sur le territoire du Congo (République démocratique du Congo c. Ouganda)*
116. *Armed Activities on the Territory of the Congo (Democratic Republic of the Congo* v. *Uganda)*

Barbour, Stephanie A.: "The tangled web": the right of self-defense against non-state actors in the Armed Activities case. (In: New York University Journal of International Law and Politics, 2008, v. 40, special issue, p. 53-106.)

Cannizzaro, Enzo: La legittima difesa nei confronti di entità non statali nella sentenza della Corte internazionale di giustizia nel calo Congo c. Uganda. (Dans: Rivista di diritto internazionale, 2006, v. 89, no. 1, 120-122).

Cervell Hortal, María José: La exploitación ilegal de los recuersos naturales de un estado a la luz de la sentencia del Tribunal Internacional de Justicia sobre las Actividades armadas en el territorio de Congo (2005). (Dans: Anuario español de derecho internacional, 2006, v. 22, p. 559-577.)

Chenevier, Justin: No safe haven for Uganda in the World Court. (In: Cambridge Law Journal, 2006, v. 65, p. 263-267.)

Dufresne, Robert: Reflections and extrapolation on the I.C.J.'s approach to illegal resource exploitation in the Armed Activities case. (In: New York University Journal of International Law and Politics, 2008, v. 40, special issue, p. 171-217.)

Forlati, Serena: Protection diplomatique, droits de l'homme et réclamations "directes" devant la Cour internationale de Justice: quelques réflexions en marge de l'arrêt Congo/Ouganda. (Dans: Revue générale de droit international public, 2007, v. 111, no. 1, p. 89-116.) [C.P.J.I., p. 92; C.I.J., passim.]

Gathii, James Thuo: Armed Activities on the Territory of the Congo: Democratic Republic of the Congo v. Uganda: International Court of Justice, December 19, 2005. (In: American Journal of International Law, 2007, v. 101, no. 1, p. 142-149.)

Gutiérrez Espada, Cesáreo et Cervell Hortal, María José: La prohibición del uso de la fuerza en la sentencia de la C.I.J. de 19 de diciembre de 2005 (asunto sobre las actividades armadas en el territorio del Congo (República democrática del Congo c. Uganda). (Dans: Revista española de derecho internacional, 2006, v. 58, p. 240-256.)

Halink, Simone: All things considered: how the International Court of Justice delegated its fact-assessment to the United Nations in the Armed Activities case. (In: New York University Journal of International Law and Politics, 2008, v. 40, special issue, p. 53-106.)

Haupais, Nicolas: Les obligations de la puissance occupante au regard de la jurisprudence et de la pratique récentes. (Dans: Revue générale de droit international public, 2007, v. 111, p. 117-146.) [C.I.J., p. 117-125, 130-139, 141-145.]

Ingadóttir, Thordis : The I.C.J. Armed Activities case : reflections on States' obligation to investigate and prosecute individuals for serious human rights violations and grave breaches of the Geneva Conventions. (In : Nordic Journal of International Law, 2009, v. 78, no. 4, p. 581-598.)

Jensen, Eric Talbot: The I.C.J.'s "Uganda wall" : a barrier to the principle of distinction and an entry point for lawfare. (In : Denver Journal of International Law and Policy, 2007, v. 35, p. 241-274.)

Kabumba, Busingye: A missed opportunity: the legacy of the Armed Activities case on the right to self-defence under international law. (In: Griffin's View on International and Comparative Law, 2007, v. 8, no. 1, p. 109-116.)

Kammerhofer, Jörg: The Armed Activities case and non-state actors in self-defence law. (In: Leiden Journal of International Law, 2007, v. 20, p. 89-113.)

Kingsbury, Benedict and Weiler, J. H. H.: Preface: studying the Armed activities decision. (In : New York University Journal of International Law and Politics, 2008, v. 40, special issue, p. 1-12.) [I.C.J., passim.]

Koutroulis, Vaios: L'affaire des Activité armées sur le territoire du Congo (Congo c. Ouganda): une lecture restrictive du droit de l'occupation? (In: Revue belge de droit international, 2006, v. 39, p. 703-741.)

Lang, Andrej: "Modus operandi" and the I.C.J.'s appraisal of the Lusaka Ceasefire agreement in the Armed Activities case: the role of peace agreements in international conflict resolution. (In: New York University Journal of International Law and Politics, 2008, v. 40, p. 107-169.)

Latty, Franck: La Cour internationale de Justice face aux tiraillements du droit international: les arrêts dans les affaires des activités armées sur le territoire du Congo (RDC c. Ouganda, 19 décembre 2005; RDC c. Rwanda, 3 février 2006. (Dans: Annuaire français de droit international, 2005, v. 51, p. 205-236.) [C.P.J.I., p. 236; C.I.J., passim.]

Mollel, Andrew L.: Judicial settlement of armed conflicts in international law: reflecting the 2005 International Court of Justice decision in the Democratic Republic of Congo. (In: Nordic Journal of International Law, 2007, v. 76, no. 4, p. 407-434.)

Ntoubandi, Faustin Z.: The Congo/Uganda case: a comment on the main legal issues. (In: African Human Rights Law Journal, 2007, v. 7, no. 3, p. 162-190.)

Oellers-Frahm, Karin: Der I.G.H. und die "Lücke" zwischen Gewaltverbot und Selbstverteidigungsrecht: neues im Fall "Kongo gegen Uganda"? (In: Zeitschrift für europarechtliche Studien (ZEUS), 2007, v. 10, p. 71-92.) [I.C.J., p. 74-90.]

Okowa, Phoebe N.: International Court of Justice: case concerning armed activities on the territory of the Congo (Democratic Republic of the Congo v. Uganda). (In: International and Comparative Law Quarterly, 2006, v. 55, p. 742-753.)

Piotrowicz, Ryszard: The Easter bunny, the tooth fairy, Santa Claus and the Security Council: a heart of darkness at the ICJ in Democratic Republic of Congo v. Uganda. (In: Australian Law Journal, 2006, v. 80, no. 3, p. 162-166.)

Raab, Dominic: Force of law. (In: World Today, 2006, v. 62, no. 6, p. 22-23.)

Ruys, Tom: D.R.C. v. Uganda: the applicability of international humanitarian law and human rights law in occupied territories. (In: International humanitarian law and human rights law: towards a new merger in international law, ed. by Roberta Arnold; Noëlle Quénivet. 2008, p. 155-195.)

Sinclair, Guy Fiti: "The ghosts of colonialism in Africa": silences and shortcomings in the I.C.J.'s 2005 Armed Activities decision. (In: ILSA Journal of International and Comparative Law, 2007, v. 14, p. 121-143.)

Sinclair, Guy Fiti: Don't mention the war (on terror): framing the issues and ignoring the obvious in the ICJ's 2005 Armed Activities Decision. (In: Melbourne Journal of International Law, 2007, v. 8, no. 1, p. 124-141.)

Van Steenberghe, Raphaël: L'arrêt de la Cour internationale de Justice dans l'affaire des Activités armées sur le territoire du Congo et le recours à la force: conclusions (implicites) de la Cour. (Dans: Revue belge de droit international, 2006, v. 39, p. 671-702.)

Verhoeven, Sten: Gewapende activiteiten op het grondgebied van de Democratische Republiek Congo (DCR t. Oeganda): het Internationaal Gerechtshof zoekt zijn weg in een juridische jungle. (In: Wereldbeeld: tijdschrift voor de Verenigde Naties, 2006, v. 30, no. 2, p. 8-16.)

Zegbe Zegs, Fidèle: Activités armées sur le territoire du Congo (R.D.C. c. Ouganda): plaidoyer pour une commission nationale d'indemnisation de victimes. (Dans: Revue de droit africain: doctrine and jurisprudence, 2007, v. 11, no. 43, p. 217-252.)

Ziccardi Capaldo, Giuliana (ed.): Decisions of international courts and tribunals in 2005: International Court of Justice: case concerning Armed Activities on the Territory of the Congo (Democratic Republic of the Congo v. Uganda): judgment, 19 December 2005. (In: Global Community: Yearbook of International Law and Jurisprudence, 2006, v. 6, no. 1, p. 235-270.)

118. *Application de la convention pour la prévention et la répression du crime de génocide (Croatie c. Yougoslavie)*

118. *Application of the Convention on the Prevention and Punishment of the Crime of Genocide (Croatia* v. *Yugoslavia)*

Bijelic, Ana et Dumont, Hélène et Boisvert, Anne-Marie : Le système de justice des pays de l'ex-Yougoslavie et les défis de l'administration de la justice pénale internationale. (Dans : La voie vers la Cour pénale internationale : tous les chemins mènent à Rome = The highway to the International Criminal Court : all roads lead to Rome, sous la dir. de Dumont, Hélène ; Boisvert, Anne-Marie. Montréal : Editions Thémis, 2004, p. 255-313.) [C.I.J., p. 261, 295-305, 313.]

Blum, Yehuda Zvi : Consistently inconsistent : the International Court of Justice and the former Yugoslavia (Croatia v. Serbia). (In : American Journal of International Law, 2009, v. 103, no. 2, p. 264-271.)

Lagrange, Evelyne : La cohérence de la chose jugée (l'affaire du génocide devant la CIJ). (Dans : Annuaire français de droit international, 2007, v. 53, p. 1-42.)

Vaurs-Chaumette, Anne-Laure : "Si le fait l'accuse, le résultat l'excuse" : l'arrêt de la CIJ sur les exceptions préliminaires dans l'affaire Croatie/Serbie. (Dans : Annuaire français de droit international, 2008, v. 54, p. 275-304.)

Weckel, Philippe (sous la dir. de) : Chronique de jurisprudence internationale. (Dans : Revue générale de droit international public, 2009, v. 113, no. 1, p. 193-224.) [C.I.J., p. 193-205.]

Werner, Wouter G. : Preliminary objections in the Croatia v. Serbia case : a commentary : application of the Convention on the Prevention and Punishment of the Crime of Genocide (Croatia v. Serbia) : preliminary objections : judgment of 18 November 2008. (In : Hague Justice Journal, 2009, v. 4, p. 51-54.)

119. *Incident aérien du 10 août 1999 (Pakistan c. Inde)*
119. *Aerial Incident of 10 August 1999 (Pakistan* v. *India)*

Case concerning the Aerial Incident of 10 August 1999 (Pakistan v. India). (In : Kokusaiho Gaiko Zassi, 2006, v. 105, p. 123-132.)

120. *Délimitation maritime entre le Nicaragua et le Honduras dans la mer des Caraïbes (Nicaragua c. Honduras)*
120. *Maritime Delimitation between Nicaragua and Honduras in the Caribbean Sea (Nicaragua* v. *Honduras)*

Honduras-Nicaragua. Report Number 2-24. Case Concerning Maritime Delimitation in the Caribbean Sea. (In : International maritime boundaries, 2005, v. 5, 3575.)

Kirk, Elizabeth A. : Case concerning Territorial and Maritime Dispute between Nicaragua and Honduras in the Caribbean Sea (Nicaragua v. Honduras), judgment of 8 October 2007. (In : International and Comparative Law Quarterly, 2008, v. 57, no. 3, p. 701-709.)

Lathrop, Coalter : Territorial and maritime dispute between Nicaragua and Honduras in the Caribbean Sea (Nicaragua v. Honduras) : International

Court of Justice, October 8, 2007. (In : American Journal of International Law, 2008, v. 102, no. 1, p. 113-119.)

Tanaka, Yoshifumi : Reflections on maritime delimitation in the Nicaragua/Honduras case. (In : Zeitschrift für ausländisches öffentliches Recht und Völkerrecht, 2008, v. 68, p. 903-937.)

Weckel, Philippe (sous la dir. de) : Chronique de jurisprudence internationale. (Dans : Revue générale de droit international public, 2008, v. 112, no. 1, p. 179-199.) [C.I.J., p. 179-189.]

121. *Mandat d'arrêt du 11 avril 2000 (République démocratique du Congo c. Belgique)*
121. *Arrest Warrant of 11 April 2000 (Democratic Republic of the Congo* v. *Belgium)*

Bollo Arocena, María Dolores : Soberanía, justicia universal e inmunidad de jurisdicción en los asuntos : República democrática del Congo c. Bélgica y República del Congo c. Francia. (Dans : Revista española de derecho internacional, 2004, v. 56, no. 1, p. 91-127.)

Bula-Bula, Sayeman : Les immunités pénales et l'inviolabilité du ministre des affaires étrangères en droit international : principes, caractères, portée, exceptions, limites, sanctions (Affaire du mandat du 11 avril 2000. R D du Congo c. Royaume de Belgique, C.I.J., arrêt du 14 février 2002). Kinshasa : Presses de l'Université de Kinshasa, 2004.

Carnerero Castilla, Rubén : Un paso atrás en la lucha contra la impunidad : la sentencia de la Corte Internacional de Justicia de 14 de febrero de 2002 en el asunto relativo a la Orden de arresto de 11 de abril de 2000 (República Democrática del Congo c. Bélgica). (Dans : Cuadernos de jurisprudencia internacional, 2004, v. 1, p. 83-104.)

Day, Adam : Crimes against humanity as a nexus of individual and State responsibility : why the I.C.J. got Belgium v. Congo wrong. (In : Berkeley Journal of International Law, 2004, v. 22, no. 3, p. 489-512.)

Kamminga, Menno T. : Universal jurisdiction after Congo v. Belgium. (In : African perspectives on international criminal justice, ed. by Anukumah, Evelyn A. ; Kwakwa, Edward K. Accra : Africa Legal Aid, 2005, p. 233-239.)

Koller, David S. : Immunities of foreign ministers : paragraph 61 of the Yerodia judgment as it pertains to the Security Council and the International Criminal Court. (In : American University International Law Review, 2004, v. 20, p. 7-42.)

Marchal, P. : Chronique de jurisprudence. (Dans : Revue de droit international et de droit comparé, 2004, v. 81, no. 2, p. 208-242.) [C.I.J., p. 208-231.]

McManus, John : Head of State immunity, or but what if it were Saddam, and we had him ? (In : La voie vers la Cour pénale internationale : tous les chemins mènent à Rome = The highway to the International Criminal Court : all roads lead to Rome, ed. by Dumont, Hélène ; Boisvert, Anne-Marie.

Montréal : Editions Thémis, 2004, p. 545-589.) [I.C.J., p. 547, 550, 567-584, 587.]

Métille, Sylvain : L'immunité des chefs d'Etat au XXIe siècle : les conséquences de l'affaire du Mandat d'arrêt du 11 avril 2000. (Dans : Revue de droit international, de sciences diplomatiques et politiques, 2004, v. 82, no. 1, p. 29-86.)

Mezjaev, A. B. : Delo ob ordere na arest (Demokratieskaja Respublika Kongo protiv Belgii). (In : Rossijskij eegodnik medunarodnogo prava, 2004, v, 2003, p. 84-99.)

O'Keefe, Roger : Universal jurisdiction : clarifying the basic concept. (In : Journal of International Criminal Justice, 2004, v. 2, p. 735-760.)

Poels, Alexander : Universal jurisdiction in absentia. (In : Netherlands Quarterly of Human Rights, 2005, v. 23, no. 1, p. 65-84.)

Prud'homme, Nancie : L'affaire Yerodia : immunités. (Dans : The measure of international law : effectiveness, fairness and validity : proceedings of the 31st annual conference of the Canadian Council on International Law, Ottawa, October 24-26, 2002 = Prendre la mesure du droit international : effectivité, équité et validité : travaux de 31e congrès annuel du Conseil canadien de droit international, Ottawa, 24 au 26 octobre 2002. The Hague [etc.] : Kluwer Law International, 2004, p. 274-296.) [C.I.J., passim.]

Reydams, Luc : Prosecuting crimes under international law on the basis of universal jurisdiction : the experience of Belgium. (In : International and national prosecution of crimes under international law : current developments, ed. by Horst Fischer ; Claus Kre ; Sascha Rolf Lüder. Berlin : Berliner Wissenschafts-Verlag, 2004, p. 799-816.) [I.C.J., p. 799, 814-815.]

Robinson, Darryl : Immunity or impunity of heads of State accused of serious international crimes. (In : La voie vers la Cour pénale internationale : tous les chemins mènent à Rome = The highway to the International Criminal Court : all roads lead to Rome, ed. by Dumont, Hélène ; Boisvert, Anne-Marie. Montréal : Editions Thémis, 2004, p. 471-481.) [I.C.J., p. 479-480.]

Strapatsas, Nicolaos : The effects of the case concerning the Arrest warrant of 11 April 2000 (Democratic Republic of the Congo v. Belgium) on the exercise of universal jurisdiction. (In : The measure of international law : effectiveness, fairness and validity : proceedings of the 31st annual conference of the Canadian Council on International Law, Ottawa, October 24-26, 2002 = Prendre la mesure du droit international : effectivité, équité et validité : travaux de 31e congrès annuel du Conseil canadien de droit international, Ottawa, 24 au 26 octobre 2002. The Hague [etc.] : Kluwer Law International, 2004, p. 297-321.) [I.C.J., passim.]

Summers, Mark A. : Diplomatic immunity ratione personae : did the International Court of Justice create a new customary law rule in Congo v. Belgium ? (In : Journal of International Law and Practice, 2007, v. 16, no. 2, p. 459-473.)

Vincent, Philippe: Jurisprudence annotée: Cour internationale de Justice, 14 février 2002. (Dans: Revue de la Faculté de droit de l'Université de Liège, 2004, v. 49, no. 3, p. 381-407.)

Walleyn, Luc: The Sabra and Shatila massacre and Belgian universal jurisdiction. (In: The case of Ariel Sharon and the fate of universal jurisdiction, ed. by John Borneman. Princeton: Princeton Institute for International and Regional Studies, 2004, p. 54-69.) [I.C.J., p. 60.]

122. *Demande en revision de l'arrêt du 11 juillet 1996 en l'affaire relative à l'*Application de la convention pour la prévention et la répression du crime de génocide (Bosnie-Herzégovine c. Yougoslavie), exceptions préliminaires *(Yougoslavie c. Bosnie-Herzégovine)*

122. *Application for Revision of the Judgment of 11 July 1996 in the* Case concerning Application of the Convention on the Prevention and Punishment of the Crime of Genocide (Bosnia and Herzegovina v. Yugoslavia), Preliminary Objections *(Yugoslavia* v. *Bosnia and Herzegovina)*

Blum, Yehuda Zvi: Was Yugoslavia a member of the United Nations in the years 1992-2000? (In: American Journal of International Law, 2007, v. 101, no. 4, p. 800-818.)

Griebel, Jörn and Plücken, Milan: New developments regarding the rules of attribution? The International Court of Justice's decision in Bosnia v. Serbia. (In: Leiden Journal of International Law, 2008, v. 21, no. 3, p. 601-622.)

Marino, Anthony: Bosnia v. Serbia and the status of rape as genocide under international law. (In: Boston University International Law Journal, 2009, v. 27, no. 1, p. 205-229.)

Ottolenghi, Michael and Prows, Peter: Res judicata in the ICJ's genocide case: implications for other courts and tribunals? (In: Pace International Law Review, 2009, v. 21, p. 37-54.)

Stoffel Vallotton, Nicole: La revisión de sentencia ante el Tribunal Internacional de Justicia y los problemas de sucesión de la nueva Yugoslavia: la sentencia de la Corte Internacional de Justicia de 3 de febrero de 2003 sobre la Demanda de revisión de la sentencia de 11 de julio de 1996 en el asunto relativo a la Aplicación de la Convención para la prevención y la represión del crimen de genocidio (Bosnia-Herzegovina c. Yugoslavia), Excepciones preliminares (Yugoslavia c. Bosnia-Herzegovina). (Dans: Cuadernos de jurisprudencia internacional, 2004, v. 1, p. 155-192.)

Tsagourias, Nicholas: International Court of Justice: Application for Revision of the Judgment of 11 July 1996 in the case concerning Application of the Convention on the Prevention and Punishment of the Crime of Genocide (Bosnia and Herzegovina v. Yugoslavia), Preliminary Objections (Yugoslavia v. Bosnia and Herzegovina), Judgment of 3 February 2003. (In: International and Comparative Law Quarterly, 2004, v. 53, no. 3, p. 731-738.)

123. *Certains biens (Liechtenstein c. Allemagne)*

123. *Certain Property (Liechtenstein* v. *Germany)*

Delmartino, Bart: The end of the road for the Prince? Sixty years after the Czechoslovak confiscation of Liechtenstein property. (In: Leiden Journal of International Law, 2006, v. 19, no. 2, p. 441-458.)

Giurisprudenza internazionale: Corte internazionale di Giustizia, 10 febbraio 2005: sentenza nell'affare relativo a taluni beni (Liechtenstein c. Germania): eccezioni preliminari. (Dans: Rivista di diritto internazionale, 2005, v. 88, p. 478-495.)

Irmscher, Tobias H.: Anmerkung zur Liechtenstein-Entscheidung des Internationalen Gerichtshofs. (In: Archiv des Völkerrechts, 2005, v. 43, no. 3, p. 375-395.)

Müller, Daniel: Procedural developments at the International Court of Justice. (In: Law and Practice of International Courts and Tribunals, 2005, v. 4, no. 2, p. 329-354.)

Toublanc, Alix: Affaire relative à certains biens (Liechtenstein c. Allemagne, exceptions préliminaires, 10 février 2005). (Dans: Annuaire français de droit international, 2004, v. 50, p. 370-388.)

Ziccardi Capaldo, Giuliana: Case concerning certain property (Liechtenstein v. Germany), preliminary objections, judgment, 10 February 2005. (In: Global Community: Yearbook of International Law and Jurisprudence, 2006, v. 6, no. 1, p. 225-234.)

124. *Différend territorial et maritime (Nicaragua c. Colombie)*
124. *Territorial and Maritime Dispute (Nicaragua* v. *Colombia)*

Abello Galvis, Ricardo, trans.: Traduccion del fallo de la Corte Internacional de Justicia en el "Diferendo Territorial y Maritimo" (Nicaragua c. Colombia). Excepciones preliminares. (Dans: Anuario Colombiano de Derecho Internacional, 2008, v. 1, p. 205-262.) [C.I.J., passim.]

Colombia-Nicaragua. Report Number 2-25. Case Concerning Title to Territory and Maritime Delimitation in the Western Caribbean Sea. (In: International maritime boundaries, 2005, v. 5, 3576.)

Díaz Martínez, Antolín: Controversia Colombia Nicaragua y diferendo colombo-venezolano. Bogotá: Universidad Cooperativa de Colombia, 2004.

Kwiatkowska, Barbara: The 2007 Nicaragua v. Colombia territorial and maritime dispute (preliminary objections) judgment: a landmark in the sound administration of international justice. (In: Hague Yearbook of International Law, 2007, v. 20, p. 75-119.)

Mills, Alex: The formalism of State sovereignty in territorial and maritime disputes. (In: Cambridge Law Journal, 2008, v. 67, no. 3, p. 443-447.) [I.C.J., passim.]

Nieto Navia, Rafael: La decisión de la Corte Internacional de Justicia sobre excepciones preliminares en el caso de Nicaragua v. Colombia. (Dans:

Anuario Colombiano de Derecho Internacional, 2009, v. 2, p. 11-57.) [C.I.J., passim.]

Weckel, Philippe: Chronique de jurisprudence internationale: CIJ, Arrêt du 13 décembre 2007, Différend territorial et maritime (Nicaragua c. Colombie) exceptions préliminaires. (Dans: Revue générale de droit international public, 2008, v. 112, p. 415-421.)

125. *Différend frontalier (Bénin/Niger)*
125. *Frontier Dispute (Benin/Niger)*

Aktypis, Spyridon: Affaire [du différend] frontalier (Bénin/Niger), arrêt du 12 juillet 2005: deux points de vue (1). (Dans: African Yearbook of International Law, 2005, v. 13, p. 235-263.)

Allen, Stephen: International Court of Justice: case concerning the Frontier Dispute (Benin/Niger). (In: International and Comparative Law Quarterly, 2006, v. 55, p. 729-742.)

Ben Mansour, Affef: Affaire frontalier (Bénin/Niger), arrêt du 12 juillet 2005: deux points de vue (2). (Dans: African Yearbook of International Law, 2005, v. 13, p. 264-280.)

Giurisprudenza internazionale: Corte internazionale di Giustizia (camera), 12 luglio 2005: sentenza nell'affare della controversia di frontiera (Benin/Niger). (Dans: Rivista di diritto internazionale, 2005, v. 88, p. 1066-1115.)

Merrills, John G.: New horizons for international adjudication. (In: Global Community: Yearbook of International Law and Jurisprudence, 2006, v. 6, no. 1, p. 47-74.) [I.C.J., p. 47, 54, 66-74.]

Norodom, Anne-Thida: L'arrêt de la chambre de la Cour internationale de Justice dans l'affaire du Différend frontalier (Bénin/Niger), 12 juillet 2005. (Dans: Annuaire français de droit international, 2005, v. 51, p. 185-204.)

Ruiz Fabri, Hélène et Sorel, Jean-Marc: Affaire du Différend frontalier (Benin/Niger) – Arrêt du 12 Juillet 2005. (Dans: Journal du droit international, 2006, v. 133, p. 1189-1197.)

Spadi, Fabio: The International Court of Justice judgment in the Benin-Niger Border dispute: the interplay of titles and "effectivités" under the uti possidetis juris principle. (In: Leiden Journal of International Law, 2005, v. 18, p. 777-794.)

Weckel, Philippe: Chronique de jurisprudence internationale: Cour internationale de Justice: arrêt du 27 juillet 2005: Différend frontalier (Bénin/Niger). (Dans: Revue générale de droit international public, 2005, v. 109, p. 939-945.)

126. *Activités armées sur le territoire du Congo (nouvelle requête: 2002) (République démocratique du Congo c. Rwanda)*
126. *Armed Activities on the Territory of the Congo (New Application: 2002) (Democratic Republic of the Congo* v. *Rwanda)*

Activités armées sur le territoire du Congo (nouvelle requête: 2002) (République démocratique du Congo c. Rwanda): arrêt du 3 février 2006 (compétence et recevabilité). (Dans: Journal du droit international, 2007, v. 134, p. 989-996.)

Cervell Hortal, María José: El asunto sobre las Actividades armadas en el territorio del Congo (nueva demanda: 2002), o la importancia de la labor didáctica de los jueces. (Dans: Revista española de derecho internacional, 2007, v. 59, no. 2, p. 417-425.)

Giurisprudenza internazionale. Corte internazionale di giustizia. (Dans: Rivista di diritto internazionale, 2006, v. 89, p. 453-496.) [C.P.J.I., p. 461, 485; C.I.J., passim.]

Henrard, K.: Hague case law: latest developments. (In: Netherlands International Law Review, 2006, v. 53, p. 163-168.)

La questione dell'ammisibilità di riserve alle clausole attributive di competenza alla luce di una recente sentenza della Corte internazionale di giustizia. (Dans: Rivista di diritto internazionale, 2006, v. 89, p. 448-451.)

Orakhelashvili, Alexander: International Court of Justice: case concerning Armed Activities on the Territory of the Congo (Democratic Republic of the Congo v. Rwanda), jurisdiction and admissibility, judgment of 3 February 2006. (In: International and Comparative Law Quarterly, 2006, v. 55, p. 753-763.)

Torres Cazorla, María Isabel: La historia jamás contada de los actos unilaterales de los Estados: de los Ensayos nucleares al asunto de la República democrática del Congo contra Ruanda. (Dans: Revista española de derecho internacional, 2006, v. 58, p. 257-269.)

Weckel, Philippe et Aréou, Guillaume: Cour internationale de Justice: arrêt du 3 février 2006, Activités armées sur le territoire du Congo (nouvelle requête) (RDC c. Rwanda). (Dans: Revue générale de droit international public, 2006, v. 110, p. 487-494.)

127. *Demande en revision de l'arrêt du 11 septembre 1992 en l'affaire du* Différend frontalier terrestre, insulaire et maritime (El Salvador/Honduras; Nicaragua (intervenant)) *(El Salvador c. Honduras)*

127. *Application for Revision of the Judgment of 11 September 1992 in the Case concerning the* Land, Island and Maritime Frontier Dispute (El Salvador/Honduras: Nicaragua intervening) *(El Salvador* v. *Honduras)*

Giurisprudenza internazionale: Corte internazionale di Giustizia (Camera), 18 dicembre 2003: Sentenza resa sulla domanda di revisione della sentenza dell'11 settembre 1992 nell'affare della controversia di frontiera terrestre, insulare e marittima (El Salvador/ Honduras; Nicaragua interveniente). (Dans: Rivista di diritto internazionale, 2004, v. 87, no. 2, p. 475-491.)

Henrard, K. (ed.): Hague case law: latest developments. (In: Netherlands International Law Review, 2004, v. 51, no. 1, p. 121-131.) [I.C.J., p. 121-122.]

International Court of Justice: International Court of Justice: application for revision of the judgment of 11 September 1992 in the Case concerning the land, island and maritime frontier dispute (El Salvador/Honduras, Nicaragua intervening) (December 18, 2003). (In: International Legal Materials, 2004, v. 43, no. 3, p. 661-685.)

López Contreras, Carlos: Misión en La Haya: la demanda de revisión presentada por El Salvador. Tegucigalpa: Litografía López, 2004.

Shaw, Malcolm N.: Application for Revision of the Judgment of 11 September 1992 in the Case concerning the Land, Island and Maritime Frontier Dispute (El Salvador/Honduras: Nicaragua Intervening), (El Salvador v Honduras), Judgment of 18 December 2003. (In: International and Comparative Law Quarterly, 2005, v. 54, no. 4, p. 1013-1022.)

Torres Ugena, Nila: Delimitación de fronteras a partir de la sucesión colonial: la demanda de revisión de la sentencia de 11 de septiembre de 1992 en el asunto de la Diferencia fronteriza, terrestre, insular y marítima (El Salvador c. Honduras; Nicaragua interviniente) (El Salvador c. Honduras). (Dans: Cuadernos de jurisprudencia internacional, 2005, v. 2, p. 97-120.)

Weckel, Philippe: Chronique de jurisprudence internationale. (Dans: Revue générale de droit international public, 2004, v. 108, no. 1, p. 215-247.) [C.I.J., p. 215-234, 236, 239-241, 243, 245.]

128. *Avena et autres ressortissants mexicains (Mexique c. Etats-Unis d'Amérique)*
128. *Avena and Other Mexican Nationals (Mexico* v. *United States of America)*

Alunni, Sylvain: La politique juridique extérieure des Etats-Unis à l'épreuve du fédéralisme: l'affaire Medellin v. Texas. (Dans: L'observateur des Nations Unies, 2008, v. 24, no. 1, p. 317-327.)

Amirfar, Catherine M.: AALS panel: Mexico v. USA (Avena): arguments of Mexico. (In: German Law Journal, 2004, v. 5, no. 4, p. 375-383.) [I.C.J., passim.]

Barrie, George N.: ICJ jurisdiction over the Vienna Convention on Consular Relations. (In: South African Yearbook of International Law, 2004, v. 29, p. 264-267.)

Bederman, David J.: Agora: Medellín: Medellín's new paradigm for treaty interpretation. (In: American Journal of International Law, 2008, v. 102, no. 3, p. 529-572.)

Benlolo-Carabot, Myriam: L'arrêt de la Cour internationale de Justice dans l'affaire Avena et autres ressortissants mexicains (Mexique c. Etats-Unis d'Amérique) du 31 mars 2004. (Dans: Annuaire français de droit international, 2004, v. 50, p. 259-291.) [C.P.J.I., p. 266, 279-280; C.I.J., passim.]

Cerna, Christina M. : The right to consular notification as a human right. (In : Suffolk Transnational Law Review, 2008, v. 31, no. 2, p. 419-469.)

Cerone, John : Making sense of the U.S. President's intervention in "Medellín". (In : Suffolk Transnational Law Review, 2008, v. 31, no. 2, p. 279-300.)

Cervell Hortal, María José : Desarollos recientes a propósito del asunto Avena (T.I.J., 2004) : la difícil relación entre el derecho internacional y el derecho interno. (Dans : Revista española de derecho internacional, 2007, v. 59, no. 2, p. 681-696.)

Clarke, Harry S. : Determining the remedy for violations of Article 36 of the VCCR : review and reconsideration and the clemency process after Avena. (In : George Washington International Law Review, 2006, v. 38, p. 131-158.)

Crook, John R. : General international and U.S. foreign relations law : U.S. strategy for responding to I.C.J.'s Avena decision. (In : American Journal of International Law, 2005, v. 99, p. 489-492.)

Culhane, Elizabeth A. : "In accordance with general principles of Comity" : President Bush's memorandum in Medellin v. Dretke and the constitutional limitations on the president's ability to enforce the ICJ's Avena Judgment at the State level. (In : Saint Louis University Law Journal, 2007, v. 51, p. 815-853.)

Culp, Emily : A father waits : Medellin v. Texas and the application of world court decisions on U.S. domestic law. (In : North Carolina Journal of International Law and Commercial Regulation, 2009, v. 35, no. 1, p. 233-261.)

Dominicé, Christian : Droits individuels et droits de l'homme : chevauchements et différences. (Dans : Diritti individuali e giustizia internazionale : liber Fausto Pocar, sous la dir. de Venturine, Gabriella ; Bariatti, Stefania. Milano : Giuffrè, 2009, v. 1, p. 301-307.) [C.I.J., passim.]

Dominicé, Christian : L'arrêt Avena et le sort judiciaire des droits individuels. (Dans : Internationale Gemeinschaft und Menschenrechte : Festschrift für Georg Ress zum 70. Geburtstag am 21. Januar 2005, sous la dir. de Bröhmer, Jürgen ; Bieber, Roland ; Calliess, Christian ; Langenfeld, Christine ; Weber, Stefan ; Wolf, Joachim. Köln [etc.] : Heymann, 2005, p. 55-62.)

Dubin, Laurence : Les garanties de non-répétition à l'aune des affaires LaGrand et Avena : la révolution n'aura pas lieu. (Dans : Revue générale de droit international public, 2005, v. 109, p. 859-888.)

Epps, Valerie : The "Medellín v. Texas" symposium : a case worthy of comment. (In : Suffolk Transnational Law Review, 2008, v. 31, no. 2, p. 209-225.)

Epstein, Paul J.: Enforcement of the Avena judgment in the United States courts: the Medellín case. (In: Global Community: Yearbook of International Law and Jurisprudence, 2005, v. 5, no. 1, p. 247-261.)

Gamble, John King and Giuliano, Christine M.: US Supreme Court, Medellín v. Texas: more than an assiduous building inspector? (In: Leiden Journal of International Law, 2009, v. 22, no. 1, p. 151-169.)

Ghandhi, Sandy: Avena and other Mexican nationals (Mexico v. United States of America), judgment of 31 March 2004. (In: International and Comparative Law Quarterly, 2005, v. 54, no. 3, p. 779-787.) [I.C.J., passim; P.C.I.J., p. 784.]

Ghandhi, Sandy: International Court of Justice: Avena and other Mexican Nationals (Mexico v. United States of America), provisional measures, order of 5 February 2003. (In: International and Comparative Law Quarterly, 2004, v. 53, no. 3, p. 738-746.)

Giurisprudenza internazionale: Corte internazionale di giustizia, 31 marzo 2004: sentenza nell'affare Avena e altri cittadini messicani (Messico c. Stati Uniti d'America). (Dans: Rivista di diritto internazionale, 2004, v. 87, no. 3, p. 773-819.)

Goodman, Jennifer: Avena and other Mexican nationals (Mex. v. U.S.): the International Court of Justice deems U.S. actions in fifty-two death penalty cases as violations of international law. (In: Tulane Journal of International and Comparative Law, 2005, v. 13, p. 379-400.)

Greffenius, Robert: Selling Medellin: the entourage of litigation surrounding the Vienna Convention on Consular Relations and the weight of International Court of Justice opinions in the domestic sphere. (In: American University International Law Review, 2008, v. 23, no. 5, p. 943-974.)

Heinrich, Denitsa Mavrova: International law and constitutional law: International Court of Justice and executive power: interpreting and implementing international treaty obligations: Medellin v. Texas, 128 S.Ct. 1346 (2008). (In: North Dakota Law Review, 2009, v. 85, no. 2, p. 435-468.)

Henrard, K. (ed.): Hague case law: latest developments. (In: Netherlands International Law Review, 2004, v. 51, no. 2, p. 329-334.) [I.C.J., p. 329-330.]

Hoppe, Carsten: Implementation of LaGrand and Avena in Germany and the United States: exploring a transatlantic divide in search of a uniform interpretation of consular rights. (In: European Journal of International Law, 2007, v. 18, p. 317-336.)

International Court of Justice: year 2004: case concerning Avena and Other Mexican Nationals (Mexico v. United States of America). (In: International Legal Materials, 2004, v. 43, no. 3, p. 581-660.)

Jackson, Craig: The anti-commandeering doctrine and foreign policy federalism: the missing issue in "Medellín v. Texas". (In: Suffolk Transnational Law Review, 2008, v. 31, no. 2, p. 335-375.)

Kadish, Mark J.: Article 36 of the Vienna Convention on Consular Relations: the International Court of Justice in Mexico v. United States (Avena) speaks emphatically to the Supreme Court of the United States about the fundamental nature of the right to consul. (In: Georgetown Journal of International Law, 2004, v. 36, no. 1, p. 1-60.)

Karamanian, Susan L.: Briefly resuscitating the great writ: the International Court of Justice and the U.S. death penalty. (In: Albany Law Review, 2005, v. 69, p. 745-770.)

Koh, Steven Arrigg: "Respectful consideration" after "Sanchez-Llamas v. Oregon": why the Supreme Court owes more to the International Court of Justice. (In: Cornell Law Review, 2007, v. 93, no. 1, p. 243-273.)

Künzli, Annemarieke: Case concerning Mexican nationals. (In: Leiden Journal of International Law, 2005, v. 18, no. 1, p. 49-64.) [I.C.J., passim; P.C.I.J., p. 51.]

MacGuinness, Margaret E.: Medellín v. Texas: 128 S.Ct. 1346 (2008): U.S. Supreme Court opinion on State courts' obligation to respect an International Court of Justice judgment and on the president's power to enforce it: United States Supreme Court, March 25, 2008. (In: American Journal of International Law, 2008, v. 102, no. 3, p. 622-628.)

MacGuinness, Margaret E.: Three narratives of "Medellín v. Texas". (In: Suffolk Transnational Law Review, 2008, v. 31, no. 2, p. 227-246.)

Martin, Pierre-Marie: Les conséquences de la non-application de la Convention de Vienne de 1963 sur les relations consulaires. (Dans: Recueil Dalloz, 2004, v. 34, p. 2446-2449.) [C.I.J., passim.]

Murphy, John F.: "Medellín v. Texas": implications of the Supreme Court's decision for the United States and the rule of law in international affairs. (In: Suffolk Transnational Law Review, 2008, v. 31, no. 2, p. 247-277.)

Naskou-Perraki, Paroula: Fairness, justice and treatment of foreign nationals before the International Court of Justice. (In: Justice in particular: festschrift in honour of professor P. J. Kozyris. Athens: Sakkoulas, 2007, p. 309-328.)

Orakhelashvili, Alexander: Judicial competence and judicial remedies in the Avena case. (In: Leiden Journal of International Law, 2005, v. 18, no. 1, p. 31-48.) [I.C.J., passim; P.C.I.J., p. 36, 43.]

Paust, Jordan J.: "Medellín", "Avena", the supremacy of treaties, and relevant executive authority. (In: Suffolk Transnational Law Review, 2008, v. 31, no. 2, p. 301-333.)

Pérez Bernárdez, Carmela: A vueltas con la asistencia consular: la sentencia de la Corte Internacional de Justicia de 31 de marzo de 2004 en el asunto Avena y otros nacionales mexicanos (México c. Estados Unidos de América). (Dans : Cuadernos de jurisprudencia internacional, 2005, v. 2, p. 121-161.)

Peyro Llopis, Ana : Après Avena : l'exécution par les Etats-Unis de l'arrêt de la Cour internationale de Justice. (Dans : Annuaire français de droit international, 2005, v. 51, p. 140-161.) [C.I.J., passim.]

Quigley, John : Avena and other Mexican nationals (Mexico v. United States of America) : must courts block executions because of a treaty ? (In : Melbourne Journal of International Law, 2004, v. 5, p. 450-461.)

Quigley, John : President Bush's directive on foreigners arrest : a critique of Medellin v. Texas. (In : Emory International Law Review, 2008, v. 22, no. 2, p. 423-454.) [IC.J., passim.]

Requena Casanova, Millán : La protección efectiva de los derechos consulares en el plano judicial : a propósito de la sentencia Avena (México c. Estados Unidos de América). (Dans : Revista española de derecho internacional, 2004, v. 56, no. 2, p. 777-792.)

Rothenberg, Laurence E. : International law, U.S. sovereignty, and the death penalty. (In : Georgetown Journal of International Law, 2004, v. 35, no. 3, p. 547-595.) [I.C.J., p. 570-592.]

Schabas, William A. : International law, the United States of America and capital punishment. (In : Suffolk Transnational Law Review, 2008, v. 31, no. 2, p. 377-418.)

Sheik, Mani : From Breard to Medellin : Supreme Court inaction or ICJ activism in the field of international law ? (In : California Law Review, 2006, v. 94, p. 531-573.)

Shelton, Dinah : Case concerning Avena and Other Mexican nationals (Mexico v. United States) : International Court of Justice, March 31, 2004. (In : American Journal of International Law, 2004, v. 98, no. 3, p. 559-566.)

Simma, Bruno and Hoppe, Carsten : From LaGrand and Avena to Medellin : a rocky road toward implementation. (In : Tulane Journal of International and Comparative Law, 2005, v. 14, no. 1, p. 7-59.)

Sloane, Robert : Measures necessary to ensure : the ICJ's provisional measures order in Avena and other Mexican nationals. (In : Leiden Journal of International Law, 2004, v. 17, p. 673-394.)

Smartt, Nancy Serano : What Breard and its progeny mean for Avena and other Mexican nationals. (In : Temple International and Comparative Law Journal, 2005, v. 19, p. 163-188.)

Sossai, Mirko : L'esecuzione della sentenza Avena negli stati uniti. (Dans : Rivista di diritto internazionale, 2006, v. 89, p. 423-477.) [C.P.J.I., p. 428; C.I.J., passim.]

Steinmark, Michael R.: The case concerning Avena and other Mexican nationals (Mexico v. United States): a Mexican perspective on the fight for consular rights. (In: Law and Business Review of the Americas, 2004, v. 10, p. 417-424.)

Tranel, Adrienne M.: The ruling of the International Court of Justice in Avena and other Mexican nationals: enforcing the right to consular assistance in U.S. jurisprudence. (In: American University International Law Review, 2004, v. 20, no. 2, p. 403-464.)

Weckel, Philippe: Chronique de jurisprudence internationale: Cour internationale de Justice, arrêt du 31 mars 2004, Avena et autres ressortissants mexicains (Mexique c. Etats-Unis). (Dans: Revue générale de droit international public, 2004, v. 108, no. 4, p. 731-752.)

Weckel, Philippe: Chronique de jurisprudence internationale: Cour internationale de Justice: ordonnance du 16 juillet 2008 (mesures conservatoires), demande en interprétation de l'arrêt du 31 mars 2004 en l'affaire Avena et autres ressortissants mexicains (Mexique c. Etats-Unis d'Amérique). (Dans: Revue générale de droit international public, 2008, v. 112, no. 4, p. 915-918.) [I.C.J., passim.]

Wojcik, Mark E.: The United States, the International Court of Justice, and the Vienna Convention on Consular Relations: Medellin v. Texas. (In: International Legal Materials, 2008, v. 47, no. 3, p. 281-321.)

Young, Laura A.: Setting sail with The Charming Betsy: enforcing the International Court of Justice's Avena judgment in federal habeas corpus proceedings. (In: Minnesota Law Review, 2004, v. 89, p. 890-915.)

129. *Certaines procédures pénales engagées en France (République du Congo c. France)*
129. *Certain Criminal Proceedings in France (Republic of the Congo* v. *France)*

Bollo Arocena, María Dolores: Soberanía, justicia universal e inmunidad de jurisdicción en los asuntos: República democrática del Congo c. Bélgica y República del Congo c. Francia. (Dans: Revista española de derecho internacional, 2004, v. 56, no. 1, p. 91-127.)

O'Donnell, Kaitlin R.: Certain criminal proceedings in France (Republic of Congo v. France) and head of State immunity: how impenetrable should the immunity veil remain? (In: Boston University International Law Journal, 2008, v. 26, no. 2, p. 375-416.) [I.C.J., passim.]

Turns, David: International Court of Justice: Certain Criminal Proceedings in France (Republic of the Congo v. France), provisional measures, order of 17 June 2003. (In: International and Comparative Law Quarterly, 2004, v. 53, no. 3, p. 747-752.)

130. *Souveraineté sur Pedra Branca/Pulau Batu Puteh, Middle Rocks et South Ledge (Malaisie/Singapour)*
130. *Sovereignty over Pedra Branca/Pulau Batu Puteh, Middle Rocks and South Ledge (Malaysia/Singapore)*

Abello Galvis, Ricardo, trans.: Traducción de la decisión de la Corte Internacional de Justicia relativa a la Soberanía sobre Pedra Branca/Pulau Batu Puteh, Middle Rocks y South Ledge (Malasia/Singapur): decisión sobre el fondo. (Dans: Anuario Colombiano de Derecho Internacional: ACDI, 2009, v. 2, p. 175-291.)

Beckman, Robert: Case between Malaysia and Singapore concerning sovereignty over Pedra Branca/Pulau Batu Puteh, Middle Rocks and South Ledge. (In: Asian Yearbook of International Law, 2008, v. 24, p. 275-287.) [I.C.J., passim.]

Beckman, Robert and Schofield, Clive: Moving beyond disputes over island sovereignty: ICJ decision sets stage for maritime boundary delimitation in the Singapore strait. (In: Ocean Development and International Law, 2009, v. 40, no. 1, p. 1-35.) [I.C.J., passim.]

Bories, Clémentine: L'arrêt de la Cour internationale de Justice du 23 mai 2008 dans l'affaire Souveraineté sur Pedra Branca/Pulau Batu Puteh, Middle Rocks et South Ledge (Malaisie/Singapour). (Dans: Annuaire français de droit international, 2008, v. 54, p. 227-236.) [C.I.J., passim.]

David, Eric: Le différend insulaire Malaisie/Singapour. (Dans: Liber amicorum Jean-Pierre Cot: le procès international. Bruxelles: Bruylant, 2009, p. 77-94.)

Faizal, Mohamed and Evangeline, Queck: The repercussions of the similarities between Sipadan/Ligitan and Pedra Branca disputes. (In: Singapore Law Review, 2004, v. 24, p. 52-65.)

Hsien-li, Tan: Case concerning Sovereignty over Pedra Branca/Pulau Batu Puteh, Middle Rocks and South Ledge (Malaysia/Singapore). (In: Singapore Yearbook of International Law, 2008, v. 12, p. 257-262.)

Jayakumar, Shunmugam and Koh, Tommy T. B.: Pedra Branca: the road to the World Court. Singapore: National University of Singapore; Ministry of Foreign Affairs Diplomatic Academy, 2009.

Lathrop, Coalter: Sovereignty over Pedra Branca/Pulau Batu Puteh, Middle Rocks and South Ledge (Malaysia/Singapore), International Court of Justice, May 23, 2008. (In: American Journal of International Law, 2008, v. 102, no. 4, p. 828-834.)

Lim, Chin L.: The uses of pacific settlement techniques in Malaysia-Singapore relations. (In: Melbourne Journal of International Law, 2005, v. 6, p. 313-341.)

Mills, Alex: The formalism of State sovereignty in territorial and maritime disputes. (In: Cambridge Law Journal, 2008, v. 67, no. 3, p. 443-447.) [I.C.J., passim.]

Xiong, Liangmin: A review of the Pedra Branca dispute. (In: China Oceans Law Review, 2008, no. 1, p. 218-227.) [I.C.J., passim.]

131. *Conséquences juridiques de l'édification d'un mur dans le Territoire palestinien occupé*
131. *Legal Consequences of the Construction of a Wall in the Occupied Palestinian Territory*

Abi-Saab, Rosemary: "Conséquences juridiques de l'édification d'un mur dans le territoire palestinien occupé": quelques réflexions préliminaires sur l'avis consultatif de la Cour internationale de Justice. (Dans: Revue internationale de la Croix-Rouge, 2004, v. 86, no. 855, p. 633-658.)

Ackerman, Erik and Bartels, Melanie: Na Arafat en Internationaal Gerechtshof: openingen in het Israelisch-Palestijns conflict? (In: Jaarboek vrede en veiligheid: bewapening, vredesbeweging en het Nederlandse veiligheidsbeleid, 2004, p. 89-109.)

Akram, Susan M. and Lynk, Michael: The wall and the law: a tale of two judgments. (In: Netherlands Quarterly of Human Rights, 2006, v. 24, no. 1, p. 61-106.)

Allain, Jean: Special dossier on the Advisory Opinion of the International Court of Justice on the Legal Consequences of the Construction of a Wall in the Occupied Palestinian Territory: introduction: a vindication of Palestinian rights. (In: Palestine Yearbook of International Law, 2004, v. 13, p. 109-132.)

Araujo, Robert John: Implementation of the ICJ advisory opinion: Legal Consequences of the Construction of a Wall in the Occupied Palestinian Territory: fences (do not) make good neighbours? (In: Boston University International Law Journal, 2004, v. 22, no. 2, p. 349-398.)

Aus dem Bereich der Vereinten Nationen: Berichte, Nachrichten, Meinungen. (In: Vereinte Nationen, 2005, v. 53, no. 1, p. 19-22.) [I.C.J., p. 19, 20.]

Aus dem Bereich der Vereinten Nationen: Berichte, Nachrichten, Meinungen. (In: Vereinte Nationen, 2005, v. 53, no. 3, p. 100-107.) [I.C.J., p. 104-107.]

Balmond, Louis et Millet-Devalle, Anne-Sophie: Chronique des faits internationaux: Israël: évolution de la situation: 15 juin – 15 septembre 2004. (Dans: Revue générale de droit international public, 2004, v. 108, no. 4, p. 1001-1006.) [C.I.J., p. 1004-1006.]

Barak-Erez, Daphne: Israel: the security barrier: between international law, constitutional law and domestic judicial review. (In: International Journal of Constitutional Law, 2006, v. 4, no. 3, p. 540-552.) [I.C.J., p. 544-548, 551-552.]

Barry, Collins: Locating sovereignty in international law: reflections on the construction of a wall in Palestine. (In: Barriers to reconciliation: case studies on Iraq and the Palestine-Israel conflict, ed. by Jacqueline S. Ismael; William W. Haddad. Lanham [etc.]: University Press of America, 2007, p. 250-273.)

Becker, Florian : IGH-Gutachten über "Rechtliche Konsequenzen des Baus einer Mauer in den besetzten palästinensischen Gebieten". (In : Archiv des Völkerrechts, 2005, v. 43, no. 2, p. 218-239.)

Bekker, Peter H. F. : The World Court's ruling regarding Israel's West Bank barrier and the primacy of international law : an insider's perspective. (In : Cornell International Law Journal, 2005, v. 38, no. 2, p. 553-568.)

Bekker, Peter H. F. : The World Court's ruling regarding Israel's West Bank barrier and the primacy of international law : an insider's perspective. (In : The Palestine question in international law, ed. by Victor Kattan. London : British Institute of International and comparative Law, 2008, p. 817-832.)

Ben-Naftali, Orna : "A la recherche du temps perdu" : rethinking Article 6 of the Fourth Geneva Convention in the light of the Legal Consequences of the Construction of a Wall in the Occupied Palestinian Territory advisory opinion. (In : Israel Law Review, 2005, v. 38, no. 1-2, p. 211-229.)

Bermejo García, Romualdo : Comentarios en torno a la opinión consultiva de la Corte Internacional de Justicia sobre el mal denominado "Muro" de Israel contra el terrorismo palestino : una opinión muy "opinable". (Dans : Uso de la fuerza y protección de los derechos humanos en un nuevo orden internacional, sous la dir. de Consuelo Ramón Chornet ; Cesáreo Gutiérrez Espada ; Romualdo Bermejo García ; Eugenia López-Jacoiste Diaz ; Antonio Remiro Brotons ; José Elías Esteve Moltó ; Pablo Antonio Fernández Sánchez ; Elena López-Almansa Beaus ; José Roberto Pérez Salom. Valencia : Publicaciones Universitat de Valencia, 2006, p. 131-172.)

Bianchi, Andrea : Dismantling the wall : the ICJ's advisory opinion and its likely impact on international law. (In : German Yearbook of International Law, 2004, v. 47, p. 343-391.)

Bockel, Alain : Le retrait israélien de Gaza et ses conséquences sur le droit international. (Dans : Annuaire français de droit international, 2005, v. 51, p. 16-26.) [C.I.J., p. 23-24.]

Bradley, Kyle K. : A mending wall : a critical look at the International Court of Justice's analysis in its Advisory Opinion on the Legal Consequences of the Construction of a Wall in the Occupied Palestinian Territory. (In : Temple International and Comparative Law Journal, 2005, v. 19, no. 2, p. 419-448.)

Broude, Tomer : The legitimacy of the ICJ's advisory competence in the shadow of the wall. (In : Israel Law Review, 2005, v. 38, no. 1-2, p. 189-210.)

Bruha, Thomas and Tams, Christian J. : Self-defence against terrorist attacks : considerations in the light of the ICJ's Israeli Wall opinion. (In : Weltinnenrecht : liber amicorum Jost Delbrück, ed. by Dicke, Klaus ; Hobe, Stephan ; Meyn, Karl-Ulrich ; Peters, Anne ; Riedel, Eibe H. ; Schütz, Hans-Joachim ; Tietje, Christian. Berlin : Duncker & Humblot, 2005, p. 85-100.)

Buergenthal, Thomas : Dissenting opinion of Judge Buergenthal. (In : Justice, 2004, v. 40, p. 26-28.) [I.C.J., passim.]

Burgis, Michelle : Discourses of division : law, politics and the ICJ Advisory Opinion on the Legal Consequences of a Wall in the Occupied Palestinian Territory. (In : Chinese Journal of International Law, 2008, v. 7, no. 1, p. 33-63.)

Calvo-Goller, Karin N. : More than a huge imbalance : the ICJ's advisory opinion on the legal consequences of the construction of the barrier. (In : Israel Law Review, 2005, v. 38, p. 165-188.) [I.C.J., passim.]

Cannizzaro, Enzo : Sui rapporti fra Consiglio di sicurezza e Assemblea generale nel campo del mantenimiento della pace. (Dans : Rivista di diritto internazionale, 2004, v. 87, no. 4, p. 1066-1068.)

Caplen, Robert A. : Mending of the "fence" : how treatment of the Israeli-Palestinian conflict by the International Court of Justice at The Hague has redefined the doctrine of self-defense. (In : Florida Law Review, 2005, v. 57, no. 3, p. 717-769.)

Cour internationale de Justice : Communiqué de presse : avis consultatif de la C.I.J. sur les Conséquences juridiques de l'édification d'un mur dans le territoire palestinien occupé (La Haye, 9 juillet 2004). (Dans : Documents d'actualité internationale, 2004, v. 17, p. 655-657.)

D'Argent, Pierre : Compliance, cessation, reparation and restitution in the Wall Advisory Opinion. (In : Völkerrecht als Wertordnung : Festschrift für Christian Tomuschat, ed. by Pierre-Marie Dupuy ; Bardo Fassbender ; Malcolm N. Shaw ; Karl-Peter Sommermann. Kehl : N. P. Engel, 2006, p. 463-477.)

Damrosch, Lori Fisler and Oxman, Bernard H. : Agora : ICJ Advisory Opinion on Construction of a Wall in the Occupied Palestinian Territory. (In : American Journal of International Law, 2005, v. 99, no. 1, p. 1-6.)

De Puy, Albero : Bringing down the barrier : a comparative analysis of the ICJ advisory opinion and the High Court of Justice of Israel's ruling on Israel's construction of a barrier in the occupied territories. (In : Tulane Journal of International and Comparative Law, 2005, v. 13, p. 275-303.)

Dennis, Michael J. : Application of human rights treaties extraterritorially in times of armed conflict and military occupation. (In : American Journal of International Law, 2005, v. 99, no. 1, p. 119-141.) [I.C.J., p. 119, 121-123, 126-129, 134, 136.]

Domb, Fania : The separation fence in the International Court of Justice and the High Court of Justice : commonalities, differences and specifics. (In : International law and armed conflict : exploring the faultlines : essays in honour of Yoram Dinstein, ed. by Michael N. Schmitt ; Jelena Pejic. Leiden ; Boston : Martinus Nijhoff, 2007, p. 509-541.)

Dominicé, Christian : L'opportunité judiciaire selon l'Avis consultatif relatif aux conséquences juridiques de l'édification d'un mur dans le territoire palestinien occupé. (Dans : Promoting justice, human rights and conflict resolution through international law : liber amicorum Lucius Caflisch, ed. by Marcelo G. Kohen. Leiden : Martinus Nijhoff, 2007, p. 837-853.)

Dragiev, Alksandr: Prejudicialni vprosi v sveatelnoto mnenie na Medunarodnija Sd na Organizacijata na Obedinenite Nacii otnosno pravnite posledici ot postrojavaneto ot Izrael na stena v okupiranata palestinska teritorija. (In: Pravna misal, 2006, v. 47, no. 2, p. 66-78.)

Dubuisson, François: La construction du mur en territoire palestinien occupé devant la Cour Suprême d'Israel: analyse d'un processus judiciaire de légitimation. (Dans: Droit du pouvoir, pouvoir du droit: mélanges offerts à Jean Salmon, 2007, p. 889-927.)

Dubuisson, François: The implementation of the I.C.J. Advisory Opinion concerning the Legal Consequences of the Construction of a Wall in the Occupied Palestinian Territory. (In: Palestine Yearbook of International Law, 2004, v. 13, p. 27-54.)

Dudai, Ron: The wall, the law and the Court: reflections on the Beit Sourik case in the Israeli Supreme Court. (In: Yearbook of Islamic and Middle Eastern Law, 2004, v. 10, p. 471-488.)

El-Kareh, Rudolph: Cour internationale de Justice: un moment historique. (Dans: Revue d'études palestiniennes, 2004, v. 93, p. 3-9.)

Falk, Richard A.: Toward authoritativeness: the ICJ ruling on Israel's security wall. (In: American Journal of International Law, 2005, v. 99, p. 42-52.)

Foster, Caroline: Legal Consequences of the Construction of a Wall in the Occupied Palestinian Territory: the advisory jurisdiction of the International Court of Justice, human security and necessity. (In: New Zealand Yearbook of International Law, 2005, v. 2, p. 51-100.)

Fuchs, Juí: Mezinárodní soudní dvur v rísi války a za zdí. (In: Právník, 2004, v. 145, no. 12, p. 1469-1485.)

Gareau, Jean-François: Shouting at the wall: self-determination and the Legal Consequences of the Construction of a Wall in the Occupied Palestinian Territory. (In: Leiden Journal of International Law, 2005, v. 18, no. 3, p. 489-521.)

Giurisprudenza internazionale: Corte internazionale di Giustizia, 9 luglio 2004: Parere relativo alle Conseguenze giuridiche della costruzione di un muro nei territori palestinesi occupati. (Dans: Rivista di diritto internazionale, 2004, v. 87, no. 4, p. 1069-1128.)

Gomez-Robledo, Juan Manuel: L'avis de la C.I.J. sur les Conséquences juridiques de l'édification d'un mur dans le territoire palestinien occupé: timidité ou prudence? (Dans: Revue générale de droit international public, 2005, v. 109, no. 3, p. 521-537.)

Gowlland-Debbas, Vera: The responsibility of the political organs of the U.N. for Palestine in light of the I.C.J.'s Wall Opinion. (In: Promoting justice, human rights and conflict resolution through international law: liber amicorum Lucius Caflisch, ed. by Marcelo G. Kohen. Leiden: Martinus Nijhoff, 2007, p. 1095-1119.)

Gray, Christine: Case and comment: the I.C.J. Advisory Opinion on Legal Consequences of the Construction of a Wall in the Occupied Palestinian Territory. (In: Cambridge Law Journal, 2004, v. 63, no. 3, p. 527-532.) [I.C.J. and P.C.I.J., passim.]

Gross, Aeyal M.: The construction of a wall between The Hague and Jerusalem: the enforcement and limits of humanitarian law and the structure of occupation. (In: Leiden Journal of International Law, 2006, v. 19, p. 393-440.)

Gross, Aeyal M.: The construction of a wall between The Hague and Jerusalem: the enforcement and limits of humanitarian law and the structure of occupation. (In: The Palestine question in international law, ed. by Victor Kattan. London: British Institute of International and comparative Law, 2008, p. 833-880.)

Haupais, Nicolas: Les obligations de la puissance occupante au regard de la jurisprudence et de la pratique récentes. (Dans: Revue générale de droit international public, 2007, v. 111, p. 117-146.) [C.I.J., p. 117-125, 130-139, 141-145.]

Henrard, K. (ed.): Hague case law: latest developments. (In: Netherlands International Law Review, 2004, v. 51, no. 3, p. 467-474.) [I.C.J., p. 467-468.]

Hirsch, Moshe: The legal status of Jerusalem following the I.C.J. advisory opinion on the separation barrier. (In: Israel Law Review, 2005, v. 38, no. 1-2, p. 298-315.)

Hogan-Doran, Justin and Stephens, Tim: Australian cases before international courts and tribunals involving questions of public international law: 2004. (In: Australian Yearbook of International Law, 2004, v. 25, p. 403-424.) [I.C.J., p. 403-409.]

Holmila, Erkki: Another brick in the wall? The decision of the Israeli Supreme Court in the case of Beit Sourik Village Council v. the Government of Israel and Commander of the IDF Forces in the West Bank (HCJ 2056/04, 30 June 2004). (In: Nordic Journal of International Law, 2005, v. 74, no. 1, p. 103-115.)

ICJ advisory opinion: Israel's written submission, special report: unofficial summary. (In: Justice, 2004, v. 38, 7-9).

Imseis, Ardi: Critical reflections on the international humanitarian law aspects of the ICJ wall advisory opinion. (In: American Journal of International Law, 2005, v. 99, no. 1, p. 102-118.)

International Court of Justice: "Contrary to international law": International Court of Justice ruling on the separation barrier. (In: The struggle for sovereignty: Palestine and Israel, 1993-2005, ed. by Joel Beinin; Rebecca L. Stein. Stanford: Stanford University Press, 2006, p. 348-349.)

International Court of Justice: Legal Consequences of the Construction of a Wall in the Occupied Palestinian Territory: Decision of the International Court of Justice: 9 July 2004, General List N° 131, Advisory Opinion. (In: Yearbook of Islamic and Middle Eastern Law, 2004, v. 10, p. 413-456.)

International Court of Justice: Legal consequences of the constructon of a wall in the occupied palestinian territory: advisory opinion. (In: Israel Law Review, 2005, v. 38, no. 1-2, 17-82).

International Court of Justice: [Special dossier on the Advisory Opinion of the International Court of Justice on the Legal Consequences of the Construction of a Wall in the Occupied Palestinian Territory:] International Court of Justice: Legal Consequences of the Construction of a Wall in the Occupied Palestinian Territory: Advisory Opinion. (In: Palestine Yearbook of International Law, 2004, v. 13, p. 337-399.)

International Court of Justice: No. 131, 9 July 2004: Legal Consequences of the Construction of a Wall in the Occupied Palestinian Territory. (In: Indian Journal of International Law, 2004, v. 44, no. 3, p. 532-669.)

Joosten, Veronique: De Israelische veiligheidsmuur: het advies van het Internationaal Gerechtshof. (In: Zoeklicht, 2004, v. 13, no. 40, p. 25-28.)

Kacowicz, Arie Marcelo: The normative dimension of international relations and the advisory opinion of the ICJ on the Separation barrier. (In: Israel Law Review, 2005, v. 38, no. 1-2, p. 348-357.)

Kahan, Rebecca: Building a protective wall around terrorists: how the International Court of Justice's ruling in the Legal Consequences of the Construction of a Wall in the Occupied Palestinian Territory made the world safer for terrorists and more dangerous for member States of the United Nations. (In: Fordham International Law Journal, 2005, v. 28, no. 3, p. 827-878.)

Kassim, Anis F.: The Advisory Opinion of the International Court of Justice on the Legal Consequences of the Construction of a Wall in the Occupied Palestinian Territory: significance and implications. (In: Yearbook of Islamic and Middle Eastern Law, 2004, v. 10, p. 457-462.)

Kattan, Victor: The legality of the West Bank wall: Israel's High Court of Justice v. the International Court of Justice. (In: Vanderbilt Journal of Transnational Law, 2007, v. 40, p. 1425-1522.)

Kattan, Victor: The legality of the West Bank wall: Israel's High Court of Justice v. the International Court of Justice. (In: The Palestine question in international law, ed. by Victor Kattan. London: British Institute of International and comparative Law, 2008, p. 881-977.)

Kattan, Victor: The wall, obligations "erga omnes" and human rights: the case for withdrawing the European Community's terms of preferential trade with Israel. (In: Palestine Yearbook of International Law, 2004, v. 13, p. 71-89.)

Kattan, Victor (ed.): The Palestine question in international law. London: British Institute of International and Comparative Law, 2008.

Keidar, Nir: An examination of the authority of the military commander to requisition privately owned land for the construction of the separation barrier. (In: Israel Law Review, 2005, v. 38, no. 1-2, p. 247-261.)

Kelly, Michael J.: Critical analysis of the International Court of Justice ruling on Israel's security barrier. (In: Fordham International Law Journal, 2005, v. 29, no. 1, p. 181-228.)

Khan, Daniel-Erasmus: Sicherheitszaun oder Apartheidmauer? Das Gutachten des Internationalen Gerichtshofes vom 9. Juli 2004 zu den israelischen Sperranlagen gegenüber dem Westjordanland. (In: Die Friedens-Warte: Blätter für internationale Verständigung und zwischenstaatliche Organisation, 2004, v. 79, no. 3-4, p. 345-370.) [I.C.J., p. 345-370.]

Kohen, Marcelo G.: L'autodétermination et l'avis consultatif sur le "mur". (Dans: Völkerrecht als Wertordnung: Festschrift für Christian Tomuschat, sous la dir. de Pierre-Marie Dupuy; Bardo Fassbender; Malcolm N. Shaw; Karl-Peter Sommermann. Kehl: N. P. Engel Verlag, 2006, p. 961-971.)

Koury, Stephanie: The I.C.J. Advisory Opinion on the Wall: a prelude to State action? (In: Yearbook of Islamic and Middle Eastern Law, 2004, v. 10, p. 463-469.)

Koury, Stephanie: Why this wall? (In: Palestine Yearbook of International Law, 2004, v. 13, p. 55-89.)

Kovács, Péter: Rather judgement than opinion? Or can we speak about a third type judicial procedure before the International Court of Justice? (In: Miskolci Nemzetközi Jogi Közlemények, 2005, v. 2, no. 1, p. 102-119.)

Kovács, Péter: Rather judgement than opinion? Or can we speak about a third type of judicial procedure before the International Court of Justice? (In: Anuario de derecho internacional, 2004, v. 20, p. 447-465.)

Kretzmer, David: The advisory opinion: the light treatment of international humanitarian law. (In: American Journal of International Law, 2005, v. 99, no. 1, p. 88-102.)

Kretzmer, David: Introduction: [to a special double issue: Domestic and international judicial review of the Construction of the Separation barrier]. (In: Israel Law Review, 2005, v. 38, no. 1-2, p. 6-16.) [I.C.J., passim.]

Lapidoth, Ruth: The advisory opinion and the Jewish settlements. (In: Israel Law Review, 2005, v. 38, no. 1-2, p. 292-297.)

Lein, Yehezkel: One big prison: freedom of movement to and from the Gaza strip on the eve of the disengagement Plan 2005. [I.C.J., p. 73.]

Litwack, Jason: A disproportionate ruling for all the right reasons: Beit Sourik Village Council v. The Government of Israel. (In: Brooklyn Journal of International Law, 2006, v. 31, no. 3, p. 857-897.)

López-Jacoiste Díaz, María Eugenia: Algunas reflexiones sobre la Opinión consultiva sobre el muro de Israel: la solución está en Ramallah y Gaza y no en La Haya ni en Manhattan. (Dans: Anuario de derecho internacional, 2004, v. 20, p. 467-491.)

Lubell, Noam: The ICJ advisory opinion and the separation barrier: a troublesome route. (In: Israel Yearbook on Human Rights, 2005, v. 35, p. 283-313.)

Mahmoudi, Said: Self-defence and international terrorism. (In: Scandinavian Studies in Law, 2005, v. 48, p. 203-213.)

Moriamé, Benjamin: La Palestine dans l'étau israélien: avant et après le mur. Paris: L'Harmattan, 2006. [C.I.J., p. 139-166.]

Murphy, Sean D.: Self-defense and the Israeli wall advisory opinion: an ipse dixit from the ICJ? (In: American Journal of International Law, 2005, v. 99, no. 1, p. 62-76.)

O'Keefe, Roger: Legal Consequences of the Construction of a Wall in the Occupied Palestinian Territory: a commentary. (In: Revue belge de droit international, 2004, v. 37, no. 1, p. 92-154.)

O'Keefe, Roger: Legal Consequences of the Construction of a Wall in the Occupied Palestinian Territory: a commentary. (In: The Palestine question in international law, ed. by Victor Kattan. London: British Institute of International and comparative Law, 2008, p. 751-815.)

Orakhelashvili, Alexander: International public order and the International Court's advisory opinion on Legal Consequences of the Construction of a Wall in the Occupied Palestinian Territory. (In: Archiv des Völkerrechts, 2005, v. 43, p. 240-256.)

Palestine: [Special dossier on the Advisory Opinion of the International Court of Justice on the Legal Consequences of the Construction of a Wall in the Occupied Palestinian Territory:] Written Statement submitted by Palestine to the International Court of Justice with respect to the Request for an Advisory Opinion Regarding Legal Consequences of the Construction of a Wall in the Occupied Palestinian Territory. (In: Palestine Yearbook of International Law, 2004, v. 13, p. 133-336.)

Pinzauti, Giulia: Aspetti problematici della legittimità del "muro" in Palestina: il caso Beit Sourik. (Dans: Rivista di diritto internazionale, 2005, v. 88, p. 441-463.) [C.I.J., p. 441-443, 459-462.]

Pinzauti, Giulia: La Corte suprema di Israele ritorna sulla questione del muro: il caso Alfei Menashe. (Dans: Rivista di diritto internazionale, 2006, v. 89, no. 1, p. 105-119.) [C.I.J., passim.]

Piotrowicz, Ryszard: Defense and defiance in international law: Israel, a wall and an advisory opinion. (In: Australian Law Journal, 2004, v. 78, no. 11, p. 710-718.)

Plessis, Max du: Seeking an advisory opinion on Israel's apartheid and colonial practices in the occupied Palestinian territories. (In: South African Yearbook of International Law, 2009, v. 34, p. 169-183.)

Pomerance, Michla: The ICJ's advisory jurisdiction and the crumbling wall between the political and the judicial. (In: American Journal of International Law, 2005, v. 99, no. 1, p. 26-42.)

Portilla Gómez, Juan Manuel: La Corte Internacional de Justicia frente al conflicto palestino-israeli. (Dans: Revista de la Facultad de Derecho y Ciencias Políticas. Universidad Pontificia Bolivariana, 2007, v. 37, no. 106, p. 155-179.)

Portilla Gómez, Juan Manuel: El derecho internacional ante la ocupación de los territorios palestinos y el muro de separación. (Dans: Anuario mexicano de derecho internacional, 2006, v. 6, p. 345-375.) [C.I.J., p. 353, 362, 365-371, 374-375.]

Pozo Serrano, María Pilar: La opinión consultiva de la CIJ sobre las consecuencias jurídicas de la construcción del muro en el territorio palestino occupado: problemas de competencia y oportunidad judicial. (Dans: Anuario de derecho internacional, 2004, v. 20, p. 493-518.) [C.I.J., passim; C.P.J.I., p. 508, 513.]

Rawaqa, Sana: L'édification du mur israélien en Palestine. Villeneuve d'Ascq: Atelier national de reproduction des thèses, c2007.

Rivier, Raphaële: Conséquences juridiques de l'édification d'un mur dans le territoire palestinien occupé. Cour internationale de Justice, avis consultatif du 9 juillet 2004. (Dans: Annuaire français de droit international, 2004, v. 50, p. 292-336.) [C.P.J.I., p. 322-323, 326-327; C.I.J., passim.]

Rostow, Nicholas: Wall of reason: Alan Dershowitz v. the International Court of Justice. (In: Albany Law Review, 2008, v. 71, no. 3, p. 953-986.)

Rotter, Manfred: The Advisory Opinion of the International Court of Justice on the Legal Consequences of the Construction of a Wall in the Occupied Palestinian Territory. (In: Rights and a Middle East peace process: analyses and case studies from a new perspective, ed. by Stefan August Lütgenau. Innsbrück [etc.]: Studien Verlag, 2007, p. 145-162.)

Sabel, Robbie: The International Court of Justice decision on the separation barrier and the green line. (In: Israel Law Review, 2005, v. 38, no. 1-2, p. 316-330.)

Salmon, Jean J.-A.: Les colonies de peuplement israéliennes en territoire palestinien occupé au regard de l'Avis consultatif de la Cour internationale de Justice du 9 juillet 2004. (Dans: Frieden in Freiheit: Festschrift für Michael Bothe zum 70. Geburtstag, sous la dir. de Fischer-Lescano,

Andreas ; Gasser, Hans-Peter ; Marauhn, Thilo ; Ronzitti, Natalino. Baden-Baden ; Zurich : Nomos Verlag ; Dike Verlag, 2008, p. 285-295.)

Sánchez Rodríguez, Luis Ignacio : De nuevo sobre la jurisdicción consultiva de la Corte : el dictamen de la Corte Internacional de Justicia de 9 de julio de 2004 relativo a las Consecuencias jurídicas de la edificación de un muro en el terrritorio palestino ocupado. (Dans : Cuadernos de jurisprudencia internacional, 2005, v. 2, p. 163-197.)

Saura Estapà, Jaume : La cuestión palestina : bases para la paz desde el derecho internacional. (Dans : Conflictos y protección de derechos humanos en el orden internacional, sous la dir. de Juan Soroeta Liceras. Bilbao : Universidad del País Vasco, 2007, v. 6, p. 149-171.) [C.I.J., p. 159-162.]

Schrijver, Nico J. : Het Internationale Gerechtshof en de Israelische muur in bezet Palestijns gebied. (In : Nederlands juristenblad, 2004, v. 79, no. 8, p. 380-381.)

Scobbie, Iain : Regarding/disregarding : the judicial rhetoric of President Barak and the International Court of Justice's wall advisory opinion. (In : Chinese Journal of International Law, 2006, v. 5, p. 269-300.)

Scobbie, Iain : Unchart(er)ed waters ? Consequences of the Advisory Opinion on the Legal Consequences of the Construction of a Wall in the Occupied Palestinian Territory for the responsibility of the UN for Palestine. (In : European Journal of International Law, 2005, v. 16, no. 5, p. 941-961.)

Scobbie, Iain : Words my mother never taught me : "in defense of the International Court". (In : American Journal of International Law, 2005, v. 99, p. 76-88.)

Shany, Yuval : Capacities and inadequacies : a look at the separation barrier cases. (In : Israel Law Review, 2005, v. 38, no. 1-2, p. 230-246.)

Smith, Adam M. : Good fences make good neighbours ? The "Wall Decision" and the troubling rise of the ICJ as a human rights court. (In : Harvard Human Rights Journal, 2005, v. 18, p. 251-263.)

Solomon, Solon : The justiciability of international disputes : the advisory opinion on Israel's security fence as a case study. Nijmegen : Wolf Legal, 2009.

Steinberg, Gerald M. : The UN, the ICJ and the separation barrier : war by other means. (In : Israel Law Review, 2005, v. 38, no. 1-2, p. 331-347.)

Strapatsas, Nicolaos : Case note on the ICJ Advisory Opinion on the Legal Consequences of the Construction of the Wall in Occupied Palestinian Territory. (In : Israel Yearbook on Human Rights, 2005, v. 35, p. 251-282.)

Supreme Court and I.C.J. rulings on security barrier. (In : Keesing's Record of World Events, 2004, v. 50, no. 7-8, p. 46138-46139.)

Tams, Christian J.: Light treatment of a complex problem: the law of self-defence in the Wall case. (In: European Journal of International Law, 2005, v. 16, no. 5, p. 963-978.)

Tashjian, Joel S.: Contentious matters and the advisory power: the ICJ and Israel's wall. (In: Chicago Journal of International Law, 2005, v. 6, no. 1, p. 427-437.)

Verbon, Harrie: Israel en internationaal recht: Barbertje moet hangen. (In: Internationale spectator, 2008, v. 62, no. 9, p. 491-494.) [I.C.J., p. 491-492.]

Verhoeven, Sten: Het advies van het Internationaal Gerechtshof over de bouw van de veiligheidsmuur. (In: Wereldbeeld: tijdschrift voor de Verenigde Naties, 2004, v. 28, no. 125, p. 30-33.)

Verhoeven, Sten: Advisory Opinion on the Legal Consequences of the Construction of a Wall in the Occupied Palestinian Territories. (In: International law Forum du droit international, 2004, v. 6, no. 3-4, p. 106-110.)

Waart, Jos de: Internationale conferentie over de Midden-Oosten politiek in het Vredespaleis. (In: VN Forum, 2004, 2004/4, v. 17, no. 4, p. 21-22.) [I.C.J., p. 21.]

Waart, Jos de: Verslag debat Algemene Ledenvergadering NVVN over de Muur: "Staat het volkenrecht in Palestina zo vast als een muur of juist voor een ondoordringbare muur?". (In: VN Forum, 2006, 2006/2, v. 19, p. 18-22.) [I.C.J., passim.]

Waart, Paul J. I. M. de: International Court of Justice firmly walled in the law of power in the Israeli-Palestinian peace process. (In: Leiden Journal of International Law, 2005, v. 18, no. 3, p. 467-487.)

Waart, Paul J. I. M. de: Israël een "muur" te ver. (In: VN Forum, 2004, 2004/1, v. 17, no. 1, p. 1-6.) [I.C.J., passim.]

Waart, Paul J. I. M. de: Israël moet muur op Palestijns gebied ontmantelen. (In: VN Forum, 2004, 2004/2, v. 17, no. 2, p. 1-6.)

Waart, Paul J. I. M. de: Verscheurd land. (In: VN Forum, 2004, 2004/4, v. 17, no. 4, p. 9-11.) [I.C.J., p. 10.]

Watson, Geoffrey R.: The "Wall" decisions in legal and political context. (In: American Journal of International Law, 2005, v. 99, no. 1, p. 6-26.)

Weckel, Philippe: Cour internationale de Justice: avis du 9 juillet 2004: conséquences juridiques de l'édification d'un mur dans le territoire palestinien occupé. (Dans: Revue générale de droit international public, 2004, v. 108, no. 4, p. 1017-1036.) [C.I.J., p. 1017-1036.]

Wedgwood, Ruth: The ICJ advisory opinion on the Israeli security fence and the limits of self-defense. (In: American Journal of International Law, 2005, v. 99, no. 1, p. 52-62.)

Ziccardi Capaldo, Giuliana: Fighting global terrorism: through global enforcement mechanisms. (In: Global Community: Yearbook of International Law and Jurisprudence, 2004, v. 4, no. 1, xv-xxvii.) [I.C.J., p. XVII-XX, XXIII.]

Zilbershats, Yaffa: The Court is not competent to hear political non-legal submissions. (In: Justice, 2004, v. 38, p. 10-13.) [I.C.J., passim.]

Zimmermann, Andreas: Uniting-for-peace und Gutachtenanfragen der Generalversammlung: Anmerkungen aus Anlaß des Gutachtens des Internationalen Gerichtshofs zur Zulässigkeit des Sicherheitszaunes zwichen Israel und den palästinensischen Gebieten. (In: Weltinnenrecht: liber amicorum Jost Delbrück, ed. by Dicke, Klaus; Hobe, Stephan; Meyn, Karl-Ulrich; Peters, Anne; Riedel, Eibe H.; Schütz, Hans-Joachim; Tietje, Christian. Berlin: Duncker & Humblot, 2005, p. 909-925.)

Zunes, Stephen: Implications of the U.S. reaction to the World Court ruling against Israel's "separation barrier". (In: Middle East Policy, 2004, v. 11, no. 4, p. 72-85.)

132. *Délimitation maritime en mer Noire (Roumanie c. Ukraine)*
132. *Maritime Delimitation in the Black Sea (Romania* v. *Ukraine)*

Anderson, David Heywood: Maritime delimitation in the Black Sea case (Romania v. Ukraine). (In: Law and Practice of International Courts and Tribunals, 2009, v. 8, p. 305-327.)

Lathrop, Coalter: Maritime delimitation in the Black Sea (Romania v. Ukraine): International Court of Justice, February 3, 2009. (In: American Journal of International Law, 2009, v. 103, no. 3, p. 543-549.)

Mühlendahl, Paul, von: L'arrêt de la Cour internationale de Justice dans l'affaire de la délimitation maritime en mer Noire (Roumanie c. Ukraine): l'aboutissement d'un processus vieux de quarante ans? (Dans: Revue québécoise de droit international, 2009, v. 22, no. 2, p. 1-24.)

Oude Elferink, Alex G.: Maritime delimination in the Black Sea (Romania v. Ukraine): case concerning Maritime Delimitation in the Black Sea (Romania v. Ukraine), Merits, Judgment, 3 February 2009. (In: Hague Justice Journal, 2009, v. 4, no. 1, p. 61-64.)

Romania-Ukraine. Report Number 8-17. Case Concerning Maritime Delimitation in the Black Sea. (In: International maritime boundaries, 2005, v. 5, 3939.)

Tanaka, Yoshifumi: Reflections on maritime delimitation in the Romania/Ukraine case before the International Court of Justice. (In: Netherlands International Law Review, 2009, v. 61, p. 397-427.)

Touzé, Sébastien: Affaire relative à la délimitation maritime en mer Noire (Roumanie / Ukraine): une clarification didactique de la règle de "l'équidistance – circonstances pertinentes". (Dans: Annuaire français de droit international, 2009, v. 55, p. 221-251.)

Weckel, Philippe (sous la dir. de): Chronique de jurisprudence internationale. (Dans: Revue générale de droit international public, 2009, v. 113, no. 2, p. 431-463.) [C.I.J., p. 431-446.]

133. *Différend relatif à des droits de navigation et des droits connexes (Costa Rica c. Nicaragua)*
133. *Dispute regarding Navigational and Related Rights (Costa Rica* v. *Nicaragua)*

Cassella, Sarah: Rééquilibrer les effets inéquitables d'une délimitation territoriale: l'arrêt de la Cour internationale de Justice du 13 juillet 2009 dans l'affaire du Différend relatif à des droits de navigation et des droits connexes (Costa Rica c. Nicaragua). (Dans: Annuaire français de droit international, 2009, v. 55, p. 253-277.)

Grossman, Nienke: Dispute regarding navigational and related rights: Costa Rica v. Nicaragua (July 13, 2009). (In: International Legal Materials, 2009, v. 48, no. 5, p. 1180-1222.)

Tanaka, Yoshifumi: Navigational rights on the San Juan River: a commentary on the "Costa Rica v. Nicaragua" case. (In: Hague Justice Journal, 2009, v. 4, no. 3, p. 215-225.)

Weckel, Philippe: Chronique de jurisprudence internationale. (Dans: Revue générale de droit international public, 2009, v. 113, no. 4, p. 931-940.) [C.I.J., passim.]

135. *Usines de pâte à papier sur le fleuve Uruguay (Argentine c. Uruguay)*
135. *Pulp Mills on the River Uruguay (Argentina* v. *Uruguay)*

Alvarez-Jiménez, Alberto: Inter-State environmental disputes, provisional measures and the International Court of Justice's order in the case concerning Pulp Mills on the River Uruguay. (In: Temple Journal of Science, Technology and Environmental Law, 2006, v. 25, p. 161-172.)

Bekker, Peter H. F.: Introductory note to Pulp Mills on the River Uruguay (Argentina v. Uruguay). International Court of Justice, Provisional measures order, January 23, 2007. (In: International Legal Materials, 2007, v. 46, p. 311-313.)

Cardoso Faria Moraes, Maira: As papeleiras na Corte Internacional de Justiça: aspectos relevantes do direito ambiental internacional. (Dans: Realidades: direitos humanos, meio ambiente e desenvolvimento, sous la dir. de Rosenite Alves de Oliveira; Yanko Marcius Alencar Xavier de; Jahyr-Philippe Bichara; Mônica Bulhões e Silva; Diogo Pignataro de Oliveira; Natália Bastos Bonavides. Natal: Editora du UFRN, 2007, p. 119-137.)

Corte internazionale di giustizia, 13 luglio 2006: ordinanza sulla domanda di misure cautelari resa nell'affare relativo alle fabbriche per la produzione di polpa di legno sul fiume Uruguay (Argentina c. Uruguay). (Dans: Rivista di diritto internazionale, 2006, v. 89, p. 790-807.)

del-Cerro, Maria Alejandra: Paper battle on the River Uruguay: the international dispute surrounding the construction of pulp mills. (In:

Georgetown International Environmental Law Review, 2007, v. 20, no. 1, p. 161-186.)

Gros Espiell, Héctor: Una reflexión sobre el diferendo argentino-uruguayo por la construcción en territorio uruguayo de dos papeleras sobre el río Uruguay. (Dans: Anuario de derecho constitucional latinoamericano, 2007, v. 2, p. 787-806.)

Hummer, Waldemar: Argentinien vs. Uruguay: ein Mehrfrontenkampf. (In: International law between universalism and fragmentation: festschrift in honour of Gerhard Hafner, ed. by Isabelle Buffard; James Crawford; Alain Pellet; Stephan Wittich. Leiden [etc.]: Martinus Nijhoff, 2008, p. 869-908.)

International Court of Justice: Pulp Mills on the River Uruguay (Argentina v. Uruguay): Request for the Indication of Provisional Measures: Order, 23 January 2007. (In: International Legal Materials, 2007, v. 46, no. 2, p. 314-336.)

Lanfranchi, Marie-Pierre: L'affaire des Usines de Pâte à Papier: un état des lieux. (Dans: L'observateur des Nations Unies, 2008, v. 24, no. 1, p. 37-63.)

Laudo del Tribunal arbitral "ad hoc" de Mercosur constituido para entender de la controversia presentada por la República oriental del Uruguay a la República Argentina sobre "omisión del Estado Argentino en adoptar medidas apropriadas para prevenir y/o hacer cesar los impedimentos a la libre circulación derivados de los cortes en territorio argentino de vías de acceso a los puentes internacionales Gral San Martín y Gral Artigas que unen la República Argentina con la República oriental del Uruguay". (Dans: Anuario argentino de derecho internacional, 2006, v. 15, p. 149-184.) [C.P.J.I., p. 170; C.I.J., p. 171.]

Liguori, Teresa: The principle of good faith in the Argentina-Uruguay pulp mills dispute. (In: The Journal of Water Law, 2009, v. 20, no. 2-3, p. 70-75.)

Manero Salvador, Ana: El Tribunal Internacional de Justicia en el ámbito iberoamericano: el asunto de las papeleras en el río Uruguay. (Dans: Tribunales internacionales y espacio iberoamericano, sous la dir. de Fernández Liesa, Carlos R.. Cizur Menor: Thomas Reuters, 2007, p. 195-214.)

Manero Salvador, Ana: Una oportunidad perdida: apreciaciones sobre el fallo del Tribunal Internacional de Justicia sobre el asunto de las Papeleras en el rio Uruguay y la proteccion internacional de medio ambiante. (Dans: Revista española de derecho internacional, 2009, v. 61, p. 318-322.)

Pavón Piscitello, Daniel: The conflict between Argentina and Uruguay concerning the installation and commissioning of pulp mills before the International Court of Justice and MERCOSUR. (In: Zeitschrift für ausländisches öffentliches Recht und Völkerrecht, 2007, v. 67, no. 1, p. 159-183.)

Ponte Iglesias, Maria Teresa: El conflicto entre Argentina y la República oriental del Uruguay por el establecimiento de plantas de celulosas sobre el río Uruguay. (Dans: Revista española de derecho internacional, 2006, v. 58, no. 2, p. 1084-1090.) [C.I.J., p. 1085, 1088-89.]

Roy, Tyson: I.C.J. maintains high evidentiary standard in granting request for indication of provisional measures: Argentina v. Uruguay: request for the indication of provisional measures, January 23, 2007. (In: Suffolk Transnational Law Review, 2008, v. 32, p. 219-229.) [I.C.J., passim.]

Saccucci, Andrea: Fond du litige et indication de mesures conservatoires: réflexions en marge des ordonnances de la C.I.J. dans l'affaire des usines de pâte à papier. (Dans: Revue générale de droit international public, 2008, v. 112, no. 4, p. 795-832.)

Tully, Stephen: Case concerning Pulp Mills on the River Uruguay (Argentina v. Uruguay): order on the request for indication of provisional measures, 2006. (In: Australian International Law Journal, 2006, v. 13, p. 281-292.)

Uruguay. (In: Keesing's Record of World Events, 2006, v. 52, no. 7/8, 47362.)

Vatna, Loïc: L'affaire des Usines de pâte à papier sur le fleuve Uruguay (Argentine c. Uruguay): un nouveau différend environnemental devant la Cour internationale de Justice. (Dans: Revue québécoise de droit international, 2009, v. 22, no. 2, p. 25-55.)

Weckel, Philippe et Aréou, Guillaume: Cour internationale de Justice. Ordonnance du 13 juillet 2006. Usines de pâte à papier sur le fleuve Uruguay (Argentine c. Uruguay). (Dans: Revue générale de droit international public, 2006, v. 110, p. 935-942.)

Wellens, Karel C.: Transboundary environmental impact disputes before the International Court of Justice: the case concerning Pulp Mills on the River Uruguay (Argentine vs. Uruguay): some preliminary remarks. (In: Een kwestie van grensoverschrijding: liber amicorum P.E.L. Janssen, ed. by Catarina Krause; Martin Scheinin. Nijmegen: Wolf Legal, 2009, p. 369-396.)

136. *Certaines questions concernant l'entraide judiciaire en matière pénale (Djibouti c. France)*
136. *Certain Questions of Mutual Assistance in Criminal Matters (Djibouti v. France)*

Briese, Robyn and Schill, Stephan W.: Djibouti v. France: self-judging clauses before the International Court of Justice. (In: Melbourne Journal of International Law, 2009, v. 10, no. 1, p. 308-328.)

Buzzini, Gionata Piero: Lights and shadows of immunities and inviolability of State officials in international law: some comments on the Djibouti v. France case. (In: Leiden Journal of International Law, 2009, v. 22, no. 3, p. 455-483.)

Fasoli, Elena: Declaratory judgment and official apologies as form of reparation of the non-material damage suffered by the State: the Djibouti-

France case. (In : Law and Practice of International Courts and Tribunals, 2008, v. 7, p. 177-192.)

Prezas, Ioannis : La répression nationale face au juge international : à propos de l'affaire de l'Entraide judiciaire en matière pénale. (Dans : Annuaire français de droit international, 2008, v. 54, p. 237-273.)

Weckel, Philippe : Chronique de jurisprudence internationale : Cour internationale de Justice : arrêt du 4 juin 2008, affaire relative à Certaines questions concernant l'entraide judiciaire en matière pénale (Djibouti c. France). (Dans : Revue générale de droit international public, 2008, v. 112, no. 4, p. 907-914.)

137. *Différend maritime (Pérou c. Chili)*
137. *Maritime Dispute (Peru* v. *Chile)*

Horna, Angel V. : Maritime dispute (Peru v. Chile) : background and preliminary thoughts. (In : Ocean Yearbook, 2009, v. 23, p. 193-229.) [I.C.J., p. 193, 200, 203-206, 218, 221, 222, 226-229.]

Illanes, Samuel Fernández : Reflexiones acerca del juicio limítrofe de Perú contra Chile, ante la Corte internacional de Justicia. (Dans : Revista Chilena de derecho, 2008, v. 35, no. 2, p. 373-383.)

Oyarce, Ximena Hinrichs : Troubled waters between Chile and Peru : early reflections on a maritime boundary claim. (In : Indian Journal of International Law, 2009, v. 49, no. 2, p. 161-212.)

139. *Demande en interprétation de l'arrêt du 31 mars 2004 en l'affaire* Avena et autres ressortissants mexicains (Mexique c. Etats-Unis d'Amérique) *(Mexique c. Etats-Unis d'Amérique)*
139. *Request for Interpretation of the Judgment of 31 March 2004 in the* Case concerning Avena and Other Mexican Nationals (Mexico v. United States of America) *(Mexico* v. *United States of America)*

Chrispin, Materneau : Arrêt de la C.I.J. sur la demande en interprétation de l'arrêt du 31 mars 2004 en l'affaire Avena et autres ressortissants mexicains : résumé et brefs commentaires. (Dans : Multipol. 2009.)

Giorgetti, Chiara : Introductory note to International Court of Justice : Request for Interpretation of the Judgment in the Case Concerning Avena and other Mexican Nationals. (In : International Legal Materials, 2008, v. 45, p. 723-739.)

Graham, James A. : Situación actual del cumplimiento por los Estados Unidos de América del fallo Avena de la CIJ. (Dans : Estudios de derecho internacional : libro homenaje al profesor Santiago Benadava, sous la dir. de Llanos Mansilla, Hugo. 2008, v. 2, p. 353-373.)

Hoppe, Carsten : A question of life and death : the Request for Interpretation of Avena and certain other Mexican Nationals (Mexico v. United States) before the International Court of Justice. (In : Human Rights Law Review, 2009, v. 9, no. 3, p. 455-464.)

Mühlendahl, Paul, von : La CIJ rejette la demande du Mexique d'interpréter Avena. (Dans : Hague Justice Portal. 2009.)

Mühlendahl, Paul, von : ICJ rejects Mexico's request to interpret Avena. (In : Hague Justice Journal, 2009, v. 4, no. 1, p. 55-59.)

Townsend, Jesse : Medellín stands alone : common law nations do not share a postratification understanding of the I.C.J. (In : Yale Journal of International Law, 2009, v. 34, p. 463-497.)

Tranchant, Baptiste : L'arrêt rendu par la C.I.J. sur la demande en interprétation de l'arrêt Avena (Mexique c. Etats-Unis d'Amérique). (Dans : Annuaire français de droit international, 2009, v. 55, p. 191-220.)

Weckel, Philippe (sous la dir. de) : Chronique de jurisprudence internationale. (Dans : Revue générale de droit international public, 2009, v. 113, no. 2, p. 431-463.) [C.I.J., p. 431-446.]

Weckel, Philippe : Chronique de jurisprudence internationale : Cour internationale de Justice : ordonnance du 16 juillet 2008 (mesures conservatoires), demande en interprétation de l'arrêt du 31 mars 2004 en l'affaire Avena et autres ressortissants mexicains (Mexique c. Etats-Unis d'Amérique). (Dans : Revue générale de droit international public, 2008, v. 112, no. 4, p. 915-918.) [I.C.J., passim.]

140. *Application de la convention internationale sur l'élimination de toutes les formes de discrimination raciale (Géorgie c. Fédération de Russie)*
140. *Application of the International Convention on the Elimination of All Forms of Racial Discrimination (Georgia* v. *Russian Federation)*

Buys, Cindy Galway : Application of the International Convention on the Elimination of All Forms of Racial Discrimination (Georgia v. Russian Federation) : International Court of Justice order on provisional measures and application of CERD as a basis of jurisdiction. (In : American Journal of International Law, 2009, v. 103, no. 2, p. 294-299.)

Ghandhi, Sandy : International Court of Justice : Application of the International Convention on the Elimination of All Forms of Racial Discrimination (Georgia v. Russian Federation) : provisional measures order of 15 October 2008. (In : International and Comparative Law Quarterly, 2009, v. 58, p. 713-725.)

Thienel, Tobias : The Georgian conflict, racial discrimination and the ICJ : the order of provisional measures of 15 October 2008. (In : Human Rights Law Review, 2009, v. 9, p. 465-472.)

Thienel, Tobias : Provisional measures in the 'Case concerning application of the International Convention on the Elimination of All Forms of Racial Discrimination' (Georgia v. Russian Federation). (In : Göttingen Journal of International Law, 2009, v. 1, p. 143-157.) [I.C.J., passim.]

Volodin, I. A. and Taratuhina, D. S. : Rossijsko-gruzinskoe razbiratelstvo v Mezunarodnom sude. (In : Russian Year Book of International Law, 2009, v, 2008, p. 28-54.)

141. *Conformité au droit international de la déclaration unilatérale d'indépendance des institutions provisoires d'administration autonome du Kosovo (requête pour avis consultatif)*
141. *Accordance with International Law of the Unilateral Declaration of Independence by the Provisional Institutions of Self-Government of Kosovo (Request for Advisory Opinion)*

Cordial, Margaret and Rosandhaug, Knut: Post-conflict property restitution: the approach in Kosovo and lessons learned for future international practice. Leiden; Boston: Martinus Nijhoff, 2009.

Corten, Olivier: Réflexions sur l'applicabilité de l'uti possidetis dans un conflit sécessionniste: le cas du Kosovo. (Dans: Liber amicorum Jean-Pierre Cot: le procès international. Bruxelles: Bruylant, 2009, p. 29-50.)

D'Argent, Pierre: Kosovo: être ou ne pas être? (Dans: Journal des tribunaux, 2008, no. 6307, p. 261-265.)

Gioia, Andrea: Kosovo's statehood and the role of recognition. (In: Italian Yearbook of International Law, 2008, v. 18, p. 3-35.)

Hilpold, Peter: The International Court of Justice's Advisory Opinion on Kosovo: perspectives of a delicate question. (In: Austrian Review of International and European Law, 2009, v. 14, p. 259-310.)

Hilpold, Peter: The Kosovo case and international law: looking for applicable theories. (In: Chinese Journal of International Law, 2009, v. 8, no. 1, p. 47-61.)

Jia, Bing Bing: The independence of Kosovo: a unique case of secession? (In: Chinese Journal of International Law, 2009, v. 8, no. 1, p. 27-46.)

Ker-Lindsay, James: Kosovo: the path to contested statehood in the Balkans. London; New York, NY: I. B. Tauris, 2009. (Library of European Studies; 11.)

Koeck, Heribert Franz and Horn, Daniela and Leidenmuehler, Franz: From protectorate to statehood: self-determination v. territorial integrity in the case of Kosovo and the position of the European Union. Antwerpen; Berlin; Wien: Intersentia: Berliner Wissenschafts Verlag: Neuer Wissenschaftlicher Verlag, 2009. (Neue juristische monografien; 56.)

Kostovicova, Denisa: Legitimacy and international administration: the Ahtisaari settlement for Kosovo from a human security perspective. (In: International Peacekeeping, 2008, v. 15, no. 5, p. 631-647.)

Muharremi, Robert: Kosovo's declaration of independence: self-determination and sovereignty revisited. (In: Review of Central and East-European Law, 2008, v. 33, p. 401-435.)

Müllerson, Rein: Precedents in the mountains: on the parallels and uniqueness of the cases of Kosovo, South Ossetia and Abkhazia. (In: Chinese Journal of International Law, 2009, v. 8, no. 1, p. 2-25.)

Nita, Irina: Ethnic conflicts and territorial solutions. Case-study: Kosovo's declaration of independence. (In: Revista romana de drept international, 2008, v. 6, p. 14-26.)

Oklopcic, Zoran: Populus interruptus: self-determination, the independence of Kosovo, and the vocabulary of peoplehood. (In: Leiden Journal of International Law, 2009, v. 22, p. 677-702.)

Orakhelashvili, Alexander: Kosovo and the pitfalls of the over-theorizing international law: observations on Hilpold's rejoinder. (In: Chinese Journal of International Law, 2009, v. 8, no. 3, p. 589-592.)

Orakhelashvili, Alexander: The Kosovo UDI between agreed law and subjective perception: a response to Hilpold. (In: Chinese Journal of International Law, 2009, v. 8, no. 2, p. 285-290.)

Orakhelashvili, Alexander: Statehood, recognition, and the United Nations system: a unilateral declaration of independence in Kosovo. (In: Max Planck Yearbook of United Nations Law, 2008, v. 12, p. 1-44.)

Pettifer, James: Albania after Kosovo independence and the NATO decision: some perspectives. Shrivenham: Advanced Research and Assessment Group; Defence Academy of the Unied Kigdom, 2008.

Ryngaert, Cedric and Griffioen, Christine: The relevance of the right to self-determination in the Kosovo matter: in partial response to the agora papers. (In: Chinese Journal of International Law, 2009, v. 8, no. 3, p. 573-587.)

Serra, Gianluca: The international civil administration in Kosovo: a commentary on some major legal issues. (In: Italian Yearbook of International Law, 2008, v. 18, p. 63-87.)

Sevastik, Per: Secession, self-determination of "peoples" and recognition: the case of Kosovo's declaration of independence and international law. (In: Law at war: the law as it was and the law as it should be: liber amicorum Ove Bring, ed. by Engdahl, Ola; Wrange, Pal. Leiden: Martinus Nijhoff, 2008, p. 231-244.)

Tancredi, Antonello: Neither authorized nor prohibited? Secession and international law after Kosovo, South Ossetia and Abkhazia. (In: The International Yearbook of International Law, 2008, v. 28, p. 37-62.)

Weller, Marc: Contested statehood: Kosovo's struggle for independence. Oxford [etc.]: Oxford University Press, 2009.

Weller, Marc: Kosovo's final status. (In: International Affairs, 2008, v. 84, p. 1223-1243.)

Weller, Marc: Negotiating the final status of Kosovo. Paris: Institute for Security Studies, European Union, 2008. (Chaillot paper; 114.)

Wet, Erika de: The governance of Kosovo: Security Council resolution 1244 and the establishment and functioning of eulex. (In: American Journal of International Law, 2009, v. 103, no. 1, p. 83-96.)

Wilde, Ralph: Kosovo 2008: independence, recognition and international law. (In: Soochow Journal of International Law, 2008, v. 5, no. 2, p. 51-81.)

Williams, Michael J.: NATO, security and risk management: from Kosovo to Kandahar. London; New York: Routledge, 2009. (Contemporary security studies.)

Wilson, Gary: Self-determination, recognition, and the problem of Kosovo. (In: Netherlands International Law Review, 2009, v. 56, p. 455-481.)

143. *Immunités juridictionnelles de l'Etat (Allemagne c. Italie)*
143. *Jurisdictional Immunities of the State (Germany* v. *Italy)*

Boysen, Siegfried: Kriegsverbrechen im Diskurs nationaler Gerichte: der Distomo-Beschluss des Bundesverfassungsgerichts vom 15. Februar 2006. (In: Archiv des Völkerrechts, 2006, v. 44, p. 363-379.) [I.C.J. p. 374.]

Moneta, Francesco: State immunity for international crimes: the case of Germany versus Italy before the I.C.J. (In: Hague Justice Journal, 2009, v. 4, p. 139-147.)

144. *Questions concernant l'obligation de poursuivre ou d'extrader (Belgique c. Sénégal)*
144. *Questions relating to the Obligation to Prosecute or Extradite (Belgium* v. *Senegal)*

Assche, Cédric van: Deux voeux formulés à l'adresse de la Cour internationale de Justice: commentaire de l'ordonnance du 28 mai 2009 dans l'affaire relative à des Questions concernant l'obligation de poursuivre ou d'extrader. (Dans: Revue belge de droit international, 2009, v. 42, p. 434-447.)

Corte internazionale di Giustizia, 28 maggio 2009: ordinanza sulle misure provvisorie nell'affare relativo a Questioni concernenti l'obligo di perseguire o estradare (Belgio c. Senegal). (Dans: Rivista di diritto internazionale, 2009, v. 92, no. 3, p. 814-829.)

Watio, Raphaël Tiwang: Affaire Hissène Habré: où en est la justice? (Dans: African Yearbook of International Law, 2009, v. 17, p. 379-409.)

148. *Chasse à la baleine dans l'Antarctique (Australie c. Japon)*
148. *Whaling in the Antarctic (Australia* v. *Japan)*

Mossop, Joanna: Australia v. Japan: whaling in the International Court of Justice. (In: New Zealand Yearbook of International Law, 2009, v. 7, p. 169-177.) [I.C.J., passim.]

151. *Demande en interprétation de l'arrêt du 15 juin 1962 en l'affaire du* Temple de Préah Vihéar (Cambodge c. Thaïlande) *(Cambodge c. Thaïlande)*

151. *Request for interpretation of the Judgment of 15 June 1962 in the case concerning the* Temple of Preah Vihear (Cambodia v. Thailand) *(Cambodia* v. *Thailand)*

Pakdeekong, Monticha: Who owns the Preah Vihear temple? A Thai position. (In: Journal of East Asia and International Law, 2009, v. 2, p. 229-237.)

Touch, Bora: Who owns the Preah Vihear temple? A Cambodian position. (In: Journal of East Asia and International Law, 2009, v. 2, p. 205-277.)

F. PROPOSITIONS TENDANT À PORTER CERTAINES QUESTIONS DEVANT LA COUR

F. PROPOSALS FOR REFERENCE OF MATTERS TO THE COURT

McHugh, Aman Mahray: Resolving international boundary disputes in Africa: a case for the International Court of Justice. (In: Howard Law Journal, 2005, v. 49, p. 209-239.)

Willard, E. Rainbow: How to get less than you bargain for: adjudicating the Guatemala-Belize territorial dispute at the I.C.J. (In: Emory International Law Review, 2009, v. 23, no. 2, p. 739-782.)

G. OUVRAGES CONTENANT DES RÉFÉRENCES À LA COUR

G. WRITINGS CONTAINING REFERENCES TO THE COURT

1. Droit international en général
1. International law in general

Ahdieh, Robert B.: Between dialogue and decree: international review of national courts. (In: New York University Law Review, 2004, v. 79, no. 6, p. 2029-2163.) [I.C.J., p. 2033-2035, 2044, 2049, 2056, 2058, 2061, 2075, 2084, 2095, 2125, 2127, 2147-2151, 2162.]

Alvarez, José E.: The public international law regime governing international investment. (In: Recueil des cours de l'Académie de droit international de La Haye, 2009, v. 344, p. 193-541.) [P.C.I.J., p. 453, 499; I.C.J., p. 204, 227, 233, 271, 324, 357, 358, 361, 376, 398, 408, 421, 432, 450, 494, 497, 498, 499, 507.]

Anand, Ram Prakash: Changing dimensions of international law: an Asian perspective. (In: Collected Courses of the Xiamen Academy of International Law, 2006, v. 1, p. 33-158.) [P.C.I.J., p. 123-125; I.C.J., p. 39, 115, 122-136.]

Ascensio, Hervé: Existe-t-il des organes du droit international? (Dans: Studi di diritto internazionale in onore di Gaetano Arangio-Ruiz, sous la dir. de Giovanni Battaglini; Paolo Benvenuti; Antonio Cassese; Giorgio Gaja. Napoli: Editoriale Scientifica, 2004, v. 1, p. 3-24.) [C.P.J.I, p. 5, 23; C.I.J., p. 8, 15, 23.]

Bachand, Rémi: L'interprétation juridictionnelle chez les internationalistes du XXe siècle. (Dans: Revue belge de droit international, 2006, v. 39, p. 173-217.) [C.P.J.I., p. 182, 184-185, 192; C.I.J., p. 186, 191, 200.]

Barnidge Jr., Robert P.: The due diligence principle under international law. (In: International Community Law Review, 2006, v. 8, p. 81-121.) [I.C.J., p. 99, 101-108, 110-112, 116, 121.]

Barsalou, Olivier: Les actes unilatéraux étatiques en droit international public: observations sur quelques incertitudes théoriques et pratiques. (Dans: Canadian Yearbook of International Law, 2006, v. 44, p. 395-420.) [I.C.J., p. 400, 401, 406, 409.]

Baudenbacher, Carl: Foreword: globalization and the judiciary. (In: Texas International Law Journal, 2005, v. 40, no. 3, p. 353-358.) [P.C.I.J. and I.C.J., p. 354.]

Bausback, Winfried and Irmscher, Tobias H.: Bericht von der 71. Konferenz der International Law Association in Berlin. (In: Archiv des Völkerrechts, 2004, v. 42, no. 4, p. 467-486.) [I.C.J., p. 483, 484.]

Bedjaoui, Mohammed: La contribution en demi-teinte de l'Afrique au développement du droit international. (Dans: German Yearbook of International Law, 2004, v. 47, p. 63-84.) [C.I.J., p. 63, 76.]

Ben Achour, Rafâa: La nouvelle charte arabe des droits de l'homme: instrument international. (Dans: La nouvelle charte arabe des droits de l'homme: dialogue italo-arabe: actes de la table ronde italo-arabe du 17-18 décembre 2004 Messina, par Claudio Zanghì; Rafâa Ben Achour. Turin: [s.n.], 2004, p. 21-32.) [C.P.J.I., p. 26; C.I.J., p. 28.]

Benzing, Markus: Community interests in the procedure of international courts and tribunals. (In: Law and Practice of International Courts and Tribunals, 2006, v. 5, p. 369-408.) [I.C.J., p. 369, 372-386, 391, 395, 396-397, 398-403, 406.]

Besselink, Leonard: Internationaal recht en nationaal recht. (In: Handboek internationaal recht, ed. by Horbach, Nathalie L. J. T.; Lefeber, René; Ribbelink, Olivier. The Hague: T.M.C. Asser Press, 2007, p. 47-80.) [I.C.J., p. 52-55.]

Bianchi, Andrea: International law and US courts: the myth of Lohengrin revisited. (In: European Journal of International Law, 2004, v. 15, no. 4, p. 751-781.) [I.C.J., p. 762-763, 766, 769-771.]

Bogdandy, Armin von: Democrazia, globalizzazione e futuro del diritto internazionale. (Dans: Rivista di diritto internazionale, 2004, v. 87, no. 2, p. 317-344.) [C.P.J.I., p. 319.]

Bogdandy, Armin von and Dellavalle, Sergio: The paradigms of universalism and particularism in the age of globalisation: Western perspectives on the premises and finality of international law. (In: Collected Courses of the Xiamen Academy of International Law, 2009, v. 2, p. 45-127.) [P.C.I.J., p. 66-67; I.C.J., p. 58, 60.]

Borba Casella, Paulo: Direito internacional dos espaços. São Paulo : Atlas, 2009. [C.P.J.I, passim ; C.I.J., passim.]

Bouchet-Saulnier, Françoise : Coutume : espace de création et d'activisme pour le juge et pour les organisations internationales. (Dans : Droit international humanitaire coutumier : enjeux et défis contemporains, sous la dir. de Tavernier, Paul ; Henckaerts, Jean-Marie. Bruxelles : Bruylant, 2008, p. 161-171.) [C.I.J., p. 165.]

Braillon, Charlotte : La théorie classique de la coutume et le rôle nouveau de l' "opinio juris" : discours de la justice en droit international et en droit interne. (Dans : Revue de la Faculté de droit de l'Université de Liège, 2009, v. 54, no. 4, p. 663-675.)

Bratspies, Rebecca M. and Miller, Russell A. (eds.): Transboundary harm in international law: lessons from the Trail Smelter arbitration. Cambridge: Cambridge University Press, 2006. [P.C.I.J., p. 35-36, 90-92, 315, 327; I.C.J., p. 3, 27, 36, 38, 42, 52, 59, 86, 90-91, 127, 135-136, 141-143, 146, 149, 156, 200, 202-203, 217-218, 226, 229-230, 232, 288, 236.]

Broude, Tomer: Fragmentation(s) of international law: on normative integration as authority allocation. (In : The shifting allocation of authority in international law: considering sovereignty, supremacy and subsidiarity: essays in honour of Professor Ruth Lapidoth, ed. by Tomer Broude ; Yuval Shany. Oxford ; Portland : Hart Publishing, 2008, p. 99-120.) [I.C.J., p. 102-103, 111, 114, 117.]

Brownlie, Ian: Principles of public international law. Oxford [etc.]: Oxford University Press, 2008. 7th ed. [I.C.J., see index p. 763-764.]

Brownlie, Ian : The work of an international lawyer. (In : Columbia Journal of Transnational Law, 2006, v. 45, p. 1-19.) [I.C.J., p. 7-8.]

Buergenthal, Thomas: Dinner speech. (In: From government to governance : the growing impact of non-state actors on the international and European legal system : proceedings of the Sixth Hague Joint Conference held in The Hague, The Netherlands, 3-5 July 2003, ed. by Heere, Wybo P. The Hague : T.M.C. Asser Press, 2004, p. 258-261.) [P.C.I.J., p. 258; I.C.J., passim.]

Buys, Cindy Galway : The United States Supreme Court misses the mark : towards better implementation of the United States' international obligations. (In : Connecticut Journal of International Law, 2008, v. 24, no. 1, p. 39-76.) [I.C.J., passim.]

Buzzini, Gionata Piero: La "généralité" du droit international général : réflexions sur la polysémie d'un concept. (Dans : Revue générale de droit international public, 2004, v. 108, no. 2, p. 381-406.) [C.I.J., p. 386, 390, 392-395.]

Caflisch, Lucius : La pratique dans le raisonnement du juge international. (Dans : La pratique et le droit international : colloque de Genève. Paris : A. Pedone, 2004, p. 125-138.) [C.I.J., p. 125-126, 128, 132-133, 137.]

Caflisch, Lucius: La pratique suisse en matière de droit international public 2003. (Dans: Schweizerische Zeitschrift für internationales und europäisches Recht, 2004, v. 14, p. 661-719.) [C.I.J., p. 687-688.]

Cameron, Peter D.: The rules of engagement: developing cross-border petroleum deposits in the North Sea and the Caribbean. (In: International and Comparative Law Quarterly, 2006, v. 55, p. 559-585.) [I.C.J., p. 562, 565, 567, 568.]

Cançado Trindade, A. A.: International law for humankind: towards a new jus gentium (I): general course on public international law. (In: Recueil des cours de l'Académie de droit international de La Haye, 2005, v. 316, p. 9-439.) [P.C.I.J., p. 46-47, 49, 73, 92-94, 148-149, 151, 154, 159, 163, 169, 174-175, 179, 185, 212, 286, 337; I.C.J., passim.]

Cançado Trindade, A. A.: International law for humankind: towards a new jus gentium (II): general course on public international law. (In: Recueil des cours de l'Académie de droit international de La Haye, 2005, v. 317, p. 9-312.) [P.C.I.J., p. 55, 92, 94, 177, 183, 191-192, 208, 217-220, 233, 236; I.C.J., passim.]

Cançado Trindade, A. A.: Los aportes latinoamericanos al derecho y a la justicia internacionales. (Dans: Doctrina latinoamericana del derecho internacional: tomo I, par A. A. Cançado Trindade; Fernando Vidal Ramírez. San José: Corte Interamericana de Derechos Humanos, 2003, p. 33-64.) [C.P.J.I., p. 49-51, 53; C.I.J., p. 51, 61.]

Cannizzaro, Enzo: La doctrine italienne et le développement du droit international dans l'après-guerre: entre continuité et discontinuité. (Dans: Annuaire français de droit international, 2004, v. 50, p. 1-23.) [C.I.J., p. 11, 19-20.]

Cardona Llorens, Jorge: Libération ou occupation? Les droits et devoirs de l'Etat vainqueur. (Dans: L'intervention en Irak et le droit international, sous la dir. de Karine Bannelier; Olivier Corten; Théodore Christakis; Pierre Klein. Paris: Pedone, 2004, p. 221-250.) [C.I.J., p. 233-235, 238-239, 244-246.]

Carreau, Dominique: Droit international. Paris: A. Pedone, 2004. 8e éd. (Etudes internationales.) [C.P.J.I. et C.I.J., voir index de la jurisprudence, p. 681-684; C.I.J., p. 630-653 et index p. 669.]

Cassese, Antonio: International law. Oxford [etc.]: Oxford University Press, 2005. 2nd ed. [P.C.I.J., p. 7, 36-38, 50, 58, 143, 153, 159, 170, 190-192, 217-218, 282, 285; I.C.J., p. 57-58, 62, 65-66, 83-87, 89-92, 117-118, 120, 122, 129, 135, 137-139, 156-159, 163-164, 167-169, 172-173, 179-180, 183-185, 187, 192-196, 200, 206-207, 209, 248-250, 265, 280, 282, 285-286, 306, 321-322, 335, 354-355, 359, 365, 373, 394, 413-414, 431, 443-444, 448, 468, 471, 488-489, 499.]

Castellino, Joshua: Territorial integrity and the "right" to self-determination: an examination of the conceptual tools. (In: Brooklyn Journal of International Law, 2008, v. 33, no. 2, p. 503-568.) [I.C.J., p. 509-510.]

Cazala, Julien : Adaptation des règles et principes probatoires au nom d'une bonne administration de la justice internationale. (Dans : L'Observateur des Nations Unies, 2009, v. 27, no. 2, p. 55-73.)

Chimni, B. S. : An outline of a marxist course on public international law. (In : Leiden Journal of International Law, 2004, v. 17, no. 1, p. 1-30.) [I.C.J., p. 11, 29.]

Christakis, Théodore : L'obligation de non-reconnaissance des situations créées par le recours illicite à la force ou d'autres actes enfreignant des règles fondamentales. (Dans : The fundamental rules of the international legal order : jus cogens and obligations erga omnes, ed. by Christian Tomuschat ; Jean-Marc Thouvenin. Leiden ; Boston : Martinus Nijhoff, 2006, p. 127-166.) [C.I.J., p. 141, 161.]

Cohen-Jonathan, Gérard et Flauss, Jean-François : Cour européenne des droits de l'homme et droit international général (2004). (Dans : Annuaire français de droit international, 2004, v. 50, p. 778-802.) [C.I.J., p. 797.]

Combacau, Jean et Sur, Serge : Droit international public. Paris : Montchrestien, 2004. 6e éd. (Domat droit public.) [C.I.J. et C.P.J.I., passim, et voir index de la jurisprudence p. 761 et index analytique p. 769.]

Condorelli, Luigi : Conclusions générales. (Dans : La pratique et le droit international : colloque de Genève. Paris : A. Pedone, 2004, p. 285-306.) [C.I.J., p. 290, 293-294, 299-300, 305.]

Conforti, Benedetto : Unité et fragmentation du droit international : "Glissez, mortels, n'appuyez pas !". (Dans : Revue générale de droit international public, 2007, v. 111, p. 5-18.) [C.P.J.I., p. 17; C.I.J., p. 9-11, 17.]

Corten, Olivier : Jean Salmon et l'héritage de l'"école de Bruxelles". (Dans : Droit du pouvoir, pouvoir du droit : mélanges offerts à Jean Salmon. Bruxelles : Bruylant, 2007, p. 3-18.) [C.I.J., p. 7, 15.]

Coulée, Frédérique : Pratique française en droit international. (Dans : Annuaire français de droit international, 2004, v. 50, p. 904-929.) [C.I.J., p. 916-917, 920-921.]

Couvreur, Philippe et Espaliú Berdud, Carlos : Convention de Vienne de 1969 : article 72 : conséquences de la suspension de l'application d'un traité. (Dans : Les Conventions de Vienne sur le droit des traités : commentaire article par article, sous la dir. d'Olivier Corten ; Pierre Klein. Bruxelles : Bruylant, 2006, v. 3, p. 2565-2585.) [I.C.J., p. 2567.]

Crawford, James : "Marbury v. Madison" at the international level. (In : George Washington International Law Review, 2004, v. 36, no. 3, p. 505-514.) [I.C.J., p. 507-508, 510-514.]

Crawford, James : Public international law in twentieth-century England. (In : Jurists uprooted : German-speaking émigré lawyers in twentieth century Britain, ed. by Beatson, Jack ; Zimmermann, Reinhard. Oxford : Oxford University Press, 2004, p. 681-707.) [P.C.I.J., p. 694, 698; I.C.J., p. 684, 698.]

Crook, John R. (ed.): Contemporary practice of the United States relating to international law. (In: American Journal of International Law, 2007, v. 101, p. 478-508.) [I.C.J., p. 478-483.]

D'Amato, Anthony: International law as an autopoietic system. (In: Developments of international law in treaty making, ed. by Rüdiger Wolfrum; Volker Röben. Berlin, [etc.]: Springer, 2005, p. 335-399.) [I.C.J., p. 350, 357, 361, 381, 389, 393, 394.]

D'Argent, Pierre: La 72ème session de l'Institut de droit international. (Dans: Revue belge de droit international, 2006, v. 39, p. 219-241.) [C.I.J., p. 222.]

D'Argent, Pierre: La réparation des dommages de guerre. (Dans: L'intervention en Irak et le droit international, sous la dir. de Karine Bannelier; Olivier Corten; Théodore Christakis; Pierre Klein. Paris: Pedone, 2004, p. 260-270.) [C.I.J., p. 265.]

d'Aspremont, Jean: The doctrinal illusion of the heterogeneity of international law-making processes. (In: Select Proceedings of the European Society of International Law, ed. by James Crawford; Sarah M. H. Nouwen. Oxford; Portland: Hart, 2008, v. 2, p. 297-312.) [I.C.J., p. 304.]

D'Orsi, Cristiano: L'obligation de réparation dans le projet d'articles sur la responsabilité de l'Etat: une analyse critique. (Dans: Revue hellénique de droit international, 2005, v. 58, p. 115-143.) [P.C.I.J., p. 119.]

Damrosch, Lori Fisler: A comparative look at domestic enforcement of international tribunal judgments. (In: Proceedings of the American Society of International Law, 2009, v. 103, p. 39-42.)

David, Eric: Cas pratiques et corrigés d'examen en droit international: (droit international public, droit des organisations internationales, droit pénal international et droit international humanitaire). Bruxelles: Bruylant, 2007. [C.P.J.I., p. 39, 51, 54, 57; C.I.J., p. 15, 27-29, 37, 40-41, 50, 57, 67, 77, 82, 94-95, 105-106, 120-121, 126-127, 138-139, 148, 218, 243, 247.]

David, Eric: L'accord, fondement du droit international? Petit conte en trois parties. (Dans: Droit du pouvoir, pouvoir du droit: mélanges offerts à Jean Salmon. Bruxelles: Bruylant, 2007, p. 291-330.) [C.P.J.I., p. 306, 307; C.I.J., p. 298, 303-308, 312-314, 317-319, 321, 327, 328.]

David, Eric: L'objecteur persistant, une règle persistante? (Dans: Droit international humanitaire coutumier: enjeux et défis contemporains, sous la dir. de Tavernier, Paul; Henckaerts, Jean-Marie. Bruxelles: Bruylant, 2008, p. 89-99.) [C.I.J., p. 90-95, 97.]

Decaux, Emmanuel: La coutume internationale comme preuve d'une pratique générale acceptée comme étant le droit. (Dans: Droit international humanitaire coutumier: enjeux et défis contemporains, sous la dir. de Tavernier, Paul; Henckaerts, Jean-Marie. Bruxelles: Bruylant, 2008, p. 217-227.) [C.I.J., passim.]

Decaux, Emmanuel et Frouville, Olivier de: Droit international public. Paris: Dalloz, 2004. 4e éd. (Hypercours.) [C.P.J.I., voir index p. 343; C.I.J., voir index p. 342-343.]

Delbrück, Jost: The Walther Schücking Institute at 90. (In: Unity and diversity in international law: proceedings of an international symposium of the Kiel Walther Schücking Institute of International Law, November 4-7, 2004, ed. by Zimmermann, Andreas; Hofmann, Rainer. Berlin: Duncker & Humblot, 2006, p. 15-19.) [P.C.I.J., p. 16.]

Delmas-Marty, Mireille: Les forces imaginantes du droit: I: le relatif et l'universel. Paris: Seuil, 2004. (La couleur des idées.) [C.I.J., voir index p. 416.]

Delmas-Marty, Mireille: Les forces imaginantes du droit: II: le pluralisme ordonné. Paris: Seuil, 2006. (La couleur des idées.) [C.I.J., voir index p. 284.]

Delmas-Marty, Mireille: Les forces imaginantes du droit: III: la refondation des pouvoirs. Paris: Seuil, 2007. (La couleur des idées.) [C.I.J., voir index p. 282.]

den Dekker, Guido and Myjer, Eric: Wapenbeheersingsrecht. (In: Handboek internationaal recht, ed. by Horbach, Nathalie L. J. T.; Lefeber, René; Ribbelink, Olivier. The Hague: T.M.C. Asser Press, 2007, p. 591-626.) [I.C.J., p. 594, 598, 601, 610.]

Donovan, Thomas W.: Challenges to the territorial integrity of Guyana: a legal analysis. (In: Georgia Journal of International and Comparative Law, 2004, v. 32, n. 3, p. 661-724.) [P.C.I.J., p. 687-688, 691, 694, 711, 715; I.C.J., p. 690-691, 697, 699-703, 713-719, 722.]

Dupuy, Pierre-Marie: La communauté internationale: une fiction? (Dans: Droit du pouvoir, pouvoir du droit: mélanges offerts à Jean Salmon. Bruxelles: Bruylant, 2007, p. 373-396.) [C.P.J.I., p. 389; C.I.J., p. 378, 380.]

Dupuy, Pierre-Marie: Droit international public. Paris: Dalloz, 2004. 7e éd. (Précis Dalloz.) [C.I.J., passim.]

Dupuy, Pierre-Marie: Les grands textes de droit international public. Paris: Dalloz, 2004. 4e éd. (Grands textes.) [C.I.J., p. 411-423.]

Dupuy, Pierre-Marie: Some reflections on contemporary international law and the appeal to universal values: a response to Martti Koskenniemi. (In: European Journal of International Law, 2005, v. 16, no. 1, p. 131-137.) [I.C.J., p. 134, 136.]

Echeverria, Gabriela: Codifying the rights of victims in international law: remedies and reparation. (In: Redressing injustices through mass claims processes: innovative responses to unique challenges, ed. by International Bureau of the Permanent Court of Arbitration. Oxford: Oxford University Press, 2006, p. 279-297.) [P.C.I.J., p. 280; I.C.J., p. 283-284.]

Economidès, Constantin P.: Le projet de la CDI sur la responsabilité de l'Etat pour fait internationalement illicite: nécessité d'une convention internationale. (Dans: Revue hellénique de droit international, 2005, v. 58, no. 1, p. 77-83.) [I.C.J., p. 78.]

Fernández Liesa, Carlos R.: Usos de la noción de justicia en el derecho internacional. (Dans: Anuario español de derecho internacional, 2006, v. 22, p. 171-203.) [C.I.J., p. 172-173, 181-191.]

Fichtelberg, Aaron: Law at the vanishing point: a philosophical analysis of international law. Aldershot; Burlington: Ashgate, 2008. (Applied legal philosophy.) [P.C.I.J. and I.C.J., see index p. 223.]

Fife, Rolf Einar: Elements of Nordic practice 2001/2003: Norway. (In: Nordic Journal of International Law, 2004, v. 73, no. 4, p. 551-575.) [I.C.J., p. 552, 563.]

Fischer-Lescano, Andreas: Völkerrechtliche Praxis der Bundesrepublik Deutschland in den Jahren 2000 bis 2002: allgemeine Fragen des Völkerrechts und Individualrechte. (In: Zeitschrift für ausländisches öffentliches Recht und Völkerrecht, 2004, v. 64, no. 1, p. 195-242.) [I.C.J., p. 220-221.]

Franck, Thomas M. and Prows, Peter: The role of presumptions in international tribunals. (In: Law and Practice of International Courts and Tribunals, 2005, v. 4, no. 2, p. 197-245.) [P.C.I.J., p. 227-228, 238; I.C.J., p. 197-199, 226-230, 238-245; P.C.I.J., p. 227-228.]

Gaja, Giorgio et Jacqué, Jean-Paul: Séance académique: 10 janvier 2006. Allocation introduction. [suivie de] La doctrine et la pratique de droit international: quelques réflexions. [suivi de] Pratique et doctrine. (Dans: Annuaire français de droit international, 2005, v. 51, ix-xxii.) [C.I.J., passim.]

Garratt, Justine: Australian practice in international law 2002. (In: Australian Yearbook of International Law, 2004, v. 23, p. 289-395.) [I.C.J., p. 301-302, 309-310.]

Gattini, Andrea: Un regard procédural sur la fragmentation du droit international. (Dans: Revue générale de droit international public, 2006, v. 110, p. 303-336.) [C.P.J.I., p. 319, 329; C.I.J., p. 305, 307-308, 312-315, 317-320, 322, 324, 327-328, 330-331.]

Gaviria Liévano, Enrique: Derecho internacional público. Bogotá: Editorial Temis, 2005. Sexta édicion, actualizada [C.I.J., p. 35, 45, 48, 109, 111, 136, 227, 246, 278, 310, 313, 345, 410, 412, 420, 430, 505, 507, 512-514, 516, 528, 537.]

Goldsmith, Jack L. and Posner, Eric A.: The limits of international law. Oxford [etc.]: Oxford University Press, 2005. [I.C.J., p. 96.]

Gorelik, A. S.: Some thoughts on the evolution of international law. (In: Symposium in commemoration of G. I. Tunkin's 100th birthday: papers delivered at a commemorative celebration held at Moscow State University,

20 October 2006, ed. by Glotova, S.; Shestakov, L. N. London: Wildy, Simmonds & Hill, 2007, p. 563-566.) [I.C.J., p. 565-566.]

Gowlland-Debbas, Vera: Comment: [on Unity and diversity in the formation and relevance of customary international law: modern concepts of customary international law as a manifestation of a value-based international order by Anja Seibert-Fohr]. (In: Unity and diversity in international law: proceedings of an international symposium of the Kiel Walther Schücking Institute of International Law, November 4-7, 2004, ed. by Zimmermann, Andreas; Hofmann, Rainer. Berlin: Duncker & Humblot, 2006, p. 285-294.) [I.C.J., p. 287-288, 290-291, 293.]

Gros Espiell, Héctor: L'application du droit international dans le droit interne en Amérique latine. (Dans: Studi di diritto internazionale in onore di Gaetano Arangio-Ruiz, sous la dir. de Giovanni Battaglini; Paolo Benvenuti; Antonio Cassese; Giorgio Gaja. Napoli: Editoriale Scientifica, 2004, v. 1, p. 529-550.) [C.P.J.I., 536; C.I.J., p. 530, 533, 537.]

Guabatz, Kurt Taylor and MacArthur, Matthew: How international is "international law"? (In: International law, ed. by Simmons, Beth A. London: SAGE, 2008, v. 4, p. 307-336.)

Guarino, Giancarlo: La charte arabe des droits de l'homme dans le système universel des droits de l'homme. (Dans: La nouvelle charte arabe des droits de l'homme: dialogue italo-arabe: actes de la table ronde italo-arabe du 17-18 décembre 2004 Messina, par Claudio Zanghì; Rafâa Ben Achour. Turin: Giappichelli editore, 2004, p. 85-130.) [C.P.J.I., p. 91; C.I.J., p. 99.]

Guillaume, Gilbert (sous la dir. de): Débats: la pratique et la règle de droit. (Dans: La pratique et le droit international: colloque de Genève. Paris: A. Pedone, 2004, p. 229-239.) [C.I.J., p. 229-232.]

Harris, D. J.: Cases and materials on international law. London: Sweet & Maxwell, 2004. 6th ed. [P.C.I.J. and I.C.J., see table of cases, p. xiii-xxxi.]

Herdegen, Matthias: Asymmetrien in der Staatenwelt und die Herausforderungen des "konstruktiven Völkerrechts". (In: Zeitschrift für ausländisches öffentliches Recht und Völkerrecht, 2004, v. 64, no. 3, p. 571-582.) [I.C.J., p. 575, 580-581.]

Hernández, Gleider I.: On multilingualism and the international legal process. (In: Select Proceedings of the European Society of International Law, 2008, v. 2, p. 412-440.) [P.C.I.J., p. 446-447, 449; I.C.J., p. 448-451.]

Higgins, Rosalyn: Policy considerations and the international judicial process. (In: International law, ed. by Malcolm D. Evans; Patrick Capps. Farnham: Ashgate, 2009, v. 1, p. 277-303.)

Hofmann, Rainer: Concluding remarks. (In: Unity and diversity in international law: proceedings of an international symposium of the Kiel Walther Schücking Institute of International Law, November 4-7, 2004, ed. by Zimmermann, Andreas; Hofmann, Rainer. Berlin: Duncker & Humblot, 2006, p. 491-494.) [I.C.J., p. 492.]

Hofmann, Rainer and Zimmermann, Andreas: Introductory remarks. (In: Unity and diversity in international law: proceedings of an international symposium of the Kiel Walther Schücking Institute of International Law, November 4-7, 2004, ed. by Zimmermann, Andreas; Hofmann, Rainer. Berlin: Duncker & Humblot, 2006, p. 21-25.) [I.C.J., p. 24.]

Jötten, Sara: Die Tätigkeit der International Law Commission im Jahre 2004. (In: German Yearbook of International Law, 2004, v. 47, p. 922-955.) [P.C.I.J., p. 943, 950; I.C.J., p. 924, 927, 931, 943, 950.]

Kadelbach, Stefan: Ethik des Völkerrechts unter Bedingungen der Globalisierung. (In: Zeitschrift für ausländisches öffentliches Recht und Völkerrecht, 2004, v. 64, no. 1, p. 1-20.) [I.C.J., p. 13.]

Kadelbach, Stefan and Kleinlein, Thomas: Überstaatliches Verfassungsrecht: zur Konstitutionalisierung im Völkerrecht. (In: Archiv des Völkerrechts, 2006, v. 44, p. 235-266.) [I.C.J. p. 252, 260-261, 263.]

Kaikobad, Kaiyan Homi: Interpretation and revision of international boundary decisions. Cambridge [etc.]: Cambridge University Press, 2007. (Cambridge Studies in International and Comparative Law.) [P.C.I.J., p. 7, 12, 46-52, 69, 74-75, 89-94, 100-101, 105-106, 109-103, 117, 123-124, 143, 162, 171, 178-179, 194-196, 205-206, 209, 243-247, 249, 253-255, 260, 263, 268, 272, 307-308, 328, 336-338; I.C.J., p. 12, 21, 41-42, 69, 73-75, 77-78, 92-94, 96, 100, 103-105, 107, 113-117, 122-126, 129-131, 134-137, 140-143, 145, 156, 159-163, 167-170, 177, 179, 231-232, 248-251, 256-259, 261-262, 264, 267-281, 283-290, 292-297, 299, 300, 302, 305, 308-315, 318, 326-329, 333, 335, 337-338.]

Kalamkarian, R. A.: The rule of law in international relations. (In: Symposium in commemoration of G. I. Tunkin's 100th birthday: papers delivered at a commemorative celebration held at Moscow State University, 20 October 2006, ed. by Glotova, S.; Shestakov, L. N. London: Wildy, Simmonds & Hill, 2007, p. 551-556.) [I.C.J., passim.]

Kamminga, Menno T.: Humanisation of international law. (In: Changing perceptions of sovereignty and human rights: essays in honour of Cees Flinterman, ed. by Ineke Boerefijn; Jenny Goldschmidt. Anvers: Intersentia, 2008, p. 29-40.)

Kieval, Michael Y.: Be reasonable ! Thoughts on the effectiveness of State criticism in enforcing international law. (In: Michigan Journal of International Law, 2005, v. 26, no. 3, p. 869-898.) [I.C.J., p. 869-876, 978, 880, 883.]

Klabbers, Jan: The commodification of international law. (In: Select Proceedings of the European Society of International Law, ed. by Hélène Ruiz Fabri; Emmanuelle Jouannet; Vincent Tomkiewicz. Oxford; Portland: Hart, 2006, v. 1, p. 341-358.) [I.C.J., p. 344.]

Klabbers, Jan: Straddling law and politics: judicial review in international law. (In: Towards world constitutionalism: issues in the legal ordering of the world community, ed. by Ronald St. John Macdonald; Douglas M. Johnston. Leiden; Boston: Martinus Nijhoff, 2005, p. 809-835.)

Klein, Pierre: Le droit international à l'épreuve du terrorisme. (Dans: Recueil des cours de l'Académie de droit international de La Haye, 2007, v. 321, p. 203-484.) [C.P.J.I., p. 224; C.I.J., p. 278, 282, 288, 333-334, 336, 371, 374, 388-393, 407-408, 412-413, 450.]

Klein, Pierre: Jean Salmon et l'école de Reims. (Dans: Droit du pouvoir, pouvoir du droit: mélanges offerts à Jean Salmon. Bruxelles: Bruylant, 2007, p. 19-38.) [C.P.J.I., p. 31; C.I.J., p. 30-33, 35.]

Kohen, Marcelo G. (ed.): Promoting justice, human rights and conflict resolution through international law: liber amicorum Lucius Caflisch. Leiden: Martinus Nijhoff, 2007. (Graduate Institute of International Studies, Geneva.) [P.C.I.J., p. 130, 604-605, 833, 899-900, 999, 1234; I.C.J., p. 131, 134, 136-137, 139-141, 158, 161, 165, 184-149, 222, 225, 251, 417, 426, 489, 504, 603-607, 619, 621, 768, 771-772, 774-775, 779, 783-786, 792, 800, 803, 830-834, 845, 899-900, 902-903, 916, 919, 921, 923, 925, 928, 930, 933-934, 999, 1021-1023, 1031, 1038, 1041-1043, 1049, 1055, 1095-1097, 1101-1102, 1105, 1108, 1110, 1113, 1115, 1118.]

Kolb, Robert: Conflits entre normes de jus cogens. (Dans: Droit du pouvoir, pouvoir du droit: mélanges offerts à Jean Salmon. Bruxelles: Bruylant, 2007, p. 481-505.) [C.P.J.I., p. 459; C.I.J., p. 456, 457, 459, 461, 470-479.]

Kolb, Robert: Note sur l'émergence d'une maxime de l'utilisation du moyen le moins fort ("civiliter uti") en droit international public. (Dans: Revue belge de droit international, 2006, v. 39, p. 599-620.) [C.P.J.I., p. 619; C.I.J., p. 609-611.]

Koroma, Abdul G.: International law and multiculturalism. (In: Multiculturalism and international law: essays in honour of Edward McWhinney, ed. by Yee, Sienho; Morin, Jacques-Yvan. Leiden; Boston: Martinus Nijhoff, 2009, p. 79-94.)

Koskenniemi, Martti et Zaragozá García, Natalia, trans. et Alberro, Paula, trans. et Falcón y Tella, Fernando, trans.: El discreto civilizador de naciones: el auge y la caída del derecho internacional 1870-1960. Buenos Aires; Madrid: Ciudad Argentina: Universidad Complutense – Facultad de Derecho, 2005. [C.P.J.I., p. 173, 241, 383; C.I.J., p. 259, 380, 382-387.]

Koskenniemi, Martti: The fate of public international law: between technique and politics. (In: Modern Law Review, 2007, v. 70, no. 1, p. 1-30.) [I.C.J., p. 4-6, 13-14, 15, 17.]

Koskenniemi, Martti and Mosley, Christopher C.: The work of the International Law Commission at its fifty-fifth session (2003). (In: Nordic Journal of International Law, 2004, v. 73, p. 99-134.) [I.C.J., p. 101-103, 105-106.]

Krisch, Nico: International law in times of hegemony: unequal power and the shaping of the international legal order. (In: European Journal of International Law, 2005, v. 16, no. 3, p. 369-408.) [I.C.J., p. 391-392.]

Krivickaité, Monika and Laufmöller, Meike: Die Tätigkeit der International Law Commission im Jahre 2006. (In: German Yearbook of International Law, 2006, v. 49, p. 665-690.) [P.C.I.J., p. 666; I.C.J., p. 666, 667, 669, 672, 675.]

Lalonde, Suzanne: The role of "uti possidetis" in determining boundaries. (In: Sovereignty and diversity, ed. by Miodrag Jovanovic; Kristin Henrard. Utrecht: Eleven International Publishing, 2008, p. 55-70.) [I.C.J., p. 60, 61.]

Lapas, Davorin: Some remarks on fragmentation of international law: disintegration or transformation? (In: Comparative and International Law Journal of Southern Africa, 2007, v. 40, no. 1, p. 1-29.) [I.C.J., p. 3, 4, 6, 8, 11, 21.]

Latty, Franck: Arbitrage transnational et droit international général. (Dans: Annuaire français de droit international, 2008, v. 54, p. 467-512.) [C.P.J.I., p. 477, 496; C.I.J., p. 474, 478, 490-491, 497, 502.]

Leathley, Christian: An institutional hierarchy to combat the fragmentation of international law: has the ILC missed an opportunity? (In: New York University Journal of International Law and Politics, 2007, v. 40, no. 1, p. 259-306.)

Leben, Charles: Un nouveau bilan des théories et réalités du droit international. (Dans: Revue générale de droit international public, 2005, v. 109, p. 75-100.) [C.I.J., p. 77, 87, 91, 95; C.P.J.I., p. 81-82.]

Lecomte, Charley: Le manuel de Tallinn au regard des principes posés dans la jurisprudence de la Cour internationale de Justice. (Dans: Internet et le droit international: colloque de Rouen. Paris: Pedone, 2009, p. 309-322.) [I.C.J., passim.]

Licková, Magdalena: European exceptionalism in international law. (In: European Journal of International Law, 2008, v. 19, no. 3, p. 463-490.) [P.C.I.J., p. 471; I.C.J., p. 466, 471.]

Lindroos, Anja: Addressing norm conflicts in a fragmented legal system: the doctrine of lex specialis. (In: Nordic Journal of International Law, 2005, v. 74, no. 1, p. 27-66.) [P.C.I.J., p. 41, 53, 63; I.C.J., p. 30-34, 37, 42-44, 47-52, 55-57, 65.]

Lowe, Vaughan: International law. Oxford [etc.]: Oxford University Press, 2007. (Clarendon Law Series.) [P.C.I.J. and I.C.J., see index p. 291.]

Lowe, Vaughan: Shadows in the cave: the nature of international law when it appears before English courts. (In: International law and power: perspectives on legal order and justice: essays in honour of Colin Warbrick, ed. by Kaiyan Homi Kaikobad; Michael Bohlander. Leiden; Boston: Martinus Nijhoff, 2009, p. 125-139.) [I.C.J., p. 129.]

Lucchini, Laurent: Le juge et l'équidistance: sense or sensibility? (Dans: L'Etat souverain dans le monde d'aujourd'hui: mélange en l'honneur de Kean-Pierre Puissochet, sous la dir. d'Edwige Belliard. Paris: Pedone, 2008, p. 175-181.)

Lukashuk, Igor Ivanovitch: Resolutions of international organizations in international law. (In: Symposium in commemoration of G. I. Tunkin's 100th birthday: papers delivered at a commemorative celebration held at Moscow State University, 20 October 2006, ed. by Glotova, S.; Shestakov, L. N. London: Wildy, Simmonds & Hill, 2007, p. 631-643.) [I.C.J., p. 633, 636-640, 642-643.]

Luker, Daniel: On the borders of justice: an examination and possible solution to the doctrine of uti possidetis. (In: Progress in international law, ed. by Russel A. Miller; Rebecca M. Bratspies. Leiden; Boston: Martinus Nijhoff, 2008, p. 151-170.) [I.C.J., passim.]

Mahiou, Ahmed: Le droit international ou la dialectique de la rigueur et de la flexibilité: cours général de droit international. (Dans: Recueil des cours de l'Académie de droit international de La Haye, 2008, v. 337, p. 9-516.) [C.P.J.I., p. 45, 118, 124, 125, 127, 134, 139, 142, 162, 265, 299, 313, 329, 330, 364, 373-375, 380-382, 388, 401, 408, 436, 444, 453, 454; C.I.J., p. 47, 57, 60, 61, 65, 72, 88, 89, 96, 111, 127-129, 135, 136, 145, 146, 170, 174, 201, 213, 260, 265, 279, 280, 283, 284, 302, 303, 307, 310, 313, 318-328, 331, 332, 344-348, 350, 354, 358-360, 371-386, 393, 398, 402-408, 417-422, 424, 429-432, 436-440, 444-446, 448, 450, 453, 454, 457, 461, 465, 467, 468, 470, 471, 474, 475, 496.]

Mälksoo, Lauri: The science of international law and the concept of politics: the arguments and lives of the international law professors at the University of Dorpat/Iur'ev/Tartu 1855-1985. (In: British Year Book of International Law, 2005, v. 76, p. 383-501.) [I.C.J., p. 490.]

Mandala, Joseph Peter: Universal civil jurisdiction: universalising civil jus cogens liability through adoption of the alien tort statute and retooling the International Criminal Court. (In: Hague Yearbook of International Law, 2009, v. 22, p. 311-355.) [I.C.J., p. 349-350.]

Mapithy-Ma Mapithy, Alban Audrey: La délicate succession d'Etats face à la reconnaissance internationale. Paris: ANRT, 2007. [C.I.J., p. 88-91, 168.]

McCorquodale, Robert: An inclusive international legal system. (In: Leiden Journal of International Law, 2004, v. 17, no. 3, p. 477-504.) [I.C.J. and P.C.I.J., p. 479, 481, 483-489, 491-492, 498-501, 504.]

McWhinney, Edward: Multi-culturalism and contemporary international law: presentation at the XJTU Silk Road Institute seminar. (In: Chinese Journal of International Law, 2007, v. 6, no. 2, p. 527-533.) [I.C.J., p. 528, 530.]

McWhinney, Edward: Multiculturalism and contemporary international law and law-making. (In: The diversity of international law: essays in honour of Professor Kalliopi K. Koufa, ed. by Aristotle Constantinides; Nikos Zaikos. Leiden [etc.]: Nijhoff, 2009, p. 47-59.)

Meza, Miguel Arenas: Los límites al recurso a la fuerza transfronteriza en el actual derecho internacional: el principio de proporcionalidad. Santiago de Compostela: Andavira, 2004. (Colección Estudios Internacionales.)

[I.C.J., p. 6-7, 29-30, 32-35, 40-45, 70, 74, 80, 156, 160-161, 181-183, 208, 242-243, 269, 284-286, 288-292, 294, 303, 308-314.]

Michel, Nicolas (sous la dir. de): Débats. (Dans: La pratique et le droit international: colloque de Genève. Paris: A. Pedone, 2004, p. 275-283.) [C.I.J., p. 277.]

Miller, Russell A. and Bratspies, Rebecca M. (eds.): Progress in international law. Leiden: Martinus Nijhoff, 2008. (Developments in International Law; 60.) [P.C.I.J., p. 13, 15-17, 45, 178, 200, 345, 407, 434, 437, 439, 440, 442, 434, 439, 446-449, 451, 453, 455-457, 459, 460-464, 493-494, 521, 522, 604, 615, 855, 885, 899, 904; I.C.J., p. xviii, xx, xxiii, xxv, 15-17, 22, 26, 45, 47, 52-53, 56, 58, 61-62, 81, 119-120, 130, 140, 156, 164-166, 168, 179-180, 182, 184, 185, 187-188, 199, 225, 232-236, 239, 277, 292, 301, 309, 341, 350, 385, 434, 436-438, 440-445, 447-448, 451-454, 458-459, 463, 464, 466-468, 470, 474, 503, 521, 533, 576, 584-549, 562, 576, 603-604, 637, 670, 682.]

Minnerop, Petra: The classification of States and the creation of status within the international community. (In: Max Planck Yearbook of United Nations Law, 2004, v. 7, p. 79-182.) [P.C.I.J., p. 95-96; I.C.J., p. 89, 91, 94-97, 104, 106-108, 115, 122, 151-153, 160-162.]

Moore, John Norton: Solving the war puzzle: beyond the democratic peace. Durham: Carolina Academic Press, 2004. [I.C.J., p. 16, 56-57, 108.]

Morrison, Fred L.: Comment: [on Unity and diversity in the formation and relevance of customary international law: modern concepts of customary international law as a manifestation of a value-based international order by Anja Seibert-Fohr]. (In: Unity and diversity in international law: proceedings of an international symposium of the Kiel Walther Schücking Institute of International Law, November 4-7, 2004, ed. by Zimmermann, Andreas; Hofmann, Rainer. Berlin: Duncker & Humblot, 2006, p. 295-297.) [I.C.J., p. 297.]

Murphy, John F.: Enforcing the law. (In: International Law Studies (Naval War College), 2006, 80, p. 311-317.) [I.C.J., p. 313.]

Murphy, Sean D.: Contemporary practice of the United States relating to international law. (In: American Journal of International Law, 2004, v. 98, no. 2, p. 349-370.) [I.C.J., p. 363-368.]

Murphy, Sean D.: Contemporary practice of the United States relating to international law. (In: American Journal of International Law, 2004, v. 98, no. 4, p. 820-831.) [I.C.J., p. 822.]

Nasu, Hitoshi: Investigation propio motu for the maintenance of international peace and security. (In: Australian Yearbook of International Law, 2004, v. 23, p. 105-134.) [I.C.J., p. 107, 111, 120, 126-127, 129.]

Nations Unies: La Commission du droit international et son oeuvre: volume I. New York: Nations Unies, 2009. 7e éd. [C.P.J.I., p. 450, 453; C.I.J., p. 12, 14, 16, 19, 22, 25, 30, 75, 94, 101-102, 104-105, 108, 152, 157, 162, 165,

167, 173-174, 179, 245-246, 263, 302, 321, 323-326, 331-333, 400-401, 403, 450-451, 453, 455-458, 461-465.]

Nations Unies: La Commission du droit international et son oeuvre: volume II: instruments. New York: Nations Unies, 2009. 7 éd. [C.I.J., p. 24, 33-34, 41, 59, 62-63, 95, 98-99, 120-122, 148, 154, 163, 200, 225, 243, 276-277, 286-287, 302-303, 306, 320, 351.]

Neate, Francis (ed.): The rule of law: perspectives from around the globe. London [etc.]: LexisNexis, 2009. [I.C.J., passim.]

Neuhold, Hanspeter and Binder, Christina and Schreuer, Christoph: Österreichisches Handbuch des Völkerrechts: v.1 Texttiel. Wien: Manz, 2004. 4., völlig überarb. Aufl. /unter Mitarb. von Christina Binder und David Rezac. (Manz Handbuch.) [I.C.J. and P.C.I.J., passim.]

Neuhold, Hanspeter and Binder, Christina and Schreuer, Christoph: Österreichisches Handbuch des Völkerrechts: v.2 Materialenteil. Wien: Manz, 2004. 4., völlig überarb. Aufl. /unter Mitarb. von Christina Binder und David Rezac. (Manz Handbuch.) [I.C.J. and P.C.I.J., passim.]

Nollkaemper, André and Villeneuve, Carel de: Recht van internationale waterlopen. (In: Handboek internationaal recht, ed. by Horbach, Nathalie L. J. T.; Lefeber, René; Ribbelink, Olivier. The Hague: T.M.C. Asser Press, 2007, p. 769-799.) [P.C.I.J., p. 774, 787; I.C.J., p. 776.]

Nota biografica di Gaetano Arangio-Ruiz. (Dans: Studi di diritto internazionale in onore di Gaetano Arangio-Ruiz, sous la dir. de Giovanni Battaglini; Paolo Benvenuti; Antonio Cassese; Giorgio Gaja. Napoli: Editoriale Scientifica, 2004, v. 1, lix-lx.) [C.I.J., p. lx.]

Orakhelashvili, Alexander: International law and geopolitics: one object, conflicting legitimacies? (In: Netherlands Yearbook of International Law, 2008, v. 39, p. 155-204.) [I.C.J., p. 166, 180-182, 184, 199, 200.]

Orford, Anne: The destiny of international law. (In: Leiden Journal of International Law, 2004, v. 17, no. 3, p. 441-476.) [I.C.J., p. 456-457.]

Overall statements. (In: Unity and diversity in international law: proceedings of an international symposium of the Kiel Walther Schücking Institute of International Law, November 4-7, 2004, ed. by Zimmermann, Andreas; Hofmann, Rainer. Berlin: Duncker & Humblot, 2006, p. 471-490.) [I.C.J., p. 474-475, 490.]

Owada, Hisashi: The rule of law in a globalising world. (In: The rule of law: perspectives from around the globe, ed. by Francis Neate. London [etc.]: LexisNexis, 2009, p. 151-162.) [I.C.J., p. 157-158, 161.]

Owada, Hisashi: Some reflections on the problem of international public order. (In: Kokusaiho Gaiko Zassi, 2003, v. 102, no. 3, p. 1-30.) [I.C.J., p. 7-9, 12, 13, 15, 22-24.]

Paulsson, Jan: Denial of justice in international law. Cambridge [etc.]: Cambridge University Press, 2006, c2005. (Hersch Lauterpacht memorial lectures ; 17.) [P.C.I.J., p. 116; I.C.J., p. 2.]

Paulus, Andreas L.: A comparative look at domestic enforcement of international tribunal judgments. (In: Proceedings of the American Society of International Law, 2009, v. 103, p. 42-48.)

Pauwelyn, Joost: Bridging fragmentation and unity: international law as a universe of inter-connected islands. (In: Michigan Journal of International Law, 2004, v. 25, p. 903-916.) [I.C.J., p. 911, 914.]

Pellet, Alain: As novas tendências do direito intercional: aspectos "macrojurídicos". (Dans: O Brasil e os novos desafios do direito internacional, sous la dir. de Brant, Leonardo Nemer Caldeira. Rio de Janeiro: Editora Forense, 2004, p. 3-25.) [C.I.J., p. 5, 8, 14-16, 20.]

Pellet, Alain: Between codification and progressive development of the law: some reflections from the ILC. (In: International Law FORUM du droit international, 2004, v. 6, no. 1, p. 15-23.) [I.C.J., p. 17, 21.]

Pellet, Alain: L'adaptation du droit international aux besoins changeants de la société internationale: conférence inaugurale, session du droit international public 2007. (Dans: Recueil des cours de l'Académie de droit international de La Haye, 2007, v. 329, p. 9-47.) [C.I.J., passim.]

Pellet, Alain: Responsabilité de l'Etat et responsabilité pénale individuelle en droit international. (Dans: Revista romana de drept international, 2007, v. 4, p. 11-20.) [C.I.J., p. 17-20.]

Peters, Anne: Compensatory constitutionalism: the function and potential of fundamental international norms and structures. (In: Leiden Journal of International Law, 2006, v. 19, p. 579-610.) [I.C.J., p. 586, 588, 594, 598, 606.]

Peyro Llopis, Ana: La place du droit international dans la jurisprudence récente de la Cour suprême des Etats-Unis. (Dans: Revue générale de droit international public, 2005, v. 109, p. 609-642.) [C.I.J., p. 616-617.]

Picchio Forlati, Laura et Palmisano, Giuseppe: La lezione di una vita: cos'è e com'è il diritto internazionale. (Dans: Studi di diritto internazionale in onore di Gaetano Arangio-Ruiz, sous la dir. de Giovanni Battaglini; Paolo Benvenuti; Antonio Cassese; Giorgio Gaja. Napoli: Editoriale Scientifica, 2004, v. 1, xvii-lviii.) [C.P.J.I, p. xxxvi, xxxvii; C.I.J., p. xxxvii, liv-lvi, lviii.]

Poulain, Michèle: Chronologie des faits internationaux d'intérêt juridique (année 2004). (Dans: Annuaire français de droit international, 2004, v. 50, p. 931-980.) [C.I.J., p. 944-945, 966-967.]

Prescott, Victor and Triggs, Gillian Doreen: International frontiers and boundaries: law, politics and geography. Leiden [etc.]: Martinus Nijhoff, 2008. [I.C.J., p. 139, 143-150, 156, 158-162, 164-166, 169, 171, 173, 175-180, 180, 183, 185, 187-188, 192, 195-198, 201-204, 206, 211, 218, 220, 228, 230, 384.]

Prost, Mario: Le droit international: son fondement, son unité. (Dans: Revue belge de droit international, 2006, v. 39, p. 621-670.) [C.P.J.I., p. 648, 661; C.I.J., p. 623, 627, 634, 641, 661, 665, 668.]

Protiere, Guillaume (sous la dir. de): Espaces du droit et droits des espaces. Paris: Harmattan, 2009. (Administration et Aménagement du Territoire.) [C.P.J.I., p. 121, 126, 148; C.I.J., p. 16-17, 111, 122-135, 143, 151-153.]

Reece Thomas, Katherine: The changing status of international law in English domestic law. (In: Netherlands International Law Review, 2006, v. 53, p. 371-398.) [I.C.J., p. 376, 385, 393, 395.]

Reinisch, August: The use and limits of res judicata and lis pendens as procedural tools to avoid conflicting dispute settlement outcomes. (In: The Law & Practice of International Courts and Tribunals, 2004, v. 3, no. 1, p. 37-77.) [P.C.I.J., p. 46, 48-51, 53, 62; I.C.J., p. 38-39, 42, 46-48, 52, 54, 65, 76.]

Reisman, William Michael and Arsanjani, Mahnoush H. and Wiessner, Siegfried and Westerman, Gayl S.: International law in contemporary perspective. New York: Foundation Press, 2004. [2nd ed.] (University Casebook Series.)

Rezek, Francisco: Direito internacional público: curso elementar. São Paulo: Saraiva, 2005. 10a ed., inteiramente rev. e atualizada. [P.C.I.J., p. 104, 335, 356; I.C.J., p. 9, 22, 91, 93, 115, 118-120, 122, 124, 132, 135-137, 141, 143-144, 146-147, 165, 172, 182, 217, 225, 237, 248, 253-254, 257, 269-270, 272-273, 278, 280-282, 335-336, 338-339, 349, 356-365.]

Richter, Dagmar: Does international jurisprudence matter in Germany? The Federal Constitutional Court's new doctrine of "factual precedent". (In: German Yearbook of International Law, 2006, v. 49, p. 51-75.) [I.C.J., p. 53-64, 66-67, 69, 70, 72-75.]

Rigaux, François: L'apport des juristes belges à la doctrine du droit international. (Dans: Droit du pouvoir, pouvoir du droit: mélanges offerts à Jean Salmon. Bruxelles: Bruylant, 2007, p. 543-553.) [C.P.J.I., p. 551, 552; C.I.J., p. 552, 553.]

Riquelme Cortado, Rosa: Derecho internacional: entre un orden global y fragmentado. Madrid: Editorial Biblioteca Nueva: Fundación José Ortega y Gasset, 2005. (Colección dirigida por el Instituto Universitario Ortega y Gasset de la Fundación José Ortega y Gasset.) [C.P.J.I., p. 63; C.I.J., p. 35, 50, 52-53, 58, 62, 67-71, 73, 75, 77-81, 85, 91, 98, 100, 140, 188, 198, 211-213, 217, 235, 237-239, 241-242, 244-250, 252, 260, 262, 268-270, 281, 284-286, 303, 318, 327, 331, 339, 345-346, 350-351, 353, 355-362.]

Röben, Volker: The role of international conventions and general international law in the fight against international terrorism. (In: Terrorism as a challenge for national and international law: security versus liberty?, ed. by Walter, Christian; Vöneky, Silja; Röben, Volker; Schorkopf, Frank. Berlin [etc.]: Springer, 2004, p. 789-821.) [I.C.J., p. 790, 816-817, 820-821.]

Ronzitti, Natalino: L'adattamento dell'ordinamento italiano alle norme imperative del diritto internazionale. (Dans: Studi di diritto internazionale in onore di Gaetano Arangio-Ruiz, sous la dir. de Giovanni Battaglini; Paolo Benvenuti; Antonio Cassese; Giorgio Gaja. Napoli: Editoriale Scientifica, 2004, v. 1, p. 633-640.) [C.I.J., p. 633.]

Rosenne, Shabtai: The perplexities of modern international law. Leiden [etc.]: Martinus Nijhoff, 2004. [I.C.J. and P.C.I.J., passim.]

Rosenne, Shabtai: The role of controversy in international legal development. (In: Essays on international law and practice, by Shabtai Rosenne. Leiden; Boston: Martinus Nijhoff, 2007, p. 559-598.)

Rosenne, Shabtai: Three central elements of modern international law. (In: Essays on international law and practice, by Shabtai Rosenne. Leiden; Boston: Martinus Nijhoff, 2007, p. 621-632.)

Rosenne, Shabtai: The three central elements of modern international law. (In: Hague Yearbook of International Law, 2004, v. 17, p. 3-13.) [I.C.J., p. 6-7.]

Rubin, Alfred P.: One world? (In: Studi di diritto internazionale in onore di Gaetano Arangio-Ruiz, ed. by Giovanni Battaglini; Paolo Benvenuti; Antonio Cassese; Giorgio Gaja. Napoli: Editoriale Scientifica, 2004, v. 1, p. 191-210.) [P.C.I.J., p. 196.]

Ruzié, David: Réflexions sur la pratique du droit de recours des fonctionnaires internationaux. (Dans: Internationale Gemeinschaft und Menschenrechte: Festschrift für Georg Ress zum 70. Geburtstag am 21. Januar 2005, sous la dir. de Bröhmer, Jürgen; Bieber, Roland; Calliess, Christian; Langenfeld, Christine; Weber, Stefan; Wolf, Joachim. Köln [etc.]: Heymann, 2005, p. 223-233.) [C.I.J., p. 224, 227.]

Sahovic, Milan: Le système normatif du droit international et la société internationale contemporaine. (Dans: Studi di diritto internazionale in onore di Gaetano Arangio-Ruiz, sous la dir. de Giovanni Battaglini; Paolo Benvenuti; Antonio Cassese; Giorgio Gaja. Napoli: Editoriale Scientifica, 2004, v. 1, p. 421-426.) [C.I.J., p. 423, 425.]

Salinas Alcega, Sergio et Tirado Robles, Carmen: Casos prácticos de derecho internacional público. Zaragoza: Real Instituto de Estudios Europeos, 2005. [C.I.J., passim.]

Samuels, Joel H.: Redrawing the map: lessons of post-colonial boundary dispute resolution in Africa. (In: Africa: mapping new boundaries in international law, by Jeremy Levitt. Oxford [etc.]: Hart, 2008, p. 227-255.) [I.C.J., passim.]

Sand, Peter H.: United States and Britain in Diego Garcia: the future of a controversial base. London: Palgrave Macmillan, 2009. [I.C.J., p. 4.]

Santulli, Carlo: Travaux de la Commission du droit international (cinquante-sixième session). (Dans: Annuaire français de droit international, 2004, v. 50, p. 564-579.) [C.I.J., p. 573.]

Sauer, Heiko: Die neue Schlagkraft der gemeineuropäischen Grundrechtsjudikatur: zur Bindung deutscher Gerichte an die Enstscheidungen des Europäischen Gerichtshofs für Menschenrechte. (In: Zeitschrift für ausländisches öffentliches Recht und Völkerrecht, 2005, v. 65, no. 1, p. 35-69.) [I.C.J., p. 61.]

Schachter, Oscar: Metaphor and realism in international law. (In: Studi di diritto internazionale in onore di Gaetano Arangio-Ruiz, ed. by Giovanni Battaglini; Paolo Benvenuti; Antonio Cassese; Giorgio Gaja. Napoli: Editoriale Scientifica, 2004, v. 1, p. 211-216.) [I.C.J., p. 214.]

Schiff Berman, Paul: From international law to law and globalization. (In: Columbia Journal of Transnational Law, 2005, v. 43, no. 2, p. 485-556.) [I.C.J., p. 535.]

Schill, Stephan W.: The multilateralization of international investment law. Cambridge: Cambridge University Press, 2009. [I.C.J., see index p. 410.]

Schilling, Theodor: Völkerkonsensrecht. (In: Internationale Gemeinschaft und Menschenrechte: Festschrift für Georg Ress zum 70. Geburtstag am 21. Januar 2005, ed. by Bröhmer, Jürgen; Bieber, Roland; Calliess, Christian; Langenfeld, Christine; Weber, Stefan; Wolf, Joachim. Köln [etc.]: Heymann, 2005, p. 235-248.) [I.C.J., p. 235, 237-238, 240-244.]

Scott, Shirley V.: International law in world politics: an introduction. Boulder [etc.]: Rienner, 2004. [I.C.J., p. 3, 10-13, 16, 18, 21, 29, 37, 41, 49-63, 66-67, 69-71, 74, 80-83, 94-102, 105, 110-113, 125-131, 135, 137, 144, 151, 154, 158, 182, 219, 293-295; P.C.I.J., p. 11, 91, 111.]

Seibert-Fohr, Anja: Unity and diversity in the formation and relevance of customary international law: modern concepts of customary international law as a manifestation of a value-based international order. (In: Unity and diversity in international law: proceedings of an international symposium of the Kiel Walther Schücking Institute of International Law, November 4-7, 2004, ed. by Zimmermann, Andreas; Hofmann, Rainer. Berlin: Duncker & Humblot, 2006, p. 257-283.) [I.C.J., p. 259-266, 271, 273-275, 277, 280-281.]

Shiner, Phil: Experiences with domestic courts: court experiences in the U.K. (In: Freedom from nuclear weapons through legal accountability and good faith: conference report, ed. by George Farebrother. Nottingham: Spokesman; World Court Project, 2007, p. 65-69.) [I.C.J., p. 67, 68.]

Simma, Bruno: Universality of international law from the perspective of a practitioner. (In: Select Proceedings of the European Society of International Law, ed. by James Crawford; Sarah M. H. Nouwen. Oxford; Portland: Hart, 2008, v. 2, p. 1-36.) [I.C.J., p. 6-10, 13, 15-24, 26-27.]

Slaughter, Anne-Marie and Burke-White, William: The future of international law is domestic (or, the European way of law). (In: Harvard International Law Journal, 2006, v. 47, p. 327-352.) [I.C.J. and P.C.I.J., p. 327.]

Somek, Alexander: Kelsen lives. (In: European Journal of International Law, 2007, v. 18, p. 409-451.) [I.C.J., p. 419.]

Spiermann, Ole: Twentieth century internationalism in law. (In: European Journal of International Law, 2007, v. 18, no. 5, p. 785-814.) [P.C.I.J., p. 788, 793, 795-796, 808, 813; I.C.J., p. 790-791, 793, 799-801, 812-814.]

Stikkelbroeck, Fredericke E. M.: Hague Conference on Private International Law: work in 2006. (In: Hague Yearbook of International Law, 2006, v. 19, p. 217-232.) [I.C.J., p. 3, 6-16.]

Strydom, Hennie: South Africa and international law: from confrontation to cooperation. (In: German Yearbook of International Law, 2004, v. 47, p. 160-213.) [I.C.J., p. 173-174, 180, 182-186, 204.]

Su, Jinyuan: XJTU Silk Road Institute seminar: multiculturalism and international law. (In: Chinese Journal of International Law, 2007, v. 6, no. 2, p. 523-525.) [I.C.J., p. 524.]

Thiele, Carmen: Fragmentierung des Völkerrechts als herausforderung für die Staatengemeinschaft. (In: Archiv des Völkerrechts, 2008, v. 46, no. 1, p. 1-41.)

Thürer, Daniel: Von der komplexen Gestalt des Völkerrechts: eine grobe Skizze. (In: Internationale Gemeinschaft und Menschenrechte: Festschrift für Georg Ress zum 70. Geburtstag am 21. Januar 2005, ed. by Bröhmer, Jürgen; Bieber, Roland; Calliess, Christian; Langenfeld, Christine; Weber, Stefan; Wolf, Joachim. Köln [etc.]: Heymann, 2005, p. 307-316.) [I.C.J., p. 312, 314.]

Tomuschat, Christian: The International Law Commission: an outdated institution? (In: German Yearbook of International Law, 2006, v. 49, p. 77-105.) [I.C.J., p. 92, 93-94, 99, 105.]

Tourme-Jouannet, Emmanuelle: Universalism and imperialism: the true-false paradox of international law? (In: European Journal of International Law, 2007, v. 18, p. 379-407.) [P.C.I.J., p. 383.]

Trakman, Leon: Ex aequo et bono: demistifying an ancient concept. (In: Chicago Journal of International Law, 2008, v. 8, no. 2, p. 621-642.)

Treves, Tullio: Judicial lawmaking in an era of "proliferation" of international courts and tribunals: development or fragmentation of international law? (In: Developments of international law in treaty making, ed. by Rüdiger Wolfrum; Volker Röben. Berlin, [etc.]: Springer, 2005, p. 587-519.) [I.C.J., passim.]

Tunkin, Grigorij Ivanovic: Fundamental principles of contemporary international law: instructional manual. (In: Symposium in commemoration of G. I. Tunkin's 100th birthday: papers delivered at a commemorative celebration held at Moscow State University, 20 October 2006, ed. by Glotova, S.; Shestakov, L. N. London: Wildy, Simmonds & Hill, 2007, p. 793-841.) [I.C.J., p. 805-807, 818, 833.]

Verdier, Pierre-Hugues: Enforcement of international judgments and decisions in Canadian courts. (In: Proceedings of the American Society of International Law, 2009, v. 103, p. 48-52.)

Villagrán Kramer, Francisco: La globalización y los principios del derecho internacional. (Dans: Anuario hispano-luso-americano de derecho internacional, 2005, v. 17, p. 337-368.) [C.P.J.I., p. 347-349; C.I.J., p. 339, 344-346, 350-351, 353, 359, 362-363.]

Voeten, Erik: The politics of international judicial appointments. (In: Chicago Journal of International Law, 2009, v. 9, no. 2, p. 387-405.)

Voina-Motoc, Iulia: Conceptions of pluralism and international law. (In: Select Proceedings of the European Society of International Law, ed. by Hélène Ruiz Fabri; Emmanuelle Jouannet; Vincent Tomkiewicz. Oxford; Portland: Hart, 2006, v. 1, p. 401-429.) [I.C.J., p. 421-424.]

Wälde, Thomas W.: Denial of justice: a review comment on Jan Paulsson, denial of justice in international law. (In: ICSID Review: Foreign Investment Law Journal, 2006, 21, p. 449-485.) [I.C.J., p. 472, 480.]

Wessel, Ramses A.: Internationaal recht in ontwikkeling. (In: Handboek internationaal recht, ed. by Horbach, Nathalie L. J. T.; Lefeber, René; Ribbelink, Olivier. The Hague: T.M.C. Asser Press, 2007, p. 1-17.) [P.C.I.J., p. 4-5, 11; I.C.J., p. 11.]

Wet, Erika de: The emergence of international and regional value systems as a manifestation of the emerging international constitutional order. (In: Leiden Journal of International Law, 2006, v. 19, p. 611-632.) [I.C.J., p. 614, 616.]

Wet, Erika de: The international constitutional order. (In: International and Comparative Law Quarterly, 2006, v. 55, p. 51-76.) [I.C.J., p. 54, 65, 66, 67, 69.]

Winkel, Laurens: The Peace Treaties of Westphalia as an instance of the reception of Roman law. (In: Peace treaties and international law in European history: from the late middle ages to World War One, ed. by Randall Lesaffer. Cambridge: Cambridge University Press, 2004, p. 222-237.) [I.C.J., p. 230.]

Wolfrum, Rüdiger: Taking and assessing evidence in international adjudication. (In: Law of the sea, environmental law and settlement of disputes: liber amicorum Judge Thomas A. Mensah, ed. by Tafsir Malick Ndiaye; Rüdiger Wolfrum. Leiden; Boston: Martinus Nijhoff, 2007, p. 341-356.) [I.C.J., passim.]

Wood, Michael C.: "Constitutionalization" of international law: a sceptical voice. (In: International law and power: perspectives on legal order and justice: essays in honour of Colin Warbrick, ed. by Kaiyan Homi Kaikobad; Michael Bohlander. Leiden; Boston: Martinus Nijhoff, 2009, p. 85-97.) [I.C.J., p. 87, 93.]

Wuerth, Ingrid: The enforcement of international decisions in U.S. courts. (In: Proceedings of the American Society of International Law, 2009, v. 103, p. 52-56.)

Yasuaki, Onuma: A transcivilizational perspective on global legal order in the twenty-first century: a way to overcome west-centric and judiciary-centric deficits in international legal thougths. (In: International Community Law Review, 2006, v. 8, p. 29-63.) [I.C.J., p. 41, 42, 49-53, 57-61.]

Young, Ernest A.: Supranational rulings as judgments and precedents. (In: Duke Journal of Comparative and International Law, 2008, v. 18, no. 2, p. 477-519.)

Yusuf, Abdulqawi A.: Communication: le conseiller juridique d'une organisation internationale face à la pratique. (Dans: La pratique et le droit international: colloque de Genève. Paris: A. Pedone, 2004, p. 253-257.) [C.I.J. et C.P.J.I., p. 255.]

Ziccardi Capaldo, Giuliana (ed.): The pillars of global law. Aldershot [etc.]: Ashgate, 2008. [I.C.J., p. 95-136 and index p. 419-420.]

Ziccardi, Piero: Il diritto internazionale visto dall'interno. (Dans: Studi di diritto internazionale in onore di Gaetano Arangio-Ruiz, sous la dir. de Giovanni Battaglini; Paolo Benvenuti; Antonio Cassese; Giorgio Gaja. Napoli: Editoriale Scientifica, 2004, v. 1, p. 655-660.) [C.I.J., p. 659.]

2. Sources du droit international
2. Sources of international law

Al Faruque, Abdullah: Creating customary international law through bilateral investment treaties: a critical appraisal. (In: Indian Journal of International Law, 2004, v. 44, no. 2, p. 292-318.) [I.C.J., p. 294, 296-300, 309-310, 315-316; P.C.I.J., p. 297-298.]

Arangio-Ruiz, Gaetano: Customary law: a few more thoughts about the theory of "spontaneous" international custom. (In: Droit du pouvoir, pouvoir du droit: mélanges offerts à Jean Salmon. Bruxelles: Bruylant, 2007, p. 93-124.) [I.C.J., p. 103-107, 110, 113, 115.]

Baker, Christopher D.: Tolerance of international espionage: a functional approach. (In: American University International Law Review, 2004, v. 19, p. 1091-1113.) [I.C.J., p. 1094.]

Bekker, Peter H. F.: The treatment of the evidentiary source of international law in U.S. Alien Tort Statute cases. (In: Globalisation and jurisdiction, ed. by Piet Jan Slot; Mielle Bulterman. Leiden: Kluwer Law International, 2004, p. 157-182.) [I.C.J., p. 168, 170, 175-181.]

Boisson de Chazournes, Laurence: Commentaire. (Dans: L'influence des sources sur l'unité et la fragmentation du droit international: travaux du séminaire tenu à Palma, les 20-21 mai 2005, sous la dir. de Rosario Huesa Vinaixa; Karel Wellens. Bruxelles: Bruylant, 2006, p. 75-80.) [C.I.J., p. 76, 78.]

Boisson de Chazournes, Laurence: Qu'est-ce que la pratique en droit international? (Dans: La pratique et le droit international: colloque de Genève. Paris: A. Pedone, 2004, p. 13-47.) [C.I.J., p. 15-21, 24-43; C.P.J.I., p. 35, 41.]

Boisson de Chazournes, Laurence: Treaty law-making and non-treaty law-making: the evolving structure of the international legal order. (In: Developments of international law in treaty making, ed. by Rüdiger Wolfrum; Volker Röben. Berlin, [etc.]: Springer, 2005, p. 463-479.) [I.C.J., p. 468, 470.]

Buffard, Isabelle et Hafner, Gerhard: Risques et fragmentation en droit international. (Dans: L'observateur des Nations Unies, 2007, v. 22, p. 29-56.) [C.I.J., p. 33-34, 47, 49, 50, 54.]

Buzzini, Gionata Piero: Abstention, silence et droit international général. (Dans: Rivista di diritto internazionale, 2005, v. 88, p. 342-382.) [C.P.J.I., p. 344-345, 348-349, 372; C.I.J., p. 344-345, 347-379, 358, 369.]

Buzzini, Gionata Piero: The development of international law: alternatives to treaty-making? Max Planck Institute, 14-15 November 2003. (In: International Law FORUM du droit international, 2004, v. 6, no. 1, p. 46-51.) [I.C.J., p. 46-48, 50-51.]

Cançado Trindade, A. A.: Foundations of international law: the role and importance of its basic principles. (In: XXX Curso de derecho internacional: organizado por el Comité Jurídico Interamericano y la Secretaría General de la OEA en agosto de 2003. Washington, D.C.: Organización de los Estados Americanos, Secretaría General, Subsecretaría de Asuntos Jurídicos, 2004, p. 359-415.) [P.C.I.J., p. 370-372; I.C.J., p. 369, 372, 376, 389, 394-397, 400, 401, 404, 410, 411.]

Cardona Llorens, Jorge: Le rôle des traités. (Dans: L'influence des sources sur l'unité et la fragmentation du droit international: travaux du séminaire tenu à Palma, les 20-21 mai 2005, sous la dir. de Rosario Huesa Vinaixa; Karel Wellens. Bruxelles: Bruylant, 2006, p. 25-48.) [C.I.J., p. 29-30, 36.]

Cazala, Julien: Le résultat manifestement absurde ou déraisonnable de l'interprétation dans l'affaire de l'Apurement des comptes (Pays-Bas c. France). (Dans: Annuaire français de droit international, 2004, v. 50, p. 624-652.) [C.P.J.I., p. 633-634, 638, 640-641, 647; C.I.J., p. 630, 633-634, 636-643, 647-648, 652.]

Cohen-Jonathan, Gérard: Le jus cogens et les droits de l'homme. (Dans: Mélanges en l'honneur de Jean Charpentier: la France, l'Europe, le monde. Paris: Pedone, 2008, p. 61-72.)

Corten, Olivier: La participation du Conseil de sécurité à l'élaboration, à la cristallisation ou à la consolidation de règles coutumières. (Dans: Revue belge de droit international, 2004, v. 37, p. 552-567.) [C.I.J., p. 554-556, 558-559, 561, 564.]

Daudet, Yves : Aspects de la question des sources du droit international. (Dans : Collected Courses of the Xiamen Academy of International Law, 2009, v. 2, p. 1-43.) [C.I.J., p. 12, 14.]

Dinstein, Yoram : The interaction between customary international law and treaties. (In : Recueil des cours de l'Académie de droit international de La Haye, 2006, v. 322, p. 243-428.) [P.C.I.J., p. 266, 269, 331; I.C.J., p. 259-260, 262-265, 267, 270, 272-274, 277, 282, 284-285, 289, 291-298, 303-310, 313, 317-326, 329, 336, 339, 353, 356-365, 370-377, 380, 384-385, 387-388, 396, 404, 409, 419, 422-424, 426.]

Dunworth, Treasa : Hidden anxieties : customary international law in New Zealand. (In : New Zealand Journal of Public and International Law, 2004, v. 2, p. 67-84.) [I.C.J., p. 78.]

Dupuy, Pierre-Marie : Formation of customary international law and general principles. (In : The Oxford handbook of international environmental law, ed. by Daniel Bodansky ; Jutta Brunnée ; Ellen Hey. Oxford : Oxford University Press, 2007, p. 449-466.) [I.C.J., p. 452-453, 457, 459-461, 464.]

Dupuy, Pierre-Marie : Préface : fragmentation du droit international ou des perceptions qu'on en a ? (Dans : L'influence des sources sur l'unité et la fragmentation du droit international : travaux du séminaire tenu à Palma, les 20-21 mai 2005, sous la dir. de Rosario Huesa Vinaixa ; Karel Wellens. Bruxelles : Bruylant, 2006, v-xxii.) [C.P.J.I., p. XVI; C.I.J., p. V-VIII, XI-XII, XIX.]

Emanuelli, Claude : L'étude du CICR sur le droit humanitaire coutumier : la coutume en question. (Dans : Revue générale de droit international public, 2006, v. 110, p. 435-444.) [C.I.J., p. 436-439, 441-444.]

Focarelli, Carlo : Customary foundations of jus gentium in Francisco Suárez's thought and the concept of international community in contemporary international law. (In : Italian Yearbook of International Law, 2006, v. 16, p. 41-56.) [I.C.J., p. 51.]

Focarelli, Carlo : I limiti dello jus cogens nella giurisprudenza più recente. (Dans : Rivista di diritto internazionale, 2007, v. 90, p. 637-656.) [C.I.J., p. 640-641, 643, 648-649.]

Forcada, Ignacio : Commentaire. (Dans : L'influence des sources sur l'unité et la fragmentation du droit international : travaux du séminaire tenu à Palma, les 20-21 mai 2005, ed. by Rosario Huesa Vinaixa ; Karel Wellens. Bruxelles : Bruylant, 2006, p. 263-269.) [I.C.J., p. 264, 269.]

Francioni, Francesco : Au-delà des traités : l'émergence d'un nouveau droit coutumier pour la protection du patrimoine culturel. (Dans : Revue générale de droit international public, 2007, v. 111, p. 19-41.) [C.I.J., p. 20.]

Franck, Thomas M. : Non-treaty law-making : when, where and how ? (In : Developments of international law in treaty making, ed. by Rüdiger Wolfrum ; Volker Röben. Berlin, [etc.] : Springer, 2005, p. 417-435.) [I.C.J., p. 417-421.]

Gärditz, Klaus Ferdinand: Ungeschriebenes Völkerrecht durch Systembildung. (In: Archiv des Völkerrechts, 2007, v. 45, p. 1-34.) [P.C.I.J., p. 13, 16, 20, 25; I.C.J., p. 5, 6, 20, 24-26, 28.]

Glennon, Michael J.: De l'absurdité du droit impératif (jus cogens). (Dans: Revue générale de droit international public, 2006, v. 110, p. 529-536.) [C.I.J., p. 533.]

Goodman, Camille: Acta sunt servanda? A regime for regulating the unilateral acts of States at international law. (In: Australian Yearbook of International Law, 2004, v. 25, p. 43-73.) [P.C.I.J., p. 49, 57, 60, 64; I.C.J., p. 43-46, 47, 49, 51, 54, 56-61, 63, 67, 70-72.]

Hansen, Peter C.: The World Bank Administrative Tribunal's external sources of law: a retrospective of the Tribunal's first quarter-century (1981-2005). (In: Law and Practice of International Courts and Tribunals, 2007, v. 6, p. 1-87.) [P.C.I.J., p. 78, 81; I.C.J., p. 2-4, 5, 15, 18, 32, 52-53, 73, 75, 78-81, 86.]

Hobe, Stephan and Khan, Rahmatullah: The role of non-state actors, in particular of NGOs, in non-contractual law-making and the development of customary international law. (In: Developments of international law in treaty making, ed. by Rüdiger Wolfrum; Volker Röben. Berlin, [etc.]: Springer, 2005, p. 319-332.) [I.C.J., p. 320, 328.]

Huesa Vinaixa, Rosario: Le rôle de l'opinio juris. (Dans: L'influence des sources sur l'unité et la fragmentation du droit international: travaux du séminaire tenu à Palma, les 20-21 mai 2005, sous la dir. de Rosario Huesa Vinaixa; Karel Wellens. Bruxelles: Bruylant, 2006, p. 55-73.) [C.I.J., p. 57-58, 60, 63-64, 66-67, 69, 71.]

Hulsroj, Peter: Jus cogens and disarmament. (In: Indian Journal of International Law, 2006, v. 46, p. 1-11.) [I.C.J., p. 2-5.]

Kaikobad, Kaiyan Homi: Non consensual aerial surveillance in the airspace over the exclusive economic zone for military and defence purposes. (In: International law and power: perspectives on legal order and justice: essays in honour of Colin Warbrick, ed. by Kaiyan Homi Kaikobad; Michael Bohlander. Leiden; Boston: Martinus Nijhoff, 2009, p. 513-572.) [P.C.I.J., p. 558, 560; I.C.J., p. 543, 555-558, 561.]

Kammerhofer, Jörg: Uncertainty in the formal sources of international law: customary international law and some of its problems. (In: European Journal of International Law, 2004, v. 15, no. 3, p. 523-553.) [I.C.J. and P.C.I.J., p. 523, 529-530, 533, 538, 541, 549, 551.]

Koch, Charles H.: Judicial dialogue for legal multiculturalism. (In: Michigan Journal of International Law, 2004, v. 25, no. 4, p. 879-902.) [I.C.J., p. 897-898.]

Kohen, Marcelo G.: La pratique et la théorie des sources du droit international. (Dans: La pratique et le droit international: colloque de Genève. Paris: A. Pedone, 2004, p. 81-111.) [C.I.J., p. 81-83, 85-86, 88-90, 93-96, 98, 100-101, 104-106, 109, 110; C.P.J.I., p. 96.]

Kolb, Robert: La maxime "qui habet commoda, ferre debet onera et contra" (celui qui jouit des avantages doit supporter aussi les charges et vice versa) en droit international public. (Dans: Revue belge de droit international, 2004, v. 37, p. 12-36.) [C.I.J., p. 19-22, 31; C.P.J.I., p. 29, 32.]

Kolb, Robert: Principles as sources of international law (with special reference to good faith). (In: Netherlands International Law Review, 2006, v. 53, no. 1, p. 1-36.) [P.C.I.J., p. 6, 9; I.C.J., p. 6-7, 10-12, 18, 21-23, 28, 30-31, 33-34.]

Koroma, Abdul G.: International courts and tribunals: alternatives to treaty making. (In: Developments of international law in treaty making, ed. by Rüdiger Wolfrum; Volker Röben. Berlin, [etc.]: Springer, 2005, p. 621-625.) [I.C.J., passim.]

Le rôle de la doctrine: sommaire du débat. (Dans: L'influence des sources sur l'unité et la fragmentation du droit international: travaux du séminaire tenu à Palma, les 20-21 mai 2005, sous la dir. de Rosario Huesa Vinaixa; Karel Wellens. Bruxelles: Bruylant, 2006, p. 271-272.) [C.I.J., p. 271.]

Le rôle des décisions judiciaires: sommaire du débat. (Dans: L'influence des sources sur l'unité et la fragmentation du droit international: travaux du séminaire tenu à Palma, les 20-21 mai 2005, sous la dir. de Rosario Huesa Vinaixa; Karel Wellens. Bruxelles: Bruylant, 2006, p. 231-235.) [C.I.J., p. 232-233.]

Letter from John Bellinger III, legal adviser, U.S. Dept. of State, and William J. Haynes, general counsel, U.S. Depart. of Defense, to Dr. Jakob Kellenberger, president, International Committee of the Red Cross, regarding customary international law study. (In: International Legal Materials, 2007, v. 46, p. 514-531.) [I.C.J., p. 524 (note 67), 527 (note 101).]

Lukashuk, Igor Ivanovitch: Sources of international law. (In: Russian Law: Theory and practice, 2009, no. 1, p. 91-114.) [P.C.I.J., p. 91; I.C.J., passim.]

Nasser, Salem Hikmat: Sources and norms of international law: a study on soft law. Glienicke; Madison: Galda: Wilch Verlag, 2008. English ed. (Mobility and norm change; 7.) [I.C.J., p. 57-80, 171-175; P.C.I.J., p. 54.]

Nieto Navia, Rafael: Do international courts and tribunals have the power to "create" law? (In: Global Community: Yearbook of International Law and Jurisprudence, 2006, v. 6, no. 1, p. 75-103.) [P.C.I.J., p. 75, 78-80, 83, 85; I.C.J., p. 75, 77, 79-87, 89, 99, 101-102.]

Norman, George and Trachtman, Joel P.: The customary international law game. (In: American Journal of International Law, 2005, v. 99, p. 541-580.) [P.C.I.J., p. 553; I.C.J., p. 543-544, 550, 555, 566, 570-571.]

Observations finales. (Dans: L'influence des sources sur l'unité et la fragmentation du droit international: travaux du séminaire tenu à Palma, les 20-21 mai 2005, sous la dir. de Rosario Huesa Vinaixa; Karel Wellens. Bruxelles: Bruylant, 2006, p. 273-278.) [C.I.J., p. 276.]

Ong, David M.: International environmental law's 'customary' dilemma: betwixt general principles and treaty rules. (In: Irish Yearbook of International Law, 2006, v. 1, p. 3-60.) [I.C.J., p. 8, 12, 15-17, 19, 24, 27-29, 34, 35, 37, 38, 47, 48, 50, 59.]

Orrego Vicuña, Francisco: Creación del derecho internacional en una sociedad global: ¿ Importa todavía el consentimiento? (Dans: Anuario hispano-luso-americano de derecho internacional, 2005, v. 17, p. 61-86.) [C.I.J., p. 61, 65, 79, 81-82.]

Orrego Vicuña, Francisco: Law making in a global society: does consent still matter? (In: Internationale Gemeinschaft und Menschenrechte: Festschrift für Georg Ress zum 70. Geburtstag am 21. Januar 2005, ed. by Bröhmer, Jürgen; Bieber, Roland; Calliess, Christian; Langenfeld, Christine; Weber, Stefan; Wolf, Joachim. Köln [etc.]: Heymann, 2005, p. 191-206.) [I.C.J., p. 202-204.]

Pazartzis, Photini: Le rôle de la pratique dans le droit coutumier. (Dans: L'influence des sources sur l'unité et la fragmentation du droit international: travaux du séminaire tenu à Palma, les 20-21 mai 2005, sous la dir. de Rosario Huesa Vinaixa; Karel Wellens. Bruxelles: Bruylant, 2006, p. 81-102.) [C.I.J., p. 82, 92, 93-94, 96-98, 100.]

Pellet, Alain: Complementarity of international treaty law, customary law, and non-contractual law-making. (In: Developments of international law in treaty making, ed. by Rüdiger Wolfrum; Volker Röben. Berlin, [etc.]: Springer, 2005, p. 409-415.) [I.C.J., p. 410-411, 413-415.]

Raimondo, Fabián O.: General principles of law in the decisions of international criminal courts and tribunals. Leiden: Martinus Nijhoff, 2008. [P.C.I.J. and I.C.J., p. 5, 17-43, 45-47, 49-52, 57, 58, 60, 63, 64, 71, 72.]

Rao, Pemmaraju Sreenivasa: The Indian position on some general principles of international law. (In: India and international law, ed. by Bimal N. Patel. Leiden [etc.]: Martinus Nijhoff, 2005, p. 33-65.) [P.C.I.J., p. 34; I.C.J., p. 33, 35-37, 39-41, 45, 47, 51, 55, 56, 59, 60, 64.]

Reisman, William Michael and Arsanjani, Mahnoush H.: The question of unilateral governmental statements as applicable law in investment disputes. (In: ICSID Review: Foreign Investment Law Journal, 2004, v. 19, no. 2, p. 328-343.) [P.C.I.J., p. 329-332; I.C.J., passim.]

Reisman, William Michael and Arsanjani, Mahnoush H.: The question of unilateral governmental statements as applicable law in investment disputes. (In: Völkerrecht als Wertordnung: Festschrift für Christian Tomuschat, sous la dir. de Pierre-Marie Dupuy; Bardo Fassbender; Malcolm N. Shaw; Karl-Peter Sommermann. Kehl: N. P. Engel, 2006, p. 409-422.) [P.C.I.J., p. 410-412; I.C.J., passim.]

Riedel, Eibe: The development of international law: alternatives to treaty-making? International organizations and non-state actors. (In: Developments of international law in treaty making, ed. by Rüdiger Wolfrum; Volker Röben. Berlin, [etc.]: Springer, 2005, p. 301-318.) [I.C.J., p. 310, 315.]

Sandrock, Corinna: Allgemeine Rechtsgrundsätze im Verfahrensrecht der WTO: die Anwendbarkeit verfahrensrechtlicher allgemeiner Rechtsgrundsätze i.S.v. Art. 38 (1) lit. c IGH-Statut durch die streitbeilegungsorgane der WTO. Heidelberg: Verlag Recht und Wirtschaft, 2004. (Schriften zum Aussenwirtschaftsrecht.) [P.C.I.J., see index p. 354; I.C.J., see index page 353.]

Simma, Bruno: Foreword. (In: International law and sustainable development: principles and practice, ed. by Nico Schrijver; Friedl Weiss. Leiden [etc.]: Martinus Nijhoff, 2004, v-vi.) [I.C.J., p. vi.]

Suy, Eric: Unilateral acts of States as a source of international law: some new thoughts and frustrations. (In: Droit du pouvoir, pouvoir du droit: mélanges offerts à Jean Salmon. Bruxelles: Bruylant, 2007, p. 631-642.) [I.C.J., p. 634, 639-640.]

Thirlway, Hugh: The law and procedure of the International Court of Justice 1960-1989 (supplement 2005) (parts one and two). (In: British Year Book of International Law, 2005, v. 76, p. 1-119.) [P.C.I.J., p. 16, 43-44, 51, 67, 71, 115, 117; I.C.J., passim.]

Toro Huerta, Mauricio Iván del: El fenómeno del soft law y las nuevas perspectivas del derecho internacional. (Dans: Anuario mexicano de derecho internacional, 2006, v. 6, p. 513-549.) [C.P.J.I., p. 528; C.I.J., p. 526-529, 543-544.]

Tourme-Jouannet, Emmanuelle: L'ambivalence des principes généraux face au caractère étrange et complexe de l'ordre juridique international. (Dans: L'influence des sources sur l'unité et la fragmentation du droit international: travaux du séminaire tenu à Palma, les 20-21 mai 2005, sous la dir. de Rosario Huesa Vinaixa; Karel Wellens. Bruxelles: Bruylant, 2006, p. 115-154.) [C.I.J., p. 136, 140-142, 153.]

Tsagourias, Nicholas: The constitutional role of general principles of law in international and European jurisprudence. (In: Transnational constitutionalism: international and European perspectives, ed. by Nicholas Tsagourias. Cambridge: Cambridge University Press, 2007, p. 71-106.) [I.C.J., passim.]

Tsagourias, Nicholas: The will of the international community as a normative source of international law. (In: Governance and international legal theory, ed. by Dekker, Ige F.; Werner, Wouter G.. Leiden; Boston, 2004, p. 97-121.) [P.C.I.J., p. 101-102; I.C.J., p. 100, 102, 106, 117.]

Vagts, Detlev F.: International relations looks at customary international law: a traditionalist's defence. (In: European Journal of International Law, 2004, v. 15, no. 5, p. 1031-1040.) [I.C.J., p. 1035.]

Vanhamme, Jan: Formation and enforcement of customary international law: the European Union's contribution. (In: Netherlands Yearbook of International Law, 2008, v. 39, p. 127-154.) [I.C.J., p. 128, 132-137, 148-152.]

Wellens, Karel C.: Quelques réflexions d'introduction. (Dans: L'influence des sources sur l'unité et la fragmentation du droit international: travaux du séminaire tenu à Palma, les 20-21 mai 2005, sous la dir. de Rosario Huesa Vinaixa; Karel Wellens. Bruxelles: Bruylant, 2006, p. 1-21.) [C.I.J., p. 11-12, 15, 18-20.]

Wessel, Ramses A.: Editorial: the U.N., the E.U. and jus cogens. (In: International Organizations Law Review, 2006, v. 3, p. 1-6.) [I.C.J., p. 4-5.]

White, Nigel D.: The ties that bind: the EU, the UN and international law. (In: Netherlands Yearbook of International Law, 2006, v. 37, p. 57-107.) [P.C.I.J., p. 74; I.C.J., p. 66, 70-71, 74, 77, 79, 81, 86.]

Wouters, Jan: Bronnen van het internationaal recht. (In: Handboek internationaal recht, ed. by Horbach, Nathalie L. J. T.; Lefeber, René; Ribbelink, Olivier. The Hague: T.M.C. Asser Press, 2007, p. 81-122.) [P.C.I.J., p. 84, 89, 101, 104, 108; I.C.J., p. 82-84, 86-91, 98-100, 102-104, 106-111, 115-116, 118-119, 121.]

Zapatero Miguel, Pablo: Sistemas jurídicos especiales. (Dans: Revista española de derecho internacional, 2005, v. 57, no. 1, p. 187-207.) [C.I.J., p. 195-196.]

Ziemele, Ineta: Case-law of the European Court of Human Rights and Integrity of International Law. (In: L'influence des sources sur l'unité et la fragmentation du droit international: travaux du séminaire tenu à Palma, les 20-21 mai 2005, ed. by Rosario Huesa Vinaixa; Karel Wellens. Bruxelles: Bruylant, 2006, p. 187-210.) [I.C.J., p. 188, 191-193, 195, 197-198.]

3. Sujets du droit international
3. Subjects of international law

Amann, Diane Marie: The International Criminal Court and the sovereign State. (In: Governance and international legal theory, ed. by Dekker, Ige F.; Werner, Wouter G.. Leiden; Boston, 2004, p. 185-212.) [I.C.J., p. 189, 196, 208.]

Aspects of the law of State succession. (In: Reports of the Annual Conference, by International Law Association (ILA), 2006, 2006, p. 301-336.) [P.C.I.J., p. 304; I.C.J., p. 331.]

Benvenuti, Paolo: Principi generali del diritto, giurisdizioni internazionali e mutamenti sociali nella vita di relazione internazionale. (Dans: Studi di diritto internazionale in onore di Gaetano Arangio-Ruiz, sous la dir. de Giovanni Battaglini; Paolo Benvenuti; Antonio Cassese; Giorgio Gaja. Napoli: Editoriale Scientifica, 2004, v. 1, p. 295-312.) [C.P.J.I., 295, 297, 301-305; C.I.J., p. 296, 301, 305-307.]

Blank, Yishai: The city and the world. (In: Columbia Journal of Transnational Law, 2006, v. 44, p. 875-939.) [I.C.J., p. 875-939.]

Blokker, Niels: Recht van international oraganisaties. (In: Handboek internationaal recht, ed. by Horbach, Nathalie L. J. T.; Lefeber, René;

Ribbelink, Olivier. The Hague: T.M.C. Asser Press, 2007, p. 437-468.) [I.C.J., p. 443, 449, 452, 454-465.]

Brandt Ahrens, Cherylyn: Chechnya and the right of self-determination. (In: Columbia Journal of Transnational Law, 2004, v. 42, no. 2, p. 575-615.) [I.C.J., p. 576, 585-592, 612-613.]

Cahin, Gérard: L'état défaillant en droit international: quel régime pour quelle notion? (Dans: Droit du pouvoir, pouvoir du droit: mélanges offerts à Jean Salmon. Bruxelles: Bruylant, 2007, p. 177-209.) [C.I.J., p. 195, 196, 198, 200, 201, 208, 209.]

Cançado Trindade, A. A.: A consolidação da personalidade e da capacidade jurídicas do indivíduo como sujeito do direito internacional. (Dans: Justicia, libertad y derechos humanos: ensayos en homenaje a Rodolfo E. Piza Escalante. San José (Costa Rica): Instituto Interamericano de Derechos Humanos, 2003, p. 3-76.) [C.P.J.I., p. 43-48; C.I.J., 20, 43-48.]

Cançado Trindade, A. A.: Direitos humanos: personalidade e capacidade juridica internacional do individuo. (Dans: O Brasil e os novos desafios do direito internacional, sous la dir. de Brant, Leonardo Nemer Caldeira. Rio de Janeiro: Editora Forense, 2004, p. 199-263.) [C.P.J.I., p. 226; C.I.J., p. 224, 226-230.]

Cançado Trindade, A. A.: The emancipation of the individual from his own State: the historical recovery of the human person as a subject of the law of nations. (In: Human rights, democracy and the rule of law: liber amicorum Luzius Wildhaber, ed. by Stephan Breitenmoser. Zurich: Dike: Nomos, 2007, p. 151-171.) [I.C.J., p. 162, 170.]

Charnovitz, Steve: The relevance of non-State actors to international law. (In: Developments of international law in treaty making, ed. by Rüdiger Wolfrum; Volker Röben. Berlin, [etc.]: Springer, 2005, p. 543-556.) [I.C.J., p. 545, 546, 553-555.]

Cheng, Bin: Hazards in international law sharing legal terms and concepts with municipal law without sufficiently taking into account the differences in structure between the two systems: prime examples: custom and opinio juris. (In: Studi di diritto internazionale in onore di Gaetano Arangio-Ruiz, ed. by Giovanni Battaglini; Paolo Benvenuti; Antonio Cassese; Giorgio Gaja. Napoli: Editoriale Scientifica, 2004, v. 1, p. 469-494.) [P.C.I.J., p. 470, 471, 475, 481-484; I.C.J., 470-472, 475, 481, 486-488, 492.]

Cheng, Tai-Heng: State succession and commercial obligations. Ardsley, N.Y.: Transnational Publishers, 2006. [I.C.J., p. 25, 70, 76, 114-115, 153, 175, 178-187, 196, 201-202, 239, 249, 251-258, 263, 265-266, 289-290, 302, 323, 330-333, 384, 387, 402.]

Chernichenko, Stanislas V. and Kotliar, Vladimir S.: Ongoing global legal debate on self-determination and secession: main trends. (In: Secession and international law: conflict avoidance: regional appraisals, ed. by Dahlitz, Julie. The Hague: T.M.C. Asser Press, 2003, p. 75-88.) [I.C.J., p. 87.]

Ciciriello, Maria Clelia: La soggettività internazionale dell'Ordine di Malta: un problema ancora aperto? (Dans: Studi di diritto internazionale in onore di Gaetano Arangio-Ruiz, sous la dir. de Giovanni Battaglini; Paolo Benvenuti; Antonio Cassese; Giorgio Gaja. Napoli: Editoriale Scientifica, 2004, v. 1, p. 47-70.) [C.I.J., p. 50, 53.]

Cohen, Amichai: Domestic courts and sovereignty. (In: The shifting allocation of authority in international law: considering sovereignty, supremacy and subsidiarity: essays in honour of Professor Ruth Lapidoth, ed. by Tomer Broude; Yuval Shany. Oxford; Portland: Hart Publishing, 2008, p. 265-292.) [I.C.J., p. 272, 280-284, 286.]

d'Aspremont, Jean: La création internationale d'Etats démocratiques. (Dans: Revue générale de droit international public, 2005, v. 109, no. 4, p. 889-908.) [C.I.J., p. 898-899.]

d'Aspremont, Jean: Regulating statehood: the Kosovo status settlement. (In: Leiden Journal of International Law, 2007, v. 20, p. 649-668.) [I.C.J., p. 652, 662, 664, 666.]

De Kerchove, Gilles et Marquardt, Stephan: Les accords internationaux conclus par l'Union européenne. (Dans: Annuaire français de droit international, 2004, v. 50, p. 803-825.) [C.I.J., p. 11, 19-20.]

de Passalaqua, J. L. A.: Secession in North America: the United States & Puerto Rico. (In: Secession and international law: conflict avoidance: regional appraisals, ed. by Dahlitz, Julie. The Hague: T.M.C. Asser Press, 2003, p. 207-226.) [I.C.J., p. 216.]

Dekker, Ige F. and Schrijver, Nico J.: Internationale rechtssubjecten. (In: Handboek internationaal recht, ed. by Horbach, Nathalie L. J. T.; Lefeber, René; Ribbelink, Olivier. The Hague: T.M.C. Asser Press, 2007, p. 19-46.) [I.C.J., p. 24, 26, 28-30, 40, 43.]

Dinstein, Yoram: Sovereignty, the Security Council and the use of force. (In: Redefining sovereignty: the use of force after the Cold War, ed. by Michael Bothe; Mary Ellen O'Connell; Natalino Ronzitti. Ardsley: Transnational Publishers, 2005, p. 111-122.) [P.C.I.J., p. 112; I.C.J., p. 114.]

Dugard, John R.: A legal basis for secession: relevant principles and rules. (In: Secession and international law: conflict avoidance: regional appraisals, ed. by Dahlitz, Julie. The Hague: T.M.C. Asser Press, 2003, p. 89-96.) [I.C.J., p. 91, 92.]

Dumberry, Patrick: Is a new State responsible for obligations arising from internationally wrongful acts committed before its independence in the context of secession? (In: Canadian Yearbook of International Law, 2005, v. 43, p. 419-453.) [I.C.J., p. 445, 450.]

Dumberry, Patrick: L'entreprise, sujet de droit international? Retour sur la question à la lumière des développements récents du droit international des investissements. (Dans: Revue générale de droit international public, 2004, v. 108, no. 1, p. 103-122.) [C.I.J., p. 111, 115, 117-119, 121.]

Dumberry, Patrick: New State responsibility for internationally wrongful acts by an insurrectional movement. (In: European Journal of International Law, 2006, v. 17, p. 605-621.) [P.C.I.J., p. 613.]

Dumberry, Patrick: Obsolete and unjust: the rule of continuous nationality in the context of State succession. (In: Nordic Journal of International Law, 2007, v. 76, p. 153-183.) [P.C.I.J., p. 154, 160, 169, 177, 183; I.C.J., p. 160-161.]

Eudes, Marina: Retour sur une réussite passé inaperçue: l'accord de Belfast et la nouvelle lecture du droit à l'autodétermination. (Dans: Revue générale de droit international public, 2006, v. 110, p. 631-646.) [C.I.J., p. 637, 642.]

Fujioka, Yuka: Does sovereignty help us to understand international politics? Its change and robustness from the debate between realism and constructivism. (In: Kobe University Law Review, 2005, v. 39, p. 23-37.) [I.C.J., p. 31.]

Geiß, Robin: Failed States: legal aspects and security implications. (In: German Yearbook of International Law, 2004, v. 47, p. 457-501.) [I.C.J., p. 461, 470, 478-479, 487.]

Geiß, Robin: Non-State actors: their role and impact on the fragmentation of international law. (In: Unity and diversity in international law: proceedings of an international symposium of the Kiel Walther Schücking Institute of International Law, November 4-7, 2004, ed. by Zimmermann, Andreas; Hofmann, Rainer. Berlin: Duncker & Humblot, 2006, p. 303-327.) [P.C.I.J., p. 323; I.C.J., p. 305, 314-315, 323, 325-326.]

Guarino, Giancarlo: Personalità giuridica di diritto internazionale: il caso dell'Organizzaxione per la Liberazione della Palestina. (Dans: Studi di diritto internazionale in onore di Gaetano Arangio-Ruiz, sous la dir. de Giovanni Battaglini; Paolo Benvenuti; Antonio Cassese; Giorgio Gaja. Napoli: Editoriale Scientifica, 2004, v. 1, p. 85-130.) [C.I.J., p. 92, 95.]

Hamant, Hélène: La succession d'Etats de l'U.R.S.S. en matière militaire. (Dans: Annuaire français de droit international, 2004, v. 50, p. 213-230.) [C.P.J.I., p. 225.]

Higgins, Rosalyn: Self-determination and secession. (In: Secession and international law: conflict avoidance: regional appraisals, ed. by Dahlitz, Julie. The Hague: T.M.C. Asser Press, 2003, p. 21-38.) [I.C.J., p. 25.]

Hilpold, Peter: What role for academic writers in interpreting international law? A rejoinder to Orakhelashvili. (In: Chinese Journal of International Law, 2009, v. 8, no. 2, p. 291-298.) [I.C.J., p. 296, 298.]

Husain, Amin M.: Who is the legitimate representative of the Palestinian people? (In: Chinese Journal of International Law, 2003, v. 2, no. 1, p. 207-225.) [I.C.J., p. 212, 213, 214.]

Jennings, Robert Y.: Reflections on the subsidiary means for the determination of rules of law. (In: Studi di diritto internazionale in onore di

Gaetano Arangio-Ruiz, ed. by Giovanni Battaglini ; Paolo Benvenuti ; Antonio Cassese ; Giorgio Gaja. Napoli : Editoriale Scientifica, 2004, v. 1, p. 319-338.) [P.C.I.J., p. 333-335; I.C.J., p. 319-321, 325-329, 331-333, 335.]

Kamto, Maurice : La volonté de l'Etat en droit international. (Dans : Recueil des cours de l'Académie de droit international de La Haye, 2004, v. 310, p. 9-428.) [C.P.J.I., p. 61-62, 74-75, 102, 106, 113, 122, 126-129, 135, 154, 166-167, 171-172, 212-213, 236, 260, 264, 282-283, 287, 293, 297, 302, 304-305, 307, 331, 349, 386, 393-395, 399; C.I.J., p. 65-66, 72-74, 75, 78, 81, 82-84, 87-89, 91-93, 96, 99-101, 104-107, 109, 111-114, 116-124, 129-133, 135-140, 142-147, 149-150, 152, 157-158, 163-168, 172, 184, 204-205, 209, 211, 213-215, 217, 223-225, 234-238, 263, 265, 269-270, 272-273, 275-279, 282, 283-296, 298-302, 308-310, 321, 323-328, 333-335, 337-338, 340, 342-344, 346-349, 351-353, 362-363, 365-366, 377-378, 381-382, 386-426.]

Kandeh, Jimmy D. : Civil-military relations. (In : West Africa's security challenges : building peace in a troubled region, ed. by Adekeye Adebajo ; Ismail Rashid. Boulder : Lynne Rienner Publishers, 2004, p. 145-168.) [I.C.J., p. 154.]

Kattan, Victor : The nationality of denationalized Palestinians. (In : Nordic Journal of International Law, 2005, v. 74, p. 67-102.) [P.C.I.J., p. 72; I.C.J., p. 70.]

Kohen, Marcelo G. (ed.) : Secession : international law perspectives. New York, NY [etc.] : Cambridge University Press, 2006. [P.C.I.J., p. 72, 475; I.C.J., p. 10-11, 27, 34, 36, 38-40, 44, 57, 69, 71, 73, 77-78, 81, 85, 156, 169-170, 191, 195, 197, 200-201, 203, 206, 212, 214, 217-221, 234, 241, 244-245, 250, 253, 264, 500.]

Miele, Alberto : L'indipendenza degli stati. (Dans : Studi di diritto internazionale in onore di Gaetano Arangio-Ruiz, sous la dir. de Giovanni Battaglini ; Paolo Benvenuti ; Antonio Cassese ; Giorgio Gaja. Napoli : Editoriale Scientifica, 2004, v. 1, p. 169-190.) [C.P.J.I., p. 171.]

Miller, Russell A. : Legitimacy, blind spots and paradoxes of personality. (In : Select Proceedings of the European Society of International Law, ed. by James Crawford ; Sarah M. H. Nouwen. Oxford ; Portland : Hart, 2008, v. 2, p. 267-293.) [I.C.J., p. 270.]

Minnerop, Petra : Paria-Staaten im Völkerrecht? Berlin : Springer, 2004. (Beiträge zum ausländischen öffentlichen Recht und Völkerrecht ; 178.) [P.C.I.J., p. 59, 341, 343, 352; I.C.J., p. 8-9, 43, 66, 333-334, 342, 344, 346, 348, 361-362, 365, 369, 378, 387, 405-409, 453-455, 466-469, 484-485, 487-488, 490.]

Neukirchen, Mathias : Taiwan : eigenständig, aber nicht souverän : zur Frage der Aufnahme der Republik China in die Vereinten Nationen. (In : Vereinte Nationen, 2005, v. 53, no. 2, p. 50-55.) [I.C.J., p. 52, 53.]

Oeter, Stefan : The dismemberment of Yugoslavia : an update on Bosnia and Herzegovina, Kosovo and Montenegro. (In : German Yearbook of

International Law, 2007, v. 50, p. 457-521.) [I.C.J., p. 458, 460, 462-463, 470, 472-474.]

Organization of American States: The OAS in transition 1994-2004. [S.l.]: OAS: [s.n.], 2004. [I.C.J., p. 93-95.]

Paust, Jordan J.: Comment: [on Non-State actors: their role and impact on the fragmentation of international law by Robin Geiß]. (In: Unity and diversity in international law: proceedings of an international symposium of the Kiel Walther Schücking Institute of International Law, November 4-7, 2004, ed. by Zimmermann, Andreas; Hofmann, Rainer. Berlin: Duncker & Humblot, 2006, p. 325-338.) [I.C.J., p. 325-326.]

Permanent Court of Arbitration (PCA), Eritrea-Ethiopia Claims Commissions: partial award, civilian claims-Ethiopia's claim 5 (December 17, 2004). (In: International Legal Materials, 2005, v. 44, p. 545-568.) [I.C.J., p. 550.]

Pietrobon, Alessandra: Dalla comity all'opinio iuris: note sull'elemento psicologico nella formazione della consuetudine. (Dans: Studi di diritto internazionale in onore di Gaetano Arangio-Ruiz, sous la dir. de Giovanni Battaglini; Paolo Benvenuti; Antonio Cassese; Giorgio Gaja. Napoli: Editoriale Scientifica, 2004, v. 1, p. 355-374.) [C.P.J.I., p. 355, 356; C.I.J., p. 355, 356, 373.]

Pinto, M. C. W.: Power and preference: participation in the making of international law. (In: Studi di diritto internazionale in onore di Gaetano Arangio-Ruiz, ed. by Giovanni Battaglini; Paolo Benvenuti; Antonio Cassese; Giorgio Gaja. Napoli: Editoriale Scientifica, 2004, v. 1, p. 375-419.) [I.C.J., p. 376.]

Puoti, Paola: La questione jugoslava davanti alla Corte internazionale di giustizia: contributi alla ricostruzione degli istituti della successione, della causa comune, della cancellazione della causa dal ruolo e delle misure cautelari. Napoli: Editorale scientifica, 2004. (Studi di diritto internazionale e dell'Unione europea; 3.)

Rabkin, Jeremy A.: Law without nations? Why constitutional government requires sovereign States. Princeton; Oxford: Princeton University Press, 2007. [P.C.I.J., p. 121, 123; I.C.J., p. 163, 170, 220.]

Röben, Volker: Proliferation of actors. (In: Developments of international law in treaty making, ed. by Rüdiger Wolfrum; Volker Röben. Berlin, [etc.]: Springer, 2005, p. 511-536.) [I.C.J., p. 535.]

Ronen, Yaël: Recognition of divorce without recognition of statehood. (In: Cambridge Law Journal, 2004, v. 63, p. 268-271.) [I.C.J., p. 269.]

Rosenne, Shabtai: Israel: some legal aspects of the transition from mandate to independence: December 1947 – 15 May 1948. (In: Essays on international law and practice, by Shabtai Rosenne. Leiden; Boston: Martinus Nijhoff, 2007, p. 649-682.)

Roucounas, Emmanuel: Civil society and its international dimension. (In: Droit du pouvoir, pouvoir du droit: mélanges offerts à Jean Salmon. Bruxelles: Bruylant, 2007, 555--567.) [I.C.J., p. 561.]

Sanchez, José: 1993-2003: dix ans de souveraineté andorrane. (Dans: Revue générale de droit international public, 2005, v. 109, p. 123-146.) [C.I.J., p. 136.]

Schrijver, Nico J.: Secession and the ban on the use of force: some reflections. (In: Secession and international law: conflict avoidance: regional appraisals, ed. by Dahlitz, Julie. The Hague: T.M.C. Asser Press, 2003, p. 97-108.) [I.C.J., p. 98.]

Seidel, Gerhard: Die Palästinafrage und das Völkerrecht. (In: Archiv des Völkerrechts, 2006, v. 44, p. 121-158.) [I.C.J. p. 123, 129, 131, 133, 136, 138, 145, 151.]

Shaw, Malcolm N.: The role of recognition and non-recognition with respect to secession: notes on some relevant issues. (In: Secession and international law: conflict avoidance: regional appraisals, ed. by Dahlitz, Julie. The Hague: T.M.C. Asser Press, 2003, p. 243-257.) [I.C.J., p. 251.]

Shelton, Dinah: Self-determination and secession: the jurisprudence of international human rights tribunals. (In: Secession and international law: conflict avoidance: regional appraisals, ed. by Dahlitz, Julie. The Hague: T.M.C. Asser Press, 2003, p. 47-72.) [I.C.J., p. 68.]

Sina, Stephan: Der völkerrechtliche Status des Westjordanlandes und des Gaza-Streifens nach den Osloer Verträgen. Berlin [etc.]: Springer, 2004. (Beiträge zum ausländischen öffentlichen Recht und Völkerrecht; 167.) [I.C.J., p. 23, 117, 128, 155, 271, 292.]

Strawson, John: British (and international) legal foundations for the Israeli wall: international law and multi-colonialism. (In: Palestine Yearbook of International Law, 2004, v. 13, p. 1-26.) [I.C.J., p. 1, 18-19, 26.]

Summers, James J.: The rhetoric and practice of self-determination: a right of all peoples or political institutions. (In: Nordic Journal of International Law, 2004, v. 73, no. 3, p. 325-363.) [I.C.J., p. 341.]

Talmon, Stefan: The constitutive versus the declaratory theory of recognition: tertium non datur? (In: British Year Book of International Law, 2004, v. 75, p. 101-182.) [P.C.I.J., p. 108, 111, 128, 138; I.C.J., passim.]

Tavernier, Paul: Variations sur le thème de l'autodétermination des peuples (de Reims à La Haye). (In: Droit du pouvoir, pouvoir du droit: mélanges offerts à Jean Salmon. Bruxelles: Bruylant, 2007, p. 1095-1110.) [C.I.J., p. 1096, 1101, 1103, 1105-1110.]

Thürer, Daniel: Comment: [on Non-State actors: their role and impact on the fragmentation of international law by Robin Geiß]. (In: Unity and diversity in international law: proceedings of an international symposium of the Kiel Walther Schücking Institute of International Law, November 4-7,

2004, ed. by Zimmermann, Andreas; Hofmann, Rainer. Berlin: Duncker & Humblot, 2006, p. 339-344.) [I.C.J., p. 341.]

Tupaz, A. Edsel C. F.: Self-determination as "defined" under the United Nations draft declaration on the rights of indigenous peoples: secession or autonomy? (In: Ateneo law journal, 2007, v. 51, no. 4, p. 1039-1078.) [I.C.J., p. 1062-1063, 1075-1076.]

Vermeulen, Mathias: Kosovo's future status: opening a Pandora's box of secessionist's claims or a precedent for the "responsibility to protect"? (In: Studia diplomatica, 2006, 59, p. 77-92.) [I.C.J., p. 78-79.]

Vidmar, Jure: International legal responses to Kosovo's declaration of independence. (In: Vanderbilt Journal of Transnational Law, 2009, v. 42, p. 779-851.) [I.C.J., p. 783, 813, 826.]

Wafa-Mohammed, Achraf: Effet de la succession d'Etats sur la mise en oeuvre du droit international privé. (In: Revue égyptienne de droit international, 2005, v. 61, p. 213-328.) [C.P.J.I., p. 245, 265.]

Wang, Zhi-an: The creation of States and the function of international law: defining a new status for the recognition of States. (In: Kokusaiho Gaiko Zassi, 2003, v. 102, no. 3, p. 31-58.) [I.C.J., p. 46, 48, 49.]

Weckel, Philippe: Plaidoyer pour le processus d'indépendance du Kosovo: réponse à Olivier Corten. (Dans: Revue générale de droit international public, 2009, v. 113, no. 2, p. 257-271.) [C.I.J., p. 257, 258, 266.]

4. Compétences de l'Etat
4. State jurisdiction

Abraham, Garth: "Lines upon maps": Africa and the sanctity of African boundaries. (In: African Journal of International and Comparative Law, 2007, v. 15, no. 1, p. 61-84.) [I.C.J., p. 61-62, 71-75, 78-79.]

Alves Pereira, Antonio Celso: Soberania e pós-modern idade. (Dans: O Brasil e os novos desafios do direito internacional, sous la dir. de Brant, Leonardo Nemer Caldeira. Rio de Janeiro: Editora Forense, 2004, p. 619-662.) [C.P.J.I., p. 638; C.I.J., p. 656.]

Beinin, Joel: Histories and futures of a failed peace. (In: The struggle for sovereignty: Palestine and Israel, 1993-2005, ed. by Joel Beinin; Rebecca L. Stein. Stanford: Stanford University Press, 2006, p. 1-17.) [I.C.J., p. 11.]

Biehler, Gernot: Procedures in international law. Berlin: Springer, 2008. [P.C.I.J., p. 40, 273, 281, 289; I.C.J., see index p. 346.]

Boeglin Naumovic, Nicolas: De l'usage des cours d'eau internationaux comme frontières. (Dans: Les ressources en eau et le droit international, sous la dir. de Laurence Boisson de Chazournes; Salman M. A. Salman. Leiden; Boston: Martinus Nijhoff, 2005, p. 133-165.) [C.P.J.I., p. 136, 156, 164; C.I.J., p. 134-136, 141-144, 146, 149, 154, 163-164.]

D'Orsi, Cristiano: Les spécificités du droit international en Afrique sub-saharienne avec une particulière référence à l'intégration du droit international dans l'ordre juridique interne des pays d'Afrique sub-saharienne. (Dans: Revue hellénique de droit international, 2005, v. 58, no. 2, p. 593-615.) [C.I.J., p. 600, 607-608.]

Dutta, Anatol: Public policy und die Wirkungen des Völkerrechts im englischen Internatiolen Privatrecht: die Enstcheidung des House of Lords in Kuwait Airways Corp v. Iraqi Airways Co. (Nos. 4 and 5). (In: Rabels Zeitschrift für ausländisches und internationales Privatrecht, 2005, v. 69, no. 1, p. 101-123.) [I.C.J., p. 113.]

Gray, Christine: The Eritrea/Ethiopia Claims Commission oversteps its boundaries: a partial award? (In: European Journal of International Law, 2006, v. 17, no. 4, p. 699-721.) [I.C.J., p. 713-714, 715-721.]

Hammami, Rema and Tamari, Salim: Anatomy of another rebellion: from intifada to interregnum. (In: The struggle for sovereignty: Palestine and Israel, 1993-2005, ed. by Joel Beinin; Rebecca L. Stein. Stanford: Stanford University Press, 2006, p. 263-281.) [I.C.J., p. 281.]

Hoogh, André J. J. de and Molier, Gelijn: Jurisdictie. (In: Handboek internationaal recht, ed. by Horbach, Nathalie L. J. T.; Lefeber, René; Ribbelink, Olivier. The Hague: T.M.C. Asser Press, 2007, p. 195-229.) [P.C.I.J., p. 199, 206, 216; I.C.J., p. 196, 202, 204, 210-211, 222, 225-226.]

Inazumi, Mitsue: Universal jurisdiction in modern international law: expansion of national jurisdiction for prosecuting serious crimes under international law. Antwerpen: Intersentia, 2005. (School of human rights research; 19.)

Köck, Heribert Franz: Grundsätzliches zu Primat und Vorrang des Unions-bzw: Gemeinschaftsrechts im Verhältnis zum mitgliedstaatlichen Recht oder als die Frösche keinen König haben wollten. (In: Internationale Gemeinschaft und Menschenrechte: Festschrift für Georg Ress zum 70. Geburtstag am 21. Januar 2005, ed. by Bröhmer, Jürgen; Bieber, Roland; Calliess, Christian; Langenfeld, Christine; Weber, Stefan; Wolf, Joachim. Köln [etc.]: Heymann, 2005, p. 557-576.) [I.C.J., p. 562, 570-571.]

Kolb, Robert: Du domaine réservé: réflexions sur la théorie de la compétence nationale. (Dans: Revue générale de droit international public, 2006, v. 110, p. 597-630.) [C.P.J.I., p. 615; C.I.J., p. 619-622.]

Lange-Bertalot, Nils: Weltbürgerliches Völkerrecht: Kantianische Brücke zwischen konstitutioneller Souveränität und humanitärer Intervention. Berlin: Duncker & Humblot, 2005. (Schriften zum Völkerrecht; 169.) [P.C.I.J. p. 116; I.C.J. p. 82, 137, 142, 150, 155, 164, 184, 214, 415, 425, 447, 457-462, 493-494, 5.]

Lenzerini, Federico: Sovereignty revisited: international law and parallel sovereignty of indigenous peoples. (In: Texas International Law Journal, 2006, v. 42, p. 155-189.) [I.C.J., p. 164, 167, 187.]

Mangu, André Mbata B.: States' revenge against people in international law: requiem for universal jurisdiction? (In: Indian Journal of International Law, 2004, v. 44, no. 2, p. 324-346.) [I.C.J., p. 324, 328, 329, 332, 334-336.]

Mbengue, Makane Moïse: Le statut du fleuve Sénégal: visages actuels. (Dans: Les ressources en eau et le droit international, sous la dir. de Laurence Boisson de Chazournes; Salman M. A. Salman. Leiden; Boston: Martinus Nijhoff, 2005, p. 473-532.) [C.P.J.I., p. 488-490, 494, 500, 521; C.I.J., p. 497, 499-500, 506, 509.]

McGinnis, John O.: Medellin and the future of international delegation. (In: Yale Law Journal, 2009, v. 118, no. 8, p. 1712-1760.) [I.C.J., p. 1715-1716, 1725-1730, 1734-1736.]

McGregor, Lorna: Torture and State immunity: deflecting impunity, distorting sovereignty. (In: European Journal of International Law, 2007, v. 18, p. 903-919.) [P.C.I.J., p. 911; I.C.J., p. 907-908, 916.]

Michaels, Ralf: Territorial jurisdiction after territoriality. (In: Globalisation and jurisdiction, ed. by Piet Jan Slot; Mielle Bulterman. Leiden: Kluwer Law International, 2004, p. 105-130.) [P.C.I.J., p. 106.]

Nagan, Winston P. and Hammer, Craig: The changing character of sovereignty in international law and international relations. (In: Columbia Journal of Transnational Law, 2004, v. 43, no. 1, p. 141-187.) [I.C.J., p. 157-159, 162; P.C.I.J., p. 154, 159.]

Nishimura, Mika: Constraints on sovereignty in the Chemical Weapons Convention from the perspective of international law. (In: Sovereignty and the global community: the quest for order in the international system, ed. by Hensel, Howard M. Aldershot [etc.]: Ashgate, 2004, p. 55-82.) [I.C.J., p. 63-64, 70-71.]

Paulus, Andreas L.: From territoriality to functionality? Towards a legal methodology of globalization. (In: Governance and international legal theory, ed. by Dekker, Ige F.; Werner, Wouter G.. Leiden; Boston, 2004, p. 59-95.) [P.C.I.J., p. 72; I.C.J., p. 63-66, 70, 79, 86, 93.]

Pedersen, Morten Peschardt: Territorial jurisdiction in Article 1 of the European Convention on Human Rights. (In: Nordic Journal of International Law, 2004, v. 73, p. 279-305.) [I.C.J. and P.C.I.J., p. 280, 284, 287.]

Popovski, Vesselin: Sovereignty as duty to protect human rights. (In: United Nations chronicle, 2004, v. 41, no. 4, p. 16-18.) [I.C.J., p. 18.]

Querol, María: Rethinking international rivers and lakes as boundaries. (In: Les ressources en eau et le droit international, ed. by Laurence Boisson de Chazournes; Salman M. A. Salman. Leiden; Boston: Martinus Nijhoff, 2005, p. 97-132.) [I.C.J., p. 109-110, 115-116, 127-128.]

Rodrigo Hernández, Angel J.: Soberanía y administración de territorios. (Dans: Anuario de derecho internacional, 2004, v. 20, p. 279-326.) [C.I.J., p. 305-306.]

Roht-Arriaza, Naomi: Universal jurisdiction: steps forward, steps back. (In: Leiden Journal of International Law, 2004, v. 17, no. 2, p. 375-389.) [I.C.J., p. 376, 385-386.]

Rossi, Matthias: Extraterritorial geschlossene Verwaltungsverträge. (In: Archiv des Völkerrechts, 2007, v. 45, p. 115-135.) [P.C.I.J. p. 119-120, 123; I.C.J. p. 119, 134.]

Salerno, Francesco: Il neo-dualismo della Corte costituzionale nei rapporti tra diritto internazionale e diritto interno. (Dans: Rivista di diritto internazionale, 2006, v. 89, p. 340-383.) [C.P.J.I., p. 371-372; C.I.J., p. 341, 380.]

Sciacovelli, Annita Larissa: La controversia confinaria tra Eritrea ed Etiopia. (Dans: Rivista di diritto internazionale, 2004, v. 87, no. 3, p. 730-751.) [C.I.J., p. 743, 746-747, 749.]

Shany, Yuval: Jurisdictional competition between national and international courts: could international jurisdiction-regulating rules apply? (In: Netherlands Yearbook of International Law, 2006, v. 37, p. 3-56.) [P.C.I.J., p. 4, 21, 24, 29, 33, 35, 39-40, 48; I.C.J., p. 8, 17, 19, 22, 24-25, 40-42, 51-54.]

Shaw, Malcolm N.: The acquisition of title in nineteenth century Africa: some thoughts. (In: Völkerrecht als Wertordnung: Festschrift für Christian Tomuschat, ed. by Pierre-Marie Dupuy; Bardo Fassbender; Malcolm N. Shaw; Karl-Peter Sommermann. Kehl: N. P. Engel, 2006, p. 1029-1049.)

Shaw, Malcolm N.: Territorial administration by non-territorial sovereigns. (In: The shifting allocation of authority in international law: considering sovereignty, supremacy and subsidiarity: essays in honour of Professor Ruth Lapidoth, ed. by Tomer Broude; Yuval Shany. Oxford; Portland: Hart Publishing, 2008, p. 369-415.) [I.C.J., p. 371, 375-378, 383-384; P.C.I.J., p. 399.]

Shaw, Malcolm N.: Title, control, and closure? The experience of the Eritrea-Ethiopia Boundary Commission. (In: International and Comparative Law Quarterly, 2007, v. 56, no. 4, p. 755-796.) [I.C.J., p. 755, 758-759, 761-762, 776-777, 790.]

Simpson, Gerry: Great powers and outlaw States: unequal sovereigns in the international legal order. Cambridge: Cambridge University Press, 2004. (Cambridge Studies in International and Comparative Law.) [P.C.I.J., p. 28-29, 43, 118, 157-158; I.C.J., p. 21-22, 27-29, 41, 43-46, 51-53, 55, 56, 78, 184, 187, 190, 196, 199-200, 204-207, 270-272, 274, 282, 2.]

Sloane, Robert: Breaking the genuine link: the contemporary international legal regulation of nationality. (In: Harvard International Law Journal, 2009, v. 50, no. 1, p. 1-60.) [I.C.J., passim.]

Stephens, Dale: Comparative Approaches to Security and Maritime Border Control. (In: International Law Studies (Naval War College), 2006, 81, p. 19-30.) [I.C.J., p. 25-26.]

Thirlway, Hugh: The law and procedure of the International Court of Justice 1960-1989 (supplement 2009) (parts seven and eight). (In: British Year Book of International Law, 2009, v. 80, p. 13-216.)

Verny, Edouard: Le principe de territorialité de l'ordre répressif français: "quand tu seras à Rome, conduis-toi en romain". (Dans: Mélanges offerts à André Decocq: une certaine idée du droit. Paris: [s.n.], 2004, p. 593-604.) [C.I.J., p. 599.]

Vinuesa, Raúl Emilio: La aplicación del derecho internacional des mar por los tribunales internos de los estados: a propósito de la gestión de recursos marinos. (Dans: La gestión de los recursos marinos y la cooperación internacional: actas del seminario, Santiago de Chile, 22-23 de marzo de 2004, sous la dir. de Del Vecchio, Angela. Roma: Instituto italo-latino americano, 2006, p. 177-202.) [C.I.J., p. 200.]

Werner, Wouter G.: De Staat. (In: Handboek internationaal recht, ed. by Horbach, Nathalie L. J. T.; Lefeber, René; Ribbelink, Olivier. The Hague: T.M.C. Asser Press, 2007, p. 159-193.) [P.C.I.J., p. 170; I.C.J., p. 160, 164, 168, 174, 186-188, 1992.]

Werner, Wouter G.: State sovereignty and international legal discourse. (In: Governance and international legal theory, ed. by Dekker, Ige F.; Werner, Wouter G. Leiden; Boston, 2004, p. 125-157.) [P.C.I.J., p. 138; I.C.J., p. 131-132, 141-142, 145-147, 149, 152, 154.]

Wittich, Stephan: Domestic implementation and the unity of international law. (In: Unity and diversity in international law: proceedings of an international symposium of the Kiel Walther Schücking Institute of International Law, November 4-7, 2004, ed. by Zimmermann, Andreas; Hofmann, Rainer. Berlin: Duncker & Humblot, 2006, p. 345-372.) [P.C.I.J., p. 352; I.C.J., p. 353, 364.]

Zhu, Lijiang: The Chinese universal jurisdiction clause: how far can it go? (In: Netherlands International Law Review, 2005, v. 52, no. 1, p. 85-107.) [I.C.J., p. 104.]

5. Droit diplomatique et consulaire
5. Diplomatic and consular law

Alebeek, Rosanne van: Staatsimmuniteit. (In: Handboek internationaal recht, ed. by Horbach, Nathalie L. J. T.; Lefeber, René; Ribbelink, Olivier. The Hague: T.M.C. Asser Press, 2007, p. 231-273.) [I.C.J., p. 254, 257-258.]

Anatolevich Kolodkin, Roman: Preliminary report on immunity of State officials from foreign criminal jurisdiction. Geneva: International Law Commission, 2008. [I.C.J., passim.]

Barker, J. Craig: The protection of diplomatic personnel. Aldershot [etc.]: Ashgate, 2006. [I.C.J., p. 23-24, 76-87, 112, 119.]

Beaud, Olivier: L'immunité du chef de l'Etat en droit constitutionnel et en droit comparé. (Dans: Le droit international des immunités: contestation ou consolidation?, sous la dir. de Verhoeven, Joe. Paris: L.G.D.J., 2004, p. 149-188.) [C.I.J., p. 162.]

Bolewski, Wilfried: Les privilèges diplomatiques dans la pratique. (Dans: Revue de droit international et de droit comparé, 2005, v. 82, no. 3, p. 295-316.) [C.I.J., p. 305, 314.]

Bordoni, Matteo: Default nel debito pubblico ed immunità dello Stato estero dalla giurisdizione civile. (Dans: Rivista di diritto internazionale, 2006, v. 89, p. 1031-1059.) [C.P.J.I. et C.I.J., p. 1056.]

Borghi, Alvaro: Corruption et immunité des dirigeants politiques. (Dans: Les traités internationaux contre la corruption: l'ONU, l'OCDE, le Conseil de l'Europe et la Suisse, par Balmelli, Tiziano; Jaggy, Bernard, eds. Lausanne [etc.]: Editions interuniversitaires suisses (Edis), 2004, p. 91-109.) [C.I.J., p. 93-94, 96.]

Bradley, Curtis and Damrosch, Lori Fisler and Flaherty, Martin: Discussion: Medellin v. Dretke: federalism and international law. (In: Columbia Journal of Transnational Law, 2005, v. 43, no. 3, p. 667-703.) [I.C.J., p. 668-673, 676-698, 700-702.]

Cançado Trindade, A. A.: The humanization of consular law: the impact of advisory opinion no. 16 (1999) of the Inter-American Court of Human Rights on international case-law and practice. (In: Chinese Journal of International Law, 2007, v. 6, p. 1-16.) [I.C.J., p. 3-6, 9, 10-12, 15.]

Cançado Trindade, A. A.: The humanization of consular law: the impact of advisory opinion no. 16 (1999) of the Inter-American Court of Human Rights on international case-law and practice. (In: Anuario hispano-luso-americano de derecho internacional, 2007, v. 18, p. 277-298.) [I.C.J., p. 280-283, 287-291, 295-296.]

Cerna, Christina M.: Impact on the right to consular notification. (In: The impact of human rights law on general international law, ed. by Kamminga, Menno T.; Scheinin, Martin. Oxford: Oxford University Press, 2009, p. 171-209.)

Coombs, Mary: Kaunda v. President of the Republic of South Africa. Case CCT 23/04. Constitutional Court of South Africa, August 4, 2004. (In: American Journal of International Law, 2005, v. 99, p. 681-686.) [I.C.J., p. 682.]

Cooper-Hill, James: The law of sovereign immunity and terrorism. [New York, N.Y.]: Oceana, 2006. (Terrorism: documents on international and local control: second series; 19.) [I.C.J., p. 116-117.]

Crespo Navarro, Elena: El proyecto de artículos de la Comisión de derecho internacional sobre la protección diplomática: la protección de las personas físicas. (Dans: Revista española de derecho internacional, 2005, v. 57, no. 1, p. 221-238.) [C.P.J.I., p. 228-231, 235; C.I.J., p. 226-227, 229-236.]

Crook, John R.: Contemporary practice of the United States relating to international law. (In: American Journal of International Law, 2005, v. 99, no. 3, p. 691-719.) [I.C.J., p. 695.]

Denza, Eileen: Diplomatic law: commentary on the Vienna Convention on Diplomatic Relations. Oxford [etc.]: Oxford University Press, 2008. 3rd ed. [I.C.J., p. 77, 141, 148, 150, 164-166, 194, 265, 267, 283, 292, 311-312, 472, 447, 478, 482-483, 498, 503, 505, 511-516, 529.]

Deysine, Anne: Sur la peine de mort aux Etats-Unis. (Dans: Le christianisme dans le monde. Paris: Documenation Française, 2008, p. 97-105.) [C.I.J., p. 105-106.]

Diplomatic protection of persons and property. (In: Reports of the Annual Conference, by International Law Association (ILA), 2006, 2006, p. 353-405.) [P.C.I.J., p. 356; I.C.J., p. 358, 360, 366, 368-369, 374, 380.]

Dugard, John R.: Diplomatic protection and human rights: the draft articles of the International Law Commission. (In: Australian Yearbook of International Law, 2005, v. 24, p. 75-91.) [P.C.I.J., p. 76; I.C.J., p. 76, 80-81, 84, 87-88.]

Fox, Hazel: In defence of State immunity: why the UN Convention on State Immunity is important. (In: International and Comparative Law Quarterly, 2006, v. 55, p. 399-406.) [I.C.J., p. 400, 402.]

Fox, Hazel: State immunity and other norms of international law: possible methods of accommodation. (In: Liber memorialis Petar Sarcevic: universalism, tradition and the individual, ed. by J. Erauw; V. Tomljenovic; P. Volken. München: Sellier, 2006, p. 545-564.) [I.C.J., p. 550-552, 556, 559-560.]

Gaeta, Paola: Immunities and genocide. (In: The UN Genocide Convention: a commentary, ed. by Paola Gaeta. Oxford [etc.]: Oxford University Press, 2009, p. 310-333.)

Gärditz, Klaus Ferdinand: Case Nos. 2 BvR2115/01, 2 BvR2132/01, & 2 BvR348/03.60 Neue Juristische Wochenschrift 499 (2007): Bundesverfassungsgericht (Federal Constitutional Court of Germany), September 19, 2006. (In: American Journal of International Law, 2007, v. 101, no. 3, p. 627-635.)

Garibian, Sévane: Vers l'émergence d'un droit individuel à la protection diplomatique? (Dans: Annuiare français de droit international, 2008, v. 54, p. 119-141.) [C.I.J., p. 120-121, 126, 133-134; C.P.I.J., p. 121-122.]

Hafner, Gerhard and Köhler, Ulrike: The United Nations Convention on Jurisdictional Immunities of States and their Property. (In: Netherlands Yearbook of International Law, 2004, v. 35, p. 3-49.) [I.C.J., p. 43, 45.]

Hartmann, Jacques: The Gillon affair. (In: International and Comparative Law Quarterly, 2005, v. 54, no. 3, p. 745-755.) [I.C.J., p. 751, 753-754.]

Honorati, Costanza: Sul tipo di attività statale preclusa ad un giudice nazionale dall'esistenza di un'immunità personale. (Dans: Immunità costituzionali e crimini internazionali: atti del Convegno, Milano, 8 e 9 febbraio 2007, sous la dir. de Bardusco, Aldo. Milan: Giuffrè, 2008, p. 253-265.) [I.C.J., p. 254, 256-260.]

Iovane, Massimo: The activity of the International Law Commission during its 58th session (2006). (In: Italian Yearbook of International Law, 2006, v. 16, p. 245-265.) [P.C.I.J., p. 245; I.C.J., p. 247, 250.]

Kamminga, Menno T.: Final report on the impact of international human rights law on general international law. (In: The impact of human rights law on general international law, ed. by Menno T. Kamminga; Martin Scheinin. Oxford [etc.]: Oxford University Press, 2009, p. 1-22.) [I.C.J., p. 3, 5-8, 11, 13-15, 17-20.]

Künzli, Annemarieke: Exercising diplomatic protection: the fine line between litigation, demarches and consular assistance. (In: Zeitschrift für ausländisches öffentliches Recht und Völkerrecht, 2006, v. 66, p. 321-350.) [P.C.I.J., p. 325-329, 349; I.C.J., p. 325-329, 337-339, 341-342, 346.]

Larson, Michael J.: Calling all consuls: U.S. Supreme Court divergence from the International Court of Justice and the shortcomings of Sanchez-Llamas v. Oregon. (In: Emory International Law Review, 2008, v. 22, no. 1, p. 317-346.)

Le Mon, Christopher J.: Post-Avena application of the Vienna Convention on Consular Relations by United States courts. (In: Leiden Journal of International Law, 2005, v. 18, no. 2, p. 215-236.) [I.C.J., p. 215, 216, 218-236.]

Marks, Jonathan H.: Mending the web: universal jurisdiction, humanitarian intervention and the abrogation of immunity by the Security Council. (In: Columbia Journal of Transnational Law, 2004, v. 42, no. 2, p. 445-490.) [I.C.J., p. 445-446, 448-463, 468, 472, 475, 478, 483, 489.]

Matheson, Michael J.: The fifty-eighth session of the International Law Commission. (In: American Journal of International Law, 2007, v. 101, p. 407-441.) [I.C.J., p. 418-419, 423, 425.]

Matheson, Michael J. and Bickler, Sara: The fifty-fifth session of the International Law Commission. (In: American Journal of International Law, 2004, v. 98, no. 2, p. 317-324.) [I.C.J., p. 317-318.]

Orakhelashvili, Alexander: State immunity and international public order revisited. (In: German Yearbook of International Law, 2006, v. 49, p. 327-365.) [P.C.I.J., p. 328, 352; I.C.J., p. 327, 353, 355.]

Pellet, Alain: The second death of Euripide Mavrommatis? Notes on the International Law Commission's draft articles of diplomatic protection. (In: Law and Practice of International Courts and Tribunals, 2008, v. 7, p. 33-58.) [P.C.I.J., p. 33-35, 38, 46-47, 56; I.C.J., p. 32, 36, 38, 41, 45, 47-50.]

Pellet, Alain: La seconde mort d'Euripide Mavrommatis (1)? Notes sur le projet de la C.D.I. sur la protection diplomatique. (Dans: Droit du pouvoir, pouvoir du droit: mélanges offerts à Jean Salmon. Bruxelles: Bruylant, 2007, p. 1359-1382.) [C.P.J.I., 1360, 1371, 1380; C.J.I., 1361-1362, 1364, 1372-1374.]

Pergantis, Vasileios: Towards a "humanization" of diplomatic protection? (In: Zeitschrift für ausländisches öffentliches Recht und Völkerrecht, 2006, v. 66, p. 351-397.) [P.C.I.J., p. 352, 361, 371, 383; I.C.J., p. 354-355, 357-361, 364, 366-368, 370, 372-374, 377, 379, 384-388, 395-396.]

Pisillo Mazzeschi, Riccardo: Impact on the law of diplomatic protection. (In: The impact of human rights law on general international law, ed. by Kamminga, Menno T.; Scheinin, Martin. Oxford: Oxford University Press, 2009, p. 211-233.)

Poirat, Florence: Les immunités des sujets du droit international (Etats et organisations internationales). (Dans: Le droit international des immunités: contestation ou consolidation?, par Beaud, Olivier [et al.]. Paris: L.G.D.J., 2004, p. 11-60.) [C.I.J., p. 18.]

Puissochet, Jean-Pierre: La pratique française de la protection diplomatique. (Dans: La protection diplomatique: mutations contemporaines et pratiques nationales: actes de la journée d'études du 30 mars 2001 organisée à la mémoire de Georges Perrin, sous la dir. de Jean-Francois Flauss. Bruxelles: Bruylant, 2003, p. 115-120.) [C.I.J., p. 115.]

Rosenfeld, Eric: Irreconcilable differences: how Sanchez-Llamas v. Oregon undermines Article 36 of the Vienna Convention on Consular Relations. (In: University of Pittsburgh Law Review, 2008, v. 69, no. 4, p. 789-808.)

Salazar Albornoz, Mariana: Legal nature and legal consequences of diplomatic protection, contemporary challenges. (In: Anuario mexicano de derecho internacional, 2006, v. 6, p. 377-417.) [P.C.I.J., p. 380, 397, 410; I.C.J., p. 379, 387-390, 398, 400-402.]

Sánchez Patrón, José Manuel: La inmunidad de ejecución de los bienes del estado extranjero: el caso Montasa/EE.UU. (Dans: Revista española de derecho internacional, 2005, v. 57, no. 1, p. 171-185.) [C.I.J., p. 179.]

Storost, Christian: Diplomatischer Schutz durch EG und EU? Die Berücksichtigung von Individualinteressen in der europäischen Aussenpolitik. Berlin: Duncker & Humblot, 2005. (Schriften zum Völkerrecht; 155.) [P.C.I.J., p. 21, 251; I.C.J., p. 21, 25, 34, 40-43, 54, 55, 64, 65, 76, 77, 92, 93, 113, 118, 149, 150, 153-154, 156, 159, 165-168.]

Storost, Christian: Der Fall Abbasi: Wegbereiter eines gemeineuropäischen Anspruchts auf diplomatischen Schutz? (In: Archiv des Völkerrechts, 2004, v. 42, no. 4, p. 411-424.) [I.C.J., p. 414.]

Strauss, Andrew: Climate change litigation: opening the door to the International Court of Justice. (In: Adjudicating climate change: State, national, and international approaches, ed. by William C. G. Burns; Hari M. Osofsky. New York {etc.]: Cambridge University Press, 2009, p. 334-356.)

Talmon, Stefan: Diplomacy under occupation: the status of diplomatic missions in occupied Iraq. (In: Anuario mexicano de derecho internacional, 2006, v. 6, p. 461-511.) [P.C.I.J., p. 484; I.C.J., p. 500-501.]

Verhoeven, Joe: Les immunités propres aux organes ou autres agents des sujets du droit international. (Dans: Le droit international des immunités: contestation ou consolidation?, sous la dir. de Verhoeven, Joe. Bruxelles: De Boeck & Larcier, 2004, p. 61-146.) [C.I.J., p. 65, 68, 74, 76-77, 83, 85-89, 91-93, 95-96, 98-99, 101, 117, 126-127, 132, 146.]

Vermeer-Künzli, Annemarieke: As if: the legal fiction in diplomatic protection. (In: European Journal of International Law, 2007, v. 18, p. 37-68.) [P.C.I.J., p. 38-39, 42, 50, 58, 61; I.C.J., p. 39, 59-60, 66-67.]

Vermeer-Künzli, Annemarieke: Restricting discretion: judicial review of diplomatic protection. (In: Nordic Journal of International Law, 2006, v. 75, p. 279-307.) [P.C.I.J., p. 279; I.C.J., p. 279-280, 282.]

Vigni, Patrizia: Accesso alla giustizia ed assistenza consolare. (Dans: Accesso alla giustizia dell'individuo nel diritto internazionale e dell'Unione Europea, sous la dir. de Francioni, Francesco; Gestri, Marco; Ronzitti, Natalino; Scovazzi, Tullio. Milano: Giuffrè, 2008, p. 175-196.) [I.C.J., p. 178-182, 184-188.]

Zhu, Lijiang: State immunity from measures of constraints for the property of foreign central banks: the Chinese perspective. (In: Chinese Journal of International Law, 2007, v. 6, p. 67-81.) [I.C.J., p. 72-73.]

Zieck, Marjoleine: Diplomatik en consulair recht. (In: Handboek internationaal recht, ed. by Horbach, Nathalie L. J. T.; Lefeber, René; Ribbelink, Olivier. The Hague: T.M.C. Asser Press, 2007, p. 275-308.) [I.C.J., p. 276, 282-283, 292-294, 300.]

6. Droit des traités
6. Law of treaties

Ascensio, Hervé: Convention de Vienne de 1969: article 70: conséquences de l'extinction d'un traité. (Dans: Les Conventions de Vienne sur le droit des traités: commentaire article par article, sous la dir. d'Olivier Corten; Pierre Klein. Bruxelles: Bruylant, 2006, v. 2, p. 2503-2539.) [C.I.J., p. 2530-2534, 2537-2539.]

Aust, Anthony: Modern treaty law and practice. Cambridge [etc.]: Cambridge University Press, 2007. 2nd ed. [I.C.J., p. 255, 291, 340, 346, 358-360, 408-409.]

Bannelier, Karine: Les effets des conflits armés sur les traités: et si la Convention de Vienne et le droit de la responsabilité suffisaient? (Dans: Droit du pouvoir, pouvoir du droit: mélanges offerts à Jean Salmon. Bruxelles: Bruylant, 2007, p. 125-159.) [C.P.J.I., p. 147; C.I.J., p. 133, 138, 143-144, 151-152, 158.]

Basedow, Jürgen: Uniform private law conventions and the law of treaties. (In: Uniform Law Review, 2006, v. 11, p. 731-747.) [I.C.J., p. 738, 742.]

Bederman, David J.: Foreign Office international legal history. (In: Time, history and international law, ed. by Matthew C. R. Craven; Malgosia A. Fitzmaurice; Maria Vogiatzi. Leiden; Boston: Martinus Nijhoff, 2007, p. 43-62.) [I.C.J., p. 58-62.]

Bedjaoui, Mohammed et Leidgens, Tamara: Convention de Vienne de 1969: article 44: divisibilité des dispositions d'un traité. (Dans: Les Conventions de Vienne sur le droit des traités: commentaire article par article, sous la dir. d'Olivier Corten; Pierre Klein. Bruxelles: Bruylant, 2006, v. 2, p. 1641-1662.) [C.P.J.I., p. 1646; C.I.J., p. 1674-1648, 1651, 1657-1658.]

Bonucci, Nicola and Kuijper, Pieter Jan and Guillaume, Gilbert and Treves, Tullio and Tulkens, Françoise: L'actualité des Conventions de Vienne sur le droit des traités: le point de vue des praticiens. (In: Revue belge de droit international, 2006, v. 39, p. 432-458.) [C.I.J., passim.]

Cachapuz de Medeiros, Antônio Paulo: O Brasil e os novos desafios do direito dos tratados. (Dans: O Brasil e os novos desafios do direito internacional, sous la dir. de Brant, Leonardo Nemer Caldeira. Rio de Janeiro: Editora Forense, 2004, p. 433-524.) [C.P.J.I., p. 440; C.I.J., p. 440, 442-443, 487.]

Cairn, David A.: Introductory note to International Centre for Settlement of Investment Disputes (ICSID): Salini Costruttori S.P.A. and Italstrade S.P.A. v. The Hashemite Kingdom of Jordan, Decision on jurisdiction. (In: International Legal Materials, 2005, v. 44, no. 3, p. 569-572.) [I.C.J., p. 571.]

Casolari, Federico: La successione degli Stati nei trattati bilaterali al vaglio della Corte di giustizia: il caso Budvar. (Dans: Rivista di diritto internazionale, 2005, v. 88, no. 1, p. 121-148.) [C.P.J.I., p. 144, 148; C.I.J., p. 125-126, 139, 144-148.]

Crawford, James: Multilateral rights and obligations in international law. (In: Recueil des cours de l'Académie de droit international de La Haye, 2006, v. 319, p. 325-482.) [P.C.I.J., p. 344, 395, 413, 429, 439; I.C.J., p. 336-338, 342, 345, 347-348, 371, 373-379, 385-387, 389-390, 392-410, 412-413, 415-420, 422-425, 428-429, 434-437, 439, 443, 447, 449-451, 452, 456, 472-477.]

Criddle, Evan: The Vienna Convention on the Law of Treaties in U.S. treaty interpretation. (In: Virginia Journal of International Law, 2004, v. 44, no. 2, p. 431-500.) [I.C.J. and P.C.I.J., p. 440, 444-447, 455-456, 460.]

Czapski, Waldemar: Application et interprétation de la Convention CMR à la lumière du droit international. (Dans: Uniform Law Review, 2006, 11, p. 545-568.) [C.P.J.I., p. 545, 547, 556, 559, 565; C.I.J., p. 545-546, 554-557, 559-562.]

Damrosch, Lori Fisler: Treaties and international regulation. (In: Proceedings of the American Society of International Law, 2004, v. 98, p. 349-351.) [I.C.J., p. 350.]

Davidson, Scott (ed.): The law of treaties. Farnham [etc.]: Ashgate, 2004. (Library of essays in international law.)

Distefano, Giovanni: Le Protocole de Londres du 17 janvier 1871: miroir du droit international. (Dans: Journal of the History of International Law, 2004, v. 6, no. 1, p. 79-142.) [C.I.J. et C.P.J.I., p. 106, 110-111, 117, 123.]

Doria, José Rodrigues: Reservations to the ICCPR and CEDAW in the light of common but differentiated responsibility: different scenarios in different States. (In: Hague Yearbook of International Law, 2004, v. 17, p. 37-75.) [I.C.J., p. 41-43, 53.]

Dörr, Oliver: Codifying and developing meta-rules: the ILC and the law of treaties. (In: German Yearbook of International Law, 2006, v. 49, p. 129-164.) [P.C.I.J., p. 134, 144-145; I.C.J., p. 132, 138, 143-147, 150, 152, 161, 163.]

Dupuy, Pierre-Marie: La Convention de Vienne sur le droit des traités à l'épreuve de la pratique: quel bilan trente ans après son entrée en vigueur? (In: Revue belge de droit international, 2006, v. 39, p. 411-431.) [C.I.J., passim.]

Engelen, F. A.: Over waarden en normen: Het beginsel van de goede trouw in het (fiscale) verdragenrecht. Deventer: Kluwer, 2006. [P.C.I.J., p. 14; I.C.J., p. 8, 10, 28, 29, 41, 42, 45-49.]

Espaliú Berdud, Carlos: The Spanish reservation to Article IX of the Convention on the Prevention and Punishment of the Crime of Genocide. (In: Spanish Yearbook of International Law, 2004, v. 10, p. 67-95.) [P.C.I.J., p. 71-72; I.C.J., passim.]

Fitzmaurice, Malgosia A.: Dynamic (evolutive) interpretation of treaties. Part I. (In: Hague Yearbook of International Law, 2008, v. 21, p. 101-153.) [I.C.J., p. 103-113, 149.]

Frouville, Olivier de: L'intangibilité des droits de l'Homme en droit international: régime conventionnel des droits de l'homme et droit des traités. Paris: Pedone, 2004. (Publications de la Fondation Marangopoulos pour les Droits de l'Homme (FMDH); no. 7.) [C.P.J.I., p. 45, 287; C.I.J., p. 3, 29, 50, 52, 53, 57, 198-201, 273, 279, 282, 284-286, 288-293, 352-356, 336-343, 353, 355-357, 377, 385-389, 392, 398, 403, 413, 416, 419, 429, 438, 461-463, 470, 476-477, 480, 483, 484, 496, 497, 499, 505-507, 512-513.]

Gardiner, Richard K.: Treaty interpretation. Oxford [etc.]: Oxford University Press, 2008. (The Oxford International Law Library.) [P.C.I.J., see index p. 403; I.C.J., see index p. 4.]

Gaurier, Dominique: Histoire du droit international: auteurs, doctrines et développement de l'Antiquité à l'aube de la période contemporaine.

Rennes : Presses universitaires de Rennes, 2005. (Collection Didact droit.) [C.P.J.I., p. 342.]

Gautier, Philippe : Les accords informels et la Convention de Vienne sur le droit des traités entre Etats. (Dans : Droit du pouvoir, pouvoir du droit : mélanges offerts à Jean Salmon. Bruxelles : Bruylant, 2007, p. 425-454.) [C.P.J.I., p. 451; C.I.J., passim.]

Georgopoulos, Théodore : Le droit intertemporel et les dispositions conventionnelles évolutives : quelle thérapie contre la vieillesse des traités ? (Dans : Revue générale de droit international public, 2004, v. 108, p. 123-148.) [C.I.J. et C.P.J.I., p. 128, 130-137, 140, 142-143, 145-147.]

Gianelli, Alessandra : Aspects of the relationship between the law of treaties and State responsibility. (In : Studi di diritto internazionale in onore di Gaetano Arangio-Ruiz, ed. by Giovanni Battaglini ; Paolo Benvenuti ; Antonio Cassese ; Giorgio Gaja. Napoli : Editoriale Scientifica, 2004, v. 2, p. 757-805.) [I.C.J., p. 757, 769.]

Glashausser, Alex : Treaties as domestic law in the United States. (In : Progress in international law, ed. by Russel A. Miller ; Rebecca M. Bratspies. Leiden [etc.] : Nijhoff, 2008, p. 219-242.)

Greig, D. W. : The time of conclusion and the time of application of treaties as points of reference in the interpretative process. (In : Time, history and international law, ed. by Matthew C. R. Craven ; Malgosia A. Fitzmaurice ; Maria Vogiatzi. Leiden [etc.] : Nijhoff, 2007, p. 163-217.) [I.C.J., passim.]

Guillaume, Gilbert : Methods and practice of treaty interpretation by the International Court of Justice. (In : The WTO at ten : the contribution of the dispute settlement system, ed. by Giorgio Sacerdoti ; Alan Yanovich ; Jan Bohanes. Cambridge : Cambridge University Press, 2006, p. 465-473.) [I.C.J., passim.]

Hall, Christopher Keith : The duty of States parties to the Convention against Torture to provide procedures permitting victims to recover reparations for torture committed abroad. (In : European Journal of International Law, 2008, v. 18, no. 5, p. 921-937.) [I.C.J., p. 928, 931.]

Heymann, Monika : Unity and diversity with regard to international treaty law. (In : Unity and diversity in international law : proceedings of an international symposium of the Kiel Walther Schücking Institute of International Law, November 4-7, 2004, ed. by Zimmermann, Andreas ; Hofmann, Rainer. Berlin : Duncker & Humblot, 2006, p. 217-239.) [I.C.J., p. 237.]

Kamto, Maurice : Le statut juridique des traités signés entre les représentants des puissances coloniales et les monarques indigènes africains en droit international. (Dans : Droit du pouvoir, pouvoir du droit : mélanges offerts à Jean Salmon. Bruxelles : Bruylant, 2007, p. 455-480.) [C.P.J.I., p. 459; C.I.J., p. 456, 457, 459, 461, 470-479.]

Klabbers, Jan : Verdragenrecht. (In : Handboek internationaal recht, ed. by Horbach, Nathalie L. J. T. ; Lefeber, René ; Ribbelink, Olivier. The Hague :

T.M.C. Asser Press, 2007, p. 123-157.) [P.C.I.J., p. 125, 135, 148, 152; I.C.J., p. 126, 135-136, 139, 142, 144, 149-150, 152-154.]

Klein, Eckart: Impact of treaty bodies on the international legal order. (In: Developments of international law in treaty making, ed. by Rüdiger Wolfrum; Röben Volker. Berlin [etc.]: Springer, 2005, p. 571-579.) [I.C.J., p. 574.]

Kohen, Marcelo G.: Comment: [on Unity and diversity with regard to international treaty law by Monika Heymann]. (In: Unity and diversity in international law: proceedings of an international symposium of the Kiel Walther Schücking Institute of International Law, November 4-7, 2004, ed. by Zimmermann, Andreas; Hofmann, Rainer. Berlin: Duncker & Humblot, 2006, p. 241-246.) [I.C.J., p. 242, 245.]

Kolb, Robert: La modification d'un traité par la pratique subséquente des parties: note sur l'affaire relative au régime fiscal des pensions versées aux fonctionnaires retraités de l'UNESCO résidant en France, sentence du 14 janvier 2003. (Dans: Schweizerische Zeitschrift für internationales und europäisches Recht, 2004, v. 14, p. 9-32.) [C.I.J. et C.P.J.I., p. 11, 14, 17-20, 28-29.]

Kolb, Robert: Note: is an obligation assumed by two different States in two different treaties binding between them? (In: Netherlands International Law Review, 2004, v. 51, no. 2, p. 185-194.) [I.C.J., p. 189.]

Krieger, Heike: A nuclear test for multilateralism: challenges to the non-proliferation treaty as a means of arms control. (In: German Yearbook of International Law, 2006, v. 49, p. 17-50.) [I.C.J., p. 24, 30.]

Laly-Chevalier, Caroline: La violation du traité. Bruxelles: Bruylant, 2005. (Collection de droit international; 59.) [C.I.J., p. 217, 221 -222, 247-250, 252, 254-256, 259, 266-267, 270-272, 274-275, 279, 281, 340, 574-575, 579.]

Lévesque, Jean-François: Traités de verre: réflexions sur l'interprétation. (In: Revue québécoise de droit international, 2006, v. 19, no. 1, p. 53-78.) [I.C.J., passim.]

Linderfalk, Ulf: Is the hierarchical structure of Articles 31 and 32 of the Vienna Convention real or not? Interpreting the rules of interpretation. (In: Netherlands International Law Review, 2007, v. 54, no. 1, p. 133-154.) [I.C.J., p. 136-137, 139, 150.]

Linderfalk, Ulf: On the interpretation of treaties: the modern international law as expressed in the 1969 Vienna Convention on the Law of Treaties. Dordrecht: Springer, 2007. (Law and Philosophy Library; 83.) [P.C.I.J., p. 84-85, 196, 243, 245, 273, 280-281, 300-302, 304-308, 313, 317-318; I.C.J., p. 14-15, 17, 23-25, 67-69, 81-84, 86, 88-91, 94, 97-100, 117--124, 129, 143-147, 157, 179-181, 183-189, 196, 201, 221-223, 250-253, 255-258, 275-276, 315.]

Matz, Nele: Wege zur Koordinierung völkerrechtlicher Verträge: völkervertragsrechtliche und institutionelle Ansätze. Berlin [etc.]: Springer,

2005. (Beiträge zum auslandischen öffentlichen Recht und Völkerrecht; 175.) [P.C.I.J., p. 304; I.C.J., p. 240, 246, 277-278, 287, 289, 300-301, 334.]

Mbuyi, Benjamin Mulamba: Droit des traités internationaux: notes de cours à l'usage des étudiants en droit. Paris: Harmattan, 2009. (Etudes africaines.) [P.C.I.J. et C.I.J., index p. 179.]

McLachlan, Campbell: The principle of systemic integration and Article 31(3)(c) of the Vienna Convention. (In: International and Comparative Law Quarterly, 2005, v. 54, no. 2, p. 279-319.) [I.C.J., p. 279-282, 288-289, 292-293, 295-296, 298, 306-309, 311-313, 317-318.]

Merkouris, Panos: Debating the ouroboros of international law: the drafting history of Article 31(3)(c). (In: International Community Law Review, 2007, v. 9, no. 1, p. 1-31.) [P.C.I.J., p. 7, 13; I.C.J., p. 7, 10, 14, 17, 21.]

Pellet, Alain: Comment: [on Unity and diversity with regard to international treaty law by Monika Heymann]. (In: Unity and diversity in international law: proceedings of an international symposium of the Kiel Walther Schücking Institute of International Law, November 4-7, 2004, ed. by Zimmermann, Andreas; Hofmann, Rainer. Berlin: Duncker & Humblot, 2006, p. 247-251.) [I.C.J., p. 248.]

Pellet, Alain: Excerpts from the second report on reservations to treaties. (In: Reservations to human rights treaties and the Vienna Convention regime: conflict, harmony or reconciliation, ed. by Ineta Ziemele. Leiden [etc.]: Martinus Nijhoff, 2004, p. 235-309.) [I.C.J., p. 258, 264, 273-275, 278, 282-283, 291, 297].]

Quilleré-Majzoub, Fabienne: La succession d'états en matière de traités relatifs à l'utilisation des cours d'eau internationaux à des fins autres que la navigation: essai de réactualisation. (Dans: Revue hellénique de droit international, 2005, v. 58, no. 2, p. 331-360.) [C.P.J.I., p. 349-350; C.I.J., p. 351-356, 360.]

Raustiala, Kal: Form and substance in international agreements. (In: American Journal of International Law, 2005, v. 99, p. 581-614.) [I.C.J., p. 587.]

Redgwell, Catherine: Universality or integrity? Some reflections on reservations to general multilateral treaties. (In: International law, ed. by Malcolm D. Evans; Patrick Capps. Farnham [etc.]: Ashgate, 2009, v. 1, p. 439-476.)

Reed, Lucy and Granoff, Ilmi: Treaties in US domestic law: Medellín v. Texas in context. (In: The Law and Practice of International Courts and Tribunals, 2009, v. 8, no. 1, p. 1-26.) [I.C.J., p. 2-3, 9-12, 15-16, 23-24.]

Reed, Lucy and Martinez, Lucy: Treaty obligations to honor arbitral awards and diplomatic protection. (In: Enforcement of arbitral awards against sovereigns, ed. by Bishop, R. Doak. Huntington, NY: Jurisnet, 2009, p. 13-34.)

Rosenne, Shabtai: Codification revisited after fifty years. (In: Essays on international law and practice, by Shabtai Rosenne. Leiden; Boston: Martinus Nijhoff, 2007, p. 599-620.)

Rosenne, Shabtai: When is a final clause not a final clause? (In: Essays on international law and practice, by Shabtai Rosenne. Leiden; Boston: Martinus Nijhoff, 2007, p. 445-447.)

Schmalenbach, Kirsten: Die rechtliche Wirkung der Vertragsauslegung durch IGH, EuGH und EGMR. (In: Zeitschrift für öffentliches Recht, 2004, v. 59, no. 3, p. 213-231.) [C.I.J., p. 215-218.]

Schöpp-Schilling, Hanna Beate: Reservations to the Convention on the Elimination of All Forms of Discrimination against Women: an unresolved issue or (no) new developments? (In: Reservations to human rights treaties and the Vienna Convention regime: conflict, harmony or reconciliation, ed. by Ineta Ziemele. Leiden [etc.]: Martinus Nijhoff, 2004, p. 3-39.) [I.C.J., p. 16, 39.]

Seibert-Fohr, Anja: The potentials of the Vienna Convention on the Law of Treaties with respect to reservations to human rights treaties. (In: Reservations to human rights treaties and the Vienna Convention regime: conflict, harmony or reconciliation, ed. by Ineta Ziemele. Leiden [etc.]: Martinus Nijhoff, 2004, p. 183-211.) [I.C.J., p. 185-188.]

Sitaraman, Srini: State participation in international treaty regimes. Surrey; Burlington: Ashgate, 2009. [I.C.J., p. 39, 120, 135, 188, 191-194.]

Tomuschat, Christian: The complementarity of international treaty law, customary international law, and non-contractual lawmaking. (In: Developments of international law in treaty making, ed. by Rüdiger Wolfrum; Volker Röben. Berlin, [etc.]: Springer, 2005, p. 401-408.) [I.C.J., p. 401, 404-406.]

Tuma, Otmar J.: The degree of default under Article 29 CMR. (In: Uniform Law Review, 2006, 11, p. 585-607.) [I.C.J., p. 605.]

Ulfstein, Geir: Treaty bodies. (In: The Oxford handbook of international environmental law, ed. by Daniel Bodansky; Jutta Brunnée; Ellen Hey. Oxford: Oxford University Press, 2007, p. 877-889.) [I.C.J., p. 881.]

Vagts, Detlev F.: Rebus revisited: changed circumstances in treaty law. (In: Columbia Journal of Transnational Law, 2005, v. 43, no. 2, p. 459-476.) [P.C.I.J., p. 468, 475; I.C.J., p. 471-473, 475.]

Villiger, Mark: Articles 31 and 32 of the Vienna Convention on the Law of Treaties in the case-law of the European Court of Human Rights. (In: Internationale Gemeinschaft und Menschenrechte: Festschrift für Georg Ress zum 70. Geburtstag am 21. Januar 2005, ed. by Bröhmer, Jürgen; Bieber, Roland; Calliess, Christian; Langenfeld, Christine; Weber, Stefan; Wolf, Joachim. Köln [etc.]: Heymann, 2005, p. 317-330.) [I.C.J., p. 317, 319, 324-327, 329.]

Villiger, Mark: The 1969 Vienna Convention on the Law of Treaties: 40 years after. (In: Recueil des cours de l'Académie de droit international de La Haye, 2009, v. 344, p. 9-192.) [P.C.I.J., p. 115, 136, 145, 161; I.C.J., passim.]

Zemanek, Karl: Appropriate instruments for codification reflections on the ILC Draft on State Responsibility. (In: Studi di diritto internazionale in onore di Gaetano Arangio-Ruiz, ed. by Giovanni Battaglini; Paolo Benvenuti; Antonio Cassese; Giorgio Gaja. Napoli: Editoriale Scientifica, 2004, v. 2, p. 897-918.) [P.C.I.J., p. 913; I.C.J., p. 899, 910-911, 913, 917.]

7. Droit de la mer
7. Law of the sea

Agreement between the Government of Australia and the Government of the Democratic Republic of Timor-Leste relating to the unitisation of the Sunrise and Troubadour Fields (Dili, 6 March 2003). (In: International maritime boundaries, ed. by Colson, David A.; Smith, Robert W. Leiden; Boston: Martinus Nijhoff, 2005, v. 5, p. 3872-3899.) [I.C.J., p. 3895-3896.]

Alcaide-Fernández, Joaquín: The contemporary high seas fisheries regime: not a free-for-all, but ... how free? (In: L'Europe et la mer: pêche, navigation et environnement marin, ed. by Rafael Casado Raigon. Bruxelles: Bruylant, 2005, p. 315-331.) [I.C.J., p. 323, 326.]

Ali, Kamal-Deen: Legal and policy dimensions of coastal zone monitoring and control: the case in Ghana. (In: Ocean Development and International Law, 2004, v. 35, no. 2, p. 179-194.)

Anderson, David Heywood: Developments in maritime boundary law and practice. (In: International maritime boundaries, ed. by David A. Colson; Robert W. Smith. Leiden; Boston: Martinus Nijhoff, 2005, v. 5, p. 3199-3222.) [I.C.J., p. 3200, 3202.]

Anderson, David Heywood: Modern law of the sea: selected essays. Leiden [etc.]: Martinus Nijhoff, 2008. (Publications on Ocean Development; 59.) [I.C.J., see index p. 609.]

Arnaut, Damir: Stormy waters on the way to the high seas: the case of the territorial sea delimitation between Croatia and Slovenia. (In: Bringing new law to ocean waters, ed. by Caron, David D.; Scheiber, Harry N. Leiden; Boston: Martinus Nijhoff, 2004, p. 427-465.) [I.C.J., p. 427-428, 441-442, 450, 454.]

Australia-East Timor, report number 6-20 (1) and (2): exchanges of notes constituting an agreement between the Government of the Democratic Republic of East Timor and the Government of Australia concerning arrangements for the exploration and exploitation of petroleum in an area of the Timor Sea, Timor Sea Treaty between the Government of East Timor and the Government of Australia. (In: International maritime boundaries, ed. by Colson, David A.; Smith, Robert W. Leiden; Boston: Martinus Nijhoff, 2005, v. 5, p. 3806-3820.) [I.C.J., p. 3809-3811, 3814, 3817.]

Aznar Gómez, Mariano J.: La protección internacional del patrimonio cultural subacuático: con especial referencia al caso de Espana. Valencia: Tirant lo blanch, 2004. (Tirant monografías; 337.) [C.I.J., p. 50, 140, 142, 152, 157, 162, 165, 179, 201, 382, 412, 635; C.P.J.I., p. 244, 635.]

Barboza, Julio: Provisional measures, or the dangers of being too exceptional. (In: Law of the sea, environmental law and settlement of disputes: liber amicorum Judge Thomas A. Mensah, ed. by Tafsir Malick Ndiaye; Rüdiger Wolfrum. Leiden; Boston: Martinus Nijhoff, 2007, p. 143-157.) [P.C.I.J., p. 145; I.C.J., 145, 147-148, 150, 153, 155.]

Becker, Michael A.: The shifting public order of the oceans: freedom of navigation and the interdiction of ships at sea. (In: Harvard International Law Journal, 2005, v. 46, no. 1, p. 131-230.) [P.C.I.J., p. 171; I.C.J., p. 167.]

Beckman, Robert and Schofield, Clive: Moving beyond disputes over island sovereignty: ICJ decision sets stage for maritime boundary delimitation in the Singapore strait. (In: Ocean Development and International Law, 2009, v. 40, no. 1, p. 1-35.) [I.C.J., passim.]

Bennouna, Mohamed: La stabilité des frontières maritimes entre Etats. (Dans: L'évolution et l'état actuel du droit international de la mer: mélanges de droit de la mer offerts à Daniel Vignes. Bruxelles: Bruylant, 2009, p. 59-67.)

Bischoff, Jan Asmus: Kriegsschiffwracks: welches Recht gilt für Fragen des Eigentums, der Beseitigung und der Haftung? (In: Zeitschrift für ausländisches öffentliches Recht und Völkerrecht, 2006, v. 66, p. 455-490.) [P.C.I.J., p. 472.]

Bölükbas, Deniz: Turkey and Greece: the Aegean disputes: a unique case in international law. London [etc.]: Cavendish, 2004. [P.C.I.J., p. 38, 814, 877, 940-941; I.C.J., p. 103-104, 144, 155-158, 205-218, 236-238, 241-246, 253-572, 725, 783-784, 790, 792-822, 863.]

Bourgeois, Marc A. et Desrosiers, Marie-Claude: Le droit maritime. Cowansville: Yvon Blais, 2005. (La common law en poche; 23.) [C.I.J., p. 9-10.]

Boyle, Alan: Further development of the Law of the Sea Convention: mechanisms for change. (In: International and Comparative Law Quarterly, 2005, v. 54, no. 3, p. 563-584.) [I.C.J., p. 567-569, 573, 575.]

Brubaker, R. Douglas: The Russian Arctic straits. Leiden [etc.]: Nijhoff, 2005. (International straits of the world; 14.) [I.C.J., p. 26-27, 37, 39, 41, 46-50, 52, 106, 111-113, 115, 119, 137, 139, 147, 149-151, 157, 159-160, 164, 166-168, 173, 176, 180, 182, 188-189; P.C.I.J., p. 47, 52.]

Caligiuri, Andrea: La lutte contre l'immigration clandestine par la mer: problèmes liés à l'exercice de la juridiction par les Etats côtiers. (Dans: L'Europe et la mer: pêche, navigation et environnement marin, sous la dir. de Rafael Casado Raigón. Bruxelles: Bruylant, 2005, p. 419-439.) [C.I.J., p. 420, 422.]

Carleton, Chris M.: Maritime delimitation in complex island situations: a case study on the Caribbean Sea. (In: Maritime delimitation, ed. by Rainer Lagoni; Daniel Vignes. Leiden; Boston: Martinus Nijhof, 2006, p. 153-188.) [I.C.J. p. 170, 171, 183, 187.]

Carleton, Chris M.: Red Sea/Persian Gulf maritime boundaries. (In: International maritime boundaries, ed. by Colson, David A.; Smith, Robert W. Leiden; Boston: Martinus Nijhoff, 2005, v. 5, p. 3467-3475.) [I.C.J., p. 3473.]

Carrera Hernández, F. Jesús: Protección internacional del patrimonio cultural submarino. Salamanca: Ediciones universidad de Salamanca, 2005. (Acta Salmanticensia Estudios Jurídicos; 84.) [C.I.J., p. 71, 117.]

Cataldi, Giuseppe: L'Italia e la delimitazione degli spazi marini: osservazioni sulla prassi recente di estensione della giurisdizione costiera nel Mediterraneo. (Dans: Rivista di diritto internazionale, 2004, v. 87, no. 3, p. 621-642.) [C.I.J., p. 622, 624-629.]

Cazala, Julien: Le principe de précaution dans le contentieux relatif au droit de la mer. (Dans: L'observateur des Nations Unies, 2007, v. 22, p. 69-87.) [C.P.J.I., p. 78, 81; C.I.J., p. 70, 78-82, 83, 85-87.]

Chang, Yen-Chiang: Good ocean governance. (In: Ocean Yearbook, 2009, v. 23, p. 89-118.) [I.C.J., p. 114, 115.]

Chircop, Aldo: The customary law of refuge for ships in distress. (In: Places of refuge for ships: emerging environmental concerns of a maritime custom, ed. by Aldo Chircop; Olof Linden. Leiden; Boston: Martinus Nijhoff, 2006, p. 163-229.) [I.C.J., p. 165-167.]

Chircop, Aldo: Law of the sea and international environmental law considerations for places of refuge for ships in need of assistance. (In: Places of refuge for ships: emerging environmental concerns of a maritime custom, ed. by Aldo Chircop; Olof Linden. Leiden; Boston: Martinus Nijhoff, 2006, p. 231-269.) [I.C.J., p. 237-238, 267-268.]

Chircop, Aldo and Dzidzornu, David M. and Guerreiro, Jose and Grilo, Catarina: The maritime zones of East African States in the law of the sea: benefits gained, opportunities missed. (In: African Journal of International and Comparative Law, 2008, v. 16, no. 2, p. 121-150.) [I.C.J., p. 125, 148.]

Churchill, Robin Rolf: The management of shared fish stocks: the neglected "other" paragraph of Article 63 of the UN Convention on the Law of the Sea. (In: Unresolved issues and new challenges to the law of the sea: time before and time after, ed. by Anastasia Strati; Maria Gavouneli; Nikolaos Skourtos. Leiden [etc.]: Martinus Nijhoff, 2006, p. 1-19.) [I.C.J., p. 17.]

Churchill, Robin Rolf: The role of the International Court of Justice in maritime boundary delimitation. (In: Oceans management in the 21st century: institutional frameworks and responses, ed. by Alex G. Oude Elferink; Donald R. Rothwell. Leiden [etc.]: Martinus Nijhoff, 2004, p. 125-141.) [I.C.J., passim.]

Clark, Hilary: Staying afloat in international law: the proliferation security initiative's implications for freedom of navigation. (In: Ocean Yearbook, 2007, v. 21, p. 441-474.) [P.C.I.J., p. 465; I.C.J., p. 461.]

Claypoole, Charles: Access to international justice: a review of the trust funds available for law of the sea-related disputes. (In: International Journal of Marine and Coastal Law, 2008, v. 23, no. 1, p. 77-94.)

Costa e Silva, Paula: A resolução de controvérsias na Convenção das Nações Unidas sobre o direito do mar. (Dans: Estudos em homenagem ao Prof. Doutor Armando M. Marques Guedes: direito constitucional, direito administrativo, direito internacional e direito do mar, direito comunitário europeu, outras áreas, sous la dir. de Miranda, Jorge. Lisbon: Coimbra Editora, 2004, p. 541-601.) [I.C.J., p. 586-591.]

Cot, Jean-Pierre: The law of the sea and the margin of appreciation. (In: Law of the sea, environmental law and settlement disputes: liber amicorum judge Thomas Mensah, ed. by Tafsir Malick Ndiaye; Rüdiger Wolfrum; Chie Kojima. Leiden; Boston: Martinus Nijhoff, 2007, p. 389-403.) [P.C.I.J., p. 390; I.C.J., p. 390-391, 395.]

Couvreur, Philippe: Le règlement juridictionnel. (Dans: Le processus de délimitation maritime: étude d'un cas fictif: colloque international, Monaco, 27-29 mars 2003, sous la dir. de Laurent Lucchini. Paris: Pedone, 2004, p. 349-388.)

Currie, John H.: Maritime boundary delimitation in a federal domestic setting: the Newfoundland and Labrador v. Nova Scotia arbitration. (In: Leiden Journal of International Law, 2004, v. 17, no. 1, p. 155-170.) [I.C.J., p. 157, 159, 161, 163-165, 169.]

Cyprus-Egypt. Report Number 8-15. Agreement between the Republic of Cyprus and the Arab Republic of Egypt on the delimitation of the exclusive economic zone. (In: International maritime boundaries, ed. by Colson, David A.; Smith, Robert W. Leiden; Boston: Martinus Nijhoff, 2005, v. 5, p. 3917-3926.) [I.C.J., p. 3920.]

Daniel, Tim: African maritime boundaries. (In: International maritime boundaries, ed. by Colson, David A.; Smith, Robert W. Leiden; Boston: Martinus Nijhoff, 2005, v. 5, p. 3429-3437.) [I.C.J., p. 3430-3434.]

Degan, Vladimir-Djuro: Consolidation of legal principles on maritime delimitation: implications for the dispute between Slovenia and Croatia in the North Adriatic. (In: Chinese Journal of International Law, 2007, v. 6, no. 3, p. 601-634.) [I.C.J., passim.]

Degan, Vladimir-Djuro: Pravni naslov i efektivnost kao osnove suverenosti nad dravnim podrujem. (In: Uporedno pomorsko pravo, 2008, v. 47, no. 162, p. 1-44.)

Dipla, Haritini: The role of the International Court of Justice and the International Tribunal for the Law of the Sea in the progressive development of the law of the sea. (In: Unresolved issues and new challenges to the law of the sea: time before and time after, ed. by Anastasia Strati; Maria

Gavouneli; Nikolaos Skourtos. Leiden [etc.]: Martinus Nijhoff, 2006, p. 235-250.) [P.C.I.J., p. 235-236; I.C.J., passim.]

Doelle, Meinhard: Climate change and the use of the dispute settlement regime of the Law of the Sea Convention. (In: Ocean Development and International Law, 2006, v. 37, no. 3-4, p. 319-337.) [I.C.J., p. 328, 331, 332.]

Dormuth, Bianca: Befugnisse des Hafenstaates. (In: Schutz der Weltmeere gegen Öltankerunfälle: das rechtliche Instrumentarium, ed. by Tomuschat, Christian. Berlin: Duncker & Humblot, 2005, p. 93-113.) [I.C.J., p. 111.]

Duff, John A.: A note on the United States and the law of the sea: looking back and moving forward. (In: Ocean Development and International Law, 2004, v. 35, no. 3, p. 195-219.) [I.C.J., p. 209.]

Dundas, Carl W.: Middle American and Caribbean maritime boundaries. (In: International maritime boundaries, ed. by Colson, David A.; Smith, Robert W. Leiden; Boston: Martinus Nijhoff, 2005, v. 5, p. 3405-3423.) [I.C.J., p. 3412-3414, 3421.]

Egede, Edwin: The outer limit of the continental shelf: African States and the 1982 Law of the Sea Convention. (In: Ocean Development and International Law, 2004, v. 35, no. 2, p. 157-178.)

Ehlers, Peter and Lagoni, Rainer (eds.): Responsibility and liability in the maritime context. Berlin [etc.]: Lit Verlag, 2009. (Schriften zum See- und Hafenrecht; 16.) [I.C.J., p. 193.]

Escher, Anne-Katrin: Release of vessels and crews before the International Tribunal for the Law of the Sea [Part I-II]. (In: Law and Practice of International Courts and Tribunals, 2004, v. 3, no. 2, p. 205-374.) [I.C.J., p. 237, 240, 253, 281-283, 288-289, 300, 343-345, 348-351, 354-358, 360-361, 366, 369-370, 372.]

Escher, Anne-Katrin: Release of vessels and crews before the International Tribunal for the Law of the Sea [Part III]. (In: Law and Practice of International Courts and Tribunals, 2004, v. 3, no. 3, p. 411-507.) [I.C.J., p. 460; P.C.I.J., p. 492.]

Espaliat Larson, Astrid: Conflictos pesqueros contemporàneos: el caso del pez espada. (Dans: La gestiôn de los recursos marinos y la cooperación internacional: actas del seminario, Santiago de Chile, 22-23 de marzo de 2004, sous la dir. de Del Vecchio, Angela. Roma: Instituto italo-latino americano, 2006, p. 111-152.) [C.I.J., p. 116, 138.]

Espaliú Berdud, Carlos: La nature juridique du passage inoffensif des navires de guerre étrangers dans la mer territoriale: régime existant en marge de la Convention. Bruxelles: Bruylant, 2005. [C.I.J., p. 390-391.]

Espaliú Berdud, Carlos et Casado Raigón, Rafael: El paso inocente de buques de guerra extranjeros por mar territorial: alcance del régimen de la

C.N.U.D.M. (Dans : Revista española de derecho internacional, 2005, v. 57, no. 2, p. 777-798.) [C.I.J., p. 782, 785, 788, 792, 795-796.]

Eto, Junichi: Consideration of relevant circumstances in maritime delimitation : the process of setting objective criteria through case law. (In : Kokusaiho Gaiko Zassi, 2008, v. 107, no. 2, p. 12-40.)

Exclusive Economic Zone Co-operation Treaty between the Republic of Guyana and the State of Barbados concerning the exercise of jurisdiction in their exclusive economic zones in the area of bilateral overlap within each of their outer limits and beyond the outer limits of the exclusive economic zones of other States. (In : International maritime boundaries, ed. by Colson, David A. ; Smith, Robert W. Leiden ; Boston : Martinus Nijhoff, 2005, v. 5, p. 3587-3597.) [I.C.J., p. 3587.]

Fanning, Lucia M.: Understanding influence : lessons from Canada's and Nova Scotia's 1999 George Bank Moratorium Decision. (In : Ocean Yearbook, 2009, 23, p. 119-159.) [I.C.J., p. 122, 128.]

Franckx, Erik: The 200-mile limit : between creeping jurisdiction and creeping common heritage? (In : German Yearbook of International Law, 2005, v. 48, p. 117-149.) [I.C.J., p. 133.]

Franckx, Erik: Multilateralism and marine issues in the Southeast Atlantic. (In : Bringing new law to ocean waters, ed. by Caron, David D. ; Scheiber, Harry N. Leiden ; Boston : Martinus Nijhoff, 2004, p. 177-197.) [I.C.J., p. 181, 189, 192.]

Freestone, David and Salman, Salman M. A.: Ocean and freshwater resources. (In : The Oxford handbook of international environmental law, ed. by Daniel Bodansky ; Jutta Brunnée ; Ellen Hey. Oxford : Oxford University Press, 2007, p. 337-361.) [I.C.J., p. 354.]

Freestone, David and Barnes, Richard and Ong, David M. (eds.): The law of the sea : progress and prospects. Oxford [etc.] : Oxford University Press, 2006.

Gabon-São Tomé and Príncipe. Report Number 4-11. Agreement on the delimitation of the maritime border between the Gabonese Republic and the Democratic Republic of São Tomé and Príncipe. (In : International maritime boundaries, ed. by Colson, David A. ; Smith, Robert W. Leiden ; Boston : Martinus Nijhoff, 2005, v. 5, p. 3683-3689.) [I.C.J., p. 3684-3685.]

García García-Revillo, Miguel: España y la jurisdicción del Corte Internacional de Justicia . La declaración de 19 de julio de 2002. (Dans : Revista española de derecho internacional, 2006, v. 58, p. 297-308.) [C.I.J., p. 297-308.]

Gautier, Philippe: The International Tribunal for the Law of the Sea : activities in 2005. (In : Chinese Journal of International Law, 2006, v. 5, p. 381-396.) [I.C.J., p. 384, 386, 388-390, 392-393.]

Gautier, Philippe: The International Tribunal for the Law of the Sea: activities in 2006. (In: Chinese Journal of International Law, 2007, v. 6, no. 2, p. 389-402.) [P.C.I.J., p. 400; I.C.J., p. 396-398, 401-402.]

Gautier, Philippe: Le réglement obligatoire des différends relatifs au droit de la mer et la pratique des Etats. (Dans: Global Community: Yearbook of International Law and Jurisprudence, 2009, v. 9, no. 1, p. 107-125.)

Gaviria Liévano, Enrique: Los archipiélagos de Estado en el derecho del mar: el caso de San Andrés y Providencia. Bogotá: Temis, 2008.

Gavouneli, Maria: From uniformity to fragmentation? The ability of the UN Convention on the Law of the Sea to accommodate new uses and challenges. (In: Unresolved issues and new challenges to the law of the sea: time before and time after, ed. by Strati, Anastasia; Gavouneli, Maria; Skourtos, Nikolaos. Leiden; Boston: Martinus Nijhoff, 2006, p. 205-234.) [I.C.J., p. 211.]

George, Mary: The regulation of maritime traffic in straits used for international navigation. (In: Oceans management in the 21st century: institutional frameworks and responses, ed. by Oude Elferink, Alex G.; Rothwell, Donald R.. Leiden; Boston: Martinus Nijhoff, p. 19-47.) [I.C.J., p. 30-31.]

Girerd, P.: De l'utilité du concept de "piraterie"? (Dans: Annuaire de droit maritime et océanique, 2005, v. 23, p. 153-177.) [C.I.J., p. 168, 176.]

González Napolitano, Silvina S.: La importancia de las medidas provisionales en las controversias relativas a la pesca. (Dans: La gestión de los recursos marinos y la cooperación internacional: actas del seminario, Santiago de Chile, 22-23 de marzo de 2004, sous la dir. de Del Vecchio, Angela. Roma: Instituto italo-latino americano, 2006, p. 169-175.) [C.I.J., p. 170-173.]

Guilfoyle, Douglas: Interdicting vessels to enforce the common interest: maritime countermeasures and the use of force. (In: International and Comparative Law Quarterly, 2007, v. 56, p. 69-82.) [P.C.I.J., p. 70; I.C.J., p. 75, 80.]

Hamukuaya, Hashali: South east Atlantic Fisheries Organization: a modern instrument to address typical fisheries management issues. (In: Ocean Yearbook, 2007, v. 21, p. 203-236.) [I.C.J., p. 236.]

Harrison, James: Judicial law-making and the developing order of the oceans. (In: Journal of Marine and Coastal Law, 2007, v. 22, no. 2, p. 283-302.)

Hayashi, Moritaka: Jurisdiction over foreign commercial ships in ports: a gap in the law of the sea codification. (In: Ocean Yearbook, 2004, v. 18, p. 488-511.) [P.C.I.J., p. 494-495.]

Heintschel von Heinegg, Wolff: Current legal issues in maritime operations: maritime interception operations in the global war on terrorism, exclusion zones, hospital ships and maritime neutrality. (In : International Law Studies (Naval War College), 2006, v. 80, p. 207-233.) [I.C.J., p. 213.]

Heintschel von Heinegg, Wolff : The United Nations Convention on the Law of the Sea and maritime security operations. (In : German Yearbook of International Law, 2005, v. 48, p. 151-185.) [P.C.I.J., p. 178; I.C.J., p. 180, 183.]

Hinojo Rosas, Manuel : Le régime juridique de la navigation par le canal de Suez. (Dans : L'Europe et la mer : pêche, navigation et environnement marin, sous la dir. de Rafael Casado Raigón. Bruxelles : Bruylant, 2005, p. 347-377.) [C.P.J.I., p. 358; C.I.J., p. 371-373.]

Iglesias Berlanga, Marta : La jurisprudencia del Tribunal Internacional del Derecho del Mar. (Dans : Cuadernos de jurisprudencia internacional, 2005, v. 2, p. 199-248.) [C.I.J., p. 202, 212, 229, 231-233, 235-237, 242-247.]

Ihraï, Saïd : La zone économique exclusive : problèmes de délimitation. (Dans : Le processus de délimitation maritime : étude d'un cas fictif : colloque international, Monaco, 27-29 mars 2003. Paris : Pedone, 2004, p. 77-97.)

Jacob, Patrick : Conseil constitutionnel, 28 avril 2005, décision no 2005-514 DC, loi relative à la création du registre international français. (Dans : Revue générale de droit international public, 2005, v. 109, p. 739-747.) [C.P.J.I., p. 743-745.]

Kamto, Maurice : Sur quelques questions techniques liées à la détermination du tracé d'une frontière maritime délimitée. (Dans : L'évolution et l'état actuel du droit international de la mer : mélanges de droit de la mer offerts à Daniel Vignes. Bruxelles : Bruylant, 2009, p. 481-505.)

Kangueu Ekeuh, Robert : Les eaux intérieures en droit public maritime au Cameroun. (Dans : Annuaire de droit maritime et océanique, 2005, v. 23, p. 217-249.) [C.P.J.I., p. 244; C.I.J., p. 225-229.]

Karagiannis, Syméon : L'article 59 de la Convention des Nations Unies sur le droit de la mer (ou les mystères de la nature juridique de la zone économique exclusive). (Dans : Revue belge de droit international, 2004, v. 37, p. 325-418.) [C.I.J., p. 330-331, 333, 337-339, 348-349, 386-387, 391-392, 396, 402.]

Karagiannis, Syméon : La succession d'Etats et le droit de la mer : les zones maritimes de l'Etat successeur. (Dans : Revue belge de droit international, 2006, v. 39, p. 459-506.) [C.I.J., p. 461, 464, 469, 479, 483, 484, 488, 490, 497.]

Kassmann, Rico : Die Bekämpfung der Meeresverschmutzung nach Tankerunglücken : Intervention und Kooperation. (In : Schutz der Weltmeere gegen Öltankerunfälle : das rechtliche Instrumentarium, ed. by Tomuschat, Christian. Berlin : Duncker & Humblot, 2005, p. 129-167.) [I.C.J., p. 160, 161, 163, 164.]

Kaye, Stuart B. : Freedom of navigation, surveillance and security : legal issues surrounding the collection of intelligence from beyond the littoral. (In :

Australian Yearbook of International Law, 2005, v. 24, p. 93-105.) [I.C.J., p. 94-95.]

Kaye, Stuart B.: Negotiation and dispute resolution: a case study in international boundary making: the Australia-Indonesia boundary. (In: Oceans management in the 21st century: institutional frameworks and responses, ed. by Oude Elferink, Alex G.; Rothwell, Donald R.. Leiden; Boston: Martinus Nijhoff, p. 143-166.) [I.C.J., p. 146, 148, 151, 154-156, 162-165.]

Kaye, Stuart B.: The proliferation security initiative in the maritime domain. (In: International Law Studies (Naval War College), 2006, v. 81, p. 141-164.) [P.C.I.J., p. 144; I.C.J., p. 146, 152.]

Kaye, Stuart B.: Territorial sea baselines along ice-covered coasts: international practice and limits of the law of the sea. (In: Ocean Development and International Law, 2004, v. 35, no. 1, p. 75-102.) [I.C.J., p. 78, 83, 86-87.]

Kim, Doo-young: Advisory proceedings before the International Tribunal for the Law of the Sea as an alternative procedure to supplement the dispute-settlement mechanism under part XV of the United Nations Convention on the Law of the Sea. (In: Issues in Legal Scholarship, 2008, v. 7, no. 1, p. 1-14.) [I.C.J., p. 2-6, 8, 10-11, 13.]

Kim, Sun Pyo: Maritime delimitation and interim arrangements in North East Asia. The Hague [etc.]: Nijhoff, 2004. (Publications on ocean development; v. 40.) [I.C.J. and P.C.I.J., p. 1, 3, 8, 10-13, 15-16, 19-25, 27, 29-30, 39, 41-42, 44-45, 47, 52, 54-61, 67-69, 71, 73, 77-78, 81, 83-88, 91-93, 95, 97, 102, 149, 154, 164, 166-167, 195-196, 205, 213-214, 216, 218-220, 222, 224, 230, 236, 240-241, 243-246, 256, 282, 298, 308.]

Klein, Natalie: Dispute settlement in the UN Convention on the Law of the Sea. Cambridge: Cambridge University Press, 2005. (Cambridge studies in international and comparative law; 39.) [I.C.J., p. 10, 14-16, 19, 24, 30, 43-44, 54-61, 74, 76, 79, 91-92, 161-162, 171, 202, 228-229, 234, 236-237, 242-243, 245-246, 257, 259, 261, 264-265, 267-269, 285, 291, 298, 367; P.C.I.J., p. 9-11, 39, 74, 160, 258-259.]

König, Doris: Questionnaire international law of the sea. (In: Unity and diversity in international law: proceedings of an international symposium of the Kiel Walther Schücking Institute of International Law, November 4-7, 2004, ed. by Zimmermann, Andreas; Hofmann, Rainer. Berlin: Duncker & Humblot, 2006, p. 27-63.) [P.C.I.J., p. 61; I.C.J., p. 41, 50-54.]

Kovats, Laszlo J.: True internationalism of the law of the sea. (In: Indian Journal of International Law, 2004, v. 44, no. 2, p. 347-369.) [I.C.J., p. 349.]

Kozyris, Phaedon John: Islands in the recent maritime adjudications: simplifying the Aegean Conundrum. (In: Ocean Development and International Law, 2008, v. 39, no. 4, p. 329-342.)

Kunoy, Bjørn: The rise of the sun: legal arguments in outer continental margin delimitations. (In: Netherlands International Law Review, 2006, v. 53, p. 247-272.) [I.C.J., p. 249, 251-252, 255-271.]

Kwiatkowska, Barbara: The 2006 UNCLOS annex VII Barbados/Trinidad and Tobago award: landmark progress in compulsory jurisdiction and equitable maritime boundary delimitation. (In: Hague Yearbook of International Law, 2006, v. 19, p. 33-86.) [I.C.J., passim.]

Kwiatkowska, Barbara: The landmark 2006 UNCLOS annex VII Barbados/Trinidad and Tobago maritime delimitation (jurisdiction and merits) award. (In: The George Washington International Law Review, 2007, v. 39, no. 3, p. 573-620.) [I.C.J., passim.]

Kwiatkowska, Barbara: Resource, navigational and environmental factors in equitable maritime boundary delimitation. (In: International maritime boundaries, ed. by Colson, David A.; Smith, Robert W. Leiden; Boston: Martinus Nijhoff, 2005, v. 5, p. 3223-3244.) [I.C.J., p. 3224-3236, 3238-3244.]

La Fayette, Louise Angélique, de: The consequences of climate change in the Arctic. (In: Ocean Yearbook, 2009, v. 23, p. 39-88.) [I.C.J., p. 57-59, 62.]

Labrecque, Georges: Les frontières maritimes internationales: géopolitique de la délimitation en mer. Paris [etc.]: L'Harmattan, 2004. 2e éd. rev. et augm. (Collection Raoul-Dandurand géopolitique.) [I.C.J., p. 17-20, 25, 30, 32, 40, 56-57, 78-79, 83-85, 87-89, 92-93, 94-101, 104-131, 135-138, 141-142, 149, 155-157, 161, 164-165, 195, 220-230, 260-261, 269, 278-281, 299-300, 310, 312-322, 330, 332, 341-356, 381, 390-403, 417, 462-471.]

Lagoni, Rainer and Vignes, Daniel (eds.): Maritime delimitation. Leiden; Boston: Martinus Nijhoff, 2006. (Publications on ocean development; 53.) [P.C.I.J., p. 22, 33-35, 48, 129; I.C.J., p. 29, 33-40, 51, 66, 71, 80-81, 88.]

Land reclamation case (Malaysia v. Singapore). (In: International Law Reports, 2005, v. 126, p. 487-535.) [I.C.J., p. 523, 524; P.C.I.J., p. 529.]

Lathrop, Coalter: Tripoint issues in maritime boundary delimitation. (In: International maritime boundaries, ed. by Colson, David A.; Smith, Robert W. Leiden; Boston: Martinus Nijhoff, 2005, v. 5, p. 3305-3375.) [I.C.J., p. 3306, 3311-3312, 3318, 3320-3322, 3324-3333, 3337, 3341, 3343.]

Leanza, Umberto: L'Italia e la scelta di rafforzare la tutela dell'ambiente marino: l'istituzione di zone di protezione ecologica. (Dans: Rivista di diritto internazionale, 2006, v. 89, p. 309-339.) [C.I.J., p. 318-319.]

Lee, Kuen-Gwan: Toward an equitable resolution of maritime delimitation disputes in East Asia: a critical perspective. (In: Kokusaiho Gaiko Zassi, 2004, v. 103, no. 1, p. 50-83.) [I.C.J., p. 51-56, 58-59, 62-71, 73-82.]

Legal issues of the outer continental shelf. (In: Reports of the Annual Conference, by International Law Association (ILA), 2004, v. 71, p. 773-825.) [I.C.J., p. 774, 787.]

Legal issues of the outer continental shelf, second report. (In: Reports of the Annual Conference, by International Law Association (ILA), 2006, 2006, p. 215-253.) [P.C.I.J., p. 240; I.C.J., p. 216-218, 246.]

Lehardy, Magali: La liberté de la pêche en haute mer et l'accord sur les stocks de poissons: principe en faillite ou en voie d'effectivité. (Dans: Annuaire de droit maritime et océanique, 2005, v. 23, p. 251-308.) [C.P.J.I., p. 263.]

Liacouras, Petros: Intelligence gathering on the high seas. (In: Unresolved issues and new challenges to the law of the sea: time before and time after, ed. by Anastasia Strati; Maria Gavouneli; Nikolaos Skourtos. Leiden [etc.]: Martinus Nijhoff, 2006, p. 123-148.) [I.C.J., p. 138.]

Lowe, Vaughan: Advocating judicial activism: the ITLOS opinions of Judge Ivan Shearer. (In: Australian Yearbook of International Law, 2005, v. 24, p. 145-157.) [I.C.J., p. 147, 153, 155.]

Lucchini, Laurent: Plaidoyer pour une ligne unique de délimitation. (Dans: L'évolution et l'état actuel du droit international de la mer: mélanges de droit de la mer offerts à Daniel Vignes. Bruxelles: Bruylant, 2009, p. 561-585.)

Marques Antunes, Nuno S.: Some thoughts on the technical input in maritime delimitation. (In: International maritime boundaries, ed. by Colson, David A.; Smith, Robert W. Leiden; Boston: Martinus Nijhoff, 2005, v. 5, p. 3377-3398.) [I.C.J., p. 3382-3384, 3389-3390, 3393, 3395.]

Martínez Pérez, Enrique: Port State measures at the WTO. (In: L'Europe et la mer: pêche, navigation et environnement marin, ed. by Rafael Casado Raigón. Bruxelles: Bruylant, 2005, p. 441-454.) [I.C.J., p. 441.]

McDorman, Ted L.: Canada ratifies the 1982 United Nations Convention on the Law of the Sea: at last. (In: Ocean Development and International Law, 2004, v. 35, no. 2, p. 105-106.)

McDorman, Ted L.: A Canadian perspective on the continued non-ratification of the Convention on the Law of the Sea by the United States. (In: Canadian Yearbook of International Law, 2005, v. 43, p. 393-417.) [I.C.J., p. 398, 405, 411-412, 415.]

McDorman, Ted L.: Central Pacific and East Asian maritime boundaries. (In: International maritime boundaries, ed. by Colson, David A.; Smith, Robert W. Leiden; Boston: Martinus Nijhoff, 2005, v. 5, p. 3439-3451.) [I.C.J., p. 3439, 3445-3446.]

McDorman, Ted L. and Bolla, Alexander J. and Johnston, Douglas M. and Duff, John A. (eds.): International ocean law: materials and commentaries. Durham: Carolina Academic Press, 2005. (Carolina Academic Press law casebook series.) [I.C.J., see index p. 425.]

Milano, Enrico: The new fisheries partnership agreement between the European Community and the Kingdom of Morocco: fishing too south? (In: Anuario español de derecho internacional, 2006, v. 22, p. 413-457.) [I.C.J., p. 415-416, 417, 429, 432, 434, 436, 445, 447, 450-451.]

Miyoshi, Masahiro: Some thoughts on maritime boundary delimitation. (In: Maritime boundary disputes, settlement processes, and the law of the sea, ed. by Seoung-Yong Hong; Jon M. Van Dyke. Leiden: Martinus Nijhoff Publishers, 2009, p. 107-118.) [I.C.J., passim.]

Momtaz, Djamchid: Le régime de passage dans le détroit d'Hormuz. (Dans: L'Europe et la mer: pêche, navigation et environnement marin, sous la dir. de Rafael Casado Raigón. Bruxelles: Bruylant, 2005, p. 167-174.) [C.I.J., p. 169.]

Nelson, L. Dolliver M.: The settlement of disputes arising from conflicting outer continental shelf claims. (In: International Journal of Marine and Coastal Law, 2009, v. 24, no. 2, p. 409-422.) [I.C.J., p. 410, 420-421.]

Ngnintedem, Jean-Claude: Le nouvel ordre maritime international et les pays en voie de développement: bilan d'une participation à l'oeuvre normative internationale. (Dans: Annuaire de droit maritime et océanique, 2005, v. 23, p. 121-152.) [C.I.J., p. 135-136.]

Nguyen, Hong Thao: Le Vietnam et ses différends maritimes dans la Mer de Bien Dong (Mer de Chine méridionale). Paris: Pedone, 2004. [C.I.J., p. 37-38, 55-56, 60-63, 67-69, 81, 113, 124-125, 128, 130, 132, 135, 163, 172, 174, 184, 198, 208, 225, 245, 250-251, 275; C.P.J.I., p. 124, 197, 250-251.]

Nigeria-São Tomé and Príncipe. Report Number 4-10. Treaty between the Federal Republic of Nigeria and the Democratic Republic of São Tomé and Príncipe on the joint development of petroleum and other resources in respect of areas of the exclusive economic zone of the two States. (In: International maritime boundaries, ed. by Colson, David A.; Smith, Robert W. Leiden; Boston: Martinus Nijhoff, 2005, v. 5, p. 3638-3648.) [I.C.J., p. 3640.]

Oceans and the law of the sea: report of the Secretary-General, 2002. (In: Ocean Yearbook, 2004, v. 18, p. 635-825.) [I.C.J., p. 756-757.]

Oceans and the law of the sea: report of the Secretary-General, 2003. (In: Ocean Yearbook, 2005, v. 19, p. 405-483.) [I.C.J., p. 412.]

Oceans and the law of the sea: report of the Secretary-General, 2003: addendum. (In: Ocean Yearbook, 2005, v. 19, p. 484-526.) [I.C.J., p. 493, 513, 516-517.]

Odeke, Ademun: From the "Constitution of the Maritime Safety Committee" to the "Constitution of the Council": will the IMCO experience repeat itself at the IMO nearly fifty years on? The juridicial politics of an international organization. (In: Texas International Law Journal, 2007, v. 43, no. 1, p. 55-113.)

Oral, Nilufer: Protection of vulnerable marine ecosystems in areas beyond national jurisdiction: can international law meet the challenge? (In: Unresolved issues and new challenges to the law of the sea: time before and time after, ed. by Anastasia Strati; Maria Gavouneli; Nikolaos Skourtos. Leiden [etc.]: Martinus Nijhoff, 2006, p. 85-108.) [I.C.J., p. 94.]

Orrego Vicuña, Francisco: The International Tribunal for the Law of the Sea and provisional measures: settled issues and pending problems. (In: International Journal of Marine and Coastal Law, 2007, v. 22, p. 451-462.) [I.C.J., p. 452-455.]

Oude Elferink, Alex G.: "Openness" and Article 76 of the Law of the Sea Convention: the process does not need to be adjusted. (In: Ocean Development and International Law, 2009, v. 40, no. 1, p. 36-50.) [I.C.J., p. 38.]

Oude Elferink, Alex G.: The continental shelf beyond 200 nautical miles: the relationship between the CLCS and third party dispute settlement. (In: Oceans management in the 21st century: institutional frameworks and responses, ed. by Alex G. Oude Elferink; Donald R. Rothwell. Leiden [etc.]: Martinus Nijhoff, 2004, p. 107-123.) [I.C.J., p. 115-116.]

Oude Elferink, Alex G.: The continental shelf in the polar regions: cold war or black-letter law? (In: Netherlands Yearbook of International Law, 2009, v. 40, p. 121-181.) [I.C.J., p. 145, 155.]

Oude Elferink, Alex G. and Soons, Alfred H. A.: Recht van de zee. (In: Handboek internationaal recht, ed. by Horbach, Nathalie L. J. T.; Lefeber, René; Ribbelink, Olivier. The Hague: T.M.C. Asser Press, 2007, p. 713-767.) [I.C.J., p. 719, 722, 728-729, 733, 737.]

Oude Elferink, Alex G.: Reviewing the implementation of the LOS Convention: the role of the United Nations General Assembly and the meeting of States parties. (In: Oceans management in the 21st century: institutional frameworks and responses, ed. by Oude Elferink, Alex G.; Rothwell, Donald R.. Leiden; Boston: Martinus Nijhoff, p. 295-312.) [I.C.J., p. 301.]

Oude Elferink, Alex G.: Submissions of coastal States to the CLCS in cases of unresolved land or maritime disputes. (In: Legal and scientific aspects of continental shelf limits, ed. by Myron H. Nordquist; John Norton Moore; Tomas H. Heidar. Leiden [etc.]: Martinus Nijhoff, 2004, p. 263-277.) [I.C.J., p. 265, 266.]

Oude Elferink, Alex G.: Third States in maritime delimitation cases: too big a role, too small a role, or both? (In: The future of ocean regime-building: essays in tribute to Douglas M. Johnston, ed. by Aldo Chircop; Ted L. McDorman; Susan J. Rolston. Leiden; Boston: Martinus Nijhoff, 2009, p. 611-641.) [I.C.J., p. 53-54, 202, 416, 453, 455, 617, 663-665, 620, 629-631, 634-639, 714-720.]

Oude Elferink, Alex G. and Rothwell, Donald R. (eds.): Oceans management in the 21st century: institutional frameworks and responses.

Leiden [etc.]: Martinus Nijhoff, 2004. (Publications on ocean development; 44.) [I.C.J., see index p. 379.]

Oude Elferink, Alex G. (ed.): Stability and change in the law of the sea: the role of the LOS Convention. Leiden [etc.]: Martinus Nijhoff, 2005. (Nova et vetera iuris gentium. Series A. Verzijl. International Law; 24.) [I.C.J., see index p. 243.]

Oxman, Bernard H.: The International Tribunal for the Law of the Sea. (In: Bringing new law to ocean waters, ed. by Caron, David D.; Scheiber, Harry N. Leiden; Boston: Martinus Nijhoff, 2004, p. 285-296.) [I.C.J., p. 285, 289, 292.]

Pallas, Nadine Christina: Maritimer Kulturgüterschutz. Berlin: Duncker & Humblot, 2004. (Schriften zum Völkerrecht; 154.) [P.C.I.J., p. 294; I.C.J., p. 225, 248, 249, 269, 283, 309, 324, 334-336, 342.]

Papanicolopulu, Irini: A note on maritime delimitation in a multizonal context: the case of the Mediterranean. (In: Ocean Development and International Law, 2007, v. 38, no. 4, p. 381-398.) [I.C.J., p. 388, 389.]

Park, Choon-Ho: The changeable legal status of islands and "non-islands" in the law of the sea: some instances in the Asia-Pacific region. (In: Bringing new law to ocean waters, ed. by Caron, David D.; Scheiber, Harry N. Leiden; Boston: Martinus Nijhoff, 2004, p. 483-491.) [I.C.J., p. 485.]

Pastor Palomar, Antonio: El derecho reenvía a la geografía: cayos y bancos en la delimitación marítima interestatal. (Dans: Mares y océanos en un mundo de cambio: tendencias jurídicas, actores y factores: XXI Jornadas de la Asociación Española de Profesores de Derecho Internacional y Relaciones Internacionales a Coruña, 22-24 de septiembre de 2005, sous la dir. de José Manuel Sobrino Heredia. Valencia: tirant lo blanch, 2007, p. 219-253.) [C.I.J., p. 223-230, 235-236, 247-253.]

Perry, Timothy C.: Blurring the ocean zones: the effect of the proliferation security initiative on the customary international law of the sea. (In: Ocean Development and International Law, 2006, v. 37, no. 1, p. 33-53.) [I.C.J., p. 44.]

Pinto, M. C. W.: Participation and compliance in international law. (In: Ocean Yearbook, 2004, v. 18, p. 220-245.) [I.C.J., p. 232.]

Piquemal, Alain and Lahlou, Abdelkader: The intervention of the International Ocean Institute in the prevention and settlement of maritime disputes. (In: Ocean Yearbook, 2007, v. 21, p. 23-40.) [P.C.I.J., p. 26; I.C.J., p. 26-34.]

Pratt, Martin: The role of the technical expert in maritime delimitation cases. (In: Maritime delimitation, ed. by Lagoni, Rainer; Vignes, David. Leiden; Boston: Martinus Nijhoff, 2006, p. 79-94.) [I.C.J., p. 81-82, 84-85.]

Prescott, Victor and Triggs, Gillian Doreen: Islands and rocks and their role in maritime delimitation. (In: International maritime boundaries, ed. by David A. Colson; Robert W. Smith. Leiden; Boston: Martinus Nijhoff, 2005,

v. 5, p. 3245-3280.) [I.C.J., p. 3246, 3256, 3263-3267, 3270-3274, 3276, 3279.]

Proceedings Concerning the MOX Plant (Ireland v. United Kingdom). (In: International Law Reports, 2005, v. 126, p. 259-333.) [I.C.J., p. 287-289, 296, 298-299, 325; P.C.I.J., p. 282.]

Prows, Peter: Tough love: the dramatic birth and looming demise of UNCLOS property law (and what is to be done about it). (In: Texas International Law Journal, 2007, v. 42, p. 241-309.) [I.C.J., p. 244, 252-254, 257-260, 263-265, 277.]

Quéneudec, Jean-Pierre: Les principes dégagés par le juge et le rôle des circonstances pertinentes en matière de délimitation maritime. (Dans: Le processus de délimitation maritime: étude d'un cas fictif: colloque international, Monaco, 27-29 mars 2003, sous la dir. de Laurent Lucchini. Paris: Pedone, 2004, p. 279-285.)

Rah, Sicco and Wallrabenstein, Tilo: The International Tribunal for the Law of the Sea and its future. (In: Ocean Yearbook, 2007, v. 21, p. 41-67.) [I.C.J., p. 41, 43-45, 54-56.]

Rangel, Vicente Marotta: A problemática contemporânea do direito do mar. (Dans: O Brasil e os novos desafios do direito internacional, sous la dir. de Brant, Leonardo Nemer Caldeira. Rio de Janeiro: Editora Forense, 2004, p. 323-339.) [C.I.J., p. 334-336.]

Rayfuse, Rosemary: Countermeasures and high seas fisheries enforcement. (In: Netherlands International Law Review, 2004, v. 51, no. 1, p. 41-76.) [I.C.J., p. 48, 50-52, 73.]

Rayfuse, Rosemary: Regulation and enforcement in the law of the sea: emerging assertions of a right to non-flag State enforcement in the high seas fisheries and disarmament contexts. (In: Australian Yearbook of International Law, 2005, v. 24, p. 181-200.) [I.C.J., p. 197.]

Reisman, William Michael and Arsanjani, Mahnoush H.: Some reflections on the effect of artisanal fishing on maritime boundary delimitation. (In: Law of the sea, environmental law and settlement of disputes: liber amicorum Judge Thomas A. Mensah, ed. by Tafsir Malick Ndiaye; Rüdiger Wolfrum. Leiden; Boston: Martinus Nijhoff, 2007, p. 629-665.)

Robineau, Daniel: Une histoire de la chasse à la baleine. Paris: Vuibert, 2007. (Planète vivante.) [C.P.J.I., p. 133.]

Romano, Cesare P. R.: The settlement of disputes under the 1982 Law of the Sea Convention: how entangled can we get? (In: Kokusaiho Gaiko Zassi, 2004, v. 103, no. 1, p. 84-106.) [I.C.J., p. 85, 87, 89-91, 97, 102-103.]

Ronzitti, Natalino: La convenciòn de Naciones Unidas sobre el derecho del mar y el procedimiento para la pronta liberaciòn de buques y tripulantes. (Dans: La gestiòn de los recursos marinos y la cooperación internacional: actas del seminario, Santiago de Chile, 22-23 de marzo de 2004, sous la dir. de Del Vecchio, Angela. Roma : Instituto italo-latino americano, 2006, p. 153-167.) [C.I.J., p. 157.]

Ros, Nathalie : Les effectivités (rôle et place). (Dans : Le processus de délimitation maritime : étude d'un cas fictif : colloque international, Monaco, 27-29 mars 2003, sous la dir. de Laurent Lucchini. Paris : Pedone, 2004, p. 195-227.) [C.P.J.I., p. 198, 204-206, 209-210; C.I.J., p. 203-205, 207-213, 215-227.]

Ros, Nathalie : Les méthodes juridictionnelles de délimitation maritime. (Dans : L'évolution et l'état actuel du droit international de la mer : mélanges de droit de la mer offerts à Daniel Vignes. Bruxelles : Bruylant, 2009, p. 797-827.) [C.I.J., passim.]

Rosenne, Shabtai : Historic waters in the Third United Nations Conference on the Law of the Sea. (In : Essays on international law and practice, by Shabtai Rosenne. Leiden ; Boston : Martinus Nijhoff, 2007, p. 497-511.)

Rosenne, Shabtai : Reflections on fisheries management disputes. (In : L'évolution et l'état actuel du droit international de la mer : mélanges de droit de la mer offerts à Daniel Vignes. Bruxelles : Bruylant, 2009, p. 829-851.) [I.C.J., p. 830, 832-834, 837, 850.]

Rosenne, Shabtai : The United Nations Convention on the Law of the Sea, 1982 : the application of Part XI : an element of background. (In : Essays on international law and practice, by Shabtai Rosenne. Leiden ; Boston : Martinus Nijhoff, 2007, p. 457-468.)

Rosenne, Shabtai : The United Nations, the oceans and some geography. (In : Essays on international law and practice, by Shabtai Rosenne. Leiden ; Boston : Martinus Nijhoff, 2007, p. 469-495.)

Rothwell, Donald R. : Building on the strengths and adressing the challenges : the role of law of the sea institutions. (In : Ocean Development and International Law, 2004, v. 35, no. 2, p. 131-156.)

Rothwell, Donald R. and Stephens, Tim : Dispute resolution and the law of the sea : reconciling the interaction between the LOS Convention and other environmental instruments. (In : Oceans management in the 21st century : institutional frameworks and responses, ed. by Oude Elferink, Alex G. ; Rothwell, Donald R. Leiden ; Boston : Martinus Nijhoff, p. 209-229.) [I.C.J., p. 209, 212, 215.]

Rothwell, Donald R. : Oceans management and the law of the sea in the twenty-first century. (In : Oceans management in the 21st century : institutional frameworks and responses, ed. by Oude Elferink, Alex G. ; Rothwell, Donald R. Leiden ; Boston : Martinus Nijhoff, p. 329-356.) [I.C.J., p. 331, 335.]

Sakamoto, Shigeki : Japan-China dispute over maritime boundary delimitation : from a Japanese perspective. (In : Japanese Yearbook of International Law, 2008, v. 51, p. 98-118.)

Sánchez Rodríguez, Luis Ignacio: L'uti possidetis: application à la délimitation maritime. (Dans: Le processus de délimitation maritime: étude d'un cas fictif: colloque international, Monaco, 27-29 mars 2003, sous la dir. de Laurent Lucchini. Paris: Pedone, 2004, p. 303-315.) [C.I.J., passim.]

Sánchez Rodríguez, Luis Ignacio: La pêche et les intérêts espagnols. (Dans: L'Europe et la mer: pêche, navigation et environnement marin, sous la dir. de Rafael Casado Raigón. Bruxelles: Bruylant, 2005, p. 29-37.) [C.I.J., p. 34, 36.]

Schiffman, Howard S.: Marine conservation agreements: the law and policy of reservations and vetoes. Leiden [etc.]: Martinus Nijhoff, 2008. (Publications on ocean development; 60.) [I.C.J., see index p. 273.]

Schofield, Clive and Carleton, Chris M.: Technical considerations in law of the sea dispute resolution. (In: Oceans management in the 21st century: institutional frameworks and responses, ed. by Alex G. Oude Elferink; Donald R. Rothwell. Leiden [etc.]: Martinus Nijhoff, 2004, p. 231-254.) [I.C.J., p. 237-247, 251-253.]

Scott, Karen N.: International regulation of undersea noise. (In: International and Comparative Law Quarterly, 2004, v. 53, no. 2, p. 287-323.) [I.C.J., p. 293, 322.]

Scott, Shirley V.: The contribution of the LOS Convention organizations to its harmonious implementation. (In: Oceans management in the 21st century: institutional frameworks and responses, ed. by Oude Elferink, Alex G.; Rothwell, Donald R.. Leiden; Boston: Martinus Nijhoff, p. 313-327.) [I.C.J., p. 314, 316-318.]

Scovazzi, Tullio: The Mediterranean and Black Sea maritime boundaries. (In: International maritime boundaries, ed. by Colson, David A.; Smith, Robert W. Leiden; Boston: Martinus Nijhoff, 2005, v. 5, p. 3471-3491.) [I.C.J., p. 3484, 3490.]

Serdy, Andrew: Towards certainty of seabed jurisdiction beyond 200 nautical miles from the territorial sea baseline: Australia's submission to the Commission on the Limits of the Continental Shelf. (In: Ocean Development and International Law, 2005, v. 36, no. 3, p. 201-217.) [I.C.J., p. 202.]

Shearer, Ivan: Oceans management challenges for the law of the sea in the first decade of the 21st century. (In: Oceans management in the 21st century: institutional frameworks and responses, ed. by Oude Elferink, Alex G.; Rothwell, Donald R.. Leiden; Boston: Martinus Nijhoff, p. 1-18.) [I.C.J., p. 4, 13.]

Sioussiouras, Petros: The contiguous zone as a mechanism for protecting the underwater cultural heritage. (In: Unresolved issues and new challenges to the law of the sea: time before and time after, ed. by Anastasia Strati; Maria Gavouneli; Nikolaos Skourtos. Leiden [etc.]: Martinus Nijhoff, 2006, p. 63-70.) [I.C.J., p. 57.]

Sohn, Louis B. and Noyes, John E.: Cases and materials on the law of the sea. Ardsley: Transnational, 2004. [P.C.I.J. and I.C.J., see table of cases, p. lxvii-lxix.]

Stephens, Dale: The legal efficacy of freedom of navigation assertions. (In: International Law Studies (Naval War College), 2006, v. 80, p. 235-256.) [P.C.I.J., p. 238, 250; I.C.J., p. 238, 243-245, 248-251.]

Strati, Anastasia: Protection of the underwater cultural heritage: from the shortcomings of the UN Convention on the Law of the Sea to the compromises of the UNESCO Convention. (In: Unresolved issues and new challenges to the law of the sea: time before and time after, ed. by Anastasia Strati; Maria Gavouneli; Nikolaos Skourtos. Leiden [etc.]: Martinus Nijhoff, 2006, p. 21-62.) [I.C.J., p. 40.]

Strati, Anastasia and Gavouneli, Maria and Skourtos, Nikolaos (eds.): Unresolved issues and new challenges to the law of the sea: time before and time after. Leiden [etc.]: Nijhoff, 2006. (Publications on ocean development; 54.) [I.C.J., see index p. 339.]

Suarez, Suzette V.: The outer limits of the continental shelf: legal aspects of their establishment. Berlin [etc.]: Springer, 2008. (Beiträge zum auslandischen öffentlichen Recht und Völkerrecht; 199.) [I.C.J., p. 13, 104, 113, 120-122, 124, 128, 126-143, 146-148, 173, 221-225, 228-229, 238, 242-243, 247.]

Syrigos, Angelos M.: Developments on the interdiction of vessels of the high seas. (In: Unresolved issues and new challenges to the law of the sea: time before and time after, ed. by Strati, Anastasia; Gavouneli, Maria; Skourtos, Nikolaos. Leiden; Boston: Martinus Nijhoff, 2006, p. 149-201.) [I.C.J., p. 156-157, 162, 176-177.]

Tanaka, Maki: Lessons from the protracted MOX plant dispute: a proposed protocol on marine environmental impact assesment to the United Nations Convention on the Law of the Sea. Ann Arbor, MI: University of Michigan Law School, 2004. [I.C.J. and P.C.I.J., p. 343-344, 347, 353, 355.]

Tanaka, Yoshifumi: Low-tide elevations in international law of the sea: selected issues. (In: Ocean Yearbook, 2006, v. 20, p. 189-219.) [I.C.J., p. 195-209, 214-219.]

Tanaka, Yoshifumi: Prompt release in the United Nations Convention on the Law of the Sea: some reflections on the ITLOS jurisprudence. (In: Netherlands International Law Review, 2004, v. 51, p. 237-271.) [I.C.J., p. 250, 252.]

Tanaka, Yoshifumi: Quelques observations sur deux approches jurisprudentielles en droit de la délimitation maritime: l'affrontement entre prévisibilité et flexibilité. (Dans: Revue belge de droit international, 2004, v. 37, p. 419-455.) [C.I.J., passim.]

Timor Sea Treaty between the Government of East Timor and the Government of Australia (Dili, 20 May 2002). (In: International maritime boundaries, ed. by Colson, David A. ; Smith, Robert W. Leiden ; Boston : Martinus Nijhoff, 2005, v. 5, p. 3829-3866.) [I.C.J., p. 3847.]

Tomuschat, Christian : Die Internationale Seeschifffahrts-Organisation (International Maritime Organization, IMO) als Hauptakteur. (In : Schutz der Weltmeere gegen Öltankerunfälle : das rechtliche Instrumentarium, ed. by Tomuschat, Christian. Berlin : Duncker & Humblot, 2005, p. 21-30.) [I.C.J., p. 22.]

Traisbach, Knut: Haftung und Entschädigung bei Öltankerunfällen. (In : Schutz der Weltmeere gegen Öltankerunfälle : das rechtliche Instrumentarium, ed. by Tomuschat, Christian. Berlin : Duncker & Humblot, 2005, p. 169-214.) [I.C.J., p. 195.]

Treaty between the Federal Republic of Nigeria and the Democratic Republic of São Tomé and Príncipe on the joint development of petroleum and other resources, in respect of areas of the exclusive economic zone of the two States. 21 February 2001. (In : International maritime boundaries, ed. by Colson, David A. ; Smith, Robert W. Leiden ; Boston : Martinus Nijhoff, 2005, v. 5, p. 3649-3682.) [I.C.J., p. 3679.]

Treves, Tullio : The International Tribunal for the Law of the Sea and other law of the sea jurisdictions (2006). (In : Italian Yearbook of International Law, 2006, v. 16, p. 227-243.) [I.C.J., p. 230-231, 240-241.]

Treves, Tullio : The Law of the Sea Convention ten years after entry into force : positive developments and reasons for concern. (In : Bringing new law to ocean waters, ed. by Caron, David D. ; Scheiber, Harry N. Leiden ; Boston : Martinus Nijhoff, 2004, p. 349-354.) [I.C.J., p. 354.]

Treves, Tullio : La nécessité en droit de la mer. (Dans : La nécessité en droit international : colloque de Grenoble. Paris : Pedone, 2007, p. 237-246.)

Triggs, Gillian Doreen : The Timor Sea Treaty and the international unitisation agreement for greater sunrise : practical solutions in the Timor sea. (In : Australian Yearbook of International Law, 2004, v. 23, p. 161-176.) [I.C.J., p. 163, 174.]

United Kingdom of Great Britain and Northern Ireland and Norway : agreement relating to the exploitation of the Frigg field reservoir and the transmission of gas therefrom to the United Kingdom (with annexes), signed at London on 10 May 1976. (In : International maritime boundaries, ed. by Colson, David A. ; Smith, Robert W. Leiden ; Boston : Martinus Nijhoff, 2005, v. 5, p. 3950-3968.) [I.C.J., p. 3965.]

United Kingdom of Great Britain and Northern Ireland and Norway : agreement relating to the exploitation of the Murchison field reservoir and the offtake of petroleum therefrom (with annexes) : signed at Oslo on 16 October 1979. (In : International maritime boundaries, ed. by Colson, David A. ; Smith, Robert W. Leiden ; Boston : Martinus Nijhoff, 2005, v. 5, p. 3969-3985.) [I.C.J., p. 3980.]

United Nations. Office of Legal Affairs : Division for Ocean Affairs and the Law of the Sea : Digest of international cases on the law of the sea. New York : United Nations, 2007. [I.C.J., passim.]

Uprety, Kishor : The transit regime for landlocked States : international law and development perspectives. Washington, DC : World Bank, 2006. (Law, Justice and Development.) [P.C.I.J., p. 33, 40, 50, 52-55, 97, 109; I.C.J., p. 4-5, 24, 33-35, 108-111, 150.]

Van Dyke, Jon M. : An analysis of the Aegean disputes under international law. (In : Ocean Development and International Law, 2005, v. 36, no. 1, p. 63-117.) [P.C.I.J., p. 67, 108, 117; I.C.J., p. 71, 87, 89-91, 103, 105, 108-109, 111, 113-114.]

Van Dyke, Jon M. : Giving teeth to the environmental obligations in the LOS Convention. (In : Oceans management in the 21st century : institutional frameworks and responses, ed. by Oude Elferink, Alex G. ; Rothwell, Donald R.. Leiden ; Boston : Martinus Nijhoff, p. 167-186.) [I.C.J., p. 172-174.]

Van Dyke, Jon M. : Legal issues related to sovereignty over Dokdo and its maritime boundary. (In : Ocean Development and International Law, 2007, v. 38, no. 1-2, p. 157-224.) [P.C.I.J., p. 160, 180; I.C.J., p. 158, 160-165, 180, 184, 186, 187-193, 195, 198, 199-205.]

Van Dyke, Jon M. : U.S. accession to the Law of the Sea Convention. (In : Ocean Yearbook, 2008, v. 22, p. 47-59.) [I.C.J., p. 58.]

Van Dyke, Jon M. and Gardner, Emily A. and Morgan, Joseph : Whales, submarines, and active sonar. (In : Ocean Yearbook, 2004, v. 18, p. 330-363.) [I.C.J., p. 348-349, 352, 354-356, 358; P.C.I.J., p. 352.]

Vignes, Daniel : Conclusions générales. (Dans : L'Europe et la mer : pêche, navigation et environnement marin, sous la dir. de Rafael Casado Raigón. Bruxelles : Bruylant, 2005, p. 301-312.) [C.I.J., p. 303, 307, 309.]

Vinuesa, Raúl Emilio : La aplicación del derecho internacional des mar por los tribunales internos de los estados : a propósito de la gestión de recursos marinos. (Dans : La gestión de los recursos marinos y la cooperación internacional : actas del seminario, Santiago de Chile, 22-23 de marzo de 2004, sous la dir. de Del Vecchio, Angela. Roma : Instituto italo-latino americano, 2006, p. 177-202.) [C.I.J., p. 200.]

Virzo, Roberto : In tema di misure cautelari comportanti obblighi di cooperazione per la protezione dell'ambiente marino. (Dans : Rivista di diritto internazionale, 2005, v. 88, p. 383-412.) [C.I.J., p. 395, 397, 401-402, 404-405, 407, 409.]

Vukas, Budislav : The law of the sea : selected writings. Leiden [etc.] : Nijhoff, 2004. (Publications on ocean development ; 45.) [I.C.J. and P.C.I.J., p. 8-9, 17, 37, 40-41, 46, 61, 94-98, 100-102, 176-177, 188, 297-300, 302-315, 317-325, 327-333.]

Vukas, Budislav : State practice in the aftermath of the UN Convention on the Law of the Sea : the exclusive economic zone and the Mediterranean sea. (In : Unresolved issues and new challenges to the law of the sea : time before and time after, ed. by Strati, Anastasia ; Gavouneli, Maria ; Skourtos, Nikolaos. Leiden ; Boston : Martinus Nijhoff, 2006, p. 251-258.) [I.C.J., p. 253.]

Walker, George K. : Defining terms in the 1982 Law of the Sea Convention III : the International Hydrographic Organization E.C.D.I.S. glossary. (In : California Western International Law Journal, 2004, v. 34, no. 2, p. 211-271.) [I.C.J., p. 233-234, 271.]

Walker, George K. : Professionals' definitions and States' interpretative declarations (understandings, statements, or declarations) for the 1982 Law of the Sea Convention. (In : Emory International Law Review, 2007, v. 21, no. 2, p. 461-542.) [P.C.I.J., p. 475, 535; I.C.J., p. 468-479, 481, 493-494, 499-500, 502-505, 512, 516, 522-524, 528, 532, 534-536, 541.]

Wasum-Rainer, Susanne and Schlegel, Daniela : The UNCLOS dispute settlement system : between Hamburg and The Hague. (In : German Yearbook of International Law, 2005, v. 48, p. 187-222.) [P.C.I.J., p. 211; I.C.J., p. 188-189, 194, 196-200, 202-213, 216, 218-222.]

Weckel, Philippe (ed.) : Tribunal arbitral de la mer (Annexe VII CNUDM). Sentence du 11 avril 2006. Délimitation de la ZEE et du plateau continental (Barbade c. Trinité-et-Tobago). (Dans : Revue générale de droit international public, 2006, v. 110, p. 711-721.) [C.I.J., p. 712, 714, 716-717, 719-721.]

Wegelein, Florian H. Th : Marine scientific research : the operation and status of research vessels and other platforms in international law. Leiden ; Boston : Martinus Nijhoff, 2005. (Publications on ocean development ; 49.) [P.C.I.J., p. 106-108, 145-146, 343-344, 346; I.C.J., p. 3, 100-102, 105, 145-146, 170, 223, 266, 272, 274, 282, 327, 329, 347-349.]

Wei Su, Steven : The territorial dispute over the Tiaoyu/Senkaku Islands : an update. (In : Ocean Development and International Law, 2005, v. 36, no. 1, p. 45-61.) [P.C.I.J., 50; I.C.J., p. 49-53, 57, 60-61.]

Wolfrum, Rüdiger : The delimitation of the outer continental shelf : procedural considerations. (In : Liber amicorum Jean-Pierre Cot : le procès international. Bruxelles : Bruylant, 2009, p. 349-366.) [C.I.J., p. 355, 358.]

Wood, Michael C. : Northern and Western European maritime boundaries. (In : International maritime boundaries, ed. by Colson, David A. ; Smith, Robert W. Leiden ; Boston : Martinus Nijhoff, 2005, v. 5, p. 3493-3505.) [I.C.J., p. 3495-3498, 3500-3502, 3504.]

Yacouba, Cissé and McRae, Donald : The legal regime of maritime boundary agreements. (In : International maritime boundaries, ed. by Colson, David A. ; Smith, Robert W. Leiden ; Boston : Martinus Nijhoff, 2005, v. 5, p. 3281-3304.) [I.C.J., p. 3287, 3291, 3299.]

Zou, Keyuan : China's marine legal system and the law of the sea. Leiden ; Boston : Martinus Nijhoff, 2005. (Publications on ocean development ; 48.) [I.C.J., p. 74-76, 241, 306-307.]

8. Droit aérien et droit de l'espace
8. Air and space law

Adolph, John: The recent boom in private space development and the necessity of an international framework embracing private property rights to encourage investment. (In: International Lawyer, 2006, v. 40, p. 961-985.) [I.C.J., p. 970, 982.]

Bourbonnière, Michel and Lee, Ricky J.: Legality of deployment of conventional weapons in earth orbit: balancing space law and the law of armed conflict. (In: European Journal of International Law, 2007, v. 18, p. 873-901.) [P.C.I.J., p. 880; I.C.J., p. 879, 886-888, 897, 899.]

Cheng, Bin: A new era in the law of international carriage by air: from Warsaw (1929) to Montreal (1999). (In: International and Comparative Law Quarterly, 2004, v. 53, no. 4, p. 833-859.) [P.C.I.J., p. 852.]

Dempsey, Paul Stephen: Flights of fancy and fights of fury: arbitration and adjudication of commercial and political disputes in international aviation. (In: Georgia Journal of International and Comparative Law, 2004, v. 32, no. 2, p. 231-305.) [I.C.J., passim.]

Goh, Gérardine Meishan: Dispute settlement in international space law: a multi-door courthouse for outer space. Leiden [etc.]: Martinus Nijhoff, 2007. (Studies in Space Law; 2.) [I.C.J., p. 5, 26, 27, 44, 50, 52, 55, 57, 70, 85-87, 89, 90, 94, 95, 112, 123, 124, 126-130, 132, 133, 187, 196, 198, 199, 202, 203, 212, 218, 229-231, 233, 234, 272, 288, 293, 295, 320.]

Leon, Pablos Mendes de: Luchtrecht. (In: Handboek internationaal recht, ed. by Horbach, Nathalie L. J. T.; Lefeber, René; Ribbelink, Olivier. The Hague: T.M.C. Asser Press, 2007, p. 801-838.) [P.C.I.J., p. 806; I.C.J., p. 823, 828.]

Nakatani, Kazuhiro: International adjudication concerning the economic aspects of international air transport. (In: Kokusaiho Gaiko Zassi, 2004, v. 103, no. 2, p. 31-57.) [I.C.J., p. 33, 34, 39.]

Quilleré-Majzoub, Fabienne: "A qui appartiennent les nuages?" (Essai de définition d'un statut des nuages en droit international public). (Dans: Annuaire français de droit international, 2004, v. 50, p. 653-667.) [C.I.J., p. 660.]

Talmon, Stefan: Luftverkehr mit nicht anerkannten Staaten: der Fall Nordzypern. (In: Archiv des Völkerrechts, 2005, v. 43, no. 1, p. 1-42.) [I.C.J., p. 12.]

9. Droit économique
9. Economic law

ADF Group Inc. v. United States of America (Case No. ARB(AF)/00/1): procedural order no. 2 concerning the place of arbitration, 11 July 2001, procedural order no. 3 concerning the production of documents, 4 October 2001, award, 9 January 2003. (In: ICSID Reports, 2004, v. 6, p. 450-537.) [I.C.J., p. 522.]

Al Faruque, Abdullah: Creating customary international law through bilateral investment treaties: a critical appraisal. (In: Indian Journal of International Law, 2004, v. 44, no. 2, p. 292-318.) [I.C.J., p. 294, 296-300, 309-310, 315-316; P.C.I.J., p. 297-298.]

Andenas, Mads and Zleptnig, Stefan: Proportionality: WTO law: in comparative perspective. (In: Texas International Law Journal, 2007, v. 42, p. 371-427.) [I.C.J., p. 399, 401-402.]

Atteritano, Andrea: La "jurisdiction" del giudice statale nei procedimenti di "enforcement" dei lodi arbitrali stranieri disciplinati dalla convenzione di New York del 1958. (Dans: Rivista di diritto internazionale privato e processuale, 2007, v. 43, p. 115-136.) [C.I.J., p. 123.]

Azurix Corp. v. Argentine Republic (ICSID Case No. ARB/01/12). Decisions on Jurisdiction, 8 December 2003. (In: International Centre for Settlement of Investment Disputes (ICSID) – Reports, 2006, 10, p. 413-442.) [I.C.J., p. 434.]

Ben Hamida, Walid: L'arbitrage Etat-investisseur face à un désordre procédural: la concurrence des procédures et les conflits de juridictions. (Dans: Annuaire français de droit international, 2005, v. 51, p. 564-602.) [C.P.J.I., p. 589; C.I.J., p. 566, 572-573, 589.]

Benvenisti, Eyal and Downs, George W.: Distributive politics and international institutions: the case of drugs. (In: Case Western Reserve Journal of International Law, 2004, v. 36, no. 1, p. 21-51.) [I.C.J., p. 31, 41; P.C.I.J., p. 30.]

Casado and President Allende Foundation v. Republic of Chile (Case No. ARB/98/2): decision on provisional measures, 25 September 2001. (In: ICSID Reports, 2004, v. 6, p. 373-397.) [I.C.J., p. 374, 379-381, 387, 392-393; P.C.I.J., p. 377, 379, 382, 392.]

Cazala, Julien: Les renvois opérés par le droit de l'Organisation mondiale du commerce à des instruments extérieurs à l'Organisation. (Dans: Revue belge de droit international, 2005, v. 38, p. 527-558.) [C.I.J., p. 549, 551-552, 555-556.]

Champion Trading Company, Ameritrade International Inc., J.T., J.B. and T.T. Wahba v. Arab Republic of Egypt (ICSID Case No. ARB/02/9). Decision on Jurisdiction, 21 October 2003. (In: International Centre for Settlement of Investment Disputes (ICSID) – Reports, 2006, 10, p. 398-411.) [I.C.J., p. 407-409.]

Cheng, Tai-Heng: State succession and commercial obligations. Ardsley, N.Y.: Transnational Publishers, 2006. [I.C.J., p. 25, 70, 76, 114-115, 153, 175, 178-187, 196, 201-202, 239, 249, 251-258, 263, 265-266, 289-290, 302, 323, 330-333, 384, 387, 402.]

CMS Gas Transmission Company v. Republic of Argentina (ICSID Case No. ARB/01/8). (In: ICSID Reports, 2005, v. 7, p. 492-522.) [I.C.J., p. 502-503.]

Compañia de Aguas del Aconquija SA and Vivendi Universal v. Argentine Republic (Case No. ARB/97/3): decision on the challenge to the President of the Committee, 3 October 2001, decision on annulment, 3 July 2002. (In: ICSID Reports, 2004, v. 6, p. 327-372.) [I.C.J., p. 366.]

Cruz Miramontes, Rodolfo: Derecho internacional del comercio, derecho del comercio internacional o derecho del comercio exterior? (Dans: Anuario mexicano de derecho internacional, 2006, v. 6, p. 619-650.) [C.I.J., p. 643.]

Cuniberti, Gilles: Parallel litigation and foreign investment dispute settlement. (In: ICSID Review: Foreign Investment Law Journal, 2006, 21, p. 381-426.) [P.C.I.J., p. 392-393; I.C.J., p. 396.]

Dahinden, Erwin: Neue Regelungen für Nichtexplodierte Munitionsrückstände (NEMR). (In: Krisensicherung und humanitärer Schutz: Festschrift für Dieter Fleck, ed. by Horst Fischer; Ulrike Froissart; Wolff Heintschel von Heinegg. Berlin: Berliner Wissenschafts-Verlag, 2004, p. 59-79.) [I.C.J., p. 68.]

Dammann, Jens C.: Amerikanische Gesellschaften mit Sitz in Deutschland: Zugleich eine Anmerkung zu BGH 29.1.2003-VIII ZR 155/02. (In: Rabels Zeitschrift für ausländisches und internationales Privatrecht, 2004, v. 68, no. 4, p. 607-653.) [I.C.J., p. 644.]

Davey, William J.: Compliance problems in WTO dispute settlement. (In: Cornell International Law Journal, 2009, v. 42, no 1, p. 119-128.) [I.C.J., p. 119.]

Dolzer, Rudolf: Fair and equitable treatment: a key standard in investment treaties. (In: International Lawyer, 2005, v. 39, no. 1, p. 87-106.) [I.C.J., p. 87-88, 93, 105; P.C.I.J., p. 102, 105.]

Dolzer, Rudolf: Meistbegünstigungsklauseln in Investitionsschutzverträgen. (In: Internationale Gemeinschaft und Menschenrechte: Festschrift für Georg Ress zum 70. Geburtstag am 21. Januar 2005, ed. by Bröhmer, Jürgen; Bieber, Roland; Calliess, Christian; Langenfeld, Christine; Weber, Stefan; Wolf, Joachim. Köln [etc.]: Heymann, 2005, p. 47-54.) [I.C.J., p. 48.]

El Boudouhi, Saïda: L'intérêt général et les règles substantielles de protection des investissements. (Dans: Annuaire français de droit international, 2005, v. 51, p. 542-563.) [C.I.J., p. 560.]

El Paso Energy International Company v. Argentine Republic (ICSID Case No. ARB/03/15). (In: ICSID Review: Foreign Investment Law Journal, 2006, 21.) [P.C.I.J., p. 511; I.C.J., p. 505, 509-511, 560, 565-567.]

Finke, Jasper: Competing jurisdiction of international courts and tribunals in light of the MOX Plant Dispute. (In: German Yearbook of International Law, 2006, v. 49, p. 307-326.) [P.C.I.J., p. 317; I.C.J., p. 309, 312, 316-317, 319.]

Fortier, Yves and Drymer, Stephen L.: Indirect expropriation in the law of international investment: I know it when I see it, or caveat investor. (In:

ICSID Review: Foreign Investment Law Journal, 2004, v. 19, p. 293-327.) [I.C.J., p. 301, 309.]

Generation Ukraine Inc. v. Ukraine (ICSID Case No. ARB/00/9). Award, 16 September 2003. (In: International Centre for Settlement of Investment Disputes (ICSID) – Reports, 2006, 10, p. 236-308.) [P.C.I.J., p. 266, 300.]

Genin and others v. Republic of Estonia (Case No. ARB/99/2): award, 25 June 2001, decision on claimants' request for supplementary decisions and rectification, 4 April 2002. (In: ICSID Reports, 2004, v. 6, p. 236-307.) [I.C.J., p. 301.]

Goetz and others v. Republic of Burundi (Case No. ARB/95/3): award, 10 February 1999. (In: ICSID Reports, 2004, v. 6, p. 3-51.) [I.C.J., p. 11, 21-22, 25-26, 34; P.C.I.J., p. 24.]

Gotanda, John Yukio: Recovering lost profits in international disputes. (In: Georgetown Journal of International Law, 2004, v. 36, p. 61-112.) [I.C.J., p. 105.]

Grazziotin Noschang, Patrícia: O caso das papeleras na Corte internacional de Justiça: direito ambiental versus direito econômico? (Dans: Revista de direito da Unigranrio, 2008, v. 1, no. 1, p. 1-14.) [I.C.J., passim.]

Happ, Richard and Rubins, Noah: Awards and decisions of ICSID tribunals in 2004. (In: German Yearbook of International Law, 2004, v. 47, p. 878-921.) [P.C.I.J., p. 903; I.C.J., p. 881, 916, 919.]

Henckels, Caroline: Overcoming jurisdictional isolationism at the WTO-FTA Nexus: a potential approach for the WTO. (In: European Journal of International Law, 2008, v. 19, no. 3, p. 571-599.) [I.C.J., p. 573, 583, 585-587, 589, 591-592, 594-597.]

Hildering, Antoinette: Water as an economic good. (In: Les ressources en eau et le droit international, ed. by Laurence Boisson de Chazournes; Salman M. A. Salman. Leiden; Boston: Martinus Nijhoff, 2005, p. 209-238.) [P.C.I.J., p. 215; I.C.J., p. 211.]

Horchani, Ferhat: Le droit international des investissements à l'heure de la mondialisation. (Dans: Journal du droit international, 2004, v. 131, p. 367-417.) [C.I.J., p. 382, 409.]

International Center for Settlement of Investment Disputes: International Center for the Settlement of Investment Disputes (ICSID): PSEG Global Inc., the North American Coal Corporation, and Konya Ilgin Electrik Uretim ve Ticaret Limited Sirketi v. The Republic of Turkey. [June 4, 2004]. (In: International Legal Materials, 2005, v. 44, p. 465-497.) [I.C.J. and P.C.I.J., p. 487.]

International Center for Settlement of Investment Disputes: International Centre for Settlement of Investment Disputes (ICSID): Salini Costruttori S.P.A. and Italsprade S.P.A. v. The Hashemite Kingdom of Jordan, ICSID Case No. ARB/02/03, Decision on jurisdiction (November 29,

2004). (In: International Legal Materials, 2005, v. 44, p. 573-600.) [I.C.J., p. 591, 595-596.]

International Center for Settlement of Investment Disputes: International Centre for the Settlement of Investment Disputes (ICSID): Plama Consortium Limited v. The Republic of Bulgaria, decision on jurisdiction (February 8, 2005). (In: International Legal Materials, 2005, v. 44, p. 721-758.) [I.C.J., p. 738, 740-741, 745, 754.]

International Center for Settlement of Investment Disputes: Técnicas Medioambientales Tecmed, S. A. v. United Mexican States (Case No. ARB(AF)/00/2). (Dans: ICSID Review: Foreign Investment Law Journal, 2004, v. 19, no. 1, p. 154-271.) [I.C.J., p. 239.]

International Centre for Settlement of Investment Disputes. (In: Global Community: Yearbook of International Law and Jurisprudence, 2006, v. 6, no. 2, p. 1447-1676.) [P.C.I.J., p. 1464, 1470-1471, 1519, 1559, 1575, 1584, 1640-1641, 1646-1647; I.C.J., p. 1449, 1464, 1470-1471, 1491-1492, 1508-1510, 1519, 1551, 1566-1567, 1577, 1580-1583, 1608, 1612, 1613-1614, 1616, 1640-1642, 1646, 1652.]

International law on sustainable development. (In: Reports of the Annual Conference, by International Law Association (ILA), 2006, 2006, p. 467-522.) [I.C.J., p. 477, 492.]

Judin, J. Michael and Kassim, Hisham and Marin, Daniel and Massot, Alejandro M. and Franco, Isabel C. and Garcia, Alessandra and Giantomasi, Thiago and Inglez de Souza, Ricardo and Ríos, Marcos and Chabaneix, Jean-Paul and Pate, John R.: International investment. (In: International Lawyer, 2007, v. 41, p. 415-425.) [I.C.J., p. 416.]

Kaufmann-Kohler, Gabrielle and Boisson de Chazournes, Laurence and Bonnin, Victor and Mbengue, Makane Moïse: Consolidation of proceedings in investment arbitration: how can multiple proceedings arising from the same or related situations be handled efficiently? Final report on the Geneva Colloquium held on 22 April 2006. (In: ICSID Review: Foreign Investment Law Journal, 2006, v. 21, p. 59-125.) [P.C.I.J., p. 104-108; I.C.J., p. 64-65, 66, 76, 104-110, 117-119.]

Kentin, Esther: Sustainable development in international investment dispute settlement: the I.C.S.I.D. and N.A.F.T.A. experience. (In: International law and sustainable development: principles and practice, ed. by Nico Schrijver; Friedl Weiss. Leiden [etc.]: Martinus Nijhoff, 2004, p. 309-338.) [I.C.J., p. 309-310, 318, 323, 328.]

Kofele-Kale, Ndiva: Presumed guilty: balancing competing rights and interests in combating economic crimes. (In: International Lawyer, 2006, v. 40, p. 909-944.) [I.C.J., p. 935.]

Lakehal, Djamel-Eddine: Quelques réflexions sur les contrats pétroliers algériens à la lumière de la théorie des contrats d'Etat en droit international. (Dans: Droit du pouvoir, pouvoir du droit: mélanges offerts à Jean Salmon. Bruxelles: Bruylant, 2007, p. 507-517.) [C.P.J.I., p. 516.]

López-Ayllón, Sergio et Posadas Urtusuástegui, Alejandro: Inversión y derecho internacional de la inversión extranjera: reflexión sobre algunas disciplinas adoptadas por México. (Dans: Anuario mexicano de derecho internacional, 2006, v. 6, p. 301-344.) [C.I.J., p. 320-323.]

Meng, Werner: Wirtschaftssanktionen wegen Menschenrechtsverletzungen: Problems im WTO-Recht. (In: Internationale Gemeinschaft und Menschenrechte: Festschrift für Georg Ress zum 70. Geburtstag am 21. Januar 2005, ed. by Bröhmer, Jürgen; Bieber, Roland; Calliess, Christian; Langenfeld, Christine; Weber, Stefan; Wolf, Joachim. Köln [etc.]: Heymann, 2005, p. 165-190.) [P.C.I.J., p. 188; I.C.J., p. 174.]

Mondev International Ltd v. United States of America (Case No. ARB(AF)/99/2): miscellaneous procedural orders, award, 11 October 2002. (In: ICSID Reports, 2004, v. 6, p. 180-235.) [I.C.J., p. 203, 205, 211, 213, 219-220, 225; P.C.I.J., p. 213.]

Montt Oyarzún, Santiago: Aplicación de los tratados bilaterales de protección de inversiones por tribunales chilenos: responsabilidad del estado y expropriaciones regulatorias en un mundo crecientemente globalizado. (Dans: Revista chilena de derecho, 2005, v. 32, no. 1, p. 19-78.) [C.P.J.I., p. 30.]

Muchlinski, Peter: "Caveat investor"? The relevance of the conduct of the investor under the fair and equitable treatment standard. (In: International and Comparative Law Quarterly, 2006, v. 55, p. 527-557.) [P.C.I.J., p. 547; I.C.J., p. 529, 532, 542, 546, 554.]

Muchlinski, Peter: The diplomatic protection of foreign investors: a tale of judicial caution. (In: International investment law for the 21st century: essays in honour of Christoph Schreuer, ed. by Christina Binder. New York: Oxford University Press, 2009, p. 341-362.) [I.C.J., passim.]

Muchlinski, Peter: Multinational enterprises and the law. Oxford [etc.]: Oxford University Press, 2007. 2nd ed. [P.C.I.J. and I.C.J., see index p. 747.]

NAFTA Chapter Eleven Tribunal: Gami Investments, Inc. v. The Government of the United Mexican States (November 15, 2004). (In: International Legal Materials, 2005, v. 44, p. 545-568.) [I.C.J., p. 550.]

Nanetti, Francesco et Squillante, Francesca: Recenti sviluppi dell'ordinamento internazionale in materia di concorrenza fiscale dannosa. (Dans: Studi di diritto internazionale in onore di Gaetano Arangio-Ruiz, sous la dir. de Giovanni Battaglini; Paolo Benvenuti; Antonio Cassese; Giorgio Gaja. Napoli: Editoriale Scientifica, 2004, v. 3, p. 2263-2285.) [C.P.J.I., p, 2281, 2282; C.I.J., p. 2009.]

Nowrot, Karsten: Nun sag, wie hast du's mit den Global Players? Fragen an die Völkerrechtsgemeinschaft zur internationalen Rechtsstellung transnationaler Unternehmen. (In: Die Friedens-Warte: Blätter für internationale Verständigung und zwischenstaatliche Organisation, 2004, v. 79, no. 1-2, p. 119-150.) [I.C.J., p. 123, 133.]

O'Keefe, Roger: A bit justiciable. (In: Cambridge Law Journal, 2006, v. 65, p. 259-263.) [P.C.I.J. and I.C.J., p. 261.]

Osteneck, Kathrin: Die Umsetzung von UN-Wirtschaftssanktionen durch die Europäische Gemeinschaft: völker- und europarechtliche Rahmenbedingungen für ein Tätigwerden der Europäischen Gemeinschaft im Bereich von UN-Wirtschaftssanktionsregimen unter besonderer Berücksichtigung der Umsetzungspraxis der EG-Organe. Berlin [etc.]: Springer, 2004. (Beiträge zum ausländischen öffentlichen Recht und Völkerrecht; 168.) [I.C.J., p. 24, 34-35, 80-82, 84, 97, 101, 299, 315.]

Osuna, Orianne: L'apport de la jurisprudence internationale en matière de nécessité économique et financière avant 1945. (Dans: La nécessité en droit international: colloque de Grenoble. Paris: Pedone, 2007, p. 355-366.)

Pakistan. Supreme Court: Société Générale de Surveillance SA v. Pakistan, through Secretary, Ministry of Finance. (In: ICSID Reports, 2005, v. 8, p. 352-451.) [I.C.J., p. 437, 445.]

Pastor Palomar, Antonio: Protección de inversiones con conceptos indeterminados: el trato justo y equitativo en los appris celebrados por España. (Dans: Revista española de derecho internacional, 2006, v. 58, p. 271-287.) [C.I.J., p. 272, 279.]

Petersmann, Ernst-Ulrich: Justice in international economic law? From the "international law among States" to "international integration law" and "constitutional law". (In: Global Community: Yearbook of International Law and Jurisprudence, 2006, v. 6, no. 1, p. 105-146.) [I.C.J., p. 129.]

Pratap, Ravindra: Sovereign economic freedom and interests of other States. (In: India and international law, ed. by Bimal N. Patel. Leiden; Boston: Martinus Nijhoff, 2005, p. 117-139.) [P.C.I.J., p. 119; I.C.J., p. 120-122, 124, 127, 132, 137.]

Radi, Yannick: The application of the most-favoured-nation clause to the dispute settlement provisions of bilateral investment treaties: Domesticating the "Trojan Horse". (In: European Journal of International Law, 2007, v. 18, p. 757-774.) [P.C.I.J., p. 764; I.C.J., p. 759, 763, 770.]

Reinisch, August: Introductory note to International Centre for the Settlement of Investment Disputes (ICSID): Plama Consortium Limited v. Republic of Bulgaria. (In: International Legal Materials, 2005, v. 44, p. 717-720.) [I.C.J., p. 717-719.]

Reisman, William Michael and Arsanjani, Mahnoush H.: The question of unilateral governmental statements as applicable law in investment disputes. (In: ICSID Review: Foreign Investment Law Journal, 2004, v. 19, no. 2, p. 328-343.) [P.C.I.J., p. 329-332; I.C.J., passim.]

Reisman, William Michael and Arsanjani, Mahnoush H.: The question of unilateral governmental statements as applicable law in investment disputes. (In: Völkerrecht als Wertordnung: Festschrift für Christian Tomuschat, sous la dir. de Pierre-Marie Dupuy; Bardo Fassbender;

Malcolm N. Shaw; Karl-Peter Sommermann. Kehl: N. P. Engel, 2006, p. 409-422.) [P.C.I.J., p. 410-412; I.C.J., passim.]

Reusch, Ralf: Die Legitimation des WTO-Streitbeilegungsverfahrens. Berlin: Duncker & Humblot, 2007. (Tübinger Schriften zum internationalen und europäischen Recht; 87.) [I.C.J., p. 118, 172, 179, 184, 192, 194, 199.]

Rigo Sureda, Andres: The law applicable to the activities of international development banks. (In: Recueil des cours de l'Académie de droit international de La Haye, 2004, v. 308, p. 9-252.) [I.C.J., p. 28, 51, 151-154; P.C.I.J., p. 114, 115.]

S.D. Myers Inc. v. Government of Canada: NAFTA Arbitration Tribunal under the UNCITRAL Rules. (In: ICSID Reports, 2005, v. 8, p. 3-193.) [P.C.I.J., p. 63, 119, 185.]

Schlemmer-Schulte, Sabine: Building an international grievance system: the World Bank inspection panel: selected issues. (In: Internationale Gemeinschaft und Menschenrechte: Festschrift für Georg Ress zum 70. Geburtstag am 21. Januar 2005, ed. by Bröhmer, Jürgen; Bieber, Roland; Calliess, Christian; Langenfeld, Christine; Weber, Stefan; Wolf, Joachim. Köln [etc.]: Heymann, 2005, p. 249-284.) [I.C.J., p. 262.]

Schreuer, Christoph: Calvo's grandchildren: the return of local remedies in investment arbitration. (In: Law and Practice of International Courts and Tribunals, 2005, v. 4, no. 1, p. 1-17.) [I.C.J., p. 16.]

Schreuer, Christoph: Shareholder protection in international investment law. (In: Völkerrecht als Wertordnung: Festschrift für Christian Tomuschat, sous la dir. de Pierre-Marie Dupuy; Bardo Fassbender; Malcolm N. Shaw; Karl-Peter Sommermann. Kehl: N. P. Engel, 2006, p. 601-619.) [I.C.J., p. 603, 604, 616.]

SGS Société Générale de Surveillance SA v. Republic of the Philippines (ICSID Case No. ARB/02/6). (In: ICSID Reports, 2005, v. 8, p. 515-571.) [I.C.J., p. 523, 524, 561, 562.]

Shadikhodjaev, Sherzod and Park, No-hyoung: Cessation and reparation in the GATT/WTO legal system: a view from the law of State responsibility. (In: Journal of World Trade, 2007, v. 41, no. 6, p. 1237-1258.) [P.C.I.J., p. 1242; I.C.J., p. 1249, 1256.]

Shany, Yuval: Consolidation and tests for application: is international law relevant? (In: ICSID Review: Foreign Investment Law Journal, 2006, 21, p. 135-149.) [I.C.J., p. 140, 141, 146.]

Simma, Bruno and Kill, Theodore: Harmonizing investment protection and international human rights: first steps towards a methodology. (In: International investment law for the 21st century: essays in honour of Christoph Schreuer, ed. by Christina Binder. New York: Oxford University Press, 2009, p. 678-707.)

Sinclair, Anthony C.: The substance of nationality requirements in investment treaty arbitration. (In: ICSID Review: Foreign Investment Law Journal, 2005, v. 20, p. 357-388.) [P.C.I.J., p. 364; I.C.J., p. 360, 366-367.]

Smutney, Abby Cohen: Claims of shareholders in international investment law. (In: International investment law for the 21st century: essays in honour of Christoph Schreuer, by Christina Binder. New York: Oxford University Press, 2009, p. 363-376.) [I.C.J., passim.]

Snodgrass, Elizabeth: Protecting investors' legitimate expectations: recognizing and delimiting a general principle. (In: ICSID Review: Foreign Investment Law Journal, 2006, 21, p. 1-58.) [P.C.I.J., p. 11, 13-14, 21, 40; I.C.J., p. 2, 12-13, 15-17, 21, 23-25.]

Sornarajah, Muthucumaraswamy: Economic neo-liberalism and the international law on foreign investment. (In: The third world and international order: law, politics and globalization, ed. by Anghie, Antony. Leiden: Martinus Nijhoff, 2003, p. 173-190.) [I.C.J., p. 179.]

Técnicas Medioambientales Tecmed SA v. United Mexican States (ICSID Case No. ARB(AF)/00/2). Award, 29 May 2003. (In: International Centre for Settlement of Investment Disputes (ICSID) – Reports, 2006, 10, p. 130-212.) [P.C.I.J., p. 189, 193; I.C.J., p. 210.]

Van Den Bossche, Peter and Denters, Erik: International economisch recht. (In: Handboek internationaal recht, ed. by Horbach, Nathalie L. J. T.; Lefeber, René; Ribbelink, Olivier. The Hague: T.M.C. Asser Press, 2007, p. 627-679.) [P.C.I.J., p. 662.]

Verma, Surinder Kaur: Trade in services, World Trade Organisation and India. (In: India and International Law, ed. by Bimal N. Patel. Leiden; Boston: Martinus Nijhoff, 2005, p. 67-91.) [I.C.J., p. 75.]

Vinuesa, Raúl Emilio: Jurisdictional objections to ICSID arbitration under bilateral investment treaties. (In: Internationale Gemeinschaft und Menschenrechte: Festschrift für Georg Ress zum 70. Geburtstag am 21. Januar 2005, ed. by Bröhmer, Jürgen; Bieber, Roland; Calliess, Christian; Langenfeld, Christine; Weber, Stefan; Wolf, Joachim. Köln [etc.]: Heymann, 2005, p. 331-355.) [I.C.J., p. 331-355.]

Waibel, Michael: Two worlds of necessity in ICSID arbitration: CMS and LG&E. (In: Leiden Journal of International Law, 2007, v. 20, p. 637-648.) [I.C.J., p. 640-641, 643, 647.]

Waste Management Inc. v. United Mexican States (No. 2) (Case No. ARB(AF)/00/3): decision on venue of the arbitration, 26 September 2001, decision on the preliminary objection, 26 June 2002. (In: ICSID Reports, 2004, v. 6, p. 538-563.) [I.C.J., p. 558-559.]

Wena Hotels Ltd v. Arab Republic of Egypt (Case No. ARB/98/4): decision on jurisdiction, 29 June 1999, award, 8 December 2000, decision on annulment, 5 February 2002. (In: ICSID Reports, 2004, v. 6, p. 69-153.) [I.C.J., p. 138-139.]

Whitsitt, Elizabeth: Application of most-favoured-nation clauses to the dispute settlement provisions of bilateral investment treaties: an assessment of the jurisprudence. (In: Journal of Energy & Natural Resources Law: the journal of the Section on Energy and Natural Resources Law of the International Bar Association, 2009, v. 27, no 4, p. 527-557.) [I.C.J., p. 532.]

WTO dispute settlement system. (In: Global Community: Yearbook of International Law and Jurisprudence, 2006, v. 6, no. 1, p. 273-389.) [I.C.J., passim.]

Yaung Chi Oo Trading Pte Ltd v. Government of the Union of Myanmar (ASEAN ID Case No. ARB/01/1). (In: ICSID Reports, 2005, v. 8, p. 452-488.) [I.C.J., p. 459, 463.]

Zapatero Miguel, Pablo: Coherencia y coordinación en Bretton Woods. (Dans: Anuario de derecho internacional, 2004, v. 20, p. 326-371.) [C.I.J., p. 348.]

Zhinvali Development Limited v. Republic of Georgia (ICSID Case No. ARB/00/1). Award, 24 January 2003. (In: International Centre for Settlement of Investment Disputes (ICSID) – Reports, 2006, 10, p. 1-113.) [I.C.J., p. 69.]

10. Droit du développement
10. Law of development

Barstow Magraw, Daniel and Hawke, Lisa D.: Sustainable development. (In: The Oxford handbook of international environmental law, ed. by Daniel Bodansky; Jutta Brunnée; Ellen Hey. Oxford: Oxford University Press, 2007, p. 613-638.) [I.C.J., p. 624, 626, 631.]

El Boudouhi, Saïda: L'intérêt général et les règles substantielles de protection des investissements. (Dans: Annuaire français de droit international, 2005, v. 51, p. 542-563.) [C.I.J., p. 560.]

Ellis, Jaye: Sustainable development as a legal principle: a rhetorical analysis. (In: Select Proceedings of the European Society of International Law, ed. by James Crawford; Sarah M. H. Nouwen. Oxford; Portland: Hart, 2008, v. 2, p. 641-660.) [I.C.J., p. 644-646.]

Kentin, Esther: Sustainable development in international investment dispute settlement: the I.C.S.I.D. and N.A.F.T.A. experience. (In: International law and sustainable development: principles and practice, ed. by Nico Schrijver; Friedl Weiss. Leiden [etc.]: Martinus Nijhoff, 2004, p. 309-338.) [I.C.J., p. 309-310, 318, 323, 328.]

Salacuse, Jeswald W. and Sullivan, Nicholas P.: Do BITs really work? An evaluation of bilateral investment treaties and their grand bargain. (In: Harvard International Law Journal, 2005, v. 46, no. 1, p. 67-130.) [I.C.J., p. 68, 83, 113.]

Srinivasan, T. N.: Development: domestic constraints and external opportunities from globalization. (In: Michigan Journal of International Law, 2004, v. 26, no. 1, p. 63-98.) [I.C.J., p. 85.]

11. Droit de l'environnement
11. Environmental law

Anglés Hernández, Marisol: Los cursos de agua compartidos entre México y los Estados Unidos de América y la variable medioambiental. Una aproximación. (Dans: Anuario mexicano de derecho internacional, 2006, v. 6, p. 89-166.) [C.I.J., p. 118, 124-126.]

Arnauld, Andreas von: Völkerrechtliche Informationspflichten bei Naturkatastrophen. (In: Archiv des Völkerrechts, 2005, v. 43, no. 3, p. 279-311.) [P.C.I.J., p. 309; I.C.J., p. 286, 287, 291, 302-306, 309, 312.]

Barral, Virginie: La sentence du Rhin de fer, une nouvelle étape dans la prise en compte du droit de l'environnement par la justice internationale. (Dans: Revue générale de droit international public, 2006, v. 110, p. 647-668.) [C.I.J., p. 654-656, 657-659, 663-665.]

Barsh, Russel Lawrence: Indigenous peoples. (In: The Oxford handbook of international environmental law, ed. by Daniel Bodansky; Jutta Brunnée; Ellen Hey. Oxford: Oxford University Press, 2007, p. 829-852.) [P.C.I.J., p. 834; I.C.J., p. 849.]

Beyerlin, Ulrich: Different types of norms in international environmental law: policies, principles and rules. (In: The Oxford handbook of international environmental law, ed. by Daniel Bodansky; Jutta Brunnée; Ellen Hey. Oxford: Oxford University Press, 2007, p. 425-448.) [I.C.J., p. 443-444.]

Birnie, Patricia W.: Might future generations conclude that their interests in whale stocks would have been better safeguarded by a body considering ocean space holistically? (In: Ocean Yearbook, 2004, v. 18, p. 284-329.) [I.C.J., p. 285-286, 323, 325.]

Böckenförde, Markus: Grüne Gentechnik und Welthandel: das Biosafety-Protokoll und seine Auswirkungen auf das Regime der WTO: genetic engineering and world trade (English summary). Berlin [etc.]: Springer, 2004. (Beiträge zum ausländischen öffentlichen Recht und Völkerrecht; 171.) [P.C.I.J., p. 440, 452; I.C.J., p. 9, 230, 312, 318, 357, 418-422, 433, 435, 440, 452.]

Boisson de Chazournes, Laurence: Eaux internationales et droit international: vers l'idée de gestion commune. (Dans: Les ressources en eau et le droit international, sous la dir. de Laurence Boisson de Chazournes; Salman M. A. Salman. Leiden; Boston: Martinus Nijhoff, 2005, p. 3-43.) [C.P.J.I., p. 9, 15-16, 20; C.I.J., p. 12-14, 20.]

Boisson de Chazournes, Laurence: Technical and financial assistance and compliance: the interplay. (In: Ensuring compliance with multilateral environmental agreements: a dialogue between practitioners and academia, ed. by Ulrich Beyerlin; Peter-Tobias Stoll; Rüdiger Wolfrum. Leiden; Boston: Martinus Nijhoff, 2006, p. 273-300.) [I.C.J., p. 289-290, 291-292.]

Bouvet, Jean-Pierre: L'unité de gisement: [hydrocarbures et autres matières minérales]. Paris [etc.]: L'Harmattan, 2004. (Logiques juridiques.) [C.P.J.I., p. 55, 65, 168, 286, 327, 330-331, 337-338, 350, 353, 371, 387, 389, 395; C.I.J., p. 12, 15, 19-20, 33, 60, 76-86, 89-90, 92-103, 106-108, 116-129, 131, 165, 167, 179-180, 194, 202-203, 205, 209, 323-324, 326-327, 329-332, 336-338, 340-341, 348-354, 358-361, 367-373, 376, 382-383, 385, 388, 391-395, 430.]

Boyle, Alan: Relationship between international environmental law and other branches of international law. (In: The Oxford handbook of international environmental law, ed. by Daniel Bodansky; Jutta Brunnée; Ellen Hey. Oxford: Oxford University Press, 2007, p. 125-146.) [I.C.J., p. 128-130, 135, 143-144.]

Brunnée, Jutta: Common areas, common heritage, and common concern. (In: The Oxford handbook of international environmental law, ed. by Daniel Bodansky; Jutta Brunnée; Ellen Hey. Oxford: Oxford University Press, 2007, p. 550-573.) [I.C.J., p. 551-552, 555-558, 570-571.]

Brunnée, Jutta: Enforcement mechanisms in international law and international environmental law. (In: Ensuring compliance with multilateral environmental agreements: a dialogue between practitioners and academia, ed. by Ulrich Beyerlin; Peter-Tobias Stoll; Rüdiger Wolfrum. Leiden; Boston: Martinus Nijhoff, 2006, p. 1-23.) [I.C.J., p. 4-5.]

Brunnée, Jutta: The United States and international environmental law: living with an elephant. (In: European Journal of International Law, 2004, v. 15, no. 4, p. 617-649.) [P.C.I.J., p. 633.]

Campins-Eritja, Mar and Gupta, Joyeeta: The role of "sustainability labelling" in the international law of sustainable development. (In: International law and sustainable development: principles and practice, ed. by Nico Schrijver; Friedl Weiss. Leiden [etc.]: Martinus Nijhoff, 2004, p. 251-270.) [I.C.J., p. 256-257, 259.]

Capaldo, Griselda D.: The Rio de la Plata basin. (In: The evolution of the law and politics of water, ed. by Dellapenna, Joseph W.; Gupta, Joyeeta. Dordrecht: Springer, 2009, p. 299-315.) [I.C.J., p. 312.]

Castillo-Laborde, Lilian del: Case law on international watercourses. (In: The evolution of the law and politics of water, ed. by Dellapenna, Joseph W.; Gupta, Joyeeta. Dordrecht: Springer, 2009, p. 319-335.) [P.C.I.J., p. 320-323, 325, 329; I.C.J., p. 320-321, 325-326, 329, 331.]

Cazala, Julien: Le droit international de l'eau et les différends relatifs au Tigre et à l'Euphrate. (Dans: Les ressources en eau et le droit international, sous la dir. de Laurence Boisson de Chazournes; Salman M. A. Salman. Leiden; Boston: Martinus Nijhoff, 2005, p. 533-575.) [C.P.J.I., p. 565-566; C.I.J., p. 539, 548, 554, 557, 560-562.]

Cazala, Julien: Le principe de précaution en droit international. Louvain-la-Neuve: Anthemis, 2006. (Bibliothèque de l'Institut des hautes études internationales de Paris.) [C.P.I.J. et C.I.J., passim.]

Chetan, Cosmina et Bojin, Lucian : Le test de nécessité environnementale et le principe de précaution comme éléments du droit de l'eau douce. (Dans : Revue québécoise de droit international, 2006, v. 19, no. 2, p. 125-158.) [C.P.J.I., p. 153, 156; C.I.J., p. 141, 143-149, 153, 155, 157.]

Craik, Neil : The international law of environmental impact assessment. Cambridge : Cambridge University Press, 2008. (Cambridge Studies in International and Comparative Law.) [I.C.J., p. 60, 62-63, 67, 70, 75, 80-81, 89, 108, 111-114, 117, 119-120, 124, 128, 144, 153-154, 196, 200, 203, 259, 261, 263.]

Décisions judiciaires et arbitrales : décisions internationales : affaire concernant l'Apurement des comptes entre le Royaume des Pays-Bas et la République française en application du Protocole du 25 septembre 1991 additionnel à la Convention relative à la protection du Rhin contre la pollution par les chlorures du 3 décembre 1976, sentence arbitrale du 12 mars 2004. (Dans : Revue générale de droit international public, 2004, v. 108, no. 4, p. 775-836.) [C.I.J. et C.P.J.I., p. 797-800, 802-803, 810, 834-835.]

DeGarmo, Denise : International environmental treaties and State behaviour : factors influencing cooperation. London ; New York : Routledge, 2009. (Studies in international relations.) [I.C.J., p. 48, 142.]

Denters, Erik : Free riders, claims and countermeasures in combating climate change. (In : International law and sustainable development : principles and practice, ed. by Nico Schrijver ; Friedl Weiss. Leiden [etc.] : Martinus Nijhoff, 2004, p. 231-250.) [I.C.J., p. 238-239.]

Dominguez Matés, Rosario : La protección del medio ambiente en el derecho internacional humanitario. Valencia : Tirant lo Blanch [etc.], 2005. [C.P.J.I., p. 126; C.I.J., p. 297-299, 310, 347-349, 356, 372, 387, 394-397, 429, 456, 470-471, 487.]

Doumbé-Billé, Stéphane : Force du droit et droit de la force en droit international de l'environnement. (Dans : Le droit international à la croisée des chemins : force du droit et droit de la force : VIe rencontre internationale de la Faculté des Sciences juridiques, politiques et sociales de Tunis, 14, 15 et 16 avril 2004, sous la dir. de Rafâa Ben Achour ; Slim Laghmani. Paris : Pedone, 2004, p. 367-383.) [C.P.J.I., p. 373; C.I.J., p. 369, 371, 373, 375-377, 379, 381-382.]

Dupuy, Pierre-Marie : Formation of customary international law and general principles. (In : The Oxford handbook of international environmental law, ed. by Daniel Bodansky ; Jutta Brunnée ; Ellen Hey. Oxford : Oxford University Press, 2007, p. 449-466.) [I.C.J., p. 452-453, 457, 459-461, 464.]

Edeson, William R. : Practice of compliance control within the framework of the protection of marine living resources. (In : Ensuring compliance with multilateral environmental agreements : a dialogue between practitioners and academia, ed. by Ulrich Beyerlin ; Peter-Tobias Stoll ; Rüdiger Wolfrum. Leiden ; Boston : Martinus Nijhoff, 2006, p. 151-173.) [I.C.J., p. 166.]

Epiney, Astrid: The role of NGOs in the process of ensuring compliance with MEAs. (In: Ensuring compliance with multilateral environmental agreements: a dialogue between practitioners and academia, ed. by Ulrich Beyerlin; Peter-Tobias Stoll; Rüdiger Wolfrum. Leiden; Boston: Martinus Nijhoff, 2006, p. 319-352.) [I.C.J., p. 331.]

Farrajota, Maria Manuela: Notification and consultation in the law applicable to international watercourses. (In: Les ressources en eau et le droit international, ed. by Laurence Boisson de Chazournes; Salman M. A. Salman. Leiden; Boston: Martinus Nijhoff, 2005, p. 281-339.) [P.C.I.J., p. 329; I.C.J., p. 289, 309, 314, 317, 322, 327.]

Fitzmaurice, Malgosia A.: Contemporary issues in international environmental law. Cheltenham: Edward Elgar, 2009. [I.C.J., p. 20-22.]

Fitzmaurice, Malgosia A.: The International Court of Justice and the environment. (In: Non-State actors and international law, 2004, v. 4, no. 3, p. 173-197.)

Fitzmaurice, Malgosia A.: International responsibility and liability. (In: The Oxford handbook of international environmental law, ed. by Daniel Bodansky; Jutta Brunnée; Ellen Hey. Oxford: Oxford University Press, 2007, p. 1010-1035.) [P.C.I.J., p. 1015-1016; I.C.J., p. 1013, 1020-1021.]

Footer, Mary E.: Our agricultural heritage: sustainability, common heritage and intergenerational equity. (In: International law and sustainable development: principles and practice, ed. by Nico Schrijver; Friedl Weiss. Leiden [etc.]: Martinus Nijhoff, 2004, p. 433-466.) [I.C.J., p. 457.]

French, Duncan: The role of the State and international organisations in reconciling sustainable development and globalisation. (In: International law and sustainable development: principles and practice, ed. by Nico Schrijver; Friedl Weiss. Leiden [etc.]: Martinus Nijhoff, 2004, p. 53-71.) [I.C.J., p. 67.]

Fuentes, Ximena: International law-making in the field of sustainable development: the unequal competition between development and the environment. (In: International law and sustainable development: principles and practice, ed. by Nico Schrijver; Friedl Weiss. Leiden [etc.]: Martinus Nijhoff, 2004, p. 7-37.) [I.C.J., p. 21-24.]

Gandhi, M.: State responsibility and international environmental law. (In: India and international law, ed. by Bimal N. Patel. Leiden; Boston: Martinus Nijhoff, 2005, p. 223-247.) [I.C.J., p. 225, 227, 233-234.]

Gautier, Philippe: Mesures conservatoires, préjudice irréparable et protection de l'environnement. (Dans: Liber amicorum Jean-Pierre Cot: le procès international. Bruxelles: Bruylant, 2009, p. 131-154.)

Gillespie, Alexander: Whaling diplomacy: defining issues in international environmental law. Cheltenham; Northampton: Edward Elgar, 2005. (New horizons in environmental law.) [I.C.J., see index p. 485.]

Giorgetta, Sueli: The right to a healthy environment. (In: International law and sustainable development: principles and practice, ed. by Nico Schrijver;

Friedl Weiss. Leiden [etc.]: Martinus Nijhoff, 2004, p. 379-404.) [I.C.J., p. 381-382.]

Giuffrida, Roberto: Lo sviluppo sostenibile: i caratteri delle norme internationali e il loro operare nella soluzione delle controversie. (Dans: Studi di diritto internazionale in onore di Gaetano Arangio-Ruiz, sous la dir. de Giovanni Battaglini; Paolo Benvenuti; Antonio Cassese; Giorgio Gaja. Napoli: Editoriale Scientifica, 2004, v. 2, p. 1039-1094.) [C.I.J., p. 1046, 1059-1072, 1080.]

Goote, Maas and Hey, Ellen: Internationaal milieurecht. (In: Handboek internationaal recht, ed. by Horbach, Nathalie L. J. T.; Lefeber, René; Ribbelink, Olivier. The Hague: T.M.C. Asser Press, 2007, p. 681-711.) [I.C.J., p. 698-702, 706, 708.]

Gray, Kevin R.: Transboundary environmental disputes along the Canada-US frontier: revisiting the efficacy of applying the rules of State responsibility. (In: Canadian Yearbook of International Law, 2005, v. 43, p. 333-391.) [P.C.I.J., p. 337, 360, 370-371; I.C.J., p. 334, 337, 339-340, 341-343, 348, 371.]

Grazziotin Noschang, Patrícia: O caso das papeleras na Corte internacional de Justiça: direito ambiental versus direito econômico? (Dans: Revista de direito da Unigranrio, 2008, v. 1, no. 1, p. 1-14.) [I.C.J., passim.]

Gros Espiell, Héctor: Las medidas cautelares (provisionales) en los tribunales internacionales: el caso de la Corte Internacional de Justicia y el medio ambiente. (Dans: Anuario hispano-luso-americano de derecho internacional, 2007, v. 18, p. 383-403.)

Handl, Günther: Transboundary impacts. (In: The Oxford handbook of international environmental law, ed. by Daniel Bodansky; Jutta Brunnée; Ellen Hey. Oxford: Oxford University Press, 2007, p. 531-549.) [I.C.J., p. 533, 542.]

Happold, Matthew: Dams and international law. (In: Les ressources en eau et le droit international, ed. by Laurence Boisson de Chazournes; Salman M. A. Salman. Leiden; Boston: Martinus Nijhoff, 2005, p. 577-604.) [I.C.J., p. 601-602.]

Harrison, James: Significant international environmental law cases. (In: Journal of Environmental Law, 2006, v. 18, no. 3, p. 505-516.) [I.C.J., p. 507, 508.]

Helal, Mohammed S.: Sharing blue gold: the 1997 UN Convention on the Law of Non-navigational uses of International Watercourses ten years on. (In: Colorado Journal of International Environmental Law and Policy, 2007, v. 18, no. 2, p. 337-378.) [I.C.J., p. 343-344, 357, 365.]

Hey, Ellen: Exercising delegated public powers: multilateral environmental agreements and multilateral funds. (In: Developments of international law in treaty making, ed. by Rüdiger Wolfrum; Volker Röben. Berlin, [etc.]: Springer, 2005, p. 437-461.) [I.C.J., p. 451, 461.]

Hey, Ellen : Global environmental law. (In : Finnish Yearbook of International Law, 2008, v. 19, p. 5-27.)

Hey, Ellen : International institutions. (In : The Oxford handbook of international environmental law, ed. by Daniel Bodansky ; Jutta Brunnée ; Ellen Hey. Oxford : Oxford University Press, 2007, p. 749-769.) [I.C.J., p. 751.]

Hildering, Antoinette : The right of access to freshwater resources. (In : International law and sustainable development : principles and practice, ed. by Nico Schrijver ; Friedl Weiss. Leiden [etc.] : Martinus Nijhoff, 2004, p. 405-429.) [I.C.J., p. 406-407, 418.]

Holtwisch, Christoph : Das Nichteinhaltungsverfahren des Kyoto-Protokolls : Entstehung – Gestalt – Wirkung. Berlin : Duncker & Humblot, 2006. (Schriften zum Völkerrecht ; 167.) [I.C.J., p. 111, 218, 219, 220, 221, 261.]

Hutchison, Cameron : Coming in from the shadow of the law : the use of law by States to negotiate international environmental disputes in good faith. (In : Canadian Yearbook of International Law, 2005, v. 43, p. 101-143.) [P.C.I.J., p. 117; I.C.J., p. 102-103, 109-114, 117-118, 120, 123, 131, 135, 139.]

Idris : Prinsip-Prinsip Pemban gunan Berkelanjutan dan Implikasinya Bagi Pengelolaan Sumber Daya Alam Hayati Perikanan dan Kehutanan Indonesia. (In : Jurnal hukum internasional UNPAD, 2007, v. 6, no. 1, p. 90-103.) [C.I.J., p. 90, 101, 102.]

Kiss, Alexandre-Charles et Beurier, Jean-Pierre : Droit international de l'environnement. Paris : Pedone, 2004. 3e éd. (Etudes internationales ; 3.) [C.P.J.I., p. 435; C.I.J., p. 51, 58, 60-61, 79, 120, 137-138, 145-146, 221, 241-250, 439.]

Klabbers, Jan : Compliance procedures. (In : The Oxford handbook of international environmental law, ed. by Daniel Bodansky ; Jutta Brunnée ; Ellen Hey. Oxford : Oxford University Press, 2007, p. 995-1009.) [I.C.J., p. 1002.]

Kulovesi, Kati : Fragmented landscapes, troubled relationships, the WTO dispute settlement system and international environmental law. (In : Finnish Yearbook of International Law, 2008, v. 19, p. 29-62.)

Kurukulasuriya, Lal : Training manual on international environmental law. Nairobi : UNEP, 2006. [I.C.J., p. 1, 18, 24, 25, 42, 47, 67, 68, 170, 213, 266, 282.]

Laly-Chevalier, Caroline : Les catastrophes maritimes et la protection des côtes françaises. (Dans : Annuaire français de droit international, 2004, v. 50, p. 581-606.) [C.I.J., p. 593.]

Lammers, Johan G. : Equity in international environmental law and the special position of developing countries. (In : Hague Yearbook of International Law, 2008, v. 20, p. 9-40.) [I.C.J., p. 11-12, 21-22.]

Lavieille, Jean-Marc: Droit international de l'environnement. Paris: Ellipses, 2004. 2e éd. [mise à jour]. (Le droit en questions.) [C.I.J., p. 17-18, 48, 65-66, 68, 89-90.]

Loibl, Gerhard: The evolving regime on climate change and sustainable development. (In: International law and sustainable development: principles and practice, ed. by Nico Schrijver; Friedl Weiss. Leiden [etc.]: Martinus Nijhoff, 2004, p. 97-118.) [I.C.J., p. 98.]

Maljean-Dubois, Sandrine: L'O.N.U. et la protection de l'environnement: éléments pour un bilan. (Dans: L'observateur des Nations Unies, 2006, v. 20-21, p. 315-328.) [C.I.J., p. 320, 326-327.]

Malone, Linda A. and Pasternack, Scott: Defending the environment: civil society strategies to enforce international environmental law. Ardsley: Transnational, 2004. [I.C.J., p. 26, 29, 42, 141-142, 153-154, 175-179, 186, 192.]

Matsui, Yoshiro: The principle of "common but differentiated responsibilities". (In: International law and sustainable development: principles and practice, ed. by Nico Schrijver; Friedl Weiss. Leiden [etc.]: Martinus Nijhoff, 2004, p. 73-96.) [I.C.J., p. 74.]

Melkas, Eriika: Equitable as equal: the Kyoto Protocol project based flexibility mechanisms in a unequal world. (In: International Community Law Review, 2007, v. 9, no. 3, p. 263-289.) [P.C.I.J., p. 279.]

Menselijke leefomgeving. (In: VN Forum, 2004, 2004/3, v. 17, no. 3, p. 21-24.) [I.C.J., p. 21.]

Morgera, Elisa: Whale sanctuaries: an evolving concept within the International Whaling Commission. (In: Ocean Development and International Law, 2004, v. 35, no. 4, p. 319-338.) [I.C.J., p. 328.]

Mushkat, Roda: The principle of public participation: an Asia-Pacific perspective. (In: International law and sustainable development: principles and practice, ed. by Nico Schrijver; Friedl Weiss. Leiden [etc.]: Martinus Nijhoff, 2004, p. 607-630.) [I.C.J., p. 613.]

Nanda, Ved P.: International environmental norms applicables to nuclear activities, with particular focus on decisions of international tribunals and international settlements. (In: Denver Journal of International Law and Policy, 2006, v. 35, p. 47-65.) [I.C.J., p. 54-60, 62.]

Ochoa Ruiz, Natalia: Dispute settlement over non-navigational uses of international watercourses: theory and practice. (In: Les ressources en eau et le droit international, ed. by Laurence Boisson de Chazournes; Salman M. A. Salman. Leiden; Boston: Martinus Nijhoff, 2005, p. 343-387.) [P.C.I.J., p. 346, 361, 379, 382; I.C.J., p. 344, 347, 350, 362, 372-374, 379-386.]

Okowa, Phoebe N.: Natural resources in situations of armed conflict: is there a coherent framework for protection? (In: International Community Law Review, 2007, v. 9, no. 3, p. 237-262.) [I.C.J., p. 246, 248-249, 253-256, 259-260.]

Olivier, Juliette : L'Union Mondiale pour la Nature (UICN) : une organisation singulière au service du droit de l'environnement. Bruxelles : Bruylant, 2005. (Travaux du CERIC ; 6.) [C.P.J.I., p. 138; C.I.J., p. 127-128, 137-139, 141, 147, 158, 192-193.]

Ong, David M. : International environmental law's 'customary' dilemma : betwixt general principles and treaty rules. (In : Irish Yearbook of International Law, 2006, v. 1, p. 3-60.) [I.C.J., p. 8, 12, 15-17, 19, 24, 27-29, 34, 35, 37, 38, 47, 48, 50, 59.]

Owada, Hisashi : International environmental law and the International Court of Justice. (In : Iustum Aequum Salutare, 2006, v. 3-4, p. 5-32.) [I.C.J., passim.]

Pavoni, Riccardo : Environmental rights, sustainable development, and investor-State case law : a critical appraisal. (In : Human rights in international investment law and arbitration, ed. by Pierre-Marie Dupuy ; Francesco Francioni ; Ernst-Ulrich Petersmann. Oxford : Oxford University Press, 2009, p. 525-556.)

Pinto, Christopher : Some thoughts on the making of international environmental law : a cautionary tale. (In : International law and sustainable development : principles and practice, ed. by Nico Schrijver ; Friedl Weiss. Leiden [etc.] : Martinus Nijhoff, 2004, p. 39-51.) [I.C.J., p. 40, 41.]

Puvimanasinghe, Shyami : Public interest litigation, human rights and the environment in the experience of Sri Lanka. (In : International law and sustainable development : principles and practice, ed. by Nico Schrijver ; Friedl Weiss. Leiden [etc.] : Martinus Nijhoff, 2004, p. 652-676.) [I.C.J., p. 662, 671.]

Quilleré-Majzoub, Fabienne : Pour une méthodologie de l'utilisation équitable et raisonnable des cours d'eau internationaux : (lex, calculus, casus et exemplaris mathematici). (Dans : Revue de droit international et de droit comparé, 2006, v. 83, p. 323-353.) [C.I.J., p. 339-340.]

Rainne, Juha : The work of the International Law Commission on shared natural resources : the pursuit of competence and relevance. (In : Nordic Journal of International Law, 2006, v. 75, p. 321-338.) [I.C.J., p. 323, 326.]

Redgwell, Catherine : National implementation. (In : The Oxford handbook of international environmental law, ed. by Daniel Bodansky ; Jutta Brunnée ; Ellen Hey. Oxford : Oxford University Press, 2007, p. 922-946.) [I.C.J., p. 933, 939.]

Reynaers Kini, Els : The precautionary principle, multilateral treaties and the formation of customary international law : a symptom of a larger conundrum ? Lugano [etc.] : Editions interuniversitaires suisses (Edis), 2008. [I.C.J., p. 54-60, 83-93, 141-156 and passim.]

Romano, Cesare P. R. : International dispute settlement. (In : The Oxford handbook of international environmental law, ed. by Daniel Bodansky ; Jutta Brunnée ; Ellen Hey. Oxford : Oxford University Press, 2007, p. 1036-1056.) [I.C.J., p. 1040, 1044, 1046, 1053-1055.]

Romi, Raphaël: Risques et droit international de l'environnement. (Dans: L'observateur des Nations Unies, 2007, v. 22, p. 57-67.) [C.I.J., p. 64, 66-67.]

Salman, Salman M. A.: Evolution and context of international water resources law. (In: Les ressources en eau et le droit international, ed. by Laurence Boisson de Chazournes; Salman M. A. Salman. Leiden; Boston: Martinus Nijhoff, 2005, p. 45-94.) [P.C.I.J., p. 56, 91; I.C.J., p. 57, 60, 86, 89, 91.]

Sands, Philippe: Developing environmental law: where we are. (In: Environmental Policy and Law, 2007, v. 37, p. 293-296.) [I.C.J., p. 294, 295.]

Sands, Philippe: Litigating environmental disputes: courts, tribunals and the progressive development of international environmental law. (In: Law of the sea, environmental law and settlement of disputes: liber amicorum Judge Thomas A. Mensah, ed. by Tafsir Malick Ndiaye; Rüdiger Wolfrum. Leiden; Boston: Martinus Nijhoff, 2007, p. 313-325.) [I.C.J., p. 315, 318-319.]

Schrijver, Nico J. and Weiss, Friedl: Introductory note by the editors to part II. (In: International law and sustainable development: principles and practice, ed. by Nico Schrijver; Friedl Weiss. Leiden [etc.]: Martinus Nijhoff, 2004, p. 153-157.) [I.C.J., p. 153.]

Scovazzi, Tullio: Some remarks on international responsibility in the field of environmental protection. (In: International responsibility today: essays in memory of Oscar Schachter, ed. by Maurizio Ragazzi. Leiden; Boston: Martinus Nijhoff, 2005, p. 209-222.) [I.C.J., p. 210, 214.]

Setear, John K.: Can legalization last? Whaling and the durability of national (executive) discretion. (In: Virginia Journal of International Law, 2004, v. 44, no. 3, p. 711-757.) [I.C.J., p. 719.]

Shelton, Dinah: Equity. (In: The Oxford handbook of international environmental law, ed. by Daniel Bodansky; Jutta Brunnée; Ellen Hey. Oxford: Oxford University Press, 2007, p. 639-662.) [I.C.J., p. 646-648.]

Sitack Yombatina, Béni: Le principe de précaution en droit de l'environnement: règle juridique obligatoire ou simple principe destiné à ... (Dans: Revue de droit africain: doctrine et jurisprudence, 2006, v. 10, no. 40, p. 383-399.) [I.C.J., p. 384.]

Soares, Guido Fernando Silva: A evolução do dereito internacional do meio ambiente. (Dans: O Brasil e os novos desafios do direito internacional, sous la dir. de Brant, Leonardo Nemer Caldeira. Rio de Janeiro: Editora Forense, 2004, p. 341-377.) [C.P.J.I., p. 362; C.I.J., p. 362.]

Sohnle, Jochen: Nouvelles tendances en matière de règlement pacifique des différends relatifs aux ressources en eau douce internationales. (Dans: Les ressources en eau et le droit international, sous la dir. de Laurence Boisson de Chazournes; Salman M. A. Salman. Leiden; Boston: Martinus

Nijhoff, 2005, p. 389-426.) [C.P.J.I., p. 407-408; C.I.J., p. 396-399, 401-404, 406-408.]

Spielmann, Dean: La Cour internationale de Justice et le droit de l'environnement. (Dans: Annuaire international des droits de l'homme, 2006, v. 1, p. 39-56.)

Stephens, Tim: Multiple international courts and the "fragmentation" of international environmental law. (In: Australian Yearbook of International Law, 2004, v. 25, p. 227-271.) [I.C.J., p. 230-231, 233, 238-240, 251.]

Stoll, Peter-Tobias: Questionnaire international environmental law. (In: Unity and diversity in international law: proceedings of an international symposium of the Kiel Walther Schücking Institute of International Law, November 4-7, 2004, ed. by Zimmermann, Andreas; Hofmann, Rainer. Berlin: Duncker & Humblot, 2006, p. 135-168.) [I.C.J., p. 141, 146, 163-164.]

Strauss, Andrew: Climate change litigation: opening the door to the International Court of Justice. (In: Adjudicating climate change: State, national, and international approaches, ed. by William C. G. Burns; Hari M. Osofsky. New York {etc.]: Cambridge University Press, 2009, p. 334-356.)

Tanaka, Maki: Lessons from the protracted MOX plant dispute: a proposed protocol on marine environmental impact assesment to the United Nations Convention on the Law of the Sea. Ann Arbor, MI: University of Michigan Law School, 2004. [I.C.J. and P.C.I.J., p. 343-344, 347, 353, 355.]

Tarlock, Dan: Ecosystems. (In: The Oxford handbook of international environmental law, ed. by Daniel Bodansky; Jutta Brunnée; Ellen Hey. Oxford: Oxford University Press, 2007, p. 574-596.) [I.C.J., p. 583-584.]

Trouwborst, Arie: The precautionary principle in general international law: combating the Babylonian confusion. (In: Review of European Community and International Environmental Law, 2007, v. 16, no. 2, p. 185-195.) [I.C.J., p. 187-188, 194.]

Trouwborst, Arie: Precautionary rights and duties of States. Leiden; Boston: Martinus Nijhoff, 2006. 2006 (Nova et Vetera Iuris Gentium: Series A: Modern International Law; 25.) [I.C.J., p. 9-10, 34, 53, 115, 199, 208-209, 219.]

Ulfstein, Geir: Treaty bodies. (In: The Oxford handbook of international environmental law, ed. by Daniel Bodansky; Jutta Brunnée; Ellen Hey. Oxford: Oxford University Press, 2007, p. 877-889.) [I.C.J., p. 881.]

Van Dyke, Jon M.: The evolution and international acceptance of the precautionary principle. (In: Bringing new law to ocean waters, ed. by Caron, David D.; Scheiber, Harry N. Leiden; Boston: Martinus Nijhoff, 2004, p. 357-379.) [I.C.J., p. 370-371.]

Van Dyke, Jon M.: Liability and compensation for harm caused by nuclear activities. (In: Denver Journal of International Law and Policy, 2006, v. 35, p. 13-46.) [P.C.I.J., p. 17, 37; I.C.J., p. 14-15, 17-18, 20, 22.]

Varuhas, Jason N. E.: One person can make a difference: an individual petition system for international environmental law. (In: New Zealand Journal of Public and International Law, 2005, v. 3, p. 329-372.) [P.C.I.J. and I.C.J., p. 366.]

Wälde, Thomas W.: Natural resources and sustainable development: from "good intentions" to "good consequences". (In: International law and sustainable development: principles and practice, ed. by Nico Schrijver; Friedl Weiss. Leiden [etc.]: Martinus Nijhoff, 2004, p. 119-150.) [I.C.J., p. 120.]

Wang, Hanling: Ecosystem management and its application to large marine ecosystems: science, law, and politics. (In: Ocean Development and International Law, 2004, v. 35, no. 1, p. 41-74.) [I.C.J., p. 50.]

Wolfrum, Rüdiger and Friedrich, Jürgen: The Framework Convention on Climate Change and the Kyoto Protocol. (In: Ensuring compliance with multilateral environmental agreements: a dialogue between practitioners and academia, ed. by Ulrich Beyerlin; Peter-Tobias Stoll; Rüdiger Wolfrum. Leiden; Boston: Martinus Nijhoff, 2006, p. 53-68.) [I.C.J., p. 62.]

12. Responsabilité internationale
12. International responsibility

Abass, Ademola: Consent precluding State responsibility: a critical analysis. (In: International and Comparative Law Quarterly, 2004, v. 53, no. 1, p. 211-225.) [I.C.J., p. 211, 213-215, 220-222.]

Abi-Saab, Georges: Que reste-t-il du "crime international"? (Dans: Droit du pouvoir, pouvoir du droit: mélanges offerts à Jean Salmon. Bruxelles: Bruylant, 2007, p. 69-91.) [C.I.J., p. 69, 82.]

Ahmed, Tawhida and Jesús Butler, Israel de: The European Union and human rights: an international law perspective. (In: European Journal of International Law, 2006, v. 17, no. 4, p. 771-801.) [I.C.J., p. 779, 785.]

Alcaide-Fernández, Joaquín: Contre-mesures et règlement des différends. (Dans: Revue générale de droit international public, 2004, v. 108, no. 2, p. 347-380.) [C.I.J., p. 351, 354, 358, 361, 369, 374.]

Annoni, Alessandra: La responsabilità internazionale dello Stato per sparizioni forzate. (Dans: Rivista di diritto internazionale, 2005, v. 88, no. 3, p. 667-702.) [C.I.J., p. 675-677.]

Aust, Helmut Philipp: Through the prism of diversity: the articles on State responsibility in the light of the ILC fragmentation report. (In: German Yearbook of International Law, 2006, v. 49, p. 165-200.) [P.C.I.J., p. 170, 188; I.C.J., p. 170-171, 179, 186, 188, 192, 193, 197.]

Bank, Roland and Schwager, Elke: Is there a substantive right to compensation for individual victims of armed conflicts against a State under international law? (In: German Yearbook of International Law, 2006, v. 49, p. 367-412.) [P.C.I.J., p. 384, 392, 394-395, 400, 404; I.C.J., p. 383-385, 393, 394-395, 397, 398-400.]

Barboza, Julio: Legal injury: the tip of the iceberg in the law of State responsibility? (In: International responsibility today: essays in memory of Oscar Schachter, ed. by Maurizio Ragazzi. Leiden; Boston: Martinus Nijhoff, 2005, p. 7-22.) [I.C.J., p. 13, 18, 20; P.C.I.J., p. 9.]

Brownlie, Ian: The responsibility of States for the acts of international organizations. (In: International responsibility today: essays in memory of Oscar Schachter, ed. by Maurizio Ragazzi. Leiden; Boston: Martinus Nijhoff, 2005, p. 355-362.) [I.C.J., p. 357, 361.]

Brunnée, Jutta: International legal accountability through the lens of the law of State responsibility. (In: Netherlands Yearbook of International Law, 2005, v. 36, p. 21-56.) [I.C.J., p. 26-27, 29, 32, 34-35, 40, 42, 48.]

Brunnée, Jutta: Of sense and sensibility: reflections on international liability regimes as tools for environmental protection. (In: International and Comparative Law Quarterly, 2004, v. 53, no. 2, p. 351-367.) [P.C.I.J., p. 352; I.C.J., p. 353.]

Christakis, Théodore: Les "circonstances excluant l'illicéité": une illusion optique? (Dans: Droit du pouvoir, pouvoir du droit: mélanges offerts à Jean Salmon. Bruxelles: Bruylant, 2007, p. 223-270.) [C.I.J., p. 243, 264, 265.]

Christakis, Théodore: "Nécessité n'a pas de loi"? La nécessité en droit international. (Dans: La nécessité en droit international: colloque de Grenoble. Paris: Pedone, 2007, p. 11-63.)

Clément, Sophie et Tranchez, Elodie: Risque et responsabilité en droit international. (Dans: L'observateur des Nations Unies, 2007, v. 22, p. 3-26.) [C.P.J.I., p. 17; C.I.J., p. 15-16, 23, 26.]

Cohen-Jonathan, Gérard: Responsabilité internationale pour atteinte aux droits de l'homme. (Dans: Studi di diritto internazionale in onore di Gaetano Arangio-Ruiz, sous la dir. de Giovanni Battaglini; Paolo Benvenuti; Antonio Cassese; Giorgio Gaja. Napoli: Editoriale Scientifica, 2004, v. 2, p. 675-702.) [C.P.J.I., p. 691; C.I.J., passim.]

Corporate responsibility for human rights and environmental damage: issues of transnational justice litigations including international jurisdiction. (In: From government to governance: the growing impact of non-state actors on the international and European legal system: proceedings of the Sixth Hague Joint Conference held in The Hague, The Netherlands, 3-5 July 2003, ed. by Heere, Wybo P. The Hague: T.M.C. Asser Press, 2004, p. 202-243.) [I.C.J., p. 210, 212, 242.]

Corten, Olivier: Quels droits et quels devoirs pour les Etats tiers? Les effets juridiques d'une assistance à un acte d'agression. (Dans: L'intervention en Irak et le droit international, sous la dir. de Karine Bannelier; Olivier Corten; Théodore Christakis; Pierre Klein. Paris: Pedone, 2004, p. 105-128.) [C.I.J., p. 111.]

Cortese, Bernardo: International economic sanctions as a component of public policy for conflict-of-laws purposes. (In: Les sanctions économiques en droit international, ed. by Laura Picchio Forlati; Linos-Alexandre

Sicilianos. Leiden [etc.]: Martinus Nijhoff, 2004, p. 717-759.) [I.C.J., p. 719, 720, 754.]

D'Argent, Pierre: Le droit de la responsabilité internationale complété? Examen des principes fondamentaux et directives concernant le droit à un recours et à réparation des victimes de violations flagrantes du droit international des droits de l'homme et de violations graves du droit international humanitaire. (Dans: Annuaire français de droit international, 2005, v. 51, p. 27-55.) [C.P.J.I., p. 50; C.I.J., p. 43-44, 50-51.]

d'Aspremont, Jean: Abuse of legal responsibility of international organizations and the responsibility of member States. (In: International Organizations Law Review, 2007, v. 4, p. 91-119.) [I.C.J., p. 113-114, 117.]

D'Orsi, Cristiano: L'obligation de réparation dans le projet d'articles sur la responsabilité de l'Etat: une analyse critique. (Dans: Revue hellénique de droit international, 2005, v. 58, p. 115-143.) [P.C.I.J., p. 119.]

De Vittor, Francesca: La partecipazione del pubblico ufficiale quale elemento della definizione del crimine di tortura: in margine al caso Kunarac. (Dans: Rivista di diritto internazionale, 2004, v. 87, no. 2, p. 426-451.) [C.I.J., p. 443.]

Dekker, Ige F.: Making sense of accountability in international institutional law. An analysis of the Final Report of the ILA Committee on Accountability of International Organizations from a conceptual legal perspective. (In: Netherlands Yearbook of International Law, 2005, v. 36, p. 83-118.) [I.C.J., p. 102.]

Diggelmann, Oliver: Fault in the law of State responsibility: pragmatism ad infinitum? (In: German Yearbook of International Law, 2006, v. 49, p. 293-305.) [P.C.I.J., p. 298; I.C.J., p. 299.]

Dominicé, Christian: A la recherche des droits erga omnes. (Dans: Droit du pouvoir, pouvoir du droit: mélanges offerts à Jean Salmon. Bruxelles: Bruylant, 2007, p. 357-371.) [C.I.J., p. 357-360, 364, 366-368, 371.]

Dominicé, Christian: Personne privé et responsabilité internationale des Etats. (Dans: Studi di diritto internazionale in onore di Gaetano Arangio-Ruiz, sous la dir. de Giovanni Battaglini; Paolo Benvenuti; Antonio Cassese; Giorgio Gaja. Napoli: Editoriale Scientifica, 2004, v. 2, p. 729-745.) [C.P.J.I., p. 731; C.I.J., p. 732.]

Dumberry, Patrick: The controversial issue of State succession to international responsibility revisited in light of recent State practice. (In: German Yearbook of International Law, 2006, v. 49, p. 413-447.) [I.C.J., p. 427-429, 444-446.]

Dumberry, Patrick: Is a new State responsible for obligations arising from internationally wrongful acts committed before its independence in the context of secession? (In: Canadian Yearbook of International Law, 2005, v. 43, p. 419-453.) [I.C.J., p. 445, 450.]

Dumberry, Patrick: New State responsibility for internationally wrongful acts by an insurrectional movement. (In: European Journal of International Law, 2006, v. 17, p. 605-621.) [P.C.I.J., p. 613.]

Espósito Massicci, Carlos: Comment: [on Unity and diversity in the law of State responsibility by Christian J. Tams]. (In: Unity and diversity in international law: proceedings of an international symposium of the Kiel Walther Schücking Institute of International Law, November 4-7, 2004, ed. by Zimmermann, Andreas; Hofmann, Rainer. Berlin: Duncker & Humblot, 2006, p. 461-462.) [I.C.J., p. 461.]

Fitzmaurice, Malgosia A.: International responsibility and liability. (In: The Oxford handbook of international environmental law, ed. by Daniel Bodansky; Jutta Brunnée; Ellen Hey. Oxford: Oxford University Press, 2007, p. 1010-1035.) [P.C.I.J., p. 1015-1016; I.C.J., p. 1013, 1020-1021.]

Fitzmaurice, Malgosia A. and Sarooshi, Danesh (eds.): Issues of State responsibility before international judicial institutions. Oxford; Portland, OR: Hart Publishing, 2004. (The Clifford Chance lectures; 7.)

Forteau, Mathias: La levée et la suspension des sanctions internationales. (Dans: Annuaire français de droit international, 2005, v. 51, p. 57-84.) [C.P.J.I., p. 73; C.I.J., p. 58-61, 67, 71, 73, 78-79, 82.]

Frumer, Philippe: De l'incidence du temps sur la réalisation de l'illicite: quelques observations relatives à l'arrêt Blecic c. Croatie de la Cour européenne des droits de l'homme (8 mars 2006). (Dans: Droit du pouvoir, pouvoir du droit: mélanges offerts à Jean Salmon. Bruxelles: Bruylant, 2007, p. 396-416.) [C.P.I.J., p. 404; C.I.J., p. 402.]

Gaeta, Paola: On what conditions can a State be held responsible for genocide? (In: European Journal of International Law, 2007, v. 18, p. 631-648.) [I.C.J., passim.]

Gaja, Giorgio: Do States have a duty to ensure compliance with obligations erga omnes by other States? (In: International responsibility today: essays in memory of Oscar Schachter, ed. by Maurizio Ragazzi. Leiden; Boston: Martinus Nijhoff, 2005, p. 31-36.) [I.C.J., p. 31-34, 36.]

Gaja, Giorgio: La possibilité d'invoquer l'état de nécessité pour protéger les intérêts de la communauté internationale. (Dans: Droit du pouvoir, pouvoir du droit: mélanges offerts à Jean Salmon. Bruxelles: Bruylant, 2007, p. 417-424.) [C.I.J., p. 419, 421, 423.]

Garcia, Thierry: Le sommet de Saint-Petersbourg des 15-17 juillet 2006: le G 8, un directoire mondial? (Dans: Revue générale de droit international public, 2006, v. 110, p. 891-896.) [C.I.J., p. 894.]

Gattini, Andrea: La renonciation au droit d'invoquer la responsabilité. (Dans: Völkerrecht als Wertordnung: Festschrift für Christian Tomuschat, sous la dir. de Pierre-Marie Dupuy; Bardo Fassbender; Malcolm N. Shaw; Karl-Peter Sommermann. Kehl: N. P. Engel Verlag, 2006, p. 317-340.)

Gazzini, Tarcisio: The legal nature of WTO obligations and the consequences of their violation. (In: European Journal of International Law, 2006, v. 17, no. 4, p. 723-742.) [P.C.I.J., p. 735-736; I.C.J., p. 724-727, 734-736, 741.]

Geslin, Albane: Réflexions sur la répartition de la responsabilité entre l'organisation internationale et ses Etats membres. (Dans: Revue générale de droit international public, 2005, v. 109, p. 539-579.) [C.I.J., p. 540, 556-559, 571, 574; C.P.J.I., p. 568.]

Gianelli, Alessandra: Crimini internazionali ed immunità degli Stati dalla giurisdizione nella sentenza Ferrini. (Dans: Rivista di diritto internazionale, 2004, v. 87, no. 3, p. 643-684.) [C.I.J., p. 665, 675-676.]

Giardina, Andrea: Responsabilità internazionale, esaurimento dei mezzi interni di ricorso e carattere sussidiario della tutela internazionale dei diritti dell'uomo. (Dans: Studi di diritto internazionale in onore di Gaetano Arangio-Ruiz, sous la dir. de Giovanni Battaglini; Paolo Benvenuti; Antonio Cassese; Giorgio Gaja. Napoli: Editoriale Scientifica, 2004, v. 2, p. 1019-1037.) [C.I.J., p. 1019, 1026.]

Gray, Kevin R.: Transboundary environmental disputes along the Canada-US frontier: revisiting the efficacy of applying the rules of State responsibility. (In: Canadian Yearbook of International Law, 2005, v. 43, p. 333-391.) [P.C.I.J., p. 337, 360, 370-371; I.C.J., p. 334, 337, 339-340, 341-343, 348, 371.]

Greenwood, Christopher J.: State responsibility for the decisions of national courts. (In: Issues of State responsibility before international judicial institutions, ed. by Malgosia A. Fitzmaurice; Danesh Sarooshi. Oxford [etc.]: Hart, 2004, p. 55-73.) [I.C.J., p. 64, 71.]

Gutiérrez Espada, Cesáreo: El estado de necesidad cabalga de nuevo. (Dans: Revista española de derecho internacional, 2004, v. 56, no. 2, p. 669-704.) [PC.I.J., p. 673; I.C.J., p. 670-677, 680, 690-691, 695-697, 700, 704.]

Higgins, Rosalyn: The International Court of Justice: selected issues of State responsibility. (In: International responsibility today: essays in memory of Oscar Schachter, by Maurizio Ragazzi. Leiden; Boston: Martinus Nijhoff, 2005, p. 271-286.) [P.C.I.J., p. 271, 280; I.C.J., passim.]

Horbach, Nathalie L. J. T. and Lefeber, René: Staatsaansprakelijkheid. (In: Handboek internationaal recht, ed. by Horbach, Nathalie L. J. T.; Lefeber, René; Ribbelink, Olivier. The Hague: T.M.C. Asser Press, 2007, p. 309-345.) [P.C.I.J., p. 312, 314, 321, 325, 330; I.C.J., p. 312, 314, 316, 319-322, 326, 328, 329-330, 333, 337, 339-342.]

Hulsroj, Peter: To the rescue, all hands: the good neighbour principle in international law. (In: Irish Yearbook of International Law, 2006, v. 1, p. 167-189.)

Iovane, Massimo: The activity of the International Law Commission during its 58th session (2006). (In: Italian Yearbook of International Law, 2006, v. 16, p. 245-265.) [P.C.I.J., p. 245; I.C.J., p. 247, 250.]

Johnstone, Rachael Lorna: State responsibility: a concerto for court, council and committee. (In: Denver Journal of International Law and Policy, 2008, v. 37, no. 1, p. 63-117.)

Kaplan, Margo: Using collective interests to ensure human rights: an analysis of the articles on State responsibility. (In: New York University Law Review, 2004, v. 79, p. 1902-1933.) [I.C.J., p. 1909-1913, 1928-1929.]

Karagiannis, Syméon: Du non étatique à l'étatique: la cruciale question de l'imputabilité d'actes de particuliers en droit international. (Dans: Acteurs non étatiques et droit international: VIIe rencontre internationale de la Faculté des Sciences juridiques, politiques et sociales de Tunis: 6, 7 et 8 avril 2006, sous la dir. de Rafâa Ben Achour; Slim Laghmani. Paris: Pedone, 2007, p. 161-195.) [C.P.J.I., p. 163; C.I.J., 165, 167-168, 172-175, 181-182, 184, 190, 193.]

Kiss, Alexandre-Charles: State responsibility and liability for nuclear damage. (In: Denver Journal of International Law and Policy, 2006, v. 35, p. 67-83.) [I.C.J., p. 68-70.]

Klein, Natalie: State responsibility for international humanitarian law violations and the work of the Eritrea Ethiopia Claims Commission so far. (In: German Yearbook of International Law, 2004, v. 47, p. 214-266.) [P.C.I.J., p. 239; I.C.J., p. 224, 231-232, 235, 239, 246, 266.]

Kolb, Robert: La proportionnalité dans le cadre des contre-mesures et des sanctions: essai de clarification conceptuelle. (Dans: Les sanctions économiques en droit international, sous la dir. de Laura Picchio Forlati; Linos-Alexandre Sicilianos. Leiden [etc.]: Martinus Nijhoff, 2004, p. 379-443.) [C.P.J.I., p. 400, 419, 428, 436; C.I.J., p. 393-394, 397-398, 400, 406, 425, 428-430, 437, 438, 441.]

Kontos, Alexis P.: "Private" security guards: privatized force and State responsibility under international human rights law. (In: Non-state actors and international law, 2004, v. 4, no. 2, p. 199-238.) [I.C.J., p. 216.]

Lagerwall, Anne: L'administration du territoire irakien: un exemple de reconnaissance et d'aide au maintien d'une occupation résultant d'un acte d'agression? (Dans: Revue belge de droit international, 2006, v. 39, p. 249-273.) [C.I.J., p. 251, 255, 259, 268, 273.]

Larsen, Kjetil Mujezinovic: Attribution of conduct in peace operations: the "ultimate authority and control" test. (In: European Journal of International Law, 2008, v. 19, no. 3, p. 509-531.) [I.C.J., p. 514-515, 517-518, 521.]

Leben, Charles: La responsabilité internationale de l'Etat sur le fondement des traités de promotion et de protection des investissements. (Dans: Annuaire français de droit international, 2004, v. 50, p. 683-714.) [C.P.J.I. et C.I.J., p. 713.]

Lowe, Vaughan: Some comments on procedural weaknesses in international law. (In: ASIL, Proceedings of the 98th Annual Meeting, March 31-April 3, 2004, 2004, v. 98, p. 37-39.) [P.C.I.J., p. 37.]

Mamadou, Hébié: L'attribution aux Etats des actes des sociétés militaires privées et de leurs employés à la lumière de l'article 4 du projet d'articles sur la responsabilité internationale des Etats de 2001. (Dans: Select Proceedings of the European Society of International Law, ed. by James Crawford; Sarah M. H. Nouwen. Oxford; Portland: Hart, 2008, v. 2, p. 598-623.) [C.P.J.I., p. 616; C.I.J., p. 600, 603, 606-607, 609, 618.]

Mampuya, Auguste: Responsabilité et réparations dans le conflit des Grands-Lacs au Congo-Zaïre. (Dans: Revue générale de droit international public, 2004, v. 108, no. 4, p. 679-707.) [C.I.J. et C.P.J.I., p. 682, 687-688, 690, 692-696, 705, 707.]

Mazzeschi, Riccardo Pisillo: Responsabilité de l'état pour violation des obligations positives relatives aux droits de l'homme. (Dans: Recueil des cours de l'Académie de droit international de La Haye, 2008, v. 333, p. 175-506.) [C.I.J., p. 218, 219, 252, 253, 270, 286, 287, 312, 313, 366, 367, 369, 390, 391.]

McCorquodale, Robert and Simons, Penelope: Responsibility beyond borders: State responsibility for extraterritorial violations by corporations of international human rights law. (In: Modern Law Review, 2007, v. 70, no. 4, p. 598-625.) [I.C.J., p. 601, 605, 608-610, 611, 616.]

Mendelson, Maurice H.: State responsibility for breach of interim protection orders of the International Court of Justice. (In: Issues of State responsibility before international judicial institutions, ed. by Malgosia A. Fitzmaurice; Danesh Sarooshi. Oxford: Hart, 2004, p. 35-53.)

Milanovic, Marko: State responsibility for acts of non-state actors: a comment on Griebel and Plücken. (In: Leiden Journal of International Law, 2009, v. 22, no. 2, p. 307-324.)

Milanovic, Marko: State responsibility for genocide. (In: European Journal of International Law, 2006, v. 17, p. 553-604.) [I.C.J., p. 553-555, 558-560, 564-567, 568, 570-571, 575-581, 584, 587, 588-592, 594-598, 600-604.]

Nakatani, Kazuhiro: Diplomacy and State responsibility. (In: International responsibility today: essays in memory of Oscar Schachter, ed. by Maurizio Ragazzi. Leiden; Boston: Martinus Nijhoff, 2005, p. 37-47.) [I.C.J., p. 47.]

Nanda, Ved P. and Van Dyke, Jon M.: International nuclear law: an introduction. (In: Denver Journal of International Law and Policy, 2006, v. 35, p. 1-12.) [I.C.J., p. 2-4.]

Nieminen, Katja: The rules of attribution and the private military contractors at Abu Ghraib: private acts or public wrongs? (In: Finnish Yearbook of International Law, 2004, v. 15, p. 289-319.) [P.C.I.J., p. 294; I.C.J., p. 304-312.]

O'Connell, Mary Ellen: Controlling countermeasures. (In: International responsibility today: essays in memory of Oscar Schachter, ed. by Maurizio Ragazzi. Leiden; Boston: Martinus Nijhoff, 2005, p. 49-62.) [I.C.J., p. 50, 60-61; P.C.I.J., p. 52.]

O'Keefe, Roger: World cultural heritage: obligations to the international community as a whole? (In: International and Comparative Law Quarterly, 2004, v. 53, no. 1, p. 189-209.) [I.C.J., p. 190-191, 205.]

Ohlin, Jens David: State responsibility for conspiracy, incitement, and attempt to commit genocide. (In: The UN Genocide Convention: a commentary, ed. by Paola Gaeta. Oxford [etc.]: Oxford University Press, 2009, p. 374-380.)

Orrego Vicuña, Francisco: The protection of shareholders under international law: making State responsibility more accessible. (In: International responsibility today: essays in memory of Oscar Schachter, ed. by Maurizio Ragazzi. Leiden; Boston: Martinus Nijhoff, 2005, p. 161-170.) [I.C.J., p. 161-165, 168, 169.]

Paasivirta, Esa and Kuijper, Pieter Jan: Does one size fit all? The European Community and the responsibility of international organizations. (In: Netherlands Yearbook of International Law, 2005, v. 36, p. 169-226.) [I.C.J., p. 182.]

Pechota, Vratislaw: The limits of international responsibility in the protection of foreign investments. (In: International responsibility today: essays in memory of Oscar Schachter, ed. by Maurizio Ragazzi. Leiden; Boston: Martinus Nijhoff, 2005, p. 171-182.) [P.C.I.J., p. 173, 174; I.C.J., p. 176.]

Peirano, Jorge: International responsibility and cooperation for development. (In: International responsibility today: essays in memory of Oscar Schachter, ed. by Maurizio Ragazzi. Leiden; Boston: Martinus Nijhoff, 2005, p. 183-195.) [I.C.J., p. 190, 192, 194.]

Petculescu, Ioana: Droit international de la responsabilité et droits de l'homme: à propos de l'arrêt de la Cour européenne des droits de l'homme du 8 juillet 2004 dans l'affaire Ilascu et autres c. la République de Moldova et la Fédération de Russie. (Dans: Revue générale de droit international public, 2005, v. 109, p. 581-607.) [C.I.J., p. 588, 592.]

Petman, Jarna: Resort to economic sanctions by not directly affected States. (In: Les sanctions économiques en droit international, ed. by Laura Picchio Forlati; Linos-Alexandre Sicilianos. Leiden [etc.]: Martinus Nijhoff, 2004, p. 309-377.) [I.C.J., p. 310-311, 318, 321, 329, 332, 341-342, 348-350, 352, 358-359.]

Picchio Forlati, Laura: The legal core of international economic sanctions. (In: Les sanctions économiques en droit international, ed. by Laura Picchio Forlati; Linos-Alexandre Sicilianos. Leiden [etc.]: Martinus Nijhoff, 2004, p. 99-207.) [I.C.J., p. 101-102, 121-124, 128, 135, 138-139, 141, 143, 149, 152, 155, 157, 160, 163, 164.]

Picone, Paolo: Obblighi erga omnes e codificazione della responsabilità degli Stati. (Dans: Rivista di diritto internazionale, 2005, v. 88, p. 893-954.) [C.I.J., p. 899, 904, 921-922, 931, 935, 942.]

Pisillo Mazzeschi, Riccardo: The marginal role of the individual in the ILC's articles on State responsibility. (In: Italian Yearbook of International Law, 2004, v. 14, p. 39-51.) [I.C.J., p. 42.]

Pulkowski, Dirk: Testing compliance theories: towards US obedience of international law in the Avena case. (In: Leiden Journal of International Law, 2006, v. 19, p. 511-554.) [I.C.J., passim.]

Quigley, John: Must treaty violations be remedied? A critique of Sanchez-Llamas v. Oregon. (In: Georgia Journal of International and Comparative Law, 2008, v. 36, no. 2, p. 355-380.) [P.C.I.J., p. 367, 369; I.C.J., p. 365-369, 371-372, 378-379.]

Rao, Pemmaraju Sreenivasa: International crimes and State responsibility. (In: International responsibility today: essays in memory of Oscar Schachter, ed. by Maurizio Ragazzi. Leiden; Boston: Martinus Nijhoff, 2005, p. 63-80.) [I.C.J., p. 66, 68, 74, 77, 79.]

Rigaux, François: International responsibility and the principle of causality. (In: International responsibility today: essays in memory of Oscar Schachter, ed. by Maurizio Ragazzi. Leiden; Boston: Martinus Nijhoff, 2005, p. 81-91.) [I.C.J., p. 83-86, 91.]

Ronzitti, Natalino: L'eccezione dello ius cogens alla regola dell'immunità degli Stati dalla giurisdizione è compatibile con la Convenzione delle Nazioni Unite del 2005? (Dans: Accesso alla giustizia dell'individuo nel diritto internazionale e dell'Unione Europea, sous la dir. de Francioni, Francesco; Gestri, Marco; Ronzitti, Natalino; Scovazzi, Tullio. Milano: Giuffrè, 2008, p. 45-67.) [I.C.J., p. 48.]

Rosenne, Shabtai: Breach of treaty in the codification of the law of State responsibility. (In: Essays on international law and practice, ed. by Shabtai Rosenne. Leiden; Boston: Martinus Nijhoff, 2007, p. 515-531.)

Rosenne, Shabtai: Decisions of the International Court of Justice and the new law of State responsibility. (In: International responsibility today: essays in memory of Oscar Schachter, ed. by Maurizio Ragazzi. Leiden; Boston: Martinus Nijhoff, 2005, p. 297-309.)

Rosenne, Shabtai: State responsibility: festina lente. (In: Essays on international law and practice, by Shabtai Rosenne. Leiden; Boston: Martinus Nijhoff, 2007, p. 533-541.)

Roucounas, Emmanuel: Non-State actors: areas of international responsibility in need of further exploration. (In: International responsibility today: essays in memory of Oscar Schachter, ed. by Maurizio Ragazzi. Leiden; Boston: Martinus Nijhoff, 2005, p. 391-404.) [I.C.J., p. 401.]

Sand, Peter H.: "Scientific whaling": whither sanctions for non-compliance with international law? (In: Finnish Yearbook of International Law, 2008, v. 19, p. 93-124.)

Sand, Peter H.: Sanctions in case of non-compliance and State responsibility: pacta sunt servanda – or else? (In: Ensuring compliance with multilateral environmental agreements: a dialogue between practitioners and academia, ed. by Ulrich Beyerlin; Peter-Tobias Stoll; Rüdiger Wolfrum. Leiden; Boston: Martinus Nijhoff, 2006, p. 259-272.) [I.C.J., p. 268.]

Schaus, Annemie: Les entités fédérées sont-elles susceptibles d'encourir une responsabilité internationale? (Dans: Droit du pouvoir, pouvoir du droit: mélanges offerts à Jean Salmon. Bruxelles: Bruylant, 2007, p. 599-629.) [C.I.J., p. 601, 602, 622.]

Seibert-Fohr, Anja: State responsibility for genocide under the Genocide Convention. (In: The UN Genocide Convention: a commentary, ed. by Paola Gaeta. Oxford [etc.]: Oxford University Press, 2009, p. 349-373.)

Sellers, M. N. S.: Economic sanctions against human rights violations. (In: Les sanctions économiques en droit international, ed. by Laura Picchio Forlati; Linos-Alexandre Sicilianos. Leiden [etc.]: Martinus Nijhoff, 2004, p. 477-526.) [I.C.J., p. 477, 479, 487, 489, 492, 494, 504, 506.]

Shaw, Malcolm N.: The International Court, responsibility and remedies. (In: Issues of State responsibility before international judicial institutions, ed. by Malgosia A. Fitzmaurice; Dan Sarooshi. Oxford [etc.]: Hart, 2004, p. 19-33.)

Sicilianos, Linos-Alexandre: Sanctions institutionnelles et contre-mesures: tendances récentes. (Dans: Les sanctions économiques en droit international, sous la dir. de Laura Picchio Forlati; Linos-Alexandre Sicilianos. Leiden [etc.]: Martinus Nijhoff, 2004, p. 3-98.) [C.I.J., p. 7-8, 11, 15, 38-39, 48-49, 51, 53, 55, 85-86, 92-94.]

Simma, Bruno: Comment: [on Unity and diversity in the law of State responsibility by Christian J. Tams]. (In: Unity and diversity in international law: proceedings of an international symposium of the Kiel Walther Schücking Institute of International Law, November 4-7, 2004, ed. by Zimmermann, Andreas; Hofmann, Rainer. Berlin: Duncker & Humblot, 2006, p. 467-470.) [I.C.J., p. 468, 470.]

Simma, Bruno and Pulkowski, Dirk: Of planets and the universe: self-contained regimes in international law. (In: European Journal of International Law, 2006, v. 17, p. 483-529.) [P.C.I.J., p. 486, 491; I.C.J., p. 483, 486, 487, 488, 491, 501, 512, 513, 514, 515, 516, 524.]

Simma, Bruno and Folz, Hans-Peter: Restitution und Entschädigung im Völkerrecht: die Verpflichtungen der Republik Österreich nach 1945 im Lichte ihrer aussenpolitischen Praxis. Wien: Oldenbourg Verlag, 2004. (Veröffentlichungen der Österreichischen Historikerkommission; 6.)

Steinberger, Eva: The WTO Treaty as a mixed agreement: problems with the EC's and the EC member States' membership of the WTO. (In:

European Journal of International Law, 2006, v. 17, no. 4, p. 837-862.) [I.C.J., p. 841, 851, 860.]

Stern, Brigitte: A plea for "reconstruction" of international responsibility based on the notion of legal injury. (In: International responsibility today: essays in memory of Oscar Schachter, ed. by Maurizio Ragazzi. Leiden; Boston: Martinus Nijhoff, 2005, p. 93-106.) [I.C.J., p. 96.]

Tams, Christian J.: Unity and diversity in the law of State responsibility. (In: Unity and diversity in international law: proceedings of an international symposium of the Kiel Walther Schücking Institute of International Law, November 4-7, 2004, ed. by Zimmermann, Andreas; Hofmann, Rainer. Berlin: Duncker & Humblot, 2006, p. 437-460.) [P.C.I.J., p. 446; I.C.J., p. 438, 442, 447, 453, 456-457.]

Thirlway, Hugh: The law and procedure of the International Court of Justice 1960-1989 (supplement 2009) (parts seven and eight). (In: British Year Book of International Law, 2009, v. 80, p. 13-216.)

Tomuschat, Christian: Conclusions générales. (Dans: La nécessité en droit international: colloque de Grenoble. Paris: Pedone, 2007, p. 377-382.)

Tomuschat, Christian: Unilateral acts under international law. (In: Droits et culture: mélanges en l'honneur du doyen Yadh Ben Achour, ed. by Kalthoum Meziou. Tunis: Centre de Publication Universitaire, 2008, p. 1487-1507.) [I.C.J., p. 1493, 1498-1500.]

Treves, Tullio: The International Law Commission's articles on State responsibility and the settlement of disputes. (In: International responsibility today: essays in memory of Oscar Schachter, ed. by Maurizio Ragazzi. Leiden; Boston: Martinus Nijhoff, 2005, p. 223-234.) [I.C.J., p. 231-233.]

Treves, Tullio: La nécessité en droit de la mer. (Dans: La nécessité en droit international: colloque de Grenoble. Paris: Pedone, 2007, p. 237-246.)

Trouwborst, Arie: Precautionary rights and duties of States. Leiden; Boston: Martinus Nijhoff, 2006. 2006 (Nova et Vetera Iuris Gentium: Series A: Modern International Law; 25.) [I.C.J., p. 9-10, 34, 53, 115, 199, 208-209, 219.]

Vázquez, Carlos M.: Direct vs. indirect obligations of corporations under international law. (In: Columbia Journal of Transnational Law, 2005, v. 43, no. 3, p. 927-959.) [I.C.J., p. 934.]

Watts, Arthur: The art of apology. (In: International responsibility today: essays in memory of Oscar Schachter, ed. by Maurizio Ragazzi. Leiden; Boston: Martinus Nijhoff, 2005, p. 107-116.) [I.C.J., p. 111, 115-116.]

Weil, Prosper and Richemond, Daphné: The Oil Platforms case before the International Court of Justice: a non-case of international responsibility. (In: International responsibility today: essays in memory of Oscar Schachter, ed. by Maurizio Ragazzi. Leiden; Boston: Martinus Nijhoff, 2005, p. 329-340.)

Werner, Wouter G.: Responding to the undesired, State responsibility, risk management and precaution. (In: Netherlands Yearbook of International Law, 2005, v. 36, p. 57-82.) [P.C.I.J., p. 67.]

Wittich, Stephan: Non-material damage and monetary reparation in international law. (In: Finnish Yearbook of International Law, 2004, v. 15, p. 321-368.) [I.C.J., p. 327, 335, 340-342, 352, 361, 367.]

Wolfrum, Rüdiger: State responsibility for private actors: an old problem of renewed relevance. (In: International responsibility today: essays in memory of Oscar Schachter, ed. by Maurizio Ragazzi. Leiden; Boston: Martinus Nijhoff, 2005, p. 423-434.) [I.C.J., p. 426, 428, 430.]

Yamada, Chusei: Revisiting the International Law Commission's draft articles on State responsibility. (In: International responsibility today: essays in memory of Oscar Schachter, ed. by Maurizio Ragazzi. Leiden; Boston: Martinus Nijhoff, 2005, p. 117-123.) [I.C.J., p. 118, 121, 123.]

Yang, Xiaodong: Jus cogens and State immunity. (In: New Zealand Yearbook of International Law, 2006, v. 3, p. 131-179.) [I.C.J., p. 134, 145.]

Yee, Sienho: The responsibility of States members of an international organization for its conduct as a result of membership of their normal conduct associated with membership. (In: International responsibility today: essays in memory of Oscar Schachter, ed. by Maurizio Ragazzi. Leiden; Boston: Martinus Nijhoff, 2005, p. 435-454.) [P.C.I.J., p. 436, 445-447; I.C.J., p. 436-437, 440, 442, 444, 449.]

Zemanek, Karl: Does the prospect of incurring responsibility improve the observance of international law? (In: International responsibility today: essays in memory of Oscar Schachter, ed. by Maurizio Ragazzi. Leiden; Boston: Martinus Nijhoff, 2005, p. 125-134.) [I.C.J., p. 131.]

13. Droits de l'homme
13. Human rights

Abad Castelos, Montserrat: ¿ Una alternativa solidaria frente a la barbarie? Las ONG en la nueva sociedad global. Madrid: CIDEAL – Fundación Asistencia Técnica para el Desarollo (ATD), 2004. [C.P.J.I., p. 337; C.I.J., p. 330, 336-3.]

Abikhzer, Franck: La notion juridique d'humanité. Aix-Marseille: Presses Universitaires d'Aix-Marseille, 2005. [C.P.J.I., p. 439; C.I.J., p. 20, 414, 421, 437, 453, 455-456, 470, 475, 476, 477-479, 489, 534-535.]

Abresch, William: A human rights law of internal armed conflict: the European Court of Human Rights in Chechnya. (In: European Journal of International Law, 2005, v. 16, no. 4, p. 741-767.) [I.C.J., p. 741, 743-744.]

Aguirre, Daniel: Multinational corporations and the realisation of economic, social and cultural rights. (In: California Western International Law Journal, 2004, v. 35, no. 1, p. 53-82.) [I.C.J., p. 58.]

Ahmad, Nafees: Refugees: State responsibility, country of origin and human rights. (In: Asia-Pacific Journal on Human Rights and the Law, 2009, v. 10, no. 2, p. 1-22.) [P.C.I.J., p. 6; I.C.J., p. 5, 17-19.]

Ahmed, Tawhida and Jesús Butler, Israel de: The European Union and human rights: an international law perspective. (In: European Journal of International Law, 2006, v. 17, no. 4, p. 771-801.) [I.C.J., p. 779, 785.]

Al Faruque, Abdullah and Begum, Najnin: Conceptualising indigenous peoples' rights: an emerging new category of third-generation rights. (In: Asia-Pacific Journal on Human Rights and the Law, 2004, v. 5, no. 2, p. 1-29.) [P.C.I.J. and I.C.J., p. 9.]

Albrecht, Lawrence G. and Apt, Benjamin L. and Fitzpatrick, Robert B.: International human rights. (In: International Lawyer, 2006, v. 40, p. 467-485.) [I.C.J., p. 468.]

Albrecht, Lawrence G. and Apt, Benjamin L. and Condon, Elizabeth-Merry and Gloria Jean, Garland and Giampolo, Angela D. and Hansel, Mary and Kerr, Russell S. and Mascarenhas, Viren and Shields, Leslie J.: International human rights. (In: International Lawyer, 2007, v. 41, p. 643-669.) [I.C.J., p. 652-653.]

Altiparmak, Kerem: Bankovic: an obstacle to the application of the European Convention on Human Rights in Iraq? (In: Journal of Conflict and Security Law, 2004, v. 9, no. 2, p. 213-251.) [P.C.I.J., p. 228; I.C.J., p. 214, 216, 218-219, 222, 225, 227, 235-236, 247.]

Aminzadeh, Sara C.: A moral imperative: the human rights implications of climate change. (In: Hastings International and Comparative Law Review, 2007, v. 30, p. 231-265.) [I.C.J., p. 245.]

Anaya, S. James: Self-determination as a collective human right under contemporary international law. (In: Operationalizing the right of indigenous peoples to self-determination, ed. by Pekka Aikio; Martin Scheinin. Turku: Institute for Human Rights, Abo Akademi University, 2005, p. 3-18.) [I.C.J., p. 7-8.]

Arnold, Roberta: Human rights in times of terrorism. (In: Zeitschrift für ausländisches öffentliches Recht und Völkerrecht, 2006, v. 66, p. 297-319.) [I.C.J., p. 302.]

Barnes, Richard: Refugee law at sea. (In: International and Comparative Law Quarterly, 2004, v. 53, no. 1, p. 47-77.) [I.C.J., p. 57, 63.]

Bedi, Shiv R. S.: The development of human rights law by the judges of the International Court of Justice. Oxford [etc.]: Hart Publishing, 2007. (Studies in International Law; 10.)

Bernhardt, Rudolf: Judgments of international human rights courts and their effects in the internal legal order of States. (In: Studi di diritto internazionale in onore di Gaetano Arangio-Ruiz, ed. by Giovanni Battaglini; Paolo Benvenuti; Antonio Cassese; Giorgio Gaja. Napoli: Editoriale Scientifica, 2004, v. 1, p. 429-440.) [I.C.J., p. 431, 432.]

Bettoni, Giangaleazzo: Spunti, ragguagli e riflessioni sui sistemi attuali di tutela dei diritti umani nel mondo. (Dans: Studi di diritto internazionale in onore di Gaetano Arangio-Ruiz, sous la dir. de Giovanni Battaglini; Paolo Benvenuti; Antonio Cassese; Giorgio Gaja. Napoli: Editoriale Scientifica, 2004, v. 3, p. 1819-1856.) [C.P.J.I., p, 1828; C.I.J., p. 1827.]

Bianchi, Andrea: Human rights and the magic of jus cogens. (In: European Journal of International Law, 2008, v. 19, no. 3, p. 491-508.) [I.C.J., p. 502-505.]

Boukongou, Jean Didier: The appeal of the African system for protecting human rights. (In: African Human Rights Law Journal, 2006, v. 6, p. 268-298.) [I.C.J., p. 297.]

Broomhall, Bruce: State actors in an international definition of terrorism from a human rights perspective. (In: Case Western Reserve Journal of International Law, 2004, v. 36, no. 2-3, p. 421-441.) [I.C.J., p. 438.]

Buchanan, Allen: Justice, legitimacy, and self-determination: moral foundations for international law. Oxford [etc.]: Oxford University Press, 2004. (Oxford political theory.) [I.C.J., p. 48.]

Bulterman, Mielle: Fundamental rights and the United Nations financial sanction regime: the Kadi and Yusuf judgments of the Court of First Instance of the European Communities. (In: Leiden Journal of International Law, 2006, v. 19, p. 753-772.) [I.C.J., p. 768-770.]

Burgorgue-Larsen, Laurence et Úbeda de Torres, Amaya (sous la dir. de): Les grandes décisions de la Cour interaméricaine des droits de l'homme. Bruxelles: Bruylant, 2008. [C.I.J., voir index page 948.]

Burra, Srinivas: India's reservations to human rights treaties. (In: Indian Journal of International Law, 2004, v. 44, no. 4, p. 749-787.) [I.C.J., p. 755, 758-761, 763-764, 782, 784-785.]

Buyse, Antoine: A lifeline in time – non-retroactivity and continuing violations under the ECHR. (In: Nordic Journal of International Law, 2006, v. 75, p. 63-88.) [P.C.I.J., p. 64, 73; I.C.J., p. 64.]

Caflisch, Lucius et Cançado Trindade, A. A.: Les Conventions américaine et européenne des droits de l'homme et le droit international général. (Dans: Revue générale de droit international public, 2004, v. 108, no. 1, p. 5-62.) [C.I.J. et C.P.J.I., p. 6-7, 41.]

Cançado Trindade, A. A.: La capacité juridique internationale de l'individu dans le système interaméricain de protection des droits de la personne humaine. (Dans: Soberanía del Estado y derecho internacional: homenaje al profesor Juan Antonio Carrillo Salcedo. Sevilla: Universidad de Sevilla, 2005, v. 1, p. 293-316.) [C.I.J., p. 299.]

Cançado Trindade, A. A.: The case-law of the Inter-American Court of Human Rights: an overview. (In: Studi di diritto internazionale in onore di Gaetano Arangio-Ruiz, ed. by Giovanni Battaglini; Paolo Benvenuti; Antonio

Cassese; Giorgio Gaja. Napoli: Ed. Scientifica, 2004, v. 3, p. 1873-1898.) [I.C.J., p. 1892-1893.]

Cançado Trindade, A. A. et Cohen-Jonathan, Gérard et Decaux, Emmanuel et Engel, Norbert et Condorelli, Luigi: Débats. (Dans: Mesures conservatoires et droits fondamentaux, sous la dir. de Gérard Cohen-Jonathan; Jean-Francois Flauss. Bruxelles: Bruylant; Nemesis, 2005, p. 57-62.) [C.I.J., p. 57-58, 60-61.]

Cançado Trindade, A. A.: El derecho de acceso a la justicia en su amplia dimensión. Santiago, Chile: Librotecnia, 2008. [C.I.J., passim.]

Cançado Trindade, A. A.: A humanização do direito internacional. Belo Horizonte: Del Rey, 2006. [C.I.J., voir index p. 419.]

Cançado Trindade, A. A.: The international standards of protection of the human person in the developing case-law of the Inter-American Court of Human Rights (1982-2004). (In: Kokusaiho Gaiko Zassi, 2006, v. 104, p. 1-36.) [I.C.J., p. 7-8.]

Cançado Trindade, A. A.: Les mesures provisoires de protection dans la jurisprudence de la Cour interaméricaine des droits de l'homme. (Dans: Mesures conservatoires et droits fondamentaux, sous la dir. de Gérard Cohen-Jonathan; Jean-Francois Flauss. Bruxelles: Bruylant: Nemesis, 2005, p. 145-163.) [C.P.J.I., p. 146; C.I.J., p. 146, 147, 152.]

Cançado Trindade, A. A.: Les mesures provisoires de protection dans la jurisprudence de la Cour interaméricaine des droits de l'homme. (Dans: Revista do Instituto Brasileiro de Direitos Humanos, 2003, v. 4, p. 13-25.) [C.P.J.I., p. 14; C.I.J., p. 14-15.]

Cançado Trindade, A. A.: Reflexiones sobre el desarraigo como problema de derechos humanos frente a la conciencia jurídica universal. (Dans: La nueva dimensión de las necesidades de protección del ser humano en el inicio del siglo XXI, par Antônio Augusto Cançado Trindade; Jaime Ruiz de Santiago. San José: UNHCR, 2006, p. 33-92.) [C.I.J., p. 68, 70, 76.]

Cançado Trindade, A. A.: El sistema interamericano de protección de los derechos humanos (1948-2002). (Dans: La protección internacional de los derechos humanos en los albores del siglo XXI, sous la dir. de Felipe Gomez Isa. Universidad de Deusto: Bilbao, 2003, p. 549-591.)

Cassese, Antonio: La prise en compte de la jurisprudence de Strasbourg par les juridictions pénales internationales. (Dans: Le rayonnement international de la jurisprudence de la Cour européenne des droits de l'homme, sous la dir. de Gérard Cohen-Jonathan; Jean-François Flauss. Bruxelles: Bruylant, 2005, p. 29-82.) [C.I.J., p. 30, 31.]

Cassimatis, Anthony: International humanitarian law, international human rights law, and fragmentation of international law. (In: International and Comparative Law Quarterly, 2007, v. 56, p. 623-640.)

Castellino, Joshua: The "right" to land, international law and indigenous peoples. (In: International law and indigenous peoples, ed. by Joshua

Castellino; Niamh Walsh. Leiden, [etc.]: Martinus Nijhoff, 2005, p. 89-116.) [I.C.J., p. 92, 93, 98, 101-106.]

Cohen-Jonathan, Gérard: Avant-propos. (Dans: Le rayonnement international de la jurisprudence de la Cour européenne des droits de l'homme, sous la dir. de Gérard Cohen-Jonathan; Jean-François Flauss. Bruxelles: Bruylant, 2005, p. 11-28.) [C.I.J., p. 14-15, 25.]

Cohen-Jonathan, Gérard: Conclusions générales. (Dans: Mesures conservatoires et droits fondamentaux, sous la dir. de Gérard Cohen-Jonathan; Jean-Francois Flauss. Bruxelles: Bruylant; Nemesis, 2005, p. 283-307.) [C.P.J.I., p. 304-305; C.I.J., p. 285, 303-304.]

Cohen-Jonathan, Gérard et Flauss, Jean-François: Cour européenne des droits de l'homme et droit international général (2005). (Dans: Annuaire français de droit international, 2005, v. 51, p. 675-698.) [C.P.J.I., p. 697; C.I.J., p. 693, 695-697.]

Cohen-Jonathan, Gérard: Le jus cogens et les droits de l'homme. (Dans: Mélanges en l'honneur de Jean Charpentier: la France, l'Europe, le monde. Paris: Pedone, 2008, p. 61-72.)

Cohen-Jonathan, Gérard: Rapport introductif général. (Dans: Droit international, droits de l'homme et juridictions internationales: actes de la table ronde du 10 juillet 2003 organisée par l'Institut international des droits de l'homme, sous la dir. de Gérard Cohen-Jonathan; Jean-François Flauss. Bruxelles: Bruylant, 2004, p. 11-58.) [C.I.J., p. 11-12, 14, 21, 24-26, 30, 36, 38, 41-50, 53, 57-58; C.P.J.I., p. 22-23.]

Coliver, Sandra and Green, Jennie and Hoffman, Paul: Holding human rights violators accountable by using international law in U.S. courts: advocacy efforts and complementary strategies. (In: Emory International Law Review, 2005, v. 19, no. 1, p. 169-226.) [I.C.J., p. 193.]

Commission internationale de juristes: Le droit à un recours et à obtenir réparation en cas de violations graves des droits de l'homme: guide pratique. Genève: Commission internationale de juristes, 2006. (Série des guides pratiques; 2.) [C.I.J., p. 29, 57, 58, 102, 114, 115, 116, 118, 122, 123, 152.]

Condorelli, Luigi: Discussion. (Dans: Mesures conservatoires et droits fondamentaux, sous la dir. de Gérard Cohen-Jonathan; Jean-Francois Flauss. Bruxelles: Bruylant; Nemesis, 2005, p. 55-56.) [C.I.J., passim.]

Conti, Erika: The referendum for self-determination: is it still a solution? The never ending dispute over Western Sahara. (In: African Journal of International and Comparative Law, 2008, v. 16, no. 2, p. 178-196.) [I.C.J., p. 178-181, 188, 189, 191, 193, 196.]

Coomans, Fons and Kamminga, Menno T.: Rechten van de mens. (In: Handboek internationaal recht, ed. by Horbach, Nathalie L. J. T.; Lefeber, René; Ribbelink, Olivier. The Hague: T.M.C. Asser Press, 2007, p. 469-507.) [I.C.J., p. 495.]

Cosme Ladeia, André Luiz: A relativização da soberania em face da preservação dos direitos e garantias fundamentais. (Dans: Anuario de derecho constitucional latinoamericano, 2009, v. 15, p. 559-584.)

D'Argent, Pierre: Le droit de la responsabilité internationale complété? Examen des principes fondamentaux et directives concernant le droit à un recours et à réparation des victimes de violations flagrantes du droit international des droits de l'homme et de violations graves du droit international humanitaire. (Dans: Annuaire français de droit international, 2005, v. 51, p. 27-55.) [C.P.J.I., p. 50; C.I.J., p. 43-44, 50-51.]

D'Ascoli, Silvia and Scherr, Kathrin Maria: The rule of prior exhaustion of local remedies in the context of human rights protection. (In: Italian Yearbook of International Law, 2006, v. 16, p. 117-138.) [P.C.I.J., p. 120, 122-123; I.C.J., p. 120, 122-126.]

Daglish, Kristen and Nasu, Hitoshi: Towards a true incarnation of the rule of law in war-torn territories: centring peacebuilding in the will of the people. (In: Netherlands International Law Review, 2007, v. 54, p. 81-114.) [I.C.J., p. 85, 87, 112.]

Danieli, Yael: Massive trauma and the healing role of reparative justice. (In: Reparations for victims of genocide, war crimes against humanity: systems in place and systems in the making, ed. by Carla Ferstman; Mariana Goetz; Alan Andrew Stephens. Leiden: Nijhoff, 2009, p. 41-77.) [I.C.J., p. 63.]

Decaux, Emmanuel: Les formes contemporaines de l'esclavage. (Dans: Recueil des cours de l'Académie de droit international de La Haye, 2008, v. 336, p. 9-197.) [C.P.J.I., p. 104; C.I.J., p. 71, 77, 99, 104-117, 133, 166, 183.]

Doebbler, Curtis F. J.: International human rights law: cases and materials. Washington, D.C.: CDP, 2004. [I.C.J., p. 62-64, 85, 99-106, 108-113, 138-139, 173, 275-276, 454, 489, 502-538, 716-717, 729; P.C.I.J., p. 376-378, 488, 531-532.]

Doswald-Beck, Louise et Kolb, Robert: Garanties judiciaires et droits de l'homme: Nations Unies, Systèmes européen, américan et africain. Textes et résumés de la jurisprudence internationale. Strasbourg: Kehl, 2004. (Commission internationale de juristes.)

Doswald-Beck, Louise: Human rights and humanitarian law: are there some individuals bereft of all legal protection? (In: ASIL, Proceedings of the 98th Annual Meeting, March 31-April 3, 2004, 2004, v. 98, p. 353-358.) [I.C.J., p. 353.]

Drumbl, Mark A.: Sixtieth anniversary of the Genocide Convention: the power of a word. (In: Proceedings of the second international humanitarian law dialogs: august 25-26, 2008, at the Chautauqua institution, ed. by Andersen, Elisabeth; Crane, David M. Washington: American Society of International Law, 2009, p. 97-116.)

Dugard, John R.: The future of international law: a human rights perspective: with some comments on the Leiden School of International

Law. (In : Leiden Journal of International Law, 2007, v. 20, no. 4, p. 729-739.)

Dupuy, Pierre-Marie : Some reflections on contemporary international law and the appeal to universal values : a response to Martti Koskenniemi. (In : European Journal of International Law, 2005, v. 16, no. 1, p. 131-137.) [I.C.J., p. 134, 136.]

Duxbury, Alison : Bigger or better? The role of human rights and democracy in determining membership of the European institutions. (In : Nordic Journal of International Law, 2004, v. 73, no. 4, p. 421-460.) [I.C.J., p. 427-428, 435, 437.]

Ebobrah, Solomon T. : A rights-protection goldmine or a waiting volcanic eruption? Competence of, and access to, the human rights jurisdiction of the ECOWAS Community Court of Justice. (In : African Human Rights Law Journal, 2007, v. 7, p. 307-329.) [I.C.J., p. 318, 326.]

Eide, Asbjørn : Group accomodation and the challenges of education : multicultural or intercultural – or a combination of the two ? (In : Human rights law : from dissemination to application : essays in honour of Göran Melander, ed. by Jonas Grimheden ; Rolf Ring. Leiden [etc.] : Martinus Nijhoff, 2006.) [I.C.J., p. 12.]

Eide, Asbjørn : Rights of indigenous peoples : achievements in international law during the last quarter of a century. (In : Netherlands Yearbook of International Law, 2006, v. 37, p. 155-212.) [I.C.J., p. 184.]

European Court of Human Rights. (In : Global Community : Yearbook of International Law and Jurisprudence, 2006, v. 6, no. 2, p. 1181-1353.) [I.C.J., p. 1219-1220.]

European Court of Human Rights : European Court of Human Rights (ECHR) : case of Mamatkulov and Askarov v. Turkey (February 4, 2005). (In : International Legal Materials, 2005, v. 44, p. 759-795.) [I.C.J., p. 768, 781-783, 791-794.]

Feminism and international law. (In : Reports of the Annual Conference, by International Law Association (ILA), 2006, 2006, p. 601-653.) [I.C.J., p. 616-617.]

Ferrer Lloret, Jaume : La imunidad de jurisdicción del Estado ante violaciones graves de los derechos humanos. (Dans : Revista española de derecho internacional, 2007, v. 59, p. 29-63.) [C.I.J., p. 58.]

Ferstman, Carla and Rosenberg, Sheri P. : Reparations in Dayton's Bosnia and Herzegovina. (In : Reparations for victims of genocide, war crimes against humanity : systems in place and systems in the making, ed. by Carla Ferstman ; Mariana Goetz ; Alan Andrew Stephens. Leiden : Nijhoff, 2009, p. 483-513.) [I.C.J., p. 483-484.]

Flauss, Jean-François : Le droit international général dans la jurisprudence de la Cour européenne des droits de l'homme. (Dans : Droit international, droits de l'homme et juridictions internationales : actes de la table ronde du

10 juillet 2003 organisée par l'Institut international des droits de l'homme, sous la dir. de Gérard Cohen-Jonathan ; Jean-François Flauss. Bruxelles : Bruylant, 2004, p. 73-120.) [C.I.J., p. 87-88, 90-91, 110-111, 113, 119; C.P.J.I., p. 89.]

Foster, Michelle : Protection elsewhere : the legal implications of requiring refugees to seek protection in another State. (In : Michigan Journal of International Law, 2007, v. 28, p. 223-286.) [I.C.J., p. 241-242, 246, 256-257, 259-260.]

Frimpong Oppong, Richard : Trade and human rights : a perspective for agents of trade policy using a rights-based approach to development. (In : African Human Rights Law Journal, 2006, v. 6, p. 123-145.) [I.C.J., p. 128.]

Gassama, Cherifou : Le principe de restitutio in integrum dans le contentieux international des droits de l'homme. (Dans : Miskolci Nemzetközi Jogi Közlemények, 2005, v. 2, no. 1, p. 1-31.) [C.P.J.I., p, 2, 7-8; C.I.J., p. 2, 6-7, 13-14.]

Genugten, Willem J. M. van and Gestel, Rob van and Groenhuijsen, Marc and Letschert, Rianne : Loopholes, risks and ambivalences in international lawmaking : the case of a framework convention on victims' rights. (In : Netherlands Yearbook of International Law, 2006, v. 37, p. 109-154.) [I.C.J., p. 118-119.]

Gerety, Corina : The Status of the prohibition on the imposition of the death penalty on juvenile offenders under international law. (In : International crime and punishment : selected issues ed. Lanham : University Press of America, 2004, v. 2, p. 129-167.) [I.C.J., p. 164.]

González Vega, Javier : Interpretación, derecho internacional y convenio europeo de derechos humanos : a propósito de la interpretación evolutiva en materia de autodeterminación sexual. (Dans : Revista española de derecho internacional, 2004, v. 56, no. 1, p. 163-184.) [C.I.J., p. 166-167.]

Goodwin-Gill, Guy S. and McAdam, Jane : The refugee in international law. Oxford : Oxford University Press, 2007. 3rd ed. [P.C.I.J., p. 9, 451, 454, 457; I.C.J., p. 9, 241, 249, 431-433, 435, 448, 456-459.]

Gradoni, Lorenzo : "You will receive a fair trial elsewhere". The ad hoc international criminal tribunals acting as human rights jurisdictions. (In : Netherlands International Law Review, 2007, v. 54, p. 1-49.) [I.C.J., p. 26.]

Grief, Nicholas : Using Article 10 of the European Convention on Human Rights as a defence to criminal proceedings arising from non-violent direct action against nuclear weapons : the relevance of international law. (In : The International Journal of Human Rights, 2007, v. 11, no. 3, p. 327-347.) [I.C.J., p. 327-329, 335, 338, 341.]

Grimheden, Jonas : The International Court of Justice : monitoring human rights. (In : International human rights monitoring mechanisms : essays in honour of Jakob Th. Moller, ed. by Gudmundur Alfredsson. 2009, p. 249-261.)

Gross, Aeyal M.: Human proportions: are human rights the emperor's new clothes of the international law of occupation? (In: European Journal of International Law, 2007, v. 18, p. 1-35.) [I.C.J., p. 2-6, 9, 11-12, 19, 21, 31-33.]

Guellali, Amna: L'application extraterritoriale des droits de l'homme en cas de conflit armé ou d'occupation de territoire. (Dans: Revue de droit international, de sciences diplomatiques et politiques, 2006, v. 84, no. 3, p. 295-327.) [I.C.J., p. 295, 296.]

Guellali, Amna: Lex specialis, droit international humanitaire et droits de l'homme: leur interaction dans les nouveaux conflits armés. (In: Revue générale de droit international public, 2007, v. 111, no. 3, p. 539-574.) [C.I.J., p. 539, 541-549.]

Guild, Elspeth: Inside out or outside in? Examining human rights in situations of armed conflict. (In: International Community Law Review, 2007, v. 9, no. 1, p. 33-58.) [I.C.J., p. 33.]

Hakimi, Monica: The Council of Europe addresses CIA rendition and detention program. (In: American Journal of International Law, 2007, v. 101, p. 442-452.) [I.C.J., p. 449.]

Halfmeier, Axel: Menschenrechte und Internationales Privatrecht im Kontext der Globalisierung. (In: Rabels Zeitschrift für ausländisches und internationales Privatrecht, 2004, v. 68, no. 4, p. 653-686.) [I.C.J., p. 668.]

Halpin, Stanley A.: Looking over a crowd and picking your friends: civil rights and the debate over the influence of foreign and international human rights law on the interpretation of the U.S. constitution. (In: Hastings International and Comparative Law Review, 2006, v. 30, p. 1-41.) [I.C.J., p. 10.]

Heinämäki, Leena: Inherent rights of aboriginal peoples in Canada – reflections of the debate in national and international law. (In: International Community Law Review, 2006, v. 8, p. 155-202.) [I.C.J., p. 158, 179-180, 194.]

Heintze, Hans-Joachim: Konsequenzen der Konvergenz von Menschenrechtsschutz und humanitärem Völkerrecht. (In: Krisensicherung und humanitärer Schutz: Festschrift für Dieter Fleck, ed. by Horst Fischer; Ulrike Froissart; Wolff Heintschel von Heinegg. Berlin: Berliner Wissenschafts-Verlag, 2004, p. 243-265.) [I.C.J., p. 244, 250, 251.]

Heintze, Hans-Joachim: On the relationship between human rights law protection and international humanitarian law. (In: Revue internationale de la Croix-Rouge, 2004, v. 86, no. 856, p. 789-813.) [I.C.J., p. 790, 796-797, 810.]

Henry, Laurence: Les Nations Unies et le droit des peuples à disposer d'eux-mêmes. (Dans: L'observateur des Nations Unies, 2006, v. 20-21, p. 225-260.) [C.I.J., p. 232-235, 242, 250.]

Hey, Ellen: Distributive justice and procedural fairness in global water law. (In: Environmental law and justice in context, ed. by Ebbesson, Jonas; Okowa, Phoebe N.. Cambridge: Cambridge University Press, 2009, p. 351-370.) [I.C.J., p. 353-355.]

Hillgenberg, Hartmut: Incommunicado in Guantanamo. (In: Internationale Gemeinschaft und Menschenrechte: Festschrift für Georg Ress zum 70. Geburtstag am 21. Januar 2005, ed. by Bröhmer, Jürgen; Bieber, Roland; Calliess, Christian; Langenfeld, Christine; Weber, Stefan; Wolf, Joachim. Köln [etc.]: Heymann, 2005, p. 133-140.) [I.C.J., p. 135, 138-139.]

Hilpold, Peter: Neue Minderheiten im Völkerrecht und im Europarecht. (In: Archiv des Völkerrechts, 2004, v. 42, no. 1, p. 80-110.) [I.C.J. and P.C.I.J., p. 82, 85.]

Hobbins, A. J. and Steward, Ann H.: Bringing individual human rights issues to the United Nations: John Humphrey and the quest for compensation. (In: Canadian Yearbook of International Law, 2004, v. 41, p. 187-223.) [I.C.J., p. 196, 199, 204.]

Hulsroj, Peter: To the rescue, all hands: the good neighbour principle in international law. (In: Irish Yearbook of International Law, 2006, v. 1, p. 167-189.)

International Commission of Jurists: The right to a remedy and to reparation for gross human rights violations: a practioners' guide. Geneva: International Commission of Jurists, 2006. (Practioners' guide series; 2.) [I.C.J., p. 26, 51, 52, 53, 94, 105, 106, 107, 113, 141, 143, 162.]

International human rights law and practice. (In: Reports of the Annual Conference, by International Law Association (ILA), 2006, 2006, p. 457-465.) [I.C.J., p. 459-461.]

Internationale bescherming mensenrechten. (In: VN Forum, 2004, 2004/3, v. 17, no. 3, p. 9-14.) [I.C.J., p. 13.]

Internationale rechtshandhaving. (In: VN Forum, 2004, 2004/3, v. 17, no. 3, p. 42-46.) [I.C.J., p. 42, 44, 45.]

Isanga, Joseph: Counter-terrorism and human rights: the emergence of a rule of customary int'l law from the U.N. resolutions. (In: Denver Journal of International Law and Policy, 2009, v. 37, no. 2, p. 233-255.)

Jaguttis, Malte: Freier Hafenzugang für Flüchtlingsschiffe? (In: Archiv des Völkerrechts, 2005, v. 43, no. 1, p. 90-128.) [I.C.J., p. 93, 95, 98, 103, 112.]

Jung, Youngjin: In pursuit of reconstructing Iraq: does self-determination matter? (In: Denver Journal of International Law and Policy, 2005, v. 33, no. 3, p. 391-410.) [I.C.J., p. 400-401.]

Kalshoven, Frits: Remarks. (In: ASIL, Proceedings of the 98th Annual Meeting, March 31-April 3, 2004, 2004, v. 98, p. 363-365.) [I.C.J., p. 364.]

Kamminga, Menno T.: Human rights treaties and State succession. (In: The status of international treaties on human rights. Strasbourg: Council of Europe Publishing, 2006, p. 31-41.) [I.C.J., p. 33.]

Kingsbury, Benedict: Reconstructing self-determination: a relational approach. (In: Operationalizing the right of indigenous peoples to self-determination, ed. by Pekka Aikio; Martin Scheinin. Turku: Institute for Human Rights, Abo Akademi University, 2005, p. 19-37.) [I.C.J., p. 22.]

Kinley, David and Tadaki, Junko: The emergence of human rights responsibilities for corporations at international law. (In: Virginia Journal of International Law, 2004, v. 44, no. 4, p. 931-1023.) [I.C.J., p. 945-946.]

Klein, Eckart: A comment on the issue of reservations to the provisions of the Covenant Representing (Peremptory) Rules of General International Law. (In: Reservations to human rights treaties and the Vienna Convention regime: conflict, harmony or reconciliation, ed. by Ineta Ziemele. Leiden, [etc.]: Martinus Nijhoff, 2004, p. 59-65.) [I.C.J., p. 62.]

Klein, Eckart: Menschenrechte und Ius cogens. (In: Internationale Gemeinschaft und Menschenrechte: Festschrift für Georg Ress zum 70. Geburtstag am 21. Januar 2005, ed. by Bröhmer, Jürgen; Bieber, Roland; Calliess, Christian; Langenfeld, Christine; Weber, Stefan; Wolf, Joachim. Köln [etc.]: Heymann, 2005, p. 151-163.) [I.C.J., p. 151-153, 159, 162.]

Koivurova, Timo: The International Court of Justice and peoples. (In: International Community Law Review, 2007, v. 9, no. 2, p. 157-180.) [I.C.J., passim.]

Kooijmans, Pieter H.: Is the right to diplomatic protection a human right? (In: Studi di diritto internazionale in onore di Gaetano Arangio-Ruiz, ed. by Giovanni Battaglini; Paolo Benvenuti; Antonio Cassese; Giorgio Gaja. Napoli: Editoriale Scientifica, 2004, v. 3, p. 1975-1984.) [P.C.I.J., p. 1975, 1976; I.C.J., p. 1976, 1978-1980.]

Lattanzi, Flavia: Il confine fra diritto internazionale umanitario e diritti dell'uomo. (Dans: Studi di diritto internazionale in onore di Gaetano Arangio-Ruiz, sous la dir. de Giovanni Battaglini; Paolo Benvenuti; Antonio Cassese; Giorgio Gaja. Napoli: Editoriale Scientifica, 2004, v. 3, p. 1985-2036.) [C.I.J., p. 2009.]

Leanza, Umberto: Il rafforzamento della tutela internazionale del patrimonio culturale in tempo di guerra nel nuovo diritto dei conflitti armati. (Dans: Studi di diritto internazionale in onore di Gaetano Arangio-Ruiz, sous la dir. de Giovanni Battaglini; Paolo Benvenuti; Antonio Cassese; Giorgio Gaja. Napoli: Editoriale Scientifica, 2004, v. 3, p. 2037-2064.) [C.I.J., p. 2045.]

Lee, Katie: China and the International Covenant on Civil and Political Rights: prospects and challenges. (In: Chinese Journal of International Law, 2007, v. 6, no. 2, p. 445-474.) [I.C.J., p. 448.]

Lenzerini, Federico: Sovereignty revisited: international law and parallel sovereignty of indigenous peoples. (In: Texas International Law Journal, 2006, v. 42, p. 155-189.) [I.C.J., p. 164, 167, 187.]

Lerner, Natan: Religion, secular beliefs and human rights: 25 years after the 1981 declaration. Leiden; Boston: Martinus Nijhoff, 2006. (Studies in Religion, Secular Beliefs and Human Rights; 2.) [P.C.I.J., p. 46, 61; I.C.J., p. 102-103, 106, 140.]

Malcontent, Peter: Human rights and peace: two sides of the same coin. (In: From sovereign impunity to international accountability: the search for justice in a world of States, ed. by Ramesh Thakur; Peter Malcontent. Tokyo, [etc.]: United Nations University Press, 2004, p. 1-12.) [I.C.J., p. 5.]

Malone, Andrew R.: Water now: the impact of Israel's security fence on Palestinian water rights and agriculture in the West Bank. (In: Case Western Reserve Journal of International Law, 2004, v. 36, no. 2-3, p. 639-671.) [I.C.J., p. 642, 652-653.]

Månsson, Katarina: Reviving the "spirit of San Francisco": the lost proposals on human rights, justice and international law to the UN Charter. (In: Nordic Journal of International Law, 2007, v. 76, p. 217-239.) [I.C.J., p. 233-234.]

McCrudden, Christopher: Human dignity and judicial interpretation of human rights. (In: European Journal of International Law, 2008, v. 19, no. 4, p. 655-724.) [I.C.J., p. 682-683.]

McGregor, Lorna: Torture and State immunity: deflecting impunity, distorting sovereignty. (In: European Journal of International Law, 2007, v. 18, p. 903-919.) [P.C.I.J., p. 911; I.C.J., p. 907-908, 916.]

Mei, Anne Pieter van der: The advisory jurisdiction of the African Court on Human and People's Rights. (In: African Human Rights Law Journal, 2005, v. 5, no. 1, p. 27-46.) [I.C.J., p. 33, 40-41.]

Milanovic, Marko: Norm conflict in international law: whither human rights? (In: Select Proceedings of the European Society of International Law, ed. by James Crawford; Sarah M. H. Nouwen. Oxford; Portland: Hart, 2008, v. 2, p. 331-355.) [I.C.J., p. 335, 345.]

Mirski, Yehudah: Human rights, democracy, and the inescapability of politics, or, human dignity thick and thin. (In: Israel Law Review, 2005, v. 38, no. 1-2, p. 358-377.)

Moore, David H.: Agency costs in international human rights. (In: Columbia Journal of Transnational Law, 2004, v. 42, no. 2, p. 491-519.) [I.C.J., p. 493.]

Mubangizi, John C.: Some reflections on recent and current trends in the promotion and protection of human rights in Africa: the pains and the gains. (In: African Human Rights Law Journal, 2006, v. 6, p. 146-165.)

Mukherjee, Amrita: Torture and the United Nations: Charter and treaty-based monitoring. London: Cameron May, 2008. reprint [I.C.J., p. 14.]

Muzny, Petr: La technique de proportionnalité et le juge de la Convention européenne des droits de l'homme: essai sur un instrument nécessaire dans une société démocratique. Aix-en-provence: Press Universitaires d'Aix-Marseille – PUAM, 2005. [C.P.J.I., p. 388; C.I.J., p. 21, 317, 530.]

Myntti, Kristian: The right of indigenous peoples to self-determination and effective participation. (In: Operationalizing the right of indigenous peoples to self-determination, ed. by Pekka Aikio; Martin Scheinin. Turku: Institute for Human Rights, Åbo Akademi University, 2005, p. 85-130.) [I.C.J., p. 94.]

Naldi, Gino J.: Interim measures in the U.N. Human Rights Committee. (In: International and Comparative Law Quarterly, 2004, v. 53, no. 2, p. 445-454.) [I.C.J., p. 453.]

Narula, Smita: The right to food: holding global actors accountable under international law. (In: Columbia Journal of Transnational Law, 2006, v. 44, p. 691-800.) [I.C.J., p. 733-734, 760-761, 772, 777, 779, 796.]

Nigro, Raffaella: Giurisdizione e obblighi positivi degli Stati parti della convenzione europea dei diritti dell'uomo: il caso Ilascu. (Dans: Rivista di diritto internazionale, 2005, v. 88, p. 413-440.) [C.I.J., p. 421.]

Norchi, Charles: Human rights: a global common interest. (In: The United Nations: confronting the challenges of a global society, by Jean E. Krasno. Boulder; London: Lynne Rienner, 2004, p. 79-115.) [I.C.J., p. 86, 96-98.]

Normand, Roger and Zaidi, Sarah: Human rights at the UN: the political history of universal justice. Bloomington: Indiana University Press, 2008. (United Nations Intellectual History Project.) [I.C.J., see index p. 459.]

North, Anthony M. and Chia, Joyce: Towards convergence in the interpretation of the Refugee Convention: a proposal for the establishment of an international judicial commission for refugees. (In: Australian Yearbook of International Law, 2004, v. 25, p. 105-137.) [I.C.J., p. 119, 123, 125, 130.]

Nowak, Manfred: U.N. Covenant on Civil and Political Rights: CCPR commentary. Kehl [etc.]: N. P. Engel, 2005. 2nd rev. ed. [P.C.I.J., p. 659; I.C.J., p. xxiii, 97, 685, 690, 694, 696, 704, 761-762, 792, 802, 805, 816.]

Ochoa Ruiz, Natalia: Los mecanismos convencionales de protección de los derechos humanos en las Naciones Unidas. Madrid: Civitas, 2004. [C.I.J., p. 33-36, 78-79, 87, 209-210, 271, 282, 284, 390, 394, 401.]

Olivier, Clémentine: Human rights law and the international fight against terrorism: how do Security Council Resolutions impact on States' obligations under international human rights law? (Revisiting Security Council Resolution 1373). (In: Nordic Journal of International Law, 2004, v. 73, no. 4, p. 399-419.) [I.C.J., p. 406-407, 410-412.]

Pastor Ridruejo, José Antonio: Droit international des droits de l'homme et droit international humanitaire: leurs rapports à la lumière de la jurisprudence de la Cour internationale de Justice. (Dans: Promoting justice, human rights and conflict resolution through international law: liber amicorum Lucius Caflisch, ed. by Marcelo G. Kohen. Leiden: Martinus Nijhoff, 2007, p. 399-407.)

Pedersen, Morten Peschardt: Territorial jurisdiction in Article 1 of the European Convention on Human Rights. (In: Nordic Journal of International Law, 2004, v. 73, p. 279-305.) [I.C.J. and P.C.I.J., p. 280, 284, 287.]

Pentassuglia, Gaetano: Evolving protection of minority groups: global challenges and the role of international jurisprudence. (In: International Community Law Review, 2009, v. 11, no. 2, p. 185-218.) [P.C.I.J., p. 187, 195; I.C.J., p. 195.]

Piotrowicz, Ryszard and van Eck, Carina: Subsidiary protection and primary rights. (In: International and Comparative Law Quarterly, 2004, v. 53, no. 1, p. 107-138.) [I.C.J., p. 134.]

Pisciotta, Linda: La tutela dei diritti umani in tempo di conflitti armati non internazionali: la giurisprudenza di due corti a confronto. (Dans: Rivista di diritto internazionale, 2006, v. 89, p. 736-755.) [C.I.J., p. 738.]

Pitea, Cesare: The non-compliance procedure of the Aarhus Convention: between environmental and human rights control mechanisms. (In: Italian Yearbook of International Law, 2006, v. 16, p. 85-116.) [P.C.I.J., p. 113; I.C.J., p. 90-91, 111, 113.]

Ramcharan, Bertrand G.: The Security Council and the protection of human rights. (In: Racism and human rights, ed. by Raphael Walden. Leiden, [etc.]: Martinus Nijhoff, 2004, p. 15-30.) [I.C.J., p. 18, 19.]

Ress, Georg: The effect of decisions and judgments of the European Court of Human Rights in the domestic legal order. (In: Texas International Law Journal, 2005, v. 40, no. 3, p. 359-382.) [I.C.J., p. 362, 370.]

Ress, Georg: Supranationaler Menschenrechtsschutz und der Wandel der Staatlichkeit. (In: Zeitschrift für ausländisches öffentliches Recht und Völkerrecht, 2004, v. 64, no. 3, p. 621-639.) [I.C.J. and P.C.I.J., p. 624, 634.]

Riedel, Eibe: Questionnaire human rights and the unity-diversity divide. (In: Unity and diversity in international law: proceedings of an international symposium of the Kiel Walther Schücking Institute of International Law, November 4-7, 2004, ed. by Zimmermann, Andreas; Hofmann, Rainer. Berlin: Duncker & Humblot, 2006, p. 111-133.) [I.C.J., p. 122-123.]

Ringelheim, Julie: Diversité culturelle et droits de l'homme: l'émergence de la problématique des minorités dans le droit de la Convention européenne des droits de l'homme. Bruxelles: Bruylant, 2006. (Centre des droits de l'homme de l'université catholique de Louvain; 4.) [C.P.J.I., p. 14, 271-272.]

Robbins, Melissa: Powerful States, customary law and the erosion of human rights through regional enforcement. (In: California Western International Law Journal, 2005, v. 35, no. 2, p. 275-302.) [P.C.I.J., p. 295; I.C.J., p. 292-295, 299.]

Roberts, Adam: Transformative military occupation: applying the laws of war and human rights. (In: American Journal of International Law, 2006, v. 100, p. 580-622.) [I.C.J., p. 594, 595, 597.]

Roberts, Anthea: Righting wrongs or wronging rights? The United States and human rights post-September 11. (In: European Journal of International Law, 2004, v. 15, no. 4, p. 721-749.) [I.C.J., p. 731, 740.]

Rodríguez-Rivera, Luis E.: The human rights to environment and the peaceful use of nuclear energy. (In: Denver Journal of International Law and Policy, 2006, v. 35, p. 173-192.) [I.C.J., p. 180-182, 187-188.]

Rubenstein, Kim: "As a woman I want no country": citizenship, nationality, international law and globalization: lessons for and from women? (In: The measure of international law: effectiveness, fairness and validity: proceedings of the 31st annual conference of the Canadian Council on International Law, Ottawa, October 24-26, 2002 = Prendre la mesure du droit international: effectivité, équité et validité: travaux de 31e congrès annuel du Conseil canadien de droit international, Ottawa, 24 au 26 octobre 2002. The Hague [etc.]: Kluwer Law International, 2004, p. 11-20.) [I.C.J., p. 19-20.]

Ruiz Miguel, Carlos: El acuerdo de pesca UE-Marruecos o el intento español de considerar a Marruecos como "potencia administradora" del Sahara Occidental. (Dans: Anuario español de derecho internacional, 2006, v. 22, p. 395-412.) [C.I.J., p. 399.]

Ruys, Tom and Heyndrickx, Isabelle: Ondervragingstechnieken en het verbod op foltering onmenselijke en vernederende behandeling: een overzicht van internationale jurisprudentie. (In: Revue belge de droit international, 2006, v. 39, p. 99-150.) [I.C.J., p. 135.]

Saccucci, Andrea: Il caso Mamatkulov dinanzi alla Corte europea dei diritti umani: un problematico revirement in tema di efficacia delle misure provvisorie. (Dans: Rivista di diritto internazionale, 2004, v. 87, no. 1, p. 70-146.) [C.P.J.I., p. 71-72; C.I.J. p. 71-72, 75, 86, 105, 111-113, 116-119, 145.]

Sandoval-Villalba, Clara: The concepts of "injured party" and "victim" of gross human rights violations in the jurisprudence of the Inter-American Court of Human Rights: a commentary on their implications for reparations. (In: Reparations for victims of genocide, war crimes against humanity: systems in place and systems in the making, ed. by Carla Ferstman; Mariana Goetz; Alan Andrew Stephens. Leiden: Nijhoff, 2009, p. 243-282.) [I.C.J., p. 246, 251.]

Saroléa, Sylvie: Droits de l'homme et migrations: de la protection du migrant aux droits de la personne migrante. Bruxelles: Bruylant, 2006. (Collection du Centre des droits de l'Homme de l'Université catholique de

Louvain ; 3.) [C.P.J.I., p. 20-22, 24, 41-42, 51-52, 79, 464-465; C.I.J., p. 16-18, 21-22, 33, 52-55, 59, 79, 148, 369, 460-461, 465-466, 477.]

Schabas, William A. : Balancing the rights of the accused with the imperatives of accountability. (In : From sovereign impunity to international accountability : the search for justice in a world of States, ed. by Ramesh Thakur ; Peter Malcontent. Tokyo, [etc.] : United Nations University Press, 2004, p. 154-168.) [I.C.J., p. 159.]

Schabas, William A. : Cultural genocide and the protection of the right of existence of aboriginal and indigenous groups. (In : International law and indigenous peoples, ed. by Joshua Castellino ; Niamh Walsh. Leiden, [etc.] : Martinus Nijhoff, 2005, p. 117-132.) [I.C.J., p. 128, 128, 130.]

Schabas, William A. : Discussion. (Dans : Mesures conservatoires et droits fondamentaux, sous la dir. de Gérard Cohen-Jonathan ; Jean-Francois Flauss. Bruxelles : Bruylant ; Nemesis, 2005, p. 77-90.) [C.P.J.I., p. 77; C.I.J., p. 77-79, 89.]

Scheinin, Martin : The ICJ and the individual. (In : International Community Law Review, 2007, v. 9, no. 2, p. 123-137.) [I.C.J., passim.]

Schilling, Theodor : Der Schutz der Menschenrechte gegen Beschlüsse des Sicherheitsrats : Möglichkeiten und Grenzen. (In : Zeitschrift für ausländisches öffentliches Recht und Völkerrecht, 2004, v. 64, no. 2, p. 343-362.) [I.C.J., p. 344, 350, 356, 358.]

Schoiswohl, Michael : Status and (human rights) obligations of non-recognized de facto regimes in international law : the case of 'Somaliland' : the resurrection of Somaliland against all international "odds" : State collapse, secession, non-recognition and human rights. Leiden ; Boston : Martinus Nijhoff, 2004. [P.C.I.J., p. 18; I.C.J., p. 13-14, 30, 62-63, 175, 198, 242, 254, 266, 272, 286.]

Schöpp-Schilling, Hanna Beate : Reservations to the Convention on the Elimination of All Forms of Discrimination against Women : an unresolved issue or (no) new developments ? (In : Reservations to human rights treaties and the Vienna Convention regime : conflict, harmony or reconciliation, ed. by Ineta Ziemele. Leiden [etc.] : Martinus Nijhoff, 2004, p. 3-39.) [I.C.J., p. 16, 39.]

Seibert-Fohr, Anja : The potentials of the Vienna Convention on the Law of Treaties with respect to reservations to human rights treaties. (In : Reservations to human rights treaties and the Vienna Convention regime : conflict, harmony or reconciliation, ed. by Ineta Ziemele. Leiden [etc.] : Martinus Nijhoff, 2004, p. 183-211.) [I.C.J., p. 185-188.]

Shany, Yuval : Faraway, so close : the legal status of Gaza after Israel's disengagement. (In : Yearbook of International Humanitarian Law, 2005, v. 8, p. 369-383.) [I.C.J., p. 370, 373, 377-378, 382.]

Shelton, Dinah : Are there differentiations among human rights ? Jus cogens, core human rights, obligations erga omnes and non-derogability. (In : The status of international treaties on human rights. Strasbourg : Council of Europe Publishing, 2006, p. 159-186.) [I.C.J., p. 159, 160, 163, 164, 170, 180.]

Shelton, Dinah: Human rights and the environment: what specific environmental rights have been recognized. (In: Denver Journal of International Law and Policy, 2006, v. 35, p. 129-171.) [I.C.J., p. 131.]

Shelton, Dinah: Self-determination and secession: the jurisprudence of international human rights tribunals. (In: Secession and international law: conflict avoidance: regional appraisals, ed. by Dahlitz, Julie. The Hague: T.M.C. Asser Press, 2003, p. 47-72.) [I.C.J., p. 68.]

Siehr, Angelika: Derogation measures under Article 4 ICCPR, with special consideration of the "war against international terrorism". (In: German Yearbook of International Law, 2004, v. 47, p. 545-593.) [I.C.J., p. 578.]

Silva de Sousa, Denise: Corte Interamericana de Direitos Humanos. (Dans: Tribunais internacionais: mecanismos contemporâneos de solução de controvérsias, sous la dir. de Welber Barral. Florianópolis: Fundação Boiteux, 2004, p. 295-312.) [C.I.J., p. 309.]

Simma, Bruno and Kill, Theodore: Harmonizing investment protection and international human rights: first steps towards a methodology. (In: International investment law for the 21st century: essays in honour of Christoph Schreuer, ed. by Christina Binder. New York: Oxford University Press, 2009, p. 678-707.)

Simma, Bruno: Human rights and State responsibility. (In: The law of international relations: liber amicorum Hanspeter Neuhold, ed. by August Reinisch; Ursula Kriebaum. Utrecht: Eleven International Publishing, 2007, p. 359-381.) [I.C.J., p. 362, 373.]

Sinkondo, M.: Le fabuleux destin de l'article 13 de la C.E.D.H. et ses suites heureuses pour les garanties individuelles. (Dans: Revue de droit international et de droit comparé, 2004, v. 81, no. 4, p. 367-417.) [C.I.J. et C.P.J.I., p. 374, 377, 384.]

Stubbs, Matthew T.: Arbitrary detention in Australia: detention of unlawful non-citizens under the Migration Act 1958 (Cth). (In: Australian Yearbook of International Law, 2004, v. 25, p. 273-308.) [P.C.I.J., p. 287; I.C.J., p. 286, 292-293.]

Sun, Shiyan: The understanding and interpretation of the ICCPR in the context of China's possible ratification. (In: Chinese Journal of International Law, 2007, v. 6, p. 17-42.) [I.C.J., p. 19-20, 22.]

Tancredi, Antonello: L'emersione dei diritti fondamentali "assoluti" nella giurisprudenza comunitaria. (Dans: Rivista di diritto internazionale, 2006, v. 89, p. 644-692.) [C.I.J., p. 652, 670, 673.]

Thornberry, Patrick: The Convention on the Elimination of Racial Discrimination, indigenous peoples and caste: descent-based discrimination. (In: International law and indigenous peoples, ed. by Joshua

Castellino; Niamh Walsh. Leiden, [etc.]: Martinus Nijhoff, 2005, p. 17-52.) [P.C.I.J., p. 23.]

Tomuschat, Christian: The applicability of human rights law to insurgent movements. (In: Krisensicherung und humanitärer Schutz: Festschrift für Dieter Fleck, ed. by Horst Fischer; Ulrike Froissart; Wolff Heintschel von Heinegg. Berlin: Berliner Wissenschafts-Verlag, 2004, p. 573-591.) [I.C.J., p. 575.]

Tomuschat, Christian: L'immunité des Etats en cas de violations graves des droits de l'homme. (Dans: Revue générale de droit international public, 2005, v. 109, p. 51-74.) [C.I.J., p. 51-52, 59, 61-62.]

Tomuschat, Christian: Der Sommerkrieg des Jahres 2006 im Nahen Osten, Eine Skizze. (In: Die Friedens-Warte: Blätter für internationale Verständigung und zwischenstaatliche Organisation, 2006, v. 81, p. 179-190.) [I.C.J., p. 181-183, 186.]

Tondini, Matteo: UN peace operations: the last frontier of the extraterritorial application of human rights. (In: Studia diplomatica, 2005, 68, p. 75-138.) [I.C.J., p. 81, 85, 89-90, 101, 104-106, 109-111.]

Torroja Mateu, Helena: La "protección diplomática" de los "derechos humanos" de los nacionales en el extranjero: ¿ Situaciones jurídicas subjetivas en tensión? (Dans: Revista española de derecho internacional, 2006, v. 58, p. 205-237.) [C.P.J.I., p. 215, 227, 229, 232; C.I.J., p. 205-206, 210-211, 216, 219-220, 223-226, 230-231, 235.]

Tully, Stephen: The contribution of human rights as an additional perspective on climate change impacts within the Pacific. (In: New Zealand Journal of Public and International Law, 2007, v. 5, p. 169-200.) [I.C.J., p. 183-184, 190, 198-199.]

Van Bueren, Geraldine: Slavery as piracy: the legal case for reparations for slavery. (In: Racism and human rights, ed. by Raphael Walden. Leiden, [etc.]: Martinus Nijhoff, 2004, p. 41-53.) [P.C.I.J., p. 50-51.]

van den Bogaert, Sina: State duty towards minorities: positive or negative? (In: Zeitschrift für ausländisches öffentliches Recht und Völkerrecht, 2004, v. 64, no. 1, p. 37-64.) [P.C.I.J., p. 40, 44-45; I.C.J., p. 41.]

Vandenhole, Wouter: Third State obligations under the ICESCR: a case study of EU sugar policy. (In: Nordic Journal of International Law, 2007, v. 76, p. 73-100.) [I.C.J., p. 87-88.]

Varennes, Fernand de: The fallacies in the "universalism versus cultural relativism" debate in human rights law. (In: Asia-Pacific Journal on Human Rights and the Law, 2006, v. 7, no. 1, p. 67-84.) [I.C.J., p. 78.]

Villiger, Mark: Articles 31 and 32 of the Vienna Convention on the Law of Treaties in the case-law of the European Court of Human Rights. (In: Internationale Gemeinschaft und Menschenrechte: Festschrift für Georg Ress zum 70. Geburtstag am 21. Januar 2005, ed. by Bröhmer, Jürgen;

Bieber, Roland; Calliess, Christian; Langenfeld, Christine; Weber, Stefan; Wolf, Joachim. Köln [etc.]: Heymann, 2005, p. 317-330.) [I.C.J., p. 317, 319, 324-327, 329.]

Wachira, George Mukundi: Twenty years of elusive enforcement of the recommendations of the Africa Commission on Human and Peoples' Rights: a possible remedy. (In: African Human Rights Law Journal, 2006, v. 6, p. 465-492.) [P.C.I.J., p. 472; I.C.J., p. 475.]

Warbrick, Colin: The European response to terrorism in an age of human rights. (In: European Journal of International Law, 2004, v. 15, no. 5, p. 989-1018.) [I.C.J., p. 992.]

Weckel, Philippe et Condorelli, Luigi et Malinverni, Giorgio et Schabas, William A. et Condorelli, Luigi: Débats. (Dans: Mesures conservatoires et droits fondamentaux, sous la dir. de Gérard Cohen-Jonathan; Jean-Francois Flauss. Bruxelles: Bruylant; Nemesis, 2005, p. 91-92.) [C.I.J., p. 91.]

Weckel, Philippe: L'apport récent des juridictions internationales non spécialisées à la protection des droits de l'homme. (Dans: Droit international, droits de l'homme et juridictions internationales: actes de la table ronde du 10 juillet 2003 organisée par l'Institut international des droits de l'homme, sous la dir. de Gérard Cohen-Jonathan; Jean-François Flauss. Bruxelles: Bruylant, 2004, p. 139-152.) [C.I.J., p. 149.]

Weckel, Philippe: Les mesures conservatoires devant les juridictions internationales de caractère universel. (Dans: Mesures conservatoires et droits fondamentaux, sous la dir. de Gérard Cohen-Jonathan; Jean-Francois Flauss. Bruxelles: Bruylant; Nemesis, 2005, p. 33-53.) [C.I.J., p. 34, 36, 37-41, 44-52.]

Wet, Erika de: The prohibition of torture as an international norm of jus cogens and its implications for national and customary law. (In: European Journal of International Law, 2004, v. 15, n. 1, p. 97-121.) [C.I.J., p. 113.]

Wilson, Barbara: Le rôle des mesures conservatoires dans la protection internationale des droits de l'homme. (Dans: Schweizerische Zeitschrift für internationales und europäisches Recht, 2005, v. 15, p. 509-521.) [I.C.J., p. 510, 514-517, 520.]

Wojcik, Mark E. and Lord, Melinda: Human rights law. (In: International Lawyer, 2004, v. 38, no. 2, p. 499-508.) [I.C.J., p. 501.]

Wouters, Jan and Verhoeven, Sten: The prohibition of genocide as a norm of ius cogens and its implications for the enforcement of the law of genocide. (In: International Criminal Law Review, 2005, v. 5, p. 401-416.) [I.C.J., p. 404, 406, 407.]

Ziemele, Ineta: Editor's preface. (In: Reservations to human rights treaties and the Vienna Convention regime: conflict, harmony or reconciliation, ed. by Ineta Ziemele. Leiden [etc.]: Martinus Nijhoff, 2004, xiii-xv.) [I.C.J., p. XIII-XIV.]

Zyberi, Gentian: The development and interpretation of international human rights and humanitarian law rules and principles through the case-law of the International Court of Justice. (In: Netherlands Quarterly of Human Rights, 2007, v. 25, no. 1, p. 117-139.)

14. Droit pénal
14. Criminal law

Abline, Gaël: La désignation des juges et du procureur de la Cour pénale internationale. (Dans: Journal du droit international, 2004, v. 131, p. 465-490.) [C.I.J., p. 467, 470-471, 474-476, 484, 488.]

Abou al-Wafa, Ahmed: Criminal international law (with special reference to Islamic criminal international law). (In: Revue égyptienne de droit international, 2006, v. 62, p. 1-299.) [P.C.I.J., p. 44, 48, 102; I.C.J., p. 29, 35-40, 58, 70-73, 85-89, 91, 94-96, 99, 103-104, 115, 122, 128, 140, 153-154, 159-160, 162-163, 176, 199-201, 206-207, 215, 220, 248-249, 276, 291.]

Abtahi, Hirad and Webb, Philippa: The Genocide Convention: the travaux préparatoires. Leiden: Brill, 2008. (The Travaux Préparatoires of Multilateral Treaties; 2.) [I.C.J., passim.]

Ailincai, Mihaela: La justification devant le Tribunal pénal international pour l'ex-Yougoslavie des pertes civiles ou de la destruction de biens civils par l'argument de nécessité militaire. (Dans: La nécessité en droit international: colloque de Grenoble. Paris: Pedone, 2007, p. 337-348.)

Akande, Dapo: The application of international law immunities in prosecutions for international crimes. (In: Bringing power to justice? The prospects of the International Criminal Court, ed. by Joanna Harrington; Michael Milde; Richard Vernon. Montreal [etc.]: McGill-Queen's University Press, 2006, p. 47-98.) [I.C.J., p. 51-52, 56, 58, 62.]

Amann, Diane Marie: The International Criminal Court and the sovereign State. (In: Governance and international legal theory, ed. by Dekker, Ige F.; Werner, Wouter G.. Leiden; Boston, 2004, p. 185-212.) [I.C.J., p. 189, 196, 208.]

Ambos, Kai and Wirth, Steffen: Genocide and war crimes in the Former Yugoslavia before German criminal courts. (In: International and national prosecution of crimes under international law: current developments, ed. by Horst Fischer; Claus Kreß; Sascha Rolf Lüder. Berlin: Berliner Wissenschafts-Verlag, 2004, p. 769-797.) [P.C.I.J., p. 780.]

Ambos, Kai: La parte general del derecho penal internacional: bases para una elaboración dogmática. Montevideo [etc.]: Fundación Konrad-Adenauer, Oficina Uruguay [etc.], 2005. [C.I.J., p. 91.]

Anatolevich Kolodkin, Roman: Preliminary report on immunity of State officials from foreign criminal jurisdiction. Geneva: International Law Commission, 2008. [I.C.J., passim.]

Arnold, Roberta: The prosecution of terrorism as a crime against humanity. (In: Zeitschrift für ausländisches öffentliches Recht und Völkerrecht, 2004, v. 64, no. 4, p. 979-1000.) [I.C.J., p. 995.]

Ascensio, Hervé et Maison, Rafaëlle: L'activité des juridictions pénales internationales (2005). (Dans: Annuaire français de droit international, 2005, v. 51, p. 237-269.) [C.I.J., p. 427, 428.]

Bassiouni, M. Cherif: The legislative history of the International Criminal Court: vol. 1: introduction, analysis and integrated text of the Statute, elements of crimes and Rules of procedure and evidence. Ardsley: Transnational, 2005. (International and Comparative Criminal Law Series.) [I.C.J., p. 4, 37, 79, 147-148, 165, 244, 406.]

Bassiouni, M. Cherif: The legislative history of the International Criminal Court: vol. 2: an article-by-article evolution of the Statute from 1994-1998. Ardsley: Transnational, 2005. (International and Comparative Criminal Law Series.) [I.C.J., p. 35, 42, 126, 128, 179, 264, 327, 759-760.]

Bassiouni, M. Cherif: The legislative history of the International Criminal Court: vol. 3: summary records of the 1998 diplomatic conference. Ardsley: Transnational, 2005. (International and Comparative Criminal Law Series.) [I.C.J., p. 207, 243-245, 251, 344, 345, 350, 415, 472.]

Bassiouni, M. Cherif: Universal jurisdiction for international crimes: historical perspectives and contemporary practice. (In: International criminal law, ed. by Cherif Bassiouni. Leiden: Nijhoff, 2008, v. 2, p. 153-199.) [I.C.J., p. 946, 948, 953, 984-985, 992-994.]

Baudenbacher, Carl: Judicialization: can the European model be exported to other parts of the world? (In: Texas International Law Journal, 2004, v. 39, no. 3, p. 381-399.) [I.C.J., p. 383, 397.]

Beigbeder, Yves: International justice against impunity: progress and new challenges. Boston; Leiden: Martinus Nijhoff, 2005. [I.C.J., p. 3, 8, 9, 49-52, 60, 151, 154, 163, 165, 205, 211-223, 226-227, 232; P.C.I.J., p. 3, 226.]

Benzing, Markus and Bergsmo, Morten: Some tentative remarks on the relationship between internationalized criminal jurisdictions and the International Criminal Court. (In: Internationalized criminal courts and tribunals: Sierra Leone, East Timor, Kosovo and Cambodia, ed. by Cesare P. R. Romano; André Nollkaemper; Jann K. Kleffner. Oxford: Oxford University Press, 2004, p. 407-416.) [I.C.J., p. 415.]

Boeving, James Nicholas: Aggression, international law, and the ICC: an argument for the withdrawal of aggression from the Rome Statute. (In: Columbia Journal of Transnational Law, 2005, v. 43, no. 2, p. 557-611.) [P.C.I.J., p. 604, 607; I.C.J., p. 580-581.]

Bonafè, Beatrice I.: Imputazione all'individuo di crimini internazionali e immunità dell'organo. (Dans: Rivista di diritto internazionale, 2004, v. 87, no. 2, p. 393-426.) [C.I.J., p. 396-398, 410-411.]

Bottigliero, Ilaria: Redress for victims of crimes under international law. Leiden [etc.]: Martinus Nijhoff, 2004. [I.C.J., p. 49, 50.]

Bou Franch, Valentín: El crimen de genocido según el Tribunal internacional penal para Ruanda. (Dans: Anuario hispano-luso-americano de derecho internacional, 2005, v. 17, p. 133-158.) [C.I.J., p. 134, 146.]

Brody, Reed and Duffy, Helen: Prosecuting torture universally: Hissène Habré, Africa's Pinochet? (In: International and national prosecution of crimes under international law: current developments, ed. by Horst Fischer; Claus Kreß; Sascha Rolf Lüder. Berlin: Berliner Wissenschafts-Verlag, 2004, p. 817-842.) [I.C.J., p. 818.]

Burgorgue-Larsen, Laurence: Les Etats-Unis d'Amérique et la justice internationale: entre l'utilisation et l'instrumentalisation du droit international. (Dans: Le droit international à la croisée des chemins: force du droit et droit de la force: VIe rencontre internationale de la Faculté des Sciences juridiques, politiques et sociales de Tunis, 14, 15 et 16 avril 2004, sous la dir. de Rafâa Ben Achour; Slim Laghmani. Paris: Pedone, 2004, p. 233-269.) [C.P.J.I., p. 235-236, 238; C.I.J., p. 235-243, 246, 259, 264-266.]

Cassese, Antonio: State sovereignty v. international criminal justice. (In: Studi di diritto internazionale in onore di Gaetano Arangio-Ruiz, ed. by Giovanni Battaglini; Paolo Benvenuti; Antonio Cassese; Giorgio Gaja. Napoli: Editoriale Scientifica, 2004, v. 1, p. 25-46.) [I.C.J., p. 34, 35, 43.]

Cassese, Antonio: Taking stock of the Genocide Convention and looking ahead. (In: The UN Genocide Convention: a commentary, ed. by Paola Gaeta. Oxford [etc.]: Oxford University Press, 2009, p. 531-544.)

Cerone, John: Dynamic equilibrium: the evolution of US attitudes toward international criminal courts and tribunals. (In: European Journal of International Law, 2007, v. 18, p. 277-315.) [I.C.J., p. 294.]

Chetail, Vincent: La banalité du mal de Dachau au Darfour: réflexion sur l'évolution du concept de génocide depuis 1945. (Dans: Relations internationales, 2007, 131, p. 49-72.) [C.I.J., p. 51, 61, 72.]

Ciampi, Annalisa: The International Criminal Court. (In: Law and Practice of International Courts and Tribunals, 2005, v. 4, no. 1, p. 165-170.) [I.C.J., p. 169.]

Clark, Roger S.: Drafting a general part to a penal code: some thoughts inspired by the negotiations on the Rome statute of the International Criminal Court and by the Court's first substantive law discussion in the Lubanga Dyilo confirmation proceedings. (In: Criminal Law Forum, 2007, v. 19, p. 519-552.) [I.C.J., p. 549.]

Clark, Roger S.: The Rome Statute of the International Criminal Court and weapons of a nature to cause superfluous injury or unnecessary suffering, or which are inherently indiscriminate. (In: International humanitarian law: challenges, ed. by John Carey; William V. Dunlap; R. John Pritchard. Ardsley: Transnational, 2004, p. 259-281.) [I.C.J., p. 265, 268, 275, 278-279.]

Compétence des tribunaux répressifs français et de la loi pénale française. (Dans : Recueil périodique des juris-classeurs : droit international, 2004, v. 182, p. 403-10.) [C.I.J., p. 2, 5; C.P.J.I., p. 14.]

Cryer, Robert: Neither here nor there? The status of international criminal jurisprudence in the international and UK legal orders. (In: International law and power: perspectives on legal order and justice: essays in honour of Colin Warbrick, ed. by Kaiyan Homi Kaikobad; Michael Bohlander. Leiden; Boston: Martinus Nijhoff, 2009, p. 183-206.) [I.C.J., p. 189-191, 192, 200.]

Cullen, Holly: The nature of State obligations in relation to child labour: choosing prosecution over protection. (In: International law and power: perspectives on legal order and justice: essays in honour of Colin Warbrick, ed. by Kaiyan Homi Kaikobad; Michael Bohlander. Leiden; Boston: Martinus Nijhoff, 2009, p. 99-123.) [I.C.J., p. 109.]

D'Argent, Pierre: L'expérience belge de la compétence universelle: beaucoup de bruit pour rien? (Dans: Revue générale de droit international public, 2004, v. 108, no. 4, p. 597-632.) [C.I.J., p. 599-601, 618-621, 624-626, 629.]

Danieli, Yael: Massive trauma and the healing role of reparative justice. (In: Reparations for victims of genocide, war crimes against humanity: systems in place and systems in the making, ed. by Carla Ferstman; Mariana Goetz; Alan Andrew Stephens. Leiden: Nijhoff, 2009, p. 41-77.) [I.C.J., p. 63.]

David, Eric: La Cour pénale internationale. (Dans: Recueil des cours de l'Académie de droit international de La Haye, 2005, v. 313, p. 325-454.) [C.I.J., p. 353, 394, 422, 427, 442.]

David, Eric: La responsabilité pénale: quelles poursuites pour quels crimes? (Dans: L'intervention en Irak et le droit international, sous la dir. de Karine Bannelier; Olivier Corten; Théodore Christakis; Pierre Klein. Paris: Pedone, 2004, p. 271-298.) [C.I.J., p. 277, 289.]

Davidson, H. Ron: The International Criminal Tribunal for Rwanda's decision in the Prosecutor v. Ferdinand Nahimara et al.: the past, present, and future of international incitement law. (In: Leiden Journal of International Law, 2004, v. 17, no. 3, p. 505-519.) [I.C.J., p. 506.]

Davies, Thomas E.: How the Rome Statute weakens the international prohibition on incitement to genocide. (In: Harvard Human Rights Journal, 2009, v. 22, no. 2, p. 245-270.)

Decaux, Emmanuel: La crise du Darfour: chronique d'un génocide annoncé. (Dans: Annuaire français de droit international, 2004, v. 50, p. 731-754.) [C.I.J., p. 11, 19-20.]

Deen-Racsmány, Zsuzsanna: Prosecutor v. Taylor: the status of the Special Court for Sierra Leone and its implications for immunity. (In: Leiden Journal of International Law, 2005, v. 18, no. 2, p. 299-322.) [I.C.J., p. 300-308, 314-319, 322.]

Degan, Vladimir-Djuro: International crimes and international criminal justice. (In: Studi di diritto internazionale in onore di Gaetano Arangio-Ruiz, ed. by Giovanni Battaglini; Paolo Benvenuti; Antonio Cassese; Giorgio Gaja. Napoli: Editoriale Scientifica, 2004, v. 2, p. 703-728.) [I.C.J., p. 710, 721, 725, 726.]

Degan, Vladimir-Djuro: Zlocin genocida pred medunarodnim sudovima. (In: Zbornik pravnog Fakulteta u Zagrebu, 2008, v. 58, no. 1-2, p. 77-95.)

Dobovsek, José: Breves consideraciones sobre el derecho internacional penal general y sus relaciones con los sistemas penales particulares. (Dans: Anuario argentino de derecho internacional, 2006, 15, p. 45-68.) [C.I.J., p. 49, 51, 56-60.]

Donnedieu de Vabres, Henri: Les principes modernes du droit pénal international. Paris: Editions Panthéon-Assas, 2004. (Les introuvables.) [C.P.J.I., p. 42, 46, 90-91, 108-109, 128, 190-191, 364, 371, 389, 404-441.]

Durham, Helen: We the people: the position of NGOs in gathering evidence and giving witness at international criminal trials. (In: From sovereign impunity to international accountability: the search for justice in a world of States, ed. by Ramesh Thakur; Peter Malcontent. Tokyo, [etc.]: United Nations University Press, 2004, p. 169-186.) [I.C.J., p. 181.]

Eboe-Osuji, Chile: Murder as a crime against humanity at the ad hoc tribunals: reconciling differing languages. (In: Canadian Yearbook of International Law, 2005, v. 43, p. 145-195.) [I.C.J., p. 168.]

El Zeidy, Mohamed: Some remarks on the question of the admissibility of a case during arrest warrant proceedings before the International Criminal Court. (In: Leiden Journal of International Law, 2006, v. 19, p. 741-751.) [I.C.J., p. 746.]

Elberling, Björn: The work of the International Criminal Court in 2006. (In: German Yearbook of International Law, 2006, v. 49, p. 529-548.) [I.C.J., p. 533.]

Esteve Moltó, José Elías: El auto de admisión a trámite de 10 de enero de 2006 de la audiencia nacional: la aplicación de la jurisdicción universal al caso del genocidio del Tíbet. (Dans: Anuario español de derecho internacional, 2006, v. 22, p. 579-607.) [C.I.J., p. 590.]

Fairlie, Megan A.: Rulemaking from the bench: a place for minimalism at the ICTY. (In: Texas International Law Journal, 2004, v. 39, no. 2, p. 257-285.) [I.C.J., p. 263-265.]

Fallah, Katherine: Perpetrators and victims: prosecuting children for the commission of international crimes. (In: African Journal of International and Comparative Law, 2006, 14, p. 83-103.) [I.C.J., p. 92.]

Ferencz, Benjamin B. and Cassese, Antonio and Verrijn Stuart, Heikelina and Simons, Marlise: The prosecutor and the judge: interviews and writings. Amsterdam: Pallas Publications, 2009. (Praemium

Erasmianum; 2009.) [I.C.J., p. 55, 57-58, 96, 99, 109, 173, 179-182, 184-187.]

Fernández Sánchez, Pablo Antonio: Naturaleza jurídica de la jurisdicción universal. (Dans: Anuario hispano-luso-americano de derecho internacional, 2007, 18, p. 333-381.) [C.P.J.I., p. 353; C.I.J., p. 340-341, 343, 345, 353, 365.]

Fernández-Sánchez, Pablo Antonio (ed.): International legal dimension of terrorism. Leiden [etc.]: Martinus Nijhoff, 2009. (International Humanitarian Law Series; 23.)

Ferstman, Carla and Rosenberg, Sheri P.: Reparations in Dayton's Bosnia and Herzegovina. (In: Reparations for victims of genocide, war crimes against humanity: systems in place and systems in the making, ed. by Carla Ferstman; Mariana Goetz; Alan Andrew Stephens. Leiden: Nijhoff, 2009, p. 483-513.) [I.C.J., p. 483-484.]

Fofe Djofia Malewa, Jean-Pierre: La question de la preuve devant le Tribunal pénal international pour le Rwanda: le cas Cyangugu. Paris: l'Harmattan, 2006. (Points de Vue Concrets.) [C.I.J., p. 1.]

Fois, Paolo: Sul rapporto tra i crimini internazionali dello stato e i crimini internazionali dell'individuo. (Dans: Rivista di diritto internazionale, 2004, v. 87, no. 4, p. 929-954.) [C.I.J., p. 942, 944, 946, 949.]

Forsythe, David P.: International criminal justice and the United States: law, culture, power. (In: From sovereign impunity to international accountability: the search for justice in a world of States, ed. by Ramesh Thakur; Peter Malcontent. Tokyo, [etc.]: United Nations University Press, 2004, p. 61-79.) [I.C.J., p. 66, 77.]

Fox, Hazel: Imputability and immunity as separate concepts: the removal of immunity from civil proceedings relating to the commission of an international crime. (In: International law and power: perspectives on legal order and justice: essays in honour of Colin Warbrick, ed. by Kaiyan Homi Kaikobad; Michael Bohlander. Leiden; Boston: Martinus Nijhoff, 2009, p. 165-181.) [I.C.J., p. 166-167, 170, 171, 177, 180.]

Freeland, Steven: How open should the door be? Declaration by non-States parties under Article 12(3) of the Rome Statute of the International Criminal Court. (In: Nordic Journal of International Law, 2006, v. 75, p. 211-241.) [I.C.J., p. 232, 238-239.]

Freeland, Steven: Towards universal justice: why countries in the Asia-Pacific region should embrace the International Criminal Court. (In: New Zealand Journal of Public and International Law, 2007, v. 5, p. 49-76.) [I.C.J., p. 75.]

Gaeta, Paola: Immunities and genocide. (In: The UN Genocide Convention: a commentary, ed. by Paola Gaeta. Oxford [etc.]: Oxford University Press, 2009, p. 310-333.)

Gaeta, Paola: National prosecution of international crimes: international rules on grounds of jurisdiction. (In: Studi di diritto internazionale in onore di Gaetano Arangio-Ruiz, ed. by Giovanni Battaglini; Paolo Benvenuti; Antonio Cassese; Giorgio Gaja. Napoli: Editoriale Scientifica, 2004, v. 3, p. 1923-1943.) [P.C.I.J., p. 1926, 1929; I.C.J., p. 1927, 1928.]

Gaeta, Paola: On what conditions can a State be held responsible for genocide? (In: European Journal of International Law, 2007, v. 18, p. 631-648.) [I.C.J., passim.]

Gaeta, Paola: War crimes trials before Italian criminal courts: new trends. (In: International and national prosecution of crimes under international law: current developments, ed. by Horst Fischer; Claus Kreß; Sascha Rolf Lüder. Berlin: Berliner Wissenschafts-Verlag, 2004, p. 751-768.) [I.C.J., p. 757.]

García San José, Daniel: El derecho a la justicia de las víctimas de los crímenes más graves de trascendencia para la comunidad internacional. (Dans: Revista española de derecho internacional, 2006, v. 58, p. 119-145.) [C.P.J.I., p. 124, 126.]

Garraway, Charles H. B.: Accountability and reconciliation: squaring the circle in situations of internal violence. (In: Krisensicherung und humanitärer Schutz: Festschrift für Dieter Fleck, ed. by Horst Fischer; Ulrike Froissart; Wolff Heintschel von Heinegg. Berlin: Berliner Wissenschafts-Verlag, 2004, p. 125-138.) [I.C.J., p. 138.]

Gilbert, Geoff: Responding to international crime. Leiden; Boston: Martinus Nijhoff, 2006. (International Studies in Human Rights; 88.) [P.C.I.J., p. 12, 78, 266, 379; I.C.J., p. 7, 25, 31, 95-97, 190, 274-275, 294, 297, 298, 307, 308, 380, 390-391, 398, 413.]

Gioia, Federica: State sovereignty, jurisdiction, and "modern" international law: the principle of complementarity in the International Criminal Court. (In: Leiden Journal of International Law, 2006, v. 19, p. 1095-1123.) [I.C.J., p. 1097, 1102, 1105.]

Gradoni, Lorenzo: "You will receive a fair trial elsewhere". The ad hoc international criminal tribunals acting as human rights jurisdictions. (In: Netherlands International Law Review, 2007, v. 54, p. 1-49.) [I.C.J., p. 26.]

Grote, Rainer: Between crime prevention and the laws of war: are the traditional categories of international law adequate for assessing the use of force against international terrorism? (In: Terrorism as a challenge for national and international law: security versus liberty?, ed. by Walter, Christian; Vöneky, Silja; Röben, Volker; Schorkopf, Frank. Berlin [etc.], Springer, 2004, p. 951-985.) [I.C.J., p. 956-959, 962-964, 972, 974, 977.]

Guillaume, Gilbert: Terrorism and international law. (In: International and Comparative Law Quarterly, 2004, v. 53, no. 3, p. 537-548.) [I.C.J., p. 537, 543-545.]

Guillaume, Gilbert: Terrorismo e justiça internacional. (Dans: O Brasil e os novos desafios do direito internacional, sous la dir. de Brant, Leonardo

Nemer Caldeira. Rio de Janeiro : Editora Forense, 2004, p. 27-37.) [C.I.J., p. 31-32.]

Gutiérrez Posse, Hortensia D. T. : El ejercicio de la jurisdicción en el ámbito del derecho internacional penal. (Dans : Anuario hispano-luso-americano de derecho internacional, 2007, 18, p. 405-444.) [C.P.J.I., p. 412; C.I.J., p. 415.]

Hague Academy of International Law. Centre for studies and research in international law and international relations : International criminal justice. Leiden : Brill, 2008. (Centre d'étude et de recherche de droit international et de relations internationales.) [I.C.J., p. 76.]

Heeck, Stefan, van : Die Weiterentwicklung des formellen Völkerstrafrechts : von den ad hoc Tribunalen der Vereinten Nationen zum ständigen Internationalen Strafgerichtshof unter besonderer Berücksichtigung des Ermittlungsverfahrens. Berlin : Duncker & Humblot, 2006. (Schriften zum Völkerrecht ; 168.) [I.C.J., p. 37.]

Henzelin, Marc : L'immunité pénale dans le domaine économique, bancaire et financier. Un état de la pratique suisse et internationale. (Dans : Le droit international des immunités : contestation ou consolidation ?, sous la dir. de Verhoeven, Joe. Bruxelles : De Boeck & Larcier, 2004, p. 219-251.) [C.I.J., p. 248-250.]

Herik, Larissa van den : The contribution of the Rwanda Tribunal to the development of international law. Leiden ; Boston : Martinus Nijhoff, 2005. (Developments in International Law ; 53.) [I.C.J., p. 33-34, 39, 71, 92, 94-95, 99, 120, 128-129, 134, 204, 222-224, 226, 274-276.]

Inazumi, Mitsue : Universal jurisdiction in modern international law : expansion of national jurisdiction for prosecuting serious crimes under international law. Antwerpen : Intersentia, 2005. (School of human rights research ; 19.)

Ingadóttir, Thordis : The financing of internationalized criminal courts and tribunals. (In : Internationalized criminal courts and tribunals : Sierra Leone, East Timor, Kosovo and Cambodia, ed. by Cesare P. R. Romano ; André Nollkaemper ; Jann K. Kleffner. Oxford : Oxford University Press, 2004, p. 271-289.) [I.C.J., p. 277, 279.]

International Criminal Tribunal for the former Yugoslavia (ICTY) : Prosecutor v. Galic (December 5, 2003). (In : International Legal Materials, 2004, v. 43, p. 794-879.) [I.C.J., p. 806, 835-836.]

Jain, Neha : A separate law for peacekeepers : the clash between the Security Council and the International Criminal Court. (In : European Journal of International Law, 2005, v. 16, no. 2, p. 239-254.) [I.C.J., p. 243-244, 251.]

Jansen, Carel H. : Internationaal Strafhof worstelt met immuniteiten. (In : VN Forum, 2004, 200/1, v. 17, no. 1, p. 7-27.) [I.C.J., p. 17, 19-21.]

Jørgensen, Nina H. B.: Genocide as a fact of common knowledge. (In: International and Comparative Law Quarterly, 2007, v. 56, no. 4, p. 899-906.) [I.C.J., p. 897.]

Katansi, Lwamba: Cour pénale internationale et tribunaux pénaux internationaux: un dispositif d'encerclement de criminels de guerre dans la région des Grands Lacs africains. Kinshasa: Publications des Facultés de Droit des Universités du Congo, 2005. [C.I.J., p. 24, 34, 44, 50-51, 56, 60, 120-121, 194, 199, 206.]

Khan, Daniel-Erasmus: Die individuelle (völker-)strafrechtliche Verantwortlichkeit für eine völkerrechtswidrige militärische Aggression gegen den Irak. (In: Der Irak-Krieg und das Völkerrecht, ed. by Kai Ambos; Jörg Arnold. Berlin: Berliner Wissenschafts-Verlag, 2004, p. 449-470.) [I.C.J., p. 451-452, 455, 459, 466, 468; P.C.I.J., p. 469.]

King, Hugh: Immunities and bilateral immunity agreements: issues arising from Articles 27 and 98 of the Rome Statute. (In: New Zealand Journal of Public and International Law, 2006, v. 4, p. 269-310.) [I.C.J., p. 273-274, 277-279, 281, 305.]

Klein, Eckart: Die Herausforderung durch den internationalen Terrorismus – Hört hier das Völkerrecht auf? (In: Der Terror, der Staat und das Recht, by Eckart Klein; Christian Hacke; Bernd Grzeszick. Berlin: Duncker & Humblot, 2004, p. 9-39.) [I.C.J., p. 12, 13, 23-25, 32, 36, 37.]

Knoops, Geert-Jan: The prosecution and defense of peacekeepers under international criminal law. Ardsley: Transnational, 2004. (International and comparative criminal law series.) [I.C.J., p. 48, 52, 71-72, 80, 83-84, 88-91, 97, 131, 179, 181, 206, 256, 270, 272, 286-287, 289-290, 294, 327, 331, 334.]

Kontorovich, Eugene: The piracy analogy: modern universal jurisdiction's hollow foundation. (In: Harvard International Law Journal, 2004, v. 45, no. 1, p. 183-237.) [P.C.I.J., p. 183, 188, 191.]

Kreß, Claus: The International Court of Justice and the elements of the crime of genocide. (In: European Journal of International Law, 2007, v. 18, p. 619-629.)

Lagot, Daniel: Justice ou injustice internationale? Paris [etc.]: Harmattan, 2009. (Questions Contemporaines.) [C.I.J., p. 43, 46, 52, 67, 77, 80-81, 83, 86.]

Larsaeus, Nina: The relationship between safeguarding internal security and complying with international obligations of protection: the unresolved issue of excluded asylum seekers. (In: Nordic Journal of International Law, 2004, v. 73, no. 1, p. 69-97.) [I.C.J., p. 84, 88-90.]

Lee, Roy S.: States' responses: issues and solutions. (In: States' responses to issues arising from ICC Statute: constitutional, sovereignty, judicial cooperation and criminal law, ed. by Lee, Roy S. Ardsley, NY: Transnational Publishers, 2005, p. 1-55.) [I.C.J., p. 16.]

Lemonde, Lucie: La Cour pénale internationale: l'aboutissement d'une longue lutte et encore bien des défis pour les ONG. (Dans: La voie vers la Cour pénale internationale: tous les chemins mènent à Rome = The highway to the International Criminal Court: all roads lead to Rome, sous la dir. de Dumont, Hélène; Boisvert, Anne-Marie. Montréal: Editions Thémis, 2004, p. 179-192.) [C.I.J., p. 184--185.]

Lijun, Yang: Some critical remarks on the Rome Statute of the International Criminal Court. (In: States' responses to issues arising from ICC Statute: constitutional, sovereignty, judicial cooperation and criminal law, ed. by Lee, Roy S.. Ardsley, NY: Transnational Publishers, 2005, p. 281-304.) [I.C.J., p. 304.]

Lirola Delgado, Isabel et Martínez, Magdalena Ma Martín: La cooperación penal internacional en la detención y entrega de personas: el estatuto de Roma y la orden europea. (Dans: Anuario de derecho internacional, 2004, v. 20, p. 173-240.) [C.I.J., p. 187.]

Lister, Charles: What's in a name? Labels and the Statute of the International Criminal Tribunal for the former Yugoslavia. (In: Leiden Journal of International Law, 2005, v. 18, no. 1, p. 77-92.) [I.C.J., p. 77, 84, 87-88.]

Lüder, Sascha Rolf: Some preliminary thoughts on the legal nature of the International Criminal Court. (In: International and national prosecution of crimes under international law: current developments, ed. by Horst Fischer; Claus Kreß; Sascha Rolf Lüder. Berlin: Berliner Wissenschafts-Verlag, 2004, p. 47-57.) [I.C.J., p. 48.]

Maison, Rafaëlle: Les poursuites pénales internationales comme modalité de réparation du crime d'Etat. (Dans: Studi di diritto internazionale in onore di Gaetano Arangio-Ruiz, sous la dir. de Giovanni Battaglini; Paolo Benvenuti; Antonio Cassese; Giorgio Gaja. Napoli: Editoriale Scientifica, 2004, v. 2, p. 807-826.) [I.C.J., p. 823.]

Manzini, Pietro: Il principio di legalità nella giurisprudenza del Tribunale penale internazionale per la ex Iugoslavia. (Dans: Rivista di diritto internazionale privato e processuale, 2005, v. 41, no. 3, p. 679-698.) [C.I.J., p. 685.]

Marqués Rueda, Efrén Gustavo: El acto y crimen de agresión en el derecho internacional público y su repercusión en las relaciones políticas internacionales. (Dans: Anuario mexicano de derecho internacional, 2009, v. 9, p. 323-372.)

McGregor, Lorna: Addressing the relationship between State immunity and jus cogens norms: a comparative assessment. (In: International prosecution of human rights crimes, ed. by Wolfgang Kaleck; Michael Ratner; Tobias Singelnstein; Peter Weiss. Berlin [etc.]: Springer, 2007, p. 69-84.) [P.C.I.J., p. 70; I.C.J., p. 69-71, 77.]

McManus, John: A new era of accountability through domestic enforcement of international law. (In: La voie vers la Cour pénale internationale: tous les chemins mènent à Rome = The highway to the International Criminal Court: all roads lead to Rome, ed. by Dumont,

Hélène ; Boisvert, Anne-Marie. Montréal : Editions Thémis, 2004, p. 503-543.) [I.C.J., p. 510n 535.]

Ménard, Bruno : L'émergence de nouvelles institutions en droit pénal international : le cas du Timor Oriental, du Sierra Léone et du Cambodge. (Dans : La voie vers la Cour pénale internationale : tous les chemins mènent à Rome = The highway to the International Criminal Court : all roads lead to Rome, sous la dir. de Dumont, Hélène ; Boisvert, Anne-Marie. Montréal : Editions Thémis, 2004, p. 207-230.) [C.I.J., p. 221.]

Meron, Theodor : Judicial independence and impartiality in international criminal tribunals. (In : American Journal of International Law, 2005, v. 99, p. 359-369.) [I.C.J., p. 361-362.]

Milanovic, Marko : Territorial application of the Genocide Convention and State succession. (In : The UN Genocide Convention : a commentary, ed. by Paola Gaeta. Oxford [etc.] : Oxford University Press, 2009, p. 473-493.)

Negri, Stefania : Equality of arms : guiding lights or empty shell? (In : International criminal justice : a critical analysis of institutions and procedures, ed. by Michael Bohlander. London : Cameron May, 2007, p. 13-73.) [I.C.J., p. 14-19, 70.]

Nilsson, Cecilia : Contextualizing the agreement on the privileges and immunities of the International Criminal Court. (In : Leiden Journal of International Law, 2004, v. 17, no. 3, p. 559-578.) [I.C.J., p. 570, 574.]

Nollkaemper, André : Multi-level accountability : a case study of accountability in the aftermath of the Srebrenica massacre. (In : The shifting allocation of authority in international law : considering sovereignty, supremacy and subsidiarity : essays in honour of Professor Ruth Lapidoth, ed. by Tomer Broude ; Yuval Shany. Oxford ; Portland : Hart Publishing, 2008, p. 345-367.) [I.C.J., p. 345, 349, 353, 355, 359-360.]

Ntanda Nsereko, Daniel David : Triggering the jurisdiction of the International Criminal Court. (In : African Human Rights Law Journal, 2004, v. 4, p. 256-274.) [I.C.J., p. 269.]

O'Brien, Roderick : Amnesty and international law. (In : Nordic Journal of International Law, 2005, v. 74, no. 2, p. 261-278.) [I.C.J., p. 266.]

O'Keefe, Roger : The ILC's contribution to international criminal law. (In : German Yearbook of International Law, 2006, v. 49, p. 201-257.) [P.C.I.J., p. 256.]

Otshudi Okondjo, Léon : L'immunité de juridiction pénale des dirigeants étrangers accusés des crimes contre l'humanité. Paris : Publibook, 2009. (Droit.) [C.P.J.I., p. 87, 114; C.I.J., p. 25, 77, 79-80, 95, 112-115, 118, 122, 124, 128-129, 131-132, 139-141, 145-147, 148-154, 187-188, 190, 230-231.]

Pack, Melissa : Developments at the Special Court for Sierra Leone. (In : Law and Practice of International Courts and Tribunals, 2005, v. 4, no. 1, p. 171-192.) [I.C.J., p. 182.]

Padelletti, Maria Luisa : Repressione dei crimini internazionali di individui e tribunali internazionali : il caso della Corte speciale per la Sierra Leone. (Dans : Rivista di diritto internazionale, 2005, v. 88, no. 1, p. 76-105.) [C.I.J., p. 77, 86, 105.]

Page, Mitchell G. : Article 29 of the Rome Statute as a crystallization of customary international law. (In : International crime and punishment : selected issues ed. Lanham : University Press of America, 2004, v. 2, p. 1-53.) [I.C.J., p. 4-5, 30-34, 40, 43, 46, 49, 52; P.C.I.J., p. 30.]

Pina Delgado, José Manuel A. de et Kiyomi Tiujo, Liriam : Tribunais penais internacionais. (Dans : Tribunais internacionais : mecanismos contemporâneos de solução de controvérsias, sous la dir. de Welber Barral. Florianópolis : Fundação Boiteux, 2004, p. 57-87.) [C.I.J., p. 68.]

Pineschi, Laura : Forze delle Nazioni unite e obblighi di cooperazione con i tribunali penali ad hoc in materia di testimonianza. (Dans : Studi di diritto internazionale in onore di Gaetano Arangio-Ruiz, sous la dir. de Giovanni Battaglini ; Paolo Benvenuti ; Antonio Cassese ; Giorgio Gaja. Napoli : Editoriale Scientifica, 2004, v. 3, p. 1647-1688.) [C.I.J., p. 1654-1655, 1678, 1688.]

Prezas, Ioannis : La justice pénale internationale à l'épreuve du maintien de la paix : à propos de la relation entre la Cour pénale internationale et le Conseil de sécurité. (Dans : Revue belge de droit international, 2006, v. 39, p. 57-98.) [C.I.J., p. 74, 82, 96.]

Priotti de Monreal, Anahí : La jurisdicción penal internacional y la Corte penal internacional. (Dans : Anuario hispano-luso-americano de derecho internacional, 2007, 18, p. 487-505.) [C.I.J., p. 489.]

Raab, Dominic and Bevers, Hans : The International Criminal Court and the separation of powers. (In : International Organizations Law Review, 2006, v. 3, p. 93-135.) [I.C.J., p. 99-102, 104.]

Reisman, William Michael : Acting before victims become victims : preventing and arresting mass murder. (In : Case Western Reserve Journal of International Law. 2007-2008, v. 40, no. 1-2, p. 57-85.) [I.C.J., p. 73, 77-78, 80-81.]

Report of the inquiry into the alleged commission of war crimes by coalition forces in the Iraq war during 2003. (In : Indian Journal of International Law, 2004, v. 44, no. 2, p. 382-418.) [I.C.J., p. 398, 400, 407-408, 414.]

Romano, Cesare P. R. : The judges and prosecutors of internationalized criminal courts and tribunals. (In : Internationalized criminal courts and tribunals : Sierra Leone, East Timor, Kosovo and Cambodia, ed. by Cesare P. R. Romano ; André Nollkaemper ; Jann K. Kleffner. Oxford : Oxford University Press, 2004, p. 235-270.) [I.C.J., p. 236, 246, 247, 252, 253, 260.]

Rosenne, Shabtai : Antecedents of the Rome Statute of the International Criminal Court revisited. (In : Essays on international law and practice, by Shabtai Rosenne. Leiden ; Boston : Martinus Nijhoff, 2007, p. 391-422.)

Rosenne, Shabtai: The jurisdiction of the International Criminal Court. (In: Essays on international law and practice, by Shabtai Rosenne. Leiden; Boston: Martinus Nijhoff, 2007, p. 367-389.)

Rounding up the usual suspects while America gets away with murder. (In: La voie vers la Cour pénale internationale: tous les chemins mènent à Rome = The highway to the International Criminal Court: all roads lead to Rome, ed. by Dumont, Hélène; Boisvert, Anne-Marie. Montréal: Editions Thémis, 2004, p. 193-205.) [I.C.J., p. 199, 204.]

Saiki, Naoko: Japan's view on the International Criminal Court and some of its issues of implementation. (In: States' responses to issues arising from ICC Statute: constitutional, sovereignty, judicial cooperation and criminal law, ed. by Lee, Roy S.. Ardsley, NY: Transnational Publishers, 2005, p. 259-273.) [I.C.J., p. 264.]

Salinas Burgos, Hernán: El principio de jurisdicción universal ¿ Lex lata o lex desiderata? (Dans: Revista chilena de derecho, 2007, v. 34, p. 107-134.) [C.P.J.I., p. 108-109, 115; C.I.J., p. 111-113, 115-116, 118.]

Sandoval-Villalba, Clara: The concepts of "injured party" and "victim" of gross human rights violations in the jurisprudence of the Inter-American Court of Human Rights: a commentary on their implications for reparations. (In: Reparations for victims of genocide, war crimes against humanity: systems in place and systems in the making, ed. by Carla Ferstman; Mariana Goetz; Alan Andrew Stephens. Leiden: Nijhoff, 2009, p. 243-282.) [I.C.J., p. 246, 251.]

Saul, Ben: Defending "terrorism": justifications and excuses for terrorism in international criminal law. (In: Australian Yearbook of International Law, 2004, v. 25, p. 177-226.) [P.C.I.J., p. 224; I.C.J., p. 186, 187, 192, 214, 216-218, 223-224.]

Saul, Ben: Reasons for defining and criminalizing "terrorism" in international law. (In: Anuario mexicano de derecho internacional, 2006, v. 6, p. 419-459.) [I.C.J., p. 457.]

Schabas, William A.: The crime of genocide in the jurisprudence of the International Criminal Tribunals for the former Yugoslavia and Rwanda. (In: International and national prosecution of crimes under international law: current developments, ed. by Horst Fischer; Claus Kreß; Sascha Rolf Lüder. Berlin: Berliner Wissenschafts-Verlag, 2004, p. 447-471.) [I.C.J., p. 451; P.C.I.J., p. 453.]

Schmahl, Stefanie: Specific methods of prosecuting terrorists in national law. (In: Terrorism as a challenge for national and international law: security versus liberty?, ed. by Walter, Christian; Vöneky, Silja; Röben, Volker; Schorkopf, Frank. Berlin [etc.], Springer, 2004, p. 81-118.) [I.C.J. and P.C.I.J., p. 100.]

Shahabuddeen, Mohamed: Some aspects of the I.C.T.Y. (In: Studi di diritto internazionale in onore di Gaetano Arangio-Ruiz, ed. by Giovanni Battaglini; Paolo Benvenuti; Antonio Cassese; Giorgio Gaja. Napoli:

Editoriale Scientifica, 2004, v. 3, p. 2147-2168.) [P.C.I.J., p, 2155, 2156; I.C.J., p, 2147, 2148, 2150, 2153, 2154, 2156, 2157.]

Sharma, Vishnu Dutt: International criminal law: crime prevention and punishment. (In: India and international law, ed. by Bimal N. Patel. Leiden; Boston: Martinus Nijhoff, 2005, p. 189-222.) [I.C.J., p. 201, 202, 213-214.]

Sluiter, Göran: Co-operation with the International Criminal Tribunals for the former Yugoslavia and Rwanda. (In: International and national prosecution of crimes under international law: current developments, ed. by Horst Fischer; Claus Kreß; Sascha Rolf Lüder. Berlin: Berliner Wissenschafts-Verlag, 2004, p. 680-725.) [P.C.I.J and I.C.J., p. 719.]

Steiner, Sylvia Helena: Implementation of the Rome Statute in Brazil. (In: States' responses to issues arising from ICC Statute: constitutional, sovereignty, judicial cooperation and criminal law, ed. by Lee, Roy S.. Ardsley, NY: Transnational Publishers, 2005, p. 179-214.) [I.C.J., p. 191.]

Stoett, Peter J.: Guilty by association? Western involvement in transnational crimes against humanity. (In: La voie vers la Cour pénale internationale: tous les chemins mènent à Rome = The highway to the International Criminal Court: all roads lead to Rome, ed. by Dumont, Hélène; Boisvert, Anne-Marie. Montréal: Editions Thémis, 2004, p. 407-432.) [I.C.J., p. 416.]

Strydom, Hennie: South Africa's implementation of the Rome Statute. (In: States' responses to issues arising from ICC Statute: constitutional, sovereignty, judicial cooperation and criminal law, ed. by Lee, Roy S.. Ardsley, NY: Transnational Publishers, 2005, p. 105-120.) [I.C.J., p. 108.]

Timmermann, Wibke Kristin: The relationship between hate propaganda and incitement to genocide: a new trend in international law towards criminalization of hate propaganda? (In: Leiden Journal of International Law, 2005, v. 18, no. 2, p. 257-282.) [I.C.J., p. 272-274, 281.]

Tobin, John: Seeking clarity in relation to the principle of complementarity: reflections on the recent contributions of some international bodies. (In: Melbourne Journal of International Law, 2007, v. 8, no. 2, p. 356-372.)

Tomás Ortíz de la Torre, José Antonio: La competencia jurisdiccional penal internacional: pasado y presente. (Dans: Anuario hispano-luso-americano de derecho internacional, 2007, 18, p. 51-126.) [C.P.J.I., p. 62-64, 66, 68, 72, 78, 105-107, 114; C.I.J., p. 86, 88-89.]

Torres Pérez, María et Bou Franch, Valentín: La contribución del Tribunal Internacional Penal para Ruanda a la configuración jurídica de los crímenes internacionales. Valencia: Tirant lo Blanch, 2004. [C.I.J., p. 370-371.]

Ueki, Toshiya: International terrorism and the theory of international law [in Japanese]. (In: Kokusaiho Gaiko Zassi, 2007, v. 105, no. 4, p. 1-20.) [I.C.J., p. 8, 11-12, 15.]

van der Wilt, Harmen: Bilateral agreements between the United States and States parties to the Rome Statute: are they compatible with the object and purpose of the Statute? (In: Leiden Journal of International Law, 2005, v. 18, no. 1, p. 93-111.) [I.C.J., p. 101.]

van der Wilt, Harmen: International strafrecht. (In: Handboek internationaal recht, ed. by Horbach, Nathalie L. J. T.; Lefeber, René; Ribbelink, Olivier. The Hague: T.M.C. Asser Press, 2007, p. 509-551.) [P.C.I.J., p. 510; I.C.J., p. 547, 550.]

Verweij, Harry and Groenleer, Martijn: The Netherlands' legislative measures to implement the ICC Statute. (In: States' responses to issues arising from ICC Statute: constitutional, sovereignty, judicial cooperation and criminal law, ed. by Lee, Roy S.. Ardsley, NY: Transnational Publishers, 2005, p. 83-103.) [I.C.J., p. 93, 99, 103.]

Volevodz, V. A.: Doktrinalnye i pravovye predposylki formirovanija sovremennoj sistemy medunarodnogo ugolovnogo pravosudija. (In: Medunarodnoe ugolovnoe pravosudie: sovremennye preoblemy, ed. by Borua, G. I.; Trikoz, E. N. Moskva: Inst. prava i publinoj politiki, 2009, p. 324-343.)

Volevodz, V. A.: Sovremennaja sistema medunarodnoj ugolovnoj justicii: ponjatie, pravovye osnovy, struktura i priznaki. (In: Medunarodnoe ugolovnoe pravosudie: sovremennye preoblemy, ed. by Borua, G. I.; Trikoz, E. N. Moskva: Inst. prava i publinoj politiki, 2009, p. 305-323.)

Warbrick, Colin: Public international law: immunity and international crimes in English law. (In: International and Comparative Law Quarterly, 2004, v. 53, no. 3, p. 769-774.) [I.C.J., passim.]

Wet, Erika de: The relation between the International Criminal Court and ad hoc criminal tribunals: competition or symbiosis? (In: Die Friedens-Warte: Blätter für internationale Verständigung und zwischenstaatliche Organisation, 2008, v. 83, no. 4, p. 63-75.) [I.C.J., p. 35.]

Williams, Sarah: The Cambodian extraordinary chambers: a dangerous precedent for international justice? (In: International and Comparative Law Quarterly, 2004, v. 53, no. 1, p. 227-245.) [I.C.J., p. 233.]

Williams, Sarah: Internationalized tribunals: a search for their legal bases. (In: International law and power: perspectives on legal order and justice: essays in honour of Colin Warbrick, ed. by Kaiyan Homi Kaikobad; Michael Bohlander. Leiden; Boston: Martinus Nijhoff, 2009, p. 455-484.) [I.C.J., p. 463, 469.]

Wilmshurst, Elizabeth: The crime of aggression: custom, treaty and prospects for international prosecution. (In: International law between universalism and fragmentation: festschrift in honour of Gerhard Hafner, ed. by Buffard, Isabelle; Crawford, James; Pellet, Alain; Wittich, Stephan. Leiden [etc.]: Martinus Nijhoff, 2008, p. 603-623.)

Wippman, David: Exaggerating the ICC. (In: Bringing power to justice? The prospects of the International Criminal Court, ed. by Joanna Harrington; Michael Milde; Richard Vernon. Montreal [etc.]: McGill-Queen's University Press, 2006, p. 99-140.) [P.C.I.J. and I.C.J., p. 100.]

Wolfrum, Rüdiger: Prosecution of international crimes by international and national criminal courts: concurring jurisdiction. (In: Studi di diritto internazionale in onore di Gaetano Arangio-Ruiz, ed. by Giovanni Battaglini; Paolo Benvenuti; Antonio Cassese; Giorgio Gaja. Napoli: Editoriale Scientifica, 2004, v. 3, p. 2199-2209.) [P.C.I.J., p, 2199, 2200.]

Yee, Sienho: The "tu quoque" argument as a defence to international crimes, prosecution or punishment. (In: Chinese Journal of International Law, 2004, v. 3, no. 1, p. 87-133.) [I.C.J., p. 88, 116-118, 124.]

Yokaris, Angelos: La répression pénale en droit international public. Athènes; Bruxelles: Sakkoulas: Bruylant, 2005. [C.P.J.I., p. 13, 37, 43, 95-97; C.I.J., p. 6, 8, 13, 16, 41, 46-47, 55, 59, 75-76, 90-92.]

Zimmermann, Robert: La coopération judiciaire internationale en matière pénale. Berne: Stæmpfli, 2004. 2e éd. [C.I.J., p. 88, 493-495, 546, 548-550.]

15. *Jus ad bellum* et *jus in bello*
15. *Jus ad bellum* and *jus in bello*

Abi-Saab, Georges: Conclusions générales. (Dans: Le droit international à la croisée des chemins: force du droit et droit de la force: VIe rencontre internationale de la Faculté des Sciences juridiques, politiques et sociales de Tunis, 14, 15 et 16 avril 2004. Paris: Pedone, 2004, p. 421-442.) [C.I.J., p. 430, 439.]

Abresch, William: A human rights law of internal armed conflict: the European Court of Human Rights in Chechnya. (In: European Journal of International Law, 2005, v. 16, no. 4, p. 741-767.) [I.C.J., p. 741, 743-744.]

Acosta Estévez, José B.: La operación Libertad duradera y la legítima defensa a la luz de los atentados del 11 de septiembre de 2001. (Dans: Anuario mexicano de derecho internacional, 2006, v. 6, p. 13-61.) [C.I.J., p. 40-41, 43.]

Allen, Craig H.: Limits on the use of force in maritime operations in support of WMD counter-proliferation initiatives. (In: International Law Studies, 2006, v. 81, p. 77-139.) [P.C.I.J., p. 95; I.C.J., p. 89, 95.]

Amerasinghe, Chittharanjan Felix: The conundrum of recourses to force: to protect persons. (In: International Organizations Law Review, 2006, v. 3, p. 7-53.) [P.C.I.J., p. 26-27; I.C.J., p. 39, 41-46, 49, 53.]

Andrés Sáenz de Santa María, María Paz: Spain and the war on Iraq. (In: Spanish Yearbook of International Law, 2004, v. 10, p. 39-66.) [I.C.J., p. 65-66.]

Antonopoulos, Constantine: Some thoughts on the NATO position in relation to the Iraqi crisis. (In: Leiden Journal of International Law, 2004, v. 17, no. 1, p. 171-183.) [I.C.J., p. 177-178, 181.]

Arafat Abou Hijaza, Achraf: Cohérence des résolutions du Conseil de sécurité adoptées conformément au chapitre 7 de la Charte, et leur mise en oeuvre dans les ordres juridiques internes aux Etats membres. (In: Revue égyptienne de droit international, 2006, v. 61, p. 329-468.) [C.I.J., p. 338, 345, 349-350, 356, 381, 400-401.]

Aurescu, Bogdan: Le conflit libanais de 2006. Une analyse à la lumière de tendances contemporaines en matière de recours à la force. (Dans: Annuaire français de droit international, 2006, v. 52, p. 137-159.) [C.I.J., p. 145-147.]

Ben Achour, Rafâa: Le droit international à la croisée des chemins (force du droit et droit de la force). (Dans: Le droit international à la croisée des chemins: force du droit et droit de la force: VIe rencontre internationale de la Faculté des Sciences juridiques, politiques et sociales de Tunis, 14, 15 et 16 avril 2004, sous la dir. de Rafâa Ben Achour; Slim Laghmani. Paris: Pedone, 2004, p. 13-39.) [C.I.J., p. 18-20, 29, 32-34.]

Ben-Naftali, Orna and Michaeli, Keren: Public Committee Against Torture in Israel v. Government of Israel: case No. HCJ 769/02, Supreme Court of Israel, sitting as the High Court of Justice, December 13, 2006. (In: American Journal of International Law, 2007, v. 101, p. 459-465.) [I.C.J., p. 463-464.]

Bergeal, Catherine: La coutume et la conduite des hostilités. (Dans: Droit international humanitaire coutumier: enjeux et défis contemporains, sous la dir. de Tavernier, Paul; Henckaerts, Jean-Marie. Bruxelles: Bruylant, 2008, p. 101-113.) [C.I.J., p. 107.]

Berman, Nathaniel: Privileging combat? Contemporary conflict and the legal construction of war. (In: Columbia Journal of Transnational Law, 2004, v. 43, no. 1, p. 1-71.) [I.C.J., p. 12.]

Biad, Abdelwahab: Désarmement et maîtrise des armements: entre rupture et continuité. (Dans: La sécurité internationale entre rupture et continuité: mélanges en l'honneur du professeur Jean-François Guilhaudis. Bruxelles: Bruylant, 2007, p. 37-51.) [C.I.J., p. 41, 51.]

Biehler, Gernot: Property rights for individuals under international humanitarian law. (In: Archiv des Völkerrchts, 2007, v. 45, no. 3, p. 432-441.) [P.C.I.J., p. 435; I.C.J., p. 440-441.]

Blokker, Niels: The crime of aggression and the United Nations Security Council. (In: Leiden Journal of International Law, 2007, v. 20, p. 867-894.) [I.C.J., p. 879-880, 883-887, 891-893.]

Boldt, Nicki: Outsourcing war: private military companies and international humanitarian law. (In: German Yearbook of International Law, 2004, v. 47, p. 502-544.) [P.C.I.J., p. 541; I.C.J., p. 520, 540.]

Bourbonnière, Michel and Lee, Ricky J.: Legality of deployment of conventional weapons in earth orbit: balancing space law and the law of armed conflict. (In: European Journal of International Law, 2007, v. 18, p. 873-901.) [P.C.I.J., p. 880; I.C.J., p. 879, 886-888, 897, 899.]

Boysen, Siegfried: Kriegsverbrechen im Diskurs nationaler Gerichte: der Distomo-Beschluss des Bundesverfassungsgerichts vom 15. Februar 2006. (In: Archiv des Völkerrechts, 2006, v. 44, p. 363-379.) [I.C.J. p. 374.]

Bruha, Thomas: Standpunkt. (In: Der Irak-Krieg und das Völkerrecht, ed. by Kai Ambos; Jörg Arnold. Berlin: Berliner Wissenschafts-Verlag, 2004, p. 242-246.) [I.C.J., p. 244.]

Brunnée, Jutta and Toope, Stephen J.: Slouching towards new 'just' wars: international law and the use of force after September 11th. (In: Netherlands International Law Review, 2004, v. 51, no. 3, p. 363-392.) [I.C.J., p. 377.]

Brunnée, Jutta and Toope, Stephen J.: The use of force: international law after Iraq. (In: International and Comparative Law Quarterly, 2004, v. 53, p. 785-806.) [I.C.J., p. 791, 794-796, 805.]

Bugnion, François: Le droit international humanitaire coutumier et les conflits armés non internationaux. (Dans: Droit international humanitaire coutumier: enjeux et défis contemporains, sous la dir. de Tavernier, Paul; Henckaerts, Jean-Marie. Bruxelles: Bruylant, 2008, p. 179-190.) [C.I.J., p. 181-182.]

Buttlar, Christian von: Rechtsstreit oder Glaubensstreit? Anmerkungen zur Debatte um die präventive Selbstverteidigung im Völkerrecht. (In: Internationale Gemeinschaft und Menschenrechte: Festschrift für Georg Ress zum 70. Geburtstag am 21. Januar 2005, ed. by Bröhmer, Jürgen; Bieber, Roland; Calliess, Christian; Langenfeld, Christine; Weber, Stefan; Wolf, Joachim. Köln [etc.]: Heymann, 2005, p. 15-28.) [I.C.J., p. 20-21.]

Cabasso, Jacqueline: Negotiating in "good faith". (In: Freedom from nuclear weapons through legal accountability and good faith: conference report, ed. by George Farebrother. Nottingham: Spokesman; World Court Project, 2007, p. 51-56.) [I.C.J., p. 54.]

Cançado Trindade, A. A.: Post scriptum: el primado del derecho sobre la fuerza como imperativo del jus cogens. (Dans: Doctrina latinoamericana del derecho internacional: tomo II, par A. A. Cançado Trindade; Fernando Vidal Ramírez. San José: Corte Interamericana de Derechos Humanos, 2003, p. 49-66.) [I.C.J., p. 54.]

Cançado Trindade, A. A.: The primacy of international law over force. (In: Promoting justice, human rights and conflict resolution through international law: liber amicorum Lucius Caflisch, ed. by Kohen, Marcelo G.. Leiden: Martinus Nijhoff, 2007, p. 1037-1056.) [I.C.J., p. 1041-1043, 1055.]

Cardona Llorens, Jorge: Le maintien de la paix et le recours à la force: entre l'autorisation des opérations de maintien de la paix et l'externalisation. (Dans: Le droit international à la croisée des chemins: force du droit et droit de la force: VIe rencontre internationale de la Faculté des Sciences juridiques, politiques et sociales de Tunis, 14, 15 et 16 avril 2004, sous la dir. de Rafâa Ben Achour; Slim Laghmani. Paris: Pedone, 2004, p. 77-103.) [C.I.J., p. 81.]

Challenge of international terrorism to the international security system: designing responses within the UN charter and treaty framework for regional security. (In: From government to governance: the growing impact of non-state actors on the international and European legal system: proceedings of the Sixth Hague Joint Conference held in The Hague, The Netherlands, 3-5 July 2003, ed. by Heere, Wybo P. The Hague: T.M.C. Asser Press, 2004, p. 265-300.) [I.C.J., p. 274, 286, 289-290, 292, 295.]

Christakis, Théodore et Bannelier, Karine: Acteur vigilant ou spectateur impuissant? Le contrôle exercé par le Conseil de sécurité sur les Etats autorisés à recourir à la force. (Dans: Revue belge de droit international, 2004, v. 37, p. 498-527.) [C.I.J., p. 501, 512.]

Christakis, Théodore: Vers une reconnaissance de la notion de guerre préventive? (Dans: L'intervention en Irak et le droit international, sous la dir. de Karine Bannelier; Olivier Corten; Théodore Christakis; Pierre Klein. Paris: Pedone, 2004, p. 9-45.) [C.I.J., p. 18, 31-32, 40-43; C.P.J.I., p. 14.]

Christakis, Théodore et Bannelier, Karine: Volenti non fit injuria? Les effets du consentement à l'intervention militaire. (Dans: Annuaire français de droit international, 2004, v. 50, p. 102-137.) [C.P.J.I., p. 114, 118; C.I.J., p. 103, 113-115, 118-119, 127, 135.]

Compensation for victims of war. (In: Reports of the Annual Conference, by International Law Association (ILA), 2006, 2006, p. 761-814.) [I.C.J., p. 770, 780, 803.]

Condorelli, Luigi: La place de la coutume dans la justice pénale internationale au regard, en particulier, du TPIY et du TPIR. (Dans: Droit international humanitaire coutumier: enjeux et défis contemporains, sous la dir. de Tavernier, Paul; Henckaerts, Jean-Marie. Bruxelles: Bruylant, 2008, p. 191-201.) [C.I.J., p. 197.]

Condorelli, Luigi: Vers une reconnaissance d'un droit d'ingérence à l'encontre des "Etats voyous"? (Dans: L'intervention en Irak et le droit international, sous la dir. de Karine Bannelier; Olivier Corten; Théodore Christakis; Pierre Klein. Paris: Pedone, 2004, p. 47-57.) [C.I.J., p. 51.]

Consigli, José A. et Lavopa, Federico: Dos aspectos de la legítima defensa frente a la amenaza terrorista. (Dans: Anuario argentino de derecho internacional, 2006, 15, p. 25-43.) [C.I.J., p. 37-43.]

Corten, Olivier: Les arguments avancés par la Belgique pour justifier son soutien aux Etats-Unis dans le cadre de la guerre contre l'Irak. (Dans: Revue belge de droit international, 2005, v. 38, p. 417-446.) [C.I.J., p. 426.]

Corten, Olivier: Le droit contre la guerre: l'interdiction du recours à la force en droit international contemporain. Paris: Pedone, 2008. [C.P.J.I., p. 46, 206, 397; C.I.J., p. 21, 25, 35-36, 38-41, 43-44, 46, 51-53, 55-56, 58-59, 83, 85, 89-91, 93-96, 98-99, 101, 105-109, 117, 120, 128-130, 135-138, 144-145, 147-148, 150, 154-155, 160-161, 178, 203, 205, 207-208, 222, 224, 230, 233, 254-263, 266, 269, 291, 306-307, 311-312, 322-326, 350, 358-361, 370-374, 380-382, 398, 404, 407, 416, 419, 422, 424-426, 451, 505,

515, 588, 601, 609, 623, 625, 667-668, 679-680, 682-684, 690, 700-703, 705-706, 711-712, 717, 719-723, 726-728, 787, 802.]

Corten, Olivier: L'état de nécessité peut-il justifier un recours à la force non constitutif d'agression? (Dans: Global Community: Yearbook of International Law and Jurisprudence, 2004, v. 4, no. 1, p. 11-50.) [C.I.J., p. 16, 18, 37, 41, 49-50.]

Corten, Olivier: L'interdiction du recours à la force dans les relations internationales est-elle opposable aux groupes "terroristes"? (Dans: Acteurs non étatiques et droit international: VIIe rencontre internationale de la Faculté des Sciences juridiques, politiques et sociales de Tunis: 6, 7 et 8 avril 2006, sous la dir. de Rafâa Ben Achour; Slim Laghmani. Paris: A. Pedone, 2007, p. 129-159.)

Corten, Olivier: La nécessité et le jus ad bellum. (Dans: La nécessité en droit international: colloque de Grenoble. Paris: Pedone, 2007, p. 127-150.)

Cottier, Michael: Did N.A.T.O. forces commit war crimes during the Kosovo conflict? Reflections on the prosecutor's report of 13 June 2000. (In: International and national prosecution of crimes under international law: current developments, ed. by Horst Fischer; Claus Kreß; Sascha Rolf Lüder. Berlin: Berliner Wissenschafts-Verlag, 2004, p. 505-537.) [I.C.J., p. 512.]

Crook, John R.: Fact-finding in the fog: determining the facts of upheavals and wars in inter-State disputes. (In: The future of investment arbitration, ed. by Rogers, Catherine A.; Alford, Roger P.. New York [etc.]: Oxford University Press, 2009, p. 313-337.) [I.C.J., p. 320-336.]

D'Argent, Pierre: Le droit de la responsabilité internationale complété? Examen des principes fondamentaux et directives concernant le droit à un recours et à réparation des victimes de violations flagrantes du droit international des droits de l'homme et de violations graves du droit international humanitaire. (Dans: Annuaire français de droit international, 2005, v. 51, p. 27-55.) [C.P.J.I., p. 50; C.I.J., p. 43-44, 50-51.]

Daillier, Patrick: Les opérations multinationales consécutives à des conflits armés en vue du rétablissement de la paix. (Dans: Recueil des cours de l'Académie de droit international de La Haye, 2005, v. 314, p. 245-431.) [C.I.J., p. 326, 363.]

Débats. (Dans: Droit international humanitaire coutumier: enjeux et défis contemporains, sous la dir. de Tavernier, Paul; Henckaerts, Jean-Marie. Bruxelles: Bruylant, 2008, p. 229-254.) [C.I.J., p. 238-239.]

Deiseroth, Dieter: Deutschland im U.S.-Irak-Krieg – N.A.T.O.-Bündnisverpflichtungen im Konflikt mit Verfassungs- und Völkerrecht? (In: Der Irak-Krieg und das Völkerrecht, ed. by Kai Ambos; Jörg Arnold. Berlin: Berliner Wissenschafts-Verlag, 2004, p. 131-157.) [I.C.J., p. 134.]

Delcourt, Barbara: The doctrine of "responsibility to protect" and the EU stance: critical appraisal. (In: Studia diplomatica, 2006, 59, p. 69-93.) [I.C.J., p. 73, 80.]

Di Blase, Antonietta: La "dottrina Bush" e il diritto internazionale. (Dans: Studi di diritto internazionale in onore di Gaetano Arangio-Ruiz, sous la dir. de Giovanni Battaglini; Paolo Benvenuti; Antonio Cassese; Giorgio Gaja. Napoli: Editoriale Scientifica, 2004, v. 3, p. 1587-1621.) [C.I.J., p. 1593, 1595-1596, 1598-1599, 1607-1609, 1612-1613, 1618.]

Dinstein, Yoram: The Gulf War: 1990-2004 (and still counting). (In: International Law Studies (Naval War College), 2006, 81, p. 337-350.) [I.C.J., p. 344.]

Dinstein, Yoram: The ICRC customary international humanitarian law study. (In: The law of war in the 21st century: weaponry and the use of force, ed. by Helm, Anthony M. Newport, RI: Naval War College, 2006, p. 99-112.) [I.C.J., p. 102, 107, 109.]

Dinstein, Yoram: Jus in bello issues arising in the hostilities in Iraq in 2003. (In: International Law Studies (Naval War College), 2006, 80, p. 43-56.) [I.C.J., p. 49.]

Dinstein, Yoram: Sovereignty, the Security Council and the use of force. (In: Redefining sovereignty: the use of force after the Cold War, ed. by Michael Bothe; Mary Ellen O'Connell; Natalino Ronzitti. Ardsley: Transnational Publishers, 2005, p. 111-122.) [P.C.I.J., p. 112; I.C.J., p. 114.]

Dinstein, Yoram: War, aggression and self-defence. Cambridge [etc.]: Cambridge University Press, 2005. 4th ed. [P.C.I.J., p. 104; I.C.J., p. xi, xiii, 6-7, 17, 40-41, 69, 70, 72, 73, 86, 88, 90, 92, 93-97, 98, 100-102, 105, 109, 113, 127, 145, 148-149, 161-162, 164, 169, 175, 181-183, 193, 194-199, 201-206, 208-211, 212-213, 216-217, 220-222, 229, 230, 234, 236, 239, 244, 254, 256, 268-272, 289, 291, 306-307, 316, 318-325.]

Dörmann, Knut and Colassis, Laurent: International humanitarian law in the Iraq conflict. (In: German Yearbook of International Law, 2004, v. 47, p. 293-342.) [I.C.J., p. 296, 307, 323, 331.]

Doswald-Beck, Louise: Developments in customary international humanitarian law. (In: Schweizerische Zeitschrift für internationales und europäisches Recht, 2005, v. 15, p. 471-498.) [I.C.J., p. 473-486, 497.]

Dubuisson, François: La guerre du Liban de l'été 2006 et le droit à la légitime défense. (Dans: Revue belge de droit international, 2006, v. 39, p. 529-564.) [C.I.J., p. 529, 539-545, 553, 557, 558, 562.]

Dubuisson, François et Lagerwall, Anne: Que signifie encore l'interdiction de recourir à la menace de la force? (Dans: L'intervention en Irak et le droit international, sous la dir. de Karine Bannelier; Olivier Corten; Théodore Christakis; Pierre Klein. Paris: Pedone, 2004, p. 83-104.) [C.I.J., p. 84, 86-92.]

Dupuy, Pierre-Marie: Sécurité collective et coopération multilatérale. (Dans: Le droit international à la croisée des chemins: force du droit et droit de la force: VIe rencontre internationale de la Faculté des Sciences juridiques, politiques et sociales de Tunis, 14, 15 et 16 avril 2004, sous la dir. de Rafâa Ben Achour; Slim Laghmani. Paris: Pedone, 2004, p. 61-76.) [C.I.J., p. 74.]

Dupuy, Pierre-Marie and Tomuschat, Christian: Warten auf den Schlag gegen Bagdad. (In: Der Irak-Krieg und das Völkerrecht, ed. by Kai Ambos; Jörg Arnold. Berlin: Berliner Wissenschafts-Verlag, 2004, p. 247-250.) [I.C.J., p. 248.]

Evans, Gareth: The responsibility to protect: ending mass atrocity crimes once and for all. Washington, DC: Brookings Institution Press, 2008. [I.C.J., p. 20, 99, 116, 195.]

Fazal, Tanisha M.: State death: the politics and geography of conquest, occupation, and annexation. Princeton; Woodstock: Princeton University Press, 2007. [I.C.J., p. 248-249.]

Fisher, W. Jason: Targeted killing, norms, and international law. (In: Columbia Journal of Transnational Law, 2007, v. 45, p. 711-758.) [I.C.J., p. 720.]

Florent, Jean-Luc: Opposabilité de l'étude du CICR sur le droit international humanitaire coutumier aux Etats. (Dans: Droit international humanitaire coutumier: enjeux et défis contemporains, sous la dir. de Tavernier, Paul; Henckaerts, Jean-Marie. Bruxelles: Bruylant, 2008, p. 75-80.) [C.P.J.I., p. 79; C.I.J., p. 77-78.]

Frigessi di Rattalma, Marco: Qualche riflessione sull'azione bellica in Afghanistan e la legittima difesa. (Dans: Studi di diritto internazionale in onore di Gaetano Arangio-Ruiz, sous la dir. de Giovanni Battaglini; Paolo Benvenuti; Antonio Cassese; Giorgio Gaja. Napoli: Editoriale Scientifica, 2004, v. 3, p. 1623-1645.) [C.I.J., p. 1631-1632, 1635, 1637-1638.]

Garcia, Thierry: De la transgression du droit international par le recours à la force. (Dans: Revue de droit international et de droit comparé, 2005, v. 82, no. 1, p. 52-67.) [C.I.J., p. 60-61, 66.]

Gardam, Judith Gail: Necessity, proportionality and the use of force by States. Cambridge [etc.]: Cambridge University Press, 2004. (Cambridge studies in international and comparative law; 35.) [I.C.J., p. 3, 4, 11, 18, 20, 72, 73, 76, 93, 96, 107, 143-145, 151-152, 158-159, 165, 167, 169-170, 174-175, 178, 190-192, 200, 203-207, 212, 223, 225-228.]

Gardam, Judith Gail: A role for proportionality in the war on terror. (In: Nordic Journal of International Law, 2005, v. 74, no. 1, p. 3-25.) [I.C.J., p. 4, 7-8, 10, 12-14, 17-22, 24.]

Garraway, Charles H. B.: "England does not love coalitions": does anything change? (In: The law of war in the 21st century: weaponry and the use of force, ed. by Helm, Anthony M. Newport, RI: Naval War College, 2006, p. 233-244.) [I.C.J., p. 238, 240, 241.]

Gärtner, Veronika: The Brussels Convention and reparations: remarks on the judgment of the European Court of Justice in Lechouritou and others v.

the State of the Federal Republic of Germany. (In: German Law Journal, 2007, v. 8, no. 4, p. 417-442.) [I.C.J., p. 432.]

Garwood-Gowers, Andrew: Pre-emptive self-defence: a necessary development or the road to international anarchy? (In: Australian Yearbook of International Law, 2004, v. 23, p. 51-72.) [I.C.J., p. 53-55.]

Gassama, Ibrahim J.: International law at a Grotian moment: the invasion of Iraq in context. (In: Emory International Law Review, 2004, v. 18, no. 1, p. 1-52.) [I.C.J. and P.C.I.J., p. 26, 33.]

Geiß, Robin: "Weltbürger in Uniform": Anmerkungen zum Urteil des 2. Wehrdienstsenats des Bundesverwaltungsgerichts vom 21. Juni 1995, BVerwG 2 WD 12.04. (In: Archiv des Völkerrechts, 2006, v. 44, p. 217-233.) [I.C.J. p. 227.]

Geiß, Robin: Military necessity: a fundamental "principle" fallen into oblivion. (In: Select Proceedings of the European Society of International Law, ed. by James Crawford; Sarah M. H. Nouwen. Oxford; Portland: Hart, 2008, v. 2, p. 554-568.) [I.C.J., p. 557-558.]

Gill, Terry D.: Humanitarian intervention: legality, justice and legitimacy. (In: Global Community: Yearbook of International Law and Jurisprudence, 2004, v. 4, no. 1, p. 51-75.) [I.C.J., p. 57, 59, 67, 69-70.]

Glennon, Michael J.: The rise and fall of the U.N. Charter's use of force rules. (In: Hastings International and Comparative Law Review, 2004, v. 27, no. 3, p. 497-510.) [I.C.J., p. 504.]

Gray, Christine: The Bush doctrine revisited: the 2006 national security strategy of the USA. (In: Chinese Journal of International Law, 2006, v. 5, p. 555-578.) [I.C.J., p. 568-569, 571-572.]

Green, James A.: Self-defence: a state of mind for States? (In: Netherlands International Law Review, 2008, v. 55, no. 2, p. 181-206.) [P.C.I.J., p. 194; I.C.J., p. 199, 201-206.]

Green, Leslie C.: Is there a "new" law of intervention and occupation? (In: International Law Studies (Naval War College), 2006, 81, p. 167-200.) [I.C.J., p. 168.]

Greenwood, Christopher J.: Belligerent reprisals in the jurisprudence of the International Criminal Tribunal for the former Yugoslavia. (In: International and national prosecution of crimes under international law: current developments, ed. by Horst Fischer; Claus Kreß; Sascha Rolf Lüder. Berlin: Berliner Wissenschafts-Verlag, 2004, p. 539-557.) [I.C.J., p. 541, 550, 552-554.]

Greppi, Edoardo: Aggressione e crimine di aggressione: accertamento politico e riflessi giurisdizionali internazionali. (Dans: Diritti individuali e giustizia internazionale: liber Fausto Pocar, sous la dir. de Venturine, Gabriella; Bariatti, Stefania. Milano: Giuffrè, 2009, v. 1, p. 367-382.) [C.I.J., p. 375, 377-381.]

Grote, Rainer: Between crime prevention and the laws of war: are the traditional categories of international law adequate for assessing the use of force against international terrorism? (In: Terrorism as a challenge for national and international law: security versus liberty?, ed. by Walter, Christian; Vöneky, Silja; Röben, Volker; Schorkopf, Frank. Berlin [etc.], Springer, 2004, p. 951-985.) [I.C.J., p. 956-959, 962-964, 972, 974, 977.]

Gueldish, Hajer: L'ingérence humanitaire entre droit et force. (Dans: Le droit international à la croisée des chemins: force du droit et droit de la force: VIe rencontre internationale de la Faculté des Sciences juridiques, politiques et sociales de Tunis, 14, 15 et 16 avril 2004, sous la dir. de Rafâa Ben Achour; Slim Laghmani. Paris: Pedone, 2004, p. 185-203.) [C.I.J., p. 197.]

Gutiérrez Espada, Cesáreo: Del uso de la fuerza en las relaciones internacionales (práctica versus jurisprudencia). (Dans: El proceso de reforma de las Naciones Unidas: la dimensión institucional y el mantenimiento de la paz y la seguridad internacionales, sous la dir. d'Antonio Blanc Altemir. Madrid [etc.]: Tecnos etc, 2009, p. 227-248.)

Gutiérrez Espada, Cesáreo et Bermejo García, Romualdo: El programa nuclear iraní en el ojo del huracán. (Dans: Revista española de derecho internacional, 2005, v. 57, no. 1, p. 105-119.) [C.I.J., p. 118.]

Heintze, Hans-Joachim: Konsequenzen der Konvergenz von Menschenrechtsschutz und humanitärem Völkerrecht. (In: Krisensicherung und humanitärer Schutz: Festschrift für Dieter Fleck, ed. by Horst Fischer; Ulrike Froissart; Wolff Heintschel von Heinegg. Berlin: Berliner Wissenschafts-Verlag, 2004, p. 243-265.) [I.C.J., p. 244, 250, 251.]

Henckaerts, Jean-Marie: Customary international humanitarian law: a rejoinder to Judge Aldrich. (In: British Year Book of International Law, 2005, v. 76, p. 525-532.) [I.C.J., p. 529-530.]

Henckaerts, Jean-Marie: Etude du CICR sur le droit international humanitaire coutumier: objet, caractéristiques, conclusions et pertinence. (Dans: Droit international humanitaire coutumier: enjeux et défis contemporains, sous la dir. de Tavernier, Paul; Henckaerts, Jean-Marie. Bruxelles: Bruylant, 2008, p. 25-67.) [C.I.J., p. 35-38, 40-42, 50, 55-57.]

Henckaerts, Jean-Marie: Study on customary international humanitarian law: a contribution to the understanding and respect for the rule of law in armed conflict. (In: The law of war in the 21st century: weaponry and the use of force, ed. by Helm, Anthony M. Newport, RI: Naval War College, 2006, p. 37-79.) [P.C.I.J., p. 44; I.C.J., p. 40-45, 55-56.]

Hilpold, Peter: Die Vereinten Nationen und das Gewaltverbot: die Reformvorschläge des High-level Panels sind wenig hilfreich. (In: Vereinte Nationen, 2005, v. 53, no. 3, p. 81-88.) [I.C.J., p. 82-83, 87-88.]

Hofmeister, Hannes: Preemptive strikes: a new normative framework. (In: Archiv des Völkerrechts, 2006, v. 44, p. 187-200.) [I.C.J. p. 188.]

Hoppe, Carsten: Who was calling whose shots? Hezbollah and Lebanon in the 2006 armed conflict with Israel. (In: Italian Yearbook of International Law, 2006, v. 16, p. 21-40.) [I.C.J., p. 28-30, 32, 39.]

Hulme, Karen: Radiation warfare: a review of the legality of depleted uranium weaponry. (In: Canadian Yearbook of International Law, 2005, v. 43, p. 197-296.) [P.C.I.J., p. 229; I.C.J., p. 233, 238, 240, 244, 256, 270-271, 273.]

Israel Supreme Court: Public Committee against Torture in Israel v. Israel. (In: International Legal Materials, 2007, v. 46, p. 375-408.) [I.C.J., p. 387.]

Jaworski, Eric: "Military necessity" and "civilian immunity": where is the balance? (In: International crime and punishment: selected issues ed. Lanham: University Press of America, 2004, v. 2, p. 87-127.) [I.C.J., p. 191.]

Jinks, Derek: The declining significance of POW status. (In: Harvard International Law Journal, 2004, v. 45, no. 2, p. 367-442.) [I.C.J., p. 402.]

Johnstone, Ian: The plea of "necessity" in international legal discourse: humanitarian intervention and counter-terrorism. (In: Columbia Journal of Transnational Law, 2005, v. 43, no. 2, p. 337-388.) [I.C.J., p. 340-341, 343, 355, 362-363, 366-370, 374-375.]

Kaduski, Marcin: On the Martens clause in international law today. (In: Wspóczesne problemy praw czowieka i midzynarodowego prawa humanitarnego, ed. by Tadeusza Jasudowicza; Michaa Balcerzaka; Julii Kapelaskiej-Prgowskiej. Torun: TNOiK, 2009, p. 295-313.)

Kammerhofer, Jörg: Uncertainties of the law on self-defence in the United Nations Charter. (In: Netherlands Yearbook of International Law, 2004, v. 35, p. 143-204.) [I.C.J., p. 145, 149, 150, 152, 153, 158-167, 187, 189-193.]

Karagiannis, Syméon: La légalisation des situations illégales en droit international: l'exemple du recours illégal à la force. (Dans: Le droit international à la croisée des chemins: force du droit et droit de la force: VIe rencontre internationale de la Faculté des Sciences juridiques, politiques et sociales de Tunis, 14, 15 et 16 avril 2004, sous la dir. de Rafâa Ben Achour; Slim Laghmani. Paris: Pedone, 2004, p. 105-136.) [C.P.J.I., p. 112; C.I.J., p. 107, 108, 117, 119-121, 125.]

Kennedy, David: War and international law: distinguishing military and humanitarian professions. (In: The law of war in the 21st century: weaponry and the use of force, ed. by Helm, Anthony M. Newport, RI: Naval War College, 2006, p. 3-33.) [I.C.J., p. 11.]

Kleffner, Jann K.: From "belligerents" to "fighters" and civilians directly participating in hostilities – on the principle of distinction in non-international armed conflicts one hundred years after the Second Hague Peace Conference. (In: Netherlands International Law Review, 2007, v. 54, p. 315-336.) [I.C.J., p. 318.]

Klein, Natalie: State responsibility for international humanitarian law violations and the work of the Eritrea Ethiopia Claims Commission so far. (In: German Yearbook of International Law, 2004, v. 47, p. 214-266.) [P.C.I.J., p. 239; I.C.J., p. 224, 231-232, 235, 239, 246, 266.]

Kolb, Robert: Ius contra bellum: le droit international relatif au maintien de la paix: précis. Bruxelles: Bâle: Bruylant: Helbing Lichtenhahn, 2009. 2e éd. (Collection de droit international public.)

Kolb, Robert: La nécessité militaire dans le droit des conflits armés: essai de clarification conceptuelle. (Dans: La nécessité en droit international: colloque de Grenoble. Paris: Pedone, 2007, p. 151-186.)

Koller, David S.: The moral imperative: toward a human rights-based law of war. (In: Harvard International Law Journal, 2005, v. 46, no. 1, p. 231-264.) [I.C.J., p. 232, 234-235, 241, 259-263.]

Kramer, Daniel: Rechtliche Regulierung asymmetrischer Konflikte? Völkerrecht und empirische Realität. (In: Die Friedens-Warte: Blätter für internationale Verständigung und zwischenstaatliche Organisation, 2006, v. 81, p. 96-100.) [I.C.J., p. 96.]

Kretzmer, David: The Supreme Court of Israel: judicial review during armed conflict. (In: German Yearbook of International Law, 2004, v. 47, p. 392-456.) [I.C.J., p. 392, 399-400, 424-425, 441-442, 445-451, 454.]

Kretzmer, David: Targeted killing of suspected terrorists: extra-judicial executions or legitimate means of defence? (In: European Journal of International Law, 2005, v. 16, no. 2, p. 171-212.) [I.C.J., p. 185-187, 196, 205-206, 209.]

Krieger, Heike: Der privatisierte Krieg: Private Militärunternehmen im bewaffneten Konflikt. (In: Archiv des Völkerrechts, 2006, v. 44, p. 159-186.) [I.C.J. p. 173-174.]

Laghmani, Slim: La doctrine américaine de la "preemptive self-defense". (Dans: Le droit international à la croisée des chemins: force du droit et droit de la force: VIe rencontre internationale de la Faculté des Sciences juridiques, politiques et sociales de Tunis, 14, 15 et 16 avril 2004, sous la dir. de Rafâa Ben Achour; Slim Laghmani. Paris: Pedone, 2004, p. 137-184.) [C.P.J.I., p. 173; C.I.J., p. 150-151, 154-156, 167, 172.]

Lavalle, Roberto: A novel, if awkward, exercise in international law-making: Security Council Resolution 1540 (2004). (In: Netherlands International Law Review, 2004, v. 5, no. 3, p. 411-437.) [I.C.J., p. 423, 424, 432.]

Le Boeuf, Romain: La saisine de la Cour internationale de Justice pour faits de guerre. (Dans: Revue belge de droit international, 2009, v. 42, no. 1, p. 52-77.)

Lijnzaad, Liesbeth and Zwanenburg, Marten: Internationaal humanitair recht. (In: Handboek internationaal recht, ed. by Horbach, Nathalie L. J. T.;

Lefeber, René ; Ribbelink, Olivier. The Hague : T.M.C. Asser Press, 2007, p. 553-589.) [I.C.J., p. 556, 564, 575-576, 581.]

López-Jacoiste Díaz, María Eugenia : La responsabilidad de proteger : reflexiones sobre su fundamento y articulación. (Dans : Anuario español de derecho internacional, 2006, v. 22, p. 285-315.) [C.I.J., p. 291-292, 303.]

Lowe, Vaughan : "Clear and present danger" : responses to terrorism. (In : International and Comparative Law Quarterly, 2005, v. 54, no. 1, p. 185-196.) [I.C.J., p. 192.]

M'rad, Hatem : La Cour internationale de Justice et le recours à la force. (Dans : Le droit international à la croisée des chemins : force du droit et droit de la force : VIe rencontre internationale de la Faculté des Sciences juridiques, politiques et sociales de Tunis, 14, 15 et 16 avril 2004. Paris : Pedone, 2004, p. 207-231.) [C.P.J.I., p. 213; C.I.J., passim.]

Mahmoudi, Said : The Islamic perception of the use of force in the contemporary world. (In : Journal of the History of International Law, 2005, v. 7, no. 1, p. 55-68.) [I.C.J., p. 61, 65.]

Mani, Vekateshwara Subramanian : Future strategies in the war against terrorism and proliferation of weapons of mass destruction : an Indian perception. (In : Indian Journal of International Law, 2004, v. 44, no. 2, p. 221-259.) [P.C.I.J., p. 254-255; I.C.J., p. 226-227, 234, 237, 250-251, 254.]

Mani, Vekateshwara Subramanian : Humanitarian intervention today. (In : Recueil des cours de l'Académie de droit international de La Haye, 2005, v. 313, p. 9-323.) [P.C.I.J., p. 150, 151, 188, 233, 234; I.C.J., p. 32, 33, 144, 151, 165-167, 171, 172, 177, 179-181, 183, 185, 190-195, 197, 200, 207, 211, 212, 215, 219, 229, 231-236, 245, 246, 259, 263, 266, 277, 301-308.]

Maogoto, Jackson Nyamuya : New frontiers, old problems : the war on terror and the notion of anticipating the enemy. (In : Netherlands International Law Review, 2004, v. 51, no. 1, p. 1-39.) [I.C.J., p. 7, 27-28.]

Martin, Jean-Christophe : Les assassinats ciblés de terroristes présumés et l'argument de la nécessité. (Dans : La nécessité en droit international : colloque de Grenoble. Paris : Pedone, 2007, p. 297-306.)

McBride, David : Who is a member? Targeted killings against members of organized armed groups. (In : Australian Yearbook of International Law, 2009, v. 30, p. 47-91.) [I.C.J., p. 75, 76, 89.]

McCormack, Timothy L. H. : An Australian perspective on the ICRC customary international humanitarian law study. (In : The law of war in the 21st century : weaponry and the use of force, ed. by Helm, Anthony M. Newport, RI : Naval War College, 2006, p. 81-97.) [I.C.J., p. 88-89, 91.]

Meessen, Karl M. : Selbstverteidigung gegen den internationalen Terrorismus als werdendes Völkergewohnheitstrecht. (In : Der Irak-Krieg und das Völkerrecht, ed. by Kai Ambos ; Jörg Arnold. Berlin : Berliner Wissenschafts-Verlag, 2004, p. 276-281.) [I.C.J., p. 277, 279, 280.]

Meza, Miguel Arenas : Los límites al recurso a la fuerza transfronteriza en el actual derecho internacional : el pricipio de proporcionalidad. Santiago de Compostela : [s.n.], 2004. (Colección Estudios internacionales.) [I.C.J., p. 6-7, 29-30, 32-33, 35, 38, 40-45, 58, 60, 70, 74-75, 80, 156, 160-161, 176, 179, 181-183, 186-188, 202, 208-209, 218, 239, 242-243, 269, 271-272, 284-286, 288-292, 294, 303, 308-314, 3.]

Molier, Gelijn : Humanitarian intervention and the responsibility to protect after 9/11. (In : Netherlands International Law Review, 2006, v. 53, p. 37-62.) [I.C.J., p. 59-60, 61.]

Momtaz, Djamchid : Les actions de secours au cours d'un conflit armé. (Dans : Studi di diritto internazionale in onore di Gaetano Arangio-Ruiz, sous la dir. de Giovanni Battaglini ; Paolo Benvenuti ; Antonio Cassese ; Giorgio Gaja. Napoli : Editoriale Scientifica, 2004, v. 3, p. 2065-2080.) [C.I.J., p, 2068, 2069.]

Moore, John Norton : Beyond the democratic peace : solving the war puzzle. (In : Virginia Journal of International Law, 2004, v. 44, no. 2, p. 341-429.) [I.C.J., p. 365.]

Moore, John Norton : The Bush administration preemption doctrine and the future of world order. (In : ASIL, Proceedings of the 98th Annual Meeting, March 31-April 3, 2004, 2004, v. 98, p. 325-337.) [I.C.J., p. 325, 334-337.]

Müller, Christoph : The right of self-defense in the global fight against terrorism. (In : International law challenges : homeland security and combating terrorism, ed. by Sparks, Thomas McK. ; Sulmasy, Glenn M. Newport, RI : Naval War College, 2006, p. 351-366.) [I.C.J., p. 354.]

Murswiek, Dietrich : Die amerikanische Praäventivkriegsstrategie und das Völkerrecht. (In : Der Irak-Krieg und das Völkerrecht, ed. by Kai Ambos ; Jörg Arnold. Berlin : Berliner Wissenschafts-Verlag, 2004, p. 285-299.) [I.C.J., p. 298.]

Neff, Stephen C. : War and the law of nations : a general history. Cambridge [etc.] : Cambridge University Press, 2005. [P.C.I.J., p. 290 ; I.C.J., p. 317-319, 332-334, 348, 352, 363-365, 371, 393.]

Nigerian Institute of Advanced Legal Studies : International humanitarian law and intra-State conflicts. Abuja : Nigerian Institute of Advanced Legal Studies Press, 2005. (Late Taslim Elias Memorial Lecture Series.) [P.C.I.J., p. 11, 16; I.C.J., p. 5-6, 9-11, 16.]

Nollkaemper, André : Attribution of forcible acts to States : connections between the law on the use of force and the law of State responsibility. (In : The Security Council and the use of force : theory and reality : a need for change ?, ed. by Niels Blokker ; Nico J. Schrijver. Leiden ; Boston : Martinus Nijhoff, 2005.) [P.C.I.J., p. 139; I.C.J., p. 134-135, 141-143, 145-148, 152, 154-155, 159-160, 162, 166-167.]

Nolte, Georg : Vorbeugende Gewaltanwendung und gezielte Tötungen : der Weg in eine andere Rechtsordnung. (In : Der Irak-Krieg und das

Völkerrecht, ed. by Kai Ambos; Jörg Arnold. Berlin: Berliner Wissenschafts-Verlag, 2004, p. 303-321.) [I.C.J., p. 314.]

O'Connell, Mary Ellen: Ad hoc war. (In: Krisensicherung und humanitärer Schutz: Festschrift für Dieter Fleck, ed. by Horst Fischer; Ulrike Froissart; Wolff Heintschel von Heinegg. Berlin: Berliner Wissenschafts-Verlag, 2004, p. 405-426.) [I.C.J., p. 410.]

O'Connell, Mary Ellen: The legal case against the global war on terror. (In: Case Western Reserve Journal of International Law, 2004, v. 36, no. 2-3, p. 349-357.) [I.C.J., p. 349, 356-357.]

Ochoa Ruiz, Natalia and Salamanca Aguado, Esther: Exploring the limits of international law relating to the use of force in self-defence. (In: European Journal of International Law, 2005, v. 16, no. 3, p. 499-524.) [I.C.J., passim.]

Oellers-Frahm, Karin: The International Court of Justice and Article 51 of the UN Charter. (In: Weltinnenrecht: liber amicorum Jost Delbrück, ed. by Dicke, Klaus; Hobe, Stephan; Meyn, Karl-Ulrich; Peters, Anne; Riedel, Eibe H.; Schütz, Hans-Joachim; Tietje, Christian. Berlin: Duncker & Humblot, 2005, p. 503-517.)

Oeter, Stefan: The dismemberment of Yugoslavia: an update on Bosnia and Herzegovina, Kosovo and Montenegro. (In: German Yearbook of International Law, 2007, v. 50, p. 457-521.) [I.C.J., p. 458, 460, 462-463, 470, 472-474.]

Okowa, Phoebe N.: Natural resources in situations of armed conflict: is there a coherent framework for protection? (In: International Community Law Review, 2007, v. 9, no. 3, p. 237-262.) [I.C.J., p. 246, 248-249, 253-256, 259-260.]

Paul, Joel R.: The Bush doctrine: making or breaking customary international law? (In: Hastings International and Comparative Law Review, 2004, v. 27, no. 3, p. 457-479.) [I.C.J., p. 465, 469-470.]

Paust, Jordan J.: Executive plans and authorizations to violate international law concerning treatment and interrogation of detainees. (In: Columbia Journal of Transnational Law, 2005, v. 43, no. 3, p. 811-863.) [I.C.J., p. 814-817, 822.]

Perrakis, Stelios: Le droit international humanitaire et ses relations avec les droits de l'Homme: quelques considérations. (Dans: Droit international humanitaire coutumier: enjeux et défis contemporains, sous la dir. de Tavernier, Paul; Henckaerts, Jean-Marie. Bruxelles: Bruylant, 2008, p. 115-137.) [C.I.J., p. 117, 119-120, 122, 128.]

Peters, Anne and Kessler, Hans Wolfram: Questionnaire international humanitarian law. (In: Unity and diversity in international law: proceedings of an international symposium of the Kiel Walther Schücking Institute of International Law, November 4-7, 2004, ed. by Zimmermann, Andreas; Hofmann, Rainer. Berlin: Duncker & Humblot, 2006, p. 65-109.) [I.C.J., p. 78-81, 84, 87, 98-102, 105.]

Pierson, Charles: Preemptive self-defense in an age of weapons of mass destruction: operation Iraqi Freedom. (In: Denver Journal of International Law and Policy, 2004, v. 33, no. 1, p. 150-178.) [P.C.I.J., p. 172.]

Pinkowski, Jakub: Der Krieg im Irak: ein neuer Weg oder eine Sackgasse? Ein paar Bemerkungen zu den neuesten Entwicklungen im Völkerrecht. (In: Krisensicherung und humanitärer Schutz: Festschrift für Dieter Fleck, ed. by Horst Fischer van der; Ulrike Froissart; Wolff Heintschel von Heinegg. Berlin: Berliner Wissenschafts-Verlag, 2004, p. 453-460.) [I.C.J., p. 454-456.]

Pinto, Mónica: L'emploi de la force dans la jurisprudence des tribunaux internationaux. (Dans: Recueil des cours de l'Académie de droit international de La Haye, 2007, v. 331, p. 9-161.) [C.I.J., passim.]

Piotrowicz, Ryszard: The Easter bunny, the tooth fairy, Santa Claus and the Security Council: a heart of darkness at the ICJ in Democratic Republic of Congo v. Uganda. (In: Australian Law Journal, 2006, v. 80, no. 3, p. 162-166.)

Puckett, Christopher B.: In this era of "smart weapons", is a State under an international legal obligation to use precision-guided technology in armed conflict? (In: Emory International Law Review, 2004, v. 18, no. 2, p. 645-723.) [I.C.J., p. 682, 684-688, 699, 701-703, 714; P.C.I.J., p. 701-703, 714.]

Rao, Pemmaraju Sreenivasa: Countermeasures in international law: the contribution of the International Law Commission. (In: Studi di diritto internazionale in onore di Gaetano Arangio-Ruiz, ed. by Giovanni Battaglini; Paolo Benvenuti; Antonio Cassese; Giorgio Gaja. Napoli: Editoriale Scientifica, 2004, v. 2, p. 853-880.) [I.C.J., p. 869, 872, 873, 875.]

Ratner, Steven R.: Foreign occupation and international territorial administration: the challenges of convergence. (In: European Journal of International Law, 2005, v. 16, no. 4, p. 695-719.) [I.C.J., p. 699, 701, 704, 712.]

Reichard, Martin: The Madrid terrorists attacks: a midwife for E.U. mutual defence? (In: Zeitschrift für Europarechtliche Studien, 2004, v. 7, no. 2, p. 313-334.) [I.C.J., p. 323.]

Reisman, William Michael and Armstrong, Andrea: Claims to pre-emptive uses of forces: some trends and projections and their implications for world order. (In: International law and armed conflict: exploring the faultlines: essays in honour of Yoram Dinstein, ed. by Michael N. Schmitt. Leiden: Martinus Nijhoff, 2007, p. 79-112.)

Reisman, William Michael and Armstrong, Andrea: The past and future of the claim of preemptive self-defense. (In: American Journal of International Law, 2006, v. 100, no. 3, p. 525-550.) [I.C.J., p. 525-526, 528, 533-539, 548.]

Riklin, Alois: Wertfreiheit, Bellum iustum und der Irak-Krieg. (In: Archiv des Völkerrechts, 2007, v. 45, p. 35-52.) [I.C.J. p. 42.]

Robert-Cuendet, Sabrina: Aspects historiques et juridiques de la crise d'août 2008 : des conflits interethniques à la guerre ouverte avec la Russie. (Dans: Annuaire français de droit international, 2008, v. 54, p. 173-195.) [C.I.J., passim.]

Roberts, Adam: Transformative military occupation: applying the laws of war and human rights. (In: American Journal of International Law, 2006, v. 100, p. 580-622.) [I.C.J., p. 594, 595, 597.]

Rodley, Nigel S.: The extraterritorial reach and applicability in armed conflict of the International Covenant on Civil and Political Rights: a rejoinder to Dennis and Surena. (In: European Human Rights Law Review, 2009, no. 5, p. 628-636.)

Ronzitti, Natalino: The 2006 conflict in Lebanon and international law. (In: Italian Yearbook of International Law, 2006, v. 16, p. 3-19.) [I.C.J., p. 6-8, 13, 18.]

Ronzitti, Natalino: The current status of legal principles prohibiting the use of force and legal justicifications of the use of force. (In: Redefining sovereignty: the use of force after the Cold War, ed. by Michael Bothe; Mary Ellen O'Connell; Natalino Ronzitti. Ardsley: Transnational Publishers, 2005, p. 91-110.) [I.C.J., p. 91-100, 102, 104, 108.]

Roscini, Marco: Targeting and contemporary aerial bombardment. (In: International and Comparative Law Quarterly, 2005, v. 54, no. 2, p. 411-444.) [I.C.J., p. 415, 427, 436.]

Roscini, Marco: Threats of armed force and contemporary international law. (In: Netherlands International Law Review, 2007, v. 54, p. 229-277.) [I.C.J., p. 234-240, 242, 246-248, 251-253, 255-258, 260-266, 270-272.]

Rosenne, Shabtai: Self-defence and the non-use of force: some random thoughts. (In: Essays on international law and practice, by Shabtai Rosenne. Leiden; Boston: Martinus Nijhoff, 2007, p. 633-647.)

Sadoff, David A.: A question of determinacy: the legal status of anticipatory self-defense. (In: Georgetown Journal of International Law, 2009, v. 40, no. 2, p. 523-583.)

Sánchez Patrón, José Manuel: Las organizaciones internacionales ante las violaciones de los derechos humanos. Oviedo: Septem, 2004. 1a ed. [C.I.J., p. 90-93, 106-107, 109-110, 119-121.]

Sandonato de León, Pablo: Titre et statut juridiques de la présence anglo-amériaine en Irak à la lumière du droit international public. (Dans: Hague Yearbook of International Law, 2004, v. 17, p. 15-36.) [C.I.J., p. 16, 20-21, 23-24, 26, 32.]

Sassòli, Marco: Legislation and maintenance of public order and civil life by occupying powers. (In: European Journal of International Law, 2005, v. 16, no. 4, p. 661-694.) [I.C.J., p. 663, 666, 671, 674, 680-681.]

Sauer, Heiko and Wagner, Niklas: Der Tschetschenien-Konflikt und das Völkerrecht: Tschetscheniens Sezession, Russlands Militärinterventionen und die Reaktionen der Staatengemeinschaft auf dem Prüfstand des internationalen Rechts. (In: Archiv des Völkerrechts, 2007, v. 45, p. 53-83.) [I.C.J. p. 56, 61, 63, 67, 74-75, 79.]

Schaller, Christian: Massenvernichtungswaffen und Präventivkrieg: Möglichkeiten der Rechtfertigung einer militärischen Intervention im Irak aus völkerrechtlicher Sicht. (In: Der Irak-Krieg und das Völkerrecht, ed. by Kai Ambos; Jörg Arnold. Berlin: Berliner Wissenschafts-Verlag, 2004, p. 329-358.) [I.C.J., p. 331, 350.]

Schmitt, Michael N.: "Change direction" 2006: Israeli operations in Lebanon and the international law of self-defense. (In: Michigan Journal of International Law, 2008, v. 29, no. 2, p. 127-164.) [I.C.J., p. 142-143, 148-151, 157, 159, 162-163.]

Schmitt, Michael N.: The legality of operation Iraqi freedom under international law. (In: International law challenges: homeland security and combating terrorism, ed. by Sparks, Thomas McK.; Sulmasy, Glenn M. Newport, RI: Naval War College, 2006, p. 367-392.) [I.C.J., p. 371-372, 373.]

Schmitt, Michael N.: Targeting and humanitarian law: current issues. (In: International Law Studies (Naval War College), 2006, 80, p. 151-194.) [P.C.I.J., p. 169; I.C.J., p. 166.]

Schmitt, Michael N.: War, technology and the law of armed conflict. (In: The law of war in the 21st century: weaponry and the use of force, ed. by Helm, Anthony M. Newport, RI: Naval War College, 2006, p. 137-182.) [I.C.J., p. 138, 156.]

Scholz, Michael: Staatliches Selbstverteidigungsrecht gegen terroristische Gewalt. Berlin: Duncker & Humblot, 2006. (Schriften zum Völkerrecht; 165.) [I.C.J., p. 24-25, 30, 33, 40-43, 45, 47, 48, 50, 51, 54, 56-58, 64-69, 78, 80, 81, 82, 83, 88, 98, 107, 113, 120, 121, 122, 124, 131-134, 139-142, 160-166, 167, 170, 171, 172, 173, 174, 175, 176, 178, 180, 181, 185, 188.]

Schrijver, Nico J.: Secession and the ban on the use of force: some reflections. (In: Secession and international law: conflict avoidance: regional appraisals, ed. by Dahlitz, Julie. The Hague: T.M.C. Asser Press, 2003, p. 97-108.) [I.C.J., p. 98.]

Schrijver, Nico J.: September 11 and challenges to international law. (In: Terrorism and the UN: before and after September 11, ed. by Jane Boulden; Thomas G. Weiss. Bloomington; Indianapolis: Indiana University Press, 2004, p. 55-73.) [I.C.J., p. 66-67.]

Scotto, Giuliana: I bombardamenti a tutela delle zone di interdizione al volo in Iraq. (Dans: Studi di diritto internazionale in onore di Gaetano Arangio-Ruiz, sous la dir. de Giovanni Battaglini; Paolo Benvenuti; Antonio Cassese; Giorgio Gaja. Napoli: Editoriale Scientifica, 2004, v. 3, p. 1723-1744.) [C.I.J., p. 1732, 1736.]

Shaker, Mohamed Ibrahim: The evolving international regime of nuclear non-proliferation. (In: Recueil des cours de l'Académie de droit international de La Haye, 2007, v. 321, p. 9-202.) [I.C.J., p. 108-111.]

Shamir-Borer, Eran: Revisiting Hamdan v. Rumsfeld's analysis of the laws of armed conflict. (In: Emory International Law Review, 2007, v. 21, no. 2, p. 601-620.) [I.C.J., p. 611-612, 615-616.]

Sicilianos, Linos-Alexandre: Entre multilatéralisme et unilatéralisme: l'autorisation par le Conseil de sécurité de recourir à la force. (Dans: Recueil des cours de l'Académie de droit international de La Haye, 2008, v. 339, p. 9-436.) [C.I.J., p. 44, 49, 53, 54, 60, 75, 121-123, 133, 146, 166, 173, 179, 192, 205, 206, 254, 255, 307, 311, 313, 315, 340, 341, 346, 361, 362, 397, 410, 413, 419.]

Sidel, Victor W.: The effects of nuclear weapons. (In: Freedom from nuclear weapons through legal accountability and good faith: conference report, ed. by George Farebrother. Nottingham: Spokesman; World Court Project, 2007, p. 8-11.) [I.C.J., p. 8, 10, 11.]

Simma, Bruno: "Gefährlicher Bumerang-Effekt". (In: Der Irak-Krieg und das Völkerrecht, ed. by Kai Ambos; Jörg Arnold. Berlin: Berliner Wissenschafts-Verlag, 2004, p. 400-405.) [I.C.J., p. 400.]

Sloane, Robert: The cost of conflation: preserving the dualism of jus ad bellum and jus in bello in the contemporary law of war. (In: Yale Journal of International Law, 2009, v. 34, no. 1, p. 47-112.)

Stahn, Carsten: "Jus ad bellum", "jus in bello" ... "jus post bellum"? Rethinking the Conception of the Law of Armed Force. (In: European Journal of International Law, 2006, v. 17, p. 921-943.) [I.C.J., p. 922.]

Stahn, Carsten: "Nicaragua is dead, long live Nicaragua": the right to self-defence under art. 51 UN Charter and international terrorism. (In: Terrorism as a challenge for national and international law: security versus liberty?, ed. by Walter, Christian; Vöneky, Silja; Röben, Volker; Schorkopf, Frank. Berlin [etc.], Springer, 2004, p. 827-877.) [I.C.J., p. 838-840, 844, 848, 853, 859-861, 863, 870.]

Svarc, Dominika: Application of international humanitarian law to contemporary peace operations: mapping the "grey areas". (In: Select Proceedings of the European Society of International Law, ed. by James Crawford; Sarah M. H. Nouwen. Oxford; Portland: Hart, 2008, v. 2, p. 529-553.) [I.C.J., p. 536, 538, 544-545.]

Tavernier, Paul: Sécurité internationale, droit international humanitaire et droits de l'homme: quelques réflexions sur le rôle des juridictions internationales. (Dans: La sécurité internationale entre rupture et continuité: mélanges en l'honneur du professeur Jean-François Guilhaudis. Bruxelles: Bruylant, 2007, p. 541-558.) [C.I.J., p. 542-550.]

The Chatham House principles of international law on the use of force in self-defence. (In: International and Comparative Law Quarterly, 2006, v. 55, p. 963-972.) [I.C.J., p. 964, 966-967, 969-971.]

Tigroudja, Hélène: Le régime d'occupation en Iraq. (Dans: Annuaire français de droit international, 2004, v. 50, p. 77-101.) [C.I.J., p. 81-2, 85, 89, 95-96.]

Tönnies, Sibylle: Im Hintergrund der Debatte: die Aporie des modernen Völkerrecht. (In: Die Friedens-Warte: Blätter für internationale Verständigung und zwischenstaatliche Organisation, 2006, v. 81, p. 67-72.) [I.C.J., p. 67.]

Trapp, Kimberley N.: Back to basics: necessity, proportionality, and the right of self-defence against non-state terrorist actors. (In: International and Comparative Law Quarterly, 2007, v. 56, p. 141-156.) [I.C.J., p. 141, 142-145, 146, 150-152.]

Tsagourias, Nicholas: Irrational governance: the use of force. (In: From government to governance: the growing impact of non-state actors on the international and European legal system: proceedings of the Sixth Hague Joint Conference held in The Hague, The Netherlands, 3-5 July 2003, ed. by Heere, Wybo P. The Hague: T.M.C. Asser Press, 2004, p. 472-478.) [I.C.J., p. 473-477.]

Tuzmukamedov, B. R.: Upredajuee primenenie sily: vozmonye kriterii dopustimosti. (In: Rossijskij eegodnik medunarodnogo prava, 2005, v, 2005, p. 36-55.) [I.C.J., p. 45-46, 54.]

United Kingdom. Ministry of Defence: The manual of the law of armed conflict. Oxford [etc.]: Oxford University Press, 2004. [I.C.J., p. 5, 32, 117.]

Van Houtte, Hans and Delmartino, Bart and Yi, lasson and Das, Hans: Post-war restoration of property rights under international law. Cambridge: Cambridge University Press, 2008. [Vol. I: I.C.J., p. 49, 184, 201, 205, 227, 243 Vol. II: 72, 104, 127, 152.]

Vermeulen, Mathias: Kosovo's future status: opening a Pandora's box of secessionist's claims or a precedent for the "responsibility to protect"? (In: Studia diplomatica, 2006, 59, p. 77-92.) [I.C.J., p. 78-79.]

Villani, Ugo: Legittima difesa e lotta al terrorismo nell'operazione enduring freedom. (Dans: Studi di diritto internazionale in onore di Gaetano Arangio-Ruiz, sous la dir. de Giovanni Battaglini; Paolo Benvenuti; Antonio Cassese; Giorgio Gaja. Napoli: Editoriale Scientifica, 2004, v. 3, p. 1771-1792.) [C.I.J., p. 1772, 1776-1777, 1780, 1784, 1792.]

Vöneky, Silja: The fight against terrorism and the rules of the law of warfare. (In: Terrorism as a challenge for national and international law: security versus liberty?, ed. by Walter, Christian; Vöneky, Silja; Röben, Volker; Schorkopf, Frank. Berlin [etc.], Springer, 2004, p. 925-949.) [I.C.J., p. 933.]

Watkin, Kenneth: Chemical agents and "expanding" bullets: limited law enforcement exceptions or unwarranted handcuffs? (In: The law of war in the 21st century: weaponry and the use of force, ed. by Helm, Anthony M. Newport, RI: Naval War College, 2006, p. 193-218.) [I.C.J., p. 200.]

Wawrzycki, Michael T.: The waining power of shared sovereignty in international law: the evolving effect of U.S. hegemony. (In: Tulane Journal of International and Comparative law, 2006, v. 14, no. 2, p. 579-622.)

Weber, Stefan: International oder nicht-international? Die Konfliktqualifikation in der Lubanga-Entscheidung des IStG. (In: Humanitäres Völkerrecht, 2009, v. 22, no. 2, p. 75-84.)

White, Nigel D.: The road to Kandahar: British military interventions and international law. (In: International law and power: perspectives on legal order and justice: essays in honour of Colin Warbrick, ed. by Kaiyan Homi Kaikobad; Michael Bohlander. Leiden; Boston: Martinus Nijhoff, 2009, p. 485-511.) [P.C.I.J., p. 487; I.C.J., p. 487, 498-500, 503, 506, 507, 510.]

Wiefelspütz, Dieter: Völkerrecht und Staatsrecht im Wandel: die Antwort auf den 11. September 2001. (In: Die Friedens-Warte: Blätter für internationale Verständigung und zwischenstaatliche Organisation, 2006, v. 81, p. 73-80.) [I.C.J., p. 77-78.]

Williams, Jack: Biting off more than it can chew? The International Criminal Court and the crime of agression. (In: Australian Yearbook of International Law, 2009, v. 30, p. 201-226.) [I.C.J., p. 205.]

Wittich, Stephan: The use of force, self-defence and the unrealism in international law. (In: Austrian Review of International and European Law, 2009, v. 14, p. 79-99.) [I.C.J., p. 81-93, 96, 98-99.]

Wood, Michael C.: Nécessité et légitime défense dans la lutte contre le terrorisme: quelle est la pertinence de l'affaire de la Caroline aujourd'hui? (Dans: La nécessité en droit international: colloque de Grenoble. Paris: Pedone, 2007, p. 281-286.)

Wood, Michael C.: Towards new circumstances in which the use of force may be authorized? The cases of humanitarian intervention, counter-terrorism, and weapons of mass destruction. (In: The Security Council and the use of force: theory and reality: a need for change?, ed. by Niels Blokker; Nico J. Schrijver. Leiden; Boston: Martinus Nijhoff, 2005, p. 75-90.) [I.C.J., p. 75, 78-79, 84-85.]

Wouters, Jan and Ruys, Tom: The legality of anticipatory military action after 9/11: the slippery slope of self-defense. (In: Studia diplomatica, 2006, v. 59, p. 45-67.) [I.C.J., p. 49, 62.]

Zelter, Angie: An exploration of people's disarmament and international law. (In: Freedom from nuclear weapons through legal accountability and good faith: conference report, ed. by George Farebrother. Nottingham: Spokesman; World Court Project, 2007, p. 105-112.) [I.C.J., p. 105, 108, 112.]

Ziccardi Capaldo, Giuliana: Fighting global terrorism: through global enforcement mechanisms. (In: Global Community: Yearbook of International Law and Jurisprudence, 2004, v. 4, no. 1, xv-xxvii.) [I.C.J., p. XVII-XX, XXIII.]

Zwanenburg, Marten: Accountability of peace support operations. Leiden; Boston: Martinus Nijhoff, 2005. (International humanitarian law series; 9.) [P.C.I.J., p. 88, 213-214, 215, 251; I.C.J., p. 3, 32, 33, 37, 52, 53, 65-66, 68-71, 95, 108, 110-111, 116-125, 134-136, 142-145, 148, 151, 153-155, 194, 200-203, 205, 212-213, 215-216, 219, 236- 237, 243, 246-248, 280-281, 288, 319, 324, 327-328.]

Zwanenburg, Marten: The law of occupation revisited: the beginning of an occupation. (In: Yearbook of International Humanitarian Law, 2007, v. 10, p. 99-130.) [I.C.J., p. 108, 115-122, 129.]

16. Règlement pacifique des différends
16. Peaceful settlement of disputes

Abi-Saab, Georges: Le principe de l'uti possidetis: son rôle et ses limites dans le contentieux territorial international. (Dans: Promoting justice, human rights and conflict resolution through international law: liber amicorum Lucius Caflisch, sous la dir. de Marcelo G. Kohen. Leiden: Martinus Nijhoff, 2007, p. 657-671.) [I.C.J., p. 657-660, 663-671.]

Alcaide-Fernández, Joaquín: Contre-mesures et règlement des différends. (Dans: Revue générale de droit international public, 2004, v. 108, no. 2, p. 347-380.) [C.I.J., p. 351, 354, 358, 361, 369, 374.]

Alexandrov, Stanimir A.: The "baby boom" of treaty-based arbitrations and the jurisdiction of ICSID tribunals: shareholders as "investors" and jurisdiction ratione temporis. (In: Law and Practice of International Courts and Tribunals, 2005, v. 4, no. 1, p. 19-59.) [I.C.J., p. 27-28, 40, 55-56.]

Alford, Roger P.: Reflections on US – Zeroing: study in judicial overreaching by the WTO Appellate Body. (In: Columbia Journal of Transnational Law, 2006, v. 45, p. 196-220.) [P.C.I.J., p. 203.]

Anand, Ram Prakash: Effectiveness of international judicial procedures in the settlement of international disputes. (In: Dynamics of international law in the new millennium, ed. by Dixit, R. K.; Jayaraj, C. New Delhi: Indian Society of International Law, 2004, p. 61-81.) [P.C.I.J., p. 64-65; I.C.J., passim.]

Barral, Welber: Organização Mundial do Comércio (O.M.C.). (Dans: Tribunais internacionais: mecanismos contemporâneos de solução de controvérsias, sous la dir. de Welber Barral. Florianópolis: Fundação Boiteux, 2004, p. 31-55.) [C.I.J., p. 32.]

Bartels, Lorand: The separation of powers in the W.T.O.: how to avoid judicial activism. (In: International and Comparative Law Quarterly, 2004, v. 53, no. 4, p. 861-895.) [P.C.I.J., p. 882-883; I.C.J., p. 869-870, 873-874, 880, 882, 885, 889.]

Broude, Tomer: "Judges shalt though make thee in all thy gates": reforming judicial office in the WTO dispute settlement system. Toronto: [s.n.], 2006. (Law and economics research paper; p. 02-06.) [I.C.J., passim.]

Broude, Tomer: International judicial bodies as sources of normativity: the WTO dispute settlement system in comparative context. (In: Governance and international legal theory, ed. by Dekker, Ige F.; Werner, Wouter G.. Leiden; Boston, 2004, p. 237-275.) [P.C.I.J., p. 245-246; I.C.J., p. 239, 242, 245-247, 248-258, 262, 264-271, 274-275.]

Brower, Charles H.: The functions and limits of arbitration and judicial settlement under private and public international law. (In: Duke Journal of Comparative and International Law, 2008, v. 18, no. 2, p. 259-309.)

Brownlie, Ian: The peaceful settlement of international disputes (the Wang Tieya lecture in public international law). (In: Chinese Journal of International Law, 2009, v. 8, no. 2, p. 267-283.)

Buergenthal, Thomas: The proliferation of disputes, dispute settlement procedures and respect for the rule of law. (In: ICSID Review: Foreign Investment Law Journal, 2006, v. 21, p. 126-131.) [P.C.I.J., p. 129; I.C.J., p. 129, 130.]

Buergenthal, Thomas: The proliferation of disputes, dispute settlement procedures and respect for the rule of law. (In: Arbitration international, 2006, v. 22, no. 4, p. 495-499.) [I.C.J., p. 496, 497.]

Burgis, Michelle: The promise of solid ground: Arab territorial diputes and the discourse of international law. (In: International Community Law Review, 2008, v. 10, no. 1, p. 73-99.)

Caflisch, Lucius: Judicial means for settling water disputes. (In: Resolution of international water disputes: papers emanating from the Sixth PCA International Law Seminar, November 8, 2002. The Hague, [etc.]: Kluwer Law International, 2003, p. 235-245.) [I.C.J., p. 237, 239-241, 244.]

Canal-Forgues, Eric: Le règlement des différends à l'OMC. Bruxelles: Bruylant, 2008. [C.I.J., p. 9, 20, 95, 97, 98, 101, 118.]

Christofides, Jack: How good offices changed the nature of the border dispute between Cameroon and Nigeria. (In: Conflict prevention in practice: essays in honour of James Sutterlin, ed. by Bertrand G. Ramcharan. Leiden, [etc.]: Martinus Nijhoff, 2005, p. 211-217.) [I.C.J., p. 211-213, 215.]

Costa e Silva, Paula: A resolução de controvérsias na Convenção das Nações Unidas sobre o direito do mar. (Dans: Estudos em homenagem ao Prof. Doutor Armando M. Marques Guedes: direito constitucional, direito administrativo, direito internacional e direito do mar, direito comunitário europeu, outras áreas, sous la dir. de Miranda, Jorge. Lisbon: Coimbra Editora, 2004, p. 541-601.) [I.C.J., p. 586-591.]

Dolzer, Rudolf: Meistbegünstigungsklauseln in Investitionsschutzverträgen. (In: Internationale Gemeinschaft und Menschenrechte: Festschrift für Georg Ress zum 70. Geburtstag am 21. Januar 2005, ed. by Bröhmer, Jürgen; Bieber, Roland; Calliess, Christian; Langenfeld, Christine; Weber, Stefan; Wolf, Joachim. Köln [etc.]: Heymann, 2005, p. 47-54.) [I.C.J., p. 48.]

East Africa Law Society: The jurisprudence on regional and international tribunals digest. Nairobi: LawAfrica, 2007. (EALS practice manual series; 5.) [P.C.I.J., p. 217; I.C.J., p. ix, x, 217-219, 221, 223-270.]

Epiney, Astrid: Durchsetzungsmechanismen im Umweltvölkerrecht: ausgewählte Aspekte und Perspektiven. (In: Schweizerische Zeitschrift für internationales und europäisches Recht, 2005, v. 15, p. 429-443.) [I.C.J., p. 436.]

Eyffinger, Arthur and Kooijmans, Pieter H.: Vreedzame geschillenbeslechting. (In: Handboek internationaal recht, ed. by Horbach, Nathalie L. J. T.; Lefeber, René; Ribbelink, Olivier. The Hague: T.M.C. Asser Press, 2007, p. 347-384.) [P.C.I.J., p. 367-368, 372, 374; I.C.J., p. 350, 354, 362, 368, 372-384.]

Finke, Jasper: Die Parallelität internationaler Streitbeilegungsmechanismen: Untersuchung der aus der Stärkung der internationalen Gerichtsbarkeit resultierenden Konflikte. Berlin: Duncker & Humblot, 2004. (Veröffentlichungen des Walther-Schücking-Instituts für Internationales Recht an der Universität Kiel; 147.) [I.C.J., p. 17, 25-31, 35, 69-70, 103-124, 152-153, 155, 164, 170, 184-185, 202-203, 206-207, 210, 241, 271, 279-280, 288-290, 292-294, 296, 300, 301-303, 307-312, 314, 320-321, 324, 327, 329-331, 341-342, 347, 349-352, 356-374; P.C.I.J., p. 18, 26, 342-346, 348, 353, 357, 365, 369-370, 374.]

Fois, Paolo: Il nuovo ordine internazionale, il regionalismo e la soluzione pacifica delle controversie. (Dans: Studi di diritto internazionale in onore di Gaetano Arangio-Ruiz, sous la dir. de Giovanni Battaglini; Paolo Benvenuti; Antonio Cassese; Giorgio Gaja. Napoli: Editoriale Scientifica, 2004, v. 2, p. 997-1018.) [C.I.J., p. 1017.]

Foucher, Michel: L'obsession des frontières. Paris: Perrin, 2007. [C.I.J., p. 45-46, 48, 59, 65-66, 69-70.]

French, Duncan: Environmental dispute settlement: the first (hesitant) signs of spring? (In: Hague Yearbook of International Law, 2006, v. 19, p. 3-32.) [I.C.J., p. 3, 6-16.]

Friedman, Mark and Laird, Ian and Mathieu, Emily J. and Michaels, Steven and O'Gorman, Kevin and Prager, Dietmar W. and Sabater, Anibal and Sheppard Jr., Ben H.: International arbitration. (In: International Lawyer, 2007, v. 41, p. 251-290.) [P.C.I.J., p. 284.]

Gaillard, Emmanuel: Centre International pour le Règlement des Différends relatifs aux Investissements (CIRDI): chronique des sentences arbitrales. (Dans: Journal du droit international, 2004, v. 131, p. 213-287.) [C.I.J., p. 225, 242, 264, 279.]

Gaillard, Emmanuel: La jurisprudence du CIRDI. Paris: Pedone, 2004. [C.I.J., p. 35, 72, 166, 171, 179-181, 197, 262, 315, 324, 327, 334, 350, 520, 534-535, 588, 660-661, 798-799, 887; C.P.J.I., p. 47, 102, 236, 308, 324, 350-351, 355-356, 368, 372, 533-534.]

Gehring, Markus W.: Strategic use of litigation to influence negotiations: the WTO, the EU and the UN: use of litigation to influence negotiations. (In: Select Proceedings of the European Society of International Law, 2008, v. 2, p. 356-377.) [I.C.J., p. 360-362, 375.]

Giardina, Andrea: Responsabilità internazionale, esaurimento dei mezzi interni di ricorso e carattere sussidiario della tutela internazionale dei diritti dell'uomo. (Dans: Studi di diritto internazionale in onore di Gaetano Arangio-Ruiz, sous la dir. de Giovanni Battaglini; Paolo Benvenuti; Antonio Cassese; Giorgio Gaja. Napoli: Editoriale Scientifica, 2004, v. 2, p. 1019-1037.) [C.I.J., p. 1019, 1026.]

González Napolitano, Silvina S.: Las medidas provisionales en derecho internacional ante las cortes y tribunales internacionales. Buenos Aires: Facultad de derecho UBA; La Ley, 2004. [C.P.J.I., p. 2, 16, 44, 48, 55, 86, 98, 130, 137-138, 166, 168, 188; C.I.J., passim.]

Haersolte-van Hof, Jacomijn J., van: The revitalization of the Permanent Court of Arbitration. (In: Netherlands International Law Review, 2007, v. 54, p. 395-413.) [P.C.I.J., p. 398, 400; I.C.J., p. 398-400, 410-411, 413.]

Happ, Richard and Rubins, Noah: Awards and Decisions of ICSID tribunals in 2006. (In: German Yearbook of International Law, 2006, v. 49, p. 623-663.) [I.C.J., p. 632, 653.]

Hoffmeister, Frank and Ondrusek, Petr: The European Community in international litigation. (In: Revue Hellénique de Droit International, 2008, v. 61, p. 205-224.) [I.C.J., p. 210-214.]

Hout, Tjaco T. van den: Resolution of international disputes: the role of the Permanent Court of Arbitration – reflections on the centenary of the 1907 Convention for the Pacific Settlement of International Disputes. (In: Leiden Journal of International Law, 2008, v. 21, no. 3, p. 643-661.)

International Center for Settlement of Investment Disputes: Case No. ARB/03/4. Empresas Lucchetti, S.A. and Lucchetti Peru, S.A. (Claimants) v. Republic of Peru (Respondent): Award. (In: ICSID Review: Foreign Investment Law Journal, 2004, v. 19, no. 2, p. 359-388.) [I.C.J. and P.C.I.J., p. 382.]

International Center for Settlement of Investment Disputes: Caso No. ARB/03-4. Empresas Lucchetti, S.A. y Lucchetti Perú, S.A. (Demandantes) v. La República del Perú (Demandada): Laudo. (Dans: ICSID Review: Foreign Investment Law Journal, 2004, v. 19, no. 2, p. 389-421.) [C.P.J.I., p. 414-415; C.I.J., p. 414.]

International Center for Settlement of Investment Disputes: In the proceeding between Joy Mining Machinery Limited (Claimant) and The Arab Republic of Egypt (Respondent) (ICSID Case No. ARB/03/11): Award on jurisdiction. (In: ICSID Review: Foreign Investment Law Journal, 2004, v. 19, no. 2, p. 486-514.) [I.C.J. and P.C.I.J., p. 521-513.]

Johnston, Angus and Powles, Edward: The kings of the world and their dukes' dilemma: globalisation, jurisdiction and the rule of law. (In:

Globalisation and jurisdiction, ed. by Piet Jan Slot; Mielle Bulterman. Leiden: Kluwer Law International, 2004, p. 13-54.) [I.C.J., p. 25, 38; P.C.I.J., p. 21.]

Justenhoven, Heinz-Gerhard: Internationale Schiedsgerichtsbarkeit: ethische Norm und Rechtswirklichkeit. Stuttgart: W. Kohlhammer, 2006. (Theologie und Frieden; 30.) [P.C.I.J., p. 23, 185, 211-214, 232; I.C.J., p. 23, 185, 217-232.]

Jütersonke, Oliver: Hans J. Morgenthau on the limits of justiciability in international law. (In: Journal of the History of International Law, 2006, v. 8, p. 181-211.) [P.C.I.J., p. 194; I.C.J., p. 190.]

Kawano, Mariko: The role of judicial procedures in the process of the pacific settlement of international disputes. (In: Recueil des cours de l'Académie de droit international de La Haye, 2009, v. 346, p. 9-473.) [P.C.I.J. and I.C.J., passim.]

Keith, Kenneth: Member of the Permanent Court of Arbitration. (In: Sir Ninian Stephen: a tribute, ed. by Timothy L. H. McCormack; Cheryl Saunders. Carlton: Miegunyah Press, 2007, p. 155-175.)

Kerbrat, Yann: Le différend relatif à l'usine MOX de Sellafield (Irlande/Royaume Uni): connexité des procédures et droit d'accès à l'information en matière environnementale. (Dans: Annuaire français de droit international, 2004, v. 50, p. 607-623.) [C.P.J.I., p. 612; C.I.J., p. 618-619, 621-623.]

Khan, Daniel-Erasmus: Max Huber as arbitrator: the Palmas (Miangas) Case and other arbitrations. (In: European Journal of International Law, 2007, v. 18, p. 145-170.) [P.C.I.J., p. 157, 170; I.C.J., p. 161-162, 168.]

Kleffner, Jann K. and Nollkaemper, André: The relationship between internationalized courts and national courts. (In: Internationalized criminal courts and tribunals: Sierra Leone, East Timor, Kosovo and Cambodia, ed. by Cesare P. R. Romano; André Nollkaemper; Jann K. Kleffner. Oxford: Oxford University Press, 2004, p. 359-378.) [I.C.J., p. 377.]

Kolb, Robert: Note sur certaines caractéristiques du différend international. (Dans: Global Community: Yearbook of International Law and Jurisprudence, 2004, v. 4, no. 1, p. 227-242.) [P.C.I.J., p. 239; I.C.J., p. 227, 230-234, 238-241.]

Kooijmans, Pieter H.: The role of non-State actors and international dispute settlement. (In: From government to governance: the growing impact of non-state actors on the international and European legal system: proceedings of the Sixth Hague Joint Conference held in The Hague, The Netherlands, 3-5 July 2003, ed. by Heere, Wybo P. The Hague: T.M.C. Asser Press, 2004, p. 21-27.) [I.C.J., passim.]

Labrecque, Georges: Les différends internationaux en Asie: règlement judiciaire. Paris: Harmattan, 2007. (Logiques Juridiques.)

Lasmar, Jorge Mascarenhas et Rangel, Leandro de Alencar: Desafios contemporâneos dos sistemas de solução de controvérsias internacionais. (Dans: O Brasil e os novos desafios do direito internacional, sous la dir. de Brant, Leonardo Nemer Caldeira. Rio de Janeiro: Editora Forense, 2004, p. 695-712.) [C.I.J., p. 704-707.]

Lauterpacht Research Centre for International Law: International dispute settlement in an evolving global society: constitutionalization, accessibility, privatization. Cambridge [etc.]: Cambridge University Press, 2004. (Hersch Lauterpacht memorial lectures; 2001.) [P.C.I.J., p. 30-31, 50, 57-58; I.C.J., p. 10, 17-22, 24-28, 33-34, 40-43, 47, 59-61, 75, 97, 100-101, 103, 111, 116, 120-122, 125.]

Lehmann, Matthias: A plea for a transnational approach to arbitrability in arbitral practice. (In: Columbia Journal of Transnational Law, 2004, v. 42, no. 3, p. 753-775.) [I.C.J., p. 754.]

LG&E Energy Corp. LG&E Capital Corp. LG&E International Inc. (Claimants) and Argentine Republic (Respondent). ICSID Case No. ARB/02/1. Decision on Liability. (In: ICSID Review: Foreign Investment Law Journal, 2006, v. 21, p. 203-268.) [P.C.I.J., p. 251; I.C.J., p. 240.]

López Escarcena, Sebastián: La falta de jurisdicción ratione temporis en el caso Lucchetti: comentario a laudo del Centro Internacional de Arreglo de Diferencias Relativas a Inversiones, 7 de febrero de 2005. (Dans: Revista chilena de derecho, 2006, v. 33, p. 159-165.) [C.P.J.I., p. 163-164; C.I.J., p. 163.]

López Martín, Ana Gemma: Una comisión arbitral singular para una compleja controversia fronteriza: la sentencia de 13 de abril de 2002 relativa a la delimitación de la frontera entre Eritrea y Etiopía. (Dans: Cuadernos de jurisprudencia internacional, 2005, v. 2, p. 7-43.) [C.I.J., p. 12-15, 22-30, 34, 40-43.]

Lucchini, Laurent: Erythrée-Ethiopie: l'enlisement. (Dans: Annuaire français de droit international, 2004, v. 50, p. 389-415.) [C.I.J., p. 394, 401-403.]

Marboe, Irmgard: Compensation and damages in international law: the limits of "fair market value". (In: The Journal of World Investment & Trade, 2006, v. 7, no. 5, p. 723-759.) [P.C.I.J., p. 727-728, 732, 751-753; I.C.J., p. 754.]

Marchi, Jean-François: Le règlement des affaires Lockerbie et du DC-10 d'UTA: indemnités et questions connexes. (Dans: Annuaire français de droit international, 2004, v. 50, p. 173-212.) [C.I.J., p. 174, 182, 184-185, 206.]

McLachlan, Campbell: The continuing controversy over provisional measures in international disputes. (In: International Law FORUM du droit international, 2005, v. 7, no. 1, p. 5-15.) [I.C.J., p. 5-6, 13-14.]

Mendelson, Maurice H.: International dispute settlement: developments and challenges. (In: Revue Hellénique de Droit International, 2008, v. 61, p. 463-475.) [I.C.J., p. 466-467, 469, 471-472, 474.]

Merck, Billy: International law and the nuclear threat in Kashmir: a proposal for a U.S.-led resolution to the dispute under UN authority. (In: Georgia Journal of International and Comparative Law, 2004, v. 32, no. 1, p. 167-197.) [I.C.J., p. 174-175, 192.]

Merrills, John G.: International dispute settlement. Cambridge [etc.]: Cambridge University Press, 2005. 4th [expanded and updated] ed. [I.C.J., see index p. 376-377.]

Merrills, John G.: The mosaic of international dispute settlement procedures: complementary or contradictory? (In: Netherlands International Law Review, 2007, v. 54, p. 361-393.) [I.C.J., p. 363-364, 367-370, 372, 374, 381-382, 385-386, 389-392.]

Methanex Corporation v. United States of America. (In: ICSID Reports, 2005, v. 7, p. 208-284.) [I.C.J., p. 233, 263-268.]

Michels, Gilson Wessler: Tribunal internacional do direito do mar. (Dans: Tribunais internacionais: mecanismos contemporâneos de solução de controvérsias, sous la dir. de Welber Barral. Florianópolis: Fundação Boiteux, 2004, p. 89-112.) [C.I.J., p. 90-91, 94, 98, 102.]

Milano, Enrico: La sentenza arbitrale fra Italia e Costa Rica relativa ad un prestito. (Dans: Rivista di diritto internazionale, 2007, v. 90, p. 161-180.) [C.P.J.I., p. 166; C.I.J., p. 166-167, 178-179.]

Mitchell, Andrew D.: Proportionality and remedies in WTO disputes. (In: European Journal of International Law, 2006, v. 17, p. 985-1008.) [I.C.J., p. 992, 1004.]

Monaghan, Henry Paul: Article III and supranational judicial review. (In: Columbia Law Review, 2007, v. 107, no. 4, p. 833-882.) [I.C.J., p. 841, 846-850, 879-881.]

Mourre, Alexis: Are amicus curiae the proper response to the public's concerns on transparency in investment arbitration? (In: Law and Practice of International Courts and Tribunals, 2006, v. 5, p. 257-271.) [I.C.J., p. 260-261.]

Oeter, Stefan: Comment: [on Unity and diversity of international law in the settlement of international disputes by Beate Rudolf]. (In: Unity and diversity in international law: proceedings of an international symposium of the Kiel Walther Schücking Institute of International Law, November 4-7, 2004, ed. by Zimmermann, Andreas; Hofmann, Rainer. Berlin: Duncker & Humblot, 2006, p. 419-423.) [I.C.J., p. 419-421.]

Orakhelashvili, Alexander: Interpretation of jurisdictional instruments in international dispute settlement. (In: Law and Practice of International Courts and Tribunals, 2007, v. 6, p. 159-188.) [P.C.I.J., p. 159, 162, 170-172; I.C.J., p. 162-169, 172-182, 184-187.]

Pancotto Bohrer Munhoz, Carolina: Centro de solução de controvérsias sobre investimentos (I.C.S.I.D.). (Dans: Tribunais internacionais: mecanismos contemporâneos de solução de controvérsias, sous la dir. de

Welber Barral. Florianópolis : Fundação Boiteux, 2004, p. 113-132.) [C.I.J., p. 124.]

Pauwelyn, Joost : The World Trade Organization. (In : L'influence des sources sur l'unité et la fragmentation du droit international : travaux du séminaire tenu à Palma, les 20-21 mai 2005, ed. by Rosario Huesa Vinaixa ; Karel Wellens. Bruxelles : Bruylant, 2006, p. 211-229.) [P.C.I.J., p. 224; I.C.J., p. 224-225.]

Poissonnier, Ghislain : Le Timor oriental et l'espoir contrarié d'un grand soleil levant. (Dans : Journal du droit international, 2005, v. 132, p. 763-783.) [C.I.J., p. 768-769, 774-778.]

Pope and Talbot Inc. v. Government of Canada. (In : ICSID Reports, 2005, v. 7, p. 43-172.) [I.C.J., p. 159, 163.]

Posner, Eric A. : The decline of the International Court of Justice. (In : International conflict resolution, ed. by Stefan Voigt ; Max Albert ; Dieter Schmidtchen. Tübingen : Mohr Siebeck, 2006, p. 111-142.)

Raymond, Gregory A. : International adjudication and conflict management. (In : Sovereignty and the global community : the quest for order in the international system, ed. by Hensel, Howard M. Aldershot [etc.] : Ashgate, 2004, p. 221-248.) [P.C.I.J., p. 223-224; I.C.J., passim.]

Rigo Sureda, Andres : Precedent in investment treaty arbitration. (In : International investment law for the 21st century : essays in honour of Christoph Schreuer, ed. by Christina Binder. New York : Oxford University Press, 2009, p. 830-842.)

Rosenne, Shabtai : The Jaffa-Jerusalem Railway arbitration (1922). (In : Essays on international law and practice, by Shabtai Rosenne. Leiden ; Boston : Martinus Nijhoff, 2007, p. 295-352.)

Rudolf, Beate : Unity and diversity of international law in the settlement of international disputes. (In : Unity and diversity in international law : proceedings of an international symposium of the Kiel Walther Schücking Institute of International Law, November 4-7, 2004, ed. by Zimmermann, Andreas ; Hofmann, Rainer. Berlin : Duncker & Humblot, 2006, p. 389-418.) [P.C.I.J., p. 396; I.C.J., p. 390, 392, 396-397, 400-402, 407-408, 413, 414, 416.]

Ruiz Abou-Nigm, Verónica : Ancillary jurisdiction for interim measures of protection in support of cross-border litigation. (In : Uniform Law Review, 2005, v. 10, no. 4, p. 759-784.)

Saccucci, Andrea : Il Protocollo istitutivo della Corte africana dei diritti dell'uomo e dei popoli : un primo confronto con le altre corti regionali. (Dans : Rivista di diritto internazionale, 2004, v. 87, no. 4, p. 1036-1065.) [C.P.J.I., p. 1062.]

Sacerdoti, Georges : Structure et fonction du système de règlement des différends de l'O.M.C. : les enseignements des dix premières années.

(Dans : Revue générale de droit international public, 2006, v. 110, p. 769-800.) [C.I.J., p. 781-782.]

Sands, Philippe : Non-compliance and dispute settlement. (In : Ensuring compliance with multilateral environmental agreements : a dialogue between practitioners and academia, ed. by Ulrich Beyerlin ; Peter-Tobias Stoll ; Rüdiger Wolfrum. Leiden ; Boston : Martinus Nijhoff, 2006, p. 353-358.) [I.C.J., p. 354, 356-358.]

Scott, Karen N. : Managing sovereignty and jurisdictional disputes in the Antarctic : the next fifty years. (In : Yearbook of International Environmental Law, 2009, v. 20, p. 3-40.) [I.C.J., p. 8-9.]

Shany, Yuval : Jurisdictional competition between national and international courts : could international jurisdiction-regulating rules apply? (In : Netherlands Yearbook of International Law, 2006, v. 37, p. 3-56.) [P.C.I.J., p. 4, 21, 24, 29, 33, 35, 39-40, 48; I.C.J., p. 8, 17, 19, 22, 24-25, 40-42, 51-54.]

Sluiter, Göran : Legal assistance to internationalized criminal courts and tribunals. (In : Internationalized criminal courts and tribunals : Sierra Leone, East Timor, Kosovo and Cambodia, ed. by Cesare P. R. Romano ; André Nollkaemper ; Jann K. Kleffner. Oxford : Oxford University Press, 2004, p. 379-406.) [I.C.J., p. 383.]

Sourgens, Frédéric Gilles : ICSID arbitration and the importance of public accountability of a private judicature : a roman law perspective. (In : International Community Law Review, 2007, v. 9, no. 1, p. 59-102.) [I.C.J., p. 73.]

Tomka, Peter : Comment : [on Unity and diversity of international law in the settlement of international disputes by Beate Rudolf]. (In : Unity and diversity in international law : proceedings of an international symposium of the Kiel Walther Schücking Institute of International Law, November 4-7, 2004, ed. by Zimmermann, Andreas ; Hofmann, Rainer. Berlin : Duncker & Humblot, 2006, p. 425-432.) [P.C.I.J., p. 425, 431; I.C.J., p. 427-431.]

United Parcel Service of America Inc. v. Government of Canada : award on jurisdiction, 22 November 2002. (In : ICSID Reports, 2005, v. 7, p. 285-317.) [I.C.J., p. 296-297, 307.]

Vereshchetin, Vladlen S. : Some reflections of a Russian scholar on the legacy of the Second Peace Conference. (In : Actualité de la Conférence de La Haye de 1907, deuxième Conférence de la Paix : colloque La Haye, 6-7 septembre 2007, ed. by Daudet, Yves. Leiden [etc.] : Martinus Nijhoff, 2008, p. 41-50.) [I.C.J., p. 41, 42, 44, 48, 49.]

Vinuesa, Raúl Emilio : Jurisdictional objections to ICSID arbitration under bilateral investment treaties. (In : Internationale Gemeinschaft und Menschenrechte : Festschrift für Georg Ress zum 70. Geburtstag am 21. Januar 2005, ed. by Bröhmer, Jürgen ; Bieber, Roland ; Calliess, Christian ; Langenfeld, Christine ; Weber, Stefan ; Wolf, Joachim. Köln [etc.] : Heymann, 2005, p. 331-355.) [I.C.J., p. 331-355.]

Vranes, Erich: Jurisdiction and applicable law in WTO dispute settlement. (In: German Yearbook of International Law, 2005, v. 48, p. 265-289.) [I.C.J., p. 269, 272.]

Wälde, Thomas W.: Methods for settling boundary disputes: escaping from the fetters of zero-sum outcomes. (In: Journal of World Investment, 2003, vol. 4, no. 1, p. 51-61.) [I.C.J., passim.]

Wasum-Rainer, Susanne and Schlegel, Daniela: The UNCLOS dispute settlement system: between Hamburg and The Hague. (In: German Yearbook of International Law, 2005, v. 48, p. 187-222.) [P.C.I.J., p. 211; I.C.J., p. 188-189, 194, 196-200, 202-213, 216, 218-222.]

Watts, Arthur: Preparation for international litigation. (In: Law of the sea, environmental law and settlement of disputes: liber amicorum Judge Thomas A. Mensah, ed. by Tafsir Malick Ndiaye; Rüdiger Wolfrum. Leiden; Boston: Martinus Nijhoff, 2007, p. 327-340.) [I.C.J., p. 333-334, 336-40.]

Wautelet, Patrick: What has international private law achieved in meeting the challenges posed by globalisation? (In: Globalisation and jurisdiction, ed. by Piet Jan Slot; Mielle Bulterman. Leiden: Kluwer Law International, 2004, p. 55-77.) [P.C.I.J., p. 59.]

Weckel, Philippe et Aréou, Guillaume: Cour permanente d'arbitrage: sentence partielle du 17 mars 2006, Saluka Investments c. République tchèque. (Dans: Revue générale de droit international public, 2006, v. 110, p. 497-502.) [C.I.J., p. 500.]

Weckel, Philippe (sous la dir. de): Cour permanente d'arbitrage. Commission des frontières (Ethiopie/Erythrée). Communication du 27 novembre 2006. (Dans: Revue générale de droit international public, 2007, v. 111, p. 189-191.) [C.I.J., p. 191.]

Wolfrum, Rüdiger: Comment: [on Unity and diversity of international law in the settlement of international disputes by Beate Rudolf]. (In: Unity and diversity in international law: proceedings of an international symposium of the Kiel Walther Schücking Institute of International Law, November 4-7, 2004, ed. by Zimmermann, Andreas; Hofmann, Rainer. Berlin: Duncker & Humblot, 2006, p. 433-435.) [I.C.J., passim.]

Yaung Chi Oo Trading Pte Ltd v. Government of the Union of Myanmar (ASEAN ID Case No ARB/01/1). (In: International Law Reports, 2005, v. 127, p. 42-87.) [I.C.J., p. 51.]

Yesilirmak, Ali: Provisional measures in international commercial arbitration. The Hague: Kluwer Law International, 2005. (International Arbitration Law Library; 13.) [P.C.I.J., p. xxxvi, 72, 201; I.C.J., p. xxxv, 167-168, 173, 175-176, 191, 201, 222.]

Zhang, Naigen: Implementation of WTO dispute settlement. (In: Manchester Journal of International Economic Law, 2008, v. 5, no. 2, p. 111-125.) [I.C.J., p. 123-124.]

17. Organisation des Nations Unies
17. United Nations Organization

Abass, Ademola: The competence of the Security Council to terminate the jurisdiction of the International Criminal Court. (In: Texas International Law Journal, 2005, v. 40, no. 2, p. 263-297.) [P.C.I.J., p. 289-290; I.C.J., p. 277, 280, 283, 285, 288, 291-292, 296-297.]

Alvarez, José E.: International organizations as law-makers. Oxford [etc.]: Oxford University Press, 2005. [P.C.I.J., p. 20-22, 77, 87-88, 93, 98, 108, 293, 464, 485, 488, 532, 601, 611; I.C.J., p. ix, xvi, 4, 8, 11-12, 36, 44, 47-49, 52, 65, 67-68, 70-71, 73, 74-81, 82, 83-84, 87-90, 92-93, 95-98, 102-108, 116, 119, 123-124, 126-127, 130-135, 140, 149, 153, 160-162, 174, 186, 188-191, 193, 226, 258, 261, 267, 316, 388-389, 393, 412, 415-416, 419-422, 424, 428-432, 439, 442-444, 446, 448-450, 454, 458-463, 480, 485-501, 503-504, 506, 510, 514, 517-520, 523-532, 535-540, 544, 545-548, 550-551, 553-554, 558, 561-565, 568, 578-582, 598, 605, 608-611, 613, 636, 638, 640.]

Annan, Kofi A.: In larger freedom: towards development, security and human rights for all: report of the Secretary-General. New York, NY: United Nations, 2005. [I.C.J., p. 50.]

Arcari, Maurizio: L'articolo 40 della Carta delle Nazioni Unite e le misure provvisorie del Consiglio di sicurezza. (Dans: Studi di diritto internazionale in onore di Gaetano Arangio-Ruiz, sous la dir. de Giovanni Battaglini; Paolo Benvenuti; Antonio Cassese; Giorgio Gaja. Napoli: Editoriale Scientifica, 2004, v. 3, p. 1469-1526.) [C.I.J., p. 1507, 1511, 1515-1516, 1523.]

Arcari, Maurizio: Observations sur les problèmes juridiques posés par les sanctions des Nations Unies et leur évolution récente. (Dans: Anuario español de derecho internacional, 2006, v. 22, p. 317-348.) [C.I.J., p. 333, 337, 343.]

Arcari, Maurizio: Remarques occasionnelles sur les contradictions de l'action du Conseil de sécurité dans le domaine des droits de l'homme. (Dans: Anuario de derecho internacional, 2004, v. 20, p. 3-33.) [C.I.J., p. 32-33.]

Ardault, Karine et Arion, Cristina-Maria et Gnamou-Petauton, Dandi et Yetongnon, Marina: L'administration internationale de territoire à l'épreuve du Kosovo et du Timor oriental: la pratique à la recherche d'une théorie. (Dans: Revue belge de droit international, 2006, v. 39, p. 300-383.) [C.P.J.I., p. 313; C.I.J., p. 304, 324, 328, 332.]

Arnauld, Andreas von: UN-Sanktionen und gemeinschaftsrechtlicher Grundrechtsschutz: die "Soweit-Rechtssprechung" des Europäischen Gerichts Erster Instanz. (In: Archiv des Völkerrechts, 2006, v. 44, p. 201-216.) [I.C.J. p. 205, 208-209.]

Aston, Jurij D.: Sekundärgesetzgebung internationaler Organisationen zwischen mitgliedstaatlicher Souveränität und Gemeinschaftsdisziplin. Berlin: Duncker & Humblot, 2004. 1. Aufl. (Schriften zum Völkerrecht; 158.)

[I.C.J., p. 25-27, 33, 39, 74, 82-84, 96, 98, 119, 121, 123, 164, 176, 200-202, 210, 212, 215, 217-221.]

Bantekas, Ilias: United Nations employment law and the causes for its failed senior female appointments record. (In: International Organizations Law Review, 2009, v. 6, no. 1, p. 225-256.) [I.C.J., p. 230, 250, 251, 253.]

Bennouna, Mohamed: Should the United Nations be changed? (In: Global Community: Yearbook of International Law and Jurisprudence, 2004, v. 4, no. 1, p. 3-9.) [I.C.J., p. 4.]

Berman, Frank: The authorization model: Resolution 678 and its effects. (In: The UN Security Council: from the Cold War to the 21st century, ed. by David M. Malone. Boulder: Lynne Rienner Publishers, 2004, p. 153-165.) [I.C.J., p. 157, 163.]

Berman, Frank: The ILC within the UN's legal framework: its relationship with the Sixth Committee. (In: German Yearbook of International Law, 2006, v. 49, p. 107-127.) [I.C.J., p. 107.]

Bianchi, Andrea: Assessing the effectiveness of the UN Security Council's anti-terrorism measures: the quest for legitimacy and cohesion. (In: European Journal of International Law, 2006, v. 17, p. 881-919.) [I.C.J., p. 887, 889-890, 912.]

Bij een zestige verjaardag. (In: VN Forum, 2004, 2004/3, v. 17, no. 4, p. 3-8.) [I.C.J., p. 5, 7.]

Blanco-Bazán, Agustín: I.M.O.: historical highlights in the life of a U.N. agency. (In: Journal of the History of International Law, 2004, v. 6, no. 2, p. 259-283.) [I.C.J., p. 265-266.]

Blatt, Henning: Rechtsschutz gegen die Vereinten Nationen: Internationale Immunitäten und die Streitbeilegung nach Section 29 des Übereinkommens über die Vorrechte und Immunitäten der Vereinten Nationen. (In: Archiv des Völkerrechts, 2007, v. 45, p. 84-114.) [I.C.J. p. 87, 89-90, 95-96, 100, 106-108, 110-111.]

Blum, Yehuda Zvi: Proposals for U.N. Security Council reform. (In: American Journal of International Law, 2005, v. 99, p. 632-649.) [I.C.J., p. 637.]

Bore Eveno, Valérie: Le contrôle juridictionnel des résolutions du Conseil de sécurité: vers un constitutionnalisme international? (Dans: Revue générale de droit international public, 2006, v. 110, p. 827-860.) [C.I.J., p. 828, 830, 832, 834-836, 839-840, 847, 851-852, 854-855, 857.]

Bot, Bernard Rudolf: Verslag van de herfstzitting van de 59e Assemblee van de Algemene Vergadering van de Verenigde Naties (September – December 2004). (In: VN Forum, 2005, 2005/1, v. 18, no. 1, p. 30-35.) [I.C.J., p. 31.]

Campanelli, Danio: The United Nations Compensation Commission (UNCC): reflections on its judicial character. (In: Law and Practice of

International Courts and Tribunals, 2005, v. 4, no. 1, p. 107-139.) [P.C.I.J., p. 122, 136; I.C.J., p. 110, 122, 124, 129, 132, 135.]

Cançado Trindade, A. A.: Direito das organizações internacionais. Belo Horizonte: Del Rey, 2009. 4a ed. revista, atualizada e ampliada [C.P.I.J. et C.I.J., voir index p. 810.]

Cannizzaro, Enzo: A machiavellian moment? The UN Security Council and the rule of law. (In: International Organizations Law Review, 2006, v. 3, p. 189-224.) [I.C.J., p. 190, 191-197, 201.]

Christakis, Théodore et Bannelier, Karine: Acteur vigilant ou spectateur impuissant? Le contrôle exercé par le Conseil de sécurité sur les Etats autorisés à recourir à la force. (Dans: Revue belge de droit international, 2004, v. 37, p. 498-527.) [C.I.J., p. 501, 512.]

Churchill, Robin Rolf: Dispute settlement under the UN Convention on the Law of the Sea: survey for 2006. (In: International Journal of Marine and Coastal Law, 2007, v. 22, no. 4, p. 463-484.)

Colavitti, Romélien: L'O.N.U. et la protection des minorités: un droit coutumier in statu nascendi? (Dans: L'observateur des Nations Unies, 2006, v. 20-21, p. 261-283.) [C.P.J.I., p. 261-262; C.I.J., p. 264, 267, 280.]

Complak, Krystian: Une propuesta posmodernista de conciliar las operaciones de paz de la ONU con la dignidad humana. (Dans: Anuario mexicano de derecho internacional, 2006, v. 6, p. 599-618.) [C.I.J., p. 603, 608-610.]

Conforti, Benedetto: The law and practice of the United Nations. Leiden; Boston: Martinus Nijhoff, 2005. 3rd rev. ed. (Legal aspects of international organization; 42.) [P.C.I.J., p. 75-76, 132-133; I.C.J., p. V, 8-10, 12-16, 34-39, 67, 75-76, 84, 93, 103-110, 112-115, 117, 121-123, 164-165, 193-195, 210, 214, 220, 268-269, 273-282, 285-286, 293, 295, 305-311.]

Corten, Olivier: La participation du Conseil de sécurité à l'élaboration, à la cristallisation ou à la consolidation de règles coutumières. (Dans: Revue belge de droit international, 2004, v. 37, p. 552-567.) [C.I.J., p. 554-556, 558-559, 561, 564.]

D'Argent, Pierre: Le droit de la responsabilité internationale complété? Examen des principes fondamentaux et directives concernant le droit à un recours et à réparation des victimes de violations flagrantes du droit international des droits de l'homme et de violations graves du droit international humanitaire. (Dans: Annuaire français de droit international, 2005, v. 51, p. 27-55.) [C.P.J.I., p. 50; C.I.J., p. 43-44, 50-51.]

d'Aspremont, Jean: Les travaux de la Commission du droit international relatifs aux actes unilatéraux des Etats. (Dans: Revue générale de droit international public, 2005, v. 109, p. 163-189.) [C.I.J., p. 173, 178-180, 183, 187-188; C.P.J.I., p. 187.]

Denis, Catherine: Le pouvoir normatif du Conseil de sécurité des Nations Unies: portée et limites. Bruxelles: Bruylant [etc.], 2004. (Collection de droit international; 58.) [C.I.J., p. 24-25, 27, 41, 51-52, 63, 75-76, 81, 86-87, 176-183, 185, 188-189, 193, 204-204, 208-209, 212, 215-216, 223-228, 239, 242, 244-245, 248, 252, 254-255, 257, 259-261, 276, 347, 370-372, 375, 378; C.P.J.I., p. 25, 63.]

Divac Öberg, Marko: The legal effects of resolutions of the UN Security Council and General Assembly in the jurisprudence of the ICJ. (In: European Journal of International Law, 2005, v. 16, no. 5, p. 879-906.)

Dokumente der Vereinten Nationen: Humanitäres Völkerrecht, Internationaler Terrorismus, Irak-Kuwait, Kleinwaffen, Konfliktfolgezeit, Menschenrechte, Nahost, Privatsektor, Verfahren des Sicherheitsrats. (In: Vereinten Nationen, 2004, v. 52, no. 1, p. 23-35.) [I.C.J., p. 33.]

Dokumente der Vereinten Nationen: Burundi, Côte d'Ivoire, Ehemaliges Jugoslawien, Guinea-Bissau, Haiti, Internationale Strafgerichte, Internationaler Gerichtshof, Irak, Libanon, Liberia, Sudan, Terrorismus, Timor-Leste, Westsahara. (In: Vereinte Nationen, 2005, v. 53, no. 2, p. 67-79.) [I.C.J., p. 74.]

Dominicé, Christian: The international responsibility of the United Nations for injuries resulting from non-military enforcement measures. (In: International responsibility today: essays in memory of Oscar Schachter, ed. by Maurizio Ragazzi. Leiden; Boston: Martinus Nijhoff, 2005, p. 363-370.) [I.C.J., p. 365.]

Dopagne, Frédéric: L'attitude des Etats tiers et de l'ONU à l'égard de l'occupation de l'Irak. (Dans: L'intervention en Irak et le droit international, sous la dir. de Karine Bannelier; Olivier Corten; Théodore Christakis; Pierre Klein. Paris: Pedone, 2004, p. 325-341.) [C.I.J., p. 331-332.]

Duplessis, Isabelle: Le recours à la constitution de l'OIT dans l'acquisition de son autonomie institutionnelle. (Dans: Revue belge de droit international, 2004, v. 37, p. 37-70.) [C.I.J., p. 48; C.P.J.I., p. 47-49.]

Dupuy, Pierre-Marie: Le droit des Nations Unies et sa pratique dans la jurisprudence de la Cour internationale de Justice. (Dans: La pratique et le droit international: colloque de Genève. Paris: A. Pedone, 2004, p. 139-157.)

Elements of Nordic practice 2003: the Nordic countries in co-ordination. (In: Nordic Journal of International Law, 2005, v. 74, no. 1, p. 131-151.) [I.C.J., p. 133.]

Engdahl, Ola: Protection of personnel in peace operations: the role of the "Safety Convention" against the background of general international law. Leiden [etc.]: Martinus Nijhoff, 2007. (International Humanitarian Law Series; 16.) [I.C.J., p. 5, 15, 26, 28, 73, 84, 88, 97, 124, 126, 128, 131, 132, 134, 139, 140, 141, 144, 149, 318, 327.]

Fassbender, Bardo: The better peoples of the United Nations? Europe's practice and the United Nations. (In: European Journal of International Law, 2004, v. 15, no. 5, p. 857-884.) [I.C.J., p. 864, 866, 879.]

Fernández Sánchez, Pablo Antonio: La comisión de consolidación de la paz. (Dans: Revista española de derecho internacional, 2005, v. 57, p. 715-743.) [C.I.J., p. 731-732, 734.]

Fry, James D.: Dionysian disarmament: Security Council WMD coercive disarmament measures and their legal implications. (In: Michigan Journal of International Law, 2008, v. 29, no. 2, p. 197-291.) [I.C.J., p. 199, 207, 221, 236, 250.]

Garcia, Thierry: La réformation des jugements des tribunaux administratifs internationaux. (Dans: Revue de droit international et de droit comparé, 2004, v. 81, no. 1, p. 59-78.) [C.I.J., p. 60-71, 75, 77.]

Gazzini, Tarcisio: The normative element inherent in economic collective enforcement measures: United Nations and European Union practice. (In: Les sanctions économiques en droit international, ed. by Laura Picchio Forlati; Linos-Alexandre Sicilianos. Leiden [etc.]: Martinus Nijhoff, 2004, p. 279-308.) [I.C.J., p. 283-285, 288-290, 293-294.]

Genugten, Willem J. M. van and Grünfeld, Fred and Leurdijk, Dick A.: Internationale rechtshandhaving. (In: Handboek internationaal recht, ed. by Horbach, Nathalie L. J. T.; Lefeber, René; Ribbelink, Olivier. The Hague: T.M.C. Asser Press, 2007, p. 385-436.) [I.C.J., p. 394, 431-432.]

Gestri, Marco: Legal remedies against Security Council targeted sanctions: de lege lata and de lege ferenda options for enhancing the protection of the individual. (In: Italian Yearbook of International Law, 2007, v. 17, p. 25-53.) [I.C.J., p. 37, 51.]

Goulding, Marrack: The UN Secretary-General. (In: The UN Security Council: from the Cold War to the 21st century, ed. by David M. Malone. Boulder: Lynne Rienner Publishers, 2004, p. 267-280.) [I.C.J., p. 269.]

Gray, Christine: A crisis of legitimacy for the UN collective security system? (In: International and Comparative Law Quarterly, 2007, v. 56, p. 157-170.) [I.C.J., p. 164.]

Hinojosa Martínez, Luis M.: Las sanciones del Consejo de seguridad contra Al Qaeda y los Talibanes: ¿ Son realmente inteligentes? (Dans: Revista española de derecho internacional, 2006, v. 58, p. 737-770.) [C.I.J., p. 750, 752-753, 756-757.]

Homan, Kees: "Goed functionerende Verenigde Naties onmisbaar". (In: VN Forum, 2006, 2006/2, v. 19, p. 9-10.) [I.C.J., p. 9.]

Hörmann, Saskia: Völkerrecht bricht Rechtsgemeinschaft? Zu den rechtlichen Folgen einer Umsetzung von Resolutionen des UN-Sicherheitsrates durch die EG. (In: Archiv des Völkerrechts, 2006, v. 44, p. 267-327.) [I.C.J. p. 274, 281-282, 284-285, 287-288, 295, 302.]

Hurd, Ian: After anarchy: legitimacy and power in the United Nations Security Council. Princeton; Oxford: Princeton University Press, 2007. [P.C.I.J., p. 182; I.C.J., see index p. 215.]

Jain, Neha: A separate law for peacekeepers: the clash between the Security Council and the International Criminal Court. (In: European Journal of International Law, 2005, v. 16, no. 2, p. 239-254.) [I.C.J., p. 243-244, 251.]

Katselli, Elena: Holding the Security Council accountable for human rights violations. (In: Human Rights & International Legal Discourse, 2007, v. 1, no. 2, p. 301-334.) [I.C.J., p. 318-324, 326, 328-329.]

Kolb, Robert: Does Article 103 of the Charter of the United Nations apply only to decisions or also to authorizations adopted by the Security Council? (In: Zeitschrift für ausländisches öffentliches Recht und Völkerrecht, 2004, v. 64, no. 1, p. 12-35.) [I.C.J., p. 28, 30.]

Kolliopoulos, Alexandros: Les comités des sanctions de l'Organisation des Nations Unies. (Dans: Les sanctions économiques en droit international, sous la dir. de Laura Picchio Forlati; Linos-Alexandre Sicilianos. Leiden [etc.]: Martinus Nijhoff, 2004, p. 567-601.) [C.I.J., p. 570-571, 584.]

Kot, Jean-Philippe: "Investir dans l'Organisation des Nations Unies pour lui donner les moyens de sa vocation mondiale": une réforme en plus ou une réforme enfin? (Dans: L'observateur des Nations Unies, 2006, v. 20-21, p. 331-343.) [C.I.J., p. 333, 334.]

Krasno, Jean E.: Founding the United Nations: an evolutionary process. (In: The United Nations: confronting the challenges of a global society, by Jean E. Krasno. Boulder London: Lynne Rienner publishers, 2004, p. 19-45.) [C.P.I.J., p. 21; I.C.J., p. 26.]

Krasno, Jean E.: The U.N. landscape: an overview. (In: The United Nations: confronting the challenges of a global society, by Jean E. Krasno. Boulder; London: Lynne Rienner, 2004, p. 3-17.) [I.C.J., p. 4, 9-10, 13.]

Lagrange, Evelyne: Le Conseil de sécurité des Nations Unies peut-il violer le droit international? (Dans: Revue belge de droit international, 2004, v. 37, p. 568-592.) [C.I.J., p. 571, 576, 581-582.]

Langer, Eva and Linde, Eva: Die Tätigkeit der International Law Commission im Jahre 2005. (In: German Yearbook of International Law, 2005, v. 48, p. 625-646.) [I.C.J., p. 631.]

Laurenti, Jeffrey: Financing the United Nations. (In: The United Nations: confronting the challenges of a global society, by Jean E. Krasno. Boulder; London: Lynne Rienner publishers, 2004, p. 278-309.) [I.C.J., p. 278, 279.]

Lavalle, Roberto: A novel, if awkward, exercise in international law-making: Security Council Resolution 1540 (2004). (In: Netherlands International Law Review, 2004, v. 5, no. 3, p. 411-437.) [I.C.J., p. 423, 424, 432.]

Lewin, André: Les Africains à l'ONU. (Dans: Relations internationales, 2006, 128, p. 55-78.) [C.I.J., p. 75-76.]

Lim, Chin L.: The great power balance, the United Nations and what the framers intended: in partial response to Hans Köchler. (In: Chinese Journal of International Law, 2007, v. 6, no. 2, p. 307-328.) [I.C.J., p. 321-322.]

MacFarlane, S. Neil: Charter values and the response to terrorism. (In: Terrorism and the UN: before and after September 11, ed. by Jane Boulden; Thomas G. Weiss. Bloomington; Indianapolis: Indiana University Press, 2004, p. 27-52.) [I.C.J., p. 32.]

Mahbubani, Kishore: The permanent and elected Council members. (In: The UN Security Council: from the Cold War to the 21st century, ed. by David M. Malone. Boulder: Lynne Rienner Publishers, 2004, p. 253-266.) [I.C.J., p. 259.]

Majlessi, M. Shervin: Economic sanctions in the United Nations security system: recent developments. (In: Les sanctions économiques en droit international, ed. by Laura Picchio Forlati; Linos-Alexandre Sicilianos. Leiden [etc.]: Martinus Nijhoff, 2004, p. 529-566.) [I.C.J., p. 538-539, 554, 558-563.]

Mani, Vekateshwara Subramanian: Six decades of the United Nations: an Indian perception. (In: Indian Journal of International Law, 2004, v. 44, no. 1, p. 1-73.) [I.C.J., p. 3, 10, 13, 23-24, 27, 41, 57-58, 60.]

Manusama, Kenneth: The United Nations Security Council in the post-Cold War era: applying the principle of legality. Leiden; Boston: Martinus Nijhoff, 2006. (Legal aspects of international organization; 47.) [P.C.I.J., p. 49, 53; I.C.J., p. 5-6, 10-11, 14, 16-17, 18-21, 23, 25, 27, 30-31, 33, 38-39, 41, 43, 44-45, 52-53, 55, 58, 77, 92, 105, 106-107, 123, 126, 135, 137, 166, 173-176, 197-198, 241-242, 243, 244, 257, 295, 300, 314, 317.]

Marchi, Jean-François: La F.I.N.U.L. renforcée. (Dans: L'observateur des Nations Unies, 2006, v. 20-21, p. 19-39.) [C.I.J., p. 34.]

Matheson, Michael J.: ICJ review of Security Council decisions. (In: The George Washington International Law Review, 2004, v. 36, no. 3, 615-622).

Matringe, Jean: Problèmes et techniques de mise en oeuvre des sanctions économiques de l'Organisation des Nations Unies en droit interne. (Dans: Les sanctions économiques en droit international, sous la dir. de Laura Picchio Forlati; Linos-Alexandre Sicilianos. Leiden [etc.]: Martinus Nijhoff, 2004, p. 637-681.) [C.P.J.I., p. 666.]

McCorquodale, Robert: International organisations and international human rights law: one giant leap for humankind. (In: International law and power: perspectives on legal order and justice: essays in honour of Colin Warbrick, ed. by Kaiyan Homi Kaikobad; Michael Bohlander. Leiden; Boston: Martinus Nijhoff, 2009, p. 141-162.) [I.C.J., p. 143-145, 148, 156.]

Mendelson, Maurice H.: The definition of "international organization" in the International Law Commission's current project on the responsibility of international organizations. (In: International responsibility today: essays in memory of Oscar Schachter, ed. by Maurizio Ragazzi. Leiden; Boston: Martinus Nijhoff, 2005, p. 371-389.) [I.C.J., p. 381-386, 388.]

Miller, Anthony: The privileges and immunities of the United Nations. (In: International Organizations Law Review, 2009, v. 6, no. 1, p. 7-115.) [I.C.J., p. 29, 91, 97-99, 102, 109, 110-113.]

Miller, Anthony: Privileges and immunities of United Nations officials. (In: International Organizations Law Review, 2007, v. 4, no. 2, p. 169-257.) [I.C.J., p. 172, 182, 193, 196-201, 204, 214, 249, 252, 255.]

Miller, Anthony: United Nations experts on mission and their privileges and immunities. (In: International Organizations Law Review, 2007, v. 4, no. 1, p. 11-56.) [I.C.J., p. 12-14, 17, 18, 24-29, 31, 33, 37-40, 42, 43, 45, 46, 49, 55.]

Mingst, Karen A. and Karns, Margaret P.: The United Nations in the 21st century. Boulder: Westview Press, 2007. 3rd ed. (Dilemmas in world politics.) [I.C.J., p. 8, 37-39.]

Neukirchen, Mathias: Taiwan: eigenständig, aber nicht souverän: zur Frage der Aufnahme der Republik China in die Vereinten Nationen. (In: Vereinte Nationen, 2005, v. 53, no. 2, p. 50-55.) [I.C.J., p. 52, 53.]

O'Donnell, Therese: Naming and shaming: the sorry tale of Security Council resolution 1530 (2004). (In: European Journal of International Law, 2006, v. 17, p. 945-968.) [I.C.J., p. 956-957, 959.]

Orakhelashvili, Alexander: The impact of peremptory norms on the interpretation and application of United Nations Security Council resolutions. (In: European Journal of International Law, 2005, v. 16, no. 1, p. 59-88.) [I.C.J., p. 60-62, 67, 71, 74, 78-79, 82, 86-88.]

Orakhelashvili, Alexander: The power of the UN Security Council to determine the existence of a 'threat to the peace'. (In: Irish Yearbook of International Law, 2006, v. 1, p. 61-99.)

Organisation des Nations Unies (ONU). (Dans: Recueil périodique des juris-classeurs: droit international, 2004, v. 182, no. 120.) [C.P.J.I., p. 21; C.I.J., p. 6, 8-11, 13-16, 18-19, 21-22.]

Organisation des Nations Unies (ONU). (Dans: Recueil périodique des juris-classeurs: droit international, 2005, v. 183, no. p. 121-10.) [C.I.J., p. 3, 6, 10-12, 19.]

Österdahl, Inger: Preach what you practice: the Security Council and the legalisation ex post facto of the unilateral use of force. (In: Nordic Journal of International Law, 2005, v. 74, no. 2, p. 231-260.) [I.C.J., p. 234, 235, 238.]

Ould Dedde Ould Hamady, Omar: Fiscalité des pensions de retraite d'anciens fonctionnaires internationaux: note sur la sentence arbitrale du 14 janvier 2003 sur la question du régime fiscal des pensions versées aux fonctionnaires retraités de l'UNESCO résidant en France. (Dans: Revue belge de droit international, 2006, v. 39, p. 742-775.) [C.I.J., p. 746, 752-754, 759, 761, 762, 769-771.]

Papastavridis, Efthymios: Interpretation of Security Council resolutions under chapter VII in the aftermath of the Iraqi crisis. (In: International and Comparative Law Quarterly, 2007, v. 56, p. 83-118.) [P.C.I.J., p. 91, 92, 102, 110; I.C.J., p. 90-91, 92, 105-107.]

Pellet, Alain: Inutile Assemblée Générale? (Dans: L'ONU. Paris: Seuil, 2004, p. 43-60.) [C.I.J., p. 45, 48-51.]

Picard, Loïc: La pratique comme fondement de l'action du Bureau international du travail? (Dans: La pratique et le droit international: colloque de Genève. Paris: A. Pedone, 2004, p. 209-228.) [C.I.J., p. 209-210.]

Pirrone, Pasquale: L'attuazione delle decisioni del Consiglio di Sicurezza tra ordinamento nazionale e ordinamento comunitario. (Dans: Studi di diritto internazionale in onore di Gaetano Arangio-Ruiz, sous la dir. de Giovanni Battaglini; Paolo Benvenuti; Antonio Cassese; Giorgio Gaja. Napoli: Editoriale Scientifica, 2004, v. 1, p. 563-592.) [C.I.J., p. 573.]

Plantey, Alain et Loriot, François: Fonction publique internationale: organisations mondiales et européennes. Paris: CNRS Editions, 2005. [C.I.J., voir index p. 483.]

Polsi, Alessandro: Storia dell'ONU. Roma: GLF Editori Laterza, 2006. (Quadrante Laterza; 134.) [C.P.J.I., p. 19-20; I.C.J., p. 16, 19.]

Ratner, Steven R.: The Security Council and international law. (In: The UN Security Council: from the Cold War to the 21st century, ed. by David M. Malone. Boulder: Lynne Rienner Publishers, 2004, p. 591-605.) [I.C.J., p. 592, 595-596, 599, 602-603, 605.]

Reinisch, August: Should judges second-guess the UN Security Council? (In: International Organizations Law Review, 2009, v. 6, p. 257-291.) [I.C.J., p. 258, 259, 282, 290.]

Reisman, William Michael: On paying the piper: financial responsibility for Security Council referrals to the International Criminal Court. (In: American Journal of International Law, 2005, v. 99, no. 3, p. 615-618.) [I.C.J., p. 617.]

Riquelme Cortado, Rosa: La interminable historia de la reforma del Consejo de seguridad. (Dans: Revista española de derecho internacional, 2005, v. 57, no. 2, p. 745-776.) [C.I.J., p. 750.]

Rittberger, Volker and Baumgärtner, Heiko: Die Reform des Weltsicherheitsrats: Stand und Perspektiven. (In: Die Friedens-Warte: Blätter für internationale Verständigung und zwischenstaatliche Organisation, 2005, v. 80, p. 307-331.) [I.C.J., p. 325.]

Rivier, Raphaële et Lagrange, Philippe: Travaux de la Commission du droit international et de la Sixième commission (cinquante-septième session; soixantième session). (Dans: Annuaire français de droit international, 2005, v. 51, p. 340-372.) [C.I.J., p. 347-349.]

Roldán Barbero, Javier: La justicia comunitaria y el control de legalidad de las resoluciones del Consejo de seguridad de Naciones Unidas, comentario a las sentencias Yusuf/Al Barakaat y Kadi, de 21 de septiembre de 2005, del Tribunal de primera instancia de la Comunidades europeas. (Dans: Revista española de derecho internacional, 2005, v. 57, no. 2, p. 869-891.) [C.I.J., p. 870, 882.]

Rosenne, Shabtai: On multilingual interpretation. (In: Essays on international law and practice, by Shabtai Rosenne. Leiden; Boston: Martinus Nijhoff, 2007, p. 449-454.)

Ruzié, David: L'indépendance des juridictions administratives internationales. (Dans: Journal du droit international, 2004, v. 131, p. 63-75.) [C.I.J., p. 66-67, 70, 74.]

Santori, Valeria: The United Nations interim administration mission in Kosovo and the sovereignty and territorial integrity of the Federal Republic of Yugoslavia. (In: Studi di diritto internazionale in onore di Gaetano Arangio-Ruiz, ed. by Giovanni Battaglini; Paolo Benvenuti; Antonio Cassese; Giorgio Gaja. Napoli: Editoriale Scientifica, 2004, v. 3, p. 1689-1721.) [P.C.I.J., p, 1703; I.C.J., p. 1695.]

Schrijver, Nico J.: Bij een zestigste verjaardag: de toekomst van het Handvest van de Verenigde Naties. (In: VN Forum, 2005, 2005/4, v. 18, p. 1-9.) [I.C.J., p. 3.]

Sicilianos, Linos-Alexandre: Après l'Irak: vers une redéfinition des pouvoirs du Conseil de sécurité? (Dans: L'intervention en Irak et le droit international, sous la dir. de Karine Bannelier; Olivier Corten; Théodore Christakis; Pierre Klein. Paris: Pedone, 2004, p. 59-82.) [C.I.J., p. 59-60, 65, 71.]

Sicilianos, Linos-Alexandre: La codification des contre-mesures par la Commission du droit international. (Dans: Revue belge de droit international, 2005, v. 38, p. 447-500.) [C.I.J., p. 451, 454, 457-459, 465-467, 469-470, 479-482, 497.]

Sills, Joe: The United Nations and the formation of global norms. (In: The United Nations: confronting the challenges of a global society, by Jean E. Krasno. boulder London: Lynne Rienner publishers, 2004, p. 47-76.) [I.C.J., p. 49-50, 73.]

Smith, Courtney B.: Politics and process at the United Nations: the global dance. Boulder: Rienner, 2006. [I.C.J., p. 64, 79, 84, 142, 145, 151, 168, 214, 285.]

Sorel, Jean-Marc: Le caractère discrétionnaire des pouvoirs du Conseil de sécurité: remarques sur quelques incertitudes partielles. (Dans: Revue belge de droit international, 2004, v. 37, p. 462-483.) [C.I.J., p. 473-477.]

Sur, Serge: Le Conseil de Sécurité: blocage, renouveau et avenir. (Dans: L'ONU. Paris: Seuil, 2004, p. 61-74.) [C.I.J., p. 62, 69.]

Tannewald, Nina: The UN and debates over weapons of mass destruction. (In: The United Nations and global security, ed. by Richard M. Price; Mark W. Zacher. New York: Palgrave Macmillan, 2004, p. 3-20.) [I.C.J., p. 16.]

Tehindrazanarivelo, Djacoba Liva: Le droit des Nations Unies et les limites au pouvoir de sanction du Conseil de sécurité. (Dans: Les sanctions économiques en droit international, sous la dir. de Laura Picchio Forlati; Linos-Alexandre Sicilianos. Leiden [etc.]: Martinus Nijhoff, 2004, p. 211-277.) [C.I.J., p. 231-235, 253-254.]

Tercinet, Josiane: Le pouvoir normatif du Conseil de sécurité: le Conseil de sécurité peut-il légiférer? (Dans: Revue belge de droit international, 2004, v. 37, p. 528-551.) [C.I.J., p. 536, 538.]

Thirlway, Hugh: The law and procedure of the International Court of Justice 1960-1989 (supplement 2009) (parts seven and eight). (In: British Year Book of International Law, 2009, v. 80, p. 13-216.)

Thomé, Nathalie: Les pouvoirs du Conseil de Sécurité au regard de la pratique récente du Chapitre VII de la Charte des Nations Unies. Aix-en-Provence: Press Universitaires d'Aix-Marseille – PUAM, 2005. [C.P.J.I., p. 32; C.I.J., p. 30, 54, 61, 63, 86, 137, 148, 158-161, 163, 187, 229, 243, 250-273, 308, 320, 332-333, 342-344, 370.]

Thornberry, Cedric: Namibia. (In: The UN Security Council: from the Cold War to the 21st century, ed. by David M. Malone. Boulder: Lynne Rienner Publishers, 2004, p. 407-422.) [I.C.J., p. 407-409, 420, 422.]

Tomuschat, Christian: Peace enforcement and law enforcement: two separate chapters on international law? (In: Studi di diritto internazionale in onore di Gaetano Arangio-Ruiz, ed. by Giovanni Battaglini; Paolo Benvenuti; Antonio Cassese; Giorgio Gaja. Napoli: Editoriale Scientifica, 2004, v. 3, p. 1745-1769.) [P.C.I.J., p. 1760; I.C.J., p. 1750-1752, 1755, 1758, 1763, 1766.]

Toublanc, Alix: L'article 103 et la valeur juridique de la Charte des Nations Unies. (Dans: Revue générale de droit international public, 2004, v. 108, no. 2, p. 439-462.) [C.I.J., p. 442-443, 445-448, 457-459.]

Trebilcock, Anne: Implications of the UN convention against Corruption for international organizations: oversight, due process, and immunities issues. (In: International Organizations Law Review, 2009, v. 6, no. 1, p. 513-540.) [I.C.J., p. 532.]

United Nations (UN). (In: Statesman's Yearbook, 2007, 2007, p. 8-13.) [I.C.J., p. 10-11.]

Veiligheidsraad als wereldautoriteit. (In: VN Forum, 2004, 20.4/3, v. 17, no. 3, p. 25-29.) [I.C.J., p. 27.]

Venet, Olivia: L'occupation du territoire irakien et l'intervention du Conseil de sécurité: conséquences sur les pouvoirs réglementaires de la puissance occupante et réflexions sur les modes d'action choisis. (Dans: Revue belge de droit international, 2006, v. 39, p. 274-299.) [C.I.J., p. 294.]

Villani, Ugo: L'ONU e la crisi del Golfo. Bari: Cacucci, 2005. 3a ed. riv. ed amp. [C.I.J., p. 22, 24, 48, 72, 85.]

Villani, Ugo: La politica europea in materia di sicurrezza e di difesa e i suoi rapporti con le Nazioni Unite. (Dans: La comunità internazionale, 2004, v. 59, no. 1, p. 63-90.) [C.I.J., p. 73.]

Wellens, Karel C.: Visits by the Security Council missions to conflict areas: a legal postcard. (In: Studi di diritto internazionale in onore di Gaetano Arangio-Ruiz, ed. by Giovanni Battaglini; Paolo Benvenuti; Antonio Cassese; Giorgio Gaja. Napoli: Editoriale Scientifica, 2004, v. 3, p. 1793-1816.) [I.C.J., p. 1812.]

Wet, Erika de: The Chapter VII powers of the United Nations Security Council. Oxford [etc.]: Hart, 2004. (Studies in International Law; 3.) [I.C.J. and P.C.I.J., passim.]

Wet, Erika de and Wood, Michael C. and Nolte, Georg: The Security Council as a law maker: the adoption of (quasi)-judicial decisions. (In: Developments of international law in treaty making, ed. by Rüdiger Wolfrum; Volker Röben. Berlin, [etc.]: Springer, 2005, p. 183-243.) [I.C.J., p. 184-186, 188, 190-191, 199, 202-204, 209-210, 218, 221-222, 227, 230, 234, 238.]

Wheatley, Steven: The Security Council, democratic legitimacy and regime change in Iraq. (In: European Journal of International Law, 2006, v. 17, no. 3, p. 531-551.) [P.C.I.J., p. 545; I.C.J., p. 532, 536, 538, 539, 542, 543, 544, 545, 549, 550, 551.]

White, Nigel D.: The will and authority of the Security Council after Iraq. (In: Leiden Journal of International Law, 2004, v. 17, no. 4, p. 645-672.) [I.C.J., p. 652.]

Yee, Sienho: The responsibility of States members of an international organization for its conduct as a result of membership of their normal conduct associated with membership. (In: International responsibility today: essays in memory of Oscar Schachter, ed. by Maurizio Ragazzi. Leiden; Boston: Martinus Nijhoff, 2005, p. 435-454.) [P.C.I.J., p. 436, 445-447; I.C.J., p. 436-437, 440, 442, 444, 449.]

Zambelli, Mirko: Les relations entre la Cour pénale internationale et le Conseil de sécurité: la nécessaire conciliation entre justice et paix internationales. (Dans: L'observateur des Nations Unies, 2006, v. 20-21, p. 197-222.) [C.I.J., p. 206-207, 211-212, 217.]

Ziccardi Capaldo, Giuliana: Trasformazione del processo decisionale mondiale: un sistema integrato per l'attuazione coercitiva del diritto internazionale "pubblico". (Dans: Studi di diritto internazionale in onore di Gaetano Arangio-Ruiz, sous la dir. de Giovanni Battaglini; Paolo Benvenuti; Antonio Cassese; Giorgio Gaja. Napoli: Editoriale Scientifica, 2004, v. 1, p. 217-262.) [C.I.J., p. 217, 218, 222, 223, 231, 240-242, 245, 252.]

18. Autres organisations internationales
18. Other international organizations

Accountability and control of international governmental organizations: principles and procedures of "good governance". (In: From government to governance : the growing impact of non-state actors on the international and European legal system : proceedings of the Sixth Hague Joint Conference held in The Hague, The Netherlands, 3-5 July 2003, ed. by Heere, Wybo P. The Hague : T.M.C. Asser Press, 2004, p. 60-94.) [I.C.J., p. 76-81, 93-94.]

Al-Qahtani, Mutlaq Majed : The Shanghai cooperation organization and the law of international organizations. (In : Chinese Journal of International Law, 2006, v. 5, p. 129-147.) [I.C.J., p. 132.]

Angelet, Nicolas : Le tiers à l'instance dans la procédure de règlement des différends de l'OMC. (Dans : Le tiers à l'instance devant les juridictions internationales, sous la dir. d'Hélène Ruiz Fabri ; Jean-Marc Sorel. Paris : A. Pedone, 2005, p. 207-238.)

Araujo, Robert John : Objective meaning of constituent instruments and responsibility of international organizations. (In : International responsibility today : essays in memory of Oscar Schachter, ed. by Maurizio Ragazzi. Leiden ; Boston : Martinus Nijhoff, 2005, p. 343-353.) [I.C.J., p. 345.]

Barkin, J. Samuel : International organization : theories and institutions. Basingstoke [etc.] : Palgrave Macmillian, 2006. [ICJ p. 23, 30, 46, 53, 56, 63-64.]

Bastid Burdeau, Geneviève : Quelques remarques sur la notion de droit dérivé en droit international. (Dans : Droit du pouvoir, pouvoir du droit : mélanges offerts à Jean Salmon. Bruxelles : Bruylant, 2007, p. 161-175.) [C.I.J., p. 170.]

Bourgeois, Jacques and Soopramanien, Ravi : The World Trade Organization dispute settlement system : embedded in public international law? (In : Dispute resolution, ed. by Carl Baudenbacher. Stuttgart : German Law Publishers, 2009, p. 311-355.) [I.C.J., p. 314, 333, 339.]

Brölmann, Catherine : The International Court of Justice and international organisations. (In : International Community Law Review, 2007, v. 9, no. 2, p. 181-186.) [I.C.J., passim.]

Broude, Tomer : The rule(s) of trade and the rhetos of development : reflections on the functional and aspirational legitimacy of the WTO. (In : Columbia Journal of Transnational Law, 2006, v. 45, p. 221-261.) [I.C.J., p. 247.]

Caggiano, Giandonato : The new approach to financial sanctions on Member States for non-compliance with judgments of the European Court of Justice. (In : Global Community : Yearbook of International Law and Jurisprudence, 2006, v. 6, no. 1, p. 149-163.) [I.C.J., p. 153.]

d'Aspremont, Jean : Abuse of the legal personality of international organizations and the responsibility of member States. (In : International Organizations Law Review, 2007, v. 4, no. 1, p. 91-119.) [I.C.J., p. 93, 113, 114, 117.]

Daillier, Patrick et Benlolo-Carabot, Myriam et Susani, Nadine et Vaurs-Chaumette, Anne-Laure (sous la dir. de) : La jurisprudence des tribunaux des organisations d'intégration latino-américaines. (Dans : Annuaire français de droit international, 2005, v. 51, p. 633-673.) [C.P.J.I., p. 643-644, 646, 667; C.I.J., p. 644-646, 654.]

Dekker, Ige F. and Wessel, Ramses A.: Governance by international organizations : rethinking the normative force of international decisions. (In : Governance and international legal theory, ed. by Dekker, Ige F. ; Werner, Wouter G.. Leiden ; Boston, 2004, p. 215-236.) [I.C.J., p. 217-218.]

Eboe-Osuji, Chile: Genocide, justice and the forensic sensibilities of the International Committee of the Red Cross. (In: Chinese Journal of International Law, 2006, v. 5, p. 149-184.) [P.C.I.J., p. 157; I.C.J., p. 158-159.]

Frischtak, Ana: Balancing judicial economy, State opportunism, and due process concerns in the WTO. (In : Michigan Journal of International Law, 2005, v. 26, no. 3, p. 869-898.) [I.C.J., p. 869-870, 873-876, 880, 883.]

Garcia-Rubio, Mariano: Unilateral measures as a means of forcible execution of W.T.O. recommendations and decisions. (In : Les sanctions économiques en droit international, ed. by Laura Picchio Forlati ; Linos-Alexandre Sicilianos. Leiden [etc.]: Martinus Nijhoff, 2004, p. 445-475.) [I.C.J., p. 445-446, 448-449, 455-457, 459, 464, 469; P.C.I.J., p. 457.]

Gazzini, Tarcisio: L'eredità problematica dell'art. VII par. 8 della Convenzione tra le parti del trattato nord-atlantico delle loro forze armate. (Dans : Rivista di diritto internazionale privato e processuale, 2004, v. 40, no. 4, p. 1313-1326.) [C.P.J.I., p. 1324; C.I.J., p. 1317-1319.]

Grard, Loïc: L'Union Européenne, sujet de droit international. (Dans : Revue générale de droit international public, 2006, v. 110, p. 337-372.) [C.I.J., p. 349.]

Hamamoto, Shotaro: Le "pouvoir" de dernier mot : des limites de la présomption de validité des actes des organisations internationales. (Dans : Kobe University Law Review, 2004, v. 38, p. 21-44.)

Hinricher, Jens: The law-making of the International Telecommunication Union (ITU) : providing a new source of international law ? (In : Zeitschrift für ausländisches öffentliches Recht und Völkerrecht, 2004, v. 64, no. 2, p. 489-501.) [I.C.J., p. 497-498.]

Hoffmeister, Frank and Ondrusek, Petr: The European Community in international litigation. (In : Revue Hellénique de Droit International, 2008, v. 61, p. 205-224.) [I.C.J., p. 210-214.]

Hörmann, Saskia: Völkerrecht bricht Rechtsgemeinschaft? Zu den rechtlichen Folgen einer Umsetzung von Resolutionen des UN-Sicherheitsrates durch die EG. (In : Archiv des Völkerrechts, 2006, v. 44, p. 267-327.) [I.C.J. p. 274, 281-282, 284-285, 287-288, 295, 302.]

Khachaturian, Alex: The new Cultural Diversity Convention and its implication on the WTO international trade regime : a critical comparative analysis. (In: Texas International Law Journal, 2006, v. 42, p. 191-209.) [I.C.J., p. 200, 203.]

Kunoy, Bjørn: The jurisdiction of the ECJ to review the legality of the transposition of an international act in the EC legal order. (In: Nordic Journal of International Law, 2007, v. 76, p. 19-37.) [P.C.I.J., p. 25; I.C.J., p. 23, 28.]

Maddalon, Philippe: Les rapports des groupes spéciaux et de l'organe d'appel de l'OMC. (Dans: Annuaire français de droit international, 2005, v. 51, p. 603-632.) [C.P.J.I., p. 603, 615; C.I.J., p. 603-605.]

Martha, Rutsel Silvestre Jacinto: International organizations and the global financial crisis: the status of their assets in insolvency and forced liquidation proceedings. (In: International Organizations Law Review, 2009, v. 6, no. 1, p. 117-154.) [I.C.J., p. 123, 142, 153.]

McCorquodale, Robert: International organisations and international human rights law: one giant leap for humankind. (In: International law and power: perspectives on legal order and justice: essays in honour of Colin Warbrick, ed. by Kaiyan Homi Kaikobad; Michael Bohlander. Leiden; Boston: Martinus Nijhoff, 2009, p. 141-162.) [I.C.J., p. 143-145, 148, 156.]

Mengozzi, Paolo: Court of First Instance and Court of Justice of the European Communities: introductory note. (In: Global Community: Yearbook of International Law and Jurisprudence, 2006, v. 6, no. 2, p. 815-835.) [I.C.J., p. 835.]

Meyer, Frank: Lost in complexity: Gedanken zum Rechtsschutz gegen Smart Sanctions in der EU. (In: Zeitschrift für europarechtliche Studien (ZEUS), 2007, v. 10, p. 1-69.) [I.C.J., p. 26, 30, 43, 68.]

Nanda, Ved P.: Accountability of international organizations. (In: Denver Journal of International Law and Policy, 2005, v. 33, no. 3, p. 379-390.) [I.C.J., p. 385-386, 388-389.]

Nanda, Ved P.: The role of international organizations in non-contractual lawmaking. (In: Developments of international law in treaty making, ed. by Rüdiger Wolfrum; Volker Röben. Berlin, [etc.]: Springer, 2005, p. 157-182.) [I.C.J., p. 159-161.]

Neframi, Eleftheria: La politique étrangère et de sécurité commune et l'identité de l'Union européenne. (Dans: Annuaire français de droit international, 2004, v. 50, p. 826-860.) [C.I.J., p. 845.]

Nilsson, Cecilia: Contextualizing the agreement on the privileges and immunities of the International Criminal Court. (In: Leiden Journal of International Law, 2004, v. 17, no. 3, p. 559-578.) [I.C.J., p. 570, 574.]

Odello, Marco: The developing legal status of the organisation for security and co-operation in Europe. (In: Anuario español de derecho internacional, 2006, v. 22, p. 351-393.) [I.C.J., p. 361-363, 366, 369, 372, 374.]

Pauwelyn, Joost: The jurisdiction of the World Trade Organization. (In: ASIL, Proceedings of the 98th Annual Meeting, March 31-April 3, 2004, 2004, v. 98, p. 135-146.) [I.C.J., p. 137, 140, 143, 145.]

Pearson, Zoe: Non-governmental organisations and international law: mapping new mechanisms for governance. (In: Australian Yearbook of International Law, 2004, v. 23, p. 73-103.) [I.C.J., p. 87.]

Prost, Mario and Clark, Paul Kingsley: Unity, diversity and the fragmentation of international law: how much does the multiplication of international organizations really matter? (In: Chinese Journal of International Law, 2006, v. 5, p. 341-370.) [I.C.J., p. 344-345, 348, 357, 359, 364-365.]

Reichard, Martin: Some legal issues concerning the EU-NATO Berlin plus agreement. (In: Nordic Journal of International Law, 2004, v. 73, no. 1, p. 37-67.) [I.C.J., p. 64.]

Reif, Timothy M. and Eckert, Julie: Courage you can't understand: how to achieve the right balance between shaping and policing commerce in disputes before the World Trade Organization. (In: Columbia Journal of Transnational Law, 2004, v. 42, no. 3, p. 657-714.) [I.C.J., p. 658.]

Reinisch, August: Editorial: how necessary is necessity for international organizations? (In: International Organizations Law Review, 2006, v. 3, p. 177-183.) [I.C.J., p. 178.]

Rossem, Jan Willem, van: Interaction between EU law and international law in the light of Intertanko and Kadi: the dilemma of norms binding the member States but not the community. (In: Netherlands Yearbook of International Law, 2009, v. 40, p. 183-227.) [I.C.J., p. 192, 218.]

Sánchez Patrón, José Manuel: La aplicación del derecho internacional general a las actuaciones de las organizaciones internacionales: la práctica de las Comunidades Europeas – Unión Europea. (Dans: Anuario mexicano de derecho internacional, 2006, v. 6.) [C.I.J., p. 794-795.]

Simon, Denys: Cour de justice et Tribunal de première instance des Communautés européennes. (Dans: Annuaire français de droit international, 2005, v. 51, p. 725-758.) [C.I.J., p. 741, 744.]

Steinberg, Gerald M. and Lassman, Simon: The use and abuse of international law by NGOs. (In: Justice, 2004, v. 38, p. 14-18.) [I.C.J., p. 15-17.]

Talmon, Stefan: Responsibility of international organizations: does the European Community require special treatment? (In: International responsibility today: essays in memory of Oscar Schachter, ed. by Maurizio Ragazzi. Leiden; Boston: Martinus Nijhoff, 2005, p. 405-421.) [P.C.I.J., p. 410; I.C.J., p. 416.]

Tancredi, Antonello: E.C. practice in the W.T.O.: how wide is the "scope for manoeuvre"? (In: European Journal of International Law, 2004, v. 15, no. 5, p. 933-961.) [I.C.J., p. 948.]

Trebilcock, Anne: Implications of the UN Convention against Corruption for international organizations: oversight, due process, and immunities issues. (In: International Organizations Law Review, 2009, v. 6, no. 1, p. 513-540.) [I.C.J., p. 532.]

Udombana, Nsongurua J.: Back to basics: the A.C.P.-E.U. Cotonou Trade Agreement and challenges for the African Union. (In: Texas International Law Journal, 2004, v. 40, no. 1, p. 59-111.) [I.C.J., p. 70-71, 92; P.C.I.J., p. 70.]

Uruena, René: The World Trade Organization and its powers to adopt a competition policy. (In: International Organizations Law Review, 2006, v. 3, p. 55-91.) [I.C.J., p. 72, 74, 81.]

Vennemann, Nicola: Country report on the European Union. (In: Terrorism as a challenge for national and international law: security versus liberty?, ed. by Walter, Christian; Vöneky, Silja; Röben, Volker; Schorkopf, Frank. Berlin [etc.], Springer, 2004, p. 217-266.) [I.C.J., p. 249.]

Voon, Tania: UNESCO and the WTO: a clash of cultures? (In: International and Comparative Law Quarterly, 2006, v. 55, p. 635-651.) [I.C.J., p. 646.]

Vranes, Erich: Jurisdiction and applicable law in WTO dispute settlement. (In: German Yearbook of International Law, 2005, v. 48, p. 265-289.) [I.C.J., p. 269, 272.]

Yee, Sienho: The responsibility of States members of an international organization for its conduct as a result of membership of their normal conduct associated with membership. (In: International responsibility today: essays in memory of Oscar Schachter, ed. by Maurizio Ragazzi. Leiden; Boston: Martinus Nijhoff, 2005, p. 435-454.) [P.C.I.J., p. 436, 445-447; I.C.J., p. 436-437, 440, 442, 444, 449.]

Zagel, Gudrun: Responsibility of international organizations for breaches of international law. (In: Symposium in commemoration of G. I. Tunkin's 100th birthday: papers delivered at a commemorative celebration held at Moscow State University, 20 October 2006, ed. by Glotova, S.; Shestakov, L. N. London: Wildy, Simmonds & Hill, 2007, p. 651-676.) [P.C.I.J., p. 664-665; I.C.J., p. 654-655, 657-659, 661, 663-664, 667-668, 672-673.]

19. Divers
19. Miscellaneous

Abdelrahman, Afifi: Sources et normes de sécurité alimentaire en droit international. (Dans: Revue égyptienne de droit international, 2005, v. 61, p. 1-54.) [C.I.J., p. 16-17, 31, 39-40.]

Akiba, Tadatoshi: Going to the I.C.J. and civil society: the mayors for Peace 2020 Vision Campaign. (In: Freedom from nuclear weapons through legal accountability and good faith: conference report, ed. by George Farebrother. Nottingham: Spokesman; World Court Project, 2007, p. 90-93.) [I.C.J., p. 91, 93.]

Aral, Berdal: An inquiry into the Turkish "school" of international law. (In: European Journal of International Law, 2005, v. 16, no. 4, p. 769-785.) [I.C.J., p. 775.]

Bacchus, James: Lone star: the historic role of the WTO. (In: Texas International Law Journal, 2004, v. 39, no. 3, p. 401-414.) [I.C.J., p. 405-406.]

Baldtschun, Jens: Der Status der Donauschifahrt im Falle bewaffneter Konflikte. Berlin: Duncker & Humblot, 2006. (Schriften zum Völkerrecht; 164.) [P.C.I.J., p. 23-25, 29, 55, 63, 135, 140, 224, 226-227, 229, 232, 236; I.C.J., p. 20, 52, 59-60, 95, 139, 144, 220-221, 239-240, 268, 287-2.]

Bogdandy, Armin von: Globalization and Europe: how to square democracy, globalization, and international law. (In: European Journal of International Law, 2004, v. 15, no. 5, p. 885-906.) [P.C.I.J., p. 887.]

Boll, Alfred Michael: Nationality and obligations of loyalty in international and municipal law. (In: Australian Yearbook of International Law, 2005, v. 24, p. 37-63.) [P.C.I.J., p. 61; I.C.J., p. 41-42.]

Boyd, K. Lee: Universal jurisdiction and structural reasonableness. (In: Texas International Law Journal, 2004, v. 40, no. 1, p. 1-58.) [I.C.J., p. 10.]

Buergenthal, Thomas: Louis B. Sohn (1914-2006). (In: American Journal of International Law, 2006, v. 100, no. 3, p. 623-625.) [P.C.I.J., p. 623-624.]

Campbell, Colm: "Wars on terror" and vicarious hegemons: the UK, international law, and the Northern Ireland conflict. (In: International and Comparative Law Quarterly, 2005, v. 54, no. 2, p. 321-355.) [I.C.J., p. 344.]

Carty, Anthony: Conservative and progressive visions in French international legal doctrine. (In: European Journal of International Law, 2005, v. 16, no. 3, p. 525-537.) [I.C.J., p. 529-530, 532.]

Corthay, Eric: Le concept de terrorisme ou la définition d'un monstre polycéphale. (Dans: L'observateur des Nations Unies, 2006, v. 20-21, p. 111-144.) [C.I.J., p. 128, 131.]

Cot, Jean-Pierre: Commentaire. (Dans: Le principe du contradictoire devant les juridictions internationales, sous la dir. d'Hélène Ruiz-Fabri; Jean-Marc Sorel. Paris: Pedone, 2004, p. 35-42.) [C.I.J., p. 35-38.]

David, Eric: La pratique du pouvoir exécutif et le contrôle des chambres législatives en matière de droit international (1999-2003). (Dans: Revue belge de droit international, 2005, v. 38, p. 5-416.) [C.I.J., p. 135, 278-279, 385-390, 395-396.]

Decisions of British courts during 2005 involving questions of public or private international law. (In: British Year Book of International Law, 2005, v. 76, p. 565-682.) [I.C.J., p. 602-603.]

Dinstein, Yoram: Comments on the presentations by Nico Krisch and Carsten Stahn. (In: Terrorism as a challenge for national and international law: security versus liberty?, ed. by Walter, Christian; Vöneky, Silja; Röben, Volker; Schorkopf, Frank. Berlin [etc.], Springer, 2004, p. 915-924.) [I.C.J., p. 915, 917-920, 922.]

Drumbl, Mark A.: Rights, culture, and crimes: the role of rule of law for the women of Afghanistan. (In: Columbia Journal of Transnational Law, 2004, v. 42, no. 2, p. 349-390.) [I.C.J., p. 370.]

Economidès, Constantin P. et Kolliopoulos, Alexandros: La clause de déconnexion en faveur du droit communautaire: une pratique critiquable. (Dans: Revue générale de droit international public, 2006, v. 110, p. 273-302.) [C.P.J.I., p. 290, 292, 299; C.I.J., p. 290.]

Emberland, Marius: The International Court of Justice and companies: is it possible to discern a "structural bias" at the Court regarding private economic enterprise? (In: International Community Law Review, 2007, v. 9, no. 2, p. 187-208.) [P.C.I.J., p. 188; I.C.J., passim.]

Feldman v. United Mexican States (ICSID Case No. ARB(AF)/99/1). (In: I.C.S.I.D. Reports, 2005, v. 7, p. 318-420.) [I.C.J., p. 333.]

Förster, Susanne: Internationale Haftungsregeln für schädliche Folgewirkungen gentechnisch veränderter Organismen: Europäische und internationale Entwicklungen und Eckwerte für ein Haftungsregime im internationalen Recht. Berlin: Springer, 2007. (Beiträge zum auslandischen öffentlichen Recht und Völkerrecht; 181.) [P.C.I.J., p. 162, 173; I.C.J., p. 164-166, 168-169, 172-173, 176, 179, 181-1.]

Gamarra, Yolanda: Los límites del multilateralismo al control de la (no) proliferación nuclear: la cuestión iraní como pretexto. (Dans: Anuario español de derecho internacional, 2006, v. 22, p. 131-169.) [C.I.J., p. 134.]

German Federal Constitutional Court: In the proceedings on the constitutional complaint of Mr. Al-M., and his motion for temporary injunction (November 5, 2003). (In: International Legal Materials, 2004, v. 43, p. 774-788.) [P.C.I.J., p. 782.]

Globalisering met een menselijk gezicht. (In: VN Forum, 2004, 2004/3, v. 17, no. 3, p. 47-52.) [I.C.J., p. 51.]

Gounelle, Max: Relations internationales. Paris: Dalloz, 2004. 6e éd. (Mémentos Dalloz. Série Droit public, science politique.) [C.I.J., p. 48, 69, 145.]

Graf Vitzthum, Wolfgang: "Wiederaufrichtung des zertretenen Rechts": ehemalige Tübinger rechtswissenschaftliche Doktoranden im Widerstand gegen das NS-Regime. (In: Krisensicherung und humanitärer Schutz: Festschrift für Dieter Fleck, ed. by Horst Fischer; Ulrike Froissart; Wolff Heintschel von Heinegg. Berlin: Berliner Wissenschafts-Verlag, 2004, p. 643-662.) [I.C.J., p. 650.]

Guzman, Andrew T.: Global governance and the WTO. (In: Harvard International Law Journal, 2004, v. 45, no. 2, p. 303-351.) [I.C.J. and P.C.I.J., p. 328, 344.]

Hakki, Murat Metin: Turkey, water and the Middle East: some issues lying ahead. (In: Chinese Journal of International Law, 2006, v. 5, p. 441-458.) [I.C.J., p. 451-452, 457.]

Herdocia Sacasa, Mauricio: Compendio: el principio emergente de la solidaridad jurídica entre los estados: edificando un nuevo orden público internacional. Managua: [s.n.], 2008. [I.C.J., p. 26, 28, 42.]

Jenschke, Christoff: Der völkerrechtliche Rückgabeanspruch auf in Kriegszeiten widerrechtlich verbrachte Kulturgüter. Berlin: Duncker & Humblot, 2005. (Schriften zum Völkerrecht; 153.) [I.C.J., p. 84, 113, 155, 211, 221, 222-238, 251, 255, 309; P.C.I.J., p. 211, 213-214, 224, 262.]

Johanson, Märta C.: Kosovo: boundaries and the liberal dilemma. (In: Nordic Journal of International Law, 2004, v. 73, no. 4, p. 535-549.) [I.C.J., p. 539.]

Johnstone, Ian: US-UN relations after Iraq: the end of the world (order) as we know it? (In: European Journal of International Law, 2004, v. 15, no. 4, p. 813-838.) [I.C.J., p. 829.]

Josephs, Hilary K.: The remedy of apology in comparative and international law: self-healing and reconciliation. (In: Emory International Law Review, 2004, v. 18, no. 1, p. 53-84.) [I.C.J. and P.C.I.J., p. 53, 60, 66, 70-74, 76, 83-84.]

Keith, Kenneth: Sovereignty at the beginning of the 21st century: fundamental or outmoded? (In: Cambridge Law Journal, 2004, v. 63, no. 3, p. 581-604.) [I.C.J., p. 584, 602.]

Keitner, Chimène I. and Reisman, William Michael: Free association: the United States experience. (In: Texas International Law Journal, 2003, v. 39, no. 1, p. 1-63.) [I.C.J., p. 3, 9-11.]

Khan, L. Ali: A theory of international terrorism: understanding Islamic militancy. Leiden/Boston: Martinus Nijhoff, 2006. (Developments in International Law; 56.) [I.C.J., p. 61, 70-71, 117, 293-294.]

Kingsbury, Benedict: Omnilateralism and partial international communities: contributions of the emerging global administrative law. (In: Kokusaiho Gaiko Zassi, 2005, v. 104, no. 1, p. 98-124.) [I.C.J., p. 112, 119-121.]

Kittrie, Orde F.: Averting catastrophe: why the Nuclear Nonproliferation Treaty is losing its deterrence capacity and how to restore it. (In: Michigan Journal of International Law, 2007, v. 28, p. 337-430.) [I.C.J., p. 349, 365.]

Knoll, Bernhard: From benchmarking to final status? Kosovo and the problem of an international administration's open-ended mandate. (In: European Journal of International Law, 2005, v. 16, no. 4, p. 637-660.) [I.C.J., p. 654-655.]

Kohen, Marcelo G.: L'administration actuelle de l'Irak: vers une nouvelle forme de protectorat? (Dans: L'intervention en Irak et le droit international, sous la dir. de Karine Bannelier ; Olivier Corten ; Théodore Christakis ; Pierre Klein. Paris : Pedone, 2004, p. 298-315.) [C.I.J., p. 304, 307.]

Koskenmäki, Riikka : Legal implications resulting from State failure in light of the case of Somalia. (In : Nordic Journal of International Law, 2004, v. 73, no. 1, p. 1-36.) [I.C.J. and P.C.I.J., p. 5, 7, 20, 24.]

Kotzur, Markus : Die Weltgemeinschaft im Ausnahmezustand ? Politische Einheitsbildung im Zeichen der Prävention – eine Skizze. (In : Archiv des Völkerrechts, 2004, v. 42, no. 4, p. 353-388.) [I.C.J., p. 371.]

Kreijen, Gerard : State failure, sovereignty and effectiveness : legal lessons from the decolonization of Sub-Saharan Africa. Leiden [etc.] : Nijhoff, 2004. (Developments in International Law ; 50.) [I.C.J. and P.C.I.J., p. 11-12, 22, 39-40, 56, 131, 176, 189, 246, 270, 327, 348-349, 360.]

Kritsiotis, Dino : Arguments of mass confusion. (In : European Journal of International Law, 2004, v. 15, no. 2, p. 233-278.) [I.C.J., p. 235-244, 248, 250, 260, 264, 271, 273-276.]

Krugmann, Michael : Der Grundsatz der Verhältnismäßigkeit im Völkerrecht. Berlin : Duncker & Humblot, 2004. (Schriften zum Völkerrecht ; 150.) [I.C.J., p. 18, 20, 21, 34, 67, 75, 91-93, 102.]

Lammers, Johan G. : The role of the legal adviser of the Ministry of Foreign Affairs : the Dutch approach and experience. (In : Hague Yearbook of International Law, 2009, v. 22, p. 33-56.) [I.C.J., p. 41-43, 50-53.]

Lesaffer, Randall : Argument from Roman law in current international law : occupation and acquisitive prescription. (In : European Journal of International Law, 2005, v. 16, no. 1, p. 25-58.) [I.C.J., p. 25, 30-31, 38-40, 44, 52-57; P.C.I.J., p. 29, 51.]

Lévy, Vincent G. : Enforcing international norms in the United States after Roper v. Simmons : the case of juvenile offenders sentenced to life without parole. (In : Columbia Journal of Transnational Law, 2006, v. 45, p. 262-311.) [P.C.I.J., p. 279; I.C.J., p. 265, 268, 271-276, 279.]

Li, Jerry Z. : The legal status of three Sino-US joint communiqués. (In : Chinese Journal of International Law, 2006, v. 5, p. 617-645.) [I.C.J., p. 620, 622-623, 625, 632, 643.]

López Martín, Ana Gemma : Clásico pero actual : el territorio estatal. (Dans : Anuario hispano-luso-americano de derecho internacional, 2005, v. 17, p. 173-206.) [C.I.J., p. 178, 180-181, 189, 191, 194-198, 200-202, 205.]

MacFarlane, S. Neil and Khong, Yuen Foong : Human security and the UN : A critical history. Bloomington : Indiana University Press, 2006. (United Nations Intellectual History Project.) [P.C.I.J., p. 164, 199; I.C.J., p. 120, 121.]

Mahncke, Hans: US steel tariffs and the WTO dispute resolution mechanism. (In: Leiden Journal of International Law, 2004, v. 17, no. 3, p. 615-624.) [I.C.J., p. 616.]

Mahouvé, M.: La répression des violations du droit international humanitaire au niveau national et international. (Dans: Revue de droit international et de droit comparé, 2005, v. 82, no. 3, p. 229-273.) [C.I.J., p. 230-231.]

Mayer, Pierre: Le phénomène de la coordination des ordres juridiques étatiques en droit privé: cours général de droit international privé (2003). (Dans: Recueil des cours de l'Académie de droit international de La Haye, 2007, v. 327, p. 9-378.) [C.P.J.I., p. 105, 209.]

Mélin, François: Jurisprudence: France: loi étrangère, application d'office, établissement du contenu, dénaturation. (Dans: Journal du droit international, 2004, v. 131, p. 520-537.) [C.I.J., p. 532.]

Mills, Alex and Stephens, Tim: Challenging the role of judges in Slaughter's liberal theory of international law. (In: Leiden Journal of International Law, 2005, v. 18, no. 1, p. 1-30.) [P.C.I.J., p. 2, 5-7, 19; I.C.J., p. 2, 7, 13, 25.]

Minnerop, Petra: Legal status of State sponsors of terrorism in US law. (In: Terrorism as a challenge for national and international law: security versus liberty?, ed. by Walter, Christian; Vöneky, Silja; Röben, Volker; Schorkopf, Frank. Berlin [etc.], Springer, 2004, p. 733-785.) [I.C.J., p. 782.]

Mosconi, Franco: La difesa dell'armonia interna dell'ordinamento del foro tra legge italiana, convenzioni internazionali e regolamenti comunitari. (Dans: Rivista di diritto internazionale privato e processuale, 2007, v. 43, p. 5-26.) [C.I.J., p. 10.]

Müllerson, Rein: Democracy after the fall of the Berlin wall: it has come, it is coming, will it come? (In: Select Proceedings of the European Society of International Law, ed. by James Crawford; Sarah M. H. Nouwen. Oxford; Portland: Hart, 2008, v. 2, p. 37-50.) [I.C.J., p. 45.]

Müllerson, Rein: Democracy promotion: institutions, international law and politics. (Dans: Recueil des cours de l'Académie de droit international de La Haye, 2008, v. 333, p. 9-173.) [I.C.J., p. 56, 167.]

O'Connell, Mary Ellen: Enhancing the status of non-State actors through a global war on terror? (In: Columbia Journal of Transnternational Law, 2005, v. 43, no. 2, p. 435-458.) [I.C.J., p. 438, 441, 449-451.]

Panken, Heidi and Ryngaert, Cedric and van Eeckhoutte, Dries: Het arrest Sharon van het Hof van Cassatie: bouwstenen voor de verdere rol van universele jurisdictie, internationale immuniteiten en de doorwerking van het internationaal gewoonterecht. (In: Revue belge de droit international, 2004, v. 37, p. 211-254.) [I.C.J., p. 213, 219, 223, 227, 231-233, 236-240, 249, 251, 253.]

Paulus, Andreas L.: From neglect to defiance? The United States and international adjudication. (In: European Journal of International Law, 2004, v. 15, no. 4, p. 783-812.) [I.C.J., p. 783-792, 794, 796, 798-812.]

Pfeil, Julia: Völkerrechtliche Praxis der Bundesrepublik Deutschland in den Jahren 2000 bis 2002, 3. Teil: Friedenssicherung. (In: Zeitschrift für ausländisches öffentliches Recht und Völkerrecht, 2004, v. 64, no. 4, p. 1105-1178.) [I.C.J., p. 1168.]

Poulain, Michèle: Chronologie des faits internationaux d'intérêt juridique (année 2005). (Dans: Annuaire français de droit international, 2005, v. 51, p. 843-908.) [C.I.J., p. 853, 860.]

Pronto, Arnold N.: Consideration at the United Nations of an international prohibition on the cloning of human beings. (In: Leiden Journal of International Law, 2007, v. 20, p. 239-265.) [I.C.J., p. 256-257.]

R (Marchiori) v. Environment Agency. (In: International Law Reports, 2005, v. 127, p. 574-651.) [I.C.J., p. 604-606, 644-646.]

Reisman, William Michael: The democratization of contemporary international law-making processes and the differentiation of their application. (In: Developments of international law in treaty making, ed. by Rüdiger Wolfrum; Volker Röben. Berlin, [etc.]: Springer, 2005, p. 15-59.) [I.C.J., p. 17, 24-27, 56.]

Rosenne, Shabtai: Acceptance speech by professor Shabtai Rosenne on receiving the first Hague prize for international law 2004. (In: The Hague legal capital? Liber in honorem W. J. Deetman, ed. by Vriesendorp, David; Nelissen, Frans A.; Wladimiroff, Michaïl. The Hague: Hague Academic Press, 2008, p. 105-116.) [I.C.J., p. 106-107, 109-110.]

Sands, Philippe: Lawless world: the whistle-blowing account of how Bush and Blair are taking the law into their own hands. London: Penguin, 2006. [P.C.I.J., p. 7; I.C.J., p. XIII-XVI, 14, 17-18, 41, 43, 114-115, 118, 168, 239, 249-250, 252.]

Sarat, Austin: At the boundaries of law: executive clemency, sovereign prerogative, and the dilemma of American legality. (In: Legal borderlands: law and the construction of American borders, ed. by Mary L. Dudziak; Leti Volpp. 2006, p. 19-39.) [I.C.J., p. 33-34.]

Sarei v. Rio Tinto (9TH CIR.), April 12, 2007. (In: International Legal Materials, 2007, v. 46, p. 589-625.) [P.C.I.J., p. 616, 617 (note 10); I.C.J., p. 615, 618, 620.]

Schachter, Madeleine: The utility of pro bono representation of U.S.-based amicus curiae in non-U.S. and multi-national courts as a means of advancing the public interest. (In: Fordham international law journal. 2004-2005, v. 28, no. 1, p. 88-144.) [I.C.J., p. 120.]

Schoen, Susanne: Der rechtliche Status von Beutekunst: eine Untersuchung am Beispiel der aufgrund des Zweiten Weltkrieges nach

Russland verbrachten deutschen Kulturgüter. Berlin: Duncker & Humblot, 2004. (Schriften zum Völkerrecht; 151.) [I.C.J., p. 45.]

Scott, Joanne: International trade and environmental governance: relating rules (and standards) in the EU and the WTO. (In: European Journal of International Law, 2004, v. 15, no. 2, p. 307-354.) [I.C.J., p. 340.]

Shelton, Dinah: The International Court of Justice and nongovernmental organizations. (In: International Community Law Review, 2007, v. 9, no. 2, p. 139-155.) [P.C.I.J. and I.C.J., passim.]

Silingardi, Stefano: Occupazione bellica e obblighi delle potenze occupanti nel campo economico. (Dans: Rivista di diritto internazionale, 2006, v. 89, p. 978-1030.) [C.I.J., p. 981, 984-986, 994-995, 997, 1001, 1006-1007, 1015, 1018-1019.]

Soons, Alfred H. A.: A sustainable career: the academic contribution of prof. Johan G. Lammers. (In: Hague Yearbook of International Law, 2009, v. 22, p. 105-109.) [I.C.J., p. 107-108.]

Sosa v. Alvarez-Machain et al.: United States of America v. Alvarez-Machain et al. (In: International Law Reports, 2005, v. 127, p. 691-816.) [I.C.J., p. 710, 797; P.C.I.J., p. 708.]

Stern, Brigitte: Summary of remarks. (In: ASIL, Proceedings of the 98th Annual Meeting, March 31-April 3, 2004, 2004, v. 98, p. 369-370.) [I.C.J., p. 370.]

Syssoeva, Elena: Kunst im Krieg: eine völkerrechtliche Betrachtung der deutsch-russischen Kontroverse um kriegsbedingt verbrachte Kulturgüter. Berlin: Duncker & Humblot, 2004. (Schriften zum Völkerrecht; 152.) [I.C.J., p. 123, 164, 165, 172, 182, 322, 323, 331, 334, 338, 361; P.C.I.J., p. 124, 174, 175, 331.]

Talmon, Stefan: Chypre: écueil pour la Turquie sur la voie de l'Europe. (Dans: Annuaire français de droit international, 2005, v. 51, p. 85-119.) [C.I.J., p. 112-113.]

Talmon, Stefan: The European Union – Turkey controversy over Cyprus or a tale of two treaty declarations. (In: Chinese Journal of International Law, 2006, v. 5, p. 579-616.) [I.C.J., p. 609.]

Tamanaha, Brian Z.: On the rule of law: history, politics, theory. Cambridge: Cambridge University Press, 2004. [I.C.J., p. 127, 128, 130, 133, 134.]

The Loewen Group Inc. and Raymond L. Loewen v. United States of America (ICSID Case No. ARB(AF)98/3). (In: I.C.S.I.D. Reports, 2005, v. 7, p. 421-491.) [I.C.J., p. 432-433, 438-439, 467, 471, 473.]

The Queen v. Seven Named Accused. (In: International Law Reports, 2005, v. 127, p. 232-309.) [I.C.J., p. 272.]

The Telders international law moot court case 2005: The 'Failed State' of Loe Dispute (Loe v. Western Kingdom). (In: Leiden Journal of International Law, 2005, v. 18, no. 1, p. 131-137.) [P.C.I.J., p. 131; I.C.J., p. 131, 136-137.]

The Telders International Law Moot Court Competition, 1977-2007. (In: Leiden Journal of International Law, 2007, v. 20, p. 267-273.) [P.C.I.J., p. 267; I.C.J., p. 267, 273.]

Tomuschat, Christian: World order models: a disputation with B. S. Chimni and Yasuaki Onuma. (In: International Community Law Review, 2006, v. 8, p. 71-79.) [I.C.J., p. 75, 77-78.]

Tonolo, Sara: Lo scioglimento delle unioni di fatto e degli accordi di convivenza nel diritto internazionale privato e processuale italiano. (Dans: Rivista di diritto internazionale, 2005, v. 88, p. 997-1021.) [C.I.J., p. 1012.]

Triggs, Gillian Doreen: The public international lawyer and the practice of international law. (In: Australian Yearbook of International Law, 2005, v. 24, p. 201-218.) [P.C.I.J., p. 202, 207; I.C.J., p. 202-204, 207-211, 213, 215.]

United States Supreme Court: Sosa v. Alvarez-Machain, June 29, 2004. (In: International Legal Materials, 2004, v. 43, no. 6, p. 1390-1408.) [I.C.J., p. 1408.]

Velázquez Elizarrarás, Juan Carlos: Orientaciones básicas acerca de la enseñanza del derecho internacional en ciencias políticas y sociales. (Dans: Anuario mexicano de derecho internacional, 2006, v. 6, p. 831-869.) [C.P.J.I. et C.I.J., p. 837.]

Vierucci, Luisa: Sulla nozione di obiettivo militare nella guerra aerea: recenti sviluppi della giurisprudenza internazionale. (Dans: Rivista di diritto internazionale, 2006, v. 89, p. 693-735.) [C.I.J., p. 698, 724.]

Waart, Paul J. I. M. de: Israel's settlement-policy stumbling-block in the Middle East peace process. (In: Leiden Journal of International Law, 2007, v. 20, no. 4, p. 825-839.)

Wismer, Peter: Bring down the walls. (In: Chinese Journal of International Law, 2006, v. 5, p. 511-553.) [I.C.J., p. 515, 519, 522, 529, 536, 538, 542, 544-548.]

Wolfrum, Rüdiger: American-European dialogue: different perceptions of international law: introduction. (In: Zeitschrift für ausländisches öffentliches Recht und Völkerrecht, 2004, v. 64, no. 2, p. 255-262.) [I.C.J., p. 257.]

Woodward, B. K.: Global civil society and international law in global governance: some contemporary issues. (In: International Community Law Review, 2006, v. 8, p. 247-355.) [P.C.I.J., p. 254-255; I.C.J., p. 257, 326, 329-330.]

Worster, William Thomas: Conflicts between United States immigration law and the General Agreement on Trade in Services: most-favored-nation obligation. (In: Texas International Law Journal, 2006, v. 42, p. 55-117.) [I.C.J., p. 67.]

INDEX ALPHABÉTIQUE DES NOMS D'AUTEURS

ALPHABETICAL INDEX OF AUTHORS' NAMES